The Anthropology of Childhood

The raising of children, their role in society, and the degree to which family and community are structured around them, vary quite significantly around the world. *The Anthropology of Childhood* provides the first comprehensive review of the literature on children from a distinctly anthropological perspective. Bringing together key evidence from cultural anthropology, history, and primate studies, it argues that our common understandings about children are narrowly culture-bound. Whereas the dominant society views children as precious, innocent, and preternaturally cute "cherubs," Lancy introduces the reader to societies where children are viewed as unwanted, inconvenient "changelings," or as desired but pragmatically commoditized "chattel." Looking in particular at family structure and reproduction, profiles of children's caretakers, their treatment at different ages, their play, work, schooling, and transition to adulthood, this volume provides a rich, interesting, and original portrait of children in past and contemporary cultures. A must-read for anyone interested in childhood.

DAVID F. LANCY is Professor of Anthropology in the Department of Sociology, Social Work, and Anthropology, Utah State University. He is author of several books on childhood, including *Studying Children and Schools: Qualitative Research Traditions* (2001) and *Playing on the Mother Ground* (1996).

The Anthropology of Childhood

Cherubs, Chattel, Changelings

David F. Lancy

Utah State University

CAMBRIDGE UNIVERSITY PRESS
Cambridge, New York, Melbourne, Madrid, Cape Town, Singapore,
São Paulo, Delhi, Dubai, Tokyo, Mexico City

Cambridge University Press
The Edinburgh Building, Cambridge CB2 8RU, UK

Published in the United States of America by Cambridge University Press, New York

www.cambridge.org
Information on this title: www.cambridge.org/9780521887731

First published 2008
Reprinted 2010

A catalogue record for this publication is available from the British Library

Library of Congress Cataloguing in Publication data
Lancy, David F.
The anthropology of childhood : cherubs, chattel, changelings / David F. Lancy.
    p.   cm.
Includes index.
ISBN 978-0-521-88773-1 (hardback)
1. Children – Cross-cultural studies.   I. Title.
GN482.L36   2008
305.23 – dc22   2008036968

ISBN 978-0-521-88773-1 Hardback
ISBN 978-0-521-71603-1 Paperback

Contents

Plates

Picture credits

Cover plate, Plates 3, 4, 7, 8 21, 26, 30, 31 Bryan Spykerman photos. Used by permission.

Plates 1, 2, 9, 12, 13, 14, 15, 16, 17, 22, 23, 25, 27, 28, 29, 31 David F. Lancy photos and graphics.

Plates 5, 6 Paul Raffaele photos. Used by permission.

Plate 8 Peabody Essex Museum photo. Used by permission.

Plate 10 Photo of Nancy Hylin and granddaughter Inger. Photo taken by grandpa Hans Jacob Hylin. Used by permission.

Plate 11 Haefeli Cartoon *The New Yorker*, June 14, 2004. Used by permission.

Plate 18 Children playing in street, New York City. Undated, photographer anonymous. Library Congress Call No. B2-674-8. I am indebted to Becky Zarger for alerting me to the digital photo archive of the Library of Congress. Photo in public domain

Plate 19 Laura Marks photo. Used by permission.

Plate 20 Eli Lucero photo. Used by permission.

Plate 24 Spinners and doffers in Mollahan Mills, Newberry, SC. Dec. 3, 1908. Photo by Lewis W. Hine. Library of Congress Call No.: LOT 7479, v. 1, no. 0371. Photo in public domain.

Plate 32 Andrée Malone photo from Marib area, Yemen. Used by permission

Plate 33 From Oonk (2000). Used by permission.

Preface

In 2002, an article entitled "Why don't anthropologists like children?" appeared in *American Anthropologist*. The author argued that anthropologists, in their comprehensive study of every society on the planet, had ignored or mishandled childhood (Hirschfeld 2002). Since I'd devoted my career to the study of children in culture, I was personally affronted. Moreover, I had had no difficulty finding dozens of accounts of children in the ethnographic record to corroborate a thesis I advanced in a book published just a few years earlier (Lancy 1996). Consequently, I wrote a careful and thorough rebuttal and submitted it as a Commentary. The journal editors rejected it as too long. I whittled and whittled but it was still over the 500 word limit. I gave up trying to shrink my rebuttal and, instead, decided to expand it. You are reading the result.

I realized that while I might be aware of a treasure trove of material in the ethnographic record, others might not. The field, in fact, seems balkanized. For example, I've noted that anthropologists who study children in schools – there are more than seven hundred members of the Council on Anthropology and Education – may not pay much attention to the work of ethnographers studying children learning to farm or to hunt. Anthropologists looking at language socialization; archaeologists studying mortuary practices; biobehavioral anthropologists studying fertility – these and numerous other lines of inquiry run in parallel, rarely crossing. Theoretical perspectives that are treated as antithetical when they might better be seen as complementary divide us as well.

This volume aims to include, therefore, the work of anthropologists interested in childhood who, heretofore, may have been unaware or at least unappreciative of each other's work. I achieve this synthesis partly through a comprehensive literature review but also by eschewing lengthy treatment of theoretical formulations that might act as a bar to the uninitiated. Ideally, this work should serve as a catalyst that promotes much greater interaction among those who study children.

The book quite consciously sets out to capture and offer at least a passing reference to most studies in anthropology where children are in the foreground.

All of the major themes – for example, infancy, children's play, and adolescent initiation – are covered at length. Furthermore, where these themes abut the disciplines of history and primatology, I draw liberally from those bodies of scholarship to strengthen and enrich the presentation.

A seminal work that provided a model for my research was Sarah Blaffer Hrdy's *Mother Nature*. In that book, Hrdy draws on the literature on motherhood outside the dominant culture, and, in constructing a more representative portrait, she also dismantles many taken-for-granted notions about the phenomenon – the maternal "instinct" to choose just one example. It has been my intent to do for childhood what Hrdy did for motherhood. Here, too, we see that many assumptions that are made about what is "normal" or natural in children's development are, in fact, quite narrowly culture-bound. Indeed, throughout this work, the formula employed in child development texts will be turned on its head. In these texts, research on middle-class Euroamerican children defines the standard and "anecdotes" from anthropological studies illustrate "deviation from the mean." In the pages that follow, common aspects of Western childhood are examined through the lens of anthropology. This lens reveals that what we take for granted as customary appears to be rather strange when compared with prevailing practices found elsewhere. The goal is not to offer a competing volume to standard child development texts but, rather, to offer a supplement or corrective.

The alliterative terms in my sub-title suggest three compass points in this landscape. Our own society views children as precious, innocent, and preternaturally cute *cherubs*. However, for much of human history, children have been seen as anything but cherubic. I will introduce readers to societies, indeed entire periods in history, where children are viewed as unwanted, inconvenient *changelings* or as desired but pragmatically commoditized *chattel*. These perspectives will be employed in the study of family structure and reproduction; profiles of children's caretakers – parental, sib, and community; their treatment at different ages; their play; their work; their schooling; and their transition to adulthood. Again and again, our views and treatment of our cherubs will stand in sharp contrast to views of children constructed by anthropologists and historians from their work in other societies.

Another audience I hope to reach is the legion of teachers, fieldworkers, and policymakers who are laboring to improve the lives of children not fortunate enough to have been born into a privileged society. All are aware of the importance of taking culture into account in their work, and "multiculturalism" has become an oft-heard mantra. But the concept is often used to provide some exotic spices to season the otherwise standard prescriptions for children's schooling and welfare. Throughout this work we'll probe deeply into the literature to discover the ways in which child development is truly shaped by culture. But *The Anthropology of Childhood* goes beyond this analysis in consistently building bridges between the rich cultural traditions documented by ethnographers in the past and the contemporary scenarios confronted by interventionists.

For those who find this book a beginning and not an ending, I urge you to visit our website to participate in a dynamic and growing community dedicated to using anthropology to understand and serve children better: http://anthropologyofchildhood.usu.edu/.

Gradually, the 500+ word Commentary has grown into a 500 lb gorilla, dominating my life and rendering me an insufferable companion. I couldn't see a play or a movie or read a novel without finding something that might fit. Joyce has not only tolerated the beast but has groomed it on regular occasions. Other family and friends fed it snacks. Thank you Nadia, Sonia, Leslie, Bob, Judy, Quinn, Rick, and Melissa. Many others often asked after the gorilla's growth and wellbeing. At Utah State, these included (among many others) my colleagues Michael Chipman, Richley Crapo, Christie Fox, Kermit Hall, Norm Jones, Rick Krannich, Pat Lambert, Lynn Meeks and Mike Sweeney. Colleagues elsewhere who joined the vigil included Katie Anderson-Levitt, Nigel Barber, Jay Black, Gary Chick, Gary Cross, Aaron Denham, Bob Edgerton, Heather Rae Espinoza, Hilary Fouts, Rob Gordon, Judy Harris, Shep Krech, Jon Marks, Jim Marten, David Olson, Aaron Podolefsky, Paul Raffaele, Deborah Reed-Danahay, Jaipaul Roopnarine, Peter Smith, Brian Sutton-Smith, Glenn Weisfeld and Becky Zarger. Thank you all for your support, guidance, and tolerance of my persistent queries.

As this project took on visible proportions I began to bring the gorilla into my Anthropology of Childhood class. Students in the class also did much to nurture it from toddlerhood on, notably Helen Brower, JeriAnn Lukens, Amy Montuoro, Tonya Stallings, Mary Sundblom and James Young. However, no one was more critical to this enterprise than Annette Grove, who evolved from stellar student into untiring and incredibly effective research assistant and editor. My debt to Annette is simply incalculable.

Many colleagues assisted in the creation of what eventually coalesced into this oversize creature, beginning before I had any idea of what was coming. Utah State's Honors Students in 1995 selected me to give the annual "Last Lecture," and I used the opportunity to develop the child-as-commodity ideas presented at the end of the book. A general outline of chapters 6 and 7 emerged at a presentation I made at UCLA in February 1999. Hosted by Alan Fiske, the talk was followed by extremely stimulating discussions with Alan, Patricia Greenfield, Tom Weisner, Candy Goodwin, and others. In April 2004, Pierre Dasen and Jean Retschitzki invited me to a symposium in Switzerland to present early versions of chapters 5 and 6 on learning and play. Sid Strauss had me speak in December 2004 to an incredibly diverse and stimulating group – sponsored by the McDonnell Foundation – on culture and children's social learning. Chapter 6 was drafted, initially, in response to an invitation from Gerd Spittler to give a presentation in Bayreuth in July 2005. Bryan Spykerman's inspired photographs of children added personality to the text. These gratefully acknowledged efforts to assist me in gestation are complemented by the work of many midwives who critically reviewed chapters and provided often extensive and invaluable feedback. Chief among these I would thank Rob Borofsky, John Gay, Barry Hewlett, Howard Kress, Mark Moritz, Barbara Polak, Ali Pomponio, Alice Schlegel, and, particularly, John Bock and Suzanne Gaskins. Two anonymous reviewers for Cambridge University Press provided extensive, on-target feedback.

This work is dedicated to the late Nancy Hylin. Our next-door neighbor, she became, in effect, a close older sibling. Nancy, in adulthood, met and married a Norwegian, Hans Jacob Hylin, settled in Norway and proceeded to raise four sons and assist in the rearing of nine grandchildren. She also enjoyed a distinguished career as a secondary school teacher. Nancy was a natural participant observer and, for nearly fifty years, she shared her observations of childhood and adolescence with me and my family through the media of long, intimate letters and photographs. So, while my research and fieldwork has been episodic, I could count on a steady stream of "field reports" emanating from Norway, year after year. In spite of her passing in 2000, Nancy served as muse throughout this project, a silent but insistent reviewer and critic. Lastly, I need to acknowledge a muse of another sort. Katherine Iris Tomlinson will turn three in a few days and, since birth, her weekly play-dates with "Uncle David" have been both therapeutic and inspirational. As you read this text, please remember that I much prefer cherubs.

April 23, 2007

1 Where do children come from?

Introduction

American psychology . . . a monocultural enterprise paying lip service to the importance of culture . . . (Gielen 2004: 10)

Rather than perceiving Third World children as having "abnormal" childhoods, it should be remembered that First World children tend to experience more privileged, protected childhoods compared to most of the world's children. (Punch 2003: 277)

. . . in Brazil childhood is a privilege of the rich and practically nonexistent for the poor. (D. M. Goldstein 1998: 389)

As Jared Diamond (1997) so effectively argues in *Guns, Germs and Steel*, European and North American supremacy in world affairs during much of the past three centuries is largely an accident of geography. Nevertheless, Euroamerican values have come to define all that is good, beautiful, and true, including our scientific and pragmatic understanding of the nature of children. The underlying theme of this book is that the way in which modern, well-to-do Westerners view and treat their children is unique in the annals of culture. But because we invent the theories and write the textbooks, our views are taken as the norm, and variations from our standards are treated as deviations, requiring explanation.

A robust tradition in anthropology, dating at least to Mead's (1928/1961) *Coming of Age in Samoa*, challenges the ethnocentric lens of Western psychology. Mead's work undermined the claim by psychologist G. Stanley Hall that stress was inevitably part of adolescence. Universal stage theories of cognitive development, such as that of Jean Piaget, met a similar fate when a cross-cultural comparative study in Papua New Guinea demonstrated profound and unpredicted influences of culture and formal schooling (Lancy and Strathern 1981; Lancy 1983; Ochs and Schieffelin 1984).[1]

---

[1] Ochs and Schieffelin's (1984) analysis of adult–child language interaction also showed that ethnographic studies in non-Western societies could be used to "de-universalize" claims made in the mainstream developmental psychology literature.

Quite recently, Bob LeVine has taken on one of psychology's most sacred cows – mother–infant attachment.[2] His observations of agrarian, East African Gusii parents suggest the possibility of weak attachment and consequent blighted development. He finds that, while mothers respond promptly to their infant's distress signals, they ignore other vocalizations such as babbling (LeVine 2004: 154). They rarely look at their infants or speak to them – even while breastfeeding. Later, when they do address their children, they use commands and threats rather than praise or interrogatives (LeVine 2004: 156). In spite of these obvious signs of "pathology" on the part of Gusii mothers, LeVine and his colleagues – who have been studying Gusii villagers for decades – find no evidence of widespread emotional crippling (LeVine 2004).[3] He argues that the problem of excessive claims of universality arises from the "child development field's dual identity as an ideological advocacy movement for the humane treatment of children and a scientific research endeavor seeking knowledge and understanding" (LeVine 2004: 151).

Another sacred cow slain by anthropologists has been "parenting style" theory (Baumrind 1971). Central African Bofi farmers fit the so-called "authoritarian" parenting style in valuing respect and obedience and exercising coercive control over their children. According to the theory, Bofi children should be withdrawn, non-empathetic, aggressive, and lack initiative. On the contrary, they display precisely the opposite set of traits, and Fouts concludes that the theory may work when applied to Americans, but "it has very little explanatory power among the Bofi" (Fouts 2005: 361). Throughout this book the reader will find similar examples of anthropologists "exercis[ing] their veto . . ." (LeVine 2007: 250).

Not only textbooks but children's books as well reveal a pervasive bias. In depictions of Native American children, one sees:

a stereotypic Western model of the child, living in a small, happy, nuclear family consisting of parents with one boy, one girl, and perhaps an additional infant, spending considerable amounts of time playing . . . prehistoric children are pictured as healthy, despite the archaeological evidence that they were often ill, and plump, despite . . . evidence that they were often malnourished. The surroundings in which they live are picturesque and clean, lacking flies, dirt, and excrement. (Kamp and Whittaker 2002: 38–39)

This account will offer a correction to the ethnocentric lens that sees children only as precious, innocent, and preternaturally cute *cherubs*.[4] Building on a firm foundation of research in history, anthropology, and primatology, I hope

---

[2] See also: Scheper-Hughes (1987a).
[3] Although not without controversy, Judith Harris' (1998) *The Nurture Assumption* offers an insider's critique of many such sacred cows.
[4] Cherub has a diversity of meanings, depending on the particular historical epoch or text one consults. In modern usage, a cherub is a plump, angelic, child-like creature that personifies innocence.

to uncover something close to the norm for children's lives and those of their parents. I will make the case for alternative lenses whereby children may be viewed as unwanted, inconvenient *changelings*[5] or as desired but pragmatically commodified *chattel*.[6] This chapter will first identify a few key ideas about children that will guide our thinking. Then, I will introduce the major themes of the book while providing a preview of the nine chapters that follow.

Is there such a thing as childhood?

"Child" is itself not an uncomplicated term. (Boswell 1988: 26)

In order to begin our work, we'll start with a clean slate. Consider the notion that childhood didn't exist at all until recently. This is the thesis of an extremely influential book by French philosopher/historian Philippe Ariès published in 1962. In it, he argues that the concept of *childhood* as a distinct state is largely absent until the past few hundred years. His case is based primarily on an analysis of figurative art.

Medieval art until about the twelfth century did not know childhood or did not attempt to portray it. It is hard to believe that this neglect was due to incompetence or incapacity; it seems more probable that there was no place for childhood in the medieval world. (Ariès 1962: 33)

And, if we limit our database to images of children in portraits, we would have to acknowledge that they often don't look very child-like. What Ariès said, in effect, was that there are two pre-adult life-stages: the baby–toddler stage when, lacking speech, manners, and proper locomotion, the individual isn't yet fully human; and the proto-adult stage when the individual is treated as a small, incompetent adult. This characterization is probably not far off the mark for peasant society throughout much of civilization, and it may fit quite a few tribal societies studied by anthropologists.

Scholars, however, quickly picked up the gauntlet Ariès had thrown down. Sommerville (1982) documents virtually continuous evidence of childhood as a distinct stage from the Egyptians onward. In fact, when Flinders Petrie excavated the Middle Kingdom (*c*.1900 BCE) village of Lahun, he found many children's toys, including balls and pull toys that wouldn't look out of place in

---

[5] Changeling is a pagan concept borrowed by medieval Christians. Like the cuckoo, trolls or elves might substitute their peculiar offspring for a human infant. The mother of the infant had recourse to a number of punitive measures designed to rid herself of the nest usurper in hopes the erstwhile parent would bring back the human child and re-exchange the two.

[6] Chattel has its origin in the Latin *capitale* or wealth, property. The closely related term cattle has a similar origin. A typical Roman patrician household might employ more than a hundred slaves so their monetary value represented a significant, if not the largest, portion of a man's estate. Even in societies that don't or didn't practice slavery, children are/were treated as the property of the head of the household.

a modern toy store. Particularly important milestones in the social construction of childhood that Sommerville notes include the following:

- The Spartans adopting the first deliberate, Skinnerian-style childrearing system.
- Roman emperor Constantine outlawing infanticide in 318 CE.
- The establishment of church-run foundling homes from the eighth century CE.
- From the thirteenth century, humanists decrying the use of corporal punishment.
- Martin Luther advocating universal schooling.

Barbara Hanawalt, exploring various textual sources, finds ample evidence of children in the medieval period, and, in fact, is able to document consistent variation in children's lives as a function of their parents' social standing: "By 1400 professional toy-makers had shops in Nuremburg and Augsburg and began to export their wares to Italy and France. Manor children also played chess and backgammon and learned falconry and fencing" (Hanawalt 1986: 208).

To be sure, as Shahar's meticulous study shows, illness, high infant mortality, and the need to become self-sufficient, or, at least, to unburden one's parents, at an early age, meant that childhood with its carefree and pampered associations must have been rather short, for example "boys and girls, designated for the monastic life, were placed in monasteries and convents at the age of 5, and, in exceptional cases, even younger . . . " (Shahar 1990: 106). Or consider this story about early medieval "childhood." In 1180 CE, Agnes, daughter of King Louis VI of France, was sent off at eight to marry the heir to the Byzantine throne. At ten, she was widowed when her thirteen-year-old husband Alexius II was strangled by the usurper Andronicus. Not long after, she was married to Andronicus, who was only a few years shy of seventy. Three years later, she was widowed again when an angry mob tore her husband to pieces (Freely 1996: 141–142).

Ironically then, Ariès' insupportable claim that childhood is a relatively recent invention spurred an army of historians to unearth evidence of childhood in the past.

But why bother with childhood?

The majority of mammals progress from infancy to adulthood seamlessly, without any intervening stages . . . (Bogin 1998: 17)

Why does the chimpanzee, our closest relative (Diamond 1992), hover on the brink of extinction while we threaten to overrun the planet? Barry Bogin found an explanation in childhood as a "unique stage of the human life cycle, a stage not to be found in the life cycle of any other living mammal" (Bogin 1998: 17). As compared with the other apes, humans have much higher fertility which Bogin attributes to the crèche-like character of childhood. Its purpose is to provide a kind of holding pattern in which the child can be weaned – freeing the mother to bear another child – while it is still somewhat dependent on others.

Relative to chimps, humans are weaned early, when they've reached about 2.1 times their birth weight, at twenty-four months or even earlier. Chimps wean at five to six years and are independent and sexually mature soon after. So while female chimps must wait at least six to seven years between babies, humans can, under favorable circumstances, have another one every two years. And, with the advent of effective supplements for breast milk, that two years may drop to less than one.

But while they may be weaned at two or earlier, human children still need adult support and provisioning. Their brains, growing rapidly and gobbling up calories like mad, are still developing (Aiello and Wheeler 1995). Indeed, nutrients that fuel body growth in other species are diverted to the brain in humans (Bogin and Smith 1996: 705). Babies lack vital skills like speech. They are small, slow, and easy prey. They can't chew or digest adult foods. So, again, unlike most chimpanzee mothers who are often their child's sole caretaker, human mothers rely upon childcare assistance from the child's closest kin – the father, older siblings, and grandparents. Because their genes are proliferating in each of their wife/mother/daughter's children, their genetic interest is almost as great as hers.

Most textbooks on childhood posit an entirely different issue as the key. The common argument is that children require a prolonged period of dependency in order to acquire all the knowledge, skills, and strength they'll need as successful adults. But this view is colored, I believe, by the contemporary situation where our offspring remain "dependants" until they've completed college at twenty-one years and beyond. In our society, it really *does* take years to learn all you need to know to function as a competent and successful citizen. However, as I discovered in a comparative study in Papua New Guinea, learning the skills required of a swidden horticulturalist, for example, is not all that taxing (Lancy 1983: 119–122). Similarly, becoming a maize-cultivating Maya farmer is "*not* demanding in terms of *either* skill or strength and can be performed proficiently by children without a long period of training and education" (Kramer 2002b: 305).

Beyond subsistence activities, there's little evidence of an intellectually taxing village curriculum the child must master:

like many other peoples in Africa, the [agrarian] Moose have no indigenous tradition of reflective analysis of their own practices. They have a rich, elaborate religion, but no theology. They have a complex society, but no . . . sociology . . . they have virtually no mythology or cosmology. They have a sophisticated political system, but no political science. They live their lives in practice, but without any great interest in reflecting on it, analyzing it, or trying to explain it. (Fiske 1997: 3)

Fiske's ethnographic account of Moose (Burkina Faso) intellectual life is complemented by comparative analyses of cognitive development documenting a similar absence of evidence that village children routinely acquire more efficient, abstract thinking strategies. I refer to the results of extensive testing of cognitive development among several pre-modern societies in Liberia (Cole *et al.* 1971) and Papua New Guinea (Lancy 1983; 1989). In these communities, children aren't rewarded for being clever, smart, "doing it in their heads," being articulate, acquiring large amounts of information, or memorizing important texts by rote. On the contrary, they're rewarded for politeness, obedience, listening and observing, being seen and not heard.

Further, while the complete repertoire of skills and knowledge in the society may be extensive, the "basic" curriculum is typically quite limited. Among the Kpelle, a horticultural society in West Africa, the *mandatory* skill inventory that every "student" must master is quite small. A Kpelle girl will "study" how to fetch water in a container, pound rice with a pestle in a mortar to remove the husk, carry an infant on her back, keep toddlers from hurting themselves, and wash clothes on a rock in the stream. Boys will be required to learn even less (Lancy 1996).

The next point is that not only may the skill inventory be reasonably easy to acquire but children may have, for certain skills, a *decade* to get the job done. Recent studies have examined, in quite close detail, what it is that children need to learn in traditional societies and how long it takes them to learn it. Children learning to forage on the reef off Mer, an island in the Torres Straits, "reach the same efficiency as the most practiced adult by ages 10–14" (R. B. Bird and D. W. Bird 2002: 262–3). For the Hadza, a Tanzanian foraging society, "There is no indication that it takes long years of practice to acquire human foraging skills" (Blurton-Jones *et al.* 1997: 279). In comparative research on contemporary foraging peoples, Blurton-Jones and Marlowe aver that improvements in skill that occur as the child matures may be as likely assigned to increases in size and strength as to practice and learning. In other words, their findings "do not support . . . the practice theory" (Blurton-Jones and Marlowe 2002: 199).

A final reason to question the argument that childhood exists to provide a long period in which children can learn their culture is that the length of childhood varies so much cross-culturally (Hawcroft and Dennell 2000).[7] Ariès

---

[7] It is interesting that childhood was shorter for Neanderthals, but then their tool technology was also simpler than that of humans and, presumably, took less time to master.

was correct in noting that childhood is as much a cultural as a biological phenomenon.

A competing theory, most fully articulated by Eric Charnov, posits that childhood is all about health, vitality, and growth because the larger and more robust the animal, the longer the expected lifespan. Humans postpone child-bearing to exploit this potential in contrast to our primate cousins who dare not delay reproduction (Charnov 2001). The fitness loss associated with a delay in mating is offset by the gain in fertility later in life. That is, individuals who delay reproduction are often healthier and more productive and are able to bear and sustain more healthy offspring. However, this theory also suggests to me that, in modern society, the ready availability of food (clothing, shelter) makes a long period for physical development superfluous. Children are now capable of reproducing many years before they are intellectually, emotionally, and financially capable of functioning effectively as parents and many, alas, do so (Kotlowitz 1991)!

Not all scholars are ready to abandon the theory that childhood equals culture acquisition in favor of the theory that childhood equals growth and John Bock, in particular, has labored to reconcile these twin theories (Bock 2002b).

Outline of the volume

Societies take what are essentially straightforward, biologically grounded dispositions, for example puberty, or pregnancy, or menstruation, and weave around them the most intricate webs of custom, attitude, and belief. (Broude 1975)

In the remainder of this chapter, I highlight the contents of the subsequent chapters. Each chapter offers numerous examples from the rich archives on childhood from cultural anthropology,[8] primatology, archaeology, and history. Whenever possible, these sources are "triangulated," in order to gauge how old or widespread the phenomenon under examination might be. Themes are drawn, inductively, from the literature. For example, while all societies acknowledge stages or milestones in the child's development, there is considerable variation in how these are identified and marked. We will need to tease out the broad commonalities among many individual cases.

As patterns are noted, an attempt is made to identify the underlying forces that shape them. In some cases, biological fitness is a proximal force, in oth-ers, subsistence systems can be linked to aspects of childhood. Childhood in foraging bands looks different from childhood in farming communities. In yet other cases – object play by very young children, for example – we find true biological universals at work. And, obviously, there are aspects of childhood

---

[8] I draw, in particular, on examples from my own fieldwork, especially in Liberia, Papua New Guinea, and Mormon Utah.

that are uniquely driven by non-instrumental aspects of culture such as the first haircutting rite of passage.

Each chapter also features contrasts drawn between dominant, modern views on a particular aspect of childhood and views derived from the sources mentioned above. Often, we will see the contemporary view as being at odds with wider, older patterns and seek to explain how changes in the nature of parenthood and the exigencies of the modern, information economy have changed the nature of childhood. Contrast will also be drawn between the children observed by anthropologists working in intact, self-sufficient villages and their contemporary counterparts living in societies racked by poverty, disease, and civil strife. While specific policy recommendations are not a feature of this book, analysis of existing policy initiatives such as *No Child Left Behind*[9] from an anthropological perspective will be found in every chapter.

How do children happen?

Much of this book is about the interplay of biology and culture. It is my fond hope that readers will discover aspects of childhood influenced profoundly by biology which they assumed were all about "nurture," and vice versa. Most people are familiar with the answer to the above question fashioned from biology; an answer from anthropology is less assessable. Consider that, while the average age of first pregnancy in the USA edges above twenty-five, in some areas of the country pregnancy at fourteen is common and socially acceptable (Kotlowitz 1991: 88; Heath 1990: 502). Biology provides great latitude for culture to shape to its ends. But, as we'll see in chapter 2, this variation is neither random nor completely free from the laws of nature. In this particular instance, we see women in one segment of society delaying childbearing until they have reached a degree of economic self-sufficiency. And, in another, very different segment of society, we see women bearing children at an early age because their poor preparation for schooling limits their chance for economic self-sufficiency. Teenage mothers also recognize that childcare and economic support from their mothers, grandmothers, and boyfriends is most forthcoming when they're younger (Geronimus 1996).

The decision *To make a child* – the title of the second chapter – will be examined in all its variation and complexity. Using contrasting cases, like the pair just cited, we will identify key stakeholders in this agreement and try and understand their agendas.

Richard Dawkins' *The Selfish Gene* (1989) brought home to a broad audience the compelling drive for each organism to reproduce itself as often as possible. He argued that, in fact, living organisms are just the means by which genes

---

[9] Information obtained from www.ed.gov/nclb; accessed 4.18.07.

replicate. One measure of the importance we attach to successful transmission of our gene bundle is explored by Robert Wright in *The Moral Animal*. He reviews several studies that show parents' expressions of grief at the death of a child peak not in early childhood but rather at adolescence. By the teen years, a parent has made nearly 100 percent of their investment in the child and will receive, if it perishes, zero genetic return (Wright 1994: 175–176).

We've already touched on the relative reproductive success of chimps and humans but, cross-culturally, there will be great inter-species variability among *Homo s. sapiens*. Societies that have reached the carrying capacity of their territory – increasingly the case – must either find ways to limit growth voluntarily or face famine, civil war, and genocide. Similarly, individuals must make difficult decisions regarding reproduction depending on their personal and material wellbeing.

Furthermore, thanks to the brilliance of Robert Trivers (1972; 1974), we now realize that mothers, fathers, and children have differing agendas. The nursing child wants to be the *last* child his mother will ever have so that he can enjoy her care and provisioning exclusively. The father will be opportunistic in seeking mating opportunities and display a similar fickleness towards the provisioning of his offspring. He will, in other words, spread his investment around to maximize the number of surviving offspring. The mother has the most difficult decisions of all. She must weigh her health and longevity and future breeding opportunities against the cost of her present offspring, including any on the way. She must also factor in any resources that might be available from her children's fathers and her own kin network.

In a majority of the world's diverse societies, women continue as workers throughout pregnancy and resume working shortly after the child is born. This work is physically demanding so, for many, there is a peak period in their lives when they have the stamina and fat reserves to do their work *and* have babies. How many babies they successfully rear will depend heavily on their access to a supportive community of relatives who can help with household work, assist with childcare, and provide supplementary resources. Hence a woman's "fitness" or the number of her offspring who survive and reproduce themselves is at least partly a function of her social skills, her ability to recruit allies.

Another factor to take into account is infant mortality. Until recently, as many as one infant in three didn't survive until its first birthday. Typically women operate from an estimate of the ideal number of offspring and increase their fertility by a factor that reflects the incipient rate of infant mortality. If the world is perceived today as overcrowded, the blame might be placed on the disconnect between public health measures, like child vaccination and sterile obstetrics procedures, which sharply reduced infant mortality, and the reproductive calculus of millions of individual mothers. These mothers continued to use the old "ideal" as the benchmark for gauging how many children to have – Olusanya (1989) refers to them as "fertility martyrs." The agencies that intervened to reduce infant mortality were not as ready with contraception and family-planning interventions and the result – masses of humanity living on the ragged edge of poverty.[10]

Adults are rewarded for having lots of offspring when certain conditions are met. First, mothers must be surrounded by supportive kin who relieve them of much of the burden of childrearing so they can concentrate their energy on bearing more children. Second, those additional offspring must be seen as "future workers," on farm or in factory. They must be seen as having the potential to pay back the investment made in them as infants and toddlers, and pretty quickly, before they begin reproducing themselves. Failing either or both these conditions, humans will reduce their fertility (Turke 1989). Foragers, for whom children are more of a burden than a help, will have far fewer children than neighboring societies that depend on agriculture for subsistence (LeVine 1988).

As a society modernizes, economic opportunity may require the loosening of ties to one's extended family. Working parents who have moved away[11] from supportive kin must shift to a strategy of bearing fewer children on whom they lavish much attention. As sole caretakers, parents must forge stronger emotional bonds with their child and these become scaffolding for the child's socialization. The net result is that parents take advantage of modern contraception options and only give birth to children they can "afford." This pattern has become a worldwide phenomenon and is referred to by demographers as the "Great" transition (Caldwell 1982) leading to dramatically lower birth rates.

Lastly, we will visit the *Brave New World* of contemporary reproduction practices including such issues as infertility treatments and teenage sex. We will see long-standing and universal relationships between marriage, reproduction, and childrearing give way to more varied arrangements.

Balancing the equation

In the fall of 2004, Martha Stewart – the fashion arbiter of middle-class American culture – may have been languishing in jail in West Virginia,[12] but she had not neglected the urgent needs of her constituents – especially those who are parents. The Halloween edition of her *Catalog for Living* had nineteen

---

[10] Although the US Congress has approved a $34 million dollar annual US contribution to the United Nations Population Fund, President George W. Bush, adhering to the fundamentalist Christian agenda, has withheld the funds throughout his term.

[11] According to *The Current Population Survey*, more than 40 million Americans moved between 2002 and 2003. Information obtained from www.census.gov; accessed 4.18.07.

[12] The case grew out of an insider trading investigation but she was convicted for perjury and obstruction of justice.

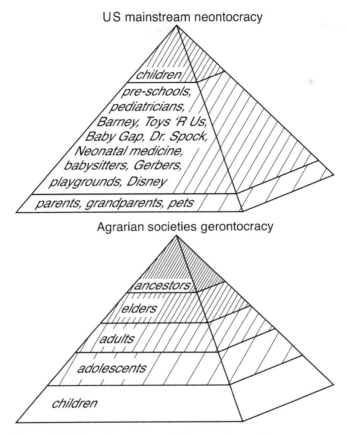

US mainstream neontocracy

children
pre-schools,
pediatricians,
Barney, Toys 'R Us,
Baby Gap, Dr. Spock,
Neonatal medicine,
babysitters, Gerbers,
playgrounds, Disney
parents, grandparents, pets

Agrarian societies gerontocracy

ancestors
elders
adults
adolescents
children

Figure 1 Child-centered versus child-supported society

pages of "ideas" for the child-centered family (e.g. Halloween character cookie cutters for joint baking activities). Featured items include "bat garlands" ($24), "pack of rats" ($24), and "ancient tombstones" ($57 for a set of three). Costumes range from "bat" ($39) to "mummy" ($49) to "chicken" ($79). The Halloween-prepared household should budget several hundred dollars for this critical undertaking.

As we will explore in chapter 3, *A child's worth* varies widely across cultures, across social classes, even within a single family. While the norm for much of human history has been a society dominated by attention to the oldest members – a gerontocracy – our society is uniquely a *neontocracy*. Figure 1 graphically depicts this distinction (Lancy 1996: 13).[13]

[13] A vivid illustration of the phenomenon is child-proof packaging which is, usually, senior-proof as well.

While evolution works on the behavior of individuals, we are subject to the dictates of society as well. In the Canadian north, Inuit adolescents are encouraged to follow the signals of their hearts and hormones and the inevitable result – an infant – will be welcomed by the community of foragers (Condon 1987: 98). For Berber adolescents, similar behavior may result in a death sentence for all concerned, including the infant. Louise Brown who, thirty years ago, became the world's first "test-tube baby" can be contrasted with the unnamed infants born to impoverished mothers in northeast Brazil studied and befriended by Nancy Scheper-Hughes. Louise might carry the title "most wanted child" considering her parents' ardent pursuit of a child and society's willingness to support their quest. In contrast, the Brazilian babies are so unwelcome that their mothers, in effect, starve them to death and no one – save the gringo anthropologist – is at all concerned (Scheper-Hughes 1987b).

In rural Bangladesh, children are expected to help out with farming and household work, and by age fifteen the breakeven point is reached: parents can now turn a "profit" on them. Girls, however, often marry before fifteen, and their marriage requires the payment of a dowry, while young men, obviously, bring in dowry when they marry. Not surprisingly then, infant/child mortality is three times higher for girls than for boys (Caine 1977).

I use admittedly extreme examples to make the point that for much of human history, children were, and still are in most of the world, treated as a commodity. Children enhance their parents' inclusive fitness (e.g. reproductive success), they assist with the care of younger siblings, and they do farmwork. They may be sold into slavery, sent to urban areas to fend for themselves in the streets, or their wages incorporated into the family's budget. In the Middle Ages, children were donated to the church as oblates to intercede with the divine on behalf of their parents. And, most extraordinary to our sensibilities, children in many societies were sacrificed to insure favorable attention of the gods.

An assortment of reliable contraceptives allow Euroamericans to "choose" how many children to have and when to have them. In much of East Asia, parents easily go one step further and choose the sex of the child they will have. This is a luxury our predecessors and those in the developing countries did not and do not have. Cruder means are used to "plan" one's family. Pregnancy creates only the potential for a new citizen, but can the community afford this new member? Under unfavorable circumstances, the mother, her husband, or the community will take the decision to withdraw their support. Is the child's paternity in doubt? Neither the husband nor his kin will be eager to provision an outsider's child. It is extremely rare to find cases of obviously deformed or sickly infants being kept alive. Even mature children may be put to death if their parents die or abandon them. Our own society has taken an extraordinary position of tolerance for costly children, yet instances of child abuse, abandonment, and murder are not unknown.

The unwanted child may be removed during pregnancy, but abortion is rare (except where protected by law and modern clinical practice) because of the danger to the mother. Removal may occur at birth (infanticide) or shortly after via abandonment – which may result in adoption or death. Abandonment was the preferred method of divesting oneself of an unwanted offspring throughout much of antiquity, was legal and, in some respects, was facilitated by the authorities.

In societies where legal constraints on these practices exist, infanticide may be delayed until a more discrete opportunity presents itself such as "accidental" suffocation in bed at night. In earlier times, the "difficult" or unwanted child might be dubbed a *"changeling"* or devil-inspired spirit, thereby providing a blanket of social acceptability to cloak its elimination (Haffter 1986). In cases where mothers are forced to rear unwanted children, the young may suffer abuse severe enough to end their life. While our society may treat such behavior by the parent as a heinous crime, "This capacity for selective removal in response to qualities both of offspring and of ecological and social environments may well be a significant part of the biobehavioral definition of *Homo sapiens*" (Dickeman 1975: 108).

Once the neonate is past the gauntlet of birth trauma, illness, and deliberate termination, it will be welcomed joyfully by its kin. On the other side of the equation, the child has inherent value as a bearer of its parents' (and extended family's) genes and as a contributor to the household economy. As soon as it is able, it will find a niche as a caretaker for its younger siblings, as a living "scarecrow" chasing birds from the ripening crop, or as a street-seller, hawking its mother's wares.

With industrialization, a child's potential worth grows as it can now augment the family account with wages it earns through regular employment. Growing wealth in the society at large also expands opportunities for the employment of the young in "domestic service."

But then, 150 years ago, the idea of the useful child began to give way to our modern notion of the useless but also priceless child (Zelizer 1985). Children become innocent and fragile *cherubs*, needing protection from adult society, including the world of work. Their value to us is no longer measured in terms of an economic payoff or even genetic fitness but in terms of complementing our own values – as book lovers, ardent travelers, athletes, or devotees of a particular sect. But I hope the reader will be brought to question attempts to export our child-centered utopia to the rest of the world, which cannot afford to ignore the economic costs and benefits of having children.

Helpers at the nest

In middle-class Euroamerican society, we take conception, pregnancy, child-birth, nursing, and infant care largely for granted. The real work of the parents, their job, if you will, begins when the child starts to become vocal, mobile, and capable of learning.

In most of the rest of the world and in the historical record, this distribution of responsibility is skewed in exactly the opposite direction. That is, conception is critical because the assurance of paternity determines whether the husband or partner and his kin will provide resources and care for the infant *or* abandon the mother and/or the child (Wilson and Daly 2002). Pregnancy is a critical period because of the threat of miscarriage, stillbirth, and birth defects. Pregnant mothers are ringed around with taboos, and among the most common is the proscription against intercourse during pregnancy or "soon" (maybe up to three years) afterwards. Childbirth is critical because of the enormous risks faced by both mother and newborn (Hern 1992: 36). Again, most cultures mark this critical rite of passage with ritual, folk medicine, and taboos. For the subsistence-farming Semai people, living in the forests of Malaysia, death in childbirth accounts for 50 percent of adult female mortality and "Puerperal blood and afterbirth are so dangerous that people use euphemisms to talk about them" (Dentan 1978: 110–111).

Nearly all societies hold very strict views on the necessity for almost constant contact between a mother or other nurturing adult and the infant. They are fed on demand, carried constantly, and sleep with their mother. Young mothers are severely chastised for any lapse in infant care. However, once the infant begins to walk, it immediately joins a social network in which its mother plays a sharply diminished role – especially if she's pregnant – and its father may play no role at all. Again, this is precisely the reverse of our views of what is normal.

The child is cosseted in a blanket of humanity, an idea captured by the African proverb *It takes a village* – the title of chapter 4. For example, an infant born to the close-knit Congolese forest-dwelling Efe may be nursed initially by its mother's relatives until she recovers from the childbirth ordeal (Tronick *et al.* 1987).

Once the infant has been judged worthy of rearing, it will be displayed to a community eager to interact with it. In particular, its older sisters will be in the forefront of those wanting to share in the nurturing process. The circle of caretakers may gradually widen to include aunts, grandmothers, and, occasionally, the father (Thomas 2001).[14] Even more distant kin can be expected

---

[14] While we all reacted with horror at the headline-making story of Andrea Yates drowning her four sons (aged two to seven) and six-month-old daughter in the bathtub, as the story unfolded it was possible to muster at least a glimmer of sympathy for her. By all accounts, Mrs. Yates

to cast a watchful eye on the child when it is playing on the "mother-ground" (Lancy 1996: 84). Indeed, the toddler must seek comfort from relatives as it may be abruptly weaned and forcibly rejected by its mother as she readies herself for the next child.

Moving from the village to the more complex societies of the ancient world, we see various "professionals," such as wet-nurses and tutors, helping at the nest. By the seventeenth and eighteenth centuries, responsibility for childrearing becomes more firmly placed on parents' shoulders. This occurs in response to increasingly modern notions that target the early years as being critical for imparting moral values and literacy. These views become accentuated by the demographic transition whereby smaller, more mobile families mitigate against sibling and grandparent caretakers. The rapid growth in knowledge pushes "education" earlier and earlier, ultimately into the nursery.

When is it a child… when does it stop being a child?

In the USA, stem cell research, considered by many as highly promising in the search for disease treatment, is hampered by funding restrictions imposed by President Bush. The rationale given is that the live human embryos from which stem cells are harvested are homunculi or persons in miniature.[15] For the fundamentalist Christians who hold this view, a human being begins at the moment of conception. In other societies, the individual isn't considered human until well after birth – as much as a year, in some cases: "among the Bororo (in Mato Grosso, Brazil) the naming process takes place only when it is detected that the baby is 'hardened' enough (usually some 5–6 months after birth). It is only through the naming ceremony that the child becomes 'socially born' and recognized" (Fabian 1990: 66). It must first be able to move steadily under its own power and communicate with other humans. Prior to being accepted as a fellow human, the child's death goes unremarked. If unwanted, it may be abandoned, smothered, or buried alive. In death, it will not be accorded burial with its kinfolk. Obviously, religion plays a part in creating these striking dichotomies of attitude but our extraordinary wealth is also a factor. We can *afford* to keep alive and nurture, at great expense, individuals that other societies would willingly let perish. Wealth is obviously relative and most Europeans and Americans don't consider themselves wealthy. But we are

was the sole caretaker and teacher (the children were home-schooled) of an infant and four active, obstreperous boys, and, at least emotionally, was not all that robust herself. A mother serving as the *exclusive* caretaker of such a large, closely spaced brood of children is almost unknown outside contemporary enclaves where fundamentalist religious values dictate family life.

[15] Julie Rovner, "Bush to veto stem-cell bill," National Public Radio, July 19, 2006: obtained from www.npr.org; accessed 4.18.07.

wealthy where it matters: we have a surplus of calories and can afford to feed (and clothe and shelter) far more mouths than we do. Contrast this with the following perspective, often recorded by anthropologists:

Regardless of how many hours they work at acquiring food, neither the Ache [of South America] nor members of any other foraging society can be shown to meet their food needs in any biological sense. Indeed, neither the Ache nor any other traditional people with whom we have worked in the past two decades agrees with the proposition that they obtain all the food they need. Instead they emphatically insist that they are hungry and would prefer more food (Hill and Hurtado 1996: 319)

We talk to our babies as if they were sentient. When the internal mechanisms of their metabolism (e.g. bowel movements) provoke a panoply of facial expressions, we rush to interpret meaningful responses. Elsewhere, societies – including European society until a few hundred years ago – treated babies as sub-human. Young children lack speech and control of bodily functions. They crawl on the ground and mouth whatever they find, all suggesting an animal of the lowest sort. For many they were seen as inherently sinful. These views tend to provoke one of two extreme responses. Benign neglect – waiting until the child can talk sensibly before acknowledging its existence – is sanctioned in many societies, as is the opposite response – ruthless suppression of all "sub-human" tendencies (e.g. bawling, crawling, thumb-sucking). And both socialization extremes work: they produce well-adjusted adults, with personae that fit their respective societies' ideals.

Two broad areas in the child's behavior may attract consistent intervention. Many societies consider it important to define unequivocally the child's gender and take various steps publicly to avow its maleness or femaleness. And a fair number of societies intervene directly to shape children's demeanor ("manners") towards those whose rank and/or kinship require appropriate recognition. Etiquette may also include notions about reciprocity and altruism towards kin – attributes which may not develop without some form of instruction. But, by and large, children are free to absorb their culture through their own initiatives, such as in make-believe play.

The shift in attitude towards children who've "gotten sense" is often quite apparent. While schooling for us may begin with the fetus (if you can believe the hype about expectant mothers listening to Mozart), most societies don't see children as readily teachable until their cognitive and linguistic skills have matured. This change usually occurs during the fifth to seventh year and may correspond to eruption of the first molars. Children become capable of following directions, attending to and copying the correct behavior of others. And, even when no one actively teaches the child, it is expected to attend to the competent actions of more mature community members and to imitate what it sees. Imperfect at first, they will keep practicing until, with perhaps the merest acknowledgment of their mastery, they are treated as useful participants in the household economy.

This readiness-to-learn transition will be of particular concern in chapter 5, *Making sense*. It will concern us because it provides a bridge to the broader issue of what we can call "folk theories of development." And differences in these folk theories, especially vis-à-vis how children become educated, in the sense of "book learning," help us to understand why many lose out in the race described in the penultimate chapter. For example, we can contrast village "incentives" to improve behavior, such as corporal punishment, shaming, teasing, and threats of demons, with the kind of encouragement, reasoning, and sympathetic scaffolding we employ to promote academic learning.

Let the play begin

The great Swiss psychologist Jean Piaget was noted for crafting ingenious experiments to tease out the child's underlying level of mental acuity. But when he wanted to describe the child's nascent ideas about morality and social convention, he focused on boys playing marbles (Piaget 1932) – hence chapter 6, on children's play, is titled *Of marbles and morals*. Piaget, however, was not alone in seeing play as a kind of "natural curriculum" for children.

Play is one of the few truly universal aspects of childhood. In the mammalian order, it is the rare species whose juveniles don't play. Gorillas at play, like many other primates, use trees as "jungle" gyms, tickle each other, play wrestle, chase each other, and play "king of the hill." Males beat their chests in imitation of their elders. A gang of juvenile mountain gorillas at play, in fact, look just like darker and hairier versions of their human counterparts (Lancy 2004).

The one thing that children can appropriate for themselves, without the sanction of culture or explicit blessing of parents, is play. It is ubiquitous. A baby will play with its mother's breast. The first glimmer of understanding about the natural world and how it works comes through play with objects. After its nurturing mother, the child's first close relationships are with its playmates – usually siblings. The child's first active engagements with the tasks which will occupy most of its adult life – hunting, cooking, house-building, baby-tending – all occur during make-believe. The games of youth are among the most mobile of cultural artifacts; "hopscotch" had diffused to every continent *before* the age of mass media and frequent flier tickets. In Puerto Ayora village, a tiny enclave of modernity in the great ocean wilderness called the Galapagos, children gather at an internet café after school to play computer games that are simultaneously engaging the attention of their counterparts in Quito, New York, and Tokyo. Growing up in the grimmest urban slum, kids will find opportunities to play with their mates. Dependants who are given a full menu of household chores from an early age still manage to weave play into their work.

Many of the child's most basic needs seem to be fed by play – their need to socialize with peers and their need for physical, sensory, and to a lesser extent, cognitive stimulation (Lancy 1980b). The demands of earning a living and reproduction gradually extinguish the desire to play. This happens earlier in girls than in boys – universally. However, where these demands are light, as, for example, with males in some segments of our society, play will continue unabated. While we take our children's play seriously, in traditional societies play's greatest value is that it keeps children distracted and out of adults' way. It is not looked upon as of special value in children's socialization.

Whatever benefits play confers, it also carries costs. Children may be injured or killed either by accident or by failing to attend to danger. They are squandering calorific energy, which, in a resource-poor society, may be in short supply. And their families may need them to assist with younger siblings or care for livestock (Lancy 2001). Children's play, in other words, looks remarkably similar over time and space but the latitude granted to children by adults will vary widely.

As in so many aspects of childhood, our society is not content to let nature take its course. The child's play is *managed* by adults. From a mother teaching an infant how to interact with "educationally oriented" objects to the highly charged atmosphere of professionally coached youth hockey, we capitalize on children's passion for play to pursue serious ends. These ends may range from inculcating the competitive ethos of the culture to fostering early literacy to affording parents cultural capital – bragging rights – with peers.

Earning your keep

Our society reacts with disapproval at the "exploitation" by parents of child models and actors. And yet, if one visits the area around Kisoro, a prosperous area in western Uganda, one will see far more young (four to eight years old) children working than playing. A four-year-old might be tending *His first goat* – the title of the seventh chapter – a proudly achieved milestone in his development. A slightly older brother drives a small flock of goats, a ten-year-old cousin tends a cow and calf, and so on up to the seventeen year old who's driving a herd of forty cattle to another pasture. Not only would the children see these "opportunities" in a positive light, their parents would wax eloquent on the many benefits to their children's character and maturation that animal husbandry provides. I've found several references in the literature to parents, semi-jokingly, referring to their "little slaves." Today, and even more so in the past, children may be treated as *chattel*. The *New York Times* recently reported numerous cases of impoverished families "marrying" pre-teen daughters to debt-holders, who conveniently forgive the debt (LaFranierie 2005).[16]

---

[16] LaFranierie (2005) article obtained from www.nytimes.com; accessed 4.18.07.

Chapter 7 will offer snapshots of children at work in a wide variety of societies leading to several critical generalizations. For example, the Hadza are more fecund than neighboring groups because children as young as four can meet a substantial part of their own nutrition by gathering and processing large quantities of baobab fruits. Since they take care of some of their own provisioning, their mothers can have another child more quickly (Blurton-Jones 1993: 405). We also note that, outside modern industrialized society, children are rarely *taught* these critical work skills. They learn them by observing older, more proficient individuals and trying out their fledging skills in make-believe play with miniature tools.

Societies vary in their need for child helpers, but most girls will be welcomed as "helpers at the nest," and a boy as young as four may be trusted with the care of a chicken. By eight or nine, a child might be working for more hours a day than it is playing, and it may be earning real money for its family through street sales and other odd jobs or a regular shift in factory, mine, or plantation. Most children are, in fact, quite eager for these opportunities to assume more adult responsibilities.

The chapter details the intricacies of various "chore" curricula from running errands/marketing to camel tending to bean cultivation. In each case we see realms of work conveniently staged into tasks of varying levels of difficulty so that even the youngest may assay to "help out." Older siblings act primarily as role models who only occasionally need to intervene in correcting a youngster's miscues. The acquisition of vital subsistence skills is a leisurely process, but, nevertheless, competency is achieved at a young age. Again our society is exceptional in that not only parents but also an army of highly paid professional teachers must devote hours each day to the child's instruction.

But what about those who don't voluntarily fall into line with expectations? For the "free spirits," truants, and "12 o'clock scholars" coercion is likely. An adult can earn no greater scorn from his/her peers than through failing to bind a child to their appointed tasks. In the hinterland Liberian village I studied, such children are said to have been born from their mother's anus (Lancy 1996: 76).

Somewhat later, the child may elect to move beyond the core skills expected of everyone to tackle more challenging endeavors such as learning pottery or weaving. S/he must demonstrate adequate strength, physical skill, and motivation before anyone will deign to spend time on his/her instruction. An apprenticeship escalates these demands and its coercive quality reinforces the high status of the master. Adults are reluctant to spend time in teaching and learners must make headway largely on their own.

Of course, in our society, schooling is the child's job. And we highlight its importance by putting our children in a classroom almost as soon as they're out of diapers. At an age when our children may be developing ever-more elaborate make-believe weddings with their Barbie dolls, girls in many societies are preparing for their arranged marriage, soon to be followed by their first pregnancy. As "Daddy's girl" accepts her college diploma, her counterpart in village Africa, pendulous breasts and wide hips testifying to her fecundity, is already bent from the strain of her heavy labors.

The central argument of the chapter is that children's work is seen by the entire society as perfectly natural and appropriate. However, as we follow this theme from the traditional village into the present, a different picture emerges. In rural areas where traditional subsistence practices are subverted by overpopulation, we see children working as virtual slaves on plantations and in mines. Alternatively, the rural village may export its surplus children to urban areas where they become street hustlers or poorly paid factory workers.

The perils of puberty

The enduring paradox of adolescence is that when children are biologically ready to claim the rights of adulthood – such as family formation – society is not prepared to grant them. But there's nevertheless the expectation that they'll give up the "games of youth." So they're *Living in limbo* (chapter 8), and they drive people crazy. Societies have devised various means for dealing with this problem. The pastoralist Masaai of East Africa send young men away from the compound to act as roving patrols; the Kpelle require youths to endure a challenging, four-year-long indoctrination in "bush school" before they're given the stamp of approval; Trobriand Islanders grant adolescents limited rights: they can have sexual relations but cannot begin to form their own households.

Like the childhood stage, adolescence is of variable length. Several factors, notably diet quality, influence the onset of puberty. Worldwide, the average age of menarche can be as low as twelve and as high as seventeen. Puberty for boys is delayed by a year or two relative to girls. Attention to and aroused feelings towards the opposite sex may begin even earlier. Indeed, by flirting with pre-pubescent girls, men may accelerate the onset of menarche and, consequently, the onset of breeding. Girls typically transition directly from their mother's "hearth" to their own; hence, adolescence as a social stage may be quite short. On the other hand, older men may resist younger men's access to post-pubescent females and/or marriage may carry steep financial requirements. In either case, delayed marriage and family formation will extend adolescence for males.

In most societies, adolescents are involuntarily assigned to their futures – as apprentices, as soldiers, as clerks in an office – and their marriages are arranged. Meanwhile, and until these new roles are assumed, their marginality can sometimes be of benefit to society. Living on the fringe of the community (literally in many cases), the risks they take may lead to the detection of useful resources or, alas, lurking dangers – a pattern found widely in the order *Primata*. "Gangs" of juvenile males are also a common sight in observations of primates.

During periods of rapid social change, adolescents may adopt new customs and survival strategies more quickly than adults and thus serve as a conduit for social change.

In our society, we are almost obsessed with marking off milestones in the child's development: birthdays, physiological events (sleeping through the night, first tooth, control of elimination), and, above all, the passage through academic grade levels. In the societies we'll be studying, such milestones are rarely noted. Nevertheless, even in the simplest societies, the child's transition to adolescence and/or adulthood may be marked by, sometimes elaborate, rites of passage. I will argue throughout the book that the norm for humans is to adopt a laissez-faire attitude towards the young – in sharp contrast to the anxious ministrations characteristic of our society. However, rites of passage signal broad and undeniable course corrections in the child's trajectory. The milestone is marked by the entire community. The child is treated differently; expectations have changed.

Circumcision rites that occur just before or after the onset of puberty apply a stamp of approval on the individual's "coming of age." Often, these signal a shift from permissive attitudes regarding the commingling of the sexes to the imposition of strict controls over – especially the girl's – sexuality. Societies where warfare is central use these rites of passage to forcibly wrench the boy from its mother's company and brutally indoctrinate him in the rigors and secrets of the male side of the culture. The process of conditioning and indoctrination may take years and, in a few cases, includes the reinforcement of a status quo where men are oppressively dominant over women.

Marriage is the succeeding rite of passage, but it may occur early in adolescence or quite late. Where virginity is highly valued, girls will be married at the onset of puberty. In warrior cultures marriage is delayed for young men. In any case, marriage is usually tightly controlled as it involves the transfer of wealth between families.

As these customs give way in the face of missionary and government intervention and the spread of modern communication, the transition to adulthood changes. Frequently this has meant a lessening of the influence of adults over the next generation, and the oral transmission of traditional culture is imperiled. In its place, adolescents appear to adopt a universal culture that is heavy on *Coca-Cola*, pop music, and, above all, school attendance.

Spelling your way to success

The enormous variety of children's pathways must all converge, in the modern era, on the school or at least the examination that measures one's progress up the academic beanstalk. The extraordinary success in the USA of Indian immigrant parents in scaffolding their children's climb up the beanstalk – as documented, for example, by ethnographer Margaret Gibson (1988) – will come as no surprise to fans of the National Spelling Bee (Blitz 2002). Indian-American children have been consistent winners; their toughest opponents usually are other Indian-Americans.[17]

While Indian-American spellers are making news, so too are child soldiers in Liberia. Their "careers" also began in school. For these youngsters, public schooling gave them aspirations without skills. They received indoctrination without any real education (Lancy 1975). Migrating to the city, after a few years of warming a bench, poorly taught in a poorly equipped classroom, they expect a wage-earning job. There are no jobs for illiterates so they drift into the hands of a rebel chieftain – always eager to recruit angry young men who don't ask questions. Having rejected their natal culture and unsuccessfully assimilated to urban society, they're in the worst sort of adolescent limbo (Lancy 1996: 194).

These two cases represent two illustrative extremes of successful and unsuccessful adoption of formal education. In chapter 9, the intervening points will be filled in. But the goal will be to apply the lessons we've learned about children in culture to try and untangle the all-too-evident patterns of success and failure in public schooling. In much of the world, including cities in the so-called Third World,[18] middle-/upper-class parents who want to shield their children from unmotivated peers and unchallenging classes can enroll them in private schools or move to a suburb with good public schools. This latter strategy is somewhat facetiously implicated in the title of chapter 9 – *How schools can raise property values*.

We will review numerous ethnographies documenting the adaptation patterns displayed cross-nationally – Japan versus the USA, for example. In addition, there are studies showing the school-adaptation strategies employed in various sub-cultures within the developed countries – immigrants versus natives, for example. Anthropologists have also been at the forefront in documenting the gradual diffusion of formal schooling around the globe and the adaptive strategies that villagers bring to this very foreign institution.

---

[17] Information obtained from National Spelling Bee website: www.spellingbee.com; accessed 4.18.07.

[18] The term "Third World" has come under attack on ideological grounds. However, there is really no objective, non-ideological term to take its place. "Developing countries" sounds better but is wildly inaccurate because many countries so designated are not "developing" in any positive sense. "Third World" remains widely used and widely understood to apply to countries where the average standard of living, if not falling, is rising very slowly. As I use it, the term does not specifically assign "blame" for this state of affairs. "First World" describes nations where the majority enjoy a high standard of living or, in a rapidly expanding economy, can anticipate improvement in the future. Of course, nearly all First World nations harbor significant minority populations who live in Third World conditions.

Should children be happy?

Popular misconception would assign anthropology the exclusive role of studying the past. On the contrary, as we pursue the study of childhood in the present and project towards the future, we see anthropologists in the forefront of such efforts. The concluding chapter – *Suffer the children* – will catalog emerging issues in the lives of children that are likely to preoccupy policymakers in the coming years.

In the penultimate chapter our focus was on the portion of the world's children who may spend much of their childhood in a school. However, a significant number – perhaps half – of the world's children will experience little or no exposure to schooling. In the last chapter, we look at street children and those who are in near full-time employment – compensated or otherwise. Changes in family structure and parental roles, provoked by the spread of AIDS as well as broad social and economic upheaval, will be examined as they influence children's lives.

We will peek behind the curtain of adverse statistics on child wellbeing in the Third World to take note of the many children who have willingly abandoned their rural families in pursuit of hard cash. However paltry and hard won, these earnings afford access to consumer goods in an urban world far more varied and exciting than the village they left behind.

Children as hustlers, rascals, hooligans, street demonstrators, pan-handlers, and, above all, "rebel" soldiers provoke mixed reactions from the public (Qin 1997). It seems the closer one gets to these children, the less sympathy is felt and the more their status as targets of urgent public intervention is questioned.

The chapter concludes by enumerating the many contrasts between our popular assumptions about the nature of childhood and the picture constructed by using the lens of anthropology.

2 To make a child

Introduction

> Humans expend considerable effort competing for status, yet those who succeed in this effort often produce fewer offspring than those who fail. This would seem to violate a fundamental assumption of evolutionary theory... (Josephson 1993: 391)

This chapter is founded on a paradox or a series of paradoxes. In our own society we expect to have few offspring and to treat them almost worshipfully – yet our children suffer from a near epidemic of psychological disorders. Other societies welcome children – lots of them – and, in those societies, children may exist on the edge of starvation. In the wealthiest communities that can "afford" lots of children, the birth rate is low and vice versa. The traditional culture of the village affords a plethora of customs and taboos for the protection of the pregnant mother and newborn and these co-exist with customs that either dictate or at least quietly sanction abortion and infanticide.

While men and women must cooperate in creating a child, they may bring diametrically opposed perspectives to the corollary task of raising the child. This lack of congruence gives rise to the variation we see in family structure and function. We will be particularly interested in polygyny, the very common pattern where a single male controls a household consisting of multiple wives and their children.

Although fertility is almost universally valued, boys are sometimes valued over girls and vice versa. These valuations are influenced by the economic roles men and women fulfill. Female babies are devalued where women are prevented from contributing to the domestic economy. Factors like birth order – first-born girls are welcome as future helpers in raising the preferred sons – also come into play. In foraging societies, where children are dependent and unproductive well into their teens, fewer children are preferred. In horticultural, pastoral, and even industrial societies where young children can undertake farmwork, shepherd flocks, or do repetitive machine-work, women are much more fertile. Children may be seen as "little slaves" (Gottlieb 2000: 87).

In recent history, changes in the economic basis of society, in particular the need for workers to spend long years in schooling, has led to a demographic transition. Families make use of effective and inexpensive methods of contraception to reduce their fertility significantly. Children have been transformed from economic assets to liabilities to personally rewarding "projects." But not all segments of the world's population have made this transition, and late in this chapter, we'll examine two instructive cases.

Life in a neontocracy

Today, as perhaps never before, we are obsessed with kids. We come close to worshipping them in our family photo albums, vacation splurges, holiday giving, and even religious services. (Cross 2004: 4)

. . . my son Rob has a driver's license, despite being only 16, which, from my perspective, is the same as being a fetus. (Dave Barry, *Miami Herald*, February 23, 1997)

Viviana Zelizer details the gradual change over the past century, in Europe, North America, and East Asia, that transformed children from future farmers or factory workers – adding their critical bit to the household economy – to economically worthless but emotionally priceless cherubs: "While in the nineteenth century a child's capacity for labor had determined its exchange value, the market price of a twentieth-century baby was set by smiles, dimples, and curls" (Zelizer 1985: 171). Viewing our culture from afar, I see a *neontocracy*, in contrast to the *gerontocracy* I found in my study of a West African village – Gbarngasuakwelle – populated primarily by members of the Kpelle tribe (Lancy 1996: 13). In a neontocracy, kids rule. For example, our entire round of holidays, passed down over millennia, have nearly all become occasions to celebrate – and spend money on – children (Cross 2004: 6). Any cruise through the supermarket will bring one face to face with a weary, overweight, and unkempt mother, accompanied by her Barbie-doll-perfect daughter. In our child-centered society, moralists hurl invectives at mothers who work in lieu of constant attention to their offspring (Eberstadt 2004).

The idea of neontocracy also encompasses the trend to steadily lengthen that part of the life-cycle we call childhood. Nowadays, twenty-somethings – who would have married, established their own domicile, and sired several children in an earlier era – are still "in the nest" (Armstrong 2004). At the other end of the continuum, medical practice and the religious right have steadily advanced the point in the life-cycle when the conglomeration of embryonic cells is defined as a child.

We deny the dictates of our hormones to delay reproduction until we've created a well-furnished and stocked nest to nurture our "treasures." And, if nature then thwarts us and we are unable to bear our own children, we go to extraordinary lengths – traveling half-way around the world and spending our life savings – to adopt a baby that isn't even remotely representative of our own genetic and cultural heritage. If we step outside the dominant cultural perspective and view childhood in other contexts our reproductive practices seem quite strange. Perhaps more representative of "humankind" is the attitude expressed by the agrarian Sebei people of Uganda as recorded by American anthropologist Walter Goldschmidt. He says, reflecting the bias of his own culture, "It would appear that progeny are desired, but children are not particularly wanted" (Goldschmidt 1976: 244). Among the farming, West African Ashanti, childless adults are taunted and "the childless . . . after death had great thorns . . . driven into the soles of the feet . . . with these words . . . 'do not return again' " (Rattray 1927: 66–67).

Sparta, always hungry for military conscripts, punished men who married late by public humiliation and rewarded those who had sired three or more children (Cartledge 2003: 171). Older husbands were encouraged to have their wives impregnated by a younger, more robust man (French 1991: 15). Additional examples underscore the high value placed on fertility alongside a low value placed on children. For Hokkien-speaking villagers in East Asia: "The dominant theme of the marriage ritual is fertility and . . . yet . . . birth is considered unclean and actually dangerous to others" (Wolf 1972: 56). "One of the duties [Roman] citizens had to the state . . . was to produce heirs, but . . . this . . . was to increase . . . the privileged classes, not to encourage a love of children" (Boswell 1988: 58).

Bearing children is bound up with a more general preoccupation with fertility. Ceremonies and symbols link childbearing to the fecundity of domestic stock, crops, and wild game (Gray 1994: 92). So powerful is this imperative to "be fruitful and multiply" that it may lead to a Malthusian nightmare.[1] Nicholas Kristof bemoans the fate of six-year-old Aberash from a village in southern Ethiopia. Obviously starving, she's the youngest of seven children and least able to secure a share of the family's meager stewpot – even though Kristof observes that her father, "Like most parents . . . didn't seem malnourished (the father almost always eats first in these villages)" (*New York Times*, May 23, 2003: A25). Ethiopia, of course, has been racked by repeated drought and famine and Aberash and her six (living) siblings were all born *since* the devastating famine of 1984–1985.[2]

In the decision to create a child – whether in an Ethiopian village or elsewhere – *their* wellbeing and happiness is rarely the issue. In fact, reproduction decisions draw in many parties who bring strikingly different interests to the table.

---

[1] Irrationally high fertility in the face of crushing obstacles is not unknown in the developed countries, as the example of the Herrin family – see note 70 below – illustrates.

[2] As Davis notes, in a neighboring area, Darfur, "famine is part and parcel of ordinary social life, and is not a breakdown of normal social experience" (Davis 1992: 151).

One big unhappy family

Mating systems are not the same as marriage systems. (Low 2005: 16)

... the behaviours that make individuals successful in mating are often mutually exclusive of the behaviours that result in successful parenting. (Bereczkei and Csanaky 2001: 501)

Popular media are replete with rhetoric on the "dysfunctional" family and this has broadened to include any form of chronic conflict – even at a low level. In the section that follows, I want to make the argument that, as much as we might wish to see families as cooperating harmoniously for the common good, especially for the sake of children, in reality, members follow different agendas that inevitably clash.

In chapter 1 two ideas were introduced: the "selfish gene" (Dawkins 1989) and the competing reproductive interests of men, women, and children (Trivers 1972). The first idea leads to a big family; the second means it will be unhappy. Haley, a no-longer-young but unabashed single mother in the play *Bad Dates*, soliloquizes about one really bad date who, nevertheless, clearly expected that the evening would end in coupling:

we clearly did not LIKE each other, but he was willing to sleep with me anyway! He was absolutely planning on it! ... Don't you think that's interesting ... about the differences between the sexes: Men will happily have sex with someone they don't like. Women won't. (Rebeck 2003: 17)

According to current thinking in human reproductive biology, Haley is absolutely right: in the absence of powerful cultural restraints, men will sleep with any willing female, whereas women "play hard to get." Men and women have evolved fundamentally different reproductive preferences. Men, under ideal circumstances, will impregnate as many women as possible and invest only enough in their offspring to keep them alive (Mulder 1992: 362). Women, ideally, want fewer children, for the children's sake and to protect their own bodies. And they'd like the father or fathers of their children to be good providers. Many societies – even the most conservative – endorse men's promiscuity (*machismo*) and women's resistance (defending her honor). Other commonsense notions that have been confirmed by science include the tendency for men to use deception ("Of course I love you"), whereas "feminine wiles" include a range of tactics designed to unmask the male's intentions (Grammer *et al.* 2000).

Men, knowing what women are looking for, are likely to "show off." In a society where whale hunters rule the roost, "young women on [Nantucket] island ... pledged to marry only men who had already killed a whale. To help ... young women identify them as hunters, boatsteerers wore chock-pins ... on their lapels. Boatsteerers, superb athletes with prospect of lucrative

captaincies, were considered the most eligible of Nantucket bachelors"
(Philbrick 2000: 13). More subtly, in several societies where men hunt,
researchers have discovered some interesting facts. First, that hunters sometimes pass up easily captured small game to pursue larger, more spectacular prey. Second, that upon returning to the community, the hunter will conspicuously share his catch with other households (Blurton-Jones *et al.* 2005:
235). Third, successful, generous hunters enjoy more mating opportunities than
unsuccessful hunters (Hawkes 1991). Even when they can earn more calories for
their families through farming, men in several South American forest-resident
tribes prefer to hunt, because game provides a much more visible indicator of
one's ability to provision a woman and her children (Kaplan and Hill 1992:
189). In southern Africa, the !Kung San[3] explain that poor hunters will remain
bachelors because "women like meat" (Biesele 1993).

In another method of showing off – "baby-parading" (Lancy and Grove
2006) – fathers, who otherwise spend little time with their offspring, in effect
"borrow" them from their mothers to take on a stroll around the village. Here
are two examples:

among the Eipo [of Papua New Guinea (PNG)], fathers pick up their baby at the women's
area and carry it . . . for half an hour or so, getting friendly attention. (Eibl-Eibesfeldt
1983: 208)

His [Fijian] father does not play with him often, but occasionally he takes the child on
his back to attend a meeting or to visit a neighbor. (Thompson 1940: 39)[4]

A man who parades his healthy infant and demonstrates his own nurturing
personality may, like a show-off hunter, improve future mating prospects.[5]

Even in otherwise simple, egalitarian societies, such as the !Kung, violent
conflict arises – usually over access to women (Edgerton 1992: 71). The unend-
ing tribal warfare that anthropologists describe in unacculturated (and "unpaci-
fied") South American (Chagnon 1968) and Papua New Guinean (Gardner
and Heider 1969) groups is often sparked by the drive to add women to the

[3] A note on African terminology. The !Kung Bushmen are among the most heavily studied group
of people in the world and will be cited often throughout this book. However, there are other
related groups that have been studied and, collectively, these foraging peoples are call *San*. The
!Kung are referred to (more accurately) as *Ju/'hoansi* in more recent literature. Moreover, they
are no longer referred to as Bushmen, partly because the term has pejorative connotations, partly
because they no longer live "in the bush."

[4] Other examples: Covarrubias (1937: 132); Paulme (1940: 439); Messing (1985: 205); Elmendorf
(1976: 94); Hewlett (1991: 148).

[5] When I asked my research assistant, Annette Grove, to search Human Relations Area Files
(HRAF) for examples of baby-parading and explained what to look for, her responses was "Oh,
it's like a chick magnet?" It was several months later that I learned that her ex-husband had been
quite attentive to their children when company came, and he actually referred to the phenomenon
as a "chick magnet." As I present the concept to various audiences, other cases are volunteered.
For example, a male student reported how effective his decision to place a photo of his young
niece and nephew on his cell phone screen had been: "Works every time."

community. By the same token, diplomacy, marriage, and filiation customs are often rooted in the necessity to exchange women who have reached breeding age and thus avoid incest (inbreeding) (Fox 1972: 309). Open conflict between competing males is also avoided by the operation of mechanisms that create and reinforce relative rank. Among the Yanomamo of South America, those who have risen to the rank of chief have significantly higher inclusive fitness (Chagnon 1979).

Almost universally, young men are blocked from access to females[6] until they have been initiated into the society of older men (Fox 1972: 308); "proven their manhood" through success as hunters (Spencer 1970); successfully pursued an arduous spiritual quest (Benedict 1922); or they and their family have amassed sufficient "bride-price" (Rappaport 1967). Meanwhile, at the top of the pecking order, wealthy and/or powerful men via the mechanism of polygyny or multiple marriages can monopolize access to young women (Low 2005: 17).

However, the dominance hierarchy, while present in our species (Weisfeld and Linkey 1985: 110), plays much less of a role in the mating process than it does among our primate relatives (Strier 2003: 168–169). Neither the harem, where the ruler sequesters (guarded by eunuchs) a large number of females, nor a Don Juan,[7] riding about the countryside deflowering damsels, is common – hence their legendary status. Rather, every society exercises some control of mating via institutions such as marriage, rules governing property, and pre-scriptions for the living arrangements of men, women, and their children. Not that these institutions are ever 100 percent successful in suppressing the mating game.[8]

The alternative offered by marriage may reduce but certainly does not elim-inate the conflict provoked by competition between males and the differing tactics of men and women. Charges of adultery filled the "docket" in the town chief's court in Gbarngasuakwelle. A very typical case pitted an older husband, whose relative wealth enabled him to acquire a young wife, against a young lover – her ace in the hole, in the likely event her aged husband died and left her without resources (Lancy 1980c).

At the other extreme from societies where the bonds of marriage are "loose" are those where pre-marital relations and adultery, with the implications of

---

[6] The Ache may attack excessively randy young men in periodic group stick fights (Hill and Hurtado 1996: 227). An interesting exception to the tendency to keep young men from mating occurs in several tropical South American foraging groups, such as the Wari, where they are paired with a pre-pubescent girl. The young man's semen is seen as essential to bringing the girl to sexual maturity, just as his semen will, later, build his offspring in the womb (Conklin 2001).

[7] From his biography, it is obvious that the basketball star Wilt Chamberlain operated like a modern Don Juan, claiming thousands of conquests (Cherry 2004).

[8] Pat Draper and Henry Harpending offer two alternative strategies – dad vs cad – that capture much of the observed variation. That is, men can achieve high fitness either by devoting themselves to their wife (wives) and children, insuring high certainty of paternity and higher survival of offspring, or by playing the field (Draper and Harpending 1982).

illegitimacy, are treated as capital crimes. "Honor" killings continue to make headlines[9] as families rid themselves of daughters whose marriage prospects have been destroyed by unsanctioned sex (including rape). Husbands who fear they've been cuckolded appeal to Islamic courts which pass sentence of death by stoning.[10] Clitoridectomy, the surgical removal of a girl's genitalia, has, rightly, become a rallying point for international human rights (Wilson and Daly 2002: 302). The ostensible purpose is to protect the virtue of women and reduce the likelihood of illegitimacy by destroying any sexual desire they might have (Ciaccio and el Shakry 1993: 47–48).

Other oppressive restrictions imposed on breeding-age women include the medieval chastity belt (Potts and Short 1999: 92); full-length clothing and head covering such as the Iranian *chador* (Ansar and Martin 2003: 177); and virtual house imprisonment (*purdah*) for higher-caste Indian wives (Deka 1993: 126). In lower-caste marriages, the wife may be terrorized into fidelity through frequent beatings (Rao 1997). Among the Dogon of Mali, monitoring a woman's sexual activity is a community affair, specifically their menses are verified to insure that, prior to marriage, they aren't already pregnant by another man (Strassmann 1993). In China, higher-class women had their feet permanently deformed (foot-binding), in part symbolizing their virtual imprisonment (Wilson and Daly 2002: 301).

Anthropologists find that there is an inverse relationship between restrictions imposed on women and their economic contribution to the household. That is, where women's labor is critical, attitudes regarding fidelity are, necessarily, more relaxed. Women suffer these restrictions to preserve their virtue, even as a society valorizes the promiscuous male. Nevertheless, given the risks and wear and tear of promiscuity, men's long-term genetic interests may be served by faithful attachment to a mate (Hrdy 1999: 231) (or multiple wives in polygyny) and anthropologists have studied the calculus that comes into play in these decisions (Hill and Reeve 2004; Kanazawa and Still 2000): "males confront a problem of how to budget their reproductive efforts between seeking, courting, and contesting new mates, on the one hand, and doing whatever it takes to monopolize the ones already acquired, on the other" (Wilson and Daly 2002: 291). A man can be expected to remain in a relationship if his mate is fertile, bears healthy young that thrive, is a hard worker who provides a significant amount of the household's needed resources (Marlowe 2004: 365), and shows little interest in other males (Apicella and Marlowe 2004: 372). A woman's commitment is leavened by similar concerns, particularly that her mate should be a "good provider" and not harm herself or her children. Research affirms

---

[9] *Christian Science Monitor*, July 7, 2004: www.csmonitor.com; accessed 4.23.07.

[10] "Afghanistan woman stoned to death," April 23, 2005: http://news.bbc.co.uk; accessed 4.23.07.

that women show a clear preference for potential mates who are depicted as enjoying children (Brase 2006: 151).

Residence is also a contributing factor. Where couples reside "patrilocally" – with the husband's family – the husband can rely on his kin to keep a close watch on his spouse(s) and aid him in insuring the legitimacy of any offspring. Studies show that the father's kin are more likely to invest in children whose paternity is certain (Huber 2006). The "family," obviously, extends well beyond the husband, wife, and nurseling. There may be multiple wives (or, rarely, husbands), which we'll discuss shortly, and extended family members such as the husband's mother in residence. Grandparents may play a vital role in childcare. Indeed, among the Ache of South America, orphans are likely to be put to death unless rescued by grandparents (Hill and Hurtado 1996: 438). On the other hand, it is the rare mother or mother-in-law who does not attempt to usurp the wife's authority, and mothers-in-law are often identified as the primary culprits in the frequent bride-burnings in India.[11] Grandfathers may not be available to assist with childcare because, at least among the Hadza of East Africa, where divorce and multiple marriages are common, a grandfather is busy siring new children on his young wife (Blurton-Jones *et al.* 2005: 224).

In our hypothetical large, unhappy family, the unhappiest member may be the child who is being weaned. Robert Trivers (1974) formulated the theoretical version of what every harried parent knows, namely, that, at a certain point in the life-cycle, the interests of the child and its mother clash. The mother may be ready to begin investing in her next baby well before this baby is willing to give up the nutrition and comfort only the breast can provide. The mother is also eager to shed what has become a heavy appendage while the toddler is reluctant to give up a free ride and locomote on her own. The result of these conflicts can set the entire family on edge: "Mothers in all societies recognize aggressive behavior by the young child towards its follower as rivalry or jealousy . . . in the [East African] Kikuyu language, the word for the adjacent younger child has a stem meaning 'rival' " (Whiting and Pope-Edwards 1988a: 173). Nisa, a !Kung woman interviewed in old age, still held vivid memories of her life's great trauma: "Some mornings I just stayed around and my tears fell and I cried and refused food. That was because I saw him (brother) nursing. I saw with my eyes the milk spilling out. I thought it was mine" (Shostak 1976: 251).

Among all the ape species, temper tantrums by displaced juveniles are both likely and effective in garnering additional attention and food (Fouts *et al.* 2001: 31). An Inuit (Arctic foragers) weanling, confronted with her nursing sister, screams and carries on until her mother makes her second breast available

---

[11] It has become increasingly common in urban, middle-class settings for receiving families to exploit the inherent power they hold over families desperate to marry off their daughters. Demands for dowry escalate and, increasingly, the young wife is murdered so the family can obtain a second dowry from the family of another wife (Stone and James 1995).

(Briggs 1970: 157). Briggs recorded fascinating interchanges between toddlers and adults in which the latter encouraged consideration of siblicide, designed, apparently, to assist the child in vocalizing its jealousy (Briggs 1990: 35).

Even the new infant may be seen as threatening to its family. Throughout West Africa, infants are seen as arriving from a "beforelife" which they are reluctant to leave. Further, they may harbor "witch spirits who complicate pregnancy, labor and delivery" (Fermé 2001: 199).

As troublesome as they are, children just may be the glue that holds the family together. Sarah Hrdy argues persuasively that humans, like a number of other species (e.g. wolves), are cooperative breeders (Hrdy 2005).[12] Following Bogin's theory, touched on in the previous chapter, human fertility is enhanced, relative to other apes, because our young, while yet immature and not entirely self-sufficient, can manage just fine without the attentions of their mother, who is free to have another child (Bogin 1998). They survive through the care of other family members, a phenomenon which we will examine in chapter 4. Another critical human trait, missing in other primate species, is the sharing of food. Older individuals – of both genders – routinely share food with younger individuals (Lancaster and Lancaster 1983). And men share food with women they'd like to mate with, who, in turn, share with their offspring. The care and feeding of children, then, may have been the *raison d'être* for the creation of families as we know them.

Love the one you're with

Females are also actively manipulating information available to males about paternity. (Hrdy 1999: 88)

... it is a wise father that knows his own child. (Shakespeare, *The Merchant of Venice*, Act II, sc. ii, 73–74)

Kpelle social fatherhood is a complex matter often involving intrigues far beyond the simple fact of biological relationships. (Bledsoe 1980a: 33)

It would be a mistake to view women as without resources in the mating game. Beauty may be in the eye of the beholder, but physical attractiveness or sex appeal has long been a woman's weapon of choice. In studies conducted in the USA, physically attractive women are more likely to delay the onset of sex and "hold out" for a higher-ranking male (Elder 1969). Mende women of West Africa "are especially proud of their full, rounded buttocks, displayed to advantage in the way they tie their clothes, and in dance ... [they] display [their] full rounded contours in a message of fecundity" (MacCormack 1994: 112).

---

[12] Referring to an Iñupiat band, Bodenhorn would concur: "In this highly mobile society, children are the most fluid" (Bodenhorn 1988: 9).

Women may have an interest in concealing their ovulation cycle to maintain discretionary control over the onset of pregnancy. Unlike other primates, female humans are never conspicuously estrous. They are almost continuously available as sex partners and reproductive targets. And this phenomenon has been used to explain the origin of male–female pair-bonding that is absent in chimpanzees, for example. That is, if men want frequent sexual access and want to prevent others from access, they had better "stick around" (Alexander and Noonan 1979) to ward off suitors. Another common tactic used by new mothers is to exaggerate the resemblance between the newborn and their husband (Apicella and Marlowe 2004: 372). Studies in our monogamous, adultery-condemning society have shown that 10 percent of men designated as the biological father of a particular child are not (Buss 1994: 66–67).

One of the more interesting and extreme manifestations of this, often deliberate, obfuscation is called "partible paternity." Among the Kpelle, the child is said to resemble "individual men in proportion to the number of times the mother has had intercourse with them" (Bledsoe 1980a: 33). In foraging societies found over a large area of South America, cutting across geographical and language barriers, babies are said to be "made" by everyone who has intercourse with the mother. While the "real" father is the individual who was most closely linked to the mother on the eve of delivery, a strategic female, once she's conceived, will seduce (Hrdy 1999: 35)[13] several good hunters (Crocker and Crocker 1994: 83–84) who will then be designated "secondary" fathers. These men constitute an insurance policy in the event the primary father dies or reneges on his obligations, and they are referred to by the same term as the primary father (Hill and Hurtado 1996: 249–250). This strategy apparently is effective: studies of the Bari – South American forest dwellers – demonstrate that children with multiple fathers have a higher survival rate than those with one (Beckerman et al. 1998; Beckerman and Valentine 2002). On the other hand, among the Ache, "too many" fathers can nullify the insurance policy in terms of men's willingness to support an orphan (Hill and Hurtado 1996: 444).

While it is always in the woman's interest to maintain a relationship with a reliable provider, it isn't necessarily in her interest to bear as many children as he would like to sire. Each pregnancy, birth, and infant nursed and carried to toddler-hood takes a huge physical toll on a woman's body. If "sex appeal" was a factor in securing her first mate, bearing multiple children will rapidly erase

---

[13] Hrdy, from her research with Hanuman langurs, noted that females were promiscuous, mating with males other than the alpha male, as opportunity permitted. Given this, coupled with the fact that newly dominant males routinely kill the infants sired by their deposed rivals, it seemed obvious that the mothers were protecting their offspring by obscuring paternity. Males rarely kill their own offspring. See also Sugiyama (1967).

that asset. Her own health and the wellbeing of present and future children may all render conception at a particular time unpropitious. If fortunate, she may have access to herbal contraception with some degree of effectiveness (Lindenbaum 1973: 251).[14] In the Sepik area (PNG), *kip*, "magic" bark from a tree, is eaten by women to successfully prevent conception (Kulick 1992: 92). The Hottentots from southern Africa had several abortifacients in their pharmacopoeia (Schapera 1930). In the high Andes of Peru, modern forms of contraception are not available; hence villagers "rely on traditional knowledge to prevent conception" (Bolin 2006: 16–17).

Abortion and infanticide, prior to the influence of Western morality, would have been widespread (Ritchie and Ritchie 1979: 39). However, the mother may need to conceal her actions from her husband and his kin because contraception or abortion is often seen as a tacit admission of promiscuity (Einarsdottir 2004: 69).[15] One strategy for family formation that may work to reduce these conflicts is polygyny.

Polygyny as the great compromise

. . . polygyny was quite common across past human societies . . . the practice had adaptive value under a range of conditions, and . . . this remains true for individuals in populations where it persists. (Sellen 1998b: 331)

. . . each wife of the [Ottoman] sultan was known as kadin, which means simply "woman," [however] the two who were the first to bear sons . . . took precedence as first (birinici) and second (ikinci) kadin. (Freely 1996: 195)

Contemporary Euroamerican society, being heavily influenced by Christian traditions, values monogamy highly. To support this "unnatural" condition, we've evolved elaborate wedding ceremonies, neolocal residence (husband and wife establish their own residence away from his/her parents), and the pervasive culture of romantic love. Polygyny, as the special form of polygamy in which a man may be legally married to more than one woman, is much more "natural," or at least far more common. Estimates range from 85 percent (Murdock 1967: 47) to 93 percent (Low 1989: 312) of all societies ever recorded (about 1,200) having practiced polygyny. The proportion might be even higher if we were to include foraging societies where egalitarian relations between and within the sexes all but preclude polygyny, but where divorce and remarriage

[14] Lindenbaum also discusses *clusters* of cultural practices that either promote or reduce overall fertility and indicates that these are mediated by resource availability. In Papua New Guinea, the Dobu and others embrace beliefs and practices that increase fertility while the Enga and others share customs that mitigate against high fertility.

[15] Similar views are characteristic of the religious right in contemporary America. Information obtained from www.theocracywatch.org; accessed 4.23.07.

are so common they are said to practice "serial monogamy" (Marlowe 2007: 179).[16]

The compromise arises because men are able to translate wealth and power into breeding opportunities while reducing the perils associated with the Don Juan model. Women in a polygynous relationship gain access to a higher-ranking, reliable provider at the cost of emotional strain in sharing resources (including the husband's affection) with others. In one study, children of senior wives were better nourished than children in monogamous unions who were, in turn, better nourished than children of later wives (Isaac and Feinberg 1982: 632). A woman must weigh the trade-offs between marrying a young man in a monogamous union or marrying an older man and joining a well-established household as a junior wife. Studies show that, if they choose monogamy, they enjoy slightly higher fertility (Josephson 2002: 378) and their children may be somewhat better nourished (Sellen 1998b: 341). However, they are, perhaps, more likely to be abandoned or divorced by their husbands.

Anthropologists have documented the, potentially negative, impact on children of the decline in polygyny. In Uganda, monogamy has led to less stable marriages. A man, rather than bringing a second wife into the household, now abandons the first wife and her children to set up a second separate household with his new mate (Ainsworth 1967: 10–11). A typical case among the Nyansongo, Kenya, describes a mother, whose childhood was spent in a large polygynous compound where multiple caretakers were always available, who must cope alone in a monogamous household. She leaves her three-year-old to mind her six-month- and two-year-old infants as she performs errands like bringing the cow in from pasture. Unfortunately, the three-year-old is simply not mature enough for this task and is, in fact, "rough and dangerously negligent" (Whiting and Pope-Edwards 1988a: 173).

Older wives in polygynous unions may find they are ignored and their share of the family larder may diminish, but they're rarely evicted. Indeed, living quarters in polygynous unions are often constructed to facilitate the rearrangement of the female pecking order (Altman and Ginat 1996: 214), as brilliantly depicted, for example, in the Chinese film *Raise the Red Lantern* (Yimou 1991). On the other hand, separate and distinct living quarters may also signal the autonomy and upward mobility available to women. West African women, in particular, often parlay their high status in polygynous households into important positions in the community. They become the managers of the, sometimes substantial, household economy and can direct the labor of their co-wives, their children, and any extended kin (Clark 1995).

---

[16] Actually, among South American foragers, sexual relations are even more fluid, and fidelity is not routinely expected of either partner (Howard Kress, personal communication, February 7, 2007).

In monogamous marriages, divorce is always a threat.[17] It is most often precipitated by infertility or loss of fertility – Henry VIII's divorce of Catherine of Aragon a well-known case in point. Adultery is almost universally considered legitimate grounds for divorce (or worse: Henry VIII had wives 2 and 5 beheaded). But far more prosaic reasons can be found. As societies become more mobile and men migrate seeking employment, the likelihood that the male will abandon (or neglect) his family in the village in order to establish a new family in the city is increasingly common (Bucher and D'Amorim 1993: 16; Timaeus and Graham 1989). And, perhaps most common of all, women whose fertility is on the decline are replaced by younger wives in peak breeding condition (Low 2000: 325), popularly referred to today as "May to December" unions.

The abandoned spouse and her children may face severe difficulties. One might think that an obviously fertile woman would be a "catch," but "Having a child towards whom a new husband will have to assume step-parental duties diminishes rather than enhances a women's marriageability" (Wilson and Daly 2002: 307).[18] In the case of a young, pregnant widow, Roman law permitted both annulment and the exposure of the infant in order to enhance her chances of remarriage (French 1991: 21). Raffaele describes an unfortunate case in a Bayaka[19] foraging band in Central Africa: "Mimba had been in a trial marriage . . . her partner's father had refused to pay the bride price and she had just been forced to return to her own family. She is two months' pregnant, and it is a disgrace for an unmarried Bayaka woman to give birth" (Raffaele 2003: 129). Fortunately for Mimba, the tribe's pharmacopoeia includes *sambolo*, a very reliable and safe herbal abortifacient[20] which she will use. Mimba will return to the pool of eligible mates and, hopefully, will find a family willing to pay bride-price so their son can join her in raising a family – something she could not accomplish by herself.

---

[17] In the USA, the divorce rate hovers around 38 percent. Information obtained from www.divorcereform.org; accessed 4.23.07.

[18] As marriage becomes more fragile, women face a classic Catch-22. If they have "too few" children, they're in danger of being divorced for low fertility. If, on the other hand, they have "many" children and are abandoned by their spouse, they face the prospect of being unable to support their "large" brood.

[19] The Bayaka are just one of several foraging peoples of the Central African rainforest to be cited in this book. Others are Efe, Aka, M'Buti, and Bofi. Aside from sharing the rainforest habitat and a minimal material culture, all these people also evince an unusually short stature, and were referred to as *pygmies* – a term now considered pejorative. All of these groups also live in a symbiotic relationship with sedentary farming peoples. Collectively, they represent several unique adaptations of special interest to students of culture and childhood.

[20] From an evolutionary perspective, abortion seems quite straightforward and predictable. Women will seek the means to abort the fetus if they are unwell, if they lack a support system, if they're living with a man who is not the father of their fetus, and, especially, if their future prospects of bringing a child into a supportive environment are favorable (Low 2000: 325).

Systems that confer/deny legitimacy on the child are complemented by elaborate customs to protect the child through pregnancy and birth.

Pregnancy and childbirth

The prenatal stage is the one in which [Chewong] parental responsibility is at its strongest since congenital malfunctions of any kind are attributed to the behaviour of one or other of the parents during this period. (Howell 1988: 155)

Childbirth is deemed an appalling sight which no [Yemeni] man should witness. (McGilvray 1994: 48)

People are also careful not to compliment a[n Enga] mother on a healthy child, for fear this may indicate their envy. (Gray 1994: 74)

On the fertile, volcanic island of New Britain, the Kaliai believe – in common with peoples around the globe – that "a successful pregnancy requires numerous acts of sexual intercourse [which] should continue until the fetus . . . quickens" (Counts 1985: 161). While that particular prescription for a healthy baby may be welcomed by parents, other Kaliai prescriptions may be less popular:

if either parent ate the flesh of the flying fox, the child might be mentally defective or it might shake and tremble as the animal does, or it might be unable to sit at the normal time because the animal does not sit erect. A pregnant woman [should] not eat wallaby because the child might develop epilepsy and have seizures during the full moon. (Counts 1985: 162)

For the Maisin in the Sepik Region of PNG:

Several species of fish are prohibited because they are too tough, and one type, a flat fish with spots which lives in salt water, is believed to produce scabies in the child of a breastfeeding mother. Eating crabs is thought to inhibit the production of milk. Mangoes and pumpkin are not eaten because of the belief that mothers who ingest them during lactation will have babies with yellow skin. (Tietjen 1985: 129)

Food taboos are often woven into a broad theory of illness and health: in Guatemala, pregnancy provokes a "hot" state so, to protect mother and fetus, cool foods are recommended (Cosminsky 1994: 201). There is little evidence that these food taboos are efficacious;[21] just the reverse may be true, especially where women are prohibited from eating fat and protein-rich meat (Einarsdottir 2004: 70). One careful study in four African societies determined that, in at least one, overall fertility was reduced by 5 percent as a result of malnourished women obeying food taboos (Aunger 1994). The Masaai (East African pastoralists) pregnancy diet is positively guaranteed to harm the fetus as "the

---

[21] A modern parallel can be found in the explosion in sales of higher-priced "organic" baby-foods to "protect" infants from pesticides and additives in regular baby-food.

woman abandons her normal diet and exists on a near starvation diet" (de Vries 1987b: 170).

Of course, foods are not the only things to be avoided. "In Fiji [Melanesia] nothing tight must be worn around the mother's neck lest the umbilical cord strangle the foetus" (Ritchie and Ritchie 1979: 43). For the same reason, Maisin mothers-to-be must not wear necklaces, make string bags, or encounter spider webs. "When going along a path towards the garden, they must either be preceded by another person or hold a large leaf in front of them to break any webs that might block the path" (Tietjen 1985: 125).

Anthropologists refer to beliefs of this sort as "sympathetic magic." A connection is made between a symptom of the child's and a similar attribute in something that may have been ingested or encountered by the mother during pregnancy. In the Kaliai epilepsy example, note that the wallaby is a small kangaroo which locomotes in sudden, rather jerky movements.

Another common element of the folk wisdom surrounding pregnancy and childbirth is the tension that may be omnipresent in the "unhappy" family. For the Mende, a difficult delivery may provoke a witch hunt – literally. When a witch is not found, the woman in labor is pressed to confess any recent adulterous mating which introduced competing sperm into her womb (MacCormack 1994: 118–119).

Witchcraft – undertaken by jealous co-wives, barren women, or rivals for the husband's affection – is a common diagnosis. Sometimes the witch is a spirit. In any case, it behooves the expectant or new mother to throw her enemies off the scent. For the people living in the Kerkennah Islands off Tunisia,

boy babies are thought to be more desirable than girl babies, so preparing for the birth of a girl is sometimes used as a ruse to disinterest the envious spirits . . . a mother . . . will go out begging from the single women in the village to buy earrings for the baby . . . [suggesting] the birth of a girl and hopefully throw[ing] the envy of the jinns (and the single women of the village) off the scent of a healthy baby boy . . . after the birth . . . a very fearful mother might publicly give [her son] a girl's name and dress him in female clothing for a period to ward off misfortune caused by envious influences. (Platt 1988: 273–274)

Women may be so concerned about potential miscarriage, deformity, or the neonate's failure to thrive that an elaborate fiction is played out. The Baganda small-scale and subsistence farmers in East Africa do not have a term for fetus and discuss pregnancy through euphemisms like " 'some disorder has caught me' or even 'syphilis has caught me'" (Kilbride and Kilbride 1990: 104). In the Himalayan kingdom of Ladakh, women "hide or conceal their pregnancy to avoid the evil eye" (Wiley 2004: 103).

Another chapter in our hypothetical folk medical handbook covers labor and delivery. In Bisayan villages in the Philippines, a woman in labor may be given a concoction including dried manure with the idea that, as her stomach violently expels this vile stuff, her uterus will expel the fetus (Hart 1965). Folklorists have collected many such customs which, sympathetically, emulate unlocking, opening, untangling, and expelling (Bates and Turner 2003).

Also common is the provision of a separate structure or a specially designated area in the forest for the actual birth. In Qiqiktamiut (Inuit) society, a tent or igloo is constructed and provisioned for use as a birth hut – where the expectant mother will be lodged at the commencement of labor (Guemple 1969: 468). Ju/'hoansi women who survive in the rugged Kalahari espouse a "cultural ideal of giving birth outdoors in the bush alone. This ideal is usually achieved after the first birth, which is attended by older female relatives" (Biesele 1997: 474). A Yanomamo woman will give birth

in the forest near the *yano*, with only the women in attendance. Man are said to become ill if they are present. The pregnant woman squats on a log, and another woman, usually the mother or a sister, holds her from behind. At birth the infant drops onto banana leaves. The baby is quickly picked up and washed with water before being given to its mother. (Peters 1998: 123)

Seclusion of the mother and new infant is an extremely common practice (Holmes 1994: 222)[22] and, while one function may be to protect them from communicable disease, another function may be to provide, in effect, a privacy curtain to allow the discreet termination of an unwanted infant's life (Caldwell and Caldwell 2005: 210; Young 2006). This function is specifically acknowledged when an Onitsha (Nigerian farming community) woman gives birth to twins, an abomination that could be discreetly erased in seclusion (Bastian 2001: 18).

The new mother may not be released from these strictures at delivery;[23] on the contrary, she and her newborn remain vulnerable. The birthing house may be their home for quite a while. For Gapun-speaking villagers in the Sepik area of PNG, a pregnant mother may be threatened by sorcerers who attack with magical substances that prevent her from expelling the infant or placenta. Continued danger, post-partum, leads them to remain in the "maternity house . . . for weeks or months" (Kulick 1992: 93). Similarly, for the Tamils of India and Sri Lanka:

The childbirth house is completely shuttered and closed during the actual delivery and . . . much of the postnatal pollution period . . . in order to protect the mother and baby from marauding spirits, ghosts, and demons which are attracted to all the blood and contamination . . . The end of the 31 days of childbirth pollution is marked . . . by

[22] The Mehinacu of Brazil are a rare case where, with the first child, *both* parents go into seclusion – for up to a year (Gregor 1970: 242).

[23] An expectant mother may be in a liminal or intermediate state and is both vulnerable and a danger to others (Rattray 1927: 187).

a purification of the house, a ritual bath for the mother, and the shaving of the child's head. (McGilvray 1994: 48–50)

Throughout most of Christian history,

the childbed was regarded with dread, even horror . . . Childbirth was exclusively women's business . . . that men were thankful to be relieved of and careful to distance themselves . . . the pain mothers endured was . . . perceived as the curse of Eve, and birth itself as a reenactment of the Fall, requiring that both mother and child be cleansed of its polluting effects [in the] rite of "churching" . . . The newborn was also regarded as a sinful polluting presence until the protective act of baptism had taken place. Even then, the "little stranger," as babies were often called, would be scrutinized for signs of original sin . . . (Gillis 2003: 88)

Comparable views are widely recorded. For example, on Taiwan, the infant is "ritually cleansed of the dirt she got from passing through 'the dirty part of a woman' by having her head and eyebrows shaved" (Wolf 1972: 57).

In some societies, such as the southern African Azande farmers, it is the father and his family that are a danger to the infant, especially if there's a hint of illegitimacy. "The birth usually takes place at the home of the husband, unless the oracles have decided that it is a dangerous place; then the wife goes to her parents' or brother's home" (Baxter 1953: 72). Women may feel threatened particularly by their co-wives and mother-in-law and elect to give birth in their natal home or a clinic offering Western medical services (Einarsdottir 2004: 73). Among the Macha Galla of Ethiopia, the mother returns to her natal home to give birth in order to avoid named (*budda* and *tolca*) harmful forces unleashed by other women in her husband's community (Batels 1969: 408). Other precautions against malevolent jealousy – common throughout the ethnographic record – include the Galla use of "bad names . . . usually those of the Mao or Nuak, the indigenous ethnic groups from whom the Galla took slaves . . . [Using] a good name may provoke the aggression of hostile people or spirits" (Batels 1969: 417).

In a matriarchal society, such as the Ashanti (Ghana), the birth will take place in the home of the mother's parents under the care of close maternal kin. Aside from the wellbeing of mother and infant, this tradition "fixes, in a very tangible way, the lineage affiliation . . . of the child" (Fortes 1950: 262). Even in patrilocal societies, such as the Aka of Africa and Rotuman of Polynesia (Howard 1970: 27), women may elect to reside in their parents' village during the birth and infancy of their children. And research confirms that "Infants residing matrilocally have significantly more alloparents and receive higher frequencies of care-giving behaviors from maternal kin" (Meehan 2005: 76). The operative force here is that the mother's kin have more certain genetic ties to the infant than do the father's kin.

Once the period of seclusion is over, the mother returns to her farmwork, and a celebratory rite of passage may follow. The Azande hold a feast in which the child is taken from the hut and passed through the smoke from a greenwood fire. The whole community is involved, prominently the kin of both parents. However, the celebration is restrained to the extent that the midwife goes unpaid and the infant unnamed until "it is certain that the child is hale" (Baxter 1953: 72). Among the Lepcha of Sikkim, the first three days of the newborn's life pass with no acknowledgment of its birth. In effect, it is still in the womb, and it is referred to as "rat-child." Only after the house and its members have been thoroughly cleansed will the infant be welcomed into the world of humans with a special feast (Gorer 1967: 289). The fourth night welcoming party on Gau Island (Fiji Islands, Melanesia) is called "*lutu na nona I vicovico* – 'falling of the umbilical cord' " (Toren 1990: 169). In Ladakh, the newborn's welcoming party (*rdun*) – celebrated by the assembled with barley beer, music, and dance – is delayed a month; even then, the child won't necessarily be named and "there appears to be no hurry to do so" (Wiley 2004: 125).

But the child may not *always* be welcomed by its kinfolk, nor even by its mother. What then? In the next section we examine the widespread practice of infanticide.

Gene roulette

[In the animal kingdom] . . . infanticide is not that unusual. (de Waal 2001: 184)[24]

Huang Liuhong, [ranking] infanticide with the failure to cultivate fruit trees and repair roads, views [it] as a violation of public order. (Waltner 1995: 209)

One of the best-established findings from the field of evolutionary anthropology is for altruism, or caring for others, to be channeled by genetics. People tend to care for related individuals. Adoptees, for example, are inevitably found living with kin (Silk 1980; 1987). Studies from the least (Hadza: Marlowe 1999) to most complex societies (urban-dwelling Xhosa – Anderson *et al.* 1999; residents of Albuquerque, NM – Anderson *et al.* 2007) consistently show that fathers are much more likely to invest in their biological – compared with step- – children. Investing in (future) stepchildren seems to be motivated by the

---

[24] Field study indicates just how common infanticide is in the animal kingdom. I observed a drama in the Galapagos Islands, where blue-footed boobies "nest" on the open ground and visitors to their rookeries must carefully pick their way among the nest sites. Many sites contained a pair of chicks, one inevitably larger and, also inevitably, consuming the majority of the food brought back by the parent and pecking its smaller sibling to death. As has been noted in numerous bird species, this "siblicide" occurs in full view of the non-intervening parents (Mock 2004). Aside from birds, the general public might be shocked to hear stories of bunny rabbits killing and devouring their young – when they are threatened – and cute pandas routinely neglecting the smaller of a pair of twins (*New York Times*, May 9, 2006).

desire to gain or maintain sexual access to the stepchild's mother.[25] Resources that flow to the mother of one's offspring are categorized as "parental effort," contrasted with "mating effort," when there are offspring from the woman's previous mate (Mulder 1992).

Step-parents often live up to their fictional reputation. Indeed, studies in the USA indicate that living with a stepfather and step-siblings leads to elevated cortisol levels, immunosuppression, and general illness (Flinn and England 1995),[26] as well as poorer educational outcomes (Lancaster and Kaplan 2000: 196). Daly and Wilson find that a child is a hundred times more likely to be killed by a step-parent than by a biological parent (Daly and Wilson 1984: 499).

Salt Lake City, Utah has nothing that could be called an "inner city." It is dominated by institutions affiliated with or owned by the Mormon church, marriage rates are high, neighborhoods are tidy, and violent crimes are rare. And yet, at least once a month, a news item like the following will appear:

Kody Frank Pahl, 26 . . . was charged Wednesday with second-degree felony child abuse for allegedly fracturing the skull of his girlfriend's 2-year-old daughter. The toddler's mother took her to the hospital Oct. 12. Pahl told his girlfriend the child had fallen off the sofa, court documents state. A doctor who later examined the girl determined her head injury was consistent with "being grabbed and her head smashed . . . " (*Salt Lake Tribune*, November 4, 2004, B2)

In some respects, contemporary children may be more vulnerable to the threat of mom's boyfriend/new husband than are their village counterparts. Highly mobile urbanites are separated from kin who could be expected to care for the child while the mother was working and to protect it from harm. Not that the killing of infants is unknown in the village – far from it. For the Yuqui (South American forest nomads) there are a variety of circumstances that might lead to abortion or infanticide.

The first pregnancy was almost always aborted since this child was considered weak.[27] Abortion was accomplished by having the woman's husband or mother kneel on her abdomen until she expelled the fetus. This was termed "breaking the child" (*taco siquio*) . . . A woman still nursing a child or who for some other reason did not want to give birth would use the same method to terminate her pregnancy. When women were angry at their husbands, they might kill their children, particularly boys, in

---

[25] On the other hand, men are more likely to divorce their wives following the birth of a child about whose paternity they are not confident (Anderson *et al.* 2007).

[26] A caveat is perhaps in order. We all know wonderful stepdads – I can think of several. However, our great wealth and the absence of any apparent need to be cared for by our children in old age permits us to defy the genetic imperative.

[27] This is mentioned as Yanomamo practice as well, suggesting that it is widespread in South America. Young mothers may be so poorly nourished that their first-born is at risk (Peters 1998: 123).

retaliation . . . In the case of a nursing child who lost its mother, sacrificing the infant to appease the mother's spirit as well as to resolve the problem of finding someone to care for the baby was common (Stearman 1989: 88–90).[28]

Many grounds for infanticide were positively sanctioned by the community including adultery (six out of fifteen cases observed among the New Guinea Eipo) (Schiefenhovel 1989). Among the Masaai, every male newborn was subject to a paternity trial. The infant was placed in the pathway of the clan's cattle returning to the homestead in the evening. "If, in this process, the baby was killed, or so badly injured that he died, he is thought to have been a bastard child" (de Vries 1987b: 171).

The Inuit, among others, were known to cull females in anticipation of high mortality among males through hunting accidents, homicide, and suicide (Dickemann 1979: 341). The birth of twins is almost always cause for terminating at least one (and sometimes both) infant's life. Mothers are unable to sustain two infants, especially where both are likely to be underweight. As Gray notes, "Even today, with the availability of western medical services it is difficult to maintain twins . . . " (Gray 1994: 73). On Bali, which is otherwise extraordinary in its elevation of babies to very high esteem, giving birth to more than one child at a time is seen as evidence of incest. Priests consider the birth of twins as sub-human or animal-like (Lansing 1994; Barth 1993; Belo 1980). Similarly, the Papel (Guinea-Bissau) believe that "it is *mufunesa* to give birth to many children at the same time like animals. Pigs have many offspring. Human beings give birth to only one each time. Therefore twins have to be thrown away. If not, the father, the mother, or somebody in the village may die . . . " (Einarsdottir 2004: 147).

Among the !Kung, Nancy Howell found that mothers whose toddlers had not been weaned might terminate the life of their newborn. In a society with high infant mortality (IM), an unweaned but otherwise thriving child is a better bet than a newcomer of unknown viability. The mother is *expected* by the band to kill one of a pair of twins or an infant with obvious defects. She would not be committing murder because, until the baby is named and formally presented in camp, it is not a person (Howell 1979: 120). We can juxtapose this picture – paralleled in pre-modern communities the world over – with the almost legendary affection and love the !Kung show their young (Konner 2005). Similarly, Trobriand Island (PNG) women, who also shower affection on their children, "were surprised that Western women do not have the right to kill an unwanted child . . . the child is not a social being yet, only a product manufactured by a woman inside her own body" (Montague 1985: 89).

---

[28] But Stearman's ethnography also makes clear the great care with which the Yuqui protect the viability of the fetus and newborn under favorable circumstances.

The historical record also indicates that the unfettered practice of infanticide is associated with improved treatment of children who "are more likely to be mourned deeply when they do die" (Golden 1990: 87).

In addition to infanticide, adoption is also widespread among sedentary peoples, especially in Oceania (Lepowsky 1985: 77) and Africa (Goody 1982). In pre-Christian Rome, surplus infants weren't necessarily killed; rather they were "exposed," placed in a public place where infertile adults might find and adopt them, a practice found in traditional societies as well (Balicki 1967). For example, on Vanatinai (Sudest) Island, "The verb 'to adopt,' *vaghan*, literally means 'to feed'" (Lepowsky 1985: 63). An unwanted infant would be placed in the crotch of a tree and anyone was then "free to retrieve the infant, wash it, and raise it as their own" (Lepowsky 1985: 63).

The decision to raise, abandon, or destroy a newborn is not only governed by immediate concerns. Fertility may be driven by a broad array of beliefs that establish an "ideal" family size as well as assigning relative value to male versus female offspring.

Pink ribbons or blue, many or few?

[In North Africa, unlike boys, Kerkenni] girls' names are not from the Qur'an. Girls' names are chosen to be pretty. (Platt 1988: 276)

What could be more startling to an imagination informed by evolutionary theory than the killing of one's own children? (Daly and Wilson 1988: 42)

In the Andes, Quechua farmers/herders have created a society in which there is relative parity of men and women. Both play critical roles in subsistence and both participate in the modern economy to some degree. This might explain why Bolin finds that South American Chillihuani parents treat their children largely the same, regardless of sex. This includes dress during infancy (Bolin 2006: 36). A display of equanimity towards the sex of one's new baby is more common among foraging peoples, again, where status differentials of any kind, but particularly between the sexes, are minimized. For example,

The Chewong are a small group of aboriginal people of the tropical rain-forest of the Malay Peninsula. Traditionally they are hunters, gatherers, and shifting cultiva-tors . . . Value judgments are not attached to gender . . . nor are these made the basis for further social or symbolic distinctions . . . There is no cultural preference for babies of either sex . . . (Howell 1988: 148, 158–159)

More commonly, we find that the infant's sex is highly salient in determining its fate. Fifteen years ago, I came across a United Nations report, on the cover of which was a picture of a mother holding on her lap a boy and girl of about the same age, possibly twins. The girl was skeletal, obviously in an advanced state of malnutrition, the boy robust and healthy. He sat erect, eyes intent on the camera, she sprawled, like a rag doll, her eyes staring into space. That picture and what it represented has haunted me ever since. In high-caste India, where daughters can neither contribute to the household economy nor find a marriage partner,[29] girls are a burden which families easily shed. One estimate put the number of "missing" women at 41 million (Deka 1993: 123) and "there are grim reports that a few villages in the northwestern plains [of India] have never raised one daughter" (Miller 1987: 99). Some hospitals in India now ban amniocentesis (and presumably ultrasound as well) because a female fetus is inevitably aborted (Miller 1987: 103) and China has prohibited such procedures altogether for the same reason.[30]

Esther Boserup first noted that, in the transition to plow agriculture, women's contribution to farming along with their relative worth and autonomy plummeted (Boserup 1970).[31] In the Highlands of Papua New Guinea, where women are the primary food producers, clans must pay an enormous bride-price in pigs and other valuables to acquire a woman in marriage. By contrast, in high-caste India, where women play almost no role in subsistence, a family must provide dowry to induce a higher-status family to take their daughter in marriage (Rao 1993).

Customary arrangements for caring for the elderly also come into play. Except in the rare matriarchy, sons are expected to inherit the family farm or business and, with these resources, care for elderly parents. Daughters marry out. They leave their parents to join their husband's family. In Bangladesh, children's farm and household labor set against their "cost" to raise have been measured by economists. The break-even age is around fifteen and sons remain in their natal home for several more years, yielding their parents a "profit." Girls

---

[29] India presents a classic Catch-22. Families use daughters to enhance their status by marrying them into higher-status families, an arrangement facilitated by the payment of dowry. Hence in families at the top of the caste structure, there is no one of higher rank to match their daughter to. On the other hand, girls aren't trained for a trade or profession because to do men's work, to venture out into the world, spoils their value as future brides. For American audiences, the film *Bend it like Beckham* conveyed this dilemma very well (Chadha 2002).

[30] Simon Parry, "Shortage of girls forces China to criminalize selective abortion," www.telegraph.co.uk, September 1, 2005. Technology became available in the mid-1980s permitting parents to identify the sex of the fetus which facilitated the selective termination of females. The result has been a sharply skewed sex ratio in China, Pakistan, and India. So, today, tens of thousands of young Asian men are "bare branches" of the family tree that won't bear fruit. They are unable to mate because they lack the means to acquire now scarce females. Social analysts believe this will have a profound destabilizing effect as bare branches are prime candidates for crime and violence (Hudson and Den Boer 2005). Further, Goodkind argues that selective abortion is preferable to selective infanticide (or abuse and neglect) which would be the likely alternative (Goodkin 1996). Interestingly, because the USA has not banned medically assisted sex selection, it has become a Mecca for foreign parents-to-be, especially from China. A couple may spend their life savings to visit the USA to have sex-specific embryos harvested from the mother's store and implanted in her uterus (*Salt Lake Tribune*, June 15, 2006: A11).

[31] Other forms of agricultural intensification, including the adoption of irrigation, diminish women's contribution to subsistence (Martin and Voorhies 1975).

are married and gone before fifteen, carrying precious family resources with them as dowry (Caine 1977). Parents, fully aware of the long-term implications of having sons and daughters, act just like Hokkien (Taiwan) villagers whose outlook was, until recently, that a girl's fate was decided shortly after her birth. "If the family had a surfeit of girls, she was simply allowed to slip into a bucket of water" (Wolf 1972: 54).

More recently on the Chinese mainland, the mother of a girl baby can expect to be "blamed, abused, or sometimes abandoned" (Johnson 2004: 5). Or, worse, they may be forced to give her up, to, more quickly, "gain another chance to produce a boy" (Johnson 2004: 30). Similarly, among the Yomut of Turkmenistan,

When a child dies, neighbors come to offer condolences, and it is customary to say to the bereaved, "May God give you another son!" This is said whether the deceased child was a boy or a girl. When a girl is born, especially if a series of births has produced girls, it is common practice to give the girl a name expressing a wish for a son. Names such as "Boy Needed" (*Oghul Gerek*) or "Last Daughter" (*Songi Qiz*) are common for girls. (Irons 2000: 230)

Nursing is another arena where sex preferences play out (Wolf 1972: 60). In rural Lebanon, girls are weaned a year earlier than their brothers, because "long nursing will pamper her. If the girl does not early learn to control herself she will later bring shame upon her family" (Williams 1968: 30). "Among the bottle-fed babies, boys were more likely to be fed from a standard store bought bottle and girls from an improvised bottle" (Williams 1968: 33).[32]

While male preference and selective female infanticide is the norm (Dickeman 1975: 129), anthropologists are finding more and more examples of *female* preference. In coastal areas of Korea, women make good money as abalone divers so girl babies are welcome (*New York Times*, July 9, 1987: C1, C10). Because girls may so effectively serve as "helpers at the nest," even in Japan, where boys are preferred, parents hope the first child will be female so she can assist with the care of her male siblings (Skinner 1987 cited in Harris 1998: 218). Several studies confirm that, if the first born is a daughter, a woman's completed fertility is increased (Turke 1988; Crognier and Hilali 2001). In Polynesia, Tongans acknowledge that girls are easier to manage than boys, they're more compliant. They also mature faster socially and physically (Morton 1996: 105). Girls are preferred in the relatively rare matriarchal society (Lepowsky 1985: 77; Clark *et al.* 1995). North American Hopi Indian mothers say "you raise up a daughter for yourself," whereas "you raise up a son for somebody else" (Schlegel 1973: 453).

---

[32] Even without such evident bias, studies find that boys are more costly, physiologically, for mothers (Blanchard and Bogaert 1997).

One thorough study compared Hungarian Gypsies (matriarchal) with mainstream Hungarian (patriarchal) society. Gender preferences were as expected and behaviors tracked preferences. Gypsy girls were extremely helpful to their mothers and tended to remain at home longer than their brothers, helping even after marriage. They were nursed longer than their brothers, while Hungarian boys were nursed longer than their sisters. "Gypsy mothers were more likely to abort after having had one or more daughters, while Hungarians are more likely to abort pregnancies when they have had sons" (Bereczkei and Dunbar 1997: 18).

Similarly in Jamaica, women are employed at much higher rates than men who are seen as troublesome pests. This attitude carries over into a preference for daughters which translates into a much lower survival rate for sons (Sargent and Harris 1998: 204). Parallel results obtain in the USA: "women with annual household incomes of less than $10,000 or without an adult male present were more likely to breast-feed their daughters an average of 5.5 months longer than their sons" (Cronk 2000: 214).

A change in subsistence patterns can affect preference for daughters or sons. The Mukogodo are an East African group studied by Lee Cronk who have made the transition from hunting and gathering to the pastoralism of their Masaai neighbors. But, as they are new to it, their herds are small and males have difficulty acquiring the necessary cattle for the bride-price. Female Mukogodo, on the other hand, are in demand from cattle-rich Masaai communities and thus serve as a conduit of wealth to their families. As a result, the gender ratio has become heavily skewed because daughters are nursed longer than sons and parents are much more likely to take their daughters for medical care than their sons (Cronk 2000: 206). However, the ancestral culture still holds sway as "Despite their behavior, most Mukogodo mothers claim to prefer sons" (Cronk 1993: 279).

Subsistence patterns also have an impact on the preferred *number* of children. For the !Kung San moving opportunistically through the Kalahari desert, children were a burden. Unable to support themselves in the harsh environment until adolescence, they were carried constantly and nursed on demand – several times an hour and throughout the night. Infants were indulged, never disciplined and permitted to wean themselves. As a result, inter-birth intervals (IBIs) were relatively long – four years (Draper 1976). Likewise for the Ache, who travel frequently through difficult terrain where placing a child on the ground exposes them to immediate hazards, children aren't "weaned from the back" before five (Konner 2005: 53). Their IBI is calculated to be slightly more than three years.[33] By contrast, the Hadza – another East African foraging

---

[33] Howard Kress reports for the Ache and the Waorani that, as these foragers settle into permanent villages with public areas cleared of creatures like snakes and bullet ants (their bite is likened

society – inhabit territory where children *can* provision themselves from an early age and are much less burdensome. They are weaned at two-and-a-half; left behind in camp from the age of three; and are often treated rather harshly by their mothers (Blurton-Jones 1993: 405).

In Central Africa, systematic comparisons have been drawn between foragers and farmers in the same region. Bofi-speaking foragers follow the !Kung model. Babies are carried or held constantly, by mothers *and* fathers, are soothed or nursed as soon as they cry, and may wean themselves after three to four years. Children are treated with the affection and respect consistent with preparing them to live in an egalitarian society where the principal subsistence strategy is *cooperative* net-hunting. Bofi-speaking farmers, on the other hand, tend not to respond as quickly to fussing and crying, are likely to pass the infant off to a slightly older sibling, and are verbally and physically abusive to children who are treated like the farmhands they are soon to be.

Bofi (farmer) mothers cover "their nipples with red fingernail polish, and/or a bandage to resemble a wound" (Fouts 2004a: 138) to initiate the weaning process which may be completed by eighteen months (Fouts 2005: 356). Not surprisingly, "Bofi forager parents criticized them for weaning children at too young an age, describing how farmer children cried so frequently when weaned" (Fouts 2004b: 71). Farmers with Darwinian attitudes towards their offspring also seem consistent with a competitive culture in which status differentials are marked. This comparative study replicated closely an earlier comparison between East African Aka foragers and their farmer-neighbors, the Ngandu (Hewlett *et al.* 2000).

These competing strategies have been referred to as "survivorship," where parents invest heavily in relatively few children, and "production," where less effort is expended on many infants – some of whom will survive (Blurton-Jones 1993: 406). The latter strategy is more likely observed where mothers work in distant fields while their young can be more easily "minded" by siblings or grandmothers in the village (Nerlove 1974)[34] *and* where children can, from an early age, help out with household chores, fieldwork, and herding (Sellen and Mace 1997: 888; Zeller 1987: 536). It also helps that domesticated foods and food-preparation options facilitate the creation of suitable "weaning" foods (Fouts 2004a: 135). Dogon (Mali) farmers can serve as an archetypal example of the "production" strategy. Their children are so poorly nourished that many

---

to the pain of a bullet wound), "birth rates explode" (Kress, personal communication February 7, 2007).

[34] There is at least one glaring exception to this pattern. Agta foragers inhabit remote mountain territory in the Philippines and, uniquely, women hunt using the tools and methods "normally" employed by men. Despite this evidence of egalitarianism, "women have many children, have short birth intervals, and lose many infants – ... approximately 49 percent of prepubescent children die" (Griffin and Griffin 1992: 300).

starve. Women are almost constantly pregnant, but when a woman secretly took contraceptives after her ninth child, her husband, thinking she'd entered menopause, took another, younger wife (Dettwyler 1994: 158). Interestingly, as the !Kung relinquished their peripatetic lifestyle to settle down as gardeners and ranch-hands during the 1970s, their reproduction strategy switched over as well (Lee 1979).

Kramer draws a comparison between a trio of South American foraging bands, where eighteen-year-olds are still dependent on relatives to supply about 20 percent of their calories (Kaplan 1994), and Mayan farming villages where:

juvenile economic dependence ends and positive net production is achieved well before males and females leave home and begin families of their own. Females achieve positive net production at age 12, the mean age at marriage is 19 . . . Males become net producers at age 17, also prior to the average age of marriage, which is 22. (Kramer 2002b: 314)

In South America the Maya value having lots of children – of either gender – whereas the Machiguenga, Piro, and Ache clearly value reproductive restraint (LeVine 1988). But, regardless of which strategy seems paramount, abortion and infanticide will be employed to eliminate unwanted children, and there will be an array of customs designed to preserve those children who are wanted.

Promoting survival

A fat baby is considered to be a healthy one. (Lepowsky 1985: 64)

In this section, we sample from among a rich array of customs that buttress infant care. One set of customs supports continuous, prolonged nursing, which provides nutrition for the current baby and may also forestall pregnancy. Daniel Sellen has created a model of the ideal infant-feeding program which includes the immediate onset of nursing so the infant benefits from immunogens found in colostrum, at least eighteen months of breastfeeding, supplemented, from six months, by appropriate foods. Unfortunately, few infants, even in developed countries, enjoy this ideal (Sellen 2005). The Datoga (East African pastoralists) believe "that the colostrum would give the infant digestive problems, because early milk was thought to be 'too heavy' for the infant's stomach" (Sellen 1998a: 485–486). Nor is this omission unusual. In a survey of fifty-seven societies, in only nine did nursing begin shortly after birth (Raphael 1966).

The length of the inter-birth interval is a key factor in an infant's survival. A minimum IBI of three to four years is ideal. In a study conducted in the USA – where we enjoy sophisticated obstetrics and calorie-rich diets – women who gave birth eighteen months or sooner after the birth of a previous child were 50 percent more likely to deliver a premature baby (*Wall Street Journal*, February 23, 2004: D1, D4) and/or a baby with "adverse perinatal outcomes" (Conde-Agudelo *et al.* 2006: 1809). In the village, early weaning replaces a sanitary, easily digestible and nutritious food with an alternative that may be none of these. A common outcome is frequent diarrhea and the attendant weakening and susceptibility to disease and parasites (Gray 1994: 72).

It turns out that frequent, prolonged nursing and permitting the infant to handle the breast freely increases production of the prolactin hormone, which, in turn, makes conception less likely (Konner and Worthman 1980). Another way in which nature contributes to increasing IBI is through post-partum depression following a miscarriage, stillbirth, or infant death. Binser notes that depression elevates cortisol and leaves the mother lethargic and sleepy, which may just serve to put off the next pregnancy until the mother has had a chance to recoup her vigor (Binser 2004).

Nature is aided by culture in promoting longer IBIs through prohibitions that mitigate against long intervals between nursing bouts and the nearly universal post-partum prohibition on intercourse between husbands and wives. In Fiji, a nursing mother must cease fishing because the cold water will sour her milk. Aside from fishing, she should avoid traveling any distance from the village as well because she may not be available when her infant is hungry. Were she to become pregnant, her nursling might develop *save* – wobbly legs. If she succumbs to the temptation to resume sexual relations, she runs the risk of falling ill herself (Maxwell West 1988: 19).

Whittemore's Mandinka (Senegal) informant explained that:

First I gave the breast to Fatu, who held it and gave it to Séku, and so on, naming her way through the ordinal sequence of her offspring. This suggests not only that her breasts define her role as mother, but also that they temporarily belong to the nursling whose milk they contain. (Whittemore 1989: 97)[35]

Frequent nursing is complemented by a concern for the *quality* of the breast milk, Kaliai parents, for example, are cautioned to avoid sex because semen poisons the milk[36] – especially the semen from a male who's not the infant's father. Nursing and the post-partum taboo on sex should continue until the child is able to recount " . . . its dreams or when it is old enough to gather shell-fish . . . about three years of age" (Counts 1985:161). Elsewhere in Papua New Guinea, the Enga see the man's semen as a component of his war magic. Were this potent substance to mix with breast milk the result for the infant could be fatal. (Gray 1994: 67)

The couple may be aided in avoiding temptation by separating. The wife may be lodged in a birthing or "lying-in" house (Lepowsky 1985: 64), or secluded in her own home, until, in the Trobriands, "mothers lost their tans and their skin color matched that of their infants" (Montague 1985: 89). She may move back

---

[35] The notion of a succession of infants "owning" the breast is complemented, in the Gambia, by the notion that a woman's age is measured not in a linear fashion but as a reservoir of life which is "used up" by successive births (Bledsoe 2001).

[36] This notion was common in Europe at least until the nineteenth century (Pollock 1983: 50).

to her natal home just prior to giving birth and remain there for a prescribed period. A new father may move into the men's house or, in a larger communal dwelling, move his sleeping mat some distance away.

A nursing mother who becomes pregnant may be treated with repugnance (Basden 1966: 188). She can expect to be publicly ridiculed by the community, by senior women, in particular (Mabilia 2005: 83). There must be considerable tension involved, nonetheless, as she must also be concerned about alienating the affections of the child's father. On the Micronesian island of Truk, when "the post-partum sexual taboo prove[s] especially frustrating, sexual relations may be arranged with wife's sisters and with brother's wives" (Fisher 1963: 532). Among Mbuti foragers in Central Africa, where polygyny is not an option, "There is no . . . prohibition against sleeping with other women, least of all unmarried girls" (Turnbull 1978: 212).

Of course nursing is not the only aspect of mother–infant relations that comes in for attention. The ethnographic record includes numerous examples of cultural traditions aimed at restoring the mother's health following childbirth. For example, the traditional Malay view – but common throughout Southeast Asia – is that pregnancy is a hot state and that with parturition the mother plunges into a dangerously cold state. Aside from diet, elaborate steps will be taken – accurately referred to as "mother roasting" – to restore her equilibrium.[37]

Other traditions highlight the fragility of infants, and urge special efforts on their caretakers to keep them alive (Guemple 1979: 42). In Sarawak villages: "The souls of children are elusive . . . [they are] never punished physically so as not to scare off their souls . . . [they] must be handled with the greatest care at least till they are about four years old when they become more secure" (Nicolaisen 1988: 199). Nearby on the Malay peninsula, Chewong (forest-dwelling bands) believe:

Children . . . are not strong . . . what is weak are the bonds between these various aspects of the person . . . not yet stabilized . . . The fact that children are ill much more often than adults is taken as proof of th[is] . . . Numerous . . . prescriptions and proscriptions exist to protect the child from a disintegration of the self and from the attacks of harmful beings. (Howell 1988: 153–154)

The Mandok (PNG) also see the "newborn's inner 'self' (*anunu*) as not yet firmly anchored inside its body . . . " As a precaution, both parents must adhere to a strict catalog of taboos such as the prohibition on hollowing canoes, wood carving, or chopping down trees. A crying child signaled the imminent departure of its *anunu*, the likely result of a taboo violation, and, in extremis, the need to bring in a ritual specialist to entice the *anunu* to return (Pomponio 1992: 77).

---

[37] Cases of third-degree burns from this treatment are not unknown (Manderson 2003:142–143).

In more complex societies, the precautionary measures undertaken after the birth may become quite elaborate. In Japan, the mother and baby emerge from her mother's house only after the viability of the newborn seems assured. Prior to a visit to the *hatsu-miyamairi* tutelary shrine for blessings, a series of ceremonies in the home solidify the child's hold on life, because "the baby's soul is believed not to be firmly implanted in its body during this period, and is therefore surrounded by many dangers" (Sofue 1965: 152). Various rites signal the infant's continued health and development, such as the *yuzome* ceremony (first hot bath), *kizome* (new clothes provided by maternal grandmother), and *kamisori* (first head shaving) (Sofue 1965: 150).

The whole village carefully scrutinizes the new mother and feels free to chastise and correct her.[38] Indeed this policing mechanism may extend to visitors. Achsah Carrier and I both did fieldwork on Ponam Island in the North Bismark Sea accompanied by our children. My experience was quite similar to hers:

> when I went back for my first visit with my son... The women began right away to correct my behavior and insist that I... feed my son, wash him, dress him and carry him properly at all times. They were angry if I did not and would tolerate no excuses... women came running out of their houses to yell at me for carrying him improperly or not holding my umbrella at the right angle to provide him with shade. (Carrier 1985: 189–190)

Pragmatic advice is mixed with appeals to the supernatural. A Mandinka mother needs to purchase from a shaman antelope horns filled with "medicine" to wear around her waist to guard her fetus against malevolent spirits during pregnancy. After the birth, it is customary to provide the child with amulets of various kinds: "the mother gathers grains of sand or earth from the birth place, a bit of charcoal from her hearth, all of which are later packed and sealed in leather sewn charms (*boro*) soon to be tied to the child's wrist" (Whittemore 1989: 86). "Among the Bofi... infants and children are adorned with magical waist cords, necklaces, bracelets, and charms to protect them from... taboos, sorcery, dangerous animals... and cold temperature" (Fouts 2005: 353).

There are reports of culturally prescribed methods for strengthening the infant. Amele (PNG) infants are "cold and soft, like their mothers, and must be strengthened by the application of warm hands heated over a fire" (Jenkins *et al.* 1985: 39). There are several reports of infants being massaged for reasons ranging from stimulating their physical development (Einarsdottir 2004: 93) to "soothing them to sleep" (Morton 1996: 62). Mandinka grandmothers massage

---

[38] Tiffany Field and colleagues, working with Haitian immigrant mothers in Miami, find they often have difficulty feeding their offspring who are hospitalized for dehydration and malnutrition at a high rate (Field *et al.* 1992: 183). I think it's possible these young women immigrants lost the opportunity to learn from older women how to care for infants.

the infant to get its "body ready for the multiple caregivers upon whom [it] will depend" (Whittemore 1989: 89). Regardless of the folk rationale, if we extrapolate from research in neonatal medicine, it's likely that this sort of stimulation *does* increase the infant's chances of survival.

Unfortunately, an objective appraisal reveals that many customs are not efficacious, if anything, they may be harmful. Not surprisingly then, we also find a lengthy catalog of beliefs that rationalize infant death and shield the parents from any accompanying emotional trauma. In the next section we will review culturally sanctioned infant- and childcare practices that are patently dysfunctional and may lead to chronic illness or death. Against a backdrop of high infant and child mortality, the ethos in many societies justifies a rather fatalistic attitude about these casualties.

Illness and death

Infancy [in the Victorian era] represented such a precarious existence that parents regarded it essentially as a state of illness. (Calvert 2003: 67)

It may seem macabre to dwell on, but the pervasiveness of infant treatments that undermine rather than enhance their health deserves at least some attention. Infants might be tightly swaddled for lengthy periods resulting in superating sores (de Mause 1974: 11) or, alternatively, repeatedly dunked into water in the middle of winter to harden them (de Mause 1974: 32). According to Bob Edgerton in *Sick Societies*, the Yoruba of Nigeria, who practice subsistence farming, treated convulsions in children with a "tonic" consisting of green tobacco leaves marinated in urine and sometimes topped off with gin. The decoction contained so much nicotine that children treated with it were "often deeply unconscious" when taken to a European hospital in Ibadan (Edgerton 1992: 106). In ancient Egypt, children in pain were treated with widely recorded nostrums the ingredients of which included an opiate and fly excrement (Halioua and Ziskind 2005: 83–84).

From her work with West African subsistence farmers, Alma Gottlieb describes the Beng practice of giving babies frequent enemas because "Mothers bear great shame if clothes are soiled due to inadequate toilet training" (Gottlieb 2000: 86). Given that diarrhea, and the consequent dehydration, is a leading cause of infant mortality (IM) worldwide (UNICEF 2004: 4), this widely reported (at least in West Africa) practice is deplorable.

A frequent diagnosis for child illness is family conflict, such as the machinations of a jealous co-wife (Strassmann 1997) or other relative. The Amele often attribute a child's chronic illness to a curse imposed by the mother's brother "because he has not received the full promised brideprice, particularly the pork component" (Jenkins *et al.* 1985: 43). In the Ecuadorian village of San Gabriel, children often died of *colerin*, caused by drinking poisoned breast milk when the mother is distraught over her husband's affair. Hence he will blamed for the death (Morgan 1998: 70). When an Ashanti child is sick, the shrine priest will focus on possible discord between the parents. Not surprisingly, such discord often emerges, and appropriate remorse and reform is supposed to effect a cure (Field 1970: 119). In my fieldwork in Gbarngasuakwelle, I lived (as a guest) in a large, polygynous household and the tensions were palpable. This was seen as harmful to children, particularly. The shaman (village blacksmith in this case) came often to divine the cause and, using appropriate rituals (inevitably involving the sacrifice of a chicken), would attempt to ameliorate it (Lancy 1996: 167). I am not suggesting that conflict reduction has no impact on child wellbeing but it so often appears to be a case of the tail wagging the dog – the child's illness providing a convenient pretext for addressing the "real" problem – disharmony.

But the greatest threat to the child is, probably, his next younger sibling. Among the Luo, an African pastoralist tribe, if a pregnant woman continues to nurse her infant, it will contract *ledho*. This illness "is characterized by a wasting away, becoming very thin, diarrhea, skin changes, and swelling of the stomach" (Cosminsky 1985: 38). We would recognize in *ledho* all the symptoms of malnutrition brought on, not by the "poisonous" milk, but by the inadequate weaning foods. As Brenda Gray notes, the most common label for child malnutrition is *Kwashiorkor* – a term native to Ghana that means "the disease of the deposed baby when the next one is born" (Gray 1994: 75–76). In Morocco, there is a term linking fetus and infant which is based on the verb "to snatch away" (Davis and Davis 1989: 80).

While many societies acknowledge the need for a "special diet" for the child who is being weaned or still nursing at twelve months or later (Lepowsky 1985: 80), the efficacy of such diets is open to question. Meat is usually among the foods kept from children. This is probably harmful, as a protein shortage, in particular, is often found in recently weaned children. However, malnutrition is rarely identified as the root of a child's illness. Katherine Dettwyler pointedly titled her study of the Dogon *Dancing Skeletons*, describing, in graphic detail, the horrific sight of severely malnourished children. She finds that, while the mothers are aware of something amiss, they attribute the problem to locally constructed folk illnesses and seek medicine from the anthropologist to effect a cure. When she tells them to provide the child with more food, they are skeptical. Children can't benefit from good food because they haven't worked hard to get it, and they don't appreciate its good taste or the feeling of satisfaction it gives. Anyway, "Old people deserve the best food, because they're going to die soon" (Dettwyler 1994: 94–95).

In the modern, industrialized world, IM is almost unknown: 5 deaths per 10,000 live-born children. By contrast, the figure for Africa is 150 per 10,000 and this is significantly higher in very poor or strife-torn areas. A recent estimate put the annual child death rate at 10.5 million (Sundberg 2006: 72). Child mortality is linked to the quality of the neonatal environment, and the prevalence of infectious and parasitic diseases. "Acute respiratory infections and diarrhea together are at the root of approximately one third of child deaths" (UNICEF 2004: 4).

Even among quite traditional and relatively affluent pastoralists such as the Datoga (Sellen 1998a: 482) and the Kashmiri Ladakh (Wiley 2004: 6), IM is at least 20 percent, with twice that classified as malnourished. The rise of urbanization did nothing to alleviate the problem. If anything, IM was higher in the first urban environments. IM is estimated at 25–35 percent in ancient Athens (Golden 1990: 83);[39] estimates for Europe in the Middle Ages were 30–50 percent (Hanawalt 2003); in late eighteenth- and early nineteenth-century Russia, the estimate was 50 percent (Dunn 1974: 385); and somewhat below 50 percent in eighteenth- and nineteenth-century Japan (Caldwell and Caldwell 2005: 213).

Humans have always had to cope with the loss of infants and societies have developed an elaborate array of "cover stories" to lessen grief and recrimination (Martin 2001: 162; Scrimshaw 1984: 443). Most importantly, by secluding the baby initially and treating it as being in a liminal state, its loss may not be widely noted. The precarious status of newborns is reflected in naming rituals common in both the historical record and the cross-cultural record of contemporary tribal societies (de Vries 1987b; Sharp 2002).[40] For example, on Vanatinai Island:

> it is not customary to name a child until a few weeks after birth, and the ritual presentation by the mother's family of shell currency necklaces or greenstone axe-blades to the father's kin to "thank him" for siring a new member of the mother's matrilineage does not take place for about six months. Presumably these delays assure that naming and "childwealth" exchanges are only performed for children who are expected to survive. (Lepowsky 1987: 78–79)[41]

In ancient Greece, children under the age of two are never (or hardly ever) said to have died *ahoros,* "untimely" (Golden 1990: 83), and in Renaissance Italy, parents waited until their child had survived a year – forgoing tax incentives to register it straightaway – because so many didn't (Klapisch-Zuber 1985:

---

[39] In a large-scale demographic survey of hundreds of well-preserved remains covering almost a 3,500-year span (2000 BCE to 1500 CE) from coastal Chile and Peru, infant and child mortality was consistently high (50 percent by age fifteen) and did not drop appreciably with the transition to sedentism and agriculture (Allison 1984).

[40] Among the Bena-Bena, a tribal society in the New Guinea Highlands, "children were often not regarded as truly human until they had survived for several years" (Langness 1981: 14).

[41] Naming is delayed among the Tamang (Fricke 1994: 133), the Ashanti (eight days: Rattray 1927: 187), Ayoreo (weeks or months: Bugos and McCarthy 1984: 508), and among the strife-torn Korowai of western New Guinea (eighteen months: Raffaele 2003: 69).

98–99). In Victorian England, a similar delay in naming and baptism was the rule (Gillis 2003: 87).[42]

Elaborate mythology undergirds community beliefs in infant vulnerability and likely death. Commonly this involves the notion that the child came from a spirit world and may, therefore, have just been "visiting." "Ashanti infants are believed to come directly from the land of the ghosts [where] a spirit mother laments the death of her child" (Rattray 1927: 187). Among peasants in Bolivia, pre-verbal children are seen as temporarily visiting from the realm of the mountain deities. Unnamed and unbaptized, should they perish, they will be "buried in a place far from the household and the community cemetery where they are 'eaten' by the mountain spirits" (Sillar 1994: 51). The Yoruba provide an interesting rationale:

One of the spiritual dangers lying in wait for pregnant women are thought to be the spirits of *abiku* who may try to usurp the child in her womb if she is foolish enough to go out at night. *Abiku* children are "born to die"; after living with their parents for only a little while, they leave to rejoin the spirit companions who have always been tempting them to return. Sometimes, it is believed, the same *abiku* child will come back time and again to torment the parents with its temporary presence, only to die in due course. (Maclean 1994: 160)

Unfortunately, the ubiquity of infant death along with well-established coping mechanisms inures people to a phenomenon which, given the state of medical knowledge and a pharmacopeia adequate to the task, shouldn't be happening.[43] The wastage of young human life and the debilitating impact this has on mothers is staggering and cannot possibly be justified. And, in the West, we remain largely oblivious of the problem of child malnutrition and death in the Third World until it reaches such proportions that the story becomes newsworthy. And the response – the provision of massive, but too little, too late, food aid – does nothing to address the underlying problems (UNICEF 2004: 2).

The extremes of high and low fertility

Sadly, child death is a common event in Biombo [Guinea-Bissau], and about one-third of all children born alive are likely to die before they reach the age of five. (Einarsdottir 1994: xi)

... change in demand for children is the prime mover behind the large and enduring decline in fertility ... that has occurred in society after society during the course of modernization ... (Turke 1989: 61)

---

[42] On the prohibition of mourning for children in Jewish culture see Pitock (1996). For Chinese, see Wu (1995: 140).

[43] For example, the role of clean water in reducing parasites and infection, or the availability of low-cost vaccines that are, nevertheless, not universally distributed. Information from Lifewater International website: www.lifewater.org; accessed 4.3.07.

As we've seen, the transition from foraging to agriculture was certainly important in influencing fertility. Demand for farm laborers creates demand for children, leading to shorter IBI, earlier weaning, higher fertility, *and* higher IM. Archaeologists studying human remains in the US Southwest find that "the amount of meat and wild plant foods in everyone's diets declined as maize became the dietary mainstay. The lesser amount of protein in women's diets . . . may have created impoverished nutrition and poor health, particularly during pregnancy and lactation . . . as women's nutritional status declined, so did the health of their unborn and newly born children" (Whittlesey 2002: 160) so that "children's health in the southwestern United States after the introduction of agriculture illustrates a pervasive pattern of high infant mortality, malnutrition, and disease infestation" (Sobolik 2002: 150).

Numerous studies have shown the deleterious effects on children's health in the agriculturalist's pursuit of the "production" strategy. However, as the land is brought fully into cultivation, population-limiting mechanisms (post-partum sex taboo) should develop to curtail further growth (Sear *et al.* 2003: 34). And this seems to have happened in many, many cases. However, Western influence in the past hundred years seems to have dismantled these mechanisms, including, especially, abortion and infanticide.[44] Improved healthcare for mothers and infants has no doubt brought improvements. But missionary efforts to stamp out "pagan" practices like polygyny also undermined the post-partum taboo on intercourse, even while they simultaneously block the introduction of modern contraceptives (Morton 1996: 53; Hern 1992: 33). Additionally, "fashion" and commercial interests pushing infant "formula" have drastically reduced the number of infants being breastfed (Small 1998: 201). The result has been, in many parts of the world, population growth outstripping opportunities for either employment or improved food production (Hern 1992: 36; Condon 1987: 35–36).

For example, from Malaita Island in the South Pacific, traditional Kwara'ae practice was to keep men separated from their nursing wives for at least a year. However, the "abolition of the *tabu* system and the ascendance of Christianity has meant that . . . ritual separation [is] no longer practiced" (Gegeo and Watson-Gegeo 1985: 240–241). As a result, fertility has jumped and families with ten to thirteen children are not uncommon.

The quality of life . . . has begun to deteriorate in the past ten years. Building materials . . . are now scarce . . . The carrying capacity of the land has almost been reached

---

[44] The impact of Western influence on reproduction patterns and children's wellbeing is not well documented. Carrier's informants on Ponam spoke about a decline in IBI and increase in birth rates following the invasive presence of foreign troops during World War II (Carrier 1985: 202). And there are similar oral history accounts that identify a sharp increase in fertility associated with the establishment of permanent Western facilities – military, mission, governmental, and commercial (plantations) – in tribal areas.

in some areas, resulting in continuously planted gardens, soil exhaustion, lower productivity, and less diversity in garden crops ... Streams and rivers have been nearly fished out ... Traditionally, food exchanges among households ensured sharing in times of ... famine or flood [but] in the past 20 years there has been a reduction in food exchanges, influenced by lower garden productivity and the growth of the cash economy. (Gegeo and Watson-Gegeo 1985: 239–240)[45]

Jonina Einarsdottir and Nancy Scheper-Hughes provide thorough case studies of the next stage in this descent into extreme poverty and environmental degradation. The former studied a very poor area of Guinea-Bissau (West Africa), the latter an even more desolate area of northeast Brazil. Both areas have been severely overpopulated for quite some time, land and job scarcity conspire to render men unable to support their families, leading to a breakdown, if not the dissolution of marriage. Einarsdottir (2004: 27) reflects: "I experienced the hopelessness and desperation of the mothers. Despite heavy and incessant work they could hardly feed themselves and their children. Their husbands, and men in general, were frequently commented on as *ka bali nada* (totally worthless)." Nevertheless, when she asked mothers how many children they would prefer, many responded: "You never have too many children" (Einarsdottir 2004: 63). Birth control is resisted in part because the motive ascribed to the use of contraceptives is an adulterous liaison (Einarsdottir 2004: 69). And in Ladeiras, northeast Brazil, a woman is said to be "used up" (*acabado*) from multiple pregnancies. Her weakness will be transferred to her fetus who will, therefore, be born weak and thin, lacking the will or strength to battle for its own survival. Locating the problem of IM in the mother's depleted body and the infant's lack of vigor justifies the mother's neglect of the child and her emotional detachment (Scheper-Hughes 1987b: 196–190).

While the plight of mothers and children in the Third World seems invisible to us, ample precedent can be found in the past. Throughout recent Euroamerican history, infant malnutrition and mortality rates were as high as they are today in Ladeiras or Biombo. However, the starvation, abuse, and neglect of children was largely invisible because it took place among the "lower orders" (Scheper-Huges 1987a: 135).

At the other end of the social scale, Hrdy finds that, in eighteenth-century Paris, inter-birth interval, fertility, and IM were all affected by the mother's social status. The richest women had the shortest inter-birth intervals, highest fertility, and lowest IM. Rich women[46] were able to hire the best wet-nurses to

---

[45] By contrast, the island peoples of Manus Province in Papua New Guinea, apparently *have* obtained access to contraceptives and are using them in the face of the overpopulation confronting them (Ataka and Ohtsuka 2006).

[46] At the upper echelons of society, fertility was probably always valued as an end in itself, unmotivated by any utility that children might have as workers.

sustain their infants as they quickly became pregnant. However, on the downside, the women's bodies suffered various symptoms related to high fecundity, including anemia and prolapsed uteruses (Hrdy 1992: 422).[47]

But something was afoot in a small corner of Europe. In seventeenth-century Netherlands, society was shifting to the forager's "survivorship" reproduction model. At this time, the Netherlands were "modern," that is, society was highly urbanized and commercial interests took precedence over courtly customs. Protestantism had been embraced along with Weber's "work ethic." The arts and literature flourished. This liberalization of society was applied to children.[48]

In the seventeenth century, foreigners were already recording their astonishment at the laxity of Dutch parents . . . they preferred to close their eyes to the faults of their children, and they refused to use corporal punishment . . . foreigners remarked on something else: since the sixteenth century, most Dutch children – girls as well as boys – had been going to school. (Kloek 2003: 53)

Among the large middle class, children were no longer viewed merely as chattel but as having inherent value. Consequently, people had fewer of them so they could afford to "pamper" and educate them. A wonderful scene painted by Jan Steen between 1663 and 1665, called *The Feast of St. Nicholas*, shows a family just after St. Nick's visit. He has left toys, candy, and cake for the children.[49] John Locke – exiled to Holland in 1685–1688 – was profoundly influenced by what he saw. His treatise on childrearing, published in 1693, brought Dutch ideas on childcare to England (Locke 1693/1964).

It took the rest of Europe a few centuries to catch up with the Netherlands – for example, "From 1730–1750, 75 percent of the [children] of greater London died by the age of five" (Sommerville 1982: 156–157) – but the change has been dramatic. Today, Italy, which had one of the world's highest birth rates, now has the world's lowest (0.07),[50] in spite of the majority of the population being at least nominal members of the Catholic church which vociferously condemns contraception.[51] In Sweden, where women postpone childbearing

---

[47] While recent research still finds a positive correlation between the number of offspring and wealth, the relationship is much weaker than in eighteenth-century bourgeois French society. Indeed, the same study finds that "better educated people have fewer biological children" (Hopcroft 2006: 106).

[48] The Dutch are still leading the way in terms of promoting liberal policies towards children. Most recently they have legalized euthanasia for terminally ill children in severe pain (*Salt Lake Tribune*, September 30, 2005: A11). In a recent survey, the top two countries ranked on child wellbeing measures were the Netherlands and Sweden . . . the bottom two (of twenty-one) were the USA and Britain (Adamson 2007).

[49] Rijksmuseum Amsterdam permanent collection. Can be viewed online: www.rijksmuseum.nl; accessed 4.23.07.

[50] Information obtained from www.cia.gov/cia/; accessed 4.23.07.

[51] Ironically, just as today the church cannot *promote* childbearing through pro-natalist policy, in the Middle Ages it was equally unsuccessful with anti-natalist policies. These were rooted in the

to their mid-late 20s, the reproduction rate is 1.6, in spite of extremely lib-eral, government-subsidized parent-support services (Wells-Nystrom 1988).[52] Worldwide, "fertility rates have fallen from an average of 4.95 children per woman in the 1960–1965 period to 2.96 children in the first half of the 1990s" (*New York Times*, June 8, 1999: A12).

Many factors have contributed to what is called the "Great" or demographic transition (Caldwell 1982). First, we have repeatedly noted that individuals – backed by consensually supported social customs – *have* found ways to limit fertility in the face of resource scarcity.[53] Second, "As societies modernize, social and economic success is increasingly achieved outside the sphere of kinship" (Turke 1989: 67). That is, one is no longer dependent on family for employment and, indeed, a characteristic of the modern economy is that it forces those who would be successful to relocate frequently. Hence families are surrounded by neighbors who are non-kin. Third, if parents no longer have easy access to extended family as part-time caretakers of their dependent children,[54] they will need to purchase childcare. The cost and quality of such services should have a depressive effect on fertility. Fourth, successful employ-ment requires years of formal education, an activity that is incompatible with childrearing; thus marriage and the age of first pregnancy are now delayed at least a decade beyond the onset of puberty.

Fifth, contemporary urban environments, unlike the village, are not con-ducive to the free-wheeling, minimally monitored playgroup.[55] Children now have to be supervised, which carries new costs and burdens for parents. Sixth, as we'll discuss in chapter 5, children in the village learn much of their cul-ture through observation and imitation with minimal instruction from adults. In contemporary society, training someone to become a competent member

Paulist philosophy that "procreation is a 'huge penitence' . . . children are the fruit of 'carnal acts' and . . . they hinder total dedication to divine worship . . . [c]hurch writers . . . lauded women and men who chose to retire from the world into a monastic order even if this entailed abandoning their children" (Shahar 1990: 9, 11). There was a comprehensive calendar of occasions when sex was prohibited by church authority: "Couples who followed these mandates would have been able to anticipate approximately twenty days per year of sexual intimacy . . . the consequences for violating these religious taboos could result in producing deformed children-changelings. Gregory of Tours (538–594) wrote of just such a child, conceived on a Sunday and consequently born with multiple birth defects" (Colón with Colón 2001: 213).

[52] Elsewhere, in Germany the average age of first marriage was 28.5 for women in 2000 (Keller and Lamm 2005: 239).

[53] Obviously, if those customs have broken down, individuals may well relinquish any attempt to ration fertility and go over completely to the "production" model. That is clearly the model that Biombo and Ladeiras mothers are following.

[54] Recent research suggests that there is considerable cross-national variation in the persistence of extended family ties and grandmother involvement with grandchildren – high in Poland, Spain, and Italy, low in the USA, Netherlands, Sweden (Harkness *et al.* 2006).

[55] As we'll see in chapter 4, villagers readily "keep an eye on" their neighbor's children. In modern sub/urban society where neighbors are not even friendly let alone related to each other, such casual supervision isn't available (Spilsbury and Korbin 2004: 197).

now requires the costly services of full-time teachers, tutors, and coaches. And parents cannot just hand their child as an unformed lump of protoplasm to these professionals (Jolivet 1997). They must invest a great deal of their precious time in prepping kids for school and other demanding but necessary institutions.

Lastly, parents may still "need" children – "A child makes a couple into a family. Childlessness is, for many, a tragedy" (Cross 2004: 5) – but the need can no longer be reckoned in terms of additional workers or augmented security in old age. In short, quality meets the current need, quantity doesn't.[56]

These and other changes all reward parents who limit reproduction and punish those who do not (Kaplan and Lancaster 2000: 283). During the economic depressions of the 1890s and 1930s, educated middle-class individuals reduced fertility – primarily by postponing marriage (Caldwell 1982).[57] This stands in sharp contrast to cases cited in this chapter – from Ethiopia and Guinea-Bissau – where fertility is not reduced in the face of famine.[58]

As widespread as this transition has been, it is by no means inevitable as the Third World cases discussed above illustrate. Mexico represents an interesting patchwork of the old and new. Among the emerging middle class, women sought birth-control medication on the black market during an era when both the church and state opposed its use (*New York Times*, June 8, 1999: A12). As the government, belatedly,[59] has begun to offer family planning, it is eagerly welcomed by women with seven or more years of education (Uribe *et al.* 1994) but rejected by women with less education.

However, the women interviewed in a rural village Browner calls San Francisco "expressed sharply negative attitudes about childbearing and childrearing" (Browner 2001: 461). They were frustrated because the mandatory school

---

[56] However, one consequence of having just one or two "precious" children is that parents exhibit what borders on paranoia in their child-directed anxiety. Many fear their child might be kidnapped and killed despite the infinitesimally small probability of that happening (Glassner 1999).

[57] Boone and Kessler (1999) make a parallel argument that applies in the longer term. That is, they show that wealthier individuals may divert resources from offspring – and elect for lower fertility – in order to invest in status enhancement or maintenance. Higher status, they demonstrate, protects the individual and his kin from periodic catastrophes such as weather-induced crop failures. Not only do higher-status families have a more secure store to draw on, their "right" to scarce resources is conceded by the community. While the majority perish, those of highest rank survive. Hence lowered fertility in the short run may lead to greater fitness in the long run.

[58] Another case of rural privation coupled with high fertility can be observed in Nepal (Baker and Panter-Brick 2000: 165–166). One important variable appears to be life expectancy which is negatively correlated with fertility. Evidently, when individuals expect a short life-span they begin bearing at puberty and continue bearing at short IBIs thereafter (Low *et al.* 2007).

[59] The Mexican economy (even when the illegal US migrant economy is included) cannot keep pace with the post-World War II exponential population growth, even though the birth rate is now falling.

Figure 2 Otavalo Market, Ecuador

attendance policy robbed them of children's labor. They were also frank about the debilitating effects on their health that frequent childbearing exacted. However, their husbands and males generally are opposed to fertility reduction and birth control. The women then "revealed an extreme reluctance to engage in socially disapproved behavior" (Browner 2001: 466).

Similarly, Kress finds that fertility has plunged among indigenous people in northern Ecuador who are enjoying great success marketing handicrafts, while it has not declined in neighboring communities not involved in craft production and sales (Kress 2005; 2007). Indeed, I visited the Otavalo market and was struck by how lavishly dressed many of the children were – they were definitely being treated as cherubs.

Even though IM rates have been falling steadily throughout the world, they're falling much more slowly or not at all in the poorest communities.[60] In 1970,

[60] These are critical times in much of the underdeveloped world. It's as if there's a race between overpopulation and environmental disaster versus investment in human capital and birth control (Caldwell *et al.* 1998).

eight times as many children perished in the world's five poorest compared with the five richest countries; by 2000 that ratio had risen to twenty (Gielen and Chumachenko 2004: 94). These trends are part of a worldwide phenomenon best captured by the aphorism "The rich get richer and the poor get [sickly] children." In Nigeria, for example, the fertility rate is 5.9, with gross national income (GNI) per capita at $260. Western Europe, on the other hand, has a fertility rate of 1.5 with a GNI of $25,300 (Gielen and Chumachenko 2004: 85).

Indeed, in the worst-off regions of the world, it's almost as if all vestiges of rationality have disappeared. Somalia has, for decades, been beset by the twin evils of rapid degradation of the subsistence system (owing to overuse of thin soils and periodic drought) and civil war. Nevertheless, Somali women vie for the title of world's most prolific breeders and when asked how many children they'd like, the *average* number desired was twelve (Dybdhal and Hundeide 1998: 139). In Burkina Faso, overpopulation has placed whole villages in jeopardy of starvation – if HIV/AIDS doesn't wipe them out first. Yet, villagers live in complete ignorance of contraception and see no connection between sexual relations and AIDS (Hampshire 2001: 117).

Madagascar is another country where the persistence of the "production" strategy has had dire consequences. Ancestor worship has always been very important and adults must depend upon their progeny to insure "the quality of their ancestral afterlife ... [A]t a wedding ... future husbands and wives [are wished] 'seven sons and seven daughters'" (Ravololomanga and Schlemmer 2000: 300). However, for decades, the island has witnessed severe erosion and spreading desertification due to land overuse. Consequently, "a large number of families can no longer even feed their children, never mind clothe them ... parents with disabled children refuse to have them fitted with artificial limbs free of charge because handicapped beggars bring in higher earnings ... " (Ravololomanga and Schlemmer 2000: 310).

For many parts of the world, modernization will come too late. Instead of the voluntary lowering of fertility associated with the "Great Transition," the effect will be accomplished via history's oldest forms of population control – famine and epidemic (Boone and Kessler 1999: 261).

Two exceptions

... infants, are much appreciated and, for the very young [African-American] mother, are much like playthings. (Field *et al.* 1992: 174)

The greatest mission of [a Mormon] woman is to give life ... to ... our Father's spirit children who anxiously desire to come to dwell here in this mortal state. (Tanner 1980: 17)

Even in the USA, the demographic transition is incomplete. I will examine two interesting cases where relatively early onset of breeding, short IBI, and high fertility prevail. In a brutally honest account, Alex Kotlowitz uses a single extended family to serve as a window into the lives of inner-city African-Americans.[61] The setting is a public housing project (*ject*) on the west side, Chicago's worst neighborhood. Violent crime and drug abuse are rampant, economic or employment opportunities nil. LaJoe Rivers and her husband, Paul, had eight children ranging in age from four (triplets) to twenty-one. Paul had abandoned the family and/or been forced out owing to womanizing and drug use. Their three oldest children were deeply involved in criminal careers. Lafayette, not yet out of grade school, acts as father figure for his younger siblings. LaJoe's parents – who'd also lived in the same projects – had thirteen children, including three sets of twins. There's every evidence that this pattern will prevail into the next generation as Terence, LaJoe's favorite, "like many of his teenage friends, [was] a father; he had three children in all, a boy and two girls. Like his mother, he had his first child when he was fourteen. As tradition dictated, the child was named after his dad, Terence, though everyone called him 'Snuggles' " (Kotlowitz 1991: 88–89).

This tendency for infants to be treated as baby-dolls, where, in effect, children are bearing children, stems, indirectly, from an accident of our evolutionary history. Because of inactive lifestyles and the cheap, easy access to high-calorie foods, girls begin accumulating body fat at a very early age. The body is "fooled" into "early biological maturation long before cognitive and social maturity are reached" (Lancaster 1986: 26). However, early and frequent child-bearing may, actually, be adaptive for these girls. The economic restructuring which triggered the demographic transition has largely passed them by. This is vividly illustrated in the education career of LaJoe's niece Dawn, who "was to be only the second of [her] generation in the Anderson family to graduate from high school. Nine children had already dropped out ... Dawn's accomplishment was made even more notable by the fact that she had, at age eighteen, four children, aged four, two, one, and three months" (Kotlowitz 1991: 126–127). Nothing in Dawn's experience suggested that postponing childbearing to complete enough education to launch a "career" was a viable option. Her graduation is largely symbolic. On the other hand, life-history factors push girls like Dawn to capitalize on their early reproductive opportunities. Anthropologist Bobbi Low lists a host of support factors that are available to a girl that aren't necessarily available to a more mature woman. At this age she's attractive to boyfriends (most of whom will be considerably older) who provide some measure of support. Her mother and even grandmother are likely to be available and

---

[61] The portrait fits most poor inner-city communities and can be extended to the Caribbean, where "Cultural norms governing mating relationships and family formation tend to be flexible and fluid" (Lange and Rodman 1992: 186).

willing to help raise her children.[62] Low reports that black "teenage mothers have about a 75 percent chance that their mothers will be alive and able to help when their child is 5 years old; for women who postpone childbearing until age 20, that figure is 40 percent" (Low 2000: 333).

In addition, poor African-American women suffer high rates of obesity (Eveleth and Tanner 1990: 74), and they "weather" early. It is thus advantageous for them to begin bearing children as teenagers, while they are still relatively healthy (Geronimus 1992; 1996). And, more generally, studies show that in a society where one's social support network may be uncertain, individuals adopt an opportunistic reproduction strategy with early onset of mating and high fertility (Belsky *et al.* 1991). Of course, the *child's* prospects may not be all that bright. Indeed, IM among lower-class African-Americans, especially in the south, has actually been on the rise and the rate (17 per 1,000: *New York Times*, April 22, 2007: A1) is more than three times the rate found in countries like Japan and Sweden.

A second US sub-culture that has, until quite recently, evaded the demographic transition is the Mormon culture in Utah.[63] The Mormons[64] have a tradition of high fertility, aided by the practice of polygyny,[65] initiated by church founder, Joseph Smith. His successor, Brigham Young – who led the harassed exiles to what would become Utah in the mid-nineteenth century – set an example by fathering at least fifty children on his many wives (Moynihan 2002: 623). The unabashed goal of the early pioneers was to populate the "Kingdom of Deseret" as quickly as possible through their own fecundity as well as through recruiting new members from the rest of the USA and Europe. They wanted to forestall the persecution they'd experienced as a minority sect in the Midwest. In this the Mormons were replicating the behavior of the Puritans (among others) who also promoted fertility (turning a blind eye to promiscuity) (Moynihan 2002: 586) as the surest means of rapidly settling a distinct and defensible territory (Reese 2000).

Even though polygyny was outlawed by the US government and abandoned by the official church in 1890 in order to pave the way to statehood, it always enhanced a man's status (Josephson 1993: 392), and has continued to the present

[62] West African societies, which were the primary source for slaves exported to the new world, have long-standing practices, including adoption and fosterage, that relieve fertile young mothers of the burden of rearing all the children they give birth to (Draper 1989).

[63] An interesting historical footnote: "When the Republican Party was founded in 1854, it consisted of a coalition of anti-slavery forces and . . . long-time anti-Mormons . . . commit[ted] to the eliminat[ation of] the 'twin relics of barbarism' – slavery and polygamy" (Lambert and Thomasson 1997: 86–87). Today Utah is a one-party state dominated by the Republican Party.

[64] The term "Mormon" is used in common parlance although it has sometimes had pejorative overtones. "LDS" is also a very common designation. However, the church authorities have striven to promote the consistent use (by non-members as well) of the official name – The Church of Jesus Christ of Latter Day Saints. I use "Mormon" for clarity and brevity.

[65] Referred to in the press as polygamy.

among the 50,000 or more members of the "Fundamentalist" LDS (FLDS) church. Like the Hutterites (Miller *et al.* 2005: 300) and other fundamentalist sects that promote "pro-natalist" lifestyles (Fogiel-Bijaoui 2005), the FLDS are isolated from the mainstream of society and self-sufficient.

As we have seen in our earlier discussion, high fertility in the polygynous household may come at a price.[66] Ethnographic study of polygynous FLDS families uncovered tensions, especially with respect to shared childcare. "Dorothy, the fourth of eight wives . . . observed that dealing with one another as mothers is very difficult – especially where disciplining the children is concerned" (Altman and Ginat 1996: 373–375). FLDS fathers – like their counterparts in the village – are distant disciplinarians who often forget the names of their children or even how many they have (Altman and Ginat 1996: 424–425). Women are given in marriage to high-ranking males in their early teen years to prevent them from forming their own attachments.[67] And young men, referred to in the press as "Lost Boys," are periodically ejected from the community to forestall their access to young women (*Salt Lake City Weekly*, September 23, 2004).

But these are fringe communities. What is more remarkable is that members of the official LDS church have managed to maintain extremely high fertility, in spite of forgoing polygyny and embracing the contemporary US economy and society. As the church weaned itself from polygyny, and the rest of the country was rapidly following the trail blazed by Margaret Sanger and others to embrace birth control and restrain fertility, Mormon women who failed to become prolific breeders were deemed unworthy of salvation (Wilcox 1987: 213).

The fact that Utah Mormons have consistently had a birth rate double the US average (Toney *et al.* 1985: 460) actually obscures the fact that truly large families (six or more children) are commonplace in the state.[68] And, again, unlike the reproduction patterns found elsewhere in modern society, in Utah fertility is *positively* related to education and income (Heaton 1988: 112–113). How have they resisted the demographic transition? It is not because

---

[66] Another cost is the high incidence of birth defects and mental retardation due to high fertility and in-breeding (Kerrigan *et al.* 2000).

[67] While civil authorities have generally turned a blind eye to polygyny in Utah and surrounding states, the marriage and impregnation of girls under 15 years old violates statutory rape laws and is sometimes prosecuted.

[68] That is, the higher birth rate derives not so much from families with three and four children instead of one or two, but from a significant number of families with six or more children. This suggests as well that there are many Utah Mormon families that, along with the rest of the nation, *have* reduced their fertility, compared with previous generations. Unlike the fertility divide in Mexico described earlier, which was based on education and urbanization, in Utah the divide separates the very devout church members from others.

their livelihoods are different: farming[69] and family businesses are no more important than in any other state, education levels are high (*Salt Lake Tribune*, March 28, 2005: A1, A8), high-tech industries and the information economy are avidly embraced. "Utahns live in the largest homes in the nation and own or lease more vehicles per household" (Lown and Rowe 2003: 118).

Obviously the LDS church exerts a tremendous influence on fertility through a variety of mechanisms.[70] First, there is the belief in pre-mortal existence whereby heaven is populated with "spirit children" who are waiting anxiously for their turn on earth before returning to the "Heavenly Father" at death (Packer 1993: 21). Unlike the zeitgeist in much of the rest of the USA and Europe where, in an overpopulated world, having children may be seen as self-indulgence,[71] in Mormon culture childless adults are labeled as selfish, not doing their part to, in effect, adopt as many of these spirit children as possible (Heaton 1988: 117). Second, there is tremendous pressure to marry early and begin bearing children shortly thereafter. And they do: roughly 80 percent are married by twenty-three and first give birth 3.5 years earlier than the US average (*The Herald Journal*, April 3, 2005: A1, A16).

Utah ranks fourth from the bottom of states in preventing unwanted pregnancies, owing to restrictive access to contraception.[72] Women are encouraged to drop out of school and quit their jobs to stay at home with their children (Holman 2002: 63). And "married women with children under age six are less likely to work than their national counterparts . . . those who do work are more likely to work part-time" (Heaton 1988: 117). Hence, "stay-at-home moms" have a strong sense of entitlement as reflected in a rather poignant essay published in the *Salt Lake Tribune* by Stephanie Milner, who holds a degree from a private junior college and is active in musical theater.

A mother of four, whose husband is working while he completes his schooling, Stephanie grudgingly concedes: "Granted, it is our fault that we didn't get masters degrees and careers before having children" (*Salt Lake Tribune*,

---

[69] Unlike other sects dedicated to high fertility, such as the Amish and Hutterites, who remain entrenched in a pre-modern agrarian economy.

[70] Apologists for the high birth rate usually cite church teachings as the primary justification. A dramatic example is provided by the Herrins, a young (both under twenty-seven, no college) couple from North Salt Lake. Their third and fourth children, born in 2002, were conjoined twins. In spite of the staggering cost – to their kin and the public – of raising (and eventually separating) the twins, the Herrins felt compelled, in 2005, to bring a second set of twins into the world, their fifth and sixth children. In the Utah and national spotlight when the first twins were surgically separated in 2006, the Herrins were treated as heroes. Information obtained from www.herrintwins.com; accessed 4.23.07.

[71] For example, having lots of babies has become a status symbol for the super-rich and a new term, "competitive birthing," has been coined to describe the phenomenon. National Public Radio, August 5, 2007: www.npr.org; accessed 9.5.2007.

[72] News release, February 28, 2006: www.guttmacher.org; accessed 4.23.07.

September 3, 2003: A3), and also acknowledges that they have benefited from many federal and state social programs including Housing and Urban Development funds for their house (which she complains is too small), Head Start for the children, and Pell grants for their education. They pay no income tax and yet the bulk of the essay is a tale of resentment that their church-promoted choices have left them "poor," unable to take their children to Disneyland.

Stephanie has plenty of company. In spite of specific church admonitions on the peril of debt, Utah's bankruptcy rate is the highest in the nation (Lown and Rowe 2003: 113),[73] and insurance fraud – as a result of the failure of children to remove themselves from their parents' policies once married – is also very high (*Salt Lake Tribune*, February 28, 2003: A1). Utah is also number one in the nation in terms of mortgage fraud (*Salt Lake Tribune*, March 29, 2007: A1), primarily by couples including in their "family income" the income of a wife who has quit her job to remain at home (*The Herald Journal*, September 19, 2004: A1). Collectively, we see a picture where the cost of Mormon high fertility is shifted, where possible, on to the general population.[74] While Mormons must tithe 10 percent of their income to the church,[75] taxes are kept low, resulting in the lowest spending on public education in the nation (LeFevre 2004).[76] The minority of non-Mormons in the state fight back via attempts to change the tax code and eliminate tax exemptions after the fourth child (*The Park Record*, February 4, 2004: B1), and to make contraception more accessible (*Salt Lake Tribune*, January 19, 2005: A8)[77] – in vain.

Not surprisingly, Mormon kids in large families receive less individualized attention from their parents (Lambert and Thomasson 1997: 91). Other signs of strain include the fact that the divorce rate is close to the national average, in spite of extensive marital counseling provided through both informal and formal

[73] However, even those who file for bankruptcy because they can't pay creditors continued to pay their tithing to the church until the bankruptcy law was recently changed (*Salt Lake Tribune*, January 9, 2005: A10). Orrin Hatch, senior Senator from Utah, has sponsored legislation that would relax those changes, permitting those in bankruptcy to continue tithing or donating to their church – in lieu of paying their creditors (*Salt Lake Tribune*, October 1, 2006: A8).

[74] Utah State University Honors Program, "Last Lecture," April 18, 2003: websites. usu.edu/politicalscience; accessed 4.23.07.

[75] In general, there's greater willingness to tithe because those funds are redistributed to fellow church members whereas tax dollars for education and social services benefit all. Subsidized daycare is strongly resisted because of the push to keep women at home with their young children.

[76] Utah State University Honors Program, "Last Lecture," April 18, 2003. In higher education, Utah is perhaps the only state where parents do not expect to pay any of their children's tuition or costs. Even wealthy parents tend to exert pressure on the state's public universities to provide "full-ride" scholarships for their offspring. When students' families fail to support them they go into debt which may also contribute to the bankruptcy problem.

[77] The Religious Right consistently lobbies – usually successfully – against any change that would relieve a woman of paying the wages of her sin. One battle they lost was a new statue to decriminalize a mother who drops her newborn off at a "safe haven," in lieu of the dumpster (*Salt Lake Tribune*, November 16, 2000: A4).

church facilities. Indeed, during the first few years of marriage, it is higher than the national average, probably due to the early and often rushed nuptials (Lambert and Thomasson 1997: 97). Because divorced women had often cast all thoughts of education and career aside upon marriage, and divorced husbands remarry and sire additional offspring quickly, divorcees are plunged into (real) poverty. In one case that made it into the newspaper only because the estranged husband tried to gain access, through the courts, to his wife's computer hard drive, the couple had seven children aged four months to seven years and, with only $700 per month in support from her ex, the divorcee was forced to begin her post-secondary education to qualify as a legal assistant (*Salt Lake Tribune*, February 12, 2005: B5). Not surprisingly, Utah has the second highest rate (11 percent of those over eighteen) of mental illness in the country – after Rhode Island – and 16 percent of the population takes anti-depressant drugs (*Salt Lake Tribune*, January 23, 2005: A4).

These two cautionary tales remind us that, in spite of the demographic transition, where favorable conditions support high fertility, large families may be the norm. In the concluding section which follows, we will take a peek into the "Brave New World" of the future. Modernization and new technologies have spawned a bewildering array of choices with respect to reproduction.

The next transition

. . . individual and even collective behavior may be directed by cultural choices towards solutions that have negative Darwinian fitness. (Cavalli-Sforza and Feldman 1981: 343)

While adults are having fewer children, the desire for children, often amounting to desperation, has increased. (Gillis 2003: 83)

. . . sex, love and childbearing have become à la carte choices rather than a package deal that comes with marriage. (*Washington Post*, March 26, 2006: B1)

(The Great) Ramses II was such a highly respected pharaoh that nine of his successors – nearly every ruler to the end of the New Kingdom – took the name Ramses. Although he had excellent spin doctors, Ramses was not a conspicuous success militarily, nor is his reign marked by innovation in religion or literature, and public art standards fell as he promoted size and quantity of monuments over quality. His chief claim to fame was his extraordinary breeding success, siring at least 150 sons (daughters weren't counted) on his many wives and concubines. His successor, Mereneptah, was his thirteenth-born son; he outlived the first twelve.

Throughout human history, men have aspired to be like Ramses II, so what about Hugh Hefner, one of the most famous and successful Americans? Hefner, the founder of the *Playboy*[78] empire of publications, nightclubs, and television

---

[78] Whose symbol is the bunny, as in "breed like rabbits."

programs, among others, has had access to as many or perhaps more nubile, breeding-age females (referred to in the Playboy culture as G.O.H.s, Girlfriends of Hef) than Ramses and yet, tabloid reports notwithstanding, he's rumored to have fathered only one child and that a girl!

Hefner should not be seen as an anomaly;[79] elective infertility is becoming commonplace. In a brilliantly researched and argued thesis, Muriel Jolivet claims Japan is becoming a "childless" society. Dramatic social and economic changes coupled with conservative traditions are driving this trend. Young women are now expected to complete an education and at least begin the pursuit of a career before marriage. This insures that they can support themselves and aging parents in case they don't find a spouse. Following marriage and pregnancy, their lives change dramatically. Leaving their parents' home to move into isolated *beddo* (bedroom) communities, they are suddenly without friends and see little of their husbands. Because they grew up in the absence of numerous younger siblings, they have had almost no experience with babies. Their lack of confidence stands in ironic contrast to cultural attitudes that identify the biological mother as the only morally acceptable caretaker. Conveniences like disposable diapers are condemned as shirking one's duty (Jolivet 1997: 1).[80] Women who try to balance work and childrearing face a barrage of subtle and not-so-subtle abuse. For example, mothers must attend monthly meetings at school where their child's "problems" are publicly aired and where blame is squarely placed on them (Mariko 1989: 83). Not surprisingly, politicians fret that "'bellies are on strike' [as a] growing number of women admit that they find motherhood tedious, exhausting and exasperating" (Jolivet 1997: 1).

Teenage pregnancy rates in the USA have dropped by one-third in the past decade (Martin *et al.* 2003), apparently due not to any success so-called abstinence-only programs may be having (Trenholm *et al.* 2007)[81] but, rather, to the substitution of casual "hooking up" for oral sex in place of the customary progression from dating to going steady to intercourse (Sax 2005: 121). A corollary trend finds that, increasingly, brief liaisons between adolescents are more likely to involve condom use compared with longer-term traditional pairing which more often resulted in pregnancy.[82] And many college coeds are

---

[79] One study, however, did show that "Higher-income men . . . had . . . marginally more children than lower-income men" (Weeden *et al.* 2006: 388).

[80] These sentiments are definitely echoed, albeit somewhat muted to be sure, in contemporary US society (Warner 2005).

[81] An eight-year study shows "virginity pledgers" to be only slightly less sexually active and, not surprisingly, more likely to engage in unprotected and riskier (oral and anal) sex (*Salt Lake Tribune*, March 19, 2005: A5).

[82] National Campaign to Prevent Teen Pregnancy, 14 and Younger, *The Sexual Behavior of Young Adolescents*, 2003, Washington, D.C.: www.teenpregnancy.org/resources/reading/pdf/12summary.pdf. Other contributing factors are the availability of more effective

becoming LUGs (lesbians until graduation) (*Salt Lake Tribune*, September 6, 2005: A9) to protect themselves from the career-stunting effects of marriage and childrearing. While the messages about the perils of pregnancy seem to be getting through, those about the perils of sex before marriage are drowned out by the siren song of puberty.[83]

While more and more heterosexual couples eschew childbearing, in the USA, the latest civil-rights movement aims to grant family status to homosexual couples and the children they're raising.[84] Another trend is motherhood among mature women who've forsworn marriage (Townsend 2001: 121).[85] The birth rate for women over forty-five doubled during the 1990s (Crandell 2005: 100). For many who are nearing the end of very successful careers raising a child becomes the ultimate retirement hobby. However,

Barbara Harris (49) discovered that "Once you're in your 40s, you . . . cannot stay up all night [with a fussy baby] and be bright-eyed the next day" . . . Tina Georgeou (53) had a similar epiphany – "Looking after a child is much more intense than being in business, where in a meeting you can sit back and gather energy." (Crandell 2005: 104)

But, as the quotation from the *Washington Post* in the epigraph to this section indicates, an array of pharmacological and medical advances undergird this latest demographic trend. Among the older mothers, fifty-something media personality Joan Lunden has employed surrogate women to gestate and bear[86] her latest children. Indeed, "having a child is so important that Americans spend $2 billion a year on fertility drugs and test-tube fertilization" (Cross 2004: 5).[87] A couple might spend $45,000–$65,000 on infertility treatments (*Salt Lake*

forms of contraception and welfare reforms that have made working more rewarding and bearing children less so (Sawhill 2003: 155).

[83] Interestingly, the Mormon church has taken note of these trends that run so directly counter to its admonitions to adolescents to marry early and have many children. Reversing a long-standing policy against teenage dating, a high-ranking official warned in a "fireside chat" aimed at youth: "we counsel you to channel your associations with the opposite sex into dating patterns that have the potential to mature into marriage, not hanging-out patterns that only have the prospect to mature into team sports like touch football. Marriage is not a group activity – at least not until the children come along in goodly numbers": Dallin H. Oaks, "Fireside broadcast for young adults," May 1, 2005, Church Education System: information from www.lds.org; accessed 4.23.07.

[84] In turn, rampant homophobia now surfs a wave of new "marriage protection" statutes (Blunt 2003).

[85] In 1992, then US Vice-President Dan Quayle enjoyed a moment of fame by denouncing TV sit-com character Murphy Brown – a no-longer-young career woman – who'd elected to have a child without benefit of marriage (*New York Times*, May 20, 1992: A20).

[86] The latest economic growth area in India is the establishment of baby factories where poor women gestate and bear the children of wealthy foreigners (*Salt Lake Tribune*, December 31, 2007: A6).

[87] It is interesting that "some Shi'ite religious authorities continue to denounce sperm and egg donation, prohibiting it for their followers. Others accept egg donation as being like polygyny (which is permitted in Islam), but decry sperm donation for its implications of polyandry (which is not allowed)" (Inhorn 2005: 14).

Tribune, January 24, 2005: A6) or upwards of $30,000 on the services of a surrogate (*Salt Lake Tribune*, January 23, 2005: A8). And while sperm donors can command only about $40 per donation, *egg* donors can expect $4,000–$5,000 (*Salt Lake Tribune*, January 23, 2005: E1, E2).[88] Ethicists wrestle with the morality of, in effect, "outsourcing" pregnancy: "Does surrogacy allow one social class to take advantage of another?" (*Salt Lake Tribune*, January 24, 2005: A7).[89] Of course this issue may quickly become moot as mechanical incubation of human embryos becomes feasible (Reynolds 2005).

The number of million-dollar babies in the USA is proliferating, as our society embraces the moral obligation to subsidize a woman's "right" to have a child, under any circumstances. For example, Eloysa Vasquez suffers from a rare disorder the effects of which are so severe she weighs only 37 lbs; she is confined to a wheelchair and her bones are so fragile a sneeze could break them. Yet, her husband, family, community, and medical personnel saw nothing wrong with her repeated pregnancies and miscarriages, and celebrated her eventual "successful" (child delivered eight weeks early by cesarean-section) birth. This phenomenally costly piece of biological and social engineering was carried out at Stanford University's hospital (*San Francisco Chronicle*, February 10, 2006: B1). Another, similar, case involves sixty-year-old New Yorker Frieda Birnbaum, who gave birth to twins – following infertility treatments in South Africa – in May 2007. She describes her action as striking a blow for women's freedom (Springer 2007).[90]

A critic castigates the medical profession for this blatant self-aggrandizement. Neonatal medicine and the neonatal intensive care unit (NICU) are seen as "growth" sectors in hospital administration that earn big bucks. High-tech advances and heroic procedures now preserve the lives of barely viable neonates. While proponents brag "we can bring a peach back from death," this aggressive attitude has led to a quintupling of cerebral palsy and its attendant life-long burden on families and society. Silvermann (2004: 403) asks: "Has opportunism overwhelmed compassion in the [medical] industry?" Another critic argues that

the NICU represents an "island" mentality . . . The clinician of today may take comfort [that] "There are infants who wouldn't be alive now if we hadn't started this unit." But future generations may instead count the lives that were not saved because our culture neglected the larger picture of life and death, and count those good-hearted souls who

---

[88] One can only wonder whether this disparity will begin to effect the sex ratio among members of the social class that has taken advantage of these new economic opportunities.

[89] Of course, history is replete with examples of infant and childcare being delegated to servants, slaves, and professional wet-nurses; why not pregnancy?

[90] "Woman defends decision to give birth at 60," MSNBC, May 24, 2007: www.msnbc.msn.com; accessed 9.3.2007.

have worked so hard to build the NICU enterprise as complicit in this shocking failure. (Jameton 1995: 430)[91]

Premature births are rapidly increasing in the USA, driven in part by elective fertility treatments and in part by our acceptance of costly ($15 billion in 2005[92]), high-tech efforts to rescue marginally viable "premies" (Isaacson 2002).[93] Our willingness to spend billions on high-tech neonatal medicine in one sector of society is offset by an unwillingness to spend far smaller sums of money on *preventing* prematurity and other gestation and birth problems. Nor do we pay enough attention to children's health needs. "Of every 100 children recently surveyed in East St. Louis, 55 were incompletely immunized for polio, diphtheria, measles and whooping cough" (Kozol 1991: 21). Compared with nations in Europe, support in the USA for family planning, including contraception, genetic counseling, and pre- and post-natal care is paltry. As a result of this ideologically motivated parsimony, our IM rate places us twenty-seven on a list of developed nations (Martin *et al.* 2003).

Meanwhile, in the Third World, many thousands of children die from measles every year because vaccine, at 57 cents per child, can't be made available by impoverished governments.[94] Overall, the World Bank estimates that 11 million children die each year before the age of five – from causes that are medically preventable (*Deseret News*, April 18, 2005: A2).

In China, the strict enforcement of the "one-child" policy – instituted by Deng Xiaoping in 1979 – has resulted in an explosion in the abandonment of female babies. As Kay Johnson documents, the authorities (prodded by international condemnation of orphanage conditions) have attempted to address the crisis by, in effect, exporting surplus children. Since 1992, adoption has been liberalized – for foreigners only – and increasing numbers of Europeans and Americans, desperate to rear a child, are spending the time and money necessary to acquire a Chinese baby (Johnson 2004: xv).[95]

In an extreme irony, China's neighbor to the west, Russia, is suffering from a dearth of children and while China punishes a woman for bearing a second child, Russia will reward her with a $10,000 check. "President Vladimir Putin declared that the primary concern of the state is now about love, women and

---

[91] We should perhaps not be surprised, given the history of progressive attitudes towards children in the Netherlands, that the Dutch do not intervene aggressively with extremely (less than twenty-five weeks' gestation) premature births (Lorenz *et al.* 2001).

[92] Information from www.marchofdimes.com; accessed 4.23.07.

[93] Neonatal medicine, while evolving into a multi-billion-dollar industry, has also fashioned an entire culture of terms and practices to humanize or "normalize" a biologically defective organism.

[94] Information from www.who.int/immunization_financing/countries; accessed 4.23.07.

[95] From a trickle of Chinese adoptions in the late 1980s, the number has grown to more than 5,000 per annum to the USA alone by 2000.

children." However, in a further irony, Russia leads the world in foreign adoptions. Orphanages are virtually self-supporting as they earn hefty fees when they successfully place a child with foreign adopters (*International Herald Tribune*, May 20–21, 2006).

Meanwhile, in Fransfontein, an impoverished rural area of Namibia, Julia Pauli finds that the breakdown of traditional marriage and family structures characteristic of impoverished urban areas is spreading to villages. She uses the term "multiple parenthoods" to describe a phenomenon whereby children may never know their father and their mother may play a minor caretaking role in their lives. Since Pauli's main informant had had ten children by at least five partners, any one of her children might discover as many as twenty "siblings." Hence children must participate in elective families, forming kin-like ties on a fraternal basis. Like street children – their urban counterparts – the children of Fransfontein find that peers are preferred as nurturers, compared with, often harsh and exploitative, adults (Pauli 2005).

The number of "foster parent" programs where donors sponsor children in Third World settings is proliferating.[96] This creates opportunities to "parent" children one never lays eyes on.

What, then, do all these disparate cases have in common? They are all evidence for the uncoupling of sex and procreation, procreation and parenting, pregnancy and parenting. In short the biological processes of reproduction are, increasingly, independent of the social processes of pair-bonding, of love-making, and caring for children (Strathern 1992). Individuals who enjoy sex don't need to be burdened with pregnancy; those who enjoy pregnancy can dispense with sex *and* childrearing (Ragone 2001: 472).[97] Single individuals can now choose "all of the above" or "none of the above." Fecundity is no longer valued, indeed, high fertility is seen as inherently anti-social.

Ironically, this evidence of "sexual freedom" has provoked an international outpouring of government scrutiny and control. We may well be on the threshold of a new era in which conception and pregnancy, which have, historically, not been closely regulated by anyone, not even the responsible parties, become highly regulated.[98] Meanwhile, sexual relations, which, historically, *have* been

---

[96] Relevant websites: www.fosterparentsplan.ca; www.savethechildren.org; www.children.org; www.christianchildrensfund.org/sponsortoday; www.warmblankets.org; all accessed 4.23.07.

[97] Although the "n" is small, I'm struck by the almost universal affirmation by surrogate mothers in the USA that they "love being pregnant," for example, "Fran, age 27, divorced with one child, described the difficulty of her delivery this way: 'I had a rough delivery, a C-section, and my lung collapsed because I had the flu but it was worth every minute of it. If I were to die from childbirth, that's the best way to die'" (Ragone 2001: 472).

[98] The fate of frozen embryos, for example, has become the business of courts, legislators, and special interest lobbyists. But, from my perspective, the greatest ethical challenge we face is to justify the Western practice of pursuing very high-cost intervention strategies for infertile individuals and defective and/or extremely premature infants. Essentially, for the fortune we

of great concern to authorities and the community at large, are now only restricted by the varied desires of individuals and the fear of STDs.

This *Brave New World* [99] has already begun in Singapore, perhaps the most restrictive non-Muslim society in the world.[100] In 1987, a class-biased eugenics policy was initiated to encourage the largely Chinese middle class to bear children while offering a bounty of $6,500 to lower-class women who agreed to be sterilized (Wee 1992: 201).[101] This incentive for the lower class was accompanied by disincentives, such as a dramatically escalating "accouchement fee" for each subsequent birth after the first. The Singaporean reproduction policy[102] is designed to increase the output of "producers of wealth" while limiting production of those who are, mainly, "consumers of wealth" (Wee 1992: 189–190). The reproduction policy is further supported by a parallel schooling policy:

the entire educational system... may be understood as a nationwide searching and testing device for innate leadership. The increasingly stressful streaming process... children have to undergo is not a mere historical accident. According to Lee Kuan Yew, "severe stress" is a mechanism for "disclosing" innate leadership qualities. At the age of nine, all school children have to take a nationwide examination that will stream them into three basic categories... "express," "normal," and "monolingual". (Wee 1992: 203)

Brave new world, indeed!

spend on a few hundred of these techno-babies, millions of Third World children could be saved from death by starvation and illnesses for which there are cheap vaccinations and treatments.

[99] Huxley (1931/1998).

[100] Chewing gum is banned and spitting in public is a serious crime (Randerson 2002: 55).

[101] An apparently similar approach has been taken by the Hungarian government since 1985, to counter a trend whereby the ethnically Hungarian birth rate was falling precipitously while the Roma (Gypsy) birth rate was, if anything, rising (Fodor 2003).

[102] The controversy that the eugenics policy aroused has led the Singaporean government to modify many aspects of the policy, cf. Kenneth Tan (personal communication, October 2007).

3   A child's worth

Introduction

My daughter is extraordinary at chess and ice skating, for which I pay through the nose. (Kusserow 2004: 82)

[West African] Ijo perceive of inheritance as flowing from sons to fathers as readily as the reverse. (Hollos and Philip 1989: 29)

Much of the extant literature on children identifies the parent–child relationship as central to the functioning of the society. Furthermore, this relationship is seen as largely uni-directional. That is, the parent has manifold obligations to her child, while the child has few, if any, to the parent. However, as we review literature on children in other societies, a very different picture emerges. As the second epigraph above suggests, the obligations may be heavily weighted in the direction of child to parent.

This chapter opens with some arresting cases from the USA and Japan that illustrate the extreme devotion expected of parents towards their adored offspring. A dramatic contrast is drawn as we then examine widespread practices in which children are sacrificed to the more important interests of their parents, families, and the community at large. These actions towards infants are not only tolerated; they may be enshrined in respected and ancient customs.

This utilitarian attitude towards children is also associated with the widely shared view that children should contribute to the welfare of their families through their labor – as farmhands, traders, and laborers. But there is one group of societies – foraging bands – which cannot make good use of children's labor. Foraging requires physical attributes they lack. Further, reproduction and childcare practices in these highly mobile societies emphasize the survival of the few offspring produced. And, as a consequence, adult–child interaction among foragers has many of the hallmarks we consider "normal." The chapter concludes with further discussion of our "priceless" children.

Expensive little cherubs

...children impose economic costs more surely than they provide benefits. (Wilson and Daly 2002: 307)

There is a lot of talk [in Japan] these days about *kodomo no pettoka*, the way parents look upon their child as they would a domestic pet. (Jolivet 1997: 57)

In the USA, children have become the ultimate "big-ticket" consumer purchase. The meter starts running long before the child is born. A well-known Los Angeles obstetrician quit his practice in 1999 to open the 3D Sonography Center of Beverly Hills where expectant parents can purchase (for $250) an 8 × 10 glossy sonogram of the fetus.[1] Another booming business devoted to children is the birthday party. Birthdayparties.com asserts: "Birthday parties for children are getting more elaborate and original everyday. Sometimes a birthday party with a simple theme just isn't enough." The website sponsors a monthly contest for "best" birthday party ideas; for example, the "Combination Kidnapping and Princess Party" for an eight-year-old daughter is typical, running to nearly 1,800 words. It is clear from a perusal of the "best" descriptions that mothers are spending upwards of a hundred hours preparing these parties.[2]

For mothers who want the net effect but lack the time to invest in creating the perfect party, there are services like "Partypoopers.com" in New York that organize a variety of themed children's parties. The "Intergalactic Odyssey," for example, is priced at $2,000 for up to twenty children, plus gratuity. Of course, the party's centerpiece is the birthday gifts. In the popular media we learn about "Yoga Mamas" who will buy only the priciest items for their cherubs: YMs "are more style- and brand-conscious than their parents...they spend like lottery winners on their babies and toddlers" (Palmeri 2005: 128).

Also in the news recently, four-year-old Maddilin (*sic*) Emmons' doting mom, Timi, kept a daily diary once she became pregnant with Maddilin, as a way to relate to and communicate with her fetus, for example, "You and I ran errands and shopped a big part of the day" (*This American Life*, National Public Radio, July 25, 2003). Mrs. Emmons resigned from her job to devote herself to "scrapbooking" (*sic*) Maddie. Despite having a room dedicated exclusively to her craft, materials have overtaken the family's dining room. She spends at least fifty hours a week memorializing her daughter,[3] working until 4 a.m. on the latest scrapbook. Nine thousand dollars' worth of supplies are lavished

---

[1] Or, if you're a movie star, you can buy your own machine and bring it home, as Tom Cruise did for his pregnant girlfriend Katie Holmes (*People Magazine*, December 5, 2005). At "Peek-a-Boo" in Cucamonga, framed "first portraits" of the fetus are supplemented by competitively priced videos, T-shirts, and web-sharing facilities (*Washington Post*, August 9, 2003: C1).

[2] Information obtained from http://birthdayparties.com; accessed 4.18.07.

[3] Those with similar motives but less time can outsource this work, contracting for a DVD scrapbook for only $4,000 (*New York Times*, November 30, 2006: E9).

on the production of at least five books for each year of her daughter's life but, as she says: "When it comes to Maddie, nothing is mundane, every little bit is important." Mrs. Emmons represents a growing cohort of mothers and grandmothers who have turned "scrapbooking" into a billion dollar a year business in the USA, with thousands of stores fueling the practice (*Houston Chronicle*, March 9, 2003: Lifestyle; *The Record* (NJ), June 5, 2003: B1).

In Kusserow's ethnography of childrearing in three communities in New York City, "Parkside" is the most exclusive:

by age three Parkside children were already considered little competitors – small but complete "little people" with their own tastes, desires, needs, and wants. All of the Parkside parents I interviewed had their children enrolled in private pre-schools... competition to get in... was fierce... Many parents experienced a great deal of angst over whether their child would perform well during the interview process [A father saw similarities]... between the venture capital business and the upbringing of a child... [and a mother]... said there was nothing that would stop her children from being the best, and though developing the child through various lessons and classes cost quite a lot, it was what must be done. (Kusserow 2004: 81, 82)

Slavish devotion to one's progeny can also be found in Japan where "mothers cater to [the] baby's every whim" (Shwalb *et al.* 1996: 170). *T'aekyo*, for example, is a complex set of practices and overarching philosophy to guide the expectant mother, who must get in synch with her unborn child. She should expose herself to uplifting thoughts and pleasing sights, sounds, and aromas while avoiding their antitheses (Kim and Choi 1994: 239–240). *T'aekyo* now includes the use of new technologies to facilitate the child's academic success, including, for example, "English-language texts to be read aloud by the mother-to-be into a sort of resonating device strapped to her belly" (White 2002: 134–135).[4]

While these parents might be seen as a trifle "over-indulgent," no one would seriously question the duty of a modern American or Japanese parent to devote a significant amount of their resources in time and money to their offspring, *with no expectation of any material or tangible return* aside from the child's love and affection.

Indeed, parents' near-obsession with their children, their paranoia about their health and safety, drives them to a state of "hyper-vigilance." Aside from "nannycams," which are enjoying record sales, children are now monitored by an array of sophisticated, Pentagon-inspired, eavesdropping equipment (Katz 2005: 109). As we will see throughout this chapter, this philosophy is at odds with virtually every pre-modern society where childcare has been studied.

---

[4] In China, fetal instruction (*taijiao*) dates from the fourth century BCE. It was seen "as a means to influence the moral development of the child at the earliest possible opportunity" (Kinney 1995: 27).

These profound differences are also evident in the treatment of deceased children. Obituaries of babies are not unusual in the *Herald Journal*, the local Logan, Utah paper.[5] With a photo of the baby and running to more than three hundred words, this one was particularly expressive:

Madyson [*sic*] wiggled her way into this world with as much heaven as she could tote. She took six months to spread it all around and then, like a sweet little ladybug, flew into her Heavenly Father's open arms . . . She spent the last 5 weeks of her life at Primary Children's Medical Center . . . She loved listening to music, sucking on her toes and had recently discovered "peek-a-boo" . . . But most of all she loved her Mommy, who loved her and gave her the best care she could possibly have given. Funeral Services will be held . . . Interment will be in "Babyland" at the Logan City Cemetery. (*Logan Herald*, August 2, 2003a: A6)[6]

Madyson, who probably suffered from some clinical risk at birth, was clearly of high value to her mother and the larger community. Her passing was noted through public acknowledgment in the newspaper, a funeral service, church service, and in a specially demarcated area of the public cemetery. Nor is this an isolated case. National organizations like SHARE assist US families in creating an elaborate mortuary response for those lost during pregnancy, at birth, or as infants. SHARE volunteers bathe, weigh, and clothe the "loved one," and provide an array of mementos, such as "casts of the babies' hands and feet . . . [all] placed in satin-covered boxes and presented to the parents" (*Herald Journal*, September 21, 2004: A3).

Our views on the treatment of fetal and infant mortality and pre-term and medically challenged infants can be contrasted with a far more common pattern: among the ancient Greeks and Romans sickly, unattractive, or unwanted infants were "exposed" or otherwise eliminated; the Chinese and Hindus of India have, since time immemorial, destroyed daughters at birth, to open the way for a new pregnancy and a more desirable male offspring; the Japanese likened infanticide to thinning the rice plants in their paddies; among foragers such as the Inuit or the Jivaro, unwanted babies are left to nature to claim; and in nineteenth-century London, infant corpses littered parks and roadsides (Scrimshaw 1984: 439).

And, lest the reader be misled by the tense employed above, epidemiological studies indicate that infanticide is still very much with us. In China, "abandonment contributes notably to the annual million-plus 'missing' female births" (Johnson 2004: 73). In *developed* nations, children under twelve months are the most likely homicide victims and upwards of 20 percent of SIDS (sudden

---

[5] The paper also runs pet obituaries.

[6] Winnie the Pooh and two heart-shaped balloons carved into stone mark a special section of Logan Cemetery for miscarried and stillborn infants and those babies whose parents can't afford burial costs (*Herald Journal*, July 27, 2002: A1).

infant death syndrome) cases may result from active smothering (*The Globe and Mail*, August 3, 1995: A5; Toufexis and Bjerklie 1994). In other words, the decision to bring the infant to term and to raise it is by no means automatic. Let's examine some of the factors that come into play.

Calculating the costs

Breast feeding is metabolically expensive, and the energetic costs of lactation are actually greater then the energetic costs of pregnancy. (Hagen 1999: 331)

A sick infant simultaneously increases the cost of parental investment and reduces the likelihood of the investment paying off. (Volk and Quinsey 2002: 439)

Just how do parents decide how much to invest in a given child? From the previous chapter, we note the importance given to the presence of the biological parents in a society's willingness to accept a new arrival. For example, the death of the mother or, in many cases, of the father is grounds for infanticide among the Ache, a Paraguyan foraging society.

The baby was small and had very little hair on its head. The Ache felt little affection for children born without hair. No woman volunteered to cradle the baby while the mother recovered from the birth. No man stepped forward to cut the umbilical cord. The signs were clear, and it took only Kuchingi's verbal suggestion to settle the point. "Bury the child," he said. "It is defective, it has no hair." "Besides, it has no father [killed by a jaguar]. Betapangi [the mother's current husband] does not want it. He will leave you if you keep it." Pirajugi [the mother] said nothing, and the old woman Kanegi began to dig silently with a broken bow stave. The child and placenta were placed in the hole and covered with red sandy soil. A few minutes later the Ache packed up their belongings and Grandpa Bepurangi began to break a trail through the undergrowth with his unstrung bow. Pirajugi was tired, but she had nothing to carry, so she was able to keep up without difficulty. (Hill and Hurtado 1996: 3)[7]

The Ache are particularly direct in disposing of surplus children (approximately one-fifth) because their peripatetic, foraging lifestyle places an enormous burden on the parents. The father provides significant food resources, and the mother provides both food and the vigilant monitoring required by their dangerous jungle environment. Both men and women face significant health and safety hazards throughout their relatively short lives, and they place their own welfare over that of their offspring.[8] A survey of several foraging societies shows a close association between the willingness to commit infanticide and the daunting challenge "to carry more than a single young child on the nomadic round" (Riches 1974: 356).

---

[7] See also Mull and Mull (1987).

[8] Wilson and Daly note that having an infant or child diminishes a woman's odds of remarrying after death or divorce of the spouse (Wilson and Daly 2002: 307).

Among other South American foragers, similar attitudes prevail.[9] The Tapirapé from central Brazil allow only three children per family; all others must be left behind in the jungle. Seasonally scarce resources affecting the entire community dictate these measures (Wagley 1977). In fact, the availability of adequate resources is most commonly the criterion for determining whether an apparently healthy infant will be kept alive (Dickeman 1975). Among the Ayoreo foragers of Bolivia, it is customary for women to have several brief affairs, often resulting in childbirth, before settling into a stable relationship equaling marriage. "Illegitimate" offspring are often buried immediately after birth. During Bugos and McCarthy's fieldwork, 54 of 141 births ended in infanticide (Bugos and McCarthy 1984).

In farming communities, additional farmhands are usually welcomed. Still, in rural Japan, a family would be subjected to considerable censure for having "too many" children and might find themselves ostracized if they failed "to get rid of the 'surplus'" (Jolivet 1997: 118).[10] In the impoverished northeast of Brazil, women can count on very little support from their child's father, and their own resources are meager. Hence, "child death *a mingua* (accompanied by maternal indifference and neglect) is understood as an appropriate maternal response to a deficiency *in* the child. Part of learning how to mother . . . include[s] learning when to 'let go'" (Scheper-Hughes 1987b: 190). Early cessation of nursing – one manifestation of the mother's minimizing her investment – is supported by an elaborate folk wisdom that breast milk can be harmful, characterized as "dirty," "bitter," "salty," or "infected." Another folk illness category, *doença de crianca*, is used flexibly by mothers in justifying a decision to surrender the child into the hands of God or, alternatively, raise it as a real "fighter." Of 686 pregnancies in a sample of 72 women, 251 infants failed to reach one year of age (Scheper-Hughes 1987a).

We see a similar fatalism among mothers living in a slum adjacent to the Kimberly (South Africa) diamond-mining concession. Their infants frequently die of *skelmsiekte* (rogue-sickness) "associated with *vuil melk* (dirty milk) – the effects of promiscuity on breast milk . . . mothers . . . engag[e] in . . . prostitution . . . to obtain money to buy food for their children . . . If one asked who was the "rogue" in *skelmsiekte*, one would invariably be told that . . . the rogue is the circumstances" (Lerer 1998: 239, 243).

Wiley has studied childbearing in the Himalayan kingdom of Ladakh and offers three insights. First, that, like the jungle, high-altitude living inposes an extra cost on the expectant mother who does farmwork throughout her

---

[9] The absence of infanticide or abortion has not been noted for any area of the world. The peoples of the South American rainforests have been singled out in this discussion only because their practices were studied in advance of missionary and government efforts to suppress infanticide.

[10] See also Neel (1970).

pregnancy. Second, her infant's life chances, owing to inevitably low birth-weight and other complications, are sharply reduced (Wiley 2004: 6). Third, that the worth of the new child will always be calculated as a tiny fraction of that of his fully mature, productive mother. While the mother's health is closely monitored and she is treated with great solicitude, her infant's fate is of less concern. Its death will be "met with sadness but also with a sense of resignation ... they are buried, not cremated like adults" (Wiley (2004: 131–132).

Are Third World mothers who neglect their infants or, more actively, expose, or kill them, acting this way because they are, somehow, "uncivilized" or lack any sense of aspiration, purpose, or pleasure in having children? Not at all. The Ache – whom we saw burying an inconvenient infant –

constantly gossip with each other about the growth of their children, and their passage through important developmental landmarks. "Chejugi knows how to sit"; "My child can walk now"; "She really knows how to talk"; "He is quite a grown up young man"; "She has almost reached menarche, she is sexually active now." These types of comments are important filler information in any casual conversation [among mothers]. (Hill and Hurtado 1996: 341)

Two anthropologists who've devoted their careers to the study of mothering, Sarah Hrdy and Nancy Scheper-Hughes, argue, respectively, that "Nurturing has to be teased out, reinforced, maintained. Nurturing itself needs to be nurtured" (Hrdy 1999: 174), and that "the usefulness of such ill-defined and culturally de-contextualized terms ... as 'bonding,' 'attachment,' 'critical period,' and so forth ... [must be questioned] ... The terms seem inadequate to describe and to contain the experiences of mothering and nurturing under conditions of extreme scarcity and high risk of child death" (Scheper-Hughes 1987a: 149).

While new mothers may be evaluating the actuarial odds,[11] we know that many are also suffering from post-partum depression or, less severely, detachment from and indifference towards their offspring. A fine argument can be made that this failure to bond immediately with the infant is adaptive in that it permits the mother to keep her options open, and also shields her emotionally from the impact of the infant's death – often, a likely outcome (de Vries 1987a; Hagen 1999). In a study undertaken in Jaipur, India, the entire sample of mothers interviewed – Hindu and Muslim – had experienced *multiple* miscarriages and child deaths (Unnithan-Kumar 2001). Among the Bajau, boat-dwellers and fishers in the Sulu Sea, "infant mortality is so high that some parents cannot even recall the number of their deceased children" (Nimmo 1970: 261).

---

[11] The latest report from UNICEF states: "In 2002, 7 of every 1,000 children in industrialized countries died before they were five. At the other extreme, in sub-Saharan Africa, 174 of every 1,000 children died before celebrating their fifth birthday. In South Asia, 97 of 1,000 children died before they were five" (UNICEF 2004: 2).

Before we've finished this chapter, we'll have cataloged an extensive list of utilities that justify the costs of bearing and raising children but, bottom line, the unstated, possibly unconscious, goal for every adult is to pass on his/her genetic inheritance. This means not only making babies but rearing them in a way that insures they will survive and themselves successfully reproduce. One's success at this fundamental enterprise is referred to as "inclusive fitness." The extended family, some of whose genes are passed on each time a new member is added, also has an interest in viability decisions. Investing in a high-risk child is often, or usually, seen as a waste of resources that might be better invested in existing, healthy offspring, the mother herself, or future offspring. Furthermore, as anyone who has observed a parent struggling to maintain a handicapped child will be aware, the effort and expense involved may be two or three times higher than that required by a "normal" child. However, as Hrdy notes: "the same mother who regretfully eliminates a poorly timed neonate will lovingly care for later ones if circumstances improve" (Hrdy 1999: 314).

Being a "calculating" mother is not synonymous with wickedness; on the contrary, it is adaptive behavior.[12] While the well-to-do mothers in the first section seem to "live for their children," in the next section, we discover just how recently these attitudes have become incorporated in Western society. We will trace the fluctuating value of infants in history and see that what we now consider horrible crimes were, in earlier periods, the principal means of birth control.

The value attached to infants in antiquity

Human growth can be explosive . . . such growth must soon initiate either internal or external limitation. (Dickeman 1975: 120)

Infanticide in . . . Japan was rationalized by maintaining that the death of a newborn was not the extinction of a life but a return to the other world, allowing for the possibility of rebirth at a more favorable future time. (Kojima 2003: 116)

Classical Greece is justly famed for its self-reflective examination of all aspects of society. For the first time, philosophers question traditional ways of doing things and offer theoretical alternatives. Infanticide was one such practice that came in for a great deal of consideration; however, no one seems to have doubted the fundamental necessity for it. Indeed, the Greeks were puzzled by the fact that in Egypt infanticide was officially discouraged (Sommerville 1982: 23). (There is evidence in Egypt of careful, ritually correct infant interment [Halioua and Ziskind 2005: 75] and Egyptian medicine was particularly advanced when

---

[12] In this sense, all stepmothers should be "wicked," in that it is adaptive for them to deny resources to their stepchildren, preferentially investing in their own offspring.

it came to women's health issues, including birth control[13]). Plato believed that, in an ideal society, parents should keep only those children that they could personally afford; the poorest should remain childless (Boswell 1988: 82).[14] Aristotle was, if anything, more adamantly an advocate of eugenics (Langer 1973–1974: 354). Undoubtedly their views were colored by the fact that Greece, unlike Egypt – where the bounteous Nile almost invariably yielded a surplus of food – was chronically short of food and exported citizens by the tens of thousands to Asia Minor and Italy, establishing thriving colonies.

The Greeks went to considerable pains to distinguish between "exposing" a neonate (*brephos*) that wasn't yet fully human and child homicide. Obviously defective infants were routinely exposed or abandoned. In utopian Sparta, where every citizen was expected to become an invincible warrior, deformity was liberally defined to include lack of vigor and unattractiveness. Parents were not at liberty to make the life or death decision, which lay with the authorities. Rejected neonates were delivered to the *Apothetai*, a pit-like area near Taygetos (Colón, with Colón 2001: 68).[15]

While culling excess offspring was probably a constant in Greece, archaeologists have noted that the perceived value of children fluctuated over time. Evidence for this is found in the well-maintained cemeteries, exclusively for infants and children, that tended to cluster near the principal city gates of Athens (*c.*720–400 BCE) contrasted with the complete absence of child burial following a shift in the political climate after 400 BCE (Houby-Nielsen 2000).[16] Langer finds that, during the Hellenistic era, "infanticide, chiefly in the form of exposure of female babies, was carried to such an extent that the average family was exceptionally small. Parents rarely reared more than one daughter" (Langer 1973–1974: 355).

---

[13] Egypt is also distinguished by evidence, from a worker's cemetery, that, not only were children formally buried, but stillborn fetuses were, at least occasionally, interred in old pottery or baskets. More striking, there are burials, complete with attractive grave goods, of obviously deformed children who had *not* been put to death at birth (Meskell 1994). And Sommerville notes: "A concern for the child's comfort can also be seen in Egyptian medical texts which prescribe opiates to get children over the rough periods" (Sommerville 1982: 23). The Chinchorro of Peru may also have ritually interred children including infants and stillborns (Arriaza 1995).

[14] Singapore appears to be the only country that explicitly adopted Plato's recommendation as noted in chapter 2, providing incentives (roughly $6,500) for poor women to undergo sterilization (Wee 1992: 201).

[15] Even children kept for rearing were subjected to an extremely stressful regimen and, no doubt, many failed to survive. Hrdy documents a variety of ordeals that some societies (where adult males typically were warriors) force infants to undergo, including ice-cold baths, to toughen them or remove them from the race to survive (Hrdy 1999: 464). In infancy, I was the "beneficiary" of such a program – devised by my ex-Hussar father – spending hours outdoors in a playpen in mid-winter sheltered only by our pet Saint Bernard.

[16] Similarly, as communities in Europe adopted Christianity, child burials become more common (Lucy 1994).

Nor was an illegitimate child likely to be kept alive: "Identity was given by the family, and without a recognized father and family, the child had no proper guardian (*kurios*) since its mother could not legally fulfill such a function. Without a father, the child had no true place in the patrilineal kin structure, no right to the family name" (Patterson 1985: 115). In the case of the loss of the husband, a pregnant woman was specifically permitted to expose her infant to facilitate a second and hopefully more enduring marriage (French 1991: 21).

The infant's vital signs were closely monitored for ten days, and if a decision to expose had been forestalled, the *amphidromia* or naming ceremony was held, welcoming the infant as a member of the family. Excavations at ancient Greek sites of myriad artifacts related to children – toys, child-size furniture, including "potty" chairs, and scenes of loving childcare inscribed on vases – reveal that the calculating attitude towards potentially surplus youth coexisted with a deeply caring and positive attitude towards those who were wanted (Golden 1990).

Roman society fully accepted the idea that each infant was subject to a valuation. It had various means to prevent conception, to abort the fetus, and several widely accepted means of disposing of unwanted children.[17] For example, the *lacteria* or "nursing column," where nursing babies were abandoned, could be found in nearly every public market (Boswell 1988: 110).

On the other hand, various ceremonies and rituals were enacted to acknowledge the valued child. "The child's father . . . (or, if still alive, his *paterfamilias*) . . . had the power to decide whether or not the child should be reared."[18] By "raising up the child (*tollere*) [he showed his] willingness to rear it" (Rawson 1991: 12). The next rite of passage occurred nine days after birth (eight for girls), the *lustratio*. The child is given a name and an official, formal identity (Rawson 1991: 13).

Attitudes in imperial China were very similar. Abortion is an ancient custom. The oldest Chinese medical text found so far, some five thousand years in age, includes reference to mercury as an abortifacient. In spite of high infant mortality, families were expected to limit growth to maintain the economic viability of the household.[19] The pictogram for "abandonment" from the Shang period shows a basket being held by two hands, ejecting a baby (Colón, with Colón 2001: 57). Another iconic image is of the "drowning bucket" kept nearby during delivery (Colón, with Colón 2001: 262).

---

[17] Excavation of a late Roman–early Byzantine sewage system at the site of Ashkelon, Israel yielded more than a hundred infant skeletons (Smith and Kahila 1992).

[18] "[C]urrent evidence suggests that men may use cues of paternity to influence the likelihood of caring for, or abusing, or abandoning, infants and children" (Volk and Quinsey 2002: 439).

[19] However, surplus sons were more often spared (Wee 1992: 192). The *contemporary* view, expressed by a county-level leader, runs: "In our opinion, abortion is not cruel. It would be much more cruel to let the population continue to grow, and to let the future generations suffer" (Potter 1987: 46).

Multiple births are typically seen as unlucky (de Vries 1987b: 171). In medieval European society, it was believed a woman could not conceive twice (simultaneously) so twins could not be from the same father. A woman might abandon twins to protect her reputation (Shahar 1990: 122). Romulus and Remus, history's most noted abandoned twins, were abducted and exposed by their uncle Amulius to eliminate them as potential rivals. Rescued by a she-wolf, and later a shepherd, they grew up to found the city of Rome. And, while this tale is an obvious myth, history is replete with child homicides routinely carried out to remove potential rivals or heirs. Octavian, for example, had Cleopatra's three children by Caesar and Anthony put to death to forestall any claims they might make on their fathers' legacies.

While I have shared with the reader a small sample of cases illustrating the phenomenon, there is every indication that, absent accessible and reliable contraception, abortion, abandonment, and infanticide always have been and will continue to be "common," at least according to modern sensibilities. Successive surveys of the ethnographic literature are consistent with this view (Ford 1964: 51). John Whiting (1977) found that in a sample of ninety-nine societies, infanticide was specifically noted in eighty-four.[20] A much larger and more complex study of nearly four hundred societies, similarly, found infanticide practiced in 80 percent (Mays 2000: 181). Given the ease of concealing the act, and the possible stigma attached, the practice is undoubtedly more widespread than these data suggest.[21] And then there's physical abuse and neglect (Das Gupta 1987), which take a toll that's almost impossible to estimate. For example, anthropologists have documented many cases of culturally sanctioned dietary taboos and feeding patterns aimed at very young children that may have the unstated effect of culling the less vigorous (Lepowsky 1987; Scrimshaw 1978; Langness 1981; Miller 1987; Cassidy 1980). In the most recent survey of infanticide, of sixty societies, thirty-nine show definite evidence of the practice (Daly and Wilson 1984: 490).

And in the USA, social critics argue that "However heinous and unnatural, [infanticide] is an extreme consequence of recognized ills: poverty, child and spousal abuse, mental instability" (*Time*, November 14, 1994: 50). Studies also show that the same cluster of variables that trigger infanticide are also implicated in post-partum depression (Hagen 1999).

While the termination of the fetus or of the infant's life is most often the parents' decision and we've seen numerous possible reasons for this behavior, societies often legitimize that decision. Overpopulation, the burden on the

---

[20] Of course, absence of a mention only means that the ethnographer did not observe and/or record the incident.

[21] Examples of "rational" infanticide and neglect leading to the death of offspring are widespread in the animal world, especially among primates (Hausfater and Hrdy 1984: xxi).

community of a hard-to-raise child, the social disharmony created by illegitimacy, all give the society a stake in this critical decision. Ultimately, also, the community must value the life and emotional wellbeing of its experienced, productive adult females over any potential value a tiny infant might have. So that, even today, when the penalties and censure for infanticide are higher than at any time, the young women who deposit their new infants in trash bins "are excused because society failed them" (Lee 1994: 74).

Little angels

As a marginal being, the [Roman] child is only partially a member of the citizen society; but that implies that he is nearer to the world of the gods than the adult. (Wiedemann 1989: 25)

To this point, we have examined the phenomenon of "selective removal" of children (Dickeman 1975: 108) from a purely utilitarian perspective, seeing the act as reducing the burden on their parents and community. But children are, in some societies, seen as pure and without the stain of sin or corrupting knowledge of the world. Their innocence makes them both worthy sacrificial offerings to the gods and potential intermediaries, carrying urgent messages from their families and community. In much of Mesoamerica,[22] for example, there was a direct association between the child's tears and rain. The Aztecs sacrificed children on the first day of the month of Atlachualo to appease Tlaloc, the rain god. According to de Sahagun, the more the sacrificial victims cried and carried on, the better the prospects for rain (Sahagun 1829/1978).

On this day, children (called "human paper streamers") with two cowlicks in their hair and favorable day signs were dressed in such colors as dark green, black striped with chili red, light blue, some set with pearls, and were sacrificed in seven different locations. The flowing and falling of the children's tears ensured rain. (Carrasco 1999: 84–85)

Aztec children were also sacrificed to the god of death. This was the fate of forty-two children – mostly boys aged around six – whose remains were analyzed by Berrelleza and Balderas (2006). All shared one feature: serious cavities, abscesses, or bone infections painful enough to make them suffer. "It

---

[22] Studies of children's remains in Mesoamerica present an extremely varied picture ranging from the Chinchorro (Peru) who mummified even fetuses – suggesting therefore that children were considered persons from birth (Arriaza et al. 1998: 195) – to forty-eight children packed into a sacrificial container at the great Aztec temple at Tenochtitlan (Berrelleza and Balderas 2006: 240), from coastal Oaxaca (Mexico) where children were excluded from house burials, suggesting low or less-than-fully-human status (S. M. King 2006: 185), to post-classical Cholula (Mexico) where children were formally buried but without the grave goods that accompanied adult interments (McCafferty and McCafferty 2006: 42).

was considered a good omen if they cried a lot at the time of sacrifice" (*Salt Lake Tribune*, January 23, 2005: A16, A17).[23]

In cases of drought or famine, Maya from all over the lowlands would gather at one of the sacred *cenotes*, natural wells, where priests officiated at sacrificial ceremonies to honor and appeal to the gods. At daybreak, children were tossed into the cenote and those who were – miraculously – still alive by midday were rescued and questioned by the priests regarding any messages they might have received from the gods (Sharer 1994: 10–11).

Child sacrifice was highly institutionalized among the Inca. Represented as *capacochas*, or "royal sins," children were destined to appease the gods who might have been inadvertently angered by the rulers. Celebrated for days of feasting and ritual, these semi-divine children were likely drugged and taken to the high (up to 6,000 meters) Andean peaks by priests to be buried alive, in effect freezing to death. They were carefully wrapped in costly textiles and interred with toy-like miniatures of animals, crops, people, and tools. Both historical and archaeological evidence suggests that the children were highly valued and, in all likelihood, were the offspring of the elite (Sillar 1994).[24] These mummified children, some in their teens, have come to light recently as disappearing snow cover allows climbers to discover them (Menon 1996; Carey 1999).

In the Pacific, children were sacrificed to attract the attention of the gods:

Two practices intended to appease angry gods . . . mentioned by many of the early European visitors to Tonga, were child strangulation (*no'osia*) and finger-joint amputation (*nima kū*) . . . carried out [as examples] when a high chief was ill, [or as] a form of atonement for the desecration of the *tapu* place . . . those chosen were the children of chiefs by "inferior" female attendant[s]. (Morton 1996: 175, 176)

Another civilization where child sacrifice was practiced on a large scale was Phoenicia. At Carthage, infants or young children up to the age of four were sacrificed – burned on an altar, then interred in a ceramic urn. And Carthage's vaunted democracy extended the privilege of sacrificing a child to all social classes (Stager and Greene 2000: 31). In times of emergency, such as the invasion by Agathocles, the tyrant of Syracuse, many children may have been sacrificed at one time to Ba'al Hammon. A special area or *Tophet* was set aside for these sacrifices and the stored remains. It was most extensively used between 750 and 146 BCE when Carthage was destroyed by Rome. Tophet interments (but not child burial in the community cemetery) often included a stele with a standardized dedicatory inscription (Lee 1994: 66). The funerary urns sometimes contained the bones of sheep and goats – as substitute offerings.

---

[23] The evidence of trauma, malnutrition, and illness suggests to me that weaker children, unpromising as warriors, were the preferred victims.

[24] Also see Cobo (1653/1990).

But this practice declines over time. Stillborn or miscarried remains are also rare, suggesting that, like the Inca, the Phoenicians were sacrificing truly valued children and not just limiting their population (Stager and Greene 2000; Stager and Wolff 1984; Stager 1982).

A Tophet, or place of sacrifice, located in Benhinnom, a valley just south of Jerusalem, has been identified (Levenson 1993: 36). Levenson argues that it wasn't until the sixth century BCE[25] that the Jews abandoned child sacrifice,[26] and he credits the prophets Ezekiel and Jeremiah with a successful campaign against it. He cites passages that suggest a change in religious practices, generally to distance Judaism from the rituals practiced by their neighbors. Nevertheless, the idea that the first-born son belonged to God persisted. The concept lived on in that sacrificial animals might be substituted for the child, the first child might be "donated" to the priesthood, and circumcision became a ritual substitution for child sacrifice. Lastly, the Jewish rite of the redemption of the first-born (*pidyôn habbēn*) continues to the present (Levenson 1993: 47).

The construction of buildings, especially those with a religious character, usually called for the ceremonial burial of "foundation deposits." And these often included sacrificed children.[27] Excavation of the Hanoi citadel (eleventh century CE) revealed the skeletons of eight-year-old children who had been interred in the foundation – probably alive – to drive off evil spirits (Sachs and Le 2005). Also fairly common was the practice of sacrificing children (and adults) to accompany the deceased in the afterlife. Women and children were sacrificed as companions for Mayan rulers as a recent royal tomb excavated in northern Honduras attests (*National Geographic News*, May 30, 2001). Hill and Hurtado describe this practice among the Ache in considerable detail, especially with respect to the process of selecting the accompanying child (Hill and Hurtado 1996: 68–69).

Children can be treated as sacred without sacrificing them! In ancient Egypt, the deceased expected to be provisioned in the afterlife by his dutiful children. Quite early in its history, Egypt transitioned from putting servants and family members to death to accompany and care for the deceased to using substitutes engraved on tomb walls or free-standing sculptures. In the tomb of necropolis inspector Nikau-Anpu from the sixth dynasty, his five children

---

[25] Archaeological evidence for child sacrifice has been pushed back to the early Bronze Age (2500 BCE) at a recently excavated site in Syria (Johansen 2007).

[26] The wording of Exodus 2 with regards to Moses' mother's actions – "And the woman conceived, and bare a son: and when she saw him that he was a goodly child, she hid him" – certainly suggests that she first verified that the child was worth preserving.

[27] Tlingit Indian: Colón with Colón (2001: 64); Iron Age: Green (1999: 65). Although a rare occurrence, children continue to be sacrificed in the name of religion. For example, to foster their *jihad*, Iraqi insurgents have started using children as decoys – knowing that vehicles carrying children aren't closely examined at checkpoints – and then, later, detonating the vehicle with the children left inside (*New York Times*, March 21, 2007: A12).

appear in wall paintings "doing all sorts of menial work: grinding and sieving grain, ladling liquid, making loaves, poking a furnace, and stirring a cooking pot... [they engage in these] exaggeratedly humble activities in order to demonstrate their humility and dependence on their father and... usefulness to him in the afterlife" (Roth 2002: 110). Young boys, for centuries, have been donated by their parents to Buddhist monasteries. In Mustang, the second-born son joins a monastery at six or seven (Peissel 1992). In the Hindu *devadasi* rite, lower-caste girls may be donated to the village temple to serve the sexual needs of the priests (Verma and Saraswathi 2002: 127).

For the Beng people of the Ivory Coast,[28] babies are ancestors who've been reincarnated and returned from *wrugbe*, the land of the dead.[29] Consequently, Beng adults not only treat infants with great respect and devotion, they talk to them as well because the child/ancestor can serve as an intermediary with powerful spirit forces. This conception of children also works to cushion the shock of infant death (Gottlieb 2000: 80–81). In Indonesia, the rice-growing Balinese hold similar beliefs.[30] Spirits of ancestors return to inhabit the infant in the womb. Following birth, the baby is believed to be divine for a period of 210 days (Suryani 1984; Eisman 1989; Hobart *et al.* 1996). A woman who marries a man from a higher-ranking family may have children who outrank her. Proper respect for the child must be shown or the child may die, choosing to return to the gods rather than remain with a disrespectful mother (Mead 1955; Suryani 1984).

The same general orientation in Japan rationalizes the often-observed public misbehavior of young children. As semi-divine, a child cannot be held to the same standards of conduct as an adult and any attempt to control his or her behavior might disrupt the transition from the world of the gods to our world (Naito and Gielen 2005: 69).

Of course, it doesn't take a huge leap of imagination to see the mothers highlighted in the vignettes that opened the chapter as treating their "cherubs" rather worshipfully. Indeed, Viviana Zelizer, whose 1985 book first called attention to the uniqueness of modern conceptions of childhood, refers to the rise of the "sacred child" (Zelizer 1985: 52).

---

[28] See also the Mende of Sierra Leone where infants remain somewhat attached to the spirit world and develop "unusual powers of vision and the powers to move across different sensory domains" (Fermé 2001: 198).

[29] Similarly, among the Yoruba: "Children are watched for the unfolding of resemblances to the ancestors they reincarnate" (Zeitlin 1996: 412). Also found among the Wolof of Senegal (Rabain 1979). An interesting belief found in ancient Greece held that, since infants were as yet empty vessels, when they died their bodies could be used to transport souls of the dead to the underworld (Liapis 2004).

[30] In Mormon theology, children are "little angels," waiting in heaven for a married couple to, in effect, adopt them. They must spend at least some time among the living (see obituary text above) in order to earn a permanent place in heaven with "their Heavenly Father."

Figure 3 Novice monk in Rangoon (Yangon)

Figure 4 Angel in Christmas parade, Oaxaca

Regardless of whether a given infant ends up in an urn in the Tophet or, eventually, gracing the recital stage, its destiny is influenced greatly by the iconified image of the child that exists in the culture. Our society is only *apparently* child-centered when compared with, say, Phoenicia, because our children, too, must fulfill *our* needs.

Save the children

Throughout all of those centuries, the popular thought in most places was that being sent to foundling homes presaged early death. (Colón, with Colón 2001: 231)

As we have seen in the case of ancient Egypt (Janssen and Janssen 1990), not all societies turn a blind eye to the wastage of children. Some have embraced policies designed to raise the value of children and, thereby, reduce infanticide. During Augustus' reign, Rome was gripped by a crisis of the family. Divorce rates had soared along with adultery and infanticide. The birth rate among the patrician class had fallen. He introduced a suite of laws designed to reward patricians for having more children. His successors also censured infanticide. Hadrian (*c.* 125 CE), in particular, undertook major reforms to protect children and the needy. The father's prerogative to expose his children was revoked, and the sale or castration of children was curtailed. However, the impact of these reforms may not have been great as they were largely unenforceable (Colón, with Colón 2001: 94).

The Jewish writer Philo of Alexandria wrote condemning infanticide in the first century CE because it implied that intercourse had been for pleasure rather than reproduction (Noonan 1970: 6). Meanwhile, as Christian influence spread throughout the Roman Empire, more and more church leaders wrote condemning abandonment and infanticide, following St. Paul's injunction that, in effect, parents may not avoid paying the "wages of sin." One of the more bizarre arguments advanced (by Clement, the patriarch of Alexandria) was the threat that a father might, inadvertently, commit incest because so many abandoned children ended up in brothels.

The first Christian emperor, Constantine, outlawed infanticide in 318 CE,[31] and the death penalty was prescribed in 374 CE (Sommerville 1982: 43), but abandonment was not effectively prohibited until 600 CE (Colón, with Colón 2001: 108). Making infanticide a sin or crime without providing the means for parents to limit conception fails to address the underlying problem. Consequently, the number of infants who were accidentally suffocated under their parents' bodies grew: "the clergy suspected ... that ... such accidents [were

---

[31] Ironically, he was to kill his own son. Putting members of one's immediate family to death was by no means out of the ordinary during Rome's imperial era.

all too convenient, yet] Infanticide was tried in church courts until very late, for it was considered a sin rather than the crime of homicide" (Nicolas 1991: 38).

The creation of hundreds of monasteries and nunneries during the late Roman Empire and the early medieval period also provided an outlet for surplus children. Mothers had been encouraged to drop off their unwanted infants at churches, and this practice grew into the officially sanctioned act known as oblation.[32]

Parents received numerous benefits: one less mouth to feed, one less claimant on family property, and the enhanced spiritual benefits of having "sacrificed" a child who could serve as a pious intermediary with God and His church. On the other hand, they were expected to make a generous donation to the church to assist with the child's upkeep – if they could afford it. They would probably never see the child again, and the child for his or her part could never elect to leave the monastery (Boswell 1988: 232). Oblation was a form of life imprisonment, and oblates were not always treated kindly.

The monastic establishments could not handle the influx, and many soon discovered that hosting a gaggle of youngsters quickly undermined the very principles upon which they were founded. So the church began to establish homes for unwanted children called *brephotrophia*, the earliest opened in Milan by the end of the eighth century CE (Sommerville 1982: 50). Supply could never keep up with demand. The Ospedale degli Innocenti in Florence (one of sixteen *brephotrophia* in Tuscany alone) admitted 100 infants in its first year, admitting as many as 1,000 in succeeding years and, ultimately, accepted 5,000 unwanted babies, two-thirds of whom perished before their first birthday (Kertzer 1993).[33]

An adequate, safe substitute for mother's milk was still not widely available,[34] and wet-nurses were preoccupied with babies whose parents wanted to keep them. Wet-nurses were no longer paid after their milk stopped but, on the other hand, they were not penalized if the infant in their care died. Not surprisingly, therefore, they usually failed to notify authorities of their changed

---

[32] Even today, residents of the Himalayan Buddhist kingdom of Nepal are expected to donate their second surviving son to the monastery by the age of six or seven (Raffaele 2003: 200).

[33] Contemporary echoes of this tragedy are heard today from Russia, where 800,000 orphans – the majority abandoned by living parents – are warehoused in unfit facilities. Eyewitness descriptions include: "Healthy babies are lying in hospital beds all day . . . completely ignored. No one plays with them or provides any kind of stimulation . . . in a central Russian hospital another patient noticed a room of abandoned babies with their mouths taped shut to stop them from crying . . . Reports of babies tied down in their cots are common . . . it's often immediately clear to visitors that abandoned babies are left to 'rot alive'" "Russia's halt on adoptions spotlights conditions," National Public Radio, April 25, 2007: www.npr.org; accessed 4.25.07.

[34] And wouldn't be until the perfection of Liebig's formula in 1860 (Sunley 1955: 154).

condition, and the infant perished (Gavitt 1990: 197).[35] Nor were the "hospitals" innocent of avarice. It appears they may have earned a net profit through fees collected once they had successfully raised children and placed them in a household – as a servant – or workshop. Until they left the home permanently, the hospital "farmed both boys and girls out during the day" (Gavitt 1990: 189).[36]

As the church grew, in spite of schisms, the interdiction against infanticide remained a prominent policy. Overseas missionary efforts targeted infanticide as a matter of priority, and the early conquerors often highlighted the native practice of infanticide and/or child sacrifice as justifying brutal treatment of subject peoples, like the Inca. Ironically, the Protestant Reformation, with its condemnation of illegitimacy – heretofore tolerated throughout Europe – likely led to an increase in infanticide. "Once societal attitudes turned ugly and condemnatory, illegitimate children became victims at the hands of the mothers . . . who killed their offspring rather than endure society's scorn" (Colón, with Colón 2001: 331). Indeed, this problem became so acute that:

Napoleon [himself] decreed (1811) that there should be hospitals in every departement of France, and that each should be equipped with a turntable (*tour*), so that the mother or her agent could place the child on one side, ring a bell, and have a nurse take the child by turning the table, the mother remaining unseen and unquestioned. (Langer 1973–1974: 358)[37]

In spite of the appalling mortality, foundling homes or charity schools were very popular throughout Europe and attracted the favorable attention of monarchs (for example, Catherine II of Russia [Ransel 1988]) and other pillars of society – Handel supported them by giving benefit concerts (Sommerville 1982: 106). They were successful at removing or limiting the unpleasant sight of dead, dying, and destitute children from public view.[38] Further, it wasn't only the unmarried or destitute who unburdened themselves of children they didn't want. The great liberal philosopher Jean Jacques Rousseau – whose favorite subject was the reform of childrearing practices – placed all five of his

---

[35] On the other hand, wet-nurses hired by aristocrats were to be carefully selected and even their speech was closely scrutinized. Moralists warned that "Deformities of complexion and character both come from the wet nurses who are loose, dissolute . . . full of putrid and noxious humors, to whom rash fathers who give the matter no thought, send to feed at the breast their noble and well-born sons" (Gavitt 1990: 280).

[36] Recently, a private adoption firm, based in Utah, has been indicted for "baby-farming." The firm provided Samoan families various incentives to give up their children to American couples who were told the children were orphans. Adoptive parents were charged $13,000 for a single child, $20,000 for a pair (*Salt Lake Tribune*, March 2, 2007: A1, A8).

[37] Updated versions of the *tour* are proliferating in Europe to accommodate the unwanted offspring of illegal immigrants: eighty have been installed in Germany since 2000 (Lange 2007).

[38] An extremely graphic, horrifying, and probably accurate picture of the lives of unwanted children in eighteenth-century France is shown in the recent film *Perfume* (2006).

offspring in public institutions; he didn't even bother recording details of their births (Kessen 1978).

Even with low survival rates, the number of children supported by the church and state grew beyond all bounds, leading the satirist Jonathan Swift (1729/1996) to suggest that excess children be used as food. Authorities began shipping boat-loads of their charges to the labor-hungry colonies, and "charity schools" began to look more like workhouses (Sommerville 1982: 103).

The situation in China was no different: orphanage mortality rates of one-third to one-half of the resident children were typical. Indeed, social reformers advanced the idea of paying mothers a stipend to keep their unwanted children (Leung 1995). However, adoption was always a possibility. "An orphanage was a logical place to go to obtain a *tongyangxi* or a servant" (Johnson 2004: 29). And parents might adopt a baby girl to raise with their infant son. As the daughter grew she could look after the son and eventually the two would be married, insuring the subservience of the daughter-in-law and saving the cost of the bride-price (Johnson 2004: 7). The practice of what we might call "strategic" adoption was probably quite common and still is in the Pacific Islands and West Africa.[39]

Parents will make decisions regarding their offspring that reflect their own personal criteria. And, if they choose *not* to raise them, it should be clear from the foregoing, that even the most sympathetic public and religious institutions are not prepared to incur anywhere near the full costs of acting *in loco parentis*. Even amid relative affluence, many children may not be afforded adequate familial care and the state/church rarely, if ever, has provided adequate substitute or supplemental care. Leaping into the twenty-first century, I describe, in chapter 9, a parallel situation today where our meager publicly provided pre-school services cannot adequately perform parental functions.

Ironically, church and government prohibition of infanticide was not accompanied by a parallel concern for infant mortality, which wasn't even recognized as a problem until the early twentieth century.[40] Fertility rates had dropped as a corollary of changing economic opportunities but infant mortality had not. One concerned politician in Britain went so far as to distribute promissory notes to newly delivered women offering them a £1 bonus if they kept their infants alive for a year. "The reverse side of these promissory notes was printed with ... advice on infant hygiene and feeding" (Dyhouse 1978: 249).

As we've seen, the church's prohibitions weren't very effective, and poor communities continued to limit population through the only means available, although these actions were often enveloped in a fog of folk beliefs.

---

[39] See, for example, Monberg (1970); Ritter (1981). And, in Sierra Leone, girls who will be trained as garrah-cloth-makers are readily fostered into cloth-making households (Isaac and Conrad 1982: 244).

[40] Punishing sin was more important than saving lives.

Little demons

The anomalies of changelings ranged from the obvious – a missing limb, a large nevus, or a deformed head – to ... a child who failed to grow or ... to those who were perceived as weak, sickly, colicky, or irritable. (Colón, with Colón 2001: 247)

A reading of *Njal's Saga* suggests that the Christian prohibition of infanticide made it difficult for the Vikings to accept the new faith. Preserving the lives of defective or surplus children was difficult for villagers who lived on a razor's edge of survival. However, the church readily granted penance for the act, "taking into account the poverty of parents, accidents, and insanity, which became a common defense" (Sommerville 1982: 59). Pagan folklore that survived well into the Christian era provided another convenient cloak for the disposal of unwanted offspring:

people convinced themselves that sickly babies were impostors left by goblins in place of healthy ones. The infant left behind became an *enfant changé* in France, a *Wechselbag* in Germany, in England a "fairy child" or changeling. In ... northern Europe, changelings were left overnight in the forest. If the fairies refused to take it back, the changeling would die during the night – but since it was not human, no infanticide could have occurred. (Hrdy 1999: 465)

Somewhat later, Satan and his minions became the perpetrators switching the true child for one that was sickly, whiny, or deformed. Strategies to reverse the switch included tormenting the infant or abandoning it in a lonely spot (Haffter 1986). Not surprisingly, the "changeling" often didn't survive these ordeals (Gies and Gies 1987; Shahar 1990; Mays 2000).

On Truk Island in Micronesia, women might give "birth to ghosts ... deformed children [who were consequently] thrown into the sea, burned or buried [as were] normal children, who exhibited peculiarities of behavior such a lack of desire to eat" (Fisher 1963: 533). Navajo beliefs identify epileptics as resulting from a family member's or ancestor's earlier violation of the incest taboo[41] which justifies their neglect. A Beng mother-to-be who breaks a taboo may have her uterus invaded by a snake. The snake takes the fetus's place and, after birth, is gradually revealed by the infant's strange behavior. "The child may be harassed and hit by stones; however, being boneless like a snake, the snake-person is thought to feel no pain" (Gottlieb 1992: 145). Similarly, in Mali, children thought to be evil spirits are taken "out into the bush and you leave them ... they turn into snakes and slither away ... You go back the next day, and they aren't there. Then you know for sure that they weren't really children at all, but evil spirits" (Dettwyler 1994: 85–86).

In many areas of New Guinea, cannibalism was widespread but it survives now only in isolated communities, such as the Korowai, where inter-group

[41] Schlegel (personal communication, April 6, 2006).

Figure 5 Korowai child accused of being a *khahkua* or witch

warfare and raiding is so common, communal houses are erected on 20-meter high platforms – for safety. The Korowai are quick to accuse, convict, and then consume individuals practicing witchcraft. *Smithsonian Magazine* author Paul Raffaele found the boy shown in figure 5 hiding among distant kin who feared for his life after he'd been accused of culpability in the death of his parents (Raffaele 2006). Of course, as we saw in the earlier discussion of the Aché, orphans – even those well beyond infancy – are often put to death because no one will be able to feed them. So accusing the boy Wawa of witchcraft might have the effect of either justifying his elimination or provoking a humanitarian rescue from his kin.

In Han China, infanticide was justified in the case of "ill-omened" children born during an inauspicious period. "The 'wolflike cries' of newborn[s] were used as evidence of their inborn wickedness . . . foreshadowing . . . future unfilial behavior" (Kinney 1995: 24–25). While these attitudes have disappeared in much of the world, in areas beset by severe overpopulation and poverty they are being revived.

Children of the street have always existed in Kinshasa, but in recent years their numbers have swollen dramatically . . . Many . . . were forced to take to the street after being singled out by family members in a witchcraft accusation . . . Increasingly, children, from babies to teenagers, are being accused of causing misfortunes and mishaps, as well as . . . illness or death . . . Often the child in question is severely beaten [or] even killed by family members. (de Boeck 2005: 190, 193, 194)

These varied examples of the *changeling* notion notwithstanding, Korbin argues, more prosaically, that "neglect . . . appears to be more frequent in the cross-cultural literature than deliberate killing, even if the end result is frequently the same" (Korbin 1987a: 36). For example, a study in Hungary finds that mothers of high-risk infants breastfed them for shorter periods than their normal infants; they also smiled less often at them, and stimulated or played with them less frequently. They also became pregnant more quickly following the birth of a high-risk infant (Bereczkei 2001). In short, they scaled back their investment in the high-risk infant and acted as if they didn't expect it to survive.[42]

But, as the child grows older, especially as it survives the pre-five period of greatest mortality, its value climbs.

Children as chattel

. . . he bought me from my father. It wasn't so much the few coins, but because it was one less mouth to feed. (Eco 2000: 30)

[Kpelle] children are a form of property that fathers must pay for and maintain if they are to be considered legal owners. (Bledsoe 1980b: 91)

Under the mid-seventh-century laws of the Visigoths, a free male baby in his first year had a blood price (wergeld) of 30 solidi, which had grown to 90 solidi by his tenth year. (Nicolas 1991: 32)[43]

If parents and the larger society can countenance the abandonment/killing/fatal neglect of children, then selling them won't seem beyond the realm of possibility. And, indeed, the prospect of providing the parent with some economic return, however small, has probably kept many children alive.

The term *chattel* can mean any kind of real property, including human beings. And children throughout much of history have been indistinguishable from slaves.[44] Their masters/parents hold the power of life or death; they can and often do use corporal punishment to discipline them; they provision them

---

[42] Janet Mann's research shows quite clearly that middle-class Europeans often display the same adaptive reactions to high-risk offspring as their counterparts in developing nations (Mann 2002: 373).

[43] Similarly, in Sikkim, only after it had passed its tenth birthday would a child be accorded a funeral. Prior to that age, a deceased child would be dumped into the river (Gorer 1967: 302).

[44] " . . . the same word, '*pais*', was used to denote both a child and a slave" (Beaumont 1994: 88).

with food and clothing and a roof over their heads (or not); they program their lives of work and leisure and determine whom or whether they'll marry. And this fate has been shared as well by children of the wealthy. Indeed, their lives are often more tightly circumscribed than their lower-class age-mates.

Slaves outnumbered every other class of society by a wide margin in ancient Rome and so, not surprisingly, there were statutes regulating the sale of children. One of the most interesting came from the "Twelve Tables . . . a father could sell and repurchase a son up to three times, but thereafter a child was free" (Colón, with Colón 2001: 91). Boswell says, however, that the statutes never quite resolved whether a free-born but abandoned child could be sold into slavery. And the rights of parents to reclaim abandoned children were also in a state of flux: biological parents often tried to reclaim their abandoned children from their adoptive parents when they were old enough to earn a wage (Sommerville 1982: 44). Also in Rome abandoned children were "rescued," reared, and then sold into slavery or prostitution, or castrated to serve as eunuchs. "Employing *expositi* as beggars, possibly even crippling them to make them more pitiful, as Seneca describes, may have been common" (Boswell 1988: 113).

The sale of human beings, including children, was a dominant feature of Western European society and around the globe for better than two thousand years. It was well entrenched in Asia, and anthropologists have studied the conditions that promote it. For example, in north India, the demand for lower-caste brides creates a scarcity exploited by child thieves. "Sales of women to become concubines, courtesans, prostitutes, bondservants, or slaves [are found] in those provinces where both female infanticide and oppressive landlordism were intense" (Dickeman 1979: 345). In Europe, from the late Middle Ages until quite recently, impecunious gentry routinely restored their fortunes by marrying off sons and daughters to social-climbing merchant families.

One might argue that the Ottoman Empire was built on a foundation of child slavery, through the practice called *devshirme* (literally "collection," also "child-tribute" or "blood tax"). In the Christian regions (for example, Greece, Caucasus, Balkans) of the empire, families had to contribute a son to the Sultan. Tens if not hundreds of thousands of eight- to ten-year-old boys were rounded up by the Janissaries and brought to Istanbul for years of intense training in martial and/or academic arts to, eventually, serve in the military or government. The constant turnover in the ranks was the Sultan's solution to the ubiquitous problems of nepotism. The blood tax may not have seemed too onerous because the majority of youths converted to Islam and could, through talent alone, rise to senior positions – enriching their families as well as themselves.[45]

---

[45] Information obtained from www.hyperhistory.net; accessed 04.21.07.

The Turk's great rivals in Venice were more "enlightened."

In 1386, moved by the plight of the children imported from Albania and sold as slaves outside town even though they were Christians (not soulless infidels!), the Venetian authorities prohibited their re-exportation and ordered their emancipation – to take effect after a period of four years. The deferral applied because it was considered that the children should nevertheless work for a certain length of time until their owners had recovered the money they had spent... the status of "temporary slaves"... was extended to ten years in 1388 at the masters' request: "These souls are so rustic and crude of intellect, four years of their labour would not suffice to cover their purchase prices." (Stella 2000: 30)

Anthropologist Woody Watson documents the common practice of selling male children in China's Canton Delta region that persisted into the twentieth century. Referred to as *hsi min* or "little people," these young adolescents were identified by itinerant rice merchants who knew which families were destitute. "At the death of a slave owner his *hsi min* were divided among the surviving heirs like any other form of property" (Watson 1976: 364–365). In rural Japan:

the most destitute families would sell their nubile daughters into prostitution. So as not to alert the whole neighbourhood to the fact that they had a daughter for sale, the parents would discreetly light a fire at night which could be seen from a long way off... 3,222 young girls from the Shimabara region had been transported in this way between 1889 and 1894... These young women... accepted their fate though a sense of filial duty and sent their parents money. (Jolivet 1997: 124)

War often presents opportunities to gain a return from one's offspring. During the American Revolutionary War, parents turned idle boys into soldiers, earning money from their pay, from their enlistment bonuses, and from payments received when they entered the service as a "substitute." Obadiah Benge, aged fifteen, "was bartered into the service by his step-father... as a substitute for one James Green, [who provided]... horse, bridle and saddle" (Cox 2007: 20).

And just as infanticide continues in spite of laws to prevent it, so, too, does the sale of children (Raffaele 2005). Many argue that slavery never ended in Africa, and reports continue to surface, especially with respect to children. Throughout West Africa, children work on plantations for little or no pay. Recently there's been a "crackdown" in Nigeria and Benin where child slaves, as young as four, worked under appalling conditions in rock quarries. The slavers obtained "the children with payments to their parents of as little as US $30" (*Associated Press*, October 22, 2003: 1–2). Until fairly recently, the Yoruba might pawn (*iwofa*) their children whose work would serve as interest on a debt. They would be bound to work for the lender until the debt was paid off. The practice has been discouraged because of its resemblance to slavery (Renne 2002).

Figure 6 Slave-girl tending goats in Niger

Although certainly not as frequent, similar hair-raising stories can be found in the developed world as well. Several bizarre cases came to my attention recently, one on the sale of children in Albania. A woman had given her three-year-old to an older, childless Italian couple in exchange for a TV set and the promise of future payments. When these were not forthcoming, she complained to the authorities. Despite living in such severe poverty that she is forced to sell her children, the woman recently gave birth to her eighth child (*Salt Lake Tribune*, November 30, 2003: A18). The second reported on a long-term undercover operation that found a widespread practice of parents renting (for cash or drugs) their infants to drug couriers who store the drugs in empty baby formula tins (*Associated Press*, January 25, 2004). The third case exposed parents who capitalize on opportunities to display demure photos of their scantily clad children on internet "modeling" – aka kiddie porn – websites (LaPlante 2005). The fourth case involved the break-up of four child prostitution rings in the USA where kidnapped or trafficked children were made available to patrons at truck stops and cheap motels. The US Justice Department unit formed to uncover and prosecute such crimes has made 500 arrests in just two years (*Associated Press*, December 16, 2005).

However, children are often treated as "chattel" in the absence of slavery. Among the Nigerian Ibo, children represent social capital: sons are initiated into the various secret societies, with credit redounding to the father, and daughters are married to cement relationships with other families. Simon Ottenberg notes that, in sub-Saharan Africa, "babies are thought of as material goods" (Ottenberg 1989: 3). The same is the case in Micronesia: "children may easily be viewed as capital goods" (Fisher 1963: 527).

Of course, the greatest material value of children comes from their assistance around the home and on the farm.

Child workers

[An Amish] baby is never spoken of as "a little stranger" but is welcomed as a "new woodchopper" or a "little dishwasher." (Hostetler and Huntington 1971/1992: 22)

[In the Seychelles] it is children's labor, rather than a man's, that makes it possible for the woman to work on the plantation. (Pederson 1987: 56)

With the exception of the children of the very rich, and modern families where children are to dedicate themselves to schooling, every society has the expectation that a child will contribute to the household economy. The word "*moço*, which originally meant 'child,' came to be used in Spanish and Portuguese for a young servant... in Italian, the term *fante*... derived from *infante* (child)... applied to the domestic servant" (Stella 2000: 33). Raroians (Polynesia) believe:

that children, like all the other members of the family, ought to make themselves useful, and they give even quite small children astonishingly heavy and difficult tasks. Children of four or five are sent regularly to fetch water from the large communal tank; many of them do as many as ten trips a day with their gallon bottles. (Danielsson 1952: 121)

The Hadza, a Tanzanian hunting and gathering society, expect children as young as three years old to begin foraging independent of their mothers. By five, they gather about half their own caloric needs (especially baobab and tamarind fruits, berries) (Blurton-Jones 1993).

Children contribute to the household through child-minding (discussed at length in the next chapter), selling products in the market on behalf of a parent, tending livestock, or chasing birds away from the crop (discussed more fully in chapter 7). When I asked Kpelle parents what constitutes a "good" child, one mother, answered, without hesitation, "What makes a child good? If you ask her to bring water, she brings water. If you ask her to cook, she cooks, if you tell her to mind the baby, she does it. When you ask her to plant rice, she doesn't complain" (Lancy 1996: 76).

Moni Nag and her colleagues took a very close look at the contribution of children to the household economy in Java and Nepal. They found that girls as young as six spend upwards of two hours per day in childcare. Teenagers (fifteen–nineteen-year-olds) spend as much as eight to eleven hours per day working (Nag *et al.* 1978: 294–296). In Java, girls continue to make an economic contribution to the household after marriage as they tend to marry endogamously or within the community. Hence, unlike in East Asia, girls are welcomed into the family as eagerly as boys, and infanticide seems rare. Indeed, the attitude seems to be to have "as many children as they can afford and find useful" (Nag *et al.* 1978: 301). This folk wisdom is born out by "Econometric analyses of fertility . . . [that] have demonstrated significant positive correlations between measures of child labor-force participation and birth rates" (Nag *et al.* 1978: 293).

Prior to the industrialization of Europe, children not only worked in the fields, but they were often able to assist their parents in craftwork as well. Examples include wool combers, spinners, and, at construction sites in Provence, masons were accompanied by children "supplying 'free' labour to parents who were looking after them" (Stella 2000: 31).

As societies are transformed and wage-earning opportunities arise, we can expect that parents will seek employment for their children, even if it means that childhood will be curtailed (for example, "higher child wages lead to decreased leisure hours of both boys and girls" [Skoufias, 1994: 346]). In places where land is scarce and surplus children cannot be absorbed in agricultural labor, they are sent to live with wealthier households that can use them (Ravololomanga and Schlemmer 2000: 301).

Urbanization creates additional opportunities for parents to realize a return for their investment. With reference to the skeletons unearthed in Ashkelon noted earlier, DNA analysis showed that the majority were male. The sewer ran beneath a public bath located in the red-light district. The researchers suggest that prostitutes, whose services were available in the bath, might have reared their daughters to follow in their footsteps and support them once they were no longer able to practice their trade (Faerman *et al.* 1998).[46]

In rural Thai villages, children, especially daughters, are seen as assets to be carefully managed. As their chores are assumed by younger siblings, they may go to school for a couple of years until they can be sent to the towns to make their living in street work, including prostitution. In a study by Lisa Taylor, families whose daughter(s) sent home a part of their earnings were distinctly better off (Taylor 2002).

Dickens' immortal *Oliver Twist* uncovers an entire hidden economy of child street workers, and long before jolly old St. Nick came down chimneys to deliver Barbie dolls, he was noted for providing girls with dowries so they wouldn't be sold into prostitution (Sommerville 1982: 64). Of course, street urchins are still very much with us – as we'll see in chapter 10.

The industrial revolution had a major impact on childrearing cost/benefit calculations as factories offered parents the opportunities to earn wages through

---

[46] By comparison, in China, "daughters in some times and places [are considered] 'luxuries'" (Waltner 1995: 197).

their children. While the size of one's landholding limited the scope for child employment, the industrial revolution loosened restraints on fertility (Sommerville 1982: 152). By the 1720s, four-year-olds were employed in French textile mills, and a hundred years later in Lancashire, one-quarter of all the ten- to fifteen-year-old girls were making cotton (Chaudhuri 1991). Restrictions were gradually imposed so that, by 1830, factory workers had to be at least eight years old, but a fourteen-hour or larger work day was the norm, and they could be beaten for tardiness (Sommerville 1982: 103). However, as Zelizer shows, the movement to sanctify children, to remove them from adult spheres of influence, was inexorable. In 1900, one-fifth of children between ten and fifteen were employed. "By 1930, the economic participation of children had dwindled dramatically" (Zelizer 1985: 56). Nevertheless, reforms were met with considerable resistance:[47]

A 1909 investigation of cotton textile mills reported that "fathers and mothers vehemently declare that the State has no right to interfere if they wish to 'put their children to work,' and that it was only fair for the child to 'begin to pay back for its keep.'" In New York canneries, Italian immigrants reportedly took a more aggressive stand . . . against a canner who attempted to exclude young children from the sheds: "[He was] besieged by angry Italian women, one of whom bit his finger 'right through.'" Parents routinely sabotaged regulatory legislation simply by lying about their child's age. (Zelizer 1985: 69)

By now I hope the reader has been persuaded of the rarity and recency of the "child as cherub" view of children. However, contemporary society is not the *only* place where we see children being treated with great care and indulgence.

Children in paradise

A consistent pattern of infant care is found among the hunter-gatherers. (Lozoff and Brittenham 1979: 480)

There is a world in which children almost always feel "wanted"[48] and where "there is no cultural preference for babies of either sex" (Howell 1988: 159). Infants are suckled on demand by their mothers and by other women in her absence. They are indulged and cosseted by their fathers, grandparents, and siblings. Children wean themselves over a long period and are given nutritious foods (Robson and Kaplan 2003: 156). They are subject to little or no restraint or coercion. Infants and toddlers are carried on long journeys and comforted when

---

[47] Even today one finds isolated incidents of parents fencing with state authorities over the use of children's labor. One family which utilized their early teenage sons in dangerous work with heavy equipment moved from Washington State to Idaho because the latter has virtually no effective child labor prohibition (*Herald Journal*, November 21, 2005: A5, A6).

[48] Note that, as we saw in the previous chapter, faithfully nurturing a "wanted" child is in no way incompatible with aborting or killing an "unwanted" infant.

distressed. They are rarely or never physically punished and rarely scolded. They are not expected to contribute to the household economy and are free to play until the mid- to late teens. Their experience of adolescence is relatively stress free. This paradise exists among a globally dispersed group of isolated societies – all of which depend primarily on foraging for their subsistence. They are also characterized by relatively egalitarian and close social relations, and relative parity between men and women (Hewlett *et al.* 1998). Let's look at a few specific cases.

In central Malaysia, small bands of Batek people survive off the forest's bounty. Batek fathers as well as mothers spend a lot of time cuddling, holding, and talking with infants of either sex. Parents are quite relaxed about discipline: one two-year-old child used a bamboo flute his father had just finished making as a hammer. The father didn't care since he could easily make another. Parents rarely strike a child or use physical force on them, since their word *sakel* means both to hit and to kill, an abhorrent concept to them (Endicott 1992).

In the Paraguayan rainforest, Ache infants are almost never separated from their mothers and may suckle whenever they choose; "they are never set down on the ground or left alone for more than a few seconds" (Hill and Hurtado 1996: 219). Among the Airo-Pai foragers of Amazonian Peru:

Men and women have explicit ideas about family size and spacing. They say that the ideal number of children is three and that a woman should not become pregnant until her last child is capable of eating and moving around independently . . . Long birth spacings are necessary to provide an adequate upbringing for young children, who are bestowed with the undivided attention of their parents. Closely spaced children are said to suffer, cry and develop angry characters. (Belaunde 2001: 136)

In the Sarawak region of Borneo, the Punan Bah explain the devoted care of infants as mediated by their belief that the child is a reincarnated ancestor. Further, its body and soul are only tenuously linked, hence it is fragile, easily harmed by the distress arising from separation from its mother. Treated with great care, at least until four years of age, children are "never punished physically so as not to scare off their souls" (Nicolaisen 1988: 198–199). The Garo, who live in the forests of Bengal, all share in infant- and childcare, and parents "seldom roughhouse with their children, but play with them quietly, intimately, and fondly" (Burling 1963: 106).

In the Northwest Territory of Canada, the Inuit would never leave a child alone or let it cry for any length of time. Infants receive a great deal of solicitous care and lots of tactile comfort, all anticipatory of "the interdependence and close interpersonal relations that are an integral part of Inuit life" (Condon 1987: 59). A similar egalitarian, collective ethos animates Bofi (Central African rainforest foragers) childcare (Fouts 2005: 355). There are no sanctions against a child who fails to heed a request nor is it "pestered" by a repeat of the request (Fouts 2005: 358).[49]

It is noteworthy that extremely attentive childcare is accompanied by a great deal of respect for the child's individuality. For the Sioux living on the Great Plains of western North America, the child was invested with a great deal of character from birth. Care was taken not to suppress or divert the natural course of the child's personhood: "there was within the . . . Sioux community a profound respect for individual autonomy" (Wax 2002: 126). Draper observed a similar mindset operating among !Kung foragers in the Kalahari:

adults are completely tolerant of a child's temper tantrums and of aggression directed by a child at an adult. I have seen a seven-year-old crying and furious, hurling sticks, nut shells, and eventually burning embers at her mother. The mother sat at her fire talking with the child's grandmothers and her own sister-in-law. Bau (the mother) put up her arm occasionally to ward off the thrown objects but carried on her conversation nonchalantly. (Draper 1978: 37)

As the examples have already suggested, the entire band may participate in nurturing the child. Typical are the forest-dwelling Canela (Brazilian foragers) who live in small-scale consanguine communities of related women and their children.

While each mother is basically oriented to taking care of her own children, she can get help from her sister, her female cousins, and her mother should she need to absent herself for whatever purpose, including an extramarital tryst. Because female kin like to help one another have a good time in this way, the domestic unit has a number of willing baby-sitters built into its social structure. The . . . domestic unit includes from 10 to 20 children of all ages. They call each other brother and sister, though some may be first or even second cousins. The domestic group provides a healthy assortment of children, with many parents looking on. (Crocker and Crocker 1994: 177)

There are a cluster of factors that undergird this pattern of infant- and childcare. Unlike agrarian and industrialized societies, among most foragers children's lack of strength and stamina render them incapable of contributing much to family subsistence or income (Kaplan 1994). Second, foraging is, by definition, the active pursuit of food resources and mothers will, of necessity, carry their newborn constantly unless they can pass it off to another caretaker. Third, as discussed in the previous chapter, foragers adopt a "survivorship" reproductive strategy. Around the clock nursing and a post-partum sex taboo combine to insure long intervals between births leading to lower fertility. Low fertility is offset by the lavish attention bestowed on the few offspring, enhancing their survival (Fouts *et al.* 2001). Fourth, there are absolutely zero alternative life courses available within a foraging community. Children will either learn what

---

[49] However, Fouts notes that Bofi forager parents rarely *play* with or *talk to* their infants (personal communication, December 2005 and February 2007).

they need to – including important social skills – to feed themselves and find a mate, or starve. So there is no need to rein them in, guide, or teach them.

This paradise for children may have been the norm for much of human prehistory but the foraging way of life has become ephemeral. Only in the modern era have we seen almost a renaissance of paradise-like conditions for childhood.[50] As discussed in the last chapter, contemporary, educated parents have also adopted a survivorship strategy, following the "Great" transition. In the next section, we'll review that recent history.

The priceless child

The emergence of this economically "worthless" but emotionally "priceless" child has created an essential condition of contemporary childhood. (Zelizer 1985: 3)

How far we've come in redefining the utility of children is evident in a recent story describing how a suburban couple in Florida, the Barnards, had gone on strike and moved into a tent in their driveway, refusing to cook, clean, or otherwise care for their teenage children until they agreed to mend their ways and help out with household chores. Earlier they had tried awarding smiley faces and withholding allowances to no avail (*Associated Press*, December 10, 2004).[51]

Nothing speaks the "times have changed" refrain more poignantly than the statistics on youth employment in the USA "[While] most high school seniors in the United States work part-time during the school year... this work is not required by their school programme, nor is it undertaken primarily to save for college or help with family finances" (Bachman *et al.* 2003: 301). They spend nearly 100 percent of their earnings on their own, conspicuous consumption.[52] Further, the more hours adolescents devote to employment, the more likely they are to smoke, drink, and use marijuana and the weaker are their plans and aspirations for college and career (Bachman *et al.* 2003: 307).

Middle- and upper-class American parents gain no return from their children's employment; in fact, they may incur a loss. How did this strange state of affairs come about? There appear to be two driving forces, the first of which is

---

[50] I'm grateful to Alan Fiske for urging me to emphasize that one very significant difference between the forager's paradise and ours is that our infants and children spend far less time in direct physical contact with others. Our cherubs are talked to and get hugs and kisses, but they are most often "held" by cribs, walkers, car seats, play pens, and strollers.

[51] Similarly, Anglo-Australian parents hold the view that they can't ask their children to do more than self-care, keeping their own spaces tidy. Chores that involved caring for other family members and their property were "extra" and deserving of pay (Goodnow 1996). In a more recent article, the author had no trouble finding parents who admit to paying their children even for self-care – such as brushing their teeth (*Salt Lake Tribune*, April 17, 2007: A11).

[52] Apparently this is not a recent phenomenon in the USA: "newsies" at the turn of the century in Chicago spent their earnings on picture shows (Nasaw 1992: 19).

the demographic transition discussed at length in the previous chapter, whereby changes in the nature of work, including especially the need for residential mobility, reduced both the need for and ability to cope with large families.

A second driving force is ably documented by Zelizer in her landmark work: *Pricing the Priceless Child*. She describes a dramatic shift in attitudes towards the young in the nineteenth century. Until then, the death of a child was no great cause for sorrow, and newborns were often referred to as "it" or "little stranger." The next child replaced the deceased; indeed, "it was a common practice to name newborns after a sibling who had recently died" (Zelizer 1985: 24–25).[53]

Others credit the Protestant Reformation with ushering in a new emphasis on the sacred duty of parents to rear all children and prepare them for a blameless life. However, in heeding admonitions from the reformers to invest more in their children (childrearing tracts were published from the fifteenth century),[54] Protestants might grow so attached to them that, when they died, they were plunged into mourning – which the church also frowned on. Martin Luther agonized over his inability to shrug off the deaths of two of his children (Colón, with Colón 2001).

The Victorian child looks more and more cherubic as parents used dress and hairstyle to render children sexless. The goal was to create an ideal "of androgynous (that is, angelic) innocence" (Calvert 1992: 109). During the immediate post-World War II period in Japan, children were romanticized "as cute, dependent, and needing much tender care . . . in contrast to the earlier utilitarian conception" (Uno 1991: 398).

Linda Pollock's analysis of diaries dating from early modern England gives us glimpses of this attitude, at least among the "gentry." Already in the eighteenth century, children were seen as expensive to maintain and rear; however, they were also

seen as a source of emotional satisfaction and as providing interest and variety in life . . . they were valued for the amusement they offered and their company. They are also viewed as offering a second chance for an individual to achieve for his children the things he did not manage to have and as providing security and pleasure in later life for their parents . . . .a "comfort in old age." (Pollock 1983: 208)

Parallel research conducted more recently shows these attitudes continuing as parents go to great lengths to socialize children to embody the "outgoing, warm, loving . . . cheerful . . . qualities one might like in a friend" (Hoffman 1988: 118).[55] These changes are intimately associated with a decline in family size.

[53] In London, in the first half of the eighteenth century, 75 percent of the population under the age of five perished (Sommerville 1982: 157).

[54] Wang Shouren (1472–1529) ushered in a change in Chinese views on children closely paralleling the changes that occurred in the West four centuries later (Wu 1995: 146).

[55] Some parents may be going well beyond this point. A recent report shows increasing use of pre-implantation genetic diagnosis, or PGD, to deliberately *increase* the odds of producing an

In Sweden, because responsible adults have accepted the necessity for strictly limiting reproduction, parents' anxiety concerning their infant's viability and the risks during childhood is much, much higher than "in sub-Saharan Africa and other places where the [actual] risks to infant survival are twenty-five times as high" (Welles-Nystrom 1988: 76).

What is noteworthy is that children are valued for their contribution to parents' *emotional* wellbeing rather than to their *material* comfort. In the early twentieth century, the death of children also becomes more and more a cause for *public* concern, with newspaper editorials chiding parents for failing to prevent their children from often fatal accidents in the burgeoning vehicular traffic. The fight to limit child labor and child insurance, indeed any practice that permitted parents to earn a return from their children, became one of the twentieth century's great civil-rights crusades, with strong moral overtones. Culpable "neglect" began to replace the fatalistic "god's will" as the most common post-mortem verdict after child death (Zelizer 1985: 37).

One might argue that this crusade on behalf of the sacred child was held in abeyance during the turmoil of successive wars at mid-century, only to be renewed with increased vigor at the end of the century, viz:

American society has been increasingly "fetally fascinated." This preoccupation with the fetus takes many forms, including ongoing debates about "fetal rights,"[56] fetal con-sciousness, fetal tissue research, fetal surgery, visualizing the fetus, and commodify-ing the fetus ... [while the] ... American understanding and classification of premature infants has changed dramatically from the late nineteenth century to the present. What were categorized previously as miscarriages, abortuses, "weaklings", or unsalvageable fetuses are now called "premature infants," subject to a variety of medical and social interventions designed to finish what nature has failed to complete. (Isaacson 2002: 89)

In chapter 2, I used the following quote: "What could be more startling to an imagination informed by evolutionary theory than the killing of one's own children?" (Daly and Wilson 1988: 42) to highlight the strangeness of infanticide. However, as we realize that our society has created what I've called a "neontocracy" (Lancy 1996: 12–13) (chapter 1), we might well ask: "What could be more startling to an imagination informed by evolutionary theory than the adoption and rearing of unrelated children?" Sarah Hrdy explains the adoption of non-kin: "Unlike other animals, humans are able to consciously make choices counter to their self-interest. Indeed, much of what we consider 'ethical behavior' falls in this category" (Hrdy 1999: 460).

offspring that shares the parent's disability such as deafness or dwarfism (*New York Times*, December 5, 2007: F5).

[56] Contrast Japanese attitudes: "It is quite alien to Japanese to think of the existence of a fetus independent of the uterine body, so independent as to claim its rights, even at the risk of its nurturer's life" (Lebra 1994: 260). Or: "The fetus is never regarded as 'alive' until after it is born, so Inuit never think of it as a person" (Guemple 1979: 40).

Anthropologist John Bock offered this explanation: "I think there is an evolved psychology that provides proximate rewards (satisfaction, happiness, joy, etc.) for parenting. I think most people experience a lot of those proximate rewards (positive emotions) from parenting regardless of whether the child being parented is a biological offspring or not. . ."[57] Another factor, undoubtedly, is the scattering of families – following from our education, employment, and marriage practices. It is no longer convenient for childless couples to share in rearing their nephews, nieces, and cousins.

My own view acknowledges these evolutionary ideas but also concedes the powerful influence of culture in guiding our behavior – sometimes in directions that make no sense in evolutionary terms. Cherubic children are so attractive, so desirable, so much a reflection of our longing for innocence and naivety – while still allowing us the pursuit of sensual indulgence and materialism – that they've become essential components of "the good life." Modern Americans and Europeans often want children even when they don't want to go through the pain and/or hassle of pregnancy or marriage. Never mind gourmet cooking, orchid cultivation, or macramé, "parenting" has become the ultimate hobby, allowing us to indulge our values and tastes in shaping a real live human being. And, as our talented cherubs gather public acclaim for their good looks, cleverness, and many accomplishments, we contentedly bask in their reflected glory.

But, by the same token, when we recoil from newspaper accounts of an unmarried mother on welfare giving birth to her sixth child; or a woman drowning her sons to make herself a more attractive match for a husband; or a couple postponing childbearing because they're in debt or lack insurance; a boyfriend shaking to death his girlfriend's infant; a husband leaving his wife and four children to marry a younger woman – aren't we being rather ethnocentric? Viewed in the broad panoply of nature, of human history and culture, these actions are both predictable and, perhaps, understandable.

[57] Personal communication, August 1, 2003.

4   It takes a village

Introduction

. . . there are very few cultures in the world where a woman's role is specialized for child minding and little else. That is a peculiar Western aberration and recent at that. (Ritchie and Ritchie 1979: 57)

. . . a child is not born to [Tahitian] parents; it is born from parents to the whanau (descent group). (Ritchie and Ritchie 1979: 48)

The notion that "It takes a village" to raise a child has, in the past two decades, become part of our national folk wisdom, immortalized in a book with that title penned by Hillary Rodham Clinton (Clinton 1996). But few people seem to have any clear sense of how the original aphorism gains its force. For many, I suspect the vision conjured up is of the child cosseted by an adoring chorus of grandmother types. As I will demonstrate, if one actually looks at real kids in real villages, either one typically sees infants and young children in a group of their peers, *untended* by an adult, or one sees a mother, a father, an older sister, or a grandmother tending the child. The rule would *not* be "Everyone's eager to have a hand in caring for the child," but, rather, "Whoever can most easily be spared from more important tasks, will take care of the child." And the next rule we might derive from our observations might be, "The mother is often too busy to tend to the child."

We'll examine the role of swaddling and similar technologies that, at least partially, relieve the mother of her burden. A contrast will be drawn between patterns of infant care and the treatment – tantamount to rejection in many cases – of toddlers (Lancy 2007b). The village is a community of caretakers and, in this chapter, we will systematically examine the roles played by the mother, father, older siblings, and grandparents as well as the community at large.

After examining the nature of childrearing in the village, we'll seek the beginnings, in history, of our own, very un-village-like ideas about raising children. We conclude with a functional analysis of the childrearing program utilized by contemporary parents in mid- to upper-echelon society.

Who's your mommy?

Most of the time spent in childcare is spent not by [Javanese] mothers, but by other household members. (Nag *et al.* 1978: 296)

Caring for a little [Peyrane] baby is considered a pleasure rather than a chore by everyone except the mother. (Wylie 1957: 42)

The primary responsibilities of seventeenth-century [American] women were managing the household and childbearing, not childrearing. (Calvert 1992: 23)

In the fall of 1973, I took up residence in the polygynous household of Chief Wolliekollie in the Liberian village of Gbarngasuakwelle (Lancy 1996). While the chief was very gracious in welcoming me, in facilitating my research – on the children of the village – and in providing me with accommodation in his sprawling house, he failed to introduce me to other members of his household. Strangers rarely visited Gbarngasuakwelle and, when they did, the chief knew they usually meant trouble and expense, so he did his best to insure their stay was short and unobtrusive. There was no protocol for dealing with a resident ethnographer.

The household consisted of three of the chief's four wives, an unmarried sister of one of them, their children, and a steady stream of temporary residents related to the chief or his wives. I gradually sorted out all the adults, and it was relatively easy to match the nursing babies with their mothers, but, then, I struggled for weeks to match up the various children to their respective mothers. Bear in mind that, initially at least, given my lack of fluency, I had to rely largely on observation. I was stymied because the children, once they were no longer attached marsupial-like to their mother's body with a length of cloth, spent far more time in each other's company and in the company of other kin, particularly grandmothers and aunts in nearby houses, than with their mothers. And as far as the chief was concerned, I just had to assume that since these were his wives, the majority of the children in the vicinity must be his as well. Aside from dandling the occasional infant on his knee during the family's evening meal, I never saw him enjoy more than the most fleeting interaction with a child.[1]

My impression was that, far from being the dominant influence in their lives, the biological parents were just two of a large cast of potential child-minders. And, even while acknowledging the mother's near constant proximity to her nursing infant, the relationship is best described as "casual nurturance [where] . . . mothers carry their babies on their backs and nurse them frequently but do so without really paying much direct attention to them; they continue working or . . . socializing" (Erchak 1992: 50). This seeming indifference may

---

[1] As much as anything else, the chief, like any polygynist, is loath to stir up the cauldron of jealousy that is usually simmering in his household. Paying attention to any of his children might be construed by the mothers of his other children as "favoritism."

Figure 7 White Karen village mother playing mouth-harp as baby nurses, north Thailand

be reinforced by custom whereby a mother is chastised by peers if she is overly fond of her child (Toren 1990: 172). Figure 7 illustrates this phenomenon quite well.

Since I was enamored of the exotic – and what anthropologist isn't – these strange family customs were exciting. And yet, twenty years after completing my work in Gbarngasuakwelle, I began to see their family arrangements and childcare customs as neither unusual nor exotic, rather as close to the norm for human societies, and, simultaneously, to see the customs of the predominantly middle-class Utah community I live in now as extraordinary. My neighbors are predominantly adherents of the LDS or Latter Day Saints church which maintains a very pronounced position on the nature of the family.

LDS doctrine and utopian ideals are reflected in the following:

- "From the beginning God has made it clear that woman is very special, and . . . Satan and his cohorts are using scientific arguments and nefarious propaganda to lure women away from their primary responsibilities as wives, mothers, and homemakers" (Tanner 1974: 7).[2]
- "A mother has far greater influence on her children than anyone else . . . every word she speaks, every act . . . even her appearance and manner of dress affect the lives of her children" (Tanner 1974: 8)
- "This divine service of motherhood can be rendered only by mothers. It may not be passed to others. Nurses cannot do it; public nurseries cannot do it; hired help cannot do it" (Packer 1993: 24).

These samples are but a fraction of the steady stream of moral injunctions that issue forth from the church hierarchy to the effect that a Christian wife's calling is the production and care of children.[3] Further, this effort should be seen as a demanding, full-time occupation.[4] While the husband is the designated breadwinner and head of the family, the LDS church goes further than perhaps any contemporary moral authority in also obligating the father to participate in childcare.[5]

In contrast to this view,[6] I hope to show that in the large and growing archive on comparative childcare patterns, the mother's role may be quite attenuated[7] and the father's role is, in many societies, perhaps in the majority, non-existent. In a telling study of West African Hausa children's ability to identify kin and construct their own genealogies, LeVine found that "some children omitted

---

[2] Tanner was first Counselor to the First Presidency when he wrote this article.

[3] Luther wrote: "If women grow weary or even die while bearing children, that does no harm. Let them bear children to death, that's what they're there for." However, Luther, unlike most theologians before and since, also believed that women had a duty to satisfy their husband's sexual needs (Moynihan 2002: 390).

[4] I don't want to imply any uniqueness in the LDS perspective. These views on the "proper" role of women are broadly representative of the political/religious right throughout the world. See, for example; Eberstadt (2004).

[5] These views on the role of parents as guardians of their children's virtue are characteristic of virtually all fundamentalist groups (Coleman 1999: 76).

[6] Judith Harris makes a very cogent argument that evolution would not favor exclusive reliance on biological parents, especially on the mother. The mother may be incompetent or she may perish; others – who are already "wired" to the child, so to speak – readily take up the slack. Also, the more caretakers the child has, the more "role models" s/he may learn from (Harris 1998: 119).

[7] When Freudian theory was in fashion, the mother was seen as potentially harmful to her children's psychological wellbeing, so, in at least one utopian community, children were placed in the care of professionals at the earliest opportunity (Siskind 1999).

their parents; more than a third of the girls failed to mention their fathers" (LeVine 1974: 41). The following are reasonably typical cases that introduce the notion that the "whole village" may share responsibility for childrearing.

- In West Africa, the expectant Mende mother moves "back home" to have her baby and returns to her husband's home only after the baby is walking. She does this in order to take advantage of the support of her own close kin (as opposed to less supportive in-laws) during the most precarious period of her child's life (Isaac and Feinberg 1982: 632).[8]
- Among the Kipsigis (Kenya) the new mother's neighbors take on many of her responsibilities, including caring for her older children, bringing firewood, and preparing meals so she can rest and recover her strength (Harkness and Super 1991: 223).
- Central African Efe mothers are not always the first to nurse their new infant who, at four months, will spend 60 percent of the time being cared for by many other band members. The child will, in fact, be "passed around the band, an average of 8.3 times per hour" (Tronick et al. 1987).[9] Life expectancy among the Efe is low, leaving many children orphaned. A child who has been nurtured from birth by others will be cared for should the parents die (Morelli and Tronick 1991).
- Typically, the new baby is only gradually introduced to the rest of the family and community[10] once all is well. Hence, the Ache from Paraguay are unusual in that the birth is witnessed by the whole band. But this facilitates a process whereby a significant fraction of the community shares in the child's care and upbringing.[11]

[Another] woman holds the child in her lap and washes it gently. She is called the *tapare* ... [and] is responsible for ... the child's care during its first few days of life ... she will sometimes adopt her godchild if the child's mother dies ... a single man ... called *mondoare,* cuts the umbilical cord of the child with a bamboo knife. He is expected to provide for his godchild in times of need, and ... other individuals who lift and hold the child, or wash it in the first few minutes after birth, are designated as *upaire,* "those who lifted it," and they too take on a godparent-like relationship. (Hill and Hurtado 1996: 66–67)

- Similar to the *mondoare,* the Inuit on Belcher Island designate a *sanaria?uk* or ritual sponsor at birth. This person assumes distinct responsibilities complementing the mother's role (Guemple 1969: 470).

---

[8] The same pattern is found among the Fulani (Dupire 1963).

[9] On Fiji, an unweaned infant is as likely to be in the arms of another as with its mother (Maxwell West 1988: 22). This phenomenon is so common cross-culturally, it has its own name – "child shifting" (Lange and Rodman 1992: 190).

[10] For example, "Visitors from outside the household are kept away from the infant, and the infant only gradually makes the acquaintance of a widening circle of others" (Howrigan 1988: 41).

[11] Obviously, as we saw in the previous chapter, the community also has a say in whether or not to preserve a child's life.

- The words for mother (*Nana*) and father (*Bafa*) are used indiscriminately with all adult women and men in Bofi society – farmers from Central Africa (Fouts 2005: 357).
- In Arab society, a special kin term, *rida'a*, denotes the relationship between a child and a woman, not its own mother, who nursed it (Altorki 1980: 233).
- In Hong Kong, "rather than experiencing the birth of a baby as a beginning, the new mother considers it as 'a project finished.' The nine-month period of symbiosis for which she is solely responsible is over. The responsibility can now be shared with others" (Martin 2001: 164).
- John Chisholm, long-time student of the Navajo, found that mothers living in large extended family households interacted *more* with their children than did those in isolated, nuclear households. The latter simply didn't have as much time available – burdened as they were by *all* the domestic and gardening chores (Chisholm 1983). The community normally lifts the burden of childcare from mothers who are, coincidentally, also at the peak of their productivity as workers.
- This fact was not lost on slave owners in the USA who employed a highly organized nursery-like system to free the mother for labor more valuable to the slave owner (Alston 1992: 211).[12]

Infant care

The added weight of carrying infants while lactating [is] much like carrying a heavy backpack. (Strier 2003: 173)

Hadza mothers are quite willing to hand their children off to anyone willing to take them. (Marlowe 2005: 188)

With very few exceptions, mothers nurse the child, "on demand".[13] Of course, this still allows for wide variability;[14] for example, one study in the Congo compared the agrarian Ngandu with their foraging neighbors the Aka and found the latter mothers nursing four times an hour, on average, and the former, twice. In addition, Aka mothers hold their infants for more of the day than do the Ngandu, in spite of the fact that for the pygmy-sized Aka, the energetic costs are higher (Hewlett *et al.* 1998). Aka youngsters are also allowed to interfere

---

[12] Obviously, the author's perspective on childcare among slaves reflects a modern, middle-class bias. These practices would not be much different than those found among the slaves' contemporaries still living in Africa. Alston also mentions that slave children had no responsibilities until at least the age of six, a rather "late" age of responsibility by comparison with traditional African society.

[13] In Euroamerican society, where babies are precious cherubs, new mothers often express amazement at how "demanding" their baby can be: "I mean really I was rooted to the sofa and she was wanting to feed all the time which I hadn't prepared for" (Murphy 2007:111).

[14] Perhaps it would be more accurate to say that infants are not fed on a "schedule."

and interrupt parents even when they're working (Hewlett 1992: 228). As noted in chapter 2, these differences may reflect differing reproduction strategies in the two societies, "production" vs "survivorship" (Hewlett *et al.* 2000).

In many societies the baby is attached to the mother with a sling, woven bag, or length of cloth and rides on her chest, her back, or her hip. The infant is simultaneously kept warm and comforted by proximity to her body, kept clean and out of harm's way, and travels with her as she moves from place to place. In short, the infant is at all times accessible to the mother should it need attention. Naturally, mothers vary their ministrations, according to perceived need. Gusii mothers "provided more protective attention in the early months of life for those infants who showed signs of being vulnerable. Those . . . rated as not well organized . . . were held more by their mothers . . . Babies who weighed less during the first nine months were held more by mother and other caregivers" (LeVine and LeVine 1988: 31–32).

Breastfeeding and carrying a growing child imposes additional (up to five times) energy costs (Lee 1996) on a woman. "Maternity leave" in traditional societies is short while the labor demands on women are typically high. My female housemates and neighbors in Gbarngasuakwelle were hard at work hoeing in the rice fields shortly after the birth of their children. Not surprisingly, mothers appreciate offspring who are wiry, agile, and early walkers (Zeitlin 1996: 412).

One convenient way to reduce this cost is to "swaddle" the child or use some device like a cradleboard that keeps the child safe and secure without being constantly tethered to its mother:

swaddling immobilizes the child. Parents can hang the bound infant up on a nail and go about their business, secure in the knowledge that he cannot crawl into the fireplace or fall down a well. (Sommerville 1982: 23)

A swaddled baby, like a little turtle in its shell, could be looked after by another, only slightly older child without too much fear of injury, since the practice of swaddling made . . . child care virtually idiot proof. (Calvert 1992: 23–24)

Undoubtedly the Navajo (North American pastoralists) were the best-known exponents of the cradleboard.[15] There were four graduated sizes designed to be lashed to a horse's saddle in such a way that a kind of awning could be stretched from the saddle bow over the cradle to shield the child. Of course, the board kept the child tranquil[16] and out of its mother's way (Chisholm 1980), but the Navajo had an elaborate rationale for its use, for example, "Babies

---

[15] But its use was widespread throughout North America, e.g. Pearsall (1950: 340).

[16] Actually, Dan Freedman's research on ethnicity and infant temperament shows that Asian and Native American babies are much more placid than Caucasian babies. He concludes: "cradle-boarding probably represents a marriage between culture and infant constitution" (Freedman 1974: 162).

are kept... in the cradle to make them straight and strong. Some women let their children lie on sheep skins and roll about, but they are always weak, sick children" (Leighton and Kluckhohn 1948: 23).[17]

There are many variations on this theme. In Bukkitingi, Sumatra, I observed unattended infants in cradle-baskets, suspended on long cords, which swung, pendulum-like, in the slightest breeze. As recently as 2007, I found cradles which immobilized the infant on sale in the markets of Uzbekistan. They featured an amazing add-on that collected the child's urine – keeping it dry and diaper-free. In an article on transhumance in Mongolia, there's a photo of an infant in a cradle-like structure strapped to the back of an ox in the middle of a milling herd. The herd is being driven over a mountain pass to winter pasture. The caption reads: "An ox-back ride is sometimes dangerous and always rough but there's no other way to go: The adults are too busy herding to babysit" (Hodges 2003: 108).

One of the most interesting baby-tenders is the *manta* pouch used by Quechua farmers who live high in the Andes. It turns out this low-tech device is quite efficacious in promoting the infant's wellbeing. In this micro-environment, heightened temperature and humidity makes breathing easier and sleep more likely than wakefulness. During nursing, the infant remains in the pouch to reduce the chance it will be aroused, thus further conserving energy that would waste precious calories (Tronick *et al.* 1994: 1009–1010). Modern substitutes, including strollers, cribs, and play pens have dispersed the cradleboard concept around the world.[18]

The infant invariably sleeps with its mother for the same reasons it's usually attached to her during the day – ease of nursing. This suggests that the mother may not be sleeping with the child's father[19] and, indeed, the post-partum taboo on intercourse is widespread. Each society will operate with tacit ideas about how long the inter-birth interval should be, but a father's threat to withhold provisions until relations resume may hasten weaning.

A lengthier nursing period is usually associated with a more casual weaning process. An Efe mother, teased because she's still nursing her three-year-old, replies: "'I've tried to wean him, but he refuses, so I guess he's not ready.' Everyone laughs" (Wilkie and Morelli 1991: 55).[20] By contrast, Kpelle mothers

---

[17] The autobiography of noted Hopi Don Talayesva includes many interesting details on life in a cradleboard (Simmons 1942: 33).

[18] And these aren't the only widely used child-management aids. Ceramic baby bottles and potty chairs are clearly depicted in Greek vase paintings (*National Geographic News*, September 12, 2003: 1–2). One can view the genuine items on display in the small museum inside the Stoa of Attalus in Athens.

[19] I believe that one of the unacknowledged reasons for separating the child from its parents at bedtime and during bathing in the USA, in contrast, say, to contemporary European and Asian custom, is concern for sexually polluting the child.

[20] A similar pattern holds for the forest-dwelling Bofi as well (Fouts *et al.* 2001).

Figure 8 Chinese child-minding device

withhold the breast and force-feed infants rice water to accelerate weaning. The abruptness and severity of weaning were studied intensively in research initiated by the Whitings during the 1960s (Whiting and Whiting 1975). In many societies, children are threatened with all sorts of terrors to discourage them from nursing (Williams 1969). It can be a traumatic experience for the child – a key element in Freud's theory of personality development.

A casual and relaxed attitude towards weaning usually signals a relaxed attitude towards toilet training. The Fore, in the Eastern Highlands of Papua New Guinea, are representative:

Although disposal of body wastes was a matter of great concern to adult Fore because of their use in sorcery, toilet training was not imposed . . . A toddler could repeatedly defecate in the hamlet yard, even during a feast, without being chastised . . . [someone] would . . . clean up . . .[21] As the child grew older, he began to adopt . . . practices governing excretion by modeling . . . on those of older children . . . who often treated . . . "errors" in behavior as a cause for amusement. (Sorenson 1976: 177)

[21] I've more commonly observed dogs fulfilling this hygienic function.

Typically, there is a prescribed menu for supplemental feeding that varies with the child's age. The efficacy of this diet is highly variable. Hadza babies are fed "rendered soft fat . . . from the zebra, and bone marrow, both raw and cooked, are introduced in the early months followed by a thin gruel-like mixture made of the . . . ground seeds, of the baobab fruit" and this diet produces clinically well-nourished babies (Jelliffe *et al.* 1962: 910). As foragers, the Hadza can provide a variety of foods, including plenty of protein, for their young. But, more generally, childhood undernutrition is widespread in the less-developed world, even as overnutrition is becoming a critical problem in the developed world (Chee 2000).

Aside from a demonstrable shortage of food (Hill and Hurtado 1996: 319), undernutrition may be attributable to customs that support a shortening of the nursing period, such as the belief by some East African pastoralists that certain babies nurse "too much" and should, therefore, be weaned early (Sellen 1995). Malnutrition could be due as well to the not uncommon custom of giving babies enemas, ostensibly to better control their elimination, but with the result that they are robbed of nourishment and dehydrated as well (Riesman 1992: 4).

Mothers tend to divert the best foods to their mates. "Wives are feeding husbands like kings, leaving leftovers and thin porridge for children" (*The Monitor* (Kampala), January 9, 2003: 11). Yoruba mothers feed children scraps that "were barely visible compared to the portions they gave themselves . . . [good] food was feared to spoil the child's moral character" (Zeitlin 1996: 418).[22] The prescription for a sick child among the Gurage tribe in southwest Ethiopia is often the sacrifice of a sheep: "The flesh of the sacrificial animal is eaten exclusively by the parents of the sick child and others who are present at the curing rite; no portion of the meat is consumed by the patient, whose illness may well stem from an inadequate diet" (Shack 1969: 296).

This tendency to feed the youngest the least nutritious remnants is treated as a childcare crisis in Uganda. Worldwide, the trend to bottle-feed babies infant formula, sometimes of dubious quality, so the mother can cease nursing earlier, is also deplored as very harmful to infant survival (Howrigan 1988; Trevarthen 1988). Overall, one has the impression that parents in resource-poor societies are investing only enough in the infant to keep it alive and, of course, as we learned in the last chapter, they may well expect every second child, on average, to fail to thrive. But recall from chapter 1, that post-industrial society is a *neontocracy* that values children highly and treats babies as delightful companions and playmates.

---

[22] However, Zeitlin notes that mothers in the Indian subcontinent are expected to martyr themselves, if necessary, eating last and least.

Peek-a-boo

... in only some cultures do mothers act as the sole, or even primary, "curators of meaning." (Bakeman *et al.* 1990: 807)

Noted child psychologist Jerome Bruner called attention to a mother playing peek-a-boo with her infant as the onset of a lengthy program to stimulate the child's intellectual development (Bruner and Sherwood 1976: 277). But our survey of mother–infant relations challenges many assumptions like this one about what is essential in childcare. Is peek-a-boo "nature" at work or "nurture?" An analysis of 186 archived ethnographies of traditional societies indicated wide variation in the amount of mother–infant play and display of affection (Barry and Paxson 1971). In a more recent comparative observational study, "Euro-American adults were much more likely than Aka or Ngandu adults to stimulate (e.g., tickle) and vocalize to their infants. As a result, Euro-American infants were significantly more likely than Aka and Ngandu infants to smile, look at, and vocalize to their care providers" (Hewlett *et al.* 2000: 164).[23] Other research shows that the *en face* position whereby the mother holds the infant facing her is common in Westernized societies but rare elsewhere, as is the tendency of the mother to talk with the infant (Field *et al.* 1981). Peek-a-boo is equally rare. Playing with, talking to, and stimulating the infant are all considered by Western developmental psychologists an essential in order to promote the mother–infant bond but, again, some scholars now question the necessity for such bonding (Scheper-Hughes 1987b: 201).[24]

The pattern of infant–caretaker interaction West describes on Fiji is quite representative with respect to who plays with the infant, how they do so, and why:

While mothers performed routine physical care of infants ... the playful interactions of the non-maternal caregivers ... or of relatives visiting ... were much more notable. Various persons, of all ages and either sex, greeted infants enthusiastically and often initiated playful slaps or clapping games, or engaged the infant in reciprocal vocal or (later) verbal routines [which] may have functioned to introduce infants to the significant others in the social matrix. (Maxwell West 1988: 22)

Similarly, Marquesan infants are rarely

cuddled into the caregiver's body ... they were held in a sitting or standing position, if they were held at all .... [Mothers] ... spent much time calling the baby's name, directing him to look and wave at others ... directing 3- to 6-year-old siblings to play

---

[23] In discussions with Barry Hewlett (Aka) and Hillary Fouts (Bofi) they affirmed (personal communications, February/March 2007) that, in their systematic observations of childminding in pygmy societies, parents rarely, if ever, play with their children.

[24] For example, among the Papel, with an infant mortality rate around 33 percent, mothers aren't supposed to talk to or get too emotionally tied to their infants (Einarsdottir 2004: 73).

with him. [Adult–infant play activities] such as tickling, singing, or tossing the infant in the air, was [rarely] observed. (Martini and Kirkpatrick 1981: 199)

Bakeman and colleagues studied carefully the nature of adult–child inter-action among the !Kung, specifically seeking to test some of our Western assumptions about what is or isn't essential to the child's normal development. As on Fiji, they, too, found that "Non-mothers . . . vocalized to and entertained infants more than mothers" (Bakeman *et al.* 1990: 802). In addition, they failed to see the parent–child interactions considered critical by psychologists for language development (Bakeman *et al.* 1990: 806). On the contrary, the !Kung believe that children learn best without adult intervention (Bakeman *et al.* 1990: 796).

This view is widely shared. It certainly characterized my Kpelle informants. Similarly, the Fore mother serves only as "home base" for her wandering infant, and she does not intervene to play with it or manage its activity in any way (Sorenson 1976: 166–167).[25] In the next section, we'll see that the infant's almost magnetic attractiveness to other members of the community is commonplace and is also typical of non-human primates as well.

Playing with dolls

All female primates find babies . . . fascinating. (Hrdy 1999: 157)

I have seen a little [West African Afikpo] girl of about five or six carrying a newly born baby over her shoulder, or sitting down and giving it water to drink. (Ottenberg 1968: 80)

The mother of an infant benefits from the fact that other women, particularly her own daughters and other younger female relatives, will find her baby irresistible. In Uganda in 2003, I observed and filmed numerous primate species and, after resting, eating, and play, "baby-trading" is the most common occupation. Often I observed what amounted to a "tug-of-war" between the nursing mother and her older daughters for possession of the infant, which may lead to what Sarah Hrdy referred to as "aunting to death" (Hrdy 1976). This phenomenon, where juvenile females eagerly vie for opportunities to carry, groom, and comfort infants, is referred to by primatologists as "allomothering" (Maestripieri 1994). By contrast, mothers tend to discourage interest shown by juvenile *males* in their offspring (Strier 2003).[26]

---

[25] The mother as "home base" phenomenon is widely noted among primates (Baldwin and Baldwin 1977: 349).

[26] Barbara King describes an episode in which a mother successfully thwarts an attempt by an older brother, who'd already demonstrated his incompetence as a caretaker, from spiriting off his infant brother (King 2005).

Several studies have documented the gender bias in "baby lust" (Hrdy 1999: 157). Females show far more interest in babies, images of babies, and even silhouettes of babies than do males. Somewhat unexpectedly, this line of research also shows such interest peaking just *before* women enter their childbearing years (Maestripieri and Pelka 2001), suggesting that they are preparing for the emotional distance required of new mothers discussed in chapter 2.

The advantages to the nursing mother of having "helpers at the nest" (Turke 1988) are numerous. She can move through the environment foraging more readily with less energetic expense and she has an additional ally or two in responding to threats of predation or attacks from, sometimes, indiscriminately aggressive males. Among cotton-topped tamarins, having a daughter to carry the infant is *the* critical variable in successfully rearing offspring (Bardo *et al.* 2001) and some daughters, influenced evidently by pheromones released by their mother, *never* ovulate. As they never had offspring of their own, they could continue to provide allomothering services to their mother until she was past childbearing (Ziegler *et al.* 1987; Savage *et al.* 1988). Jane Goodall has documented several cases of juvenile chimps who perished shortly after the death of their mother, except in one case where an older sister "adopted" the orphan (van Lawick-Goodall 1973).

While comparable research with human populations is sparse, working in rural Trinidad, Mark Flinn has demonstrated delayed pregnancy in young women who are assisting in the care of younger siblings, but also that, after age thirty, mothers "pay back" by investing in their daughters' reproduction efforts (Flinn 1988; 1989). Another critical study by Paul Turke, undertaken on Ifaluk atoll in the western Pacific, found "that parents who produce daughters early in their reproductive careers... out-reproduce parents who produce sons early" (Turke 1989: 73). Among Efe foragers in the Congo, "The number of child caregivers who assisted a mother was positively related to the time that mothers spent acquiring food away from camp"(Henry *et al.* 2005: 202).

The baby's cherub-like features also aid the mother in her quest for helpers. Young mammals, generally, but especially humans, display a suite of physical features that seem to be universally attractive to others (Lancaster and Lancaster 1983: 35; Sternglanz *et al.* 1977).[27] Also critical is the fact that human infants vocalize, make eye contact, and smile from very early on (Chevalier-Skolnikoff 1977) – unlike chimps, for example, whose mothers make more limited use of helpers.

Mothers may not always rely on the inherent cuteness of their babies; they may take pains to showcase the baby – at least among close kin.[28] The Kpelle

[27] The initial theory was proposed by ethologist Konrad Lorenz (1943).

[28] The mother always has to be on the alert for the evil influences of childless women or cuckolded males, so, depending on whom she's with, she may well make *disparaging* remarks about her child.

mothers I observed didn't stop at frequently washing and cleaning their babies. They oiled their bodies until they gleamed – an ablution carried out in public view with an appreciative audience. The Kaluli mothers studied by Bambi Schieffelin in PNG not only hold their infants facing *towards* others in the social group – a practice often noted in the ethnographic record – but they treat the baby as a ventriloquist's dummy in having him/her speak to those assembled (Schieffelin 1990: 71). In the Solomon Islands:

An infant of 6 months given a piece of fruit is immediately told to "Give some to your sister/brother,"... In helping the infant to hand the piece to its sibling, the caregiver tells the infant to say, "Here's your fruit." Infants who cry or resist sharing are gently chided, teased, or laughed at. (Watson-Gegeo and Gegeo 1989: 61)

In the Sepik area of PNG, recently weaned youngsters are encouraged to act solicitously towards the neonate, if they wish to "remain in the proximity of ... mother's breast" (Barlow 2001: 97).

These examples are typical of many one finds in the anthropological literature of mothers actively teaching their children politeness or etiquette conventions and terminology (Lancy 1996: 23). As we'll see, mothers otherwise rarely act as their children's teachers so this may be directly related to their dependence on older children and kin to assist with childcare. Whenever she can, the mother will try and "market" her children to potential caretakers. She must, however, accept the consequence that virtually anyone older than her child can scold or even discipline them (Whiting 1941). In societies like our own, where childcare is handled within the nuclear family and/or by professionals, the necessity for learning manners and kinship arcana is reduced. At the same time, we are often reluctant to concede to outsiders, even "professionals," the right to discipline our young.

That "good" mothers are those who are able to amass social capital is borne out in research with primates in the wild. Joan Silk and her colleagues conducted a study of fitness (number of surviving offspring) among savannah baboons and found that: "Females who had more social contact with other adult group members and were more fully socially integrated into their groups were more likely than other females to rear infants successfully" (Silk *et al.* 2003: 1234).[29] Other studies indicate that these socializing skills are passed on to daughters who are active in grooming higher-ranking females and, in effect, acquiring social capital within the troop (Walter 1987: 365).

Comparable research with humans is rare, but we should, for example, expect better conditions for children of higher-ranking wives in a polygynous

---

[29] Studies also show high-ranking mothers as more mellow, allowing their infants to wander more freely, trusting in their high status to insure that troop members will aid and not harm their offspring – in contrast to low-ranking mothers who must be much more protective and vigilant (Altmann 1980).

household. A study of the Mende (neighbors of the Kpelle) found that senior wives did have higher fitness while junior wives had fewer surviving children than their counterparts in monogamous unions (Isaac and Feinberg 1982). Similarly, in Botswana, children of more senior wives enjoyed nutrition and school attendance advantages (Bock and Johnson 2002: 329). Given the fact that our species in its most primitive state as foragers in a marginal environment still manages to raise roughly 50 percent of its offspring, compared with a range of 12–36 percent for other primates (Lancaster and Lancaster 1983: 37), the ability to recruit childcare assistants must be seen as central to the success of human mothers.

While the benefits to the mother are obvious, allomothering daughters also clearly benefit by learning how to care for their own infants (Fairbanks 1990).[30] A study of captive chimpanzees showed that females prevented from interacting with their mothers and younger siblings were themselves utterly incompetent as mothers (Davenport and Rogers 1970). The Canela in Brazil hold an annual round of festivals – to proclaim and reinforce values – in the center of their circular village. One "hilarious" skit in the Fish Festival mocks women who've failed to learn mothering (Crocker and Crocker 1994: 124).

Riesman, in describing the situation for the pastoral Fulani of West Africa, could be referring to almost any traditional, non-urban society in the world:

All women caring for their first babies will have had years of experience taking care of babies . . . under the watchful and sometimes severe eyes of their mothers, aunts, cousins or older sisters. The other women . . . will immediately notice, comment on, and perhaps strongly criticize any departure from customary behavior on the part of mothers. (Riesman 1992: 111)

An interesting contrast can be made with our own society where girls are *not* usually assigned sib-care duties and where young mothers labor alone without the guidance of their older female relatives.[31] The results are shown on two intriguing "reality" TV shows, Fox's "Nanny 911" and ABC's "Supernanny" in which a competent nanny brings order and harmony to dysfunctional families. A reviewer claims that: "Much of the advice is common sense, but parents don't always realize they're not following it" (*Salt Lake Tribune*, February 28, 2005: C2). However, what if the "common" in common sense is not – because prospective parents never practice or even observe child care?!

---

[30] The flip side of this coin is that there is only *one* species of primate in which juvenile *males* are consistently conscripted as helpers at the nest, Barbary macaques (Burton 1972).

[31] Programs have sprung up in the USA in which young expectant mothers with no access to competent role models are "mentored" from pregnancy through the end of their child's infancy by competent volunteers (Blinn-Pike *et al.* 1998).

Toddler rejection

The "dethronement" of the infant not only follows weaning, but is also quite commonly
coincidental with the birth of the next child. (Prothro 1961: 66)

If "peek-a-boo" or parent–infant play is spotty, parent–*toddler* play is virtually
non-existent. The toddler's mother not only faces potential conflict between
childcare and work, she's likely pregnant as well. At one end of the continuum,
Central African foragers display long inter-birth intervals (IBI) and relaxed
weaning – toddlers are indulged. Fouts documents the contrasting pattern found
among their farming neighbors where IBI are much shorter, and weaning is
forced (Fouts 2004a: 138). Commonly, the mother applies hot pepper to her
nipples and this is quite effective (Culwick 1935: 338).

Clearly, however, denying the child the breast is only one among many signs
of rejection (DuBois 1944: 51). Long-term observers of the !Kung have noted
the dramatic transformation in childhood as the foragers gave up their itinerant
lifestyle and settled down to farming. The IBI shortened, fertility increased,
and the formerly loving, indulgent mothers had ruthlessly to separate their
toddlers from themselves (Draper and Cashdan 1988; Lee 1979: 330). Native
Hawaiian mothers indulge their infants but, following the birth of a subsequent
child, the toddler's "overtures are increasingly punished and he is forced to
rely . . . on . . . older children" (Gallimore *et al.* 1969: 393). Toddler rejection[32]
is by no means limited to the mother; a common theme suggests that the
rejection is community-wide.

- " . . . one of the most striking features in the [Akan] attitude to the child is the
  contrast between the lavish affection meted out to infants . . . and the harsh
  disregard which is the lot of most older children. The adored small child has
  to suffer the trauma of growing into an object of contempt" (Field 1970: 28).
- "As they begin to become more and more children rather than babies, and
  begin to be a bit irritating and willful because they are 'thinking for themselves,' [Tahitians] begin to find children less amusing. Instead of being the
  center of the household stage, the child . . . becomes annoying" (Levy 1973:
  454).[33]

Fortunately, as the mother and other adults lose interest, the toddler is taken up
by older siblings who may be more patient and willing to "baby" him/her.

Her brother's keeper

Like many firstborn children, I learned to care for children by baby-sitting my two
younger brothers. (Clinton 1996: 9)

---

[32] Term from Weisner and Gallimore (1977: 176).
[33] Other examples: Van Stone (1965: 51); Levine (1965: 266).

. . . siblings structure play activities for their younger charges to keep them out of the way of adults and to keep them entertained and happy. (Maynard 2004: 245)

While we have certainly seen the truth of the African proverb, "It takes a village to raise a child," some members play a bigger role than others. In a landmark study, Weisner and Gallimore examined hundreds of ethnographies in the Human Relations Area Files (HRAF) archive and found that, in accounts of childcare, 40 percent of infants and 80 percent of toddlers are cared for primarily by someone other than their mother, most commonly older sisters (Weisner and Gallimore 1977). In the Ngoni (Bantu pastoralists) village, one sees "nurse girls" herding toddlers to a "playground" on the outskirts of the village where they meet peers to "practice dancing, thread beads and chatter" (Read 1960: 82).

But sib-caretakers must not let themselves get too engrossed in their own pursuits. "One of the worst things a [Hopi] girl can do is to neglect an infant charge. This can result in ostracism for days, shaming [her] deeply" (Schlegel 1973: 454). In Kipsigis' villages: "Child nurses are expected not only to carry the baby around, but also to play with it, sing lullabies to it, feed it porridge . . . and help the baby in learning to talk and walk" (Harkness and Super 1991: 227).[34]

In Gbarngasuakwelle, one often observes a trio of the nursing mother accompanied by one of her daughters who's carrying the sleeping infant on her back. At the first cry from the infant, it will be transferred to the mother to nurse, then, once sated, transferred back again to the sister – who may be as young as five (Lancy 1996: 146). The involvement of siblings in infant care also facilitates the weaning process. Among the Mandinka:

with the arrival of the next sibling, dénanola (infancy) is over. Now, play begins (tulungho be a s la) and membership in a social group of peers is taken to be critical to nyinandirangho, the forgetting of the breast to which the toddler has had free access for nearly two years or more. As one mother put it, "Now she must turn to play." (Whittemore 1989: 92)

One reason why mothers do not play with their young may be that they don't want to diminish the seductive power of the playgroup. Aside from expediting weaning, it has other functions. Marquesan mothers have a fully articulated theory of the toddler's development in the company of older siblings. The toddler wants to be with and be like older peers from whom she learns to take care of herself, proper elimination, and various household chores assigned to children (Martini and Kirkpatrick 1992).

Several authors have carefully documented the stratagems employed by sibling caretakers who are, after all, just slightly older than their charges in many cases. For the Fore, older children were expected to be tolerant towards toddlers

---

[34] See also Sigman et al. (1988: 1259).

Figure 9 Sib-care, Uganda

and accept their aggression with mild amusement (Sorenson 1976: 180). Older children usually deferred "to younger children when they both wanted the same thing" (Sorenson 1976: 187). Not surprisingly, "sibling rivalry"[35] was

---

[35] On a personal note, I didn't understand, until I wrote this chapter, why my mother, the youngest of twelve (ten who survived childhood) and nicknamed "Babe," cared least for Aunt Becky, only a year older, and was much closer to aunts Marie and Verona who were at least a decade older. I realize now that the latter would have been her primary caretakers while the former was her only rival for their attention. She was rather indifferent towards Aunt Theresa – who had married and formed her own household before she was born.

non-existent (Sorenson 1976: 162).[36] Suzanne Gaskins reports that older Maya siblings are well aware that their young bothers and sisters "must always be kept happy . . ."[37] Caretakers can expect no help from or oversight by adults except to abruptly terminate the play activity "at any time if work needs to be done, play becomes too noisy or rambunctious, or a younger player begins to cry" (Gaskins 2003: 3).

However, while the Mayan playgroup is expected to remain within earshot of the family compound, in the Marquesas the playgroup is *not* welcome in the vicinity of adults. As a consequence, caretakers are not nearly as deferential to the young ones (Martini and Kirkpatrick 1992). In Quechua-speaking areas of Ecuador, child-minders are also given a great deal of latitude in trying to control the behavior of toddlers: teasing, shaming, and threatening are all legitimate tactics.

On Gau Island (Fiji) a youngster "who disciplines one even younger with a slap or a sharpish knock with the knuckles on the side of the head is rarely rebuked" (Toren 1990: 183). Boys are occasionally recruited for sib-care duties, which include "combing their hair . . . for head lice . . . helping to toilet train them . . . [and acting as] an 'interpreter' explaining to others what his/her charge has just said" (Rindstedt and Aronsson 2003: 8).

Evidence of competent childcare by older siblings in the village setting contrasts with evidence of their incompetence in our own society (Farver 1993). Brian Sutton-Smith offered these comments on the Weisner and Gallimore sib-care study:

maximal . . . development of infants is produced by the mother . . . who interacts with them in a variety of stimulating and playful ways . . . the intelligence to do this with ever more exciting contingencies is simply not present in child caretakers. It is difficult enough to impart these ideas of infant stimulation even to mothers . . . children as major caretakers maintain social life at a much lower level. (Sutton-Smith 1977: 184)

His point is no doubt true and has received considerable empirical support (Rogoff 1990: 165). But the comment is culturally biased. He is evaluating the socialization practices of non-Western people by the standards of our society. Other researchers have demonstrated how effective sibling caretakers can be in the context of village-based, agrarian society. Indeed, they show that siblings are often more patient towards and tolerant of toddler mood swings than are adults (Zukow 1989) and more likely to use special speech forms to aid their understanding (Toren 1990: 175).

---

[36] Judith Harris argues that sibling rivalry occurs in our society because parents suppress the natural power hierarchy among siblings based on age (Harris 1998: 93–94).

[37] The contrasting state of affairs in our society, where "sibling rivalry" is a fact of life, is vividly illustrated in Barbara Rogoff's account of conflict over possession of a doll (Rogoff 2003: 145–146).

With a few noteworthy exceptions, such as the Marquesas cited above, village playgroups will be reliably found in areas of the community where watchful adults aren't far away.

Playing on the mother ground

[Gusii] children soon learn that any grownup can rebuke them and has authority over them. (LeVine 1973: 135)

One of the great facilitators of reduced workload effort for childcare is something that the Kpelle refer to as *panang leè-ma* or *mother ground*.[38] This is a flat, open area in village or garden[39] where children gather to play under the watchful eye of adults working or relaxing nearby.[40] These are not purpose-built playgrounds but areas that have been cleared to facilitate traffic, discourage snakes, and as occasional areas for work such as laying out house-building materials, drying clothing or produce. These are mixed-age playgroups with older children casually minding infants and toddlers while they engage in their own play. In the rare event of conflict or injury, or when a distressed child can't be comforted, an adult is close enough to detect a problem and intervene. Situating play areas in close proximity to adults serves two ends. It affords adults the opportunity to oversee the children, almost effortlessly, but it also gives watchful children a *source* of scenes of adult activity to incorporate into their play (Lancy 1996) (discussed more fully in chapter 6). However, adults rarely intervene in children's play except when fighting threatens to get out of hand. Interestingly, primatologists note the same watchful behavior, benign neglect, and rapid intervention on the part of mothers of actively playful primate juveniles (Baldwin and Baldwin 1978).

For the Lebou of Senegal, the *mother ground* has a constantly changing cast but, in one observational study, an average of nine two- to six-year-olds were casually supervised by a couple of adults (Bloch 1989: 143). A similar configuration can be found among the Dusun rice farmers of Borneo (Williams 1969: 75). In Chaga villages one finds "a children's play area, often at the edge of or near the village commons" (Raum 1940: 95).

---

[38] Not all societies subscribe to the *mother ground* concept. In the Marquesas, parents do not want kids "hanging around." They chase them away and are unconcerned about their exposure to manifest dangers – the sea, sharp rocks, broken glass, and knives (Martini 1994).

[39] Like the Fore gardens described by Sorenson, Kpelle gardens are a place for adult singing, dancing, and socializing, and children's games as well as hard work (Sorenson 1976: 50).

[40] We can even find something approximating the *mother ground* in non-human primates: "These [ring-tailed lemur] play groups always occurred on the ground . . . there were 6–7 juveniles . . . in the . . . playgroup . . . The young animals would generally play in the center of the group, surrounded by their mothers and other adults who formed a circle around them, while some adults rested in the trees above . . ." (Sussman 1977: 522).

It is clear from Hewlett's description that the entire Aka camp – and this would certainly be true for other foraging bands (Turnbull 1978) – functions as the *mother ground*. He describes the campsite with its maximum of twenty-five to thirty-five inhabitants as "about the size of a large Euroamerican living room" (Hewlett 1992: 225). In camp, even one-year-olds are free to roam widely within the perimeter and interact with whomever they wish. The camp isn't "child-proof": no one panics if the baby handles knives or wanders into, say, a butchering site.

Indeed, small towns in remoter corners of the USA may still offer the kind of shared responsibility noted among the Aka. This description of rural Maine fits my own childhood in Beaver County perfectly:

Children's escapades through town were observed by many eyes . . . and parents seemed comfortable with the idea that someone would contact them if their child misbehaved. Such joint, unobtrusive supervision permitted children's free-ranging play and also drew multiple other adults into the role of . . . audience for the plays, circuses, animal shows, and other productions that interviewees remembered putting on. (Beach 2003: 192)

While rarely mentioned in the literature, the *mother ground* may have been overlooked by scholars because of its very ubiquity and because, perhaps, there may be no specific term for it in the language. The most frequently observed yet unrecognized example is Peter Breughel's 1560 masterpiece "Children's Games" in the Kunsthistoriches Museum, Vienna. He depicts eighty-four distinct children's "pass-times" or games and, with few exceptions, children are playing within view or hearing of adults either in the workplace or in their homes.

However, it is sadly the case that modern society is no longer likely to provide a *mother ground*.[41] In an ethnography of a suburban neighborhood, anthropologists found that adults were reluctant to intervene in settings where children were involved, deferring to public agencies. There was also the fear that intervention might be misconstrued "as an attempt to kidnap or otherwise harm the boy or girl" (Spilsbury and Korbin 2004: 197).

Among the *mother ground* custodians in the village, we are likely to find grandparents. Aside from any concern they might feel towards their grandchildren, nieces, and nephews, they are, simply, available. That is, the relatively sedentary (their work keeps them stationary and close to home) observers at the periphery of the *mother ground* are more likely to be the children's grandparents than their parents.

---

[41] Urban centers have probably always been less hospitable to children and, as we explore early European society later in the chapter, we'll see that child mortality was often the indirect result of the absence of adult supervision.

Going to grandma's place

[Hadza] grandmothers [as caretakers of grandchildren] increase their own genetic success because their daughters can have more babies sooner. (Hawkes *et al.* 2000: 253)

[Folk wisdom of Northern India claims] None but a grandmother should oversee a child. Mothers are only fit for bearing. (Kipling 1901/2003: 120)

The ethnographic literature is replete with examples of grandmothers caring for their daughter's offspring. Grandmothers substitute as primary caretakers far more often than fathers (Black *et al.* 1999: 974). But it was Kristen Hawkes and colleagues – who study the Hadza – who first put forward the notion that this particular solution to the problem of freeing mothers from childcare may have deep evolutionary roots. They point out that, compared with other great apes, our species is unique in that women routinely live well beyond their reproductive years in menopause. Their explanation for this phenomenon is that older women, by forgoing reproduction, are preserving their bodies so they can invest their energy and skills in rearing their grandchildren, thereby increasing their own genetic fitness (Hawkes *et al.* 2000). And, in the study on Ifaluk by Paul Turke, he also found that adults whose parents were living had more offspring than those who did not have the help of grandparents (Turke 1988).[42]

Of course, the opportunity to have more children is not the mother's only concern. She must address her own personal needs and those of her mate, who may be providing critical resources for her and the children. And she will, inevitably, have a vital economic role to play. In all these endeavors, a child may literally "get in the way." For Sepik women, their principal protein source is fish and "young children are a hindrance to subsistence fishing" (Barlow 2001: 84). Aka mothers on the hunt have been observed to set a (crying) infant down on the ground to run in pursuit of their quarry (Hewlett 1991: 79–80). In the Marquesas, adults shoo away children when they're processing raw coconuts into copra because the children might interrupt the activity.[43] In many cases, then, the child may be placed in the care of a grandmother – usually more tolerant of the child's curiosity and "interference."

Grandmothers intervene at critical times in the lives of their grandchildren, particularly during weaning (Hawkes *et al.* 1997; Fouts 2004a; Raphael and Davis 1985; De Laguna 1972: 507). One grandmother is described as suckling

---

[42] In another relevant study, among the Oromo of Ethiopia, the authors found that grandmothers can enhance the survivorship of their grandchildren *indirectly* as well. In this case some grandmothers visit their daughters with small children to help them with their most arduous chores. This intervention evidently frees the mother to devote more time to childcare, increasing their viability (Gibson and Mace 2005).

[43] Parents disavow any desire to teach children these skills, arguing that, in effect, when they're old enough, they'll figure it out themselves (Martini and Kirkpatrick 1992: 205).

Figure 10 Grandma's pride and joy

the fussy baby on "her wizened breasts" (Rohner and Chaki-Sircar 1988: 71). When the child is sick or injured, they serve up a stock of comforting stories (Raum 1940: 160).[44] They are there to spell the mother when she is sick, doing critical work or caring for a subsequent infant.[45] It is not uncommon to find grandmothers moving from part- to full-time childcare (Bove *et al.* 2002: 459). For the Mende of Sierra Leone, "grannies" step in to care for babies suspected of being illegitimate whose mothers are in high school; babies whose unmarried mothers spy a marriage opportunity; or babies whose mothers are anxious to resume sexual relations with their husbands and/or get pregnant. Compared with young mothers, grannies are perceived as more knowledgeable, patient, and attentive (Bledsoe and Isiugo-Abanihe 1989: 453). On the other hand, as noted by Sutton-Smith for sibling caretakers (Sutton-Smith 1977), they have their

[44] My next-door neighbors have turned their half-acre backyard into a childcare center, with a pool, elaborate outdoor gym, and both grass and sand play areas. Supervising as many as eight grandchildren at a time, they spell their children throughout the summer.

[45] As recently as the 1950s in the French village Peyrane, it was customary for grandmothers and older sisters to play a significant caretaking role. By contrast, "the father is not expected to help much in the care of children, even when he is not working" (Wylie 1957: 42).

limits. Fijian children raised by their grandmothers acquire unattractive traits. They are "said to be *either* presumptuous and 'too inquisitive' *or* 'childish' and unable to take on the tasks proper to their age" (Toren 1990: 172).

[I]n the Mende view, grannies are notoriously lax with children. They are said to feed children upon demand and do not beat them or withhold meals from them for bad behavior or for failing to work . . . Children raised like this are said to grow up lazy and dishonest . . . children can even insult their grannies in play or in anger . . . Mende teachers . . . argue . . . that children raised by grannies perform the most poorly in school. They attend only fitfully, because grannies are said to encourage them to stay home and avoid the rigors and discipline of the classroom. (Bledsoe and Isiugo-Abanihe 1989: 454, 455)

A Mende granny may not actually be the child's biological grandmother; other relatives may also be called upon and "fosterage" is extremely common.[46] A study of fosterage among the Gonja of Ghana found that at least half the sample had spent all or a significant part of their childhood in the care of an adult other than the biological parent. It commonly occurs where one household has a surplus of children while another suffers a dearth (Goody 1982). Among the Kpelle, children are given to childless adults to raise and form ties with so the children will care for them as they age (Lancy 1996: 145).

With urbanization, there are subtle changes in fostering. In Ghana (and elsewhere in the Third World – Dube 2000), wage-earners in the city send their children to school and import children of their rural kin to do the domestic chores, like infant care, normally fulfilled by children of the household. Much of the "pocket money" they provide finds its way back to the village (Hashim 2005), or may be saved by the "little niece" for a dowry (Jacquemin 2004: 384). In fact the practice of well-off families "taking in" the children of their poorer relations has been one of history's most enduring means of transferring wealth downward.[47]

As we might expect, foster or adoptive parents tend to be closely related to the child. Among Herero herders from southwest Africa, where the proportion of fostered children is high, fewer than 4 percent were being cared for by non-kin (Pennington and Harpending 1993), a comparable figure to that found in the African-American community where fosterage is also very high (Stack 1974). Silk has pursued this question with vigor and shown the importance of kin-ties in adoption in Polynesia (Silk 1980) and the Arctic (Silk 1987). She has also shown that, in a range of primate species, animals can differentiate

[46] The other region of the world with extremely high rates of adoption or fosterage is the Arctic (Bodenhorn 1988: 12).

[47] However, the reality today may be less benign. "Under the pretext of 'helping' poor rural relatives, some women have created networks to place little maids, which under the cover of fosterage, are close to child trafficking" (Jacquemin 2006: 394).

between close kin, non-kin, and distant kin and that this awareness mediates their altruistic behavior (Silk 2002).

In fact, the expression "It takes a village . . ." might be better phrased "It takes an extended family . . ." However, we conclude this section as we concluded the last, by acknowledging that, like the *mother ground*, grandparents as child-minders may fade into history.

A recent essay by a personal finance columnist suggested that couples might save on their vacation costs and have a better time by leaving children with grandparents. He was flooded with letters castigating him for making such an outrageous suggestion, declaring "We . . . have served our time, now it's their turn" (Opdyke 2005). Many contemporary Japanese grandmothers resent being asked to assist with childcare: "Having at last got rid of their own children, they want to enjoy their new-found freedom – some would like to knit, others to do calligraphy or aikido" (Jolivet 1997: 56).

Will fathers be available to take up the slack? Let's see.

Life with(out) father

In all the human cultures that have ever been studied, males have been found to take an extremely minor direct caretaking role in relation to children and, especially, infants. (Allport 1997: 46)[48]

Strange as it may seem, it is a rare father who is accorded an important place in the [Chinese] son's autobiography. (Wu 1995: 131)

Of all the cast of characters in this melodrama, the role of father is the most subject to creative script variation. But in order to grasp the assertion made in the first quotation above, I must point out how rare it is to find a father as the head of an isolated nuclear family, or what we'd consider the "normal" father's role. In my home in Gbarngasuakwelle, the "head" of the household was clearly the chief's senior wife; the chief himself was actually a rather shadowy figure around the house. In other parts of Africa, one might find people living in large, diverse groups in a "compound." There are multiple males – brothers, cousins, and grandsons – whose relationship to the corresponding group of women in the compound is not easy to discern. In large sections of Papua New Guinea, married women live in modest huts with their younger children while men, married and single, live in dorm-like bachelor quarters where homosexuality is completely accepted.

In parts of Asia, married women remain in their natal home to which their husbands make occasional conjugal visits. In Maningkabau villages in western

---

[48] Actually, this is a bit extreme, I know of at least two cases (aside from the Aka, to be discussed shortly) where at least some fathers are quite involved and I'm sure there must be others, e.g. Barlow (2001: 84–85); Hogbin (1970a).

Sumatra, the *paterfamilias* adds sections on to the communal home, like a vertical layer-cake, to accommodate his married daughters and their offspring. Similarly, among the Nyars of southern India, husbands and wives live apart except for conjugal visits and fathers have little to do with their children (Menon 2001: 354). Among the Na, a Chinese minority group living near the border with Burma, women mate secretly with their lovers whose paternity is never acknowledged (Hua 2001).

In large parts of the world, males are absent from the household for lengthy periods herding livestock, fulfilling military service, or earning money as migrant workers. In a Caribbean Garifuna community, Munroe recorded a conversation in which the (rarely) visiting father asks the mother the name of their seven-year-old son (Munroe 2005). Under these circumstances, not only is there little opportunity for the *Ozzie and Harriet style*[49] of open display of affectionate cooperation in childcare; any and all intimate relations between husband and wife may be conducted furtively in the bush.

Looking at our primate cousins, the situation is similarly unpromising. Among orangutans, the juvenile male not only doesn't interact with its biological father, it may not even *see* another male as it grows up (Horr 1977). Gorilla fathers frequently play with their infants in the wild, whereas play is uncommon in chimpanzee fathers.[50] However, "chimpanzee paternity is usually not known either by observers or apparently the chimpanzees . . . whereas it is certain in gorilla harems" (Bard 1995: 36). Of course, humans are much more closely related to chimpanzees than to gorillas.

It is a fairly safe generalization that the father's primary contribution to children occurs at conception.[51] For example, among a forest-dwelling tribe who refer to themselves as Chewong, the father "builds up" the fetus with his semen which is, in turn, nourished by the mother during pregnancy. "The prenatal stage is the one in which parental responsibility is at its strongest since congenital malfunctions of any kind are attributed to the behaviour of one or other of the parents during this period" (Howell 1988: 155).

On Ifaluk Island, no men, not even husbands, are permitted to witness the birth of a child (Burrows and Shapiro 1957) and this prohibition is almost

---

[49] *Ozzie and Harriet* was only one among a dozen or more TV programs popular from the 1950s that portrayed life in "typical" families that consisted of a man, woman, and their two to three children. Both parents were quite engaged with the children from infancy through adolescence.

[50] The general pattern for non-human primates is for adult males to keep their distance from infants – as they are seen as potentially threatening by the mothers.

[51] In the Trobriand Islands off eastern New Guinea, intercourse and pregnancy are not linked and males aren't viewed as essential for procreation. Further, in this matrilineal society, it is the mother's brother, not her husband, who acts in a "paternal" capacity vis-à-vis the children (Malinowski 1929; Roscoe and Telban 2004: 104).

a cultural universal.[52] Post-partum, fathers are discouraged from attending on their wives and new babies, as well: "the [Kipsigis] father is forbidden to see his wife or new baby... for fear that he might be tempted to break the postpartum sex taboo, or that he might unwittingly harm the vulnerable newborn by his very presence, or even that his own masculinity might be compromised by close contact with a baby" (Harkness and Super 1991: 223). Societies construct elaborate rationalizations for the father's absence from the nursery.[53] Kwara'ae "men's degree of interaction with infants was limited by beliefs that urine and feces were polluting.[54] The infant's skin was also considered potentially polluting until it reached full pigmentation" (Gegeo and Watson-Gegeo 1985: 248).[55] For the South African Thonga (Junod 1927: 169–170) and East African Logoli (Munroe 2005), it is *taboo* for a father to pick up an infant. The Fijian child learns early "not to touch or take anything... of his father – his mat, pillow, comb, or *lavalava*... if he... disobey[s, he]... will be scolded, perhaps whipped" (Thompson 1940: 39).

Japanese "[s]ociety generally ridicules the 'kind' or 'accommodating' man who helps his wife" (Jolivet 1997: 58). And this telling anecdote is from a study in the USA:

Sandy's and Ben's images of fatherhood were quite different. Ben thought about the new baby much as an athlete might think about a trophy: After it has been won, it sits on the shelf to be viewed from a distance. Sandy thought about fatherhood in much more personal terms and imagined an active participant in Kim's childhood. When the baby arrived and Ben walked away from his responsibilities, Sandy's illusions about Ben began to crumble. (Berrick 1995: 43)

Hillary Fouts' characterization of Bofi (Central African farmers) fathers would strike a familiar chord with fieldworkers all over the globe. Although, they spend many days "at home" in the village, "they rarely perform care giving tasks for their children and instead spend the majority of their time politicking with other... men" (Fouts 2005: 358). Even when fathers "tend" children, they don't exactly replicate "maternal" behavior. Yanomamo (South American foragers) men

---

[52] As recently as 1974, my participation in Lamaze classes, prior to attending the labor and delivery of my daughter Nadia, was so extraordinary it provoked a three-part feature series in the local newspaper (*Beaver County Times*, February 5, 1974: B1).

[53] Numerous studies document the rarity of fathers as caretakers or even as companions of children (Makey 1983: 394; Munroe and Munroe 1992: 218; Hewlett 2001: 49).

[54] Malinowski's vivid description of Trobriand fatherhood shows that the father seems delighted to nurse the infant and suffer whatever indignities may occur as a consequence. But then, the matrilineal Trobrianders afford the father only a marginal role in family life. So childcare is the male's way of demonstrating his worth to the family (Malinowski 1932: 19–21).

[55] These many examples from the literature of fathers avoiding the nursery must be counterbalanced by a recent survey of the literature highlighting the numerous cases where fathers are present and do assist with some aspect of childbirth (Huber 2007: 214).

are not comfortable with infants – they are afraid, for one thing, of being urinated or defecated [on] . . . When they carry young infants [their] arms are slightly extended away from their bodies . . .[56] Women carry infants placed firmly against their own bodies. If a child cries while a man is tending it, he will quickly pass it to a woman. (Peters 1998: 89)

On forest treks, the Yanomamo mother may be carrying material in a basket secured by a sling over her forehead *and* a child, perched on the basket or attached to her hip with a sling. "All the while the husband may walk empty-handed ahead of her along the forest trail" (Peters 1998: 135).

As we noted in the previous chapter, a father's primary interest in the newborn is in deciding whether to keep it alive. And that decision is mediated not only by the physical condition of the infant and its mother but also by concerns about its paternity. "If he believes that the child is his own, he will ordinarily accept the 'minding' responsibility for the child" (Lange and Rodman 1992: 188). "Minding," in this case from the Caribbean, refers to *indirect* care or provisioning, not *direct* care of the child. The former is far more common than the latter. In one of the most thorough examinations of this issue, a study of 220 foragers in six camps, Hadza fathers brought home twice as much meat (measured in calories) to their biological offspring than to stepchildren (Hawkes 1991). Frank Marlowe describes the support of one's own children as "parenting effort" while the support of stepchildren is identified as "mating effort," whose primary purpose is to enable sexual/reproductive access to the child's mother (Marlowe 1999).

For the Ache, another well-studied foraging group, similar results to those for the Hadza are found (Hill and Hurtado 1996: 317) but the situation is more complex. Women are tactically promiscuous in order to implicate several men in the paternity of their offspring and the folk wisdom regarding conception supports this theory of "partible paternity." Called "father" by the child, these "secondary" fathers, who include all those who had intercourse with the mother during the year prior to delivery, may provide some material support and protection for the child,[57] especially if the "primary" father (the predominant mate just prior to the cessation of menses) has died or left the mother (Hill and Hurtado 1996: 249–250).

Barry Hewlett has been the most dedicated student (Hewlett 1991) of the father's role in childcare, stemming from his discovery that Aka foragers are extraordinary in the critical direct role played by fathers. He attributes this to two

---

[56] Compare to a scene from an "elaborate drinking cup . . . , Zeus . . . [delivers] the baby Dionysus to the nymphs. The proud but somewhat awkward father does not cradle the child in his arms, as mothers do, but holds him stiffly out in front of him like a trophy" (Shapiro 2003: 87).

[57] Similarly, among Hanuman langurs, where intrusive males dispatch the head male in a harem, then kill his offspring to bring the females quickly into estrous, genetically related males (uncles, cousins, fathers) will intervene to protect infants from these attacks (Borries *et al.* 1999).

general phenomena: the nature of one of their principal subsistence activities – net-hunting – and a community ethos of gender equity. Net-hunting obligates the mother to strenuous work in which a baby is especially burdensome but other women are similarly burdened. Older siblings may lack sufficient strength to carry infants and toddlers for the extended distances (8–12 km per day) required, may be unable adequately to protect children from the forest's dangers, and are actively engaged in foraging on their own. Hence, fathers spell mothers on the hunt, and in camp – where grandmothers also make a significant contribution (Hewlett 1986).

However, Hewlett, in subsequent research, also found that male status is inversely correlated with time allocated to childcare (Hewlett 1988): "males gain greater fitness returns by engaging in status maintaining or resource accu-mulation than from childcare activities" (Hames 1992: 225). In addition, he also acknowledges that new Aka (and Bofi, another Congolese foraging group) fathers are required to contribute bride-service to their new in-laws and, con-sequently, tend to absent themselves from the camp at long intervals to hunt. In these cases, grandmothers take up the slack (Hewlett 1991: 41–42).[58]

While ethnographers of the !Kung, Hadza, and Ache, among others, note the occasional direct involvement in childcare by men, there is greater evidence of indirect care or provisioning. However, because hunters tend to "spread the wealth" of their prowess widely to attract additional mates (Hawkes 1991), we find, not surprisingly, when a Hadza father dies, there is no noticeable effect on his children's survival or wellbeing (Blurton-Jones *et al.* 2000).

Divorce is extremely common in foraging societies. Divorced men invariably select younger mates with consequently greater childbearing potential than the mates they're divorcing (Low 2000). In pastoralist and horticultural societies, polygyny substitutes for the "serial polygamy" of frequent divorce but family relationships remain fluid and divorce is not uncommon. Thus, the relative lack of involvement of fathers in childcare in traditional societies may attenuate the negative impact of divorce on children.

The role of the father's close kin may also vary widely. As we've seen, many women look to their families for child support and view their husbands' families as essentially hostile. In traditional Chinese and Muslim societies and others that are profoundly patriarchal, the father literally "owns" his children. The child's mother is seen not so much as the caretaker but as an incubator. It is entirely acceptable, therefore, for the father to remove his children from their mother's care and place them in the care of his family (Fernea 1991: 450) – a phenomenon that some estranged American wives of Middle Eastern men have discovered to their horror and eternal sorrow.

---

[58] Fouts' study of the Aka and very similar Bofi society finds that father involvement is higher in the absence of the child's grandmother as the preferred caretaker (Fouts 2007).

Employment opportunities associated with modernization bring new costs and benefits for village children and their mothers. Bock and Johnson conducted a very sophisticated natural experiment in Botswana on the impact of Botswana fathers on their children. They compared children of migrant workers with children of fathers resident in the village. They reasoned that since the former were unable to enjoy the benefits – if any – of direct father involvement, they should show a decrement in traditional skill acquisition compared with their peers. No such decrement was found, indicating that fathers have little impact on children's skill acquisition. They also reasoned that the remittances sent home by migrant fathers might be used to enhance child nutrition and this prediction was confirmed for both boys and girls, who showed greater weight for their age than their peers (Bock and Johnson 2002: 329).

But it's not clear how consistently mothers and their offspring benefit from these new economic opportunities. On Java, women complain about their parasitic and irresponsible husbands, who "lack the self-discipline needed to bring money home at the end of the day instead of squandering it" (Brenner 2001: 147).

One positive role that fathers do seem to play, consistently, in their offspring's lives is that of stern disciplinarian (Munroe 2005). In Central Asia, Tajik "children fear their father for his strictness and ability to hurt them" (Harris 2006: 66). Turkish fathers "play the role of the relatively distant authority whose main duty is to establish and enforce strict rules of conduct for the children" (Kagitçibasi and Sunar 1992: 82). This role also extends to guarding the virtue of daughters (Davis and Davis 1989: 78) who, in the absence of a father figure, are likely to be promiscuous (Howard 1970: 76).[59] Absent fathers may, therefore, leave socially maladjusted adolescents in their wake.

To conclude this section, let me quote from a description of Yoruba fatherhood which strikes me as quite representative:

Fatherhood exists almost independently of any engagement with . . . a child. Simply by having impregnated a woman, a man becomes a father – and remains "the owner of the child," irrespective of whether he makes any contributions to the child's upkeep. Men retain entitlements to children they have fathered . . . and through children who are publicly acknowledged as a man's offspring, women are able to make claims on men as the fathers-of-their-children. A child without a recognized father is stigmatized and bullied, and can turn against its mother in anger and shame. Having a father, then, is important for children as having children is for men, whether or not the two have any contact. (Cornwall 2001: 147)

Next let's look at what happens to childcare as society becomes more complex, with greater social distance between classes of people.

---

[59] See also Draper and Harpending (1982).

Professional child-minders

If we turn to vase painting to look for evidence of what activities Athenian fathers shared with their young sons, the picture is meager indeed. (Shapiro 2003: 98)

The [Roman state] continually expresses . . . a low estimation of the desirability of or need for direct parental involvement in childrearing. (Boswell 1988: 82)

The most notable effect of the transition to more complex, urban society on the lives of children is that, for the well-off, biological parents are even less involved in childcare than before. Where there is wealth, leisure, and servants or slaves, mothers quickly divest themselves of any residual childcare responsibilities (Janssen and Janssen 1990). Wet-nurses, nannies, and tutors are essential and often quite valued members of the household.[60] Indeed, one of the most spectacular tombs uncovered recently in Egypt is that of Maya, King Tut's wet-nurse.

Sculpture and vase paintings give us many clues to domestic life in ancient Greek society. Graves have yielded thousands of small statuettes of women holding children; these are the *kourotrophos* or "child rearers." There's also a revealing scene on a large calyx krater (*c*.400 BCE) that depicts the death of two children. The parents look on, unconcerned, while their nurse and tutor show obvious signs of mourning (Neils and Oakley 2003).

The Romans went further than their predecessors in that abandonment and infanticide were at least loosely regulated, laws regarding the legal status and property rights of children were promulgated and, during the reign of Augustus and later emperors, childbearing was encouraged and subsidies provided to parents. But at no time did Rome consider it important to promote the notion that parents (or siblings or grandparents, for that matter) should play any direct role in childrearing. Rather:

paedagogues . . . male slaves . . . looked after young children. They played with them, took them on outings, taught them table manners, and generally baby-sat . . . the paedagogue escorted [the child] to and from school . . . baths, the theater, and social functions. The paedagogue might . . . be responsible for teaching the child some simple reading and writing . . . close bonds between upper-class children and their slave or lower-class caretakers [were guarded against because] social distance must be maintained. (Shelton 1998: 33)

The use of professionals for childcare gradually spread downward. By the Middle Ages, women married to skilled laborers could afford to hire a wet-nurse, a task consigned to peasants. Expert advice was offered on how to select a wet-nurse since the infant could acquire the nurse's personal traits through her milk. "One biographer noted that Michelangelo's nurse was a stonecutter's

---

[60] "From the Han dynasty to the Ming, there were numerous cases of emperors lavishing noble titles and other favors on their wet nurses and members of their families" (Wu 1995: 133).

wife, by way of explaining his interest in sculpture" (Sommerville 1982: 80). Infants were usually lodged with wet-nurses,[61] rarely visited, then reclaimed once weaned – if they survived. Since the wet-nurse offered her services for money and not out of a love of babies,[62] her charges were usually swaddled and tucked out of harm's way while she went about her work (Sommerville 1982: 80).

This raised little concern because infants were widely seen as insensible. Almost like plants, their care could be rudimentary and not much "was actually expected of a caretaker... virtually anyone could safely tend or carry a swaddled baby" (Calvert 1992: 23).

Of the 21,000 babies registered in Paris in 1780, only 5 percent of them were nursed by their own mothers (Sussman 1982). This statistic is brandished by Hrdy as clear evidence of maternal indifference and her "prime exhibit in the case against maternal instincts in the human species" (Hrdy 1999: 351). Nor were children, once weaned, warmly cosseted in the web of family life. Parents could not afford to devote much attention to children. Hence, nearly 60 percent of medieval English children who perished before they were a year old died in fires. "Most... accidents... happened during the workday, when parents and siblings were busy and distracted by work" (Colón, with Colón 2001: 207).[63]

From medieval times, if they didn't serve as farmhands, children left their natal home at an early age. Among the nobility, children were routinely sent to live with relatives or higher-status patrons in hopes of "advancement" (Colón, with Colón 2001: 209). Children as young as five were donated by parents to the monastic life (Shahar 1990: 191). Outside the nobility, parents sent their five- to seven-year-old children (who were, in their view, no longer actually children) to the homes of master-craftsmen or merchants as apprentices, where the first *decade* of service might well be "scut-work" rather than the acquisition of usable skills. Daughters were sent into domestic "service."

Parents in sixteenth-century England were considered particularly callous in shipping off their offspring at an early age (Anonymous Venetian Diplomat 1847). However, Linda Pollock, in her analysis of personal diaries, finds a gradual shift taking place in the seventeenth century. Cavalier attitudes give way to solicitation. Even though childrearing is still a minor occupation for mothers compared with bearing them and managing the household, they now regularly *visit* their wet-nursed infants (Calvert 1992: 23). As the century advances and

---

[61] Even a casual visitor to collections of European paintings will see many, many depictions of a mother holding and/or nursing her baby but these images are "very likely that of the Virgin and Child, rather than secular scenes of everyday intimacy between mother and child" (O'Brien 2003: 369).

[62] The pervasive use of wet-nurses persisted in the USA into the twentieth century and was commonly referred to as "baby-farming" (Riis 1890/1996: 184).

[63] And who can fail to be reminded of the number of children on playgrounds caught by a stray bullet fired by a gang-banger in a "drive-by."

over the following two hundred years, profound change will occur in notions about childrearing, fostered, in part, by the Reformation.

New metaphors for childrearing

. . . the Puritans were the first modern parents. (Sommerville 1982: 112)

From plants that just grew with little attention, popular views of infants changed, so that:

- "Newborn infants appeared as unpromising material, a shapeless 'lump of flesh,' 'a round ball' that had to be molded into human form" (Calvert 1992: 19).
- "Like wild men [or beasts], babies lacked the power to reason, speak, or stand and walk erect. [They were] nasty, brutish, and dirty, communicating in wordless cries, grunts, and screams, and were given to crawling on all fours before they could be made to walk like men" (Calvert 1992: 26).
- "Left to their own devices, they would remain selfish, animalistic, and savage. Parents[64] believed they had to coerce their babies into growing up, and they expected protests and resistance" (Calvert 1992: 34).

Swaddling remained popular, not only for the convenience of the caretaker but because it prevented the baby from crawling which was both dangerous (homes were not "child-proofed") and thought to reinforce the child's animal nature. Swaddling also served, like "standing stools" (today called "walkers," they became popular in the eighteenth century), to stretch the child's legs, which might otherwise atrophy.[65]

The Puritans were the first society to create a truly comprehensive theory of childrearing, reflected in a steady stream of advice manuals published from the seventeenth century. They believed in the child's essentially animalistic and ungodly nature, taming which was the great challenge of parents. Anticipating contemporary Mormon views as noted early in this chapter, the Puritans argued that neither professionals (e.g. wet-nurses) nor neighbors could be expected to fulfill the arduous task of raising truly righteous individuals. They even cautioned against "natural" parenting instincts, for example, that parents should not "cocker" or indulge their children or laugh at their high jinks because they'd only have to beat the waywardness out of them later in life (Sommerville 1982: 110).

The Puritans were perhaps the first anxious parents, fearing they might fail and their children would turn out badly. Many migrated to found new

---

[64] Upper-crust parents had always held this view of children and expected the various child-minders in the household to shape up the children efficiently and turn them into miniature adults as soon as possible. But the "common" folk had, heretofore, thought about their infants much as parents in tribal societies still do – as hardy plants that needed little close attention.

[65] Most probably attributable to rickets.

communities in order to isolate their children from the harmful effects of non-believing peers (Sommerville 1982: 112–113), much like parents today moving to a neighborhood because it has "good" schools (chapter 9).

But then along came Darwin, whose theory of natural selection influenced every area of thinking, including child psychology. Swaddling was condemned as protecting and restraining the child excessively, prohibiting it from being toughened up by nature's slings and arrows. Meanwhile, rapid industrialization absorbed the labor of women who, formerly, earned a living as wet-nurses and/or domestic help. So, the child's mother was faced with fewer childcare options and "many mothers turned to alcohol, opium, or other drugs to soothe a restless baby" (Calvert 1992: 76).

Entering the modern era, Western parents were discovering that they couldn't start too soon to prepare their children for the rigors of formal education. This is an imperative that had driven the childcare philosophies of East Asian societies for far longer. Since sons provided social security for elderly parents, it was in the parents' self-interest to prepare them[66] for the civil service examinations. Success demanded self-discipline, concentration, and rote memorization. Concepts like "womb education" or *t'aekyo*, and sayings – "like three [years old], like a hundred" – reflect a philosophy of childrearing emphasizing the child's malleability (Uno 1991: 396) and the parent's obligation to make the most of it.

Attitudes about the care of children have changed so dramatically! We now take for granted the "need" to stimulate the infant through physical contact, motherese, and playing games like peek-a-boo to *accelerate* physical and intellectual development. Contrast these assumptions with the pre-modern objective of keeping young children quiescent so they'd make fewer demands on caretakers and not injure themselves (LeVine *et al.* 1994). Among the Maya, the overarching goal of childcare is to keep the baby quiet. They are provided with soothing comforts and never stimulated. Opportunities to explore the environment or interact with others are limited (Howrigan 1988: 41).

If parents are to become the sole caretakers of children and, further, if this is now seen as requiring a much more interactive and demanding relationship with the child, broods can be expected to shrink.

The "Great" transition

... children become more costly to parents as societies modernize and this increased cost leads to decreased demands for [them]. (Turke 1989: 76)

Since I was sticking my nose into the lives of my neighbors in Gbarnga-suakwelle, it was only fair to open up my personal life to them. They were

---

[66] In Singapore: "with the greater education and paid employment of females, many parents now say that daughters are 'as good as sons'": Wee (1992: 192).

particularly interested in my family and were appalled that someone as old as I was (twenty-eight) and so obviously wealthy – my clothes didn't have holes, I owned a camera and leather shoes – had no children. Indeed they were surprised I had only one spouse and I had to politely deflect matchmakers throughout my fieldwork. There was nothing in my explanation of why we felt the urgent need to limit reproduction that made any sense to them. And it wouldn't have made sense to 99 percent of the world's pre-modern peoples. That evidently well-fed, clothed, and generally prosperous adults should *choose* to have few children is the paradox that scholars refer to as the "Great" or "demographic" transition, discussed at length in chapter 2.

Paul Turke's "kin hypothesis" points to the shift in the burden of childcare from a widely dispersed kin network to the biological parents (Turke 1989: 67). This chapter has been replete with documentation of the first part of that equation. All other things being equal, the more you can shift the burden of childcare on to those who don't have small children of their own to care for, the more offspring you can have, thereby increasing biological fitness. But, to participate in the modern economy, one must absent oneself from the household to attend school, accept employment at a considerable remove, and establish a separate household from one's parents,[67] so shared childcare is no longer an option.

Substitutes for kin as caretakers are both costly and unreliable (Turke 1989: 71). Kim Brathwaite faced a sixteen-year jail sentence because, when her babysitter didn't show up, the McDonald's manager went to work and left her two children to die when her Brooklyn tenement apartment was torched by an arsonist. She was charged with "reckless endangerment," even though census data show that, in any given week in the USA, three million children will be left untended by an adult (*New York Times*, October 19, 2003: N1, N40). Unfortunately, stories like this one are almost commonplace (Broughton 2003).

The demographic transition has been monitored around the globe. In Ireland rigorous enforcement of child labor and compulsory schooling laws denied parents the opportunity of earning a direct return on their children. But government gave as it took away, providing new guarantees of social security which "made it unnecessary for the poor to think of children as their main defense against misfortune, unemployment, or disability" (Sommerville 1982: 159). Fertility plummeted.[68]

[67] When I worked for the Ministry of Education in Papua New Guinea, I was initially puzzled to find that teachers begged *not* to be assigned to teach in schools in their home area. But it soon became clear that, whatever they might gain by proximity to kin, they'd lose far more as relatives would "eat" all their wages.

[68] I'm one of two children while my mother was the youngest of twelve (nine living when she was born). Her immigrant parents were from East European peasant stock and she loved telling the story of her father (who lived to ninety-seven) relieving his still-resident sons of their pay packets from the (steel) "mill" each fortnight.

Mexico has recently undertaken a national effort to check its population growth.

Like many old-style Mexican matriarchs, Emma Castro Amador bore so many children that she can't keep their birthdays straight. Sometimes she even loses track of whether Oscar, her 10th, came before David, her 11th, or vice versa. "But I never regret having so many," said Mrs. Castro, 59, who had 14 children in 25 years. Mrs. Castro's offspring, however, have a different view. In a generational divide repeated in millions of Mexican families, all 14 say they are determined to limit their families to two or three children. [Dillon 1999: A1, A12][69]

Even as women's work moves out of the home and into the public sphere, and as their dollar contribution to the household economy increases, their responsibility in the domestic sphere has not lessened (Tingey *et al.* 1996: 184). And "a baby adds about ten days' worth of tasks to the household per month" (Seiter 1998: 304). Although lip service has been paid to husbands as "partners" in the home, at best they "help out" with jobs that the wife owns (Mederer 1993). That's assuming there *is* a husband around. "The percentage of American children living with their fathers has declined steadily since the 1960s" (Black *et al.* 1999: 967).

Meanwhile, the task of childrearing has became vastly more demanding. Preparing a child to succeed in the modern economy so she can leave the nest and start a family of her own takes both time and money. Much of what we think of as routine duties of modern parents (e.g. reading bedtime stories [Lancy 1994b]) or expenses (Christmas presents, braces) are completely unknown outside modern, mainstream societies. On the other hand, the economic *benefits* of children also decline dramatically as we saw in the previous chapter.

While these social changes were taking place, seismic shifts were occurring in the culture of childhood as documented by Zelizer (1985) and discussed in chapter 3. Basically, non-economic value was added to the child to counterbalance the obviously increased costs. The child became adorable, precious, special . . . the "spittin' image of his father," his parents' "hope for the future," "Mom's best friend."

Raising children in the twenty-first century

. . . child-rearing is not physics. (Harris 1998: 86)

If children can be brought to fully competent adulthood in the hands of a crosssection of villagers, including, prominently, other children, then, following Judith Harris, childrearing surely isn't physics. Or is it? What I want to argue

---

[69] And what is especially striking about these three cases (Ireland, Eastern Europe, and Mexico) is that individuals, in limiting the number of offspring, are, quite obviously, defying the teachings of their (Catholic) church.

in the concluding section of this chapter is that, preparing children to succeed in our contemporary, fast-paced, technologically dynamic and information-charged society is extremely challenging. In East Asia, for example, the road to success passes through what is widely known as "examination hell," which the child cannot successfully navigate without the devoted attention of his mother (Lebra 1994: 264).

Unfortunately, childrearing can no longer follow the village model because, today, being raised by your older siblings probably means you're on your way to becoming a gang member (Achpal 2003; Suomi 2005). Indeed, one might reasonably argue that video games and TV have become the typical child's sibling caretakers. And, in France, in the fall of 2005, when young African immigrants on a rampage torched hundreds of vehicles, we had tragic evidence of the failure of the village-based enculturation model to transfer to a modern, urban setting. Asked why the African parents had been unable to prevent their sons from running amok, a mosque director responded: "France is a democratic country. It gives rights to women and children, now parents cannot do anything – if they hit their 12-year-old, police will come to their door. There's a hot line the kids can call to report parental abuse" (*Associated Press*, November 11, 2005).[70] In the USA, people often signal their aversion to other people's children by saying to the mother, in effect, "You are solely responsible for your kid, make sure she doesn't intrude into *our* lives." They may fear reprisal if they intervene to constrain the dangerous or illegal behavior of other people's children (Spilsbury and Korbin 2004).[71]

To gauge how demanding this task is, I scanned the parenting guides selection at Amazon.com. There are literally hundreds available, and most parents will "own a small library on the subject" (Harkness *et al.* 1992: 175), including Dr. Spock's guide, second only to the Bible in sales of 30 million plus (Sommerville 1982: 12). At Amazon, I found books for every stage and milestone of the child's life. There are books for Christian parents, Jewish parents, combos, and those who find inspiration in astrology. There are books for homosexual parents and homophobic parents; young parents and older parents; books for confident parents, anxious parents, and clueless parents. There are parenting books for every ethnic and religious group. There are books for divorced parents and for parents who want to avoid divorce. There are books to cope with underachieving kids and overachieving kids, sick kids and super-athletes. Books guide the parent in meal preparation, bedroom decoration, birthday-party organization, vacation planning, children's book choices, choosing a pre-school, a nanny, a music teacher, a team, and a teacher. The list is almost

---

[70] Information obtained from www.phillyburbs.com; accessed 4.18.07.

[71] In contrast, when I traveled with my family throughout Papua New Guinea and Indonesia, the whole village wanted to "mind" our two blond, cherubic daughters.

endless. So, rather than rely on the wisdom of grandparents, we turn to books (Harkness *et al.* 1996), newspapers, and magazines for the "latest scientific information" (Welles-Nyström 1988: 79).

While the cult of the sacred child has brought us through the demographic transition, it has, nevertheless, created a new set of problems. China's "one-child" policy, coupled with the use of ultrasound (recently banned) to aid in selectively aborting females, has led to a generation of "Little Emperors." They are highly indulged, of course, and the universal preference for junk food is leading to very high cholesterol levels and obesity (Chee 2000). Similar "worship" of Japan's sacred children means that "many young kids behave so wildly and obstreperously in supermarkets, trains, or other public places, as to annoy foreigners... mothers [find] that their children, to their regret, turn into insatiable tyrants due to their earlier indulgence" (Lebra 1994: 261).

Middle-class Asian mothers, like their village counterparts, co-sleep with their infants, nurse them longer, and toilet train them later. They also tolerate more willful behavior. By contrast, middle-class North American mothers appear eager for their charges to acquire at least a limited independence from maternal oversight and solicitation. Upwardly mobile East Asian mothers (including those who've recently migrated to North America) willingly sacrifice their careers for their children while their American and European counterparts do not (Kim and Choi 1994).

Popular opinion to the contrary, studies consistently show that "the impact of maternal employment on child wellbeing [is] negligible" (Bengston *et al.* 2002: 158). Two things *do* matter[72] a great deal: family income and mother's education (Black *et al.* 1999: 974). Income has an impact on the extent to which the mother can purchase[73] aids like playpens, walkers, high-chairs, strollers, Tommee-Tippee cups and disposable diapers that reduce the labor of infant-care. Infants in the United States are held much less than their counterparts from an African village and they "spend a considerable amount of time in various sorts of 'containers,' such as high chairs and playpens" (Richman *et al.* 1988: 70). Also, child-oriented "videos provide tired mothers time to cook dinner, feed the baby, or clean the house. Toys keep children entertained while they [ride] along... on errands" (Berk 1985: 306).

The well-off mother can purchase labor-saving devices to reduce domestic labor, for example, "very small kitchen areas... [and] lack of a dishwasher [mean that] Japanese mothers uniformly washed dishes at least three times a day; American mothers did so an average of about once a day" (Fogel *et al.*

---

[72] Other variables that don't seem to have much impact on children's successful adaptation, by themselves, are: father absence, homosexual parents, and being conceived in a test-tube (Harris 1998: 51).

[73] A quick glance at one of several web-stores devoted to infant-/childcare furnishings turned up a lovely "Classic Pink" bassinette for $1,170 and a sturdy changing table for $2,900.

1992: 38). Her up-scale home or apartment will have private recreation areas and/or be located near public playgrounds or parks where she can safely allow her children to play without supervising them while she does the chores. She can afford to pay someone to come in and do her household work.[74]

A higher income purchases quality daycare[75] – consistently shown *not* to diminish the child's life-chances – as compared with children raised by "full-time moms" (Scarr 1997). After school there is youth soccer, little league, girl scouts, as well as music, ballet, and *tai kwan do* lessons – all correlated with enhanced academic success or standing in one's peer group.

Education contributes to a mother's success in childrearing[76] in a number of, sometimes quite subtle, ways. "Getting an education" usually means delaying childbearing until one has acquired a comparably educated, supportive husband (Fogel *et al.* 1992: 38–39). Continuing one's education through college may delay childbearing until one has achieved a measure of emotional and financial stability. Better-educated women may have the learning skills and motivation to acquire the cultural capital associated with successful childrearing – even in the face of adverse circumstances, like the child's attention deficit disorder, unfavorable schools, or divorce.[77] Better-educated women make smarter choices in terms of childcare aids and personnel; they know which parenting guides to buy from Amazon.com!

Savvy parents carefully manage their children's access to food, TV, video and computer games, and, above all, peers – all of which have the potential to help or harm the child. They believe "that their investment in the 'right' education toy, software, summer camp, or home teaching program [will] help their offspring avoid the temptations of an indulgent society and gain the competitive edge to win the brass ring of success" (Cross 2004: 194). Among the "tricks of the trade" that successful parents use is to talk to their babies, which accomplishes three things. First, it stimulates cortical development during a critical period in

[74] For $200 dollars a week in New York City, a private service prepares and delivers three healthy meals and two snacks a day to children at school and at home. When asked why she couldn't prepare the meals herself, a mother responded, "I love the convenience": "New diet service," CBS Evening News, March 7, 2004.

[75] In Europe, public, surrogate caretakers loom even larger in the overall picture; northeastern Italy and Sweden, in particular, are noted for their comprehensive and effective pre-school programs. Subsidized by progressive civil authorities, they are open to all children, not just those whose parents can afford them. Public attitudes in Europe reflect a view of the family that echoes the utopian ideals of the Israeli kibbutz from the mid-twentieth century while the mother might be the primary caretaker during infancy, shortly afterwards the child should be placed in a nursery with trained staff as she returns to her job. This policy is seen as beneficial to the mother's self-esteem, the economy, and to the child itself (Corsaro 1996; Dahlberg 1992; Eibl-Eibesfeldt 1983: 181).

[76] Mother's education is an extremely powerful predictor of children's academic success and this is especially true in poorer communities in the industrialized world as well as throughout the developing world.

[77] More fully discussed in chapter 9.

brain growth (Small 1998). Second, it ties the baby to its mother emotionally, a tie which Asian mothers, in particular, exploit to manage the child (Fogel *et al.* 1992). Third, it establishes a conversational partnership between the mother and her child which will, in turn, greatly facilitate the mother's role as teacher.

In contrast, *teen* parents rarely talk with their children and in standard free-play sessions, they don't know how to play with them (Gross *et al.* 2003). Mothers who live in urban high-rise ghettos seldom converse with their small children; most verbalizations are short commands or reprimands (Heath 1990). Mothers from West Africa living in France "do not usually talk to their children during childcare or diapering, which, in contrast, are rich exchange periods for French . . . mothers" (Jamin 1994: 156).

Modern parents use "dinner-table conversations" as a forum for teaching their older children. Family dinners signal that there is structure built in to home life and this structuring (along with a regular bedtime hour, after-school events, and attending church) will help the child adapt to the highly structured school routine. An opportunity is provided for children to observe adult role models, not always available in communities where adults and children rarely interact. Moral lessons may be transmitted (Pontecorvo *et al.* 2001; Sterponi 2003). Finally, the use of various speech genres (interrogation, joking, narrative) provides a fertile training ground for the child's linguistic, cognitive, and academic development (Ochs *et al.* 1992: 38).

From her ethnographic work, Mary Martini describes a typical dinner-table conversation in an average white, middle-class home:

> parents engage children in teaching routines. Typically, a child asks "Why?" and the parent answers at length. Common topics are aspects of the physical world: sea life, animals, dinosaurs, stars, astronauts, and how everyday things work . . . parents and children invent stories, jokes, and riddles. They set up "what if" scenarios and experiment with new ways of doing things. Parents listen to, watch and comment . . . Children learn to "show off" . . . inventing songs, jokes, games or implausible situations . . . parents also laugh when children break rules or violate expectations in imaginative ways. (Martini 1996: 30)[78]

Developmental psychologist Mary Gauvain relates how she was able to "multi-task" when her four-year-old son Graeme offers to help her make a cake and she turns a chore into a teaching opportunity (Gauvain 2001: 3). Intellectuals who have the patience can be wonderfully ingenious in exploiting spontaneous teaching opportunities. According to Gauvain, anthropologist Margaret Mead's "parents prided themselves on the informal education they provided for their

---

[78] And we shouldn't be surprised to learn that French parents also use mealtimes as an opportunity for *education de gout* (Sjögren-De Beauchaine 1998, cited in Suizo 2002: 298).

children in their home [where] no aspects of life, including the most mundane acts, were taken for granted (Mead 1972; cited in Gauvain 2001: 11).

These "never miss a teaching opportunity" parents are outliers at the extreme edge of the culturally sanctioned pattern for childrearing in the twenty-first century. The further one moves from this ideal, the less we see parents acting like Mary Gauvain. However, the parent-as-(patient-) teacher role has somehow became enshrined as the gold standard (Goodnow 1990: 280), whereas studies, in fact, show *wide variability* in parents' effectiveness as teachers. If we go further beyond a hypothetical mainstream of modern parenting, the teaching role shrinks drastically. Unlike the families at dinner, "in a Mayan community . . . children are taught to avoid challenging an adult with a display of greater knowledge by telling them something" (Rogoff 1990: 60). As with village adults anywhere, West African Wolof parents never quiz their kids by asking known answer questions (Irvine 1978) – a favorite trick of Euroamerican parent-teachers. While joking relationships between adults are widely reported in the ethnographic literature, the *only* reported case of a parent–child joking relationship is found in middle-class, Euroamerican culture (Alford 1983).

Village parents don't use the same strategies we've seen as prevalent in mainstream Euroamerican society because they *don't need to*. Far less demanding routines and processes (see chapter 5) will suffice – everyone in the village is a potential teacher or role model. It is only when confronted with the challenge of preparing for the demands of a Western-style education and employment that these parents' *laissez faire* strategies can't get the job done.

At the outset of this chapter, I set up a juxtaposition. One view holds that, to succeed in life, children require the near-full-time attention of a mother who treats childrearing as a vocation and prepares herself assiduously. A contrary view is that this is a task best shared among a variety of individuals, a village. What can we conclude? I would argue that, to prepare a child for life in the village, it is neither necessary nor an efficient use of scarce resources to put the burden on any one individual. However, to prepare a child for the modern world, spreading the responsibility among a variety of individuals – none of whom is in charge – invites disaster.

Hillary Clinton, in *It Takes a Village*, tries to apply the village model to the modern situation. She argues for improvements in schools, social service agencies, an increase in library and playground facilities, after-school programs – among other things (Clinton 1996). All these proposals are helpful, but all these agents – teachers, librarians, playground supervisors, Boys & Girl club volunteers – cannot, collectively, substitute for a dedicated, resourceful parent. They are not related to the child and, in our society, *the village is not responsible*. The parent is. At best, they can only *assist* the parent in fulfilling their plan for the child (Fosburg 1982).

Having said that much, I want immediately to disavow any claim that this task requires the full-time ministrations of the child's biological mother. There is overwhelming evidence – not reviewed here – that fathers, adoptive parents, lesbian partners of the biological mothers, and grandparents can all do a fine job. Any of them, or the child's mother, can and usually do avail themselves of the service of a whole array of supplementary caretakers. A working mother, in particular, may well bring home cultural, intellectual,[79] and, certainly, economic resources that a non-working mother cannot provide.

Since at least the nineteenth century, parents have imbued their children with great psychic value. When they invest time and energy in teaching their children to appreciate literature (Taylor 1983), they aren't just insuring the child's academic/social/reproductive success; they're adding a valued member to their innermost circle of friends. The Japanese mother whose life – *ikigai* – becomes her child (Lebra 1994: 262) can expect care and devotion from the child for the rest of her life. Many parents have even more ambitious aspirations for their children, driving them (literally and figuratively), not just to acceptable standards but to excel academically or as athletes, musicians or stage performers.

So parenting in contemporary society is at least somewhat like physics, as it is tough to insure both future success and lasting friendship. But, ultimately, we come full circle in that, as long as someone smart is calling the shots, the more loving, caring, intelligent helpers surrounding the nest, the better off the twenty-first-century child will be.

[79] My mother was a full-time caretaker for two kids and she nearly lost her mind – literally – from boredom.

5   Making sense

Introduction

Learning to work was like play. We [Hopi] children tagged around with our elders and copied what they did. (Simmons 1942: 51)

. . . in an important sense, Inuit do not socialize their children. (Guemple 1979: 39)

What is desired of [Gau, Fiji Islands] village children is that they should grow up. (Toren 1990: 173)

In this chapter, we will examine the way various societies accommodate the child's growing intellectual and physical potency. We will see the interplay between the child's attempts to "make sense" of her world and her kin's very calculating contributions to that enterprise.

One of the most compelling attributes of childhood is the tendency to observe others. Imitation or make-believe (in play) seems to serve complementary and similar ends. Being a spectator and incorporating what one has observed into one's play are simultaneously entertaining and educational. Further, there is a clear expectation held by adults that children's observation/imitation predilections insure that they are learning their culture largely without explicit instruction. Unfortunately, children as keen observers of the village scene become, in the modern era, television addicts and couch potatoes.

Children also learn from their innate need to explore and handle objects – possibly as a precursor to tool handling. This tendency is less easily accommodated by adults who must balance concern for the child's safety and wellbeing, if left to explore without restraint, against the burden imposed by closely monitoring the curious creature.

In contemporary society, the child is a pupil from birth, if not before. The domains where the village child is free from adult control, during play, for instance, are co-opted by Euroamerican and Asian parents to serve very specific ends in the child's preparation for school. Whereas we intervene to accelerate the child's intellectual development, elsewhere children under the age of seven or eight are seen as lacking sense, unable to benefit from direct teaching. Nevertheless, we see parents, however infrequently, intervening to accelerate

154

the child's locomotor development, hastening his independence. We will also see numerous examples of adults "pushing" children to learn proper etiquette and kin terminology. At least one reason appears to be to make the child a more attractive candidate for shared nurturing. A polite child will find more willing child-minders to relieve the mother of this burden (Kilbride 1975: 88, 93).

Children as spectators

[In the Andes] children learn many aspects of food preparation, agricultural tasks, pot-making, and weaving without detailed instruction. (Sillar 1994: 50)

[Chillihuani] elders say that it is better to set a good example for children to follow than to do a lot of talking. (Bolin 2006: 37)

Picture if you will, the avid sports spectator, eyes glued to the TV set, consuming beer and chips with an intensity that almost matches that of the muscle-bound Olympians shown competing in Athens. How could two such extremes of behavior be found in a single species?[1] We begin training early for later Herculean feats of sloth and athleticism.

Children are great observers.[2] I can still recall vividly an episode in my life when, as an eight-year-old, I had the privilege of watching craftsmen build an addition on our house. I remember the masons stretching a horizontal string to guide the laying of blocks for the foundation, the smell of sawdust as the two-by-fours were cut to frame the walls, and the mesmerizing sight of the carpenter's unerring hammer-strokes. Hours flew by in rapt observation. Should we be surprised, then, that children watch, on average, four hours of TV a day (Anonymous 2002)?

On the other hand, as Groos (1898) noted more than a hundred years ago, children seem to have energy to burn and this was his favorite candidate as answer to the question "Why play?" A more recent argument, along these lines, posits that, because of the rich human diet, children are predisposed to obesity. Fat youngsters are slow and would have been vulnerable as prey, so children are *driven* to play to burn off those excess calories and, as an added bonus, their elevated temperature reduces the risk of infection (Barber 1991).

In Gbarngasuakwelle, both tendencies were very much in view. The average court case is just slightly more interesting than watching grass grow. And this is certainly true of the local, village court presided over by Chief Wolliekollie.

---

[1] Perhaps we need to be reminded that "the entire behavior of an individual is at all times motivated by the urge to minimize effort" (Zipf 1949: 3).

[2] Of course, the curiosity that turns every child into an avid observer now has a downside. In the USA, a significant portion of the child population with access to TV will, if not prevented from doing so, watch it for every waking hour, including mealtimes, and, indeed, will fall asleep with the TV on. And it's no secret that the growing obesity epidemic in the developed world is fueled by junk food and sedentism.

Imagine a forty-minute debate about the failure *promptly* to return a borrowed lantern or an even longer debate over the amount of compensation appropriate in the case of an adulterous liaison (the *juicy* details are discretely glossed over). And yet the court never failed to attract a good crowd of juvenile male spectators (Lancy 1980c).

Meanwhile, when court wasn't in session, those same boys could be found engaged in vigorous play. The repertoire of games is quite large but I happened to be around when football (soccer) was first introduced in the village. Almost literally from dawn to dusk, the single badly abused and out-of-round ball was "in play" in a misshapen field that was, at best, a polygon, with "goals" at, approximately, opposite ends. Indeed vigorous play was one of the few aspects of children's behavior that actually provoked notice and a (negative) response from adults (Lancy 1976).

While the boys watching the chief's court were quiet and blended in with their surroundings, it was obvious that the chief saw them as "pupils" in an open-air classroom. Targeting his youthful audience, his rhetorical questions and judicial "opinions" often reflected basic principles of Kpelle morality. Most societies are keenly aware of the child as voyeur and fully expect to use public events for their didactic value (Atran and Sperber 1991).

Elizabeth Fernea illustrates this phenomenon for the Middle East. One of the time-honored public ceremonies is the post-nuptial display of a blood-stained sheet. Signaling the bride's virginity and the husband's potency, the gesture preserves the honor of bride and groom and their families. Children are present on these occasions "so these tests of honor were made clear through observation and . . . through admonition and discussion of honor" (Fernea 1991: 454).

Simon Ottenberg describes the Igbo feast of the tortoise in West Africa as a "rite of reversal" in which normally private behavior is publicly exposed. The feast includes dancing and singing, where bawdy songs openly describe sexual practices. Children are spectators for all these events, and "the content of the songs may help children to learn sexual rules and constraints" (Ottenberg 1989: 113). Further, children continue singing these songs as they work for months afterwards.

On Fiji: "any lively gathering in the house or village hall attracts small groups of children, who range themselves outside the building and peer at the proceedings through the chinks and crevices in the bamboo slats or other material that forms the walls" (Toren 1988: 241). Could children's tendency to observe closely the actions of others convey an evolutionary advantage?[3]

---

[3] In primate studies, the Fijian case would be referred to as "local enhancement," which "refers to situations in which animals are attracted to the locations at which conspecifics are behaving . . . This then places them in a position to learn something that they would not otherwise have learned" (Boesch and Tomasello 1998: 598). In Kibale National Park in January 2003, I observed a single juvenile chimp in the near vicinity of a mature adult. Both were harvesting large green

One of the most exciting debates in biobehavioral research of the past two decades has been over whether "culture" is a uniquely human phenomenon. Studies of chimps in the wild have added the most fuel to this fire.[4] We now have a lengthy catalog of practices that are associated only with specific chimp populations, meaning they aren't hard-wired. Some of these practices include: making sponges out of leaf bundles to soak water up from puddles; using stones to crack open nuts; group-hunting of prey; and using twigs stripped of their leaves to "fish" termites out of their nests (Marks 2003). Furthermore, these practices are enduring, they are passed from one generation to the next, ergo, culture![5] And culture is extremely useful (Boyd and Richerson 1996: 78).

An idea that I have found inspirational in this context I owe to Jack Roberts, who wrote:

It is possible to regard all culture as information and to view any single culture as an "information economy" in which information is received or created, stored, retrieved, transmitted, utilized, and even lost . . . information is stored in the minds of . . . members and . . . artifacts . . . [In this view, children are seen as] . . . storage units [which] must be added to the system . . . as older members of the society disappear. (Roberts 1964: 438, 439)

If culture is information, then we can ask: how do children acquire it? There are a variety of possible mechanisms but, first and foremost, children observe and copy the behavior of more mature individuals.[6] In fact, Boyd and Richerson argue that this trait is the key facilitator for the establishment of cultural traditions. In species in which the young don't automatically observe and imitate[7] others, such as Cebus monkeys, cultural traditions don't arise (Visalberghi and Fragasky 1990). Even when individuals discover something useful, this information isn't necessarily transmitted across the group or retained from one generation to the next (Boyd and Richerson 1996). There's also some interesting cross-species variability as well (Byrne 1995: 57).[8]

---

fruits high in the clerestory. Apparently, the trick is to yank the fruit from its branch and let it plummet to earth where it breaks open and the soft flesh inside can be eaten. I think this may well have been a case of "local enhancement."

[4] Orangutans also have unique cultural traditions within populations: "in Sumatra, orangutans use sticks to pry calorie-rich seeds from prickly, hard-to-eat *Neesia* fruits, a clever trick that youngsters pick up from adults" (Knott 2003: 78).

[5] "Culture . . . [is] the non-genetic spreading of habits and information" (de Waal 2001: 30).

[6] Think about the complex defensive mechanisms that we've developed to combat academic cheating. What we are doing, in essence, is recalibrating the cost–benefit equation to favor individual effort to counteract the more "natural" approach, namely, copying the answers from a classmate. For a scholarly discussion of the trade-offs between individual and social learning, see Rogers (1989) and Richerson and Boyd (1992) who aver: "Plagiarism is usually easier than invention" (p. 65).

[7] By "imitate," I mean rough approximation rather than carbon copy.

[8] See also Toshisada (2003).

For example, Barbara King finds that adult baboons in the wild do not "donate information" to juveniles during foraging. Rather, young animals remain close to and focus their attention on the adults, even sniffing their muzzles to learn what they may be eating. In other words the onus seems to be on the juvenile to apprentice themselves diligently to the more competent adults (King 1999: 21).

Ironically, when observational or social learning (the tendency that leads us, eventually, to couch potatoes[9]) becomes firmly established in the genome, innovation is facilitated as well. It's as if all those imitators are flattering the innovator, awarding him/her a "patent" for making useful discoveries.[10]

De Waal makes the case that the drive to observe and imitate is paired with a drive to "fit in" or the "desire to be like others" (de Waal 2001: 230).[11] Other incentives for hanging around with older members of one's group include the facts that they are more likely to identify and deal with threats correctly and they are better at finding food (Johnson and Bock 2004). As noted in the previous chapter, the village brings juveniles together with older individuals on the "mother ground." Here children can be supervised and protected while they observe and imitate in play adult patterns of behavior.

We also have evidence, in the animal kingdom, of what psychologists call "one-trial learning," where the organism experiences a non-fatal encounter with a threat source – predator, treacherous stream, pitfall – or *observes* someone else's encounter (McGrew 1977).[12] The reoccurrence of these threats will, subsequently, provoke an immediate avoidance reaction.[13]

Juveniles of our species, and primates generally, are keen observers and this trait places them in a position to learn from older, more competent individuals.

---

[9] It is interesting that, in captive primate colonies, macaques in particular, when researchers showed monkey videos to animals recovering from illness or surgery to keep them calm, they became just as "zoned out" as human videophiles, evidently (O'Neill-Wagner 2003).

[10] See, for example, Whiten *et al.* (2005). However, an immediate caveat is necessary: "in contrast to the usual generalizations that one hears about the flexibility and adaptability of nonhuman primates, [they are really very conservative], for example, Gombe chimpanzees will not eat proffered mangoes, a prized chimpanzee food elsewhere in Africa, although these have been growing in the Park for decades" (McGrew 1977: 269). Boyd and Richerson describe the advantages to the imitator as opposed to an individual trying to figure something out on their own. In their view, *individual* as opposed to *social* learning takes more effort, may require more brain power, and is potentially more risky (Boyd and Richerson 1996: 70). See also McElreath (2004).

[11] A "classic" formulation of this view is found in White (1959).

[12] However, Visalberghi has shown, in a number of studies, that capuchins, who are social tool users, while quick to learn about predator threats from troop-mates, are much more self-reliant when it comes to verifying the palatability of novel foods (Visalberghi and Addessi nd).

[13] Incidentally, the driven, autonomous, curious, experimental learner so central to psychology's view of the child is absent in the accounts of anthropologists. Instead, we see individuals emulating the behavior of those more important or powerful than themselves – copycats (Henrich 2001).

Another universal human trait, with practical benefits, is the manipulation of found objects.

Exploration and play with objects

... object play in childhood is necessary for efficient adult tool use ... (Byrne 1995: 87)

Theorist Richard Byrne sees a clear connection between the predilection towards object play and later use of tools (Byrne 1995: 86). The only two species where play with objects is common are humans and chimpanzees, which also happen to be the only two species that routinely use tools. Gorillas are an interesting intermediary case. In the wild, they neither play with objects nor use tools. They don't need to – their foods can be harvested without tools. However, under circumstances where there are no age-mates to play with,[14] they do play with objects, so the capacity is certainly there; captive gorillas, in fact, show considerable tool-using ability (Byrne 1995: 86). Byrne also postulates a more general impact of object play on cortical growth, and it's worth noting that, as we age, the "decline in the rate of object play coincides with decline in synaptic density in the cerebral cortex" (Fairbanks 1995: 144).

That toddlers play with objects appears to be a species universal. Jean Piaget's (1951) theory accords a prominent role to object play during the earliest stages of the child's cognitive development and these stages at least have been validated cross-culturally (Dasen *et al.* 1978). In Piaget's theory, it is not just the physical manipulation of objects that is important. More critical is the symbolic transformation of found objects into artifacts. A stick becomes a warrior's spear, a depression in the ground becomes a soup bowl, a rag becomes a baby. That chimps also share with us at least the rudiments of symbolizing is revealed in research where they are taught to communicate with humans. Perhaps the most successful case would be Kanzi, a bonobo chimp who learned to communicate in *Yerkish* (Savage and Lewin 1994). Kanzi initially picked up the "language" – which uses icon-like symbols on an electronic touch-screen – from observing his mother's, largely unsuccessful, lessons. Kanzi's motivation to learn seemed to be supported by several traits: the desire to "fit in," the tendency to observe- and copy his caretakers, an eagerness to play with objects, and the desire to communicate – especially when it affected his own wellbeing.[15]

---

[14] In my observations of mountain gorillas in western Uganda and Rwanda, juveniles without play-partners, that is, in a troop where there's a dearth of young ones, play very little.

[15] However, even when chimp language instruction is optimized, as it was with Kanzi, the chimp learns language slowly and, at eight, his language skill approximated a two-year-old human (Byrne 1995: 171). I had a chance to visit with Kanzi in January 1998 and I was struck by how juvenile and playful his behavior was, in spite of his being of breeding age. His trainers have successfully prolonged his "youth" to permit further growth of learning, pushing the envelope, so to speak. Aside from learning to use language, an experiment by anthropologist Nick Toth

To encourage object play, *we* provide lots of toys, including safe, miniature tools, in various sizes, along with the dolls to use them. We also provide objects to play with that are specifically designed to facilitate the kind of cognitive complexity and flexibility that many assert is the *raison d'être* of object play (Power 2000). And what is perhaps most remarkable, we sometimes intervene to "teach" our children how to use their toys or nudge them into more complex uses (Haight 2003). I have found only one example of this in the ethnographic literature – a father assisting his son with a miniature canoe (Hogbin 1970b)[16] – and I am confident it occurs rarely. In research where the investigators created conditions designed to *facilitate* their involvement, East Indian and Guatemalan villagers would *not* intervene in their toddlers' play (Göncü *et al.* 2000). It's hard to escape the conclusion that our "micro-management" of children's toys and play is driven by the inexorable demands of later schooling.

Object play varies in different cultures. In the USA, children have access to a huge array of store-bought toys as well as found objects and the child's environment has been safely child-proofed. No such conditions exist in village India. The few toys are either flimsy or fragile craft objects used for display, packing containers and the like are recycled quickly, and indoor areas are crowded and dangerous (Kopp *et al.* 1977: 436–437).

There are only a few cases in the ethnographic literature of adults fashioning toys for their children (Hewlett 1991). Typical are the !Kung, among whom:

adults do not make toys for babies. Nor [do] . . . adults encourage increasingly complex forms of object manipulation or object-focused language. Indeed, the folk view of development seems to emphasize a child's need for space to explore, a view that is revealed by the !Kung phrase, *a n/tharo an/te* [he/she is teaching/learning him/herself]. (Bakeman *et al.* 1990: 796)

Village children – lacking toys – generally play with found objects, including *real* tools. There are numerous observations by anthropologists of very young children handling and playing with machetes and other sharp objects (Howard 1970: 35) and liberally sampling any and all substances in the environment to test their edibility. For example, from the Kwoma of PNG: "I once saw Suw with the blade of a twelve-inch bush knife in his mouth and the adults present paid no attention to him" (Whiting 1941: 25). On Vanatinai Island in the South Pacific, "children . . . manipulate firebrands and sharp knives without

gave him an opportunity to display something never before observed in chimps, the ability to *construct* a sharp-edged stone tool to cut a cord. Solving this problem allowed him to gain access to a box containing a treat (Schick and Toth 1993).

[16] Barry Hewlett also describes Aka pygmy parents making miniature spears or digging sticks and demonstrating their use to infants during rest stops. However, since the "pupil" is too young actually to practice any of these skills, it's hard to see this as active teaching. Rather it seems to be another example of the unusual proclivity of pygmy adults to amuse or comfort children (Hewlett 1992: 234).

remonstrance . . . one four year old girl had accidentally amputated parts of several fingers on her right hand by playing with a bush knife" (Lepowsky 1987: 79). Lepcha babies "will crawl to fire and burn or scald themselves . . . There is scarcely a grown-up who does not carry scars from childhood burns" (Gorer 1967: 297). !Kung children were filmed playing with scorpions – in full view of at least one parent (Marshall 1972)!

There is an uneasy trade-off here. On the one hand, by indulging their curiosity about the environment and the things in it, parents insure that children are learning useful information without the necessity of parental intervention.[17] This efficiency comes at a cost of the occasional damage to or loss of one's offspring:[18]

[Dogon children] will not rarely fall off the rock walls if they are playing on the outskirts of the village in a landscape that to us would seem suitable only as a training ground for mountain climbers. The oft-repeated reminder that mothers should take better care of their children is useless, for even three-year-olds are left entirely in the care of their siblings who are only slightly older. (Parin 1963: 48)[19]

On the other hand, precisely because of the dangers, infants and toddlers, in many societies, are kept off the ground and denied access to found objects (Kaplan and Dove 1987: 195). For example, to a Balinese, crawling is animal-like behavior; hence the baby "may not even touch the earth and is carried everywhere" (Covarrubias 1937: 129). This is by no means a unique reaction; on the contrary, I have the impression that societies that permit the infant free rein to crawl where it will are in a distinct minority. On Gau Island, children have the freedom to crawl but their territory is limited, and should they stray they are roughly picked up and re-placed back in the safe zone with harsh admonitions. Similar treatment is meted out to the curious child who would examine or play with an adult's possessions (Toren 1990: 172).

Once children are ambulatory, however, they are almost inevitably granted great freedom to play and explore – as long as they remain in the company of sibling or adult caretakers. Found and crudely made toys will, inevitably, be used as "props" in the elaborate make-believe scenarios, frequently recorded by anthropologists.

---

[17] For example, Tony Pellegrini demonstrated that while children could learn quite a bit about the properties of objects through play, an adult instructing them through a series of questions produced much greater learning (Pellegrini 1984–1985).

[18] In the middle-class area where I live, some of the parents encourage their young (five years and up) to ride ATVs (all-terrain vehicles) without supervision. The children are out of the way and, presumably, acquiring some skills. The slim possibility of the child's arrest (several laws are broken in this activity) or of their serious injury or death seems to be a sacrifice the parents are willing to make (*Salt Lake Tribune*, June 10, 2005: A1, A12).

[19] A similar *laissez faire* attitude towards hazardous play is found in the Marquesas (Martini and Kirkpatrick 1992).

It's only make-believe

... make-believe ... seems to be an adaptation for practicing domestic and extra-domestic subsistence tasks [including] sex-role differentiation. (Parker 1984: 282)

OK, I lied. It's not "only" make-believe![20] As anthropologists have consistently shown, in the village, make-believe play is critical. It is the "classroom" where children try on and practice their culture.

The walls of the mastaba tomb of Mereruka, an Egyptian official who died *c.*2300 BCE is a virtual "picture encyclopedia" of daily life in the Old Kingdom. The intrepid visitor will discover several reliefs depicting children playing, including boys playing at war. Some boys are dressed as soldiers, while another has his hands bound – a captive. In a lower panel, girls have formed a living merry-go-round and the inscription refers to their activity as "pressing the grapes" (Strouhal 1990).

In Ghanaian villages, you'll find scaled-down "kitchens" where four- to five-year-old girls pretend to grind grain (sand). Ten-year-old sisters build small fires and cook "soup" in small pots. Brothers take the role of husband and, characteristically, criticize the consistency and flavoring of the soup (Goody 1992). Igbo children "put grasshoppers, with their wings torn off, in these constructions, and pretend that they are people, creating scenes with them" (Ottenberg 1989: 96). East African "Ngoni boys ... played ... at law courts ... In their high squeaky voices the little boys imitated their fathers whom they had seen in the courts, and they gave judgments, imposing heavy penalties, and [kept] order in the court with ferocious severity" (Read 1960: 84).

In Gbarngasuakwelle, I recorded a lengthy, elaborate enactment of the blacksmith in his forge. What was particularly interesting was that many of the more subtle aspects of the blacksmith's role were captured as well. The children had created a mock forge with tools made of found pieces of wood; there was a smith (the oldest boy), a couple of younger male "apprentices," and two girls of eight or so who bring food to their "husbands." But the blacksmith's forge is also one of the principal loci for gossip in the village, and the children had neatly captured that aspect, including quite a bit of the adult conversational language and repartee (Lancy 1980a).

My sense is that, before the advent of television and manufactured playsets, children incorporated the entire panoply of village life into their play. And this includes rare events. I once observed a group of boys re-enacting the passage of the president's motorcade, complete with siren-sounds and Liberian flags waving from the lead "vehicles" (Lancy 1996: 185). Schieffelin (1990: 213, 217) observed and photographed boys emulating their fathers serving as porters "on patrol." A seventeenth-century parent in England noted in his diary a "mock

---

[20] Also referred to in the literature as role-playing, pretend, socio-dramatic, and fantasy play.

funeral staged by his daughters, aged 8 and 6. [They buried one of their dolls] with a great deal of formality" (Pollock 1983: 237).

By and large, however, make-believe play outside our own culture appears to be quite conservative.[21] The following assessment, of Mayan children at play, is typical: "there is little elaboration or introduction of variation or complexity during the course of play. Scripts and roles are repeated over and over, almost ritualized" (Gaskins and Göncü 1992: 32). While children's behavior is channeled by their observations of the behavior of those older than themselves (Hewlett 1992), I'm aware of only one study that actually links the type and quantity of play to specific adult skills. It was conducted in an area of Botswana where villages practice differing subsistence strategies. In some villages, adult women pound grain in a mortar and pestle to remove the outer husk. Not surprisingly, girls (not boys) play at pounding, and, in communities that derived less of their food from grains, girls were much less often observed playing at grain processing. Similarly, the "aim game," which sharpens hunting skills, was seen less often in villages that derived most of their food from agriculture. Furthermore, the ethnographers noted that children were *prohibited* from practicing with actual grain for fear they'd spill it, so that play-pounding was the only means to practice this critical skill (Bock and Johnson 2004).

If practice or some form of training is necessary for the optimal development of skilled behavior, then we must ask . . . why practice *play*? Consider the alternatives. Practice outside of the play context might be extremely dangerous. If a young animal . . . had to learn to hunt by hunting, it would starve. If it had to learn mothering by practicing on its own offspring, it would have a poor reproduction record . . . Furthermore, in all these "for real" contexts, arousal is liable to be very high, and . . . learning does not progress very well under conditions of high arousal . . . [however] learning does not occur very well when arousal is too low, and most drill-type practice is boring. Similarly, teaching is . . . inefficient because it requires an investment by a second party, the teacher. Thus, while selection favors learning over instinct in many cases, it is unlikely to favor teaching or pure practice as educational media. (Lancy 1980b: 482 emphasis added)

Aside from pragmatic routines like food preparation and blacksmithing, children readily incorporate and rehearse conventional social relationships in make-believe including marriage, kin relations, adultery, birth, and death. Arunta (aboriginal Australian hunters and gatherers) children have been observed meticulously recreating gender-appropriate domestic scenes, including "adultery, with a boy running away with the 'wife' of another boy" (Williams 1983: 202).

---

[21] This is a paradoxical issue; it is not clear which social milieu is most supportive of children's development through make-believe. On the one hand, village observers see make-believe as lacking inventiveness and fantasy – compared with observations of modern, urban children's play. Contrariwise, there is evidence that television and video games may have a dampening effect on children's fantasy play (Belton 2001).

In contemporary society, we *expect* children to wrestle with emotional problems through make-believe. Indeed, this is often seen as the *main* function of make-believe, and there's an entire branch of clinical practice – play therapy – built on this assumption.[22] However, this emotional loading is largely absent in village make-believe. Gaskins reports from her close observation of Yucatec Mayan children's play that intense emotional expression is absent. One reason may be that adults expect playgroups to function harmoniously: "the dynamics to be expressed must be pleasant and predictable enough to sustain engagement of all participants" (Gaskins and Miller 2002: 4).[23]

Mayan children are not absorbed in their *own* lives as they play. They also seem to have fewer traumas to deal with because they don't live in a neontocracy. For example, instead of feeling threatened by the arrival of a new sibling, "Mayan children are more likely to view the newcomer as an [allomothering] opportunity" (Gaskins and Miller 2002: 6). They have little access to fictional characters in storybooks, so while these characters populate Euroamerican children's play, they're absent from Mayan play (Gaskins and Miller 2002: 8).

Middle-class Americans ascribe other values to make-believe play, including the development of perspective-taking, linguistic fluency, and academic preparedness. These values are revealed in the careful management[24] of the toybox and TV menu so that the scripts children enact reflect the aspirations parents have for them. Unlike parents in other societies and, indeed, unlike lower-class parents in the USA, middle-class mothers engage in fantasy construction with their children (Morelli *et al.* 2003).

American mothers often spend time directly organizing children's play activities by providing objects and ideas for play as well as engaging in the play itself. In contrast, Mexican mothers rarely involve themselves in children's play activity. Mexican children are infrequent adult companions, and most interaction with parents takes place in shared work activity rather than child-centered play. (Farver and Howes 1993: 350)

Children's make-believe play has also been co-opted by educators. In order to promote literacy, they have designed ingenious "play centers" for pre-schools and kindergarten that feature literacy-rich settings such as a post office and a bank (Roskos and Newman 1994). These are, interestingly, settings that pre-schoolers may never have visited. Indeed, one of the most salient contrasts between the village and contemporary, urban society is that, in the former, the entire adult world is laid out for children to observe and incorporate in their play, whereas, in the latter, this is much less true (Morelli *et al.* 2003), especially in poorer communities (Lancy 1982a).

---

[22] According to its website, the Association for Play Therapy has 50,000 members: www.a4pt.org; accessed 4.18.07.

[23] Also Gaskins and Miller (in press).

[24] Göncü refers to this as "policing" (Göncü 2004).

As important as make-believe appears to be as a kind of "classroom" where village children can replicate and rehearse the culture they must adopt, the emic or folk perspective on play may be more measured. That is, at the age when make-believe flourishes in most societies, children are not supposed to be very intelligent. They have not yet reached the age of reason.

The age of reason

[Among the Punan Bah] the baby is . . . hardly considered human . . . [the] child is like an unripe fruit, it must ripen, only then will you know the taste of it. (Nicolaisen 1988: 209, 202)

. . . each human child thus grows up in something like the accumulated wisdom of its entire social group, past and present. (Tomasello 2001: 137)

In modern society, parents are informed of the necessity of "Enhancing your child's brain in the womb" (Conkling 2001: 21), and that "It's never too early to begin talking with your baby" (Conkling 2001: 65). They're provided with lists of the "best" toys and activities at one to three months and four to six months (Conkling 2001: 53), and urged to emulate Albert Einstein's mother, Pauline, whose early musical stimulation undoubtedly laid the foundation for her son's genius (Conkling 2001: 119).[25] The *really* ambitious parent can turn to "IvyBound," the mission of which is to provide "award-winning" educational products to stimulate the intellectual development of toddlers destined to attend Yale and Harvard. The IvyBound mantra prescribes no limit to the child's potential, "providing they are exposed to the core principles of the Ivy League education in the earliest stages of life."[26]

On Ifaluk Island, by contrast, before the age of two, children have no thoughts or feelings; they just eat and play. Since they lack sense or morals, it is useless to get angry or to try to control their behavior. It is believed that children do not gain *repiy* (intelligence) until they are five or six years old (Burrows and Shapiro 1957; Lutz and LeVine 1983; Lutz 1985).

Not only is the age at which children are considered teachable "delayed," there is, often, little concern about the achievement of developmental milestones. For the Chewong (Malaysia) no developmental timetable is acknowledged. There are no expectations that, at a particular age, the child should be sitting or walking, nor is the child's development a subject for discussion. The onus for learning is entirely on the children and they are never "pushed." The

[25] Research has shown that cortical development *is* enhanced in four- to six-year-olds who've had Suzuki lessons for a year (Fujioka *et al.* 2006).

[26] Information obtained from www.ivybound.org; accessed 7.15.05. Going even further, "A California obstetrician has developed courses to further the intellectual skills of his students. The students? All fetuses. The name of the school is, I kid you not, 'Prenatal University'" (Robbins 2006: 334).

Chewong aver that "'We wait for [them] to come and ask us how to make a basket, or how to say a spell.' If no one asks, then they believe that the knowledge will die out" (Howell 1988: 162).

Examples of children treated as lacking any sense, as being essentially uneducable, are legion in the ethnographic record. In Gbarngasuakwelle, I was chastised for spending my time with children because "they don't know anything, they haven't yet 'gotten sense'" (Lancy 1996: 118). Olga Nieuwenhuys (1994), conducting fieldwork in an Indian coastal village, found that adults treated her attempts to observe and analyze children's culture with derision (p. 34). "An Ayoreo [South American] forager child is not considered a complete human being [until attaining]... *aiuketaotiguei*, which means 'understanding' or 'personality'" (Bugos and McCarthy 1984: 510). For Fulani (West African) pastoralists: "It is when children begin to develop *haYYillo* (social sense) that adults in turn change their expectations and behavior" (Riesman 1992: 130). For Sisala (West African) farmers, children from six years should display *wijima* (Grindal 1972: 28). For the Kipsigis (Kenya), children are said to have sense or *ng'om* when they can not only take care of themselves but undertake certain routine chores – watering the cows, sweeping the house – without supervision (Harkness and Super 1986).

Even when the child is endangered, adults may not see the utility of a "lesson." In Yemen, children love to play around construction sites, but in spite of the obvious danger, workers only half-heartedly curtail the risky behavior. More importantly, "builders adopted the prevalent Yemeni position that 'explaining' [the dangers] to children was pointless... as they... have no *'aql* (reason)" (Marchand 2001: 91).

One of the consequences of treating young children as senseless, incomplete, and amoral is that adults feel no qualms about their exposure to sexual activity. A magnificent wooden votive figurine from the Bayombe peoples of the Congo depicts a child in his mother's lap, grasping his large erect penis in one hand and his mother's breast in the other.[27] Among the Dusun in Borneo:

> young children rarely are censured for open sexual behavior. Self-masturbation, handling of the genitals, and exhibitionism are rarely attended to by adults. Adults look upon sexual play between children under four years of age with tolerance, in much the same manner as they view sex play in young animals... In play about the house younger children sometimes discover older children in solitary or mutual sexual activities. If they keep a distance and do not tease the individuals involved, younger children can watch these activities. (Williams 1969: 102)

Among the Bajau boat-dwellers in the Sulu Sea, children "wear no clothes until the age of eight or ten... commonly explore one another's genitals... [and]

---

[27] Permanent Collection: National Museum of African Art. Washington, DC.

parents do not become upset with such behavior" (Nimmo 1970: 253). Similar attitudes prevailed in European society until

[in] the course of the seventeenth century . . . the custom of teasing small children with sex play was suppressed. At the beginning of that century, the child who became Louis XIII . . . had been masturbated by his nurses, who also kissed his genitals and had him feel theirs, and had frightened him by threats of cutting off his penis and nipples. He had observed sexual intercourse, had seen pornographic books, and had played sexually with his younger sister – all before age seven. Then, abruptly, he was thought to be old enough to be aware of what was going on, and such activity ceased. (Sommerville 1982: 94)[28]

The foregoing suggests that the child has no sense at this early age, that, in fact, nothing that happens to him/her can have a lasting impression. The late Renaissance ushered in the novel idea that children were sensible or educable at a much earlier period.[29] Perhaps this occurred as an indirect response to the explosive growth of knowledge and the spread of literacy during what historians call the "Age of Enlightenment."

What all these cases share is the notion that children, before the age of five, roughly, aren't worth teaching because they are too immature to really absorb important lessons. It isn't until ages five to seven that children really begin to tune their radar to the world of adult competencies and to begin to emulate their parents and more competent older siblings – in earnest – and not just in make-believe. As Alan Fiske notes, in the ethnographic record, there is "much less childrearing than there is *culture-seeking*" (Fiske 1997: 11).[30]

A survey of fifty societies confirmed that there are two common transitions in children's development, at five to seven and at puberty, when new duties are assigned. Further, in the West, "English common law . . . has traditionally held the child of 7 years to be . . . capable of knowing right from wrong . . . of being guilty [and] . . . legally liable to trial" (Rogoff *et al.* 1975: 356–357). On the continent, "*infantia*" described a stage of development lasting until the age of seven. Only from that age was the child able to communicate with adults and begin to learn the social conventions (Shahar 1990: 24); it had achieved the "age of reason."

Of course, "getting sense" occurs across an age span of several years. The child will have taken responsibility for a few chores; she will be noted observing

---

[28] The court doctor, Jean Heroard, kept a day-to-day diary of the infancy of the future king. As a measure of how far attitudes have changed, by the 1950s women were abandoning *breastfeeding* as too overtly sexual (Sears *et al.* 1957: 77).

[29] There are earlier manifestations of this idea. Quintilian (100 CE) in *The Training of the Orator* calls for structured play and lessons appropriate to the child's age and ability. But this advice was aimed at the tiny intelligentsia at the peak of Roman society and was honored mostly in the breach (cited in Sommerville 1982: 93).

[30] Compare: "Primate infants seem to have been selected to be information extractors" (King 1999: 21).

and attempting to replicate adult skills; and she may be sent on errands. Novel or inappropriate use of adult tools or wasting valuable materials will provoke a scolding as will failure to take care of oneself or to perform simple tasks correctly (Martini and Kirkpatrick 1992: 211). Albeit casually, adults will be sizing up the child, evaluating her potential for further learning. In an important study, Guatemalan villagers were found to rate the "intelligence" of children based on their spontaneous demonstration of initiative and competence and then assign greater responsibility to "smarter" kids (Nerlove and Roberts 1974).

"Intelligence" in the village society is associated with qualities like self-sufficiency, obedience, respect towards elders, attention to detail, willingness to work, and effective management of younger siblings and livestock (Wober 1972). Qualities *we* value, such as precocity, verbal fluency, independent and creative thought, personal expression, and ability to engage in repartee, would all be seen by villagers as defects to be curtailed as quickly as possible.[31] These are danger signs of future waywardness. We see "cognitive development" from early childhood to adulthood as some inevitable march to greater sophistication and rationality. But, as Christina Toren points out, in the Fijian society she studied, children do not grow into a more rational worldview. They learn to see the world as adults do, as populated with spirit forces, superstitions, supernatural powers, and taboos (Toren 1993). Similarly, "The ability to pray [in Yemen is] directly associated with the development of reason, and some young boys . . . assert their independence by going to the mosque with an age mate, unaccompanied by their fathers" (Marchand 2001: 98).

Over-eager children may receive the cold shoulder if they request, in effect, to "apprentice" themselves to competent practicioners of various skills. They can be rebuffed because they're considered too immature to learn rapidly, their attention span is too short, or their manual dexterity or strength is undeveloped. The targeted "expert" may feel little or no responsibility for this particular child; he or she may be too busy or just too impatient. There is no presumption whatsoever that adults have a moral obligation to serve as teachers of the young (Lancy 1996: 149–150). Among the Moose of West Africa, children who are performing a task incorrectly are not shown the correct procedure; they're told to stop or threatened with punishment (Fiske 1997: 14). One hears this common refrain: "if one asks a Chaga [agriculturalists of Tanzania] where he got his knowledge, in nine cases out of ten, the reply is: 'From nobody; I taught . . . myself!'" (Raum 1940: 246–247).

However, "the intelligent [Chaga] child is expected to ask questions. Much of the lore retained in the memory of the older people is not reproduced spon-taneously" (Raum 1940: 246). Elsewhere, however, children may be chastised

---

[31] In rural Turkey the trait most valued by parents (60 percent) was obedience, least valued (18 percent) was independence (Kagitçibasi and Sunar 1992: 81).

for asking questions: "children should be seen and not heard" is the ideal in many societies. On Borneo, village children,

even the older ones, are rarely offered straightforward explanations on social matters, beliefs, ideas, values, or rituals. They must use their eyes and ears and reason a great deal on their own. They are not encouraged to ask questions or to seek explanations on why things are the way they are. When they do so, they will usually be cut short with a remark like "that is how it is," or "that is customary." (Nicolaisen 1988: 206)

Beyond the routine tasks which are open to public scrutiny, each society also "archives" a great deal of information that is secret or guarded. Perhaps it is too complex to be learned through observation and imitation, perhaps it has intrinsic value that ought not to be squandered, such as the location of rich fishing grounds: "family ritual and religious formulae are secret property, jealously conserved" (Firth 1970: 77). On Pohnpei (Micronesia), one does not freely dispense what one knows. Only those judged respectful, intelligent, and patient will be deemed worthy of the responsibility to carry knowledge to the next generation (Falgout 1992: 37).

That is, while "scaffolding" and other forms of facilitation of the child's fledgling attempts to learn are considered a critical test of the competence of modern Euroamerican parents (Rogoff 1990), in other societies parents may actively erect barriers to keep children away from inappropriate knowledge or skill acquisition.[32]

Obviously, there are various means by which the young may learn from the old but occasions when *teaching* might be called for are exceedingly rare.

The decision to teach our children

. . . teaching is a powerful tool for promoting cultural evolution. (Boesch and Tomasello 1998: 597)

In the same way that correlation is not causation in general, the existence of parent–child correlation, in particular, does not imply direct transmission. (Cavalli-Sforza and Feldman 1981: 349)

While we can find examples of learning from the literature on primates, especially in chimps, overall the evidence for the transmission from adult to juvenile of complex, multi-step skills is quite scanty (Strier 2003: 303). Boesch's long-term study of chimpanzees learning to utilize panda nuts in the Taï Forest of

---

[32] Among some segments of US society, parents may go to extraordinary lengths to prevent their children from learning about crucial subjects like sex until late in adolescence. For example, a mother in Utah objected vociferously to the requirement that her seventeen-year-old daughter answer federally mandated questions regarding her own sexual activity (she's to remain in complete ignorance until marriage) prior to donating blood (Eddington and Lynn 2005).

the Ivory Coast is, therefore, perhaps unique. He distinguishes between "facilitation"[33] and "active teaching." Facilitation is more common. Chimp mothers might leave intact nuts for their juveniles to crack, carefully positioned near hammer stones and a suitable tree-root anvil. Normally, adults eat all the nuts they crack and take their stones with them.

Active teaching occurs rarely. Once, Boesch observed a mother "modeling" by slowing down and modifying her nut cracking, all the while watching to insure her youngster was paying attention. Once a mother modified her son's positioning of the nut. On both occasions, the mothers were responding to the juvenile's unsuccessful attempts. In fact, in spite of the enormous caloric boost the nuts provide, not all chimps learn the skill and those that do may take seven years or longer to become proficient (Boesch 1991). In a related study, there was found to be no relationship between the nut-cracking skill of the mother and that of her offspring (Matsuzawa 1994: 360).

Studies of the acquisition of the complex skill of termiting in Gombe show that female chimps learn it from their mothers roughly two years earlier than juvenile males. The females stay nearer to their mothers, watch them closely, and emulate their behavior – while males are busy playing. The mothers never actually "taught" the skill, learning depending mostly on careful observation and, secondarily, on diligent practice (Lonsdorf 2005: 680–681).

Teaching as facilitation is much more common than active teaching among humans as well. As we've seen, adults expect children to observe and attempt to imitate more mature levels of task performance. Active teaching, because it demands the patient attention of a teacher – who is, therefore, unable to pursue other ends – is used quite strategically.[34] Most societies, like the Chewong, as we've seen, are content to wait until the child has acquired more mature behavior patterns, including speech, before intervening in their development. A few – which can't afford a long period of dependency – aren't willing to wait.

Anthropologists sometimes note mothers encouraging their children to walk (Harkness and Super 1991: 226–227), for example. The Kipsigis as well as the !Xun San have been observed holding babies under the arms and jumping them on their laps. This stimulates a "stepping" reflex and if this "gymnastic"

---

[33] A roughly comparable concept is "social information donation" (King 1999: 19).

[34] In an unpublished study, Barbara Polak describes the complex sequence of skills integrated into the task of sowing peanuts, sorghum, and millet among Bamana (Mali) horticulturalists. The most difficult component involves tipping a gourd – suspended from one's wrist – and rapidly removing *just* five to seven millet seeds to drop into the hole one has dug with a hoe-strike. As-yet-unproficient boys set the gourd down before removing the seeds, thereby breaking the rhythm and slowing down the process. This particular component is the *only* piece of the process that Polak observed being *taught* by an adult. Otherwise, boys must acquire the sowing skill-set entirely through observation and repeated trial (personal communication, 9.13.2007).

exercise is kept up, the babies will walk sooner – relieving their caretakers of the burden of transporting them (Takada 2005: 290). Also in East Africa, the Ganda mother's eagerness to reduce the child's dependence – in anticipation of the next infant – leads to considerable "training." They actually dig a hole in the ground to aid in propping up the infant and place him in it for lengthening periods "until he is able to sit unsupported... Walking is [also] an important landmark... because it is... the signal that a child is old enough to be weaned" (Ainsworth 1967: 321, 326).

The Zulu of South Africa use a more direct approach; they place the child on an ant's nest to motivate it to stand and walk (Krige 1965/2005). Another society where parents push development by active teaching is found on Malaita Island:

> In comparison to the other major islands in the Solomons, Malaita is an unfor-giving environment for human survival... with little arable land, thin nutrient-poor soils... "making a living"... requires a tremendous human investment in planning and labor... children are pushed to be adult as soon as possible. (Watson-Gegeo and Gegeo 2001: 3–5)

Also in Melanesia, Gau Islanders expect children to grow up quickly and treat harshly any child who seems to be lagging behind in their developmental timetable. A two-year-old will be scolded and teased as acting baby-like if it whines to be picked up and held (Toren 1990:174). Similarly, a fourteen-month-old that is still not walking will be given a chili-pepper enema (Toren 1990: 171).

Parents will accelerate the child's motor development when an impending infant threatens to absorb all of the caretaker's attention and/or because the toddler needs to begin making a useful contribution to the household as soon as possible.

Some communities also intervene to direct children away from harmful situations. The Kwoma of Papua New Guinea teach children about poisonous plants, insects, and reptiles as they send them to forage for themselves in the bush. Children are also introduced to the dangers of sorcery early on. They are taught not to take food from strangers, nor to leave personal effects about where malevolent sorcerers might lay hands on them (Whiting 1941). Kpelle parents warn children about playing in or near streams and rivers because of dangerous water spirits (Erchak 1992: 50) – obviously a sensible precaution against drowning. Samoan children are reined in by threats to call on horrific beasts to come and eat them. A fretful baby will be distracted by: "Pig! Elenoa is here, come and eat her!" (Ochs 1988: 183).

These occasional reports of active teaching should not obscure the fact that, in traditional societies, it happens rarely. Levy describes the contrast between traditional and "modern" childrearing in Tahiti. In the village situation, "to tell anybody what to do, is intrusive"[35] and reflects an unattractive, bossy personality. Urbanites in Papeete look down upon this attitude as hopelessly quaint and backward. They wean babies early, push them to become independent, and guide their language development. After all, they "have to get them ready for school" (Levy 1996: 129–130).

The upwardly mobile Tahitians would resonate to the sort of injunctions directed at American parents, who are warned:

by the time he enters kindergarten at age 5, it may be too late to catch up. You can spot a dropout as early as kindergarten . . . This is not a time when you can just let a child be babysat until they're more alive and more interesting . . . There's a real job for parents to do, and it's not just hanging around to make sure their child doesn't eat poison. (*Salt Lake Tribune*, August 25, 1992: A14)

My sister-in-law, Judy, reports that a child in her first-grade class, not as yet fully toilet-trained, single-handedly derailed the course of instruction for the whole class. Obviously, this child's mother failed to take advantage of the many aids, available from the internet or in special mall kiosks,[36] that our society provides parents to accelerate their child's transition to the student role. A recent article ("Potty on, dude"), for example, describes new technology so the parent can "go into the battleground of potty training . . . and win" (Moon 2004).

For Judy, this particular parent had failed the most basic test of competency: she had failed to teach her child how to behave in public.

The importance of good manners

Verily a [Muslim] man teaching his child manners is better for him than giving one bushel of grain in alms. (Fernea 1991: 450)

[Fijian] children of any age should be obedient, quiet and undemanding in the presence of adults. (Toren 1988: 240)

As rare as teaching is in pre-modern society, it does commonly occur in one area, namely, instruction in etiquette and social relations. Buganda (Uganda) children, for example, are expected to be socially precocious, seeking to acquire political capital from early childhood (Kilbride 1974). Parents may initiate "lessons" in good behavior even before the child has acquired "sense," for example, "Instruction in Tikopia in matters of etiquette and decorum in the house begins . . . almost before the child can fully understand what is required of it" (Firth 1970: 79). Ifaluk "parents should begin to teach their children at

---

[35] Borofsky notes from fieldwork on Pukapuka that, in status-conscious Polynesia, to seek instruction calls attention to one's inferior status (Borofsky 1987: 99).

[36] Information obtained from www.pottytrainingsolutions.com; accessed 4.18.07.

about two or three . . . how to properly behave . . . Other adults on the island will help with this instruction" (Le 2000: 218–219). The Rotuman child is subtly instructed in kin relations: "'Why don't you go outside and play with Fatiaki, he is your *sasigi*' or 'You must show respect to Samuela, he is your *o'fa*', are the kinds of things parents might say" (Howard 1970: 37). In Melanesia, Arunta children "are informed repeatedly by adults who individuals are and how they should act towards them" (Williams 1983: 202). The Hopi (North American Puebloans) provide "deliberate instruction in kinship and community obligations" (Eggan 1956: 351).

In the mid-1970s, Bambi Schieffelin documented a fascinating practice among the Kaluli (Highlands of PNG) whereby a mother sits her infant on her lap facing away from herself and, akin to a ventriloquist's use of her dummy, she has her infant "greet" passersby – a strategy to build positive relationships with potential caretakers. So, before the baby has uttered its first word, it's being taught appropriate forms of address and the rules of kinship (Schieffelin 1990). Kwara'ae (Solomon Islands) adults use a very explicit "program":

caregivers support an infant's role as conversational partner through triadic . . . repeating routines . . . telling the child what to say, line by line . . . Encoded in repeating routines is information on kin terms and relationships and on polite ways of conversing . . . important goal[s] for conversation in a society where *enoenoanga* (delicacy) and *aroaroanga* (peacefulness) are key values . . . for maintaining harmony in the extended family and descent group . . . [the child is led through] repeating routines until at about age 5 years [they] have gained mastery over adult interactional forms. (Watson-Gegeo and Gegeo 1989: 62)[37]

In dealing with their superiors, Fijian children must also learn correct posture to go along with deferential and correct speech. As young as four, the child will be expected to bend double in exaggerated respect as he passes by adults. Failure to show sufficient respect will earn the child a scolding, "if not a blow" (Toren 2001: 166).[38]

An emphasis on teaching very young children the rules of the kin structure and appropriate behavior vis-à-vis kin is ubiquitous in the ethnographic record.[39] (A very partial list would include the following: the Rotuman (South Pacific – Howard 1970: 37), Beng (West Africa – Gottlieb 2000: 83), Navajo

---

[37] While many societies believe in starting early on children's weaving themselves into the social web, they're usually not expected to be fully cognizant of all the nuances until adolescence. Heider says of the Dani (New Guinea Highlands), "It does seem safe to say, however, that achieving social structure competence takes place between the ages of six or seven and the mid-teens, and that there is considerable individual variation" (Heider 1976: 54).

[38] See also Brison (1999: 104). Toren also found, however, that children's and adult's perceptions of social relations may differ; for example, young girls tended to see men and women as nearly equal in rank (Toren 1990).

[39] An interesting counterpoint is that, among the Tale in Ghana, Fortes found that full understanding of the kinship system isn't expected before the age of twelve (Fortes 1970).

(North America – Leighton and Kluckhohn 1948: 44), Basotho (southern Africa – Demuth 1986: 75), Chaga (East Africa – Raum 1940: 172), Arab ("most pre-schoolers could recite their genealogies on both sides, going back five or more generations" – Fernea 1991: 451), and Japan (Caudill and Weinstein 1969).

Kpelle adults do not actively teach their children manners, but they are quick to censure – either directly or via the use of proverbs – a child for any of a range of behaviors and attitudes that show lack of respect or sloth. And they are keenly aware that a bad child reflects poorly on its parents: "If a child is very bad, it is hard for his father to eat. You can't go among your friends with a bad child because you will be ashamed. Such a person's ways follow him forever" (Lancy 1996: 96).

In Asia, modernization has not diminished the pressure to socialize children. In India, parents instruct children as young as two to use the "proper" hand for post-elimination ablutions (the left) as opposed to eating (the right) (Freed and Freed 1981). In Japan, parents train children to be deferential to adults and obedient, in contrast to American parents who train children to be assertive – especially with peers (Naito and Gielen 2005: 70). In a recent *New Yorker* cartoon, a mother, grasping her young son by the shoulders – with other children at a playground as the backdrop – earnestly implores him: "You have to be sensitive to the fact that other children are inferior to you" (*New Yorker*, June 14, 2007: 55).

American anthropologist Laurence Wylie's wonderful ethnography of village life in France, recorded in the early 1950s, reveals how important it was to inculcate a fine sense of proper social behavior – *à la table* – in children:

everyone considers it important for a child to know how "*se tenir comme il faut a la table.*" He must sit up straight and keep both wrists on the edge of the table when his hands are not being used for eating. An elbow must never be on the table, and a hand must never be below the table. If a hand slips down in his lap, his parents will say, "What's that hand doing, hiding down there? Put it on the table where it belongs!" . . . if he wants to be served he must say, "Thank you, papa or maman" after he is served. If he forgets to repeat the formula, his parents will pretend to be deaf and refuse to serve him until he remembers. (Wylie 1957: 45)

Wylie ruefully acknowledges that "Even though we thought that at home our children seemed normal in social situations, we saw that in Peyrane they were *mal elevés* (badly brought up) by the standards of any of the villagers, even the most humble" (Wylie 1957: 44).

It is ironic that mainstream US society, placed at the upper extreme on a continuum from high to low incidence of active teaching by parents, pays relatively short shrift to teaching children kin terminology, politeness, and etiquette. I think the situation is neatly captured in figure 11. The cartoonist

*"I thought we had the sort of relationship where
'please' and 'thank you' were implicit."*

Figure 11 No need for politeness

suggests that our emphasis as teachers of our children seems to be on creative and fluent language use and interdependence between parent and child
to the exclusion of more distant kin. While other societies spread the burden
of childrearing among a variety of individuals, to whom the child must learn
to relate in the "proper manner," we assign near-exclusive responsibility to
mothers. And the tactic these mothers are most likely to use to insure the
child's cooperation is to establish bonds of friendship, a process that is probably *not* aided by didactic instruction on inviolable rules of etiquette and kin
relations.

Fostering conformity and altruism

Ngoni adults . . . summed up the aims of the upbringing of children in one word "respect."
(Read 1960: 36)

The Romans thought that strict discipline in the home, including corporal punishment,
prepared children for the harsh realities of adult life. (Shelton 1998: 31)

The beating constitutes a lesson in [Pukapukan] social relations. (Borofsky 1987: 97)

Chapter 2 in the village parent's childrearing manual – where chapter 1 was on kinship systems and manners – may well focus on strategies for promoting respectful and altruistic behavior towards one's elders and/or betters. But before we look at several human examples, let's review the primate literature. In its rawest form, evolutionary theory cannot accommodate altruism. After all, "survival of the fittest" at least implies a kind of "every man for himself" mentality. But altruism obviously exists and the most likely explanation is that humans and most of our primate cousins benefit from belonging to a social group. "Primates learn their mode of survival by living in a troop where they benefit from the shared knowledge and experience of the species" (Poirier 1977: 4). That benefit comes at the price of treating our conspecifics well, particularly our relatives. The universal motivation to curry favor is called "reciprocal altruism": we are nice to those who are nice to us. For example, mutual grooming is universal among group-living primates.

Grooming denotes a willingness to invest time and effort in the welfare of another: what we would normally call friendship. Animals that groom together, look after each other ... female ... monkeys who are relatives groom each other frequently, and they come to each other's aid when they are in need ... much of an individual's success depends on its networks of relatives and friends. The latter are built up over years, sometimes from childhood, and especially by using the currency of social grooming. (Byrne 1995: 200, 203)

Comparative analyses demonstrate high correlations between neocortex volume and group size, use of deception in mating, amount of social play, and so forth (Barrett *et al.* 2002: 139). Since we tend to live in larger groups than other social primates, our subsistence strategies are more complex, and mutual dependency is greater, grooming just might not get the job done for us. So, several scholars have seen language coming to our rescue (Dunbar 1999). Language, in turn, can be the most important medium in transmitting to children a reliable social map of the community. Children are inherently social creatures, but parents may intervene to accelerate the child's social development, for example, in promoting the rapid acquisition of kin terms and relations. Some societies go beyond this in training children to forgo their selfishness in favor of socially sanctioned altruism.

Among !Kung foragers, the grandmother most often takes on the task of teaching *hxaro*, their quite formal system of exchange and mutual support. The very young child is given beads and told which kin to pass them on to. Whatever they are given, they are told to share it with others, while "their first words include *na* ('give it to me') and *i* ('here, take this')" (Bakeman *et al.* 1990: 796). Among pastoralists, such as the Ngoni, generosity is demanded of even small children both directly – forcing them to donate prized resources to peers – and indirectly, through proverbs lauding generosity and condemning meanness

(Read 1960: 155). For the Chaga, another Bantu group, "During seasons of feasting, one sees little troops of children carrying pots and moving hither and thither throughout the country. They are taking supplies to their relatives" (Raum 1940: 197). On the opposite side of the continent in Cameroon, Nso caretakers begin training children in appropriate public altruism early. They give them small items and then coax them to return the "gifts" (Nsamenang 1992). Even more subtle means may be employed:

a proverb might suddenly be dropped like a stone into a pond. The conversation rippled away into silence, and the boy or girl who had refused to share some peanuts or had been boasting began to wonder to himself: "Can that be for me? No? Yes? It is me. I am ashamed." No one said anything but the shamed one took the first chance of slipping away to avoid further public notice. The use of proverbs in this way [was] an effective way of making a child learn for himself and apply the lesson. (Read 1960: 44–45)

In much of Asia, crowded living conditions have been the norm for millennia, no more so than on densely populated Bali, and not surprisingly children are taught to control their emotions at a young age; positive emotions, fear, and jealousy should be hidden. If a child throws a tantrum, even if his/her mother "borrows" another child to nurse, the child will be ignored (Bateson and Mead 1942; Jensen and Suryani 1992).

Emotional restraint, modesty, and cooperation are also inculcated early on in young Chinese. Appeals to concern for maternal feelings, shaming, and ridicule are part of the socialization arsenal (Wu *et al.* 2002). "For . . . the Chinese . . . shame is an essential social and moral emotion, a virtue. Developing a sense of shame is . . . important . . . in becoming a full member of their culture" (Li *et al.* 2004: 794; Fung 1999). Equally important is the need – dating to Confucius – to instill filial piety.[40] This means serving one's parents during their lifetimes and respecting their wishes after death. Specific injunctions for the children of the aristocracy included the convention of regular but widely spaced visits to pay homage to one's father, during which one "could not sit, stand on one foot, or lean in his presence. Neither could they spit or clear their noses" (Colón, with Colón 2001: 60).

The requirement that children learn pro-social behaviors and avoid aggression or anti-social acts was by no means limited to the upper classes. On the contrary, long periods of poverty and scarcity in China have meant that an individual was often dependent on kin for assistance (Stevenson *et al.* 1992: 23). Common themes found in elementary school readers include "such pro-social activities as altruism, collectivism, and social responsibility" (Stevenson *et al.* 1992: 24).

---

[40] Inspired by Confucian thought, Korea embraced the concept of *Hyo* in the tenth century CE. However, *Hyo* emphasizes the *reciprocal* relationship between loving parents and devoted offspring (Kim 2007).

The Kaluli use teasing and shaming to socialize children and bring them into conformity with adult expectations. For example, mothers tease toddlers in order to discourage them from nursing. Also children are teased when they fail to observe greeting etiquette (Schieffelin 1986).[41] Marquesan toddlers are teased, criticized, and attacked without provocation by adults and peers. They are provoked to anger and then punished for becoming angry (Martini 1994: 79). Village parents in Taiwan tease and roughly handle children – playfully – to toughen them up (Stafford 1995: 52).

From Borneo to the American Southwest, children are warned repeatedly that improper behavior can bring the wrath of some harmful being:

Dusun parents regularly use fear of the supernatural as a means of insuring that children conform to expected behavior. Parents tell children folktales with themes of violence (inflicted on) a child because of some error in his behavior. (Williams 1969: 114)[42]

[Navajo children] are told that if they misbehave the big gray *Yeibichai* will carry them off and eat them . . . And in children's autobiographies there is evidence that these threats are effective – "The first time I saw the *Yeibichai* I was scared. I thought they eat the children, and I cried. (Leighton and Kluckhohn 1948: 51–52)

In Papua New Guinea, Bena-Bena "boys and girls are threatened 'in fun' with axes and knives and they run crying in terror" (Langness 1981). Children in Punan Bah village on Sarawak are threatened by various evil beings, including *penjamun*, creatures that abduct and sacrifice children, and by Europeans bearing injections. Adults claim "that children should be afraid . . . or they will never take advice nor pay respect to their elders" (Nicolaisen 1988: 205).

The historical record is replete with parallel cases and the roster of demons that were invoked to frighten children from *Labartu* (Assyria) to *Mormo* (Greece) was long indeed (Colón, with Colón 2001: 47). As recently as nineteenth-century England, children "were taken on visits to the gibbet to inspect rotting corpses hanging there while being told moral stories" (deMause 1974: 14). They were whipped by their parents "on returning home to make them remember what they had seen" (Bloom-Feshbach 1981: 88).

If proverbs, shaming, teasing, and threats of the bogeyman aren't effective, many societies prescribe corporal punishment. Freeman tallies the frequency and severity of child beating on Samoa, where they "believe in the unique efficacy of pain as a means of instruction . . . severe discipline . . . is visited on children from an early age" (Freeman 1983: 206, 209–210). Corporal or physical punishment is, thus, often seen as a legitimate tool in shaping the child's

---

[41] For a similar case at the opposite side of the globe see Loudon (1970).
[42] See also Mathews (1992).

behavior.[43] The Rwala Bedu (Syria) utilize an arsenal of physical punishments ranging from spanking with a stick (small children) to slashing with a saber or dagger (older children). They hold that the rod of discipline leads to paradise (Musil 1928: 256). Ainsworth (1967) recorded several episodes of physical punishment – for a variety of misdemeanors – in her observation in several Ganda villages (p. 113).[44]

Physical punishment is particularly prevalent in societies where the violence of tribal warfare, inter-village conflict, and wife-beating are endemic (Ember and Ember 1994). It may also be more frequent in modernizing or urbanizing societies, such as the Caribbean (Lange and Rodman 1992) or Turkey (Kagitçibasi and Sunar 1992: 85), or among lower-class populations in the developed nations. The collective pressure of the "village" shaping the child's behavior is missing in contemporary society and more forceful or explicit disciplinary tactics may be necessary.[45] Furthermore, while the father is generally absent from the childrearing scene, as "disciplinarian" he is a common feature of the modern family (Kagitçibasi and Sunar 1992: 82; Roopnarine et al. 1994: 16).

As we saw in chapter 4, among small, foraging bands corporal punishment may be specifically prohibited as it is in the West.[46] For example, longhouse dwellers in the forests of Borneo never punish children "so as not to scare off their souls" (Nicolaisen 1988: 199). Similarly, in the forests of South America "Piaroa society totally disallows the display of physical violence, and children are never physically punished, the children have no model of such action. Their play, although robust, is accompanied by very little obvious dissension [or] anger" (Overing 1988: 178).[47]

Summing up, there seem to be several strategies for shaping children's behavior. The most widespread and largely implicit strategy is to promote the idea that children should monitor and attempt to replicate mature, correct behavior. A poorly behaving or immature child is scorned or scolded (Erchak 1980).

---

[43] The Tapirapé rainforest foragers of Brazil engage in frequent agonistic encounters with other tribes, yet their ethnographer claimed: "I seldom saw a Tapirapé parent use corporal punishment except in extreme irritation" (Wagley 1977: 148). On the other hand, Lee Munroe's intensive study of four contrasting societies (Garifuna, Logoli, Newar, Samoa) finds fathers, at least occasionally, beating wayward children in each case (Munroe 2005).

[44] To us it may seem perverse to punish a child for *failing* to behave altruistically. We tend to juxtapose aggression and pro-social behavior. But an important line of research finds an association between the tendency to punish selfish behavior severely and a high value attached to altruism (Henrich et al. 2006).

[45] Undoubtedly the single most salient element in our teacher-training curriculum is learning to "manage" the class and discipline the non-compliant (Cangelosi 2003).

[46] In much of Europe, "spanking" by parents is now a criminal transgression, as it is in the USA when carried out by a teacher.

[47] I don't mean to suggest that corporal punishment is absent in all small-scale societies that rely on foraging or horticulture. There are reports of Yanomamo (Venezuelan forest dwellers) mothers clubbing infants with "a piece of firewood."

The Japanese seem to let children do pretty much whatever they want and then try and shame them by calling attention to their filial obligations (Lebra 1994: 263; Fogel *et al.* 1992), for example, "You're making mommy sad." Less subtle shaming is widely used in other societies.

We have seen that the use of mythical figures, like *Yeibichai*, to coerce correct behavior is common as well. This strategy is extremely efficient. In effect it's like casting a spell that works without further intervention.[48] Verbal and/or physical abuse is common, occurring "as a frequent or typical technique of discipline in societies in all major regions of the world . . . about 40 percent of the sample" (Ember and Ember 2005: 609). However, if a parent is to any degree dependent on neighbors/kin for assistance with childcare, they certainly wouldn't want to broadcast the fact that their child is unmanageable.

The rarest strategy, favored by the Euroamerican intelligentsia, is to "reason with" children. This may not be as effective at controlling behavior but, as a side-benefit, it does give some early preparation for being an effective nego-tiator. Reasoning with children accomplishes two goals. It is a way to manage children's behavior, especially when shaping more complex skills, and it also facilitates the development of the (parent-as-) teacher–pupil relationship, which we'll explore further in the last section.

But let's now turn this discussion on its head. What do parents do when they *want* their children to behave aggressively, as the first stage in their preparation to be warriors, for example?[49]

Fostering aggression

Small children sometimes threaten adults as an extension of the encouragement [Tongan] babies are given to behave violently. (Morton 1996: 211)

The Yanomamo – made famous as the "Fierce People" for their evident enjoy-ment of fighting and warfare – encourage boys to "be 'fierce' [they] are rarely punished by their parents for inflicting blows [on each other] or on the hapless girls in the village" (Chagnon 1968/1992: 126).[50] A child that is attacked will not be defended by a parent; rather, it will be given a stick and sent back into

---

[48] I remember one of my aunts very effectively using "what Jesus wants you to do," and "that's a sin" to control the behavior of my cousins.

[49] Not that there would be many societies that would espouse such an objective, but I do think many contemporary parents who use physical and verbal punishment in their interaction with children might justify it on the basis that "It's a cruel world out there." Also note that explicit, themed "training" of children for either altruism and pacifism OR aggression is uncommon. Most societies see children learning appropriate adult social behavior the way they learn everything else – through observation and imitation.

[50] The warrior cult is often paired with extreme misogyny, even abuse of women by men, hence boys are encouraged to beat up on girls. The Bena-Bena in PNG are a case in point (Langness 1981).

the fray. "This is socialization for the fisticuff duels that are so central to the Yanomami justice system" (Peters 1998: 136–138).

In southern Africa, Xhosa tribesmen terrorized their neighbors and defeated the Europeans trying to usurp their farm land. Preparing warriors started at an early age:

> In what is called *thelelekisa*, women will catch hold of the hands of two little boys two or three years old, and make them hit each other in the face, until the children get excited and angry and start lunging out on their own account, scratching and biting for good measure. The women look on with loud laughter. Slightly older little boys are given reeds or other soft "weapons" and encouraged to have a bout together; or an adult (man or woman) will pretend to fight the child with a prodding finger, and encourage him to show how hard he can hit back. (Mayer and Mayer 1970: 165)

Don Kulick describes Gapun villagers (Sepik Region, PNG) as extremely argumentative and assertive, constantly picking fights and abusing each other. Without that understanding we might find his description of their socialization practices incredible. Like the Xhosa, mothers actively pit their three-year-olds (girls as well as boys) against each other, holding them in proximity and shouting orders to strike out at the opponent. Children are also encouraged and praised for hitting dogs and chickens, and "raising a knife at an older sibling will be rewarded with smiles and cries of 'Watch out, he's *kros* now'" (Kulick 1992: 119). Elsewhere in Papua New Guinea, the phenomenon is related to inter-village and inter-sexual conflict that is persistent and, often, vicious – including socially sanctioned rape, warfare, head-hunting, and cannibalism. In one such society, the Kwoma, children are verbally and physically abused by adults and each other, and their play is infused with violent themes. Adults continually remind children of the need to cling to kin while being vigilant towards enemies (Whiting 1941: 62).

The deliberate socialization for aggression cited in these few examples was, a few centuries ago, much more common. Inter-tribal warfare would have been more widespread and polities like those in Mesoamerica would have been dependent on a constantly renewed cadre of young, fearless fighters (Hassig 1945). Pacification efforts since European contact led, after a lag period, to the reduction and elimination of the socialization of children to be aggressive (Ember and Ember 2007).

Next we'll consider gender socialization which is much more common, cross-culturally. The third chapter in the village parent's childrearing manual (after etiquette and culture-appropriate social relations) might, therefore, be on socializing gender roles.

Socializing gender

[In the Kerkennah Islands] there is generally more ritual recognition of a male birth than of a female birth. Gifts to male babies are more lavish. (Platt 1988: 275)

In a few societies gender differences are of relatively little importance. On Vanatinai Island (formerly Sudest Island, southeast of PNG), egalitarian relations between the sexes means that "Gender identity ... is formed primarily after puberty. Children of both sexes live substantially similar lives" (Lepowsky 1998: 129). Among the Inuit "at 13 years of age ... sex distinctions took on greater significance, and young people were called either *inuuhuktuq* (boys) or *arnaruhiq* (girls). In the previous stage *nutaraq*, sex distinctions were not made" (Condon 1987: 55). At the other extreme are societies where gender is so important, it must be created through ritual action. In the New Guinea Highlands, "maleness, unlike femaleness, is not a biological given. It must be artificially induced through secret ritual" (Herdt 2001: 165).

Similarly, in the Malian worldview "children are born as androgynous beings," and only through circumcision (boys) and excision of genitalia (girls) can they become adult males and females, capable of reproduction" (Arnold 2006: 50).[51] Ceremonies – many involving circumcision – to transform children into adults will be reviewed in chapter 8. In this section we'll review some of the more subtle ways that gender is marked and shaped by the society.

Parents may act on perceived differences from birth. Commonly, babies are given gifts of miniature versions of tools they'll use in the gender-specific tasks they'll later fulfill (Greenfield *et al.* 1989: 203; Hewlett 1992: 234; Whittemore 1989: 88). Other rites include the Highland Maya custom of cutting a boy's umbilical cord over a corncob and a girl's over a grinding stone (Modiano 1973: 28). Among the Aztecs, a boy's umbilical cord would be buried in a battlefield, a girl's under the hearth (Shein 1992: 25).

In US society, observers have noted that parents are more likely to snuggle up to and comfort girl babies, more likely to toss boys around, and of course, girls will be clad in pink, boys in blue.[52] Girls only may wear "lace edging on their play clothes ... [or] hold their hair in place with a barrette" (Calvert 1992: 3). In Mexico, infant girls have their ears pierced to wear earrings. Rajput boys sport a black cord around the navel, and girls wear headscarves in imitation of their mothers (Whiting and Pope-Edwards 1988a: 221–222).

Genitalia are often treated as iconic representations of the "person-to-be." In Tunisia, male babies' genitals are displayed for all to see and their sexual potential is celebrated, while the female's are always covered. Sexual shame will be her first moral lesson and she will be discouraged from active sports to prevent damage to her hymen (Platt 1988: 280). The Haitian mother takes great care of her son's penis to insure sexual prowess; it will be stroked and given an

---

[51] Also the Dogon: Dettwyler (1972: 27).

[52] I was taken aback – but shouldn't have been – when one of my assistants – an anthropology grad – commented on the eve of her ultrasound to determine her fetus's sex: "If it's a boy we'll need to get a whole new set of baby clothes," implying that the clothes of her daughter – then fourteen months old, wouldn't be acceptable.

alluring nickname, such as "little pigeon" or "little goat." No such attention is lavished on the little girl's genitals (Douyon *et al.* 1993: 102).

Feeding is also reflective of gender roles and relative status. In the Kerkennah Islands (Tunisia), females are weaned and expected to become physically independent much sooner than boys. Even so, compared with girls, boys are seen to "be very difficult to wean" (Platt 1988: 276–277). In southwestern Ethiopia, Gurage boys are always fed before and more generously than their sisters. On ceremonial occasions, boys are invited to partake of food, girls serve but do not consume any food themselves (Shack 1969: 296).

Differences in the quality and amount of food are paralleled by differences in the way illnesses are treated. For example, in Hokkien villages on Taiwan, "illnesses contracted by girls were approached with a wait-and-see attitude, whereas similar illnesses in their brothers received prompt treatment" (Wolf 1972: 61).

Aside from clothing, food, and care, societies may accentuate gender divisions through ritual. In Tamang (Nepal) custom, the first rite of passage – for boys only – is the *chewar*, a ceremony marking the first haircut. It is performed by the mother's brother (Hogbin 1970a: 103, 114). Wogeo (Papua New Guinea) males have the distinction of playing flutes and

Each male must pass through a series of initiation ceremonies that begin in babyhood and end in later youth . . . to make certain that the boy will grow into a man . . . in his pubescent period they scarify his tongue to enable him to play the flutes . . . his first artificial menstruation . . . [to eliminate] the injurious elements absorbed from females during his infancy and childhood . . . cleansing the tongue renders it pliable and hence better fitted for coping with a woodwind instrument. (Hogbin 1970a: 103, 114)

Girls and boys are often subject to varying "tether lengths," meaning that the limits imposed on them differ. Giriama (Kenya) boys "spend more time than girls beyond the range of scrutiny . . . because the chores [they] do take them outside the homestead" (Wenger 1989: 110, 100). Tongan boys "are eager to move into the boys' huts, to be associated with the older boys, and to experience their comparative freedom" (Morton 1996: 112). Girls' behavior may also be subject to other restrictions not imposed on boys. In medieval Europe a girl had to learn obedience early as she was subservient to nearly everyone – her parents, tutor, husband, or, if she took the veil, to the rule of her monastic order (Shahar 1990: 166).

In East Asian society, "Under the principles of Confucian ideology, women [must] observe the virtues of three submissions: to their fathers, their husbands, and their sons" (Kim 1993: 188). Consequently, girls found themselves suffering under severe restrictions on movement and behavior – from an early age. Again, on Taiwan, a mother will severely scold or even beat a four-year-old girl who does something that endangers her small brother . . . She has heard from the time she could understand . . . that she was a "worthless girl," Wan-iu (a four-year-old girl) was sitting on a small stool near the well. A neighbor came out and said, "Wan-iu, let Thiam-hok (a two-and-a-half-year-old boy) sit on your stool so he won't get dirty." Wan-iu pushed him away and said, "No, you can't have my stool. Get away." Wan-iu's mother shouted at her angrily, "You are a girl! Give him that stool. I'll beat you to death!" . . . By age five most little girls have learned to step aside automatically for boys. (Wolf 1972: 65–67)

Katherine Platt, whose study of children in the Kerkennah Islands I cited earlier, observes that boys are encouraged in verbal dueling and their anger and impatience is readily tolerated. Aggression or any sign of strong emotion is discouraged in girls who are rewarded for being reticent and unassuming (Platt 1988: 279). A strikingly parallel picture emerges from Tonga where "boys' . . . cheeky and aggressive behavior is often given covert approval" (Morton 1996: 105).

Whatever contribution that adults make to gender socialization is amplified, even exceeded, by the child's peers. This description of Amhara (Ethiopia) childhood is quite representative. Peers, through hazing, mold wayward behavior. A little boy will be harassed and insulted for crying, for not defending himself, or for exhibiting soft or effeminate traits. And a "girl who shows signs of daring (k'obba) is mocked and hazed" (Messing 1985: 207).

The assignment of chores is another area where gender differences are highlighted, and we will discuss the various "chore curricula" in chapter 7. Scholars who have reviewed the ethnographic literature find great consistency in role assignments across cultures (Edwards and Whiting 1980),[53] which may be the reason parents, generally, are not expected to take special pains to insure their children adopt gender-appropriate behavior and tasks. However, suffice to note here that there are plentiful examples of boys strenuously resisting being asked to do "women's work," on the one hand, and, on the other, demanding of their sisters the same degree of deference and servitude their fathers demand of their mothers (Nicolaisen 1988: 216).

In modernizing, affluent Euroamerican society, toys were commonly used to convey messages about appropriate gender roles. In one study of portraits of boys (n = 325) and girls (n = 309) from the mid-nineteenth century, the boys were shown with a great variety of toys, especially those related to sports and the military. Girls were much less often shown in company with a toy,

---

[53] I had a personal epiphany regarding the inadvisability of assigning boys as sibling caretakers in May 2007 as I stood on a busy street in front of the Registan in Samarkand. Two boys were pushing baby carriages in the street, just barely out of traffic. The street sloped downward and the lead carriage-pusher began a game of chicken, releasing his grip on the bar, then rushing after to grab it as the carriage rolled away on its own. This game was repeated with longer intervals between the release and retrieval.

and, overwhelmingly, these were dolls or doll-related (Calvert 1992: 111–112). Nevertheless, at the turn of the twentieth century, gender roles were seen as dangerously indistinct. Mechling argues that: "The Boy Scouts of America... was founded in 1910, largely in response to the... crisis of masculinity" (Mechling 2001: xvi). A famous magazine cover also reveals this growing anxiety. The doyen of American kitsch, Norman Rockwell, painted the first of his 321 *Saturday Evening Post* covers in 1916. It depicts a scowling boy of about eleven pushing a baby in a pram. The baby's bottle is lodged in his breast pocket. His frown is provoked by the jeering expressions of two of his age-mates. The painting, on display at the Rockwell Museum in Stockbridge, Massachusetts, is captioned: "Rockwell addresses a widespread anxiety discussed in the National Press at the time, the fear of a general feminization of American life. This anxiety was prompted by a series of cultural shifts, including the women's movement... "[54]

Thorne's recent playground observations in the USA yield numerous examples of adults and children using teasing and shaming to enforce conformity with gender stereotypes (Thorne 1993: 52). However, with the Women's Liberation Movement, these attitudes began to change. Not only have the biological underpinnings of gender been denied, but cultural prescriptions for gender-stereotypical images have come under attack. Famously, the Barbie Liberation Organization in December 1989 managed to switch the voice-boxes in cartons of Barbie and GI Joe dolls before they were distributed to stores. Children who opened their soldier dolls on Christmas day heard them say "Want to go shopping?" while the Barbies came out with (in a deep voice) "Dead men tell no lies" (Greenberg 1989).[55]

At least some parents in the West behave as if maleness and femaleness can be rearranged at will. Extensive research shows these attempts are largely unsuccessful. Boys encouraged to play with dolls are no more nurturing than boys who are free to play with trucks and guns (Lytton and Romney 1991). Garrison Keillor(2005) sums it up nicely: "Little boys of sensitive, caring parents take the dolls that they have been given and rip the legs off and use them for pistols. It's just how they are wired."

A backlash – which probably also goes too far – has begun, represented by a recent mass-market book *Why Gender Matters: What Parents and Teachers Need to Know about the Emerging Science of Sex Differences* (Sax 2005). In Finland, where gender equality has a long history and the culture of schooling is dominated by women, the call of retreat has been sounded in pre-school.

---

[54] *Saturday Evening Post*, May 20, 1916: front cover. Information obtained from museum website: www.nrm.org; accessed 4.18.07.
[55] Information obtained from www.etext.org; accessed 04.21.07.

Earlier house rules for example, prohibiting war toys, have been abolished. When the rule that skipping ropes could be used only for skipping was abolished, the boys could use them for lassos and lianas, like Tarzan. Also one day a week, wrestling was allowed ... The boys ... report at home that now they can do "real men's work" at day care. (Husu and Niemela 1993: 63)

Worry about whether one's child will conform to appropriate gender roles is, perhaps, a minor issue for most modern parents – who have weightier concerns to deal with. What we will see, in the final section, is the emergence of a phenomenon that is almost totally absent from the societies we've been reviewing where babies are viewed as insensate. Among the higher echelons of contemporary society, parents, mothers particularly, hold conversations with and otherwise stimulate their wee ones. They are motivated by research and folk psychology that sees early interaction as critical in the development of cognitive and intellectual functioning.

Parent–child conversation

... conversational interaction is minimal with young [Mayan] infants. (de Leon 2000: 143)

The giving of reasons is a peculiarly Western habit ... and a habit important to increasing the "mindfulness" of schooling. (Olson 2003: 153)

It should be evident that a parent in the majority of societies discussed so far who engaged an infant in conversation would be seen as extremely strange.[56] Yet in the culture shared by most readers of this work, *failure* to treat one's infant as fully cognizant and an appropriate object of speech would be taken as evidence of neglect, if not post-partum depression. While Euroamerican parents *claim* to be training their children to be independent, in fact they "strip the infant of true independence" (Gaskins 2006: 289). Parents do this because their first priority is to train the infant to accept them as the primary mediator of their every experience. The infant must learn to focus attention on the parent who is directing, scripting, and pushing him/her into areas of endeavor where they might not go on their own. In short, the Euroamerican parent is interested in accelerating language and intellectual development, but to do this, she must first secure the compliance of the infant as a willing partner.

Subtle differences emerge even between our society and one as similar as modern Japan. The middle-/upper-class American mother, in talking to and stimulating her baby, acts on the belief that it is autonomous and eager to become a distinct social being. The Japanese mother lulls and comforts her baby

---

[56] For example, "it is rare for [Gau Island] mothers to converse with children even once they have begun to talk" (Toren 1990: 171).

(Caudill 1988: 49). She sees the baby as an appendage, "and psychologically the boundaries between the two of them are blurred" (Caudill 1988: 67).[57]

Recently, American child psychologists have fostered the idea of teaching pre-linguistic babies to use American sign language. Enthusiastic devotees offer dazzling testimonials which include the following:

Our oldest (now three) has a vocabulary more than most five-year-olds. Even our pediatrician commented on his vocabulary skills. But all of this is secondary to just being able to meet the needs of our kids. We know if they are hungry, tired, thirsty, or need a diaper change.

My son is only twelve months old and he can communicate what he wants and needs and is very patient with me by nodding "yes" or "no" when I am learning to understand his talk. No language barriers, and he talks better than most two-year-olds. Hurray for Baby Signs!

Considering how slowly babies learn even easy words like *ball* and *doggy*, let alone difficult words like *scared* or *elephant*, many months are lost that could be spent having rich and rewarding interactions, both for the child and the parent. (Acredolo and Goodwyn 2002: testimonials, 3)

In our society, it is customary to hold babies *en face* and to talk to them using a special form of language referred to as *motherese*. We respond contingently to the baby's reactions. Signs of displeasure, excitement, engagement, and distraction provoke nuanced and varied speech, including tone and non-verbal signals. In comparative studies, "American middle-class parents show the most extreme prosodic modifications . . . in infant-directed speech" (Fernald 1992: 399–400).

Additional research demonstrates convincingly that, when adults speak often to infants, they pick up certain linguistic skills, such as word segmentation, *earlier* (Thiessen *et al.* 2005: 68). The child's first words are marked as important milestones and vocabulary development is accelerated through naming games of various kinds. What is ____? questions gradually expand to the full panoply of Socratic interrogation routines.

This intense and varied early language curriculum is all the more remarkable in that it is totally unnecessary. Children become fluent speakers of their mother tongue in societies where no language instruction occurs – which is the norm.[58] Clearly Euroamerican and Asian parents are preparing children to be more

---

[57] Dan Freedman has undertaken numerous studies over the years highlighting the genetic basis for infant temperament and cautions that Japanese and American mothers behave differently, at least in part because they are responding to differences in the behavior of their infants (Freedman 2003: 226).

[58] Indeed, middle-class parents are so anxious for their children to begin communicating that they have spawned a huge "speech therapy" industry to accelerate the speech development of those whose speech onset and/or fluency is "delayed" (Quinn 2005: 479).

than merely competent native speakers. They encourage the development of narrative ability through frequent queries about the child's activity, including their subjective assessments: "mothers pick up on children's... topics, repeat and extend what their children say, and adjust their language... to support the child's projects" (Martini 1995: 54).

Toddlers are expected to hold and to voice their opinions! As parents seek "explanations" from their children, they also tolerate interruptions and contradiction (Portes *et al.* 1988). And this entire package of cultural routines is almost completely absent in the ethnographic record (Robinson 1988).

- Marquesan "children defer to elders, initiate few topics of conversation, and take only brief speaking turns" (Martini and Kirkpatrick 1992: 203).
- Fijian children are never encouraged to address adults or even to make eye contact. Rather their demeanor should express timidity, fear and self-effacement (Toren 1990: 183).
- In Israel, a stark contrast can be drawn between parent–child interaction in pastoralist Bedouin camps and middle-class communities. In the former, there is little verbal interaction between adults and children. Children are given directives and not expected to reply or discuss them. Meanwhile, middle-class Israeli "adults and children... engage in many lively two-sided conversations... around a great variety of topics" (Ariel and Sever 1980: 173).

Okagaki contrasts Turkish and American parent–child speech episodes:

At a major European airport, I notice a young Turkish family consisting of a father, mother, and two little boys. The bigger boy was trying hard to get the father's attention and to engage him in conversation, as he was repeatedly telling the father some things and asking eagerly, "Isn't it so, daddy?" The father was not responding; he was not even looking at the child. The mother did not intervene or respond in any way either. She, like her husband, was looking aimlessly into space, as if the children were not there... This behavior contrasts with Western (especially American) middle-class parental behavior. I have felt surprised and even frustrated at not being able to carry on an uninterrupted conversation with an American colleague or friend if a child was around. If the child says something, even while the other person is talking, the parent typically attends to the child, therefore tuning out the other person. (Okagaki and Sternberg 1993: 45)

Sweden is, perhaps, the most deliberately child-centered nation in the world. For Swedish parents the child is a "project," and they see the need carefully to arrange their children's lives, while at the same time engaging them in the decision-making process. In effect, the price a child must pay to negotiate its own agenda is to argue the case forcibly and eloquently (Dahlberg 1992: 133–134). Why then are parent–child conversations so critical in modern, upwardly mobile families and so unlikely elsewhere? Mary Martini argues:

Parental preferences for reporting, discussing, and analyzing produce numerous opportunities for children to hear and practice explicit, complex language forms (such as
grammatical devices used to clarify time, place, number and agency), and to structure
long text-like monologues. Familiarity with the oral forms is found to facilitate learning
to read . . . Children are tested on the grammar forms and vocabulary used to explicate
when, where, how, why, and whom; and on the formulaic expressions used to connect
stages and events in a story. Children with extensive oral practice in these features tend
to perform better on standardized tests . . . To facilitate understanding, parents relate new
information to children's existing knowledge and clarify how bits of new information
fit together. In this way, they teach metacognitive learning strategies of organizing new
knowledge and of relating new knowledge to old. (Martini 1995: 57–59, 45).

In the information society, successful parents aren't just preparing their
children to perform for the teacher, in a compliant way. They are preparing
them for something more challenging, namely to be academically successful,
in spite of the occasional bad teacher, negative peer influence, and emotional
or medical crises. Some make the extreme sacrifice of forgoing a professional
career to "home school" their children. The "successful" child not only does
well in academic terms, she is popular, has a level of talent (in a sport or art
form) sufficient to command a public audience, and is socially sophisticated.
And these nascent talents must be aroused and activated well before the onset of
puberty. If the child hasn't developed a clear public *persona* by middle school,
her peers will co-opt the formation of her character.

As we've seen, the child's caretakers in the village have, traditionally, allowed
him to reach the age of reason before raising expectations for more mature
behavior – that might require active instruction to impart. Exceptions to this
laissez faire attitude are sometimes made to insure that the young child's social
behavior doesn't offend or embarrass his parents. The child is permitted near
complete freedom to make sense of his culture and it is assumed that this will be
a long and pretty casual process. Socially, adults and children have very little to
do with each other and adults rarely feel compelled to serve as conversational
partners for children or to instruct them in any formal way (Super and Harkness
1986).

This comfortable atmosphere is severely altered when societies become so
complex that only a well-educated and knowledgeable bureaucracy can keep
things running smoothly: "schooling exploded in thirteenth-century Italy . . .
in 1333 it was decreed that public officials and judges must be able to read
and write to hold their jobs" (Olson 2003: 16). Civil service usually implies a
meritocracy which in turn implies formal means of education and assessment.
A new stratum of society is created, access to which may be open only to those
with merit. Families who aspire to place their offspring in contention must
adopt an entirely new approach to childrearing. It is no longer practical to wait
until the child is "ready." Training in self-discipline, the deferral of reward, and

verbal fluency must begin in infancy. The parent-as-teacher becomes enshrined as the norm and is viewed as perhaps the most demanding challenge an adult will face. As we saw in the previous chapter, experts proffering advice find a ready audience. Toys that facilitate the child's attempts at sense making are snapped up by anxious parents who welcome all the help they can get. Yet, on the downside, in the USA, a three-year-old may now carry the burden of failing to "make the grade" (Kusserow 2004: 81).

6   Of marbles and morals

Introduction

Girls [in rural Bolivia]... could play football but boys would be teased harshly for playing with dolls. (Punch 2003: 286)

One theme we've been pursuing throughout is the notion that high human fertility is facilitated by the child's relatively rapid transition from wholly dependent to semi-dependent status. Childhood, as a stage of development unique to our species, allows the child to develop slowly with little attention from its mother, freeing her to bear another infant. However, being a child does not just mean that she can survive well with minimal care from adults; it also means, in a more positive sense, that her life is filled with play activity. From the perspective of the harried parent, the child's deep engagement with playthings and playmates is a godsend. However, keeping busy turns out to be only one of a host of potential benefits conveyed by play. I see "play as providing a basic tool kit of activities among which various species, under varying environmental conditions, at varying points in the life-cycle, select to use, elaborate, and combine in particular ways to achieve particular ends" (Lancy 1982b: 166).

We'll take a look at the many facets and potential benefits of play in this chapter, while acknowledging its ephemeral quality. We start with what might be the quintessential "pick-up" game – marbles – and consider its role in children's "moral" development. Next we consider several extremely common types of play – object play, locomotor play, and "rough and tumble" (R & T). We consider whether their ubiquity might signal the presence of evolutionary benefits. In a section entitled "Gamesmanship," we evaluate the notion that human intelligence may be primarily social in nature and that play exercises and/or telegraphs children's Machiavellian IQ. Play is, of course, affected by environmental and cultural factors. The composition of the playgroup and emerging gender role differentiation are two areas where such factors are observed.

Play has also been analyzed as an avenue through which the traditional culture is passed on to the next generation. Even a casual observer will note children creating playlets that incorporate important cultural information and, more subtly, we can tease out moral lessons from the folk-tales, songs, and games that children are repeatedly exposed to. Cultural influences on play are also seen in the relative enthusiasm/disapproval adults display towards play, generally, and, more particularly, play that may be aggressive and competitive as compared with more egalitarian interactions. In contemporary society, a philosophy has emerged which proposes, in effect, that "Play is too critical a learning medium to be left to children." We examine the rise of parent-directed and -managed play. And, finally, we consider the "downside" of play, that is, we look at cases where society's valuation of the child – as cherub or chattel – leads to the *suppression* of play.

Marbles

Marbles is capable of infinite variation. (Opie and Opie 1997: 41)

I want to start this chapter with marbles because, as the great theoretician Jean Piaget discovered, the game captures so many developmental processes, like looking at the innards of a clock with its many gears and pinions. First we see the refinement of manual dexterity. Humans are tool users, and young humans, as a consequence, are object manipulators. In its most refined form, with perfectly polished and round orbs, marbles calls forth tremendous small motor skill and digital finesse. Then we see "gamesmanship" by which children manipulate each other to enhance both the quality of play and their own success. Lastly, we see the development of social understanding, of an appreciation of rules *qua* rules.

By at least the Roman era and probably earlier, children used knucklebones, which have faces or sides similar to dice, as projectiles to try and dislodge each other's stationary targets. In other words, the basic pattern of marbles whereby a player shoots a hard object at one or more similar objects trying to drive it or them out of a demarcated area is probably quite old. The use of perfectly round, durable spheres must be more recent as technology found inexpensive ways to produce them. Marbles, as we know them, are clearly shown in Breughel's 1560 painting *Children's Games*. In Adriaen van Ostade's *Children and Dog* from 1673 boys are playing marbles outside a tavern. Of course variations on the basic rules are being formulated even as I write this.

The lengthiest treatment of marbles in English was prepared by the Opies, the greatest child folklorists of all time, and published in *Children's Games with Things*. They document three basic versions of the game, but the variation in rules of play is staggering.

To the uninitiated, a game of marbles seems anarchic. The leaping and shouting is partly caused by excited partisans cheering the players on, and partly by the calls and counter-calls which decide whether various rules can be brought into play or not. This is instant legislation. First it must be decided whether the game is to be played "Keepsies" or "Lendsies". If a boy finds his opponent's marble is obscured by a stone, stick, or lump, a shout of "Clears" (or "Clearsies") permits him to clear them away. (Opie and Opie 1997: 42)

Furthermore, for nearly every assertive claim by the shooter, such as those above, the non-shooting player can, if he's quick about it, offer a nullifying call so that calls of "Clearsies," "Kicks," "Changeys," are cancelled.

No wonder that Piaget[1] saw marbles as a rich field to mine for clues to children's acquisition of moral standards. He was generally uninterested in the child's development as a social being, but his single foray in that direction aimed to elucidate what he called "moral development." In Piaget's view, for the child to develop "morally," he would have first to acquire the notion that society is governed by rules and then to transcend that limited view by grasping that these rules can be arbitrary, anachronistic, and changeable. He must be able to juggle two rules that may be in conflict or to read nuances in a situation that lead him to question the applicability of a particular rule. Piaget saw the urban Swiss child's gradual development as a marbles player as the perfect natural experiment to view moral development unfolding: "Children's games constitute the most admirable social institutions. The game of marbles, for instance, as played by boys, contains an extremely complex system of rules, that is to say, a code of laws, a jurisprudence of its own" (Piaget 1932/1965: 13).

Like the Opies, Piaget and his colleagues identify lots of variability in the rules and style of play (Piaget 1932/1965: 16, 17, 20). After documenting the primary dimensions of the game, Piaget begins to probe the players' cognitive representation of the rules.

You begin by asking the child if he could invent a new rule . . . Once the new rule has been formulated, you ask the child whether it could give rise to a new game . . . The child either agrees to the suggestion or disputes it. If he agrees, you immediately ask him whether the new rule is a "fair" rule, a "real" rule, one "like the others," and try to get at the various motives that enter into the answers. (Piaget 1932/1965: 25)[2]

Piaget teases out distinct age-dependent styles in children's approach to marbles. Initially the child plays with the marbles as interesting objects with no game per se. By about age four, the child can play the game, knows how to make the right moves physically, and understands the necessity for turn-taking. "The

---

[1] Jean Piaget trained as a biologist and did his earliest research on mollusks but, more fundamentally, he was a philosopher. As his intellectual biographer, Fernando Vidal, makes clear, Piaget saw a parallel between the cognitive development of the child and the historical development of morality. In particular, he would see religious fundamentalism – so popular in our times – as primitive, child-like, and, from his perspective, not particularly "moral" (Vidal 1994: 232–233).

[2] Interestingly, "Plato [thought] boys [should] be forbidden to make alterations in their games, lest they be led to disobey the laws of the State in later life" (Opie and Opie 1969: 6).

child's chief interest is no longer psycho-motor; it is social" (Piaget 1932/1965: 45). He is able to imitate the model provided by a more mature player. But he really has no sense of strategy or of what to do to increase the likelihood of winning. Then, around age seven, players focus on winning, even though their grasp of the rules – as revealed through questioning – is still vague. By age eleven, there "is remarkable concordance . . . when they are questioned on the rules of the game and their possible variations" (Piaget 1932/1965: 27). Nevertheless, the child still hasn't grasped rules *qua* rules. He still sees them as "imposed upon the younger children by the older ones . . . as sacred and untouchable" (Piaget 1932/1965: 70). But, by thirteen, boys understand the mutability of the rules (Piaget 1932/1965: 70) of marbles.[3]

Piaget did not observe (or at least did not report on) episodes where novice players learned from those who were more expert.[4] In fact, this is a rarely studied phenomenon – perhaps because in modern studies of children engaged in game-play, the players are usually of the same age and, hence, equally ignorant. But it is worth noting that, in learning to play marbles, even Swiss children follow the village learning model – no teachers, classrooms, or texts.

Children in Gbarngasuakwelle learn games through a multi-phased process.[5] First, they observe their older siblings at play. Next, they replicate what they've observed as closely as they can (drawing in the sand, manipulating stones, repeating what they've heard) but while still on the periphery. They attempt to join the game but are usually rebuffed as being not yet ready. Once they are permitted to play, they are usually forgiven for violations, and better players may self-handicap themselves. This attitude insures that play can proceed and that the novices will not be too frustrated. As their competence improves, learners will be chastised for rule violation – rather than being told what the rules are. At the last stage short of mastery, the expert players may then actually bend the rules in their own favor in order to maintain themselves as consistent winners. Finally, the novice learns all the *official* rules and will "call" a rule violation, thus completely "leveling the playing field" (Lancy 1996: 112).

Furthermore, like the Swiss marble players, I was able to plot very evident developmental trends within a particular Kpelle game and across the entire

---

[3] A strikingly parallel account is available from observation of Fijian marble players (Brison 1999: 112).

[4] A second issue left unaddressed in *The Moral Judgment of the Child* is the relationship between game-play and the development of these more general, multi-purpose cognitive skills or understandings. Piaget tended not to see any *causal* link between the child's specific experiences and development. For him, these emerging abilities were hard-wired but we should see them *unfolding* through the various pre-mature stages in activities like marbles. Other scholars have accorded a more powerful role to play than merely the display or exercise of cognitive skills (Sutton-Smith 1971). Piaget's marble players were also all male but Goodwin's study of hopscotch shows "that girls regularly test the rules disputing what can count as a proper application of one, and seeing how far they can extend certain rules to work to their advantage" (Goodwin 2006: 64).

[5] Somewhat similar observations have been made of US mixed-age playgroups (Freie 1999: 88).

village game inventory. For example, for the dominoes-like game of *kwa-tinang:* "Younger boys seemed to memorize each configuration because on each trial they proceeded a little further... Older boys showed signs of acquiring a mental map of the stones because they advanced in large jumps from try to try" (Lancy 1996: 105). *Kwa-tinang*, like many Kpelle games, utilizes stones, seeds, or other convenient counters or markers. Indeed, snapshots of village children often capture them "scavenging" for objects to incorporate into play activity.

In the next section, we will see that, even in the absence of manufactured toys, including lovely glass marbles, children seek out objects to manipulate and incorporate into their play activities.

Play with objects

A tendency to play with objects in childhood might then have the biological function of building an augmented repertoire of possible solutions. (Byrne 1995: 86)

Piaget can also be credited with calling the attention of developmental psychology to the young child's fascination with objects. From an early age, infants are wont to grasp objects, mouth them, shake them, throw them, and examine them. Indeed the child's changing relationship to the physical world, her perception and manipulation of it, forms the backbone of Piaget's entire theory of cognitive development.

Among primates, play with objects is not common and, not coincidentally, tool-use is also rare. However, among humans, the extent of the child's object play varies quite a bit. There are dangers inherent in free exploration by village infants and toddlers. Much of what they might discover lying on the ground is potentially dangerous. On the other hand, the child's tendency to play with and explore objects does have a practical side, for example, "if butchering was underway [in a Fore village], even toddlers could explore and manipulate the carcass, using whatever implements they could find" (Sorenson 1976: 198).

Objects designed specifically for object play – toys – are usually absent from the village. We find some examples of *older* children making their own toys (Edwards 2005) and capturing animals to play with (Fortes 1970; Shahar 1990: 238).[6] "Safe" toys designed specifically for very young children tend to show up in the archaeological record when societies become more complex, as the frequent examples from Egypt (Janssen and Janssen 1990), Greece (*National Geographic News*, September 12, 2003: 1–2), Rome (Rawson 1991), and pre-contact Peru (Sillar 1994: 56) attest.

---

[6] Actually, village children's play with animals looks to Westerners like cruelty or even torture and, in the West, might be considered a sign of mental pathology (Ascione 2005). Living in an African village in 1968, I rescued (by paying for it) a mongoose from its tormentors and treated it as a pet – just another example of my strangeness.

In modern, urban societies[7] there are warehouse-size toy emporia, and the plastics industry has afforded the development of toys that are safe, durable, colorful, and capable of an almost chameleon-like variability. Pre-schools offer a further cornucopia of often unfamiliar objects to play with (Pellegrini and Bjorkland 2004). These have often been designed specifically to nurture the child's development. For example, in Korea, "Toys that stimulate the baby's left brain are considered the most desirable" (Cho 1995: 148).[8]

Environmental conditions and the absence of durable toys may limit object play in many societies, especially in comparison with the play experiences of middle-class children. When we look at *physical* play, the situation is somewhat reversed. In the village there are few limits to high-energy, active play – especially of boys – while, in modern society, dangers associated with an urban environment and a more sedentary, indoor lifestyle may conspire to reduce active play sharply (Karsten 2003: 457).

Blowing off steam

... the function of play is to modify development of a portion of the brain that is involved in the fine control of motor output. (Byers 1998: 600)

One attribute of childhood that is so commonplace that it passes largely unnoticed is that children are very *active* – especially boys. And most of this activity is recognizably play. Early scholars had trouble reconciling the apparently purposeless quality of play with its ubiquity. If you ask children what they're up to, the answer is likely to be "nothin'" or "just messing around." And yet, when we learn that "Marquesans ... speak of children as devoted to play" (Martini and Kirkpatrick 1992: 205), this sounds a familiar note. Why? Most answers to this question hinge on the fact that the child is in a state of rapid development – physically, emotionally, and intellectually. An early hypothesis claimed that "animals do not play because they are young, but they have their youth because they play ... [which] serves to fit them for the tasks of later life" (Groos 1898/1976: 76, xix)

Pellegrini has offered a modern account of this idea, and he stresses that males are generally more active than females of the same age and species. He claims that males' greater activity – observed from the pre-natal stage onward – develops anatomical and behavioral systems that come into play in,

---

[7] The market for products and services specifically designed for (upper-class) children, including toys, books, pamphlets, pediatric medicine, public schools, began in the early 1800s and grew in magnitude. By about 1870 – the year Macys opened its toy department – toys had become a major industry in the West, at least in part because they were now treated as collectible, show-offable status symbols (Mergen 1992: 88). Public playgrounds date to the 1880s (Chudacoff 2007: 73).

[8] However, it is likely that manufacturers and play advocates have overestimated the potency of object play for fostering problem-solving and creativity (Smith and Simon 1984: 200).

later, male–male competition. The biological basis for these gender differences is revealed in part by the fact that females exposed, pre-natally, to abnormally high levels of androgen behave like males (Pellegrini 2004: 443).

While most scholars have focused on the long-term developmental payoffs to active play, a more immediate benefit might be: "If fat juveniles are more easily caught [by predators, then] to the extent that play behavior facilitates the loss of energy that would otherwise be stored as fat, it will be preserved by natural selection" (Barber 1991: 136). Not surprisingly, then, Bushmen girls (who *are* potentially targets of predation) were observed as much more active than girls in contemporary London (Blurton-Jones and Konner 1973: 695).

In Rwanda's Parc des Volcans, the Mahoro mountain gorilla troop first habituated by Dian Fossey now has five juveniles and play – especially after the morning feeding session – is almost non-stop. One juvenile repeatedly twirled himself in a circle, falling down in apparent dizziness. I observed youngsters climbing up and down a slender 5 meter high tree and exaggerating the swaying motion as they climbed, dangling from either hand or foot while grasping and waving large leaves they'd removed. Interspersed with solo locomotor play on the ground and in the tree was chasing and rough and tumble play, involving as many as three players at a time. They pulled each other off the tree, dropped, bomb-like, from the tree on top of their playmates, and wrestled in a rolling fur-ball. Trying to distinguish body parts among the entwined animals was impossible. In the space of forty minutes, the "jungle-gym" tree they'd been using had been utterly destroyed and the surrounding low brush had been flattened into a lawn (Lancy 2004).

While this juvenile circus is in full swing, older troop members quietly feed, ruminate, and groom one another. As the Baldwins note, adults tend to be conservative and cautious – guarding lives and cultural traditions. The young are predisposed to explore, experiment, and "take risks since they are more expendable according to bioenergetic calculations" (Baldwin and Baldwin 1977: 368).

Jane Goodall acknowledges that young chimps take real risks as they engage in games of aerial tag and suggests that what they are learning about their environment offsets the costs, and further that, at an early age, their bodies can better withstand and recover from a bad fall (van Lawick-Goodall 1976a: 159). Lynn Fairbanks sees subtler and potentially more important payoffs in active juvenile play:

the ontogenetic timing of play coincides with periods of maximal plasticity and responsiveness to experience in neurological development . . . play acts to promote adult competence in physical coordination, fighting, or food handling through its effects on the developing nervous system . . . play promotes physical coordination by influencing early neuromuscular development. (Fairbanks 1995: 142)[9]

---

[9] Many of these ideas were first advanced by Robert Fagen (1981).

Mbuti children who live in the Central African rainforest are also partial to aerial play – as are children everywhere it seems – think *jungle gym*. By age four children are already adept at tree-climbing – a favorite pastime. As they grow stronger, they use vines to haul themselves up into the forest canopy, but the "idea is never just to get to the top, it is to know more about the tree" (Turnbull 1978: 183).

Similarly, boys in Gbarngasuakwelle use a home-made *baling* to practice climbing palm trees. After some years of intermittent practice, some will be skilled enough to scale the entire trunk to harvest/tend palm nut and palm wine crops (Lancy 1996: 88).

In our society, various forces have combined to reduce the level of physically active play, but this trend is not necessarily shared with other post-industrialist societies. In Sweden, children are sent out to play daily, regardless of conditions, as "There's no bad weather only bad clothing." And, by comparison with Japan, American children's play is rather tame. Daniel Walsh describes his trepidation as he exposed his two children to the challenges of adapting to Japanese children's culture: "Japanese preschools are, compared to contemporary American preschools, raucous places, filled with loud rambunctious kids who run, wrestle, hit, roughhouse, and climb on and over everything... To be *genki* – an exuberant word meaning fit, strong, healthy, and physical – is highly valued" (Walsh 2004: 99, 102). American children in Japan stand out and receive intense hazing. Their Japanese classmates are much more active, physically, and more dextrous. They run and swim in endurance races and riding a unicycle is not out of the ordinary. Japanese children seem not to notice extreme heat and cold, and they are "expected to be loud and wild – their spirit is not to be quashed" (Walsh 2004: 105). Walsh's children adjusted to Japanese expectations and, eventually, they "sat still less and exercised more" (Walsh 2004: 103).

Aside from physical fitness and escape from predators, the give and take of playful interaction may serve social functions as well. One of the most commonly observed types of active play is characterized as "rough and tumble" (R & T) or play-fighting. This form of play has been heavily studied in the USA and Europe and there is considerable speculation on its function.

Constructing the dominance hierarchy

... youngsters seem to deliberately exploit R&T ... as a way in which to publicly exhibit their dominance over a peer. (Pellegrini 2002)

R & T play – a special sub-type of physical/locomotor play – is widespread among juvenile mammals, particularly primates. Although subtle, there are clear distinctions between play-fighting and real fighting, including the use of non-verbal signals such as displaying a "play-face" to signal a non-aggressive intent (Blurton-Jones 1967). In the Mahoro troop, older juveniles handicap themselves in order to play successfully with younger ones. In one pair I observed, the older player was more than twice the size of his partner but, nevertheless, consistently took the subordinate's role.[10] On the other hand, among peers, competition is keener and, while winners consistently relinquish their advantage so play can proceed, a dominance hierarchy or pecking order will be constructed through these bouts.

More generally, "codes of social conduct... regulate what is permissible during mammalian play, and... these codes might [point to] the evolution of social morality" (Dugatkin and Bekoff 2003: 209). Weisfeld argues that competition – usually involving the display of physical prowess – is extremely common among the young. And the outcome of this competition is a linear ranking or dominance hierarchy (Weisfeld 1999: 55).[11]

Symons has spent a great deal of time observing and reflecting on play-fighting[12] in which he sees clear precursors of the "moves" employed by adult males as they fight – for real – for their place in the dominance hierarchy. He has also noted that the likelihood that one will see play-fighting in juveniles of the species is easily predicted by knowledge of mating patterns. Where an alpha male controls a cluster of females – his harem – such as among mountain gorillas, play-fighting, and a well-established rank order among adults, will be evident (Symons 1978).

In some societies, play may take on attributes that extend beyond the need to blow off steam. For example, in Borneo, where inter-village warfare and head-hunting were once common, play-fighting may evolve into a "war with words," including taunts and insults between two groups from neighboring, hostile villages (Williams 1969: 82). In the Brazilian rainforest, where inter-group warfare is endemic,

Xavante boys... form two teams painted red and black, each with the symbol of his clan on his face. The two boys who will fight one another are chosen by the oldest boys of each clan. The children hit each other's arms with the roots of a strong grass until one of them gives up... among the Camauiri, a turbulent form of play is the *Jawari*. One of the participants throws his spear towards a fence made of poles, trying to knock down the poles. The other players are lined up behind the fence and are not allowed to leave. As the "pitcher" knocks the poles down, the other players become easy targets and must then divert the spears, without moving their feet. Some are hurt during this game. (Gosso *et al.* 2005: 232)

In two Zapotec-speaking communities in southern Mexico, children from a village with high levels of adult violence spent significantly more time engaged

---

[10] This widely observed phenomenon is called "self-handicapping" (Fagen 1981).

[11] By age three, children's cognitive repertoire seems to allow them to compete – to compare their performance with that of others (Stipek 1995).

[12] See also Aldis (1975).

in play-fighting than did children from the community where adult violence was uncommon (Fry 1987). And in a study Millard Madsen and I carried out in the Highlands of Papua New Guinea, a game (which Madsen had invented) that could be played cooperatively or competitively easily revealed whether the child players were from the same clan, distant, antagonistic clans, or intermediate. Boys from the same clan always played cooperatively whereby each of two players took turns winning a coin and, vice versa, boys from potential enemy groups never made a cooperative move (Lancy and Madsen 1981).[13] And, in Africa, anthropologists have noted an elaboration of play-fighting, including the use of weapons, in societies where warfare was endemic or at least a vivid memory (Read 1960).

Play-fighting can also be seen as the ontogenetic and historical precursor to certain types of *sport*. Simon Ottenberg has documented the high level of organization and ceremony associated with wrestling in Igbo (Nigeria) society. At the youngest grade (e.g. fifteen to eighteen = *Mkpufumgba*), participation is widespread but, gradually, at each higher age grade, the ranks of competitors are thinned. Its importance cannot be underestimated. "Wrestling is not only a sport, it is intimately associated with age organizations . . . peer group activity . . . [and, formerly] . . . directly related to warfare" (Ottenberg 1989: 85, 86). Sport-style wrestling, where the winners of the major competitions are treated as folk heroes and extremely attractive mates, is also found in northeast Nigeria (Stevens 1996: 99). Of course, most of the sports we think of as particularly Olympian – javelin, track, boxing, archery, and, of course, wrestling – have their origin in combat – or hunting. *Inzema* is a Xhosa game in which boys in teams compete to spear a rolling gourd (Wilkins 2002: 36). A similar game, played in Botswana, has been statistically linked to the degree of dependence on hunting for subsistence (Bock and Johnson 2004).[14]

A recent review suggests that, in American society, the dominance hierarchy is alive and well. R & T play and competitive sports continue to function as one of the primary means of establishing rank among males (Pellegrini 2004: 441–442). While these results were obtained in the USA, they are consistent with findings from numerous other societies (Whiting and Pope-Edwards 1988b: 289).[15]

There are less obvious but perhaps even more important play activities through which the dominance hierarchy may be constructed, including group fantasy play or make-believe (Goodwin 2006: 157) and games of strategy.

---

[13] In an earlier study, Madsen had shown that suburban kids in the USA rarely played cooperatively while Mexican village children rarely competed (Madsen 1971).

[14] Parker also credits "aimed throwing" with contributing to the boy's physical development as "at puberty . . . hormones stimulate specially primed cartilage cells in the shoulder" (Parker 1984: 278).

[15] Aside from R & T and sports such as wrestling, highly competitive games of strategy may also contribute to the structuring of the dominance hierarchy (Adriani 1951/1997).

Gamesmanship

Playing games is a very old and widespread form of learning. (Coleman 1976: 460)

For me, personally, the quintessential game is not marbles but *mancala*.

"Mancala" is an Arabic word that refers to a group of games often called "count and capture" or "pit and pebble" games [which] date back to ancient times... All mancala games involved scooping up playing pieces and dropping them around a board. Seeds were often used as playing pieces and the move was called "sowing." (Wilkins 2002: 22)

The Kpelle name for the game is *malang*. I emulated the young men in the village and, volunteering as a novice player, subjected myself to the withering scorn of older men who were expert players. There's little doubt that, because older men are the experts and own the boards, *malang* provides an excellent occasion to reinforce the village's social order. Its popularity in Gbarngasuak-welle had diminished.[16] At one time, my informants said, you could tell a man's status from the size and quality of his *malang* board. Nevertheless, there is no other village activity that demands the degree of complex place-keeping and arithmetic skill as this game.[17]

In one version,[18] a player may choose to scoop the seeds out of a cup on his side and keep them in his hand (rather than distributing them), continuing on several successive turns. When opportunity knocks, he'll play out all the seeds from his hand. The player can't count the seeds without his opponent counting them too, so he has to keep a tally, in his head, of how many seeds he has cached. Furthermore, he must be able to determine, at a glance, how the outcome will look after he has distributed his seeds. In a winning play, the very last seed distributed will bring the total in that cup to two or three. The winner captures those seeds and, if the next-to-last cup has two or three, he captures those and so on. In a real *coup*, the player has calculated perfectly and all the cups contain two or three at the end of his move and he captures them all.

As a boy, the future *malang* champ passes through a lengthy curriculum of simpler games from a large corpus (Lancy 1996: 95–109). Many games involve hiding, guessing, and memory, or using seeds, stones, or bones as counters, projectiles, dice, and place-markers. In fact the Kpelle have an entire

---

[16] Young men are, increasingly, taking up introduced games such as Ludo, checkers, and card games (Lancy 1996: 186), and women are prevented from playing the game. Referring to *mancala* in another African society: "Young girls were warned that their breasts would not develop, and no men would marry them [if they played the game]. Thus the men were assured that the game would not distract the women and girls from their assigned chores in the field and the home" (Zaslavsky 1973: 124).

[17] For a thorough and fascinating discussion of Kpelle mathematics, see Gay and Cole (1967).

[18] The most comprehensive work on the variations of the game, as played in West Africa, is Retschitzki (1990).

Figure 12 Stone play in Gbarngasuakwelle

category of games called *Koni-pele* or stone play and it includes at least ten distinct games of increasing complexity (Lancy 1996: 101–107).

Aside from any physical or cognitive skills that may be enhanced during play, numerous observers have noted the honing of what we might call diplomatic skills. For example, "Word games are . . . contests of memory, wit and fluency . . . [that] practice skills of verbal combat that are highly important in the political arena" (Parker 1984: 282).

Wenger sees, in boys' play, opportunities to develop the talents and character associated with the Giriama (Kenya) role of *mwenye mudzi*, or patriarch (Wenger 1989: 102). Note that we see Giriama *boys* improving their "gamesmanship," not girls, and one recent review shows that

as males' facility with and engagement in games increases with time, girls' actually decreases. Girls tend to interact with other girls in rather sedentary ways. Relatedly, game facility does not predict girls' peer status . . . Instead of exhibiting competitiveness in their interactions with each other, girls express relatively high levels of positive affect and nurturance. (Pellegrini 2004: 443)

Earlier research by Lever found several consistent differences between the play of US boys and girls. Specifically, girls' play tends to be more spontaneous and less rule-bound, playgroups are smaller, and girls are much less likely to display aggression (Lever 1978a; 1978b). Low adds some further observations regarding gender from the cross-cultural record, namely, that compared with girls, boys play in larger groups, more competitively, and for longer periods.[19] Play bouts last so long, apparently, because of frequent disputes regarding the rules. Indeed, it almost seems that "the negotiation of rules was as important as the game itself ... [whereas, among] girls, the occurrence of a dispute tended to end the game" (Low 1989: 318).

Candy Goodwin's insightful studies of contemporary American girls at play find considerable exception to these generalizations, at least with respect to non-white girls.[20] She observes both Hispanic and African American girls who are intensely competitive in hopscotch and well equipped to contest not only the game itself but the rules of play – much like the marbles players described earlier. These feisty girls "patrol the boundaries of their play space from boys' intrusions, delimiting their territory" (Goodwin 1998: 39). She writes:

Conflict about rules and fouls is embedded within a larger participation framework visibly constituted through playfulness and laughter. Instead of breaching relationships, the disputes engendered by the game are a central part of the fun of playing it. Rather than treating conflict and cooperation as a bipolar dichotomy, the girls build complex participation frameworks in which disputes, with their rich possibilities for cognitive organization ... are embedded within a larger ethos of playfulness. (Goodwin 1998: 25)

In comparative research on children's gamesmanship in eastern Nigeria (Igbo) and the USA (Indiana), American players were almost twice as likely as Igbo players to argue for variance to the rules or an outright rule change when things didn't go their way (Nwokah and Ikekonwu 1998: 66) – budding attorneys all! On the other hand, throughout Nigeria, it is common for losers or those whose performance is sub-par to be smacked, pinched, or beaten by the other players – of both sexes. Observers note that "roughness of play in games teaches the child emotional self-control in public even if in pain or disoriented" (Nwokah and Ikekonwu 1998: 70).

---

[19] In November 2006, I observed numerous all-male playgroups roaming throughout public areas in Shibam, a large, traditional town in the Hadramwt, Yemen. This contrasts with the single group of four girls I observed, demurely playing cards on a "stoop" attached to the house.

[20] I wonder if the findings of marked differences in play, even for Anglo children, will prevail. As Hine notes: "In 1972, the year Title IX was enacted, about one high school girl in twenty-seven participated in team sports at her school. By 1997, that figure had risen to one girl in three ... athleticism has become a desirable female attribute" (Hine 1999: 288). Also, I haven't noted a conspicuous reduction in aggression and arguments regarding rule violations in female as opposed to male sports.

Figure 13 Hide and seek in Shibam

Richard Byrne sees the development of the social skills displayed in play as the foundation of intelligence:

the essence of the Machiavellian intelligence hypothesis is that intelligence evolved in social circumstances. Individuals would be favoured who were able to use and exploit others in their social group, without causing the disruption and potential group fission liable to result from naked aggression. Their manipulations might as easily involve co-operation as conflict, sharing as hoarding – but in each case the end is exploitative and selfish. (Byrne 1995: 196)[21]

Strong confirmatory evidence for play's contribution to brain development via Machiavellian processes comes from research on captive primate colonies. Comparing across fifteen species of primates, observers found a statistically

[21] The opposite of a Machiavellian intellect may be not stupidity but autism (Baron-Cohen 1995).

reliable positive relationship between cerebellum size and time devoted to social (but not to locomotor or object) play (Lewis and Barton 2004).[22] This relationship is probably even stronger in the human species, as our cortex is "larger than that of other primates in precisely those areas that support social competencies . . . such as language, a sense of self and the ability to mentally simulate social scenarios" (Flinn *et al.* 2005: 36; Alexander 1990).

This sounds like "gamesmanship"[23] to me! I would argue that games with rules offer opportunities to develop Machiavellian intelligence.[24] Indeed, Sally Nerlove undertook a seminal study, in rural Guatemala, on the positive relationship between the child's "natural intelligence," as displayed in games for example, and the valuation made by adults in terms of assigning them responsibilities (Nerlove and Roberts 1974; Wober 1972). From that study, we might posit that villagers are more attuned to Machiavellian as opposed to, say, Piagetian or information-processing intelligence.

Gamesmanship might play a role in children's success in the all-important public school environment; for example, "peer popularity . . . is predicted by the time [spent] playing games and teacher rated facility in games" (Pellegrini 2004: 445). Games scholar Gary Chick posits another payoff for the adept player in increased mating opportunities. He believes that successful child and adolescent players are advertising many positive but nascent qualities to potential future mates (Chick 2001). These might include the ability to negotiate and to show restraint and cooperation; and, perhaps, aspects of physical prowess that forecast future foraging success.

As widespread as competitive play of various kinds seems to be, it is not universal. That is, there are various cultural forces that may constrain opportunities to improve "gamesmanship." For example, Martini points out that Polynesian children's extreme sensitivity to status leads them to *avoid* play that requires leaders or lengthy negotiation of rules or roles.[25] Children who attempt to assert their authority are rejected in favor of consensus decisions (Martini 1994: 80). More examples follow in the next section.

The playgroup

[The Mayan village playgroup] must include all those resident children who want to play, no matter their character flaws nor their limited capacity, either of which might constrain . . . play. (Gaskins *et al.* 2007: 191)

---

[22] Research on children's game involvement shows similar, if less definitive, trends (Fisher 1992).

[23] In a classic study, Maccoby characterizes exceptionally able business managers as astute "gamesmen" (Maccoby 1976).

[24] See also Boulton and Smith (1992: 435).

[25] Ironically, the studied absence of rank leads African-American girls to suppress "attempts to position oneself above others in terms of possessions or privileges" in their playgroups (Goodwin 2006: 160).

Three-year-old children are able to join in a play group, and it is in such play groups that children are truly raised. (Eibl-Eibesfeldt 1989: 600)

To build up one's reputation among peers, one needs worthy opponents but they may not be readily available. The nature of play is affected by the species and age of the animals but also by the ambient "climate" for play and the composition of the playgroup. An example of what I mean by climate comes from a study of play in two contrasting Bedouin camps. In a homogenous camp, members coexisted peacefully, and children's play was varied and unconstrained. A second camp was more diverse, less harmonious, and "children were not permitted to roam freely or to enter the tents of neighbors" (Ariel and Sever 1980: 172). Even more severe constraints are routinely found in urban ghettos where mothers forbid their children from playing outdoors or visiting friends for fear of violence or moral corruption (Kotlowitz 1991).

And there may be constraints imposed on the *composition* of the playgroup. Margaret Mead noted in Samoa that toddlers only come in contact with those children watched over by *their* caretaker's friends. Thus the playgroups of younger children are indirectly structured by the caretaker's peer associations (Mead 1928/1961: 42). However, a more powerful social influence on play is the *size* of the playgroup.

In the "B" troop of mountain gorillas in aptly named Bwindi Impenetrable Forest, there were only two juveniles between one and four years of age and one kept close to its mother. Not surprisingly, I observed only a few minutes of desultory, solo play as contrasted with the non-stop play described above for the Mahoro troop.[26]

Many of our hamlet or village field sites in Papua New Guinea were quite small. Consequently, the playgroups we observed were inevitably of mixed ages which had a ceiling effect on play complexity. Games all had to be simple enough to be played by toddlers – tag and hide and seek, as examples (Lancy 1984). Further, we should expect to see fewer effects of gender on play and, indeed, in one comparative study, predictably, girls and boys from !Kung forager bands were much more similar in their patterns of play than London boys and girls (Blurton-Jones and Konner 1973).

Variability in playgroup size and game complexity was found in John and Bea Whiting's and students' documentation of childhood in six contrasting societies around the globe. For example, "the mixed age play of Gusii (Kenya) children was not conducive to competitive games with rules, however, and only tag and dirt-throwing contests were seen" (Edwards 2005: 90; Whiting and

---

[26] Sussman noted an interesting contrast between two species of lemurs on Madagascar. Among terrestrial, ring-tailed lemurs (*Lemur catta*), juvenile playgroups are large and active, whereas closely related *Lemur fulvus* groups have few young and, consequently, adults serve as playmates (Sussman 1977).

Pope-Edwards 1988a). By contrast, Lebou (Senegal) extended kin clusters lead to a relatively large population within a "family" compound, so playgroups may be relatively homogenous in age, especially if composed exclusively of boys. Girls, because they're responsible for sib-care, are more likely to play in mixed age groups (Bloch 1989).

In Gaskins' field studies in the Yucatan, she finds that close kin connections govern playgroup size rather than the overall village population (Gaskins and Göncü 1992). She observes small, stable playgroups tethered to the family compound. Older children, functioning as sib-caretakers (chapter 4), are under an obligation, therefore, to insure harmonious relations prevail in the group which means including even the youngest members in the play activity (Gaskins *et al.* 2007: 191).

A similar picture is painted of playgroups in Rakiraki village (Fiji) but with an interesting twist:

The resentment of older children towards younger ones was evident in the way children teased and physically attacked younger children when there was no adult around to intervene... While adults operate on a model of mature wisdom benevolently guiding ignorant babyhood, among children relations based on age sometimes degenerate into a starker dominance hierarchy (particularly among boys), with older children using their authority and greater size to dominate younger ones. (Brison 1999: 109)

In Gbarngasuakwelle, toddlers were usually herded together in a crèche-like manner and supervised by one or two older siblings. Consequently, homogenous groups – of both males and females – were common. Players who are close in age and hence matched on maturity and size are more likely to engage in more complex and competitive games (Lancy 1996: 112–113). Having made this generalization, I want immediately to note the huge gulf between the village playgroup and the kind of playgroups characteristic of our contemporary nursery (or more advanced levels of formal education, obviously) school. The idea of clustering as many as twenty three- to four-year-olds together within four walls is unprecedented in the annals of human culture. That this is now commonplace is a testimonial to the childcare profession and to the toy and youth furniture industries.

Another nearly universal constraint is gender related. For example, among Fore children in the Eastern Highlands of PNG, "girls spen[d] more of their time playing in the gardens and hamlet yards, often with infants and toddlers. They d[o] not explore much beyond these arenas... Boys, on the other hand, ranged much more widely in their explorations... Much of their time was spent in... more boisterous physical play" (Sorenson 1976: 191).

Girls, compared with boys, play less overall; they play closer to home (Edwards 2005: 87), and transition from mostly playing to mostly working earlier (Lancy 2001). Among the Inuit, at eight or younger "a girl was expected to interrupt her play activities to assist her mother with such tasks as cutting fresh ice ... and gathering moss" (Condon 1987: 55). By contrast, Igbo (Nigeria) boys' greater freedom to play mirrors the leisure enjoyed by men who "spend many hours in ritual matters, political issues, and settling disputes ... while their wives do physical work" (Ottenberg 1989: 49).

In the next section, we'll see that play can be viewed as an informal means to transmit a variety of cultural information particularly during make-believe. Make-believe play, introduced in the last chapter, is one of the most commonly described aspects of childhood in the ethnography archives.

Learning one's culture

... form of buffered learning through which the child can make ... step-by-step progress towards adult behavior. (Roberts and Sutton-Smith 1962: 184)

Like their Inca ancestors, Chillihuani children work at becoming master builders. (Bolin 2006: 64)

Adults everywhere seem to be at least mildly tolerant towards and amused by children's attempts to replicate adult society in their play. In Tapirapé (Brazilian) villages:

Boys spent hours shooting at lizards with miniature bows armed with bamboo splints as arrows. They sometimes played house and included little girls as wives. Adults roared with laughter when the children imitated quarrels between husband and wife.[27] And I saw boys and girls imitating copulation without being reprimanded by adults. They even imitated the male masked dancers. On one occasion two small boys dressed in small versions of the "crying bird spirit" masks danced about the village asking the residents for food. This was found amusing, and not at all sacrilegious. (Wagley 1977: 145)

In short, children's play appears to function as an oversize vacuum sucking up everything that happens in the village and transforming it into child-sized playlets. More generally, village life is captured in make-believe play. Throughout much of Africa, children will be observed pretending to hull grain using a make-believe toy or scaled-down mortar and pestle (Lancy 1996: 85 – as in figure 14) and, like target shooting, "practice pounding" is associated with a dependence on grain processing. Further, Bock and Johnson have found that children actually improve their skill through play practice: "play is an important factor in the development of adult competency" (Bock and Johnson 2004: 63).

---

[27] Peter McLaren recorded an episode like this in an elementary school located in a lower-class Toronto neighborhood. Two girls are playing with dolls (a GI Joe and a Farrah Fawcett). Georgette suggests: "Let's pretend we're married," to which Wendy agrees, at which point Georgette takes the GI Joe doll and promptly uses it to slap the Farrah doll across the face while shouting "That's what you get for talkin' to me like that" (McLaren 1980: 173).

Figure 14 Crèche of toddlers pretending to use a mortar and pestle

Meal preparation is probably the most commonly observed theme, such as the legendary "making mud pies." Esther Goody describes the richness and complexity of make-believe cooking in a village in north Ghana. Miniature kitchens are constructed, ingredients gathered, and soup made, all the while accompanied by singing and the construction of play scripts that mimic adult discourse. And, of course, the girls must insure that their play enfolds the younger siblings who are in their care. Boys have bit parts in these playlets as "husbands," and are limited to commenting on the flavor of the soup (Goody 1992). Gender roles are thus reinforced. On Wogeo Island in PNG, Hogbin observed this scene:

Wanai was now busily making mud pies and at this point begged Kalasika to build her an oven where these might be cooked. Gwa joined in the game, and, although no fire was kindled, the grubby mess was wrapped in leaves and put into the middle of a pile of stones. Wanai next made out that water bottles were empty and told Naibula to fill them. "No, that's women's work," said Gwa. "We men don't touch such things. You go yourself." (Hogbin 1970b: 136)

In a Sri Lankan village, social rank is also rehearsed in these playlets, for example, older girls admonish their "assistants" that "You must serve the father first and a lot of food must be given to him" (Prosser *et al.* 1986: 184). Goody and others consistently note how make-believe meal preparation easily segues into for-real cooking.

Centner describes what must be the epitome of make-believe in rural Congo. During the dry season, when children are free from field work, they build an elaborate play village, called the *masansa*. All of the youthful members of the community assume a part to play in what amounts to a non-stop daytime soap opera of village life. There are several families, with a "husband" and "wife" or "wives," and "children." Husbands build the temporary huts and hunt and fish. Wives prepare meals in pots that they have made, sometimes using sand as a substitute for cassava. They may utilize real food that their mothers have given them or prepare prey (small bird or fish) caught by their husbands. A "chief" is chosen from among the older boys and he appoints sub-chiefs to assist him. One boy will be selected to serve as "town crier" and another *l'hyéne* – the ogre who comes to the village to try to steal the children. The "policeman" who arrests the disorderly and puts tax defaulters in prison is a more recent addition to the *dramatis personae*. The town court, religious rituals, divining rites, and the activities of circumcision camps are all likely plots for dramatization in the *masansa* (Centner 1963).

While domestic scenes are most frequently replicated in play, especially when girls are in charge, the entire panoply of adult society provides script material. One of the most remarkable cases comes from slave autobiographies:

slave children played games of "auction" and "master and slave," in which a child would pretend to be an auctioneer at a slave sale while others played the roles of slaves crying and begging not to be sold or traded. At other times, one child would wield a simulated whip as an owner or overseer while the others would do his or her bidding. (Alston 1992: 225–226)

Wedding ceremonies are captured in make-believe; Zapotec (Mexico) children re-enact these ceremonies, including "dancing around in small semi-circles, while throwing out sweets and fruits to the wedding guests" (Jensen de López 2003: 6). The traditional Chaga wedding included bride abduction. This custom has become obsolete but "lifting of the bride" is still part of the children's version of the wedding (Raum 1940: 251). Even more dramatic is the script used by Mehinacu (Brazilian forest dwellers) children when they play *ukitsapi* ("jealousy"). Boys and girls find new partners while their "spouses" are away. When the spouse returns from fishing, he discovers his wife in the hammock with her lover. Furious, he gives his wife a mock beating while the interloper takes off (Gregor 1988: 113). When Lepcha children play at marriage, it "always ends in simulated copulation; if the 'bride' is another boy, the[y] . . . tie their penises together" (Gorer 1967: 310).[28]

---

[28] However, adults are not always tolerant of children's make-believe. Wogeo boys who carried out a simulated sacred initiation ceremony were thrashed when the outraged village elders found out (Hogbin 1970b: 138).

Also fairly common are descriptions of children – especially boys – drama-tizing various ritual activities. Tallensi (northern Ghana agriculturalists) boys "hunt" for mice and after they've played with their captives for a while, they "sacrifice" the "dog"[29] on a miniature shrine and ask to be granted success in hunting (Fortes 1970: 68). Mehinacu (Brazil) children produce an extremely accurate replication of the complete sequence of events from initial illness to the shaman's triumphant discovery of the culpable instrument of witchcraft (Gregor 1988: 114). In the socialization of future healers in the Kalahari and in Fiji, the process begins as early as five when little boys role-play the trance-inducing dance of the adult healer (Katz 1981: 62). From southern Mexico, we have a description of children re-enacting a funeral ceremony, complete with the ritual ablutions (Jensen de López 2003: 6). Parenthetically, many an anthropologist has seen her- or himself reflected (unflatteringly) in the play of erstwhile subjects (Bascom 1969: 58).

If make-believe is a popular daytime pursuit, then story-telling fills many a quiet evening. In the section that follows we will briefly review examples of folklore that serve to entertain children, but also convey important moral lessons.

The moral lessons in folklore

It is a time of amusement, reflection and learning. (Ottenberg 1989: 91)

Folklorists have amassed whole libraries of tales, myths, and oral histories from pre-literate societies. And a significant portion of these materials will have a didactic character with children as the audience. Romans used Aesop's collection,[30] the English used Mother Goose, and the Kpelle have *Polo-Gyee*. *Polo-Gyee* may be "real" stories with fantastic elements (a talking fish) mixed in or wholly fantasy but with anthropomorphized creatures *à la* Br'er Rabbit. The themes depict characters violating social norms and getting their just desserts, the language and events having a burlesque quality (Lancy 1996: 130–132).

There are a few cases in the literature of mothers or grandmothers telling stories around the hearth in the evening – one of the few occasions when adults spend time entertaining or instructing children (Lancy 1996; Ottenberg 1989; Briggs 1970). Even rarer is the Piaroa (Orinoco River foraging group) practice whereby a "wizard . . . uses story-telling, especially episodes from the mythic past to elaborate his moral lessons . . . [;] the tales tell of characters whose out-of-control behaviour leads to their own unhappiness and personal disaster, and sometimes to danger for others" (Overing 1988: 179).

---

[29] Mice are not considered appropriate prey for adult hunters, nor are they worthy sacrifices, hence they are transformed into "dogs" by the boys.

[30] Wiedemann mentions that the tutor or *pedagogus* would be expected to use tales and fables in the curriculum (1989: 145).

Another unique and interesting use of stories in a quite explicit way to "educate" children is found in the shadow puppet plays on Bali.[31]

The stories ... are primarily drawn from the great Hindu epics, the *Mahabharata* and *Ramayana* ... Children constitute the front rows of any audience, their attention being riveted on the servants who clown around and tell spicy, bawdy jokes ... the system of morality, together with the history and cosmology represented in the plays, is ... unconsciously adopted, and the molding of the individual to the social norms occurs ... indirectly as a pleasurable "by-product." Adults place high value on their culture and are fully aware ... that its continuity depends on its transmission to their descendants ... Adults ... explained that it is on the stage that such abstract ideas as rank, good and evil, or refinement and coarseness ... are made tangible. (Hobart 1988: 118, 133–134)

The role of story-telling in imparting values to children is very much alive in contemporary society as evidenced by a media sensation in 2005. Public Broadcasting Service (PBS) had been running a series called "Postcards from Buster" in which an animated bunny travels around the country visiting real kids and filming some of their customs (clogging, barrel racing). The goal of the series is to inculcate an appreciation of cultural diversity. Then, along came an episode set in Vermont on "sugaring" that provoked a firestorm of controversy and led to its censure by the government. The controversy stemmed from the fact that one of the children Buster visits in the episode seemingly had two "moms" (*Washington Post*, January 27, 2005).[32]

Proverbs and riddles also provide subtle lessons for children and adults as well. Riddles have been explicitly identified with the demonstration of cleverness and understanding of village "lore." For the Ngoni, riddles are "a test of intelligence and of memory" (Read 1960: 98).

Proverb use among the Kpelle is common and, not surprisingly, there is a children's game called *kehlong* in which typical proverbial phrases are rehearsed in a paired association contest. Children who play and learn *kehlong* will still need further experience to decode the meaning of proverbs. They will gradually start to figure them out in their mid- to late teens (Lancy 1996: 137–139).

Yup'ik (Inuit) children carve symbols on to a wet mud palette with a knife to illustrate the unfolding story. Among the lore conveyed in story-knife tales includes kinship patterns, gender roles, and community norms and values. Their tales have a more serious quality than those from Africa and are inevitably scary. Unfortunately, like so much of children's culture, this practice has been lost as modern media intrude into the village that once practiced subsistence fishing, hunting, and gathering (de Marrais *et al.* 1992).

---

[31] Children occupy the front rows during festival theatrical performances in Bengali villages. "Themes from these plays confirm the Brahmanical ethos ... powerful mothers but passive wives are often shown as the ideal" (Rohner and Chaki-Sircar 1988: 66).

[32] Article obtained from http://pqasb.pqarchiver.com; accessed 4.18.07.

In numerous African societies, children's play incorporates the always theatrical and sometimes sacred world of masked dance. In large villages, substantial cohorts of boys and, less often, girls form into voluntary associations to
construct costumes, including masks, derived from adult models. They practice
their routines of dance and song and, on appropriate occasions, perform for an
appreciative audience in the village clearing. Adults are usually encouraging
(where they may not encourage other forms of play). For example, "Each Igede
[Nigeria] village encourages young people to form children's music and dance
associations to insure that the society of the future will have accomplished
performers at funerals, New Yam festivals, and other ritual or social occasions"
(Ottenberg 2006: 123).

There is some moral ambiguity here, as many of the masked figures are
powerful entities that function to control social relations and individual behavior
in the village. Their identity is shrouded in secrecy, and they are under the
control of the most senior men. Nevertheless, among the Kuba (Central Africa
kingdom), "some avenues are left open for the acculturation of the young boys
into mask making and masquerade performance . . . the grading of . . . masks
into a hierarchy allows certain masks to be accessible . . . to children" (Binkley
2006: 113). Boys in the masking society will have opportunities to practice
mask-making in the construction of reduced-scale masks. Or they may construct
full-size but ritually impotent masquerade figures, which they wear during
informal dance performances (Binkley 2006: 106).

In Mali, Bamana boys' masking is just the first stage in their developing
understanding of ritual.

Groups of young boys would organize their own masked performance and they exhibited a surprisingly thorough understanding of how the performance was structured
and an understanding of performance roles appropriate to men and to women at these
events. [However, while] . . . boys understand that the rites, the mask and the various
emblems are sacred, they do not fully comprehend *Ndomo's* complex symbolism. The
full meaning of the various . . . masks, the sacred emblems, rites and songs . . . [they]
will learn [as] they are initiated into adult men's associations. (Arnold 2006: 61,
53)

Many of these reports are retrospective, historical. Even in the early 1970s in
a remote village, I found that I had to pull from people's memory playforms –
especially those involving the kind of children's voluntary associations just
described – to complete my inventory of Kpelle play (Lancy 1996: 107–108).
This loss of children's culture, unfortunately, means that the question of just
how much and what aspects of their culture village children acquire through
song, story, riddles, and masked dancing will remain forever unanswered.
The most I'm prepared to assert is that the lessons are predominantly moral
ones.

How culture shapes children's play

...there is little elaboration or introduction of variation or complexity during the course of [Mayan children's] play. Scripts and roles are repeated over and over, almost ritualized. (Gaskins and Göncü 1992: 32)

The very ethos of the culture may dictate the nature of play. Earlier, I cited Martini's point that, in Polynesia, the extreme salience of inherited rank – even among children – all but nullified playful activities where status is contested. Elsewhere in Oceania, one finds examples of the other extreme, societies that are so egalitarian that, in children's play, "Competitiveness is almost never in evidence" (Hogbin 1970b: 135). Patricia Draper describes !Kung children throwing a weighted feather in the air and, as it floats down, they strike it with a stick or flick it back up into the air. The "game", called *zeni*, is played solo, and children make no attempt to compare skill or success (Draper 1976: 203).

A few societies value harmonious relations among themselves and with outsiders.[33] In these cases, R & T play is rare or attenuated. Children in Semai subsistence-farming communities in west central Malaysia, for example, rarely see aggression and one of the few times an adult will intervene in children's play is to curb fighting. R & T play is extremely mild: "two children, often of disparate sizes, put their hands on each other's shoulders and wrestle, giggling, but never quite knocking each other over ... [and] pairs of children in the 2 to 12-year age range flail at each other with sticks, but stop just before hitting each other" (Fry 2005: 68). Similarly, among the Chewong, as children play, "competition is absent and personal excellence is not commented upon ... the individual is subordinated to the society" (Howell 1988: 160). In Israel, the *kibbutz* was created as a utopian alternative to the competition and status differentials inherent in modern society. Not surprisingly, a study of children's games revealed a bias towards egalitarian outcomes – no winners, no losers (Eifermann 1971)!

Another lens we can use to view the role of culture is the dolls children play with. We expect make-believe to include dolls, but in the village, girls play with *real* dolls, as caretakers of their siblings "by adulthood they care for and handle infants with ease and expertise" (Poirier 1977: 16). Among the bourgeoisie, play mothering requires the use of dolls. The doll is arguably the most widely found toy and the range of materials used and designs employed is immense. From rags tied into a shapeless bundle to high-tech baby dolls that produce a babble of baby-talk, wet themselves, and eagerly move their limbs, the variety is fascinating (see figures 15–17).

One of my favorite dolls is the faceless doll favored by the Amish who take the biblical proscription against graven images to heart. Also of interest

---

[33] At least twenty-five, according to www.peacefulsocieties.org; accessed 4.18.07.

Figure 15 Amish doll

Figure 16 Egyptian raffia doll

Figure 17 Roman ceramic gladiator

is the fact that, while baby dolls seemed to have been a universal adjunct to Roman girls' play, lower-class girls had infant dolls which they mock nursed, comforted, and cleansed while upper-class girls, whose future as adults would *not* include childcare, dressed and primped the ancient equivalent of Barbie (Wiedemann 1989: 149–150). In figure 16 is a doll from a second millennium BCE upper-class *Egyptian* tomb. The "big hair" suggests its primary purpose. Roman boys had dolls (or should I say "action figures?") as well, such as a terracotta gladiator with articulated arms.[34]

By the latter half of the nineteenth century in America, dolls were being provided by bourgeois parents with the stated intention of introducing their daughters to principles of the culture such as fashion, etiquette, and polite gatherings like housewarmings and tea parties (Formanek-Brunell 1992: 114–116).

In the examples of make-believe discussed so far, children may seem to be creating a carbon copy, in miniature, of their society. However, as they repeat certain scenes over and over, they are exploring the sociolinguistic and psychological infrastructure of common social relationships found in their community. Hence, the anthropologist is not surprised to find two sisters

---

[34] This type of gladiator was referred to as a "murmillo," *c.*100 CE.

role-playing sisterhood (Hardman 1980: 86). Nevertheless, we find considerable cross-cultural variation in the amount, content, and purpose of make-believe. And, as we have seen so often, the most dramatic differences occur when we compare children's play in traditional versus modern, urban societies.

In Power's extensive review, he finds: "children's play in traditional cultures involves imitation of adult behavior in traditional roles and rarely involves fantastic transformations . . . [or] character roles that the child will seldom, if ever, enact or encounter in later life" (Power 2000: 272).[35] Or when Lepcha "children play together it is always an imitation of adult life" (Gorer 1967: 309). In a very recent comparative study of make-believe play in several Brazilian communities, the authors found that, in a traditional Indian village, children had much less time for play and play themes reflected village life, whereas in the wealthier, more urbanized samples, children's play was more extensive and creative – perhaps strengthening abstract and symbolic thought (Morais and Gosso 2003).

Sarah Smilansky published an important study of Israeli children's play forty years ago that uncovered a striking disparity in the amount and complexity of make-believe as a function of social class and ethnicity. Poorer, ethnic minority children played less overall and less imaginatively than middle-class children and this relationship predicted intellectual development and school readiness (Smilansky 1968).[36] In a similar study undertaken in the USA, we found that middle-class white children incorporated a wide range of male role models into their play mirroring the number and diversity of employed adult males in the community. Just the reverse was found in a poor African-American community (Lancy 1982a). Generally speaking, however, for modern children, much of the "culture" may be hidden from view. Hence, television becomes their "window on society, their village square . . . what they see on the screen . . . they incorporate into their [make-believe]" (Harris 1998: 210–211).

Further, as Helen Schwartzman argues: "children's . . . play behavior does not always serve as a socializing . . . activity . . . it may . . . challenge, reverse, and/or comment on and interpret the social order" (Schwartzman 1978: 25). In contemporary society, the transmission of culture occurs largely through formal institutions like school, church, and Little League. Consequently, play can be less conservative and there is no need to reproduce the culture in play. Our children engage in just as much – even more – make-believe than the children studied by anthropologists, but the scripts and purposes seem quite different.

Since, in Euroamerican society, class status is at least partially contested, sociodramatic play affords many opportunities to develop leadership skills including explanation, narrative (elaborating a script), and persuasion (Martini

---

[35] See also Martini (1994).

[36] Similar results were obtained in a subsequent study: Ariel and Sever (1980).

1994) – precisely what Schwartzman observed in her study of nursery school playgroups (Schwartzman 1976).

Similarly, Jensen draws a telling contrast between her observations of Zapotec children's play, which includes little negotiation, preparation, and planning, and observations of Danish kindergartners (Andersen and Kampmann 1996). In the latter case, gamesmanship skills are of central importance. Jensen goes on to relate the character of play to the demands placed on competent adults in the two societies (Jensen de López 2003: 14). In Danish society, children's play, especially make-believe, is considered critical to the child's development whereas Zapotec adults see it primarily as a means to keep children occupied and out of the way.[37]

In keeping with these differing views, village parents think nothing of diverting a child from play to carry out a chore while Westerners lose sleep over the deleterious effects of television on make-believe play because it eliminates the need for children "to think up their own creative ideas" (Greenfield et al. 1990: 239).

Implied here is that imagination as opposed to imitation is related to the development of more advanced thinking and, presumably, greater success in school. And it's probably no coincidence that "good" students remain actively involved in various kinds of make-believe, including fiction and role-playing games like Dungeons and Dragons (Fine 2002) and Pokémon (Tobin 2004) well into adolescence. Play scholar Tony Pellegrini marvels that his "13-year-old son . . . along with two or three of his friends, spends hours engaging in pretend around Lego creations" (Pellegrini and Bjorkland 2004: 34). Computers can also facilitate the prolongation of fantasy play well into adolescence (S. Calvert 2003: 2).

Smilansky's (1968) landmark research spawned dozens of separate efforts to use play, particularly make-believe, as a vehicle to stimulate children's inventive, analytical, and reasoning skills. One such intervention project – evaluated as being successful – sought to replicate the "hidden cognitive curriculum" found in middle-class homes. "Toy demonstrators" visited low-income homes and showed mothers how to play with and verbally stimulate their children (Levenstein 1976: 292).

I see the gulf between the, largely imitative, make-believe play of the village and the socially and intellectually taxing make-believe we see in middle-class suburban neighborhoods and nursery schools as very wide. It is not surprising, therefore, that reformers would see an opportunity here to improve the school

---

[37] This attitude seems to be almost universal in traditional societies. One striking exception occurs among the Ijaw of Nigeria where adults pay a great deal of attention to children's make-believe, especially when it involves an imaginary companion. It turns out that they see small children as reincarnated ancestors and view make-believe as the child's interacting with the invisible representatives of the spirit world (Leis 1982).

readiness of children from the urban ghetto or Third World village. However, several researchers have uncovered flaws in this type of intervention research and question these strong claims (Power 2000: 277; Smith 2002). In fact, it may well be that more direct methods to foster the growth of academic and social skills in these children would be more effective.

Play is shaped by the ethos of society, as we've seen, and, in the next section, we'll examine the means and reasons for the *suppression* of children's play.

Suppression of play

Under conditions of food restriction, physical activity may be markedly reduced. One economy involves reduction in the level of play. (Barber 1991: 133)

The ideal [Zinacantecan] child is hardworking, obedient, and responsible; he does not waste his time in play. (Modiano 1973: 55)

Lion cubs are no different than domestic kittens. They're extremely playful, and yet, when their mother is off hunting, the cubs snuggle down into the high grass and, remain utterly still – for hours. Upon her return, they burst out of hiding and gambol about her gleefully. Were they unable to suppress their playfulness in her absence, they would be spotted and carried off by any number of potential predators (Schaller 1976). The threat of predation is probably one of the greatest costs associated with juvenile play (Baldwin and Baldwin 1977: 384). And this example should suggest to us that there's often a downside to play – ignored by those who see it as a kind of universal elixir for a successful childhood (Lancy 2004).

While primates are quite playful, in general, those with a strictly arboreal lifestyle are less playful than those who spend quite a bit of time on the ground. And when food is scarce, juveniles must spend either more time foraging or more time resting; in either case, their play-time will shrink dramatically. This effect – of a reduction in play triggered by food shortage – has been demonstrated, empirically, for chacma baboons (Hall 1963), rhesus (Loy 1970), and langur (Sommer and Domingo 1995) macaques, squirrel monkeys (Baldwin and Baldwin 1972), and humans (Barber 1991: 133). Not surprisingly, the death of the mother usually leads to a depressive state, and play drops off sharply (van Lawick-Goodall 1973).

Juveniles seem tied to their mothers by a kind of metaphorical tether, the length of which can be varied to fit the circumstances. "When the troop is quiet – such as during a general rest period – the infant leaves its low-arousal mother and explores the environment" (Baldwin and Baldwin 1977: 349).

Chimpanzee mothers in a captive colony give their young greater freedom to play and explore than do mothers observed in the wild, presumably because there are fewer dangers (Nicolson 1977). Howler monkey mothers monitor their children's play with peers and reel in the tether, so to speak, when the play-fighting gets too rough (Baldwin and Baldwin 1978). Squirrel monkey mothers seem to be extra vigilant for predation threats when their young are playing and, therefore, less attentive to danger themselves (Biben *et al.* 1989).

Tether-length is definitely a useful concept in observing human mother–toddler interaction. As Sorenson discovered in the Fore village, the infant's "early pattern of exploratory activity included frequent returns to the mother. She served as the home base, the bastion of security but not as director or overseer of activities" (Sorenson 1976: 167). For the forest-dwelling Chewong, the tether is shorter. Toddlers are discouraged from wandering away from proximity to adults with "loud exclamations . . . 'it is hot,' or 'it is sharp,' or 'there are . . . tigers, snakes, millipedes . . . '" (Howell 1988: 163).

Of course, modern Euroamerican parents are often seen using an actual tether to control the behavior of their toddlers in dangerous urban environments.[38] In the poorest urban ghettos, public areas, including "playgrounds," are dominated by gang members and criminal activity is conducted openly. Under these circumstances, it is common for mothers to forbid their children to play outside the apartment, going so far as to lock them in when they're gone.[39] Even statistically "safe" neighborhoods may be *perceived* as dangerous by anxious parents with few offspring (Liden 2003: 128).

While mothers may be concerned for their children's safety, the public at large may frown upon play as disruptive of public order. The addition of a soccer ball to the children's play arsenal was *not* welcomed by adults in Gbarngasuakwelle as it introduced an element of mayhem in the middle of the village (Lancy 1996: 187). In the Sepik area of Papua New Guinea, Kulick (1992) found that foreign games picked up by the village children, such as marbles, were condemned by senior men, particularly, as the "root of stupidity" (p. 177).[40]

Antagonism towards children's play is seen in English history. Complaints were directed at games of shuttlecock and tipcat obstructing the streets. Children's noisy play disrupted Parliament so it was banned in the vicinity. In 1447, the Bishop of Exeter writes decrying games of "toppe, queke, penny prykki" played in the cloisters "by the which the walles of the saide Cloistre have be befowled and the glas wyndowes all to brost" (Opie and Opie 1969: 11).

---

[38] One Step Ahead advertises a "Kid Keeper" to forestall "A chance you can't afford to take." Information from www.onestepahead.com; accessed 4.18.07. For $19.95, the "Little Safety Harness" by Natalé will help one cope with the "dangerous world of traffic, crowds, and strangers": www.littlesafetyharness.com; Accessed 4.18.07.

[39] Even within the apartment, the children are cautioned to stay away from doors and windows for fear of stray bullets (Kotlowitz 1991). See also *Fresh*, a cinematic tour of street culture in a ghetto in Brooklyn as seen through the eyes of a twelve-year-old black child (Yakin 1994).

[40] A report, on Andaman fathers in repose observing and offering pointers to their sons playing hide and seek in the vicinity, is the only example I've found of fathers "playing with" their post-infant sons (Pandya 1992: 274).

Figure 18 Street urchins

We may be more sympathetic today towards children's play in public; nevertheless, this description of the gradual foreclosure of children's unsupervised play in rural Maine[41] should strike a familiar chord.

A local pasture that served older generations as an amateur hillside ski area . . . and a vacant wooded lot where boys acted out World War II battles of fantasies and younger children looked for monsters [are] now filled with residential development[s] . . . a whole network of shortcuts ("secret pathways") throughout the town is gone now, replaced by parking lots, a new bank building or, in some cases, "no trespassing" signs put up by recent in-migrants . . . Busing cut children off from a prime connection to their ecology – the walk to school . . . past interesting natural sites . . . [lingering] to catch frogs at the pond, chase snakes, or bury and hold funerals for dead animals encountered along the way. (Beach 2003: 190)

Wooded areas have been posted and fenced off as have school yards. Children's use of the latter facility is confined to supervised play on manufactured structures, rather than the trees and boulders that used to serve this purpose. New roads and increased speeds have blocked access to formerly foot-accessible public areas – such as the town "green." Beach's older informants recalled exciting and hazardous play experiences in and around barns, corrals, and agricultural equipment: "injuries and scars from their early years, evidence[d] . . . physical adventurousness now probably less widespread among children" (Beach 2003: 191).

[41] A very similar trend has been observed in East Asia (Pan 1994: 62).

Parents restrict the play of their offspring not only to protect their investment; mothers may also see play as reducing the return on their investment. In Islamic areas of Nigeria, where women are sequestered,

> children's street-trading activities facilitate the economic participation of women who trade through their daughters and pre-adolescent sons... *mothers attempt to get more work out of children by prohibiting play*, which they perceive as manifestation of indolence and hedonism that will be maladaptive in the future... full-blown play, which involves a temporary relinquishment of their trading roles... could hardly occur... without reprimand and sometimes punishment. (Oloko 1994: 211 – emphasis added)

Among the Yucatec Maya, "the opportunity for play of any sort is relatively limited... children as young as three or four are often given chores[;] by age six or seven they are kept busy with work for long periods of time" (Gaskins and Göncü 1992: 31). They will be scolded for getting dirty or telling stories they know aren't true (e.g. fantasizing) (Gaskins *et al.* 2007: 192). In Senegal, Lebou children's play is often curtailed by adults to set them an errand or chore (Bloch 1989: 141). In Kenya, "because they [have] real babies to play with and real adult work to do from early ages, [girls do] little role play" (Whiting and Pope-Edwards 1998a: 16). In comparative research in Botswana, children in agrarian communities – whose labor was in great demand – spent significantly *less* time playing, as did girls, children of junior wives, and children in school (Bock and Johnson 2004: 81–82).

In Laurence Wylie's ethnography of a farming village in France in the mid-twentieth century, children's only opportunity to play occurred on the walk home from school as all but the very youngest had chores (Wylie 1957: 69). Going back further in European history, children were sent from home at an early age (as young as five) to toil as servants, pages, or apprentices in wealthy homes or were placed under the protection of better-off kin to "improve themselves." Opportunities to play would have been, consequently, quite limited. Those placed as oblates in monasteries had even less chance to be childlike: "according to surviving monastic/conventual regulations, [they] could be permitted to play for as little as one hour, once a week or once a month" (Shahar 1990: 197).

Numerous studies affirm a positive relationship between play and affluence. In homes where there might be servants, slaves, or lower-caste individuals to labor in household and fields, the demands on offspring of the head are reduced, especially on boys. In a comparative analysis of village children in Sri Lanka, those from better-off families owned more toys, spent more time in play, and exhibited a wider range of play behaviors than those from poorer families (Prosser *et al.* 1986).

Even under conditions of relative affluence, children's play may be restricted by concern for their mortal souls. Following the Protestant Reformation, many influential authors condemned play[42] in general as well as specific kinds of play – such as solitary play or contact sports. Morality came to be equated with decorum and emotional restraint; "indulging children was a cardinal sin" (Colón, with Colón 2001: 284). The only morally acceptable text was the Bible and children were to be prevented from "reading of fayned fables, vayne fantasyes, and wanton stories" (Colón, with Colón 2001: 287).

Similar sentiments were expressed by Chinese sages: "Huo T'ao had no tolerance for play . . . as soon as a child is able to walk and talk, it must be taught not to play with other children. Children must practice treating one another as adults . . . When [children] see each other in the morning, they must be taught to bow solemnly to each other" (Dardess 1991: 76). Another sage recommended "channeling young pupils' energy for running, jumping and shouting into singing and practicing etiquette" (Bai 2005: 14). Early in the last century, moralists cautioned against the harmful effect on children of games of chance, theatrical performances, and itinerant story-tellers. Presumably these activities inflamed passions and awakened emotions better left dormant (Nasaw 1992: 22–24). Contemporary moralists are much more accepting of play, in general, while, nevertheless, condemning commercially tainted dolls and video games that expose "innocent" children to premature glimpses of sex and violence. And very recently, play-time has been compressed as summer vacation and recess are eroded by the inexorable demands of schooling.[43]

"Classic" children's pastimes, like marbles, have steadily declined in popularity (Sutton-Smith and Rosenborg 1961: 27), replaced by TV, video games, and managed activities like sports and Boy Scouts. Quasi-public spaces that drew children in as ideal venues for exploring, for make-believe episodes, and impromptu games, are fast disappearing. Concern for children's exposure to violence and sexuality has led to restrictions on children's *physical* interaction with each other. These include a ban on R & T play in the school playground – perhaps the only available play space – and boys "smooching" girls prosecuted as "sexual harassment."

But the major divide between children's play in the village and the current situation is the greatly expanded role of parents and other supervisory adults. In the last section of chapter 5, the *laissez faire* parenting in the village was transformed into the active, engaged parenting found in contemporary society. The analysis at the end of the chapter, of parent–child conversation, will be complemented, below, by an analysis of parent–child play.

[42] Although the notion that play (frivolous) and training for adulthood (serious business) are fundamentally incompatible goes back at least to Plato and Aristotle.

[43] "The case for elementary school recess," American Association for the Child's Right to Play, 2004: www.ipausa.org; accessed 4.18.07.

Parent–child play

[Efe forager] mothers play little with their 1-year-olds. (Morelli and Tronick 1991: 104)

Play themes of Taiwanese mothers and children revolve not around fantasy, but around social routines . . . appropriately addressing and responding to a teacher, or interacting with a vendor. (Gaskins *et al.* 2007: 183)

Among primates, play is universal, although, as we saw in the previous section, levels of play can be attenuated owing to hunger, predation threats, or the dangers inherent in the monkey's arboreal environment. Play between mothers and their young is almost non-existent – except among chimpanzees. At the Gombe Stream Reserve, Jane Goodall reported many episodes of mother–infant play (van Lawick-Goodall 1976b; Bard 1995) and Frans Plooij observed mothers playing with infants by tickling them vigorously. Infant chimps respond with laughter if they are being adequately, but not excessively stimulated, or whimpering and crying if stimulated too much. During the second half of its first year, the baby interacts with others who also tickle it. Plooij asks:

Why is the chimpanzee mother providing her baby with what monkey infants get from their peers? One clue in the direction of an answer may be the group structure of chimpanzees. I observed that chimpanzee mothers with babies spend most of their time alone with their babies. As a consequence it is the chimpanzee mother who has to give her baby this sort of interaction if he gets it at all. (Plooij 1979: 237)

Similar forces may promote mother–child play among humans. The small band of "Utkuhikhalingmiut [Inuit are] the sole inhabitants of an area 35,000 or more miles square" (Briggs 1970: 1). Aside from the almost total lack of other children to play with, the mother–child pair is isolated inside their igloo for days on end during the worst weather. Jean Briggs observed mothers talking to their children, making toys for them, playing with them, and encouraging their language development.

Further, there is every reason to believe that modern living conditions in which infants and toddlers are isolated from peers in single-parent or nuclear households produce a parallel effect. That is, like chimps in the wild, modern, urban youngsters *only* have access to their mothers as potential play partners. In Japan, the mother–child pair have become quite isolated, sequestered in high-rise apartment buildings. Male wage-earners are gone during the child's waking hours, drastically reduced fertility has eliminated sibling playmates, and three-generation, extended families are rare (Uno 1991: 394–395).

At the other extreme, in foraging societies where children are saturated with attention from others (see pp. 122–123), infants, at least, are frequently played with. Noted ethologist "Eibl" Eibl-Eibesfeldt traveled the globe to study patterns of infant care among less complex foraging and/or horticultural societies. He frequently notes mothers and other caretakers kissing infants, rubbing noses, playing peek-a-boo, and fondling and stimulating their genitals. "Among the Yanomami, for example, mothers and fathers alike blowkiss, lick or manually rub the vaginal orifice of baby girls and stroke the scrotum of boys or mouth his penis until the age of three" (Eibl-Eibesfeldt 1983: 194). Others who've studied foraging bands also find ample evidence of affectionate, mother–infant play (Gusinde 1937; Burling 1963). In general, Eibesfeldt reports less frequent father–infant play and Hewlett (1991), who describes high levels of Aka forager father involvement in infant care, sees very little father–infant/child play (p. 95).

Play with infants also seems generally less common among agrarian societies, for example, an Apache (North American agro-pastoralists) "mother sometimes plays with her baby . . . A father is not likely to play with a baby" (Goodwin 1942: 448). In hundreds of hours of close observation of parent–child interaction among Kipsigis (Kenyan) farmers, Harkness and Super (1986) recorded "no instances of mothers playing with their children" (p. 102). Among the !Kung, parents not only don't play with their children post-infancy, they reject the notion outright as potentially harmful to the child's development (Bakeman *et al.* 1990: 796). This view is consistent with what one finds in the entire ethnographic record. It certainly characterized my Kpelle informants (Lancy 1996).

If parent–infant play is spotty, parent–toddler play is virtually non-existent, even in societies where play with infants is observed. The mother of a toddler not only faces potential conflict between childcare and work, she's likely pregnant as well. And folk medicine tacitly supports "toddler rejection" (Weisner and Gallimore 1977: 176). I would argue that the mother's greatest ally, at this point in the childrearing process, is the magnetic attraction of the sibling or neighborhood playgroup (Parin 1963: 48). The *last* thing a pregnant mother wants is for her child to see her as an attractive play partner. Even verbal play is avoided. From the Gusii perspective, the child may attempt to solicit the mother as play or conversation partner but will be ignored because, were the mother to respond, this would seem "eccentric . . . since . . . a child is not a valid human being until he reaches the age of 'sense'" (S. LeVine and R. LeVine 1981: 43–44) at six or seven.

Similarly, on Malaita Island, where children are expected carefully to observe and report on newsworthy events in the village, children's fantasy constructions are discouraged; they "are mildly reprimanded with 'you lie' (*'oko soke*)" (Watson-Gegeo and Gegeo 2001: 5).

In spite of the dearth of evidence for mother–child play elsewhere, an American psychologist, in describing her methodology for studying the development of children's personality traits, explains, without qualification, that "Mothers were instructed to play with their children as they would at home" (Stipek 1995: 244). The assumption that all mothers play with their children is so entrenched that, when middle-class mothers discuss their role, playing with their offspring – from birth – is usually central. For guidance they may turn to "How-to" books like *The Power of Parent–Child Play*. They will be introduced to Carol, a distraught mother comforted by the author, who weeps in relief after confessing: "I've always thought that something was very wrong with me, because I don't enjoy playing with my own kids. I fear they sense that and have already been damaged" (Sargent 2003: 109).

What explains this huge gulf between societies where mothers don't play with children and those where the absence of mother–child play is seen as an indicator of clinical abnormality (Trevarthen 1983: 151)? Why do Euroamerican and Asian parents invest so much of their precious time in activity – children's play – that parents elsewhere and throughout history have looked on as a welcome distraction, keeping children out of the way so they can do their work (Lancy 2007b)?

Modern parents go to considerable lengths to bind their infants to themselves emotionally and play is used as a means to this end.[44] This powerful attachment is fundamental to several parental goals that vary somewhat between the Western and Eastern Hemispheres. In both areas, the mother is the child's first and most important teacher. She is directly responsible for insuring that the child is prepared for and strives to be successful in school (Stevenson *et al.* 1992). Asian mothers also use play, didactically, to socialize the child to restrain its own desires and adopt a cooperative and deferential attitude towards others. Failure to do so brings scorn on the parents and humiliation for the mother (Haight *et al.* 1999). Until quite recently, Asian parents had a very direct stake in their child's success as their future wellbeing depended on the caretaking zeal and largess of their grown children. Hence the mother works extremely hard to insure that her child will respond to her direction as teacher as well as to feel deep filial piety and gratitude towards both parents for the remainder of their lives and beyond (Wu 1995: 131; Uno 1991; Lebra 1994; Kim and Choi 1994).

In the West, parent–child play emphasizes the development of narrative competence. Parents actively push children into realms of fantasy where a wide vocabulary can be brought into play and the child can experiment with hypothetical characters, relationships, and situations. These children are quite likely to be precocious in acquiring literacy and in their verbal interchange with others (Haight and Miller 1993). They learn to "talk like a book" (Martini 1995: 58).

---

[44] Mother–infant play in East Asia is of unknown antiquity but in the USA, it has a short history. As recently as 1914, the *Infant Care Bulletin* of the US Department of Labor's Children's Bureau warned against the dangers of playing with a baby because "it produced unwholesome [erotic] pleasure and ruined the baby's nerves." However, from 1940 "Play, having ceased to be wicked, having become harmless and good, now becomes a duty" (Wolfenstein 1955: 172–173).

Concerned about their children's school success, mothers structure the child's play[45] to promote concentration, self-discipline, emotional self-control, persistence in the face of failure, cooperation with others, and attention to adults (as teachers). They carefully control the toy inventory to facilitate these lessons as well as expose them to the artifacts of schooling, such as letters, numbers, colors, and "staying within the lines." It is not surprising, therefore, when researchers find broad commonalities in the play of children from modern, urban communities around the world (Roopnarine *et al.* 1994; Pan 1994).

Middle-upper-class US fathers, while playing less with their offspring than mothers, nevertheless behave as if this is a natural and appropriate part of their role – a view not shared in all industrialized societies.[46] But fathers do play differently than mothers. "Mother's play ... tends to be more verbal, object mediated, and didactic, whereas father's play tends to be more physical, active and unpredictable" (Power 2000: 342). In other words, mothers play for the sake of the child, fathers for themselves.[47]

Barbara Rogoff and colleagues have done extensive cross-national research which further underscores the very limited distribution of parent–child play. Their observations have been recorded at village sites in Guatemala, Central Africa, India, and in middle-class homes in Taiwan, Turkey, and the USA. Only the middle-class, urbanized mothers routinely play with their children (Rogoff *et al.* 1991; Rogoff *et al.* 1993; Morelli *et al.* 2003). Even when village mothers were given novel objects, along with guidance and encouragement to play with their children, they persisted in the attitude that children should explore them independently while they did their work (Göncü *et al.* 2000: 322; Rogoff *et al.* 1993).

In the USA, ethnographers have noted the reduction, if not complete absence, of mother–child play in lower-class households (Ward 1971; Heath 1990; Lareau 1989). Similarly, in an industrial town in north central Italy, Rebecca New found:

At no point did any mother suggest that play was an important contributor to infant development. Fathers were also unlikely to be infant playmates ... indicat[ing] a reluctance to handle their children, purportedly out of a fear of hurting them. Their attempts at play were characterized by whistles, making faces, and other distal efforts to elicit smiles ... play with objects was not seen as necessary for optimal infant development ... Their definition of play as *una cosa naturale* (a natural thing) – something children just do – precluded any active involvement on the part of adults ... When

---

[45] The idea that the child's first lessons should be embedded in play activity first surfaces in Quintilian's (100 CE) *The Training of the Orator*, cited in Sommerville (1982: 93).

[46] Japan (Uno 1991) and Turkey (Kagitçibasi and Sunar 1992) come to mind.

[47] If fathers aren't predisposed to play with children, then, when the exigencies of modern family life thrust them into that situation, they may fall back on the "rough and tumble" play that was so central in their own childhoods.

requested to play with their toddlers during an assessment of child language, symbolic play, and mother–child discourse at thirty-one months, sample mothers [refused or claimed they didn't know how to]. (New 1994: 130–132)

Not surprisingly, therefore, from a survey of the literature, we learn that children whose play is "guided" show higher levels of curiosity, greater interest in object manipulation, and more imaginative make-believe than village children whose caretakers don't think it appropriate to intervene (Power 2000). And, in US society, parents aren't the only adults who intervene to manage children's play, as we'll see in the next section.

The adult management of play

Many aspects of Little League baseball are structured by the demands and claims of adults – coaches, umpires, and parents. (Fine 1987: 15)

Families [in the USA] move, parents work two jobs or sell their homes to fund their children's sports. Sacrifice is a word used often to describe a family's commitment. (*Salt Lake Tribune*, October 23, 2005: A10)

The idea that adults might intervene to structure and control children's play is tantamount to a contradiction in terms. Among the legion of play definitions, attributes like voluntary, purposeless, child-centered, autonomous, autotelic are highlighted (Schwartzman 1978). Yet, middle-class Euroamerican parents carefully manage their children's play – from birth (Power and Parke 1982: 162),[48] and, as Rogoff points out (Rogoff 2003), they create playgroup conditions that, compared with other traditional societies, might be called "extreme." Not only do we segregate players by age, we often tightly control the rules of engagement, so that "winners" are truly the best while practice and rigorous competition act as a grinding stone, constantly sharpening skills and building self-confidence. And, unlike the situation anthropologists working in the developing world describe, in our society, parents are avid spectators and impromptu coaches of their players/children.

Nowhere is the adult's management of children's play more evident than in team sports, Little League baseball in particular. But, before we review Gary Fine's ethnography of Little League, let's see what the *absence* of adult management might look like as described by the Opies as they observed children playing in streets and fields in the first half of the twentieth century:

[Players] seldom need an umpire, they rarely trouble to keep scores, little significance is attached to who wins or loses, they do not require the stimulus of prizes, it does not seem to worry them if a game is not finished. Indeed children like games in which there

---

[48] There has been a steady increase in adult management of children's play in the USA (Sutton-Smith and Rosenborg 1961: 27).

is a sizeable element of luck, so that individual abilities cannot be directly compared. They like games which restart almost automatically, so that everybody is given a new chance. (Opie and Opie 1969: 2)[49]

By contrast, the Opies decry the fact that middle-class American children's "playtime has become almost as completely organized and supervised as their study" (Opie and Opie 1969: 16).

In the very competitive world of Little League baseball, a *laissez faire* attitude towards rules has no place. There is an official rule book which runs to better than sixty pages, its existence precluding the negotiation of rules characteristic of Piaget's marble players (Fine 1987: 20). The coach carries the burden of shaping the Little League experience to serve in socializing preadolescent boys, for example, "coaches are expected to keep their players orderly and oriented to the serious performance of baseball, while displaying an emotional coolness" (Fine 1987: 31). The display of anger, fear, arrogance, hot-dogging, and indifference are all suppressed by the coach and one's peers. The promotion of these and other values are as important a part of the coach's brief "as teaching them proper techniques for playing baseball" (Fine 1987: 61).

The seriousness with which parents treat Little League is captured in one player's recounting that "One April day, my mother handed me [my lunch] . . . and said, 'If you don't get into Little League, you better not come home for supper'" Fine (1987: 212).[50] Stories of coaches being assaulted by irate parents are becoming more common and sports facilities feel compelled to erect signs detailing "Spectator expectations" (Pennington 2005). One amateur association in Florida, "facing a rash of violent behavior by sports parents, now requires them to take an online course on how to behave at their children's athletic events" (Relin 2005: 4).

On the other hand, Fine takes note of Little League baseball's many detractors who argue:

that children should be left alone to enjoy their leisure . . . and to develop their own social system, moral order, and culture. According to critics, adult organization destroys the vitality of preadolescent activity: "Little Leaguism" is threatening to wipe out the spontaneous culture of free play and games among American children, and . . . it is therefore robbing our children not just of their childish fun but also of some of their most valuable learning experiences. (Fine 1987: 215; see also Devereux 1976)

Interestingly, in this regard, a recent national survey suggests that children themselves *prefer* to have adults organize their lives. They think that organized

---

[49] Also, when "one team outperforms another, players will often rearrange [players] to make the matchup more even . . . so that the game would not get boring" (Freie 1999: 91).

[50] This is mild stuff by comparison with the kinds of stories making the news lately of parents committing crimes on behalf of their child-athletes. See, for example, "Hockey dad gets 6 to 10 years for fatal beating," CNN, January 25, 2002: http://archives.cnn.com; accessed 4.18.07.

Figure 19 Wrestling match

youth activity is a good thing; the alternative is to hang out with friends suffering boredom because there's "nothing to do." And "3 in 4 students agree that 'a lot of kids get into trouble when they're bored and have nothing to do'" (Duffett and Johnson 2004: 10). These findings echo the results of a survey taken nearly a hundred years ago. Even then, play "was defined as organized games; anything else was 'idling'" (Mergen 1992: 101).[51]

For some parents, Little League is only the first stage in the development of their child's talent. Fourteen-year-old Tommy Winegardner's parents have enrolled him in "IMG Academics, in Bradenton, Fla., where . . . students practice their sport four or more hours a day, at least five days a week from early September through May" (Sokolove 2004: 81). While Tommy's father is

---

[51] Original source: Johnson (1916: 48–51).

at home in Ohio earning the money to pay the $70,000 annual tuition,[52] Tommy lives with his mother and sister in a $310,000[53] condo they've purchased on the IMG campus. His mother "has changed her way of cooking – more lean meats and chicken, less starch and fat – to complement his physical training in the weight room [which] has started to build muscle definition" (Sokolove 2004: 80).

The single-minded dedication of parents and children cannot be underestimated. "Tommy . . . wants to play professional baseball . . . without stopping first in college" (Sokolove 2004: 85). This worries coach Sullivan because: "The threshold for admission is not talent but money. There are a handful of stars, many earnest strivers and a few kids who just look clueless" (Sokolove 2004: 84).[54] Sullivan contrasts the American situation with Brazil, where, as he put it:

"They play soccer in every form – on grass, cement, dirt, in the street. Our society is one of constant supervision – it doesn't allow for that." [Sullivan] sometimes finds himself teaching children how to be kids. For a change of pace, he will try to get them to organize their own games, or he'll show them stickball or some other derivative form of baseball. "They can't do it very well," he said. "And they don't like it. They're like: 'If I'm going to play baseball, I want Sully around. I want to be in uniform and I want an umpire.'" (Sokolove 2004: 84)

My own introduction to the world represented by IMG occurred a few years ago as I worked with Margaret Raitt on an ethnography of a rodeo queen clinic. The rodeo queen and her court provide a feminine counterpoint to the hypermasculine culture of rodeo. And, on the other hand, parents have an opportunity to turn their horse-loving "tom-boy" into a "lady." Competition begins in the pre-teen years, as girls vie for the crown of rodeo princess for their town or rural district, then for county, state, and regional titles. Like Little League, the clinic imparts physical skills as well as character and personality building. In the evening, the clinic presents a fashion show and girls eagerly sample from a colorful wardrobe as "$50 and $100 bills change hands" (Raitt and Lancy 1988: 272).

The pursuit of the rodeo queen's crown will consume a significant portion of her family's time and discretionary income, but then, everyone basks in the reflected glory of her success. As one mother – speaking for many – argued:

---

[52] Such sports training facilities for youth have grown to an estimated annual budget of $4 billion: Sokolove (2004: 83).

[53] While these sums seem extraordinary, more modest – but still substantial – investment in the child's sports career can pay off handsomely, if the student-athlete earns a "full-ride" college scholarship.

[54] Failing to make the grade as a professional athlete is not the worst thing that can happen either. Injuries requiring surgery are likely. A doctor in Atlanta has performed ligament repair surgery on fifty high school pitchers (*Parade*, August 7, 2005: 3).

Figure 20 Prepping rodeo princess

"They make a lot of friends, they learn poise, they learn makeup, they have to give speeches, they have to model and it just makes more of a lady out of them" (Raitt and Lancy 1988: 277).

The ancestor of all modern forms of adult management of children's leisure is the Boy Scouts. Scouting offers supervised and measured doses of the sort of "healthy and wholesome" play that the children in Maine described earlier discover on their own. As Jay Mechling notes, scouting arose as a response to a crisis of masculinity in the nineteenth century. Urbanization had deprived boys of opportunities to engage in the quintessentially masculine activities of our noble savage predecessors. Hence, from 1910, Boy Scouts were instructed in "woodcraft," a rather romanticized vision of Native American culture (Mechling 2001: 38). True to the movement's roots, the ambitious, hard-working, and adventuresome scout can still earn approximately 120 "merit badges," including "Indian lore, archery, basketry, canoeing, fishing, hiking, camping, wilderness survival, wood carving, and leatherwork".[55]

---

[55] Other merit badges: American business, architecture, computers, cooking, dentistry, electronics, engineering, entrepreneurship, home repairs, journalism, oceanography, plumbing, surveying. Details from the *Bay Scout Handbook*, 11th edn, 1998.

Boy scouts, Little League, ballet, piano, and other forms of adult-managed play offer parents multiple benefits. As we've seen, doting parents can achieve, vicariously, those fifteen minutes of fame. They can also be assured that their children are acquiring habits of behavior and thinking that, if not leading directly to a lucrative contract in the big leagues, at least do no harm and undoubtedly contribute, in a general way, to life success. Another secondary benefit of enrolling one's child in a managed play activity is to segregate her from peers whose parents fail adequately to manage their free time and who might exert a "negative influence" on her. Lastly, and this by now has become a common refrain, children under the care of coaches, teachers, employers, and scout leaders – acting *in loco parentis* – free up parents from childcare responsibility and give them time to acquire resources for themselves and family members (Hofferth *et al.* 1991).

7   His first goat

Introduction

"Run and fetch me" is one of the commonest phrases heard addressed to young children in Tikopia [Solomon Islands]. (Firth 1970: 80)

Nowhere are Euroamerican views on childhood and those of the larger world more at odds than on the issue of work. Indeed, "the dissociation of childhood from the performance of valued work is considered a yardstick of modernity, and a high incidence of child labor is considered a sign of underdevelopment" (Nieuwenhuys 1996: 237). While we hamstring our children to keep them from the labor force, fearing their loss of innocence and studiousness, the norm elsewhere is to open the pathway to adulthood. We will find that as soon as children can "help out" and make an economic contribution, they do so – eagerly, without coercion, and with minimal guidance.[1]

We will explore a wide range of situations beginning with the almost idyllic process whereby bright-eyed, eager children take up the tasks of their elders and persist until mastery. In many cases, we will note that this process is unhurried and casual. Children may take many years to become proficient and productive. In other cases, we see evidence of adults pressing children to mature quickly and assume responsible roles.

Children usually learn on their own. But, when this isn't feasible, they must persuade, or their parents must pay, an expert to serve as a model and guide. Children are as often rebuffed than encouraged in their attempts to master more complex craft-making skills. On the other hand, when parents can use their children to increase the family income or larder, they usually do so without compunction. This opportunism may extend to activities that are physically harmful such as mining and which preclude school attendance.

This pragmatic view of children has only recently given way in the West to the "sacred child" syndrome, and, indeed, it still persists in many pockets of the modern, industrialized world.

---

[1] I can't help chuckling when I recall what a struggle we had persuading daughter #2 to carry her dirty socks from her bedroom to the bathroom hamper.

The chore curriculum

Only after a [Chaga] boy has proved his reliability at herding goats is he preferred to the work of pasturing cattle. (Raum 1940: 200)

Every small [Talensi] boy of 6–7 years and upwards has a passionate desire to own a hen. (Fortes 1938: 20)

[In learning to become a Touareg camel herder] Es gibt keine systematische Ausbildung, keine institutionalisierte Lehre. (Spittler 1998: 238)[2]

Prior to the modern era, "education" was not confined to a classroom or text-books. It happened everywhere there were children to observe and emulate more proficient members of the community. It continues to happen in most traditional villages today. But education in the village isn't completely without structure. Among the universe of needed tasks, there are almost always one or two that are "just right" for a given child's age and strength. Furthermore, most realms of endeavor are conveniently "staged," that is, the component tasks are naturally graded in difficulty; hence, we can speak of a chore "curriculum."

In Tanzania, a group of Hadza children heads out to the savannah to look for baobab fruits. From the age of four, they gather, haul back to camp, and process these nourishing snacks (Blurton-Jones *et al.* 1997). In the Sepik region of PNG, Kwoma children of six eagerly embrace the piglets they're given to protect, raise, and train (Whiting 1941: 47). Pigs are of central importance throughout much of New Guinea as they provide both food and a store of capital. In Gbarngasuakwelle, a five-year-old girl gets to use a "cheater," a donut roll of cloth to help balance the small container she carries on her head. She proudly accompanies a group of five of her older sisters and cousins (containers matched to the size of each child) to troop down to the stream to fetch water for the evening's cooking and washing (Lancy 1996: 144). These milestones in the child's assumption of responsibility are widely acknowledged within the community and happily anticipated by the children themselves. Indeed, we find many societies where the terminology to age grade children references the chores that are typical for that age (Mohammad 1997).

In the Giriama language the term for a child roughly 2 through 3 years in age is *kahoho kuhuma madzi*: a youngster who can be sent to fetch a cup of water . . . Children of this age take an enormous pleasure in being sent on small errands, and everyone enjoys their satisfaction at completing the task. Mothers report that they consider these small errands to be preparation for carrying out orders that involve greater responsibility . . . A girl, from about 8 years until approximately puberty, is *muhoho wa kubunda*, a child who pounds maize; a boy of this age is a *muhoho murisa*, a child who herds. (Wenger 1989: 98)

---

[2] "There is no systematic instruction, no institutionalized apprenticeship."

Contrast this nomenclature with our commonly used expressions like: pre-schooler, kindergartner, sixth grader, sophomore.

The locus of much of children's work, especially when they are quite young, is the household. Village children in Bolivia

> get up . . . between 5 and 6 am, and begin by doing . . . chores such as fetching water and firewood, letting the animals out of their enclosures, feeding and milking them. During the day children's household jobs vary according to the season and may include: looking after and feeding animals, doing agricultural tasks, fetching more water and firewood, looking after younger siblings, washing clothes or preparing food. In the evening, the animals have to be rounded up and brought in to the paddocks for the night. Since it gets dark about 6:30 pm, kitchen tasks such as supper preparation or washing up are carried out by candlelight before children go to bed, usually between 8 and 9 pm. (Punch 2003: 284–285)

In Gaskins' ethnography of Yucatec Maya households, a graded curriculum of tasks matched to the child's strength, size, and competence is evident. An eight-year-old child might start out washing just her own clothes and gradually expand her service to include, by age twelve, the entire family's laundry (Gaskins et al. 2007).[3]

As discussed in the previous chapter, many skills that children acquire have an inherently developmental character. Also, make-believe play provides a kind of "pre-school" introduction to many adult tasks. This is especially true of domains like meal preparation and gardening that are quite transparent. For example, Fore (PNG Eastern Highlands) girls learn to garden, entirely without instruction. Their make-believe gardening evolves into, initially clumsy and even destructive, attempts to emulate the gardening activities of their elders. Gradually, these efforts "more and more resemble the . . . sustained gardening [that is] the basis of the Fore way of life" (Sorenson 1976: 200). Kwoma (Sepik Region, PNG) parents go a step further by actually setting aside an area of the garden for the child to work on their own. Any produce from this mini-garden is "put in a separate bin in the family storehouse as the child's private property" (Whiting 1941: 46).

Adults rather casually accelerate or channel the chore curriculum, sometimes by providing children with miniature or scaled-down versions of tools and utensils. The Chewong give toddlers a blunt knife in lieu of a toy (Howell 1988: 159). An Ache boy will be given his first bow at two or three but it's not until ten or twelve that the toy has become a tool with which a significant number of calories can be obtained (Hill and Hurtado 1996: 223). In the New Guinea Highlands, a play digging stick gives way to an adult-made scaled-down "real" digging stick – of the proper wood, that has been shaped and fire hardened.

---

[3] Schildkrout outlines a parallel curriculum for learning to cook (Schildkrout 1990: 225).

Figure 21 His first goat, Ladakh

On Mandok Island, just off the northeast coast of New Guinea, Ali Pomponio observed:

Young children of about four to six years played in child-sized canoes in the small harbor . . . They poled their way along the beach, played at jumping on and off the canoes, and otherwise learned while frolicking in and around the water. I saw unsupervised eight-year-old children exercising their total freedom of movement some two hours of paddling away from Mandok. (Pomponio 1992: 72)

On Ponam Island, north and west of Mandok, children play on and around an abandoned canoe. They make their own toy canoes and, at ten, are given control of their own small outrigger (Lancy 1983: 121). On Wogeo, a hundred miles or so to the west, men take a keen interest in their sons' progress in the canoe curriculum and may make coconut shell toy canoes for those too young to make their own (Hogbin 1970b). Even when the craft is a large whaling ship,

Nantucket boys – who go to sea at fourteen – already at ten were using "the waterfront as their playground. They rowed decrepit whaleboats up and down the harbor and clambered up into the rigging of the ships" (Philbrick 2000: 2).

The solicitous Wogeo father is, in fact, a fairly rare exception as children need little encouragement to emulate their "betters." Forty-five years ago, Robert White gave us the now classic theory describing a universal drive to become competent (White 1959). Looking at modern children and noting the prevalence of teaching, of rewards for success, of special places for learning and compulsory attendance, White's theory seems almost dubious. However, in the village, the notion that all children are busy trying to appropriate the skills of those older than themselves rings true.

And there is at least some evidence that others may take notice of the child's growing skill, success, and particularly strong motivation to excel. In the present, this notice takes the form of assigning the child additional responsibility (Nerlove and Roberts 1974), but sexual selection theory alerts us to the very likely possibility that these exceptional children are establishing a reputation that will pay off in improved mating opportunities in the future.

Often the very first chore assigned to children is to send them on errands. My Kpelle informants extolled the virtues of child messengers. Little children were always welcome in other people's homes and aroused no suspicions. A well-behaved, polite[4] child earned the attention of potential foster parents and praise for its family's socialization efforts (Lancy 1996: 76). Delivering messages and presents (and bringing back gossip!) segues easily into marketing. The "errand" curriculum incorporates many "grades" from carrying messages (at age five) to marketing produce, hard bargaining, and making change for customers (by age eleven – Lancy 1996: 156).

Children are favored as mobile messengers and traders because adolescents or adults seen in close proximity to neighbor's houses might be suspected of adultery, theft, or witchcraft. And boys are favored because their virtue isn't as fragile as that of girls. There are, indeed, quite a few tasks for which children are *preferred*. These include carpet-making where small fingers are advantageous, camel racing – where weight is critical – and coal-mining operations in which small bodies can more readily access narrow shafts (Sastre and Meyer 2000: 87).

Another early and ubiquitous chore is caring for one's younger relatives. Among the Hausa in northern Nigeria, nine-year-olds have full responsibility for younger siblings, keeping them safe, clean, fed, and happy (Schildkrout 1990: 225). Of course this relationship is mutually beneficial. We learn from

---

[4] There is often a complex etiquette associated with carrying out the messenger's role. "If when taking a message a child had to pass a line or group of people, he had always to go in front of them, never behind, murmuring as he went by, 'I am before your eyes'" (Read 1960: 43).

numerous sources that younger children "idolize" their older brothers and sisters and eagerly apply themselves to acquire the useful skills they possess (Read 1960: 96). Kaluli mothers direct their daughters to cooperate with and emulate their older sisters (Schieffelin 1990: 218). African pastoralist societies seem especially fruitful for examples of a graded curriculum in which older siblings serve as role models. Amhara boys trail after young males "like retainers follow a feudal lord" (Messing 1985: 213). Ngoni boys work their way up from tending a goat to a calf, to sheep to a cow, to multiple cattle – all the while observing and discussing cattle with older brothers. The "cow curriculum" is quite extensive:

The Ngoni classified their cattle according to age, sex, coloring, size and shape of horns, whether castrated or not, whether in calf or not. Knowledge of the extensive series of names used for these "classes" of cattle was part of a herd-boy's A.B.C. By the time he was old enough to be told to drive certain cattle out of the kraal, designated by their class, he knew exactly which ones were meant. He could also use the cattle terminology to be precise in telling an owner about a beast which has strayed or one that had a sore hoof, or one that was giving an exceptionally good or poor flow of milk. (Messing 1985: 133)

A second pastoralist example comes from Gerd Spittler's meticulous study of Touareg (Mali) desert caravaners. Boys who will eventually be responsible for the care of the family's camel herd during grueling treks, begin at four by helping care for the family's goats under the watchful eye of their mothers. Goats are hardy animals and Spittler reports that children play vigorously with their charges "as they would play with children" (Spittler 1998: 343).

At eight or nine, the boy will be given a baby camel and transition from goat to camel tending. Aside from feeding the young camel and keeping it from its mother's teat, the child plays with it while observing the herd and the older herdsmen. Preferentially the aspirant herder interacts with and learns from herders who are slightly older, *not* adults. Adults are too forbidding to ask questions of or display ignorance in front of. Above all, it is a hands-on experience as "The abstract explanation so typical of our schooling is completely absent" (Spittler 1998: 247). At ten, a mature, capable boy will be invited along on a caravan. Initially, he does odd chores like helping to fetch water and wood, holding the milking pot, hobbling the younger camels, and so on. As his size and strength permit, he'll assume responsibility for managing the far-from-docile adult animals. By thirteen he can be trusted to pasture the herd by himself but must still acquire further critical skills including how to diagnose and treat illnesses. The nascent herder is expected to be a diligent and eager student. He's encouraged to observe and question more competent young men while signs of disinterest or sloth will be rewarded with harsh words and a beating (Spittler 1998).

In the rainforests of Venezuela, boys are busy becoming hunters. A Yanomamo five-year-old plays with toy bow and arrow, targeting beetles and cockroaches. By eight, he'll be using a scaled-down version of an adult's bow to hunt small birds with great enthusiasm and braggadocio. At fourteen, he's allowed to go on the hunt with older family members. He will learn – from observation – what arrows to use for particular prey; he'll develop a sense of direction and learn to read spoor. As his strength and endurance develop, the size of his weapon will increase, and he will rapidly and persistently pursue wounded prey or, cleverly, smoke it out of its hiding spot. "Eventually he will be able to travel throughout the region without accompaniment" (Peters 1998: 90–91).[5]

To the west, in the tropical lowlands of Ecuador, young Conambo girls are described as playing with pottery, making clay animals and pinch pots, while assisting their mothers in the gathering of materials and observing their craft. As time passes, a girl will be permitted to assist with preparing clay, shaping a pot, or completing a painted design. By fifteen the aspirant potters can make beer bowls decorated with their own designs and, by twenty, if they've persisted, they're fully competent (Bowser and Patton 2008).

The next example in this section details the Bamana (Malian agriculturalists) "bean" curriculum. Barbara Polak found that, while children are very eager to participate in the work of grown-ups, they can do more harm than good, so their efforts have to be modulated.

They risk causing damage, for instance by using a hoe the wrong way or losing seeds, or causing extra work by making it necessary to repeat a work cycle that has been performed ineptly . . . Four-year-old Bafin has already grasped the meaning of sowing and is able to perform the various movements . . . he is entrusted with an old hoe as well as with some seeds so that he can gain some practice in this activity. However . . . he has to be allocated a certain part of the field where he neither gets in the way of the others nor spoils the rows they have already sown. Also, the others have to keep an eye on his attempts and point out his mistakes to him from time to time. As a rule, his rows have to be re-sown. (Polak 2003: 126, 129)

On the other hand, even half-hearted attempts are appreciated:

[At harvest] three-year-old Daole . . . begins to pluck beans from the tendrils. After he has filled the lid with a handful of beans, his interest fades. [He] carelessly leaves the lid with the beans lying on the ground and goes looking for some other occupation . . . Five year old Sumaèla . . . looks out for a corner not yet harvested and picks as many beans as will fill his calabash . . . [he] keeps on doing this for more than one and a half

---

[5] Descriptions of !Kung boys learning to hunt look very similar. An interesting exception is the case of a mature !Kung hunter actually teaching a young man to shoot accurately with bow and arrow. The young man being instructed had been accidentally shot with a poison arrow when young and was always considered too weak to hunt, but now that he's married and has a child, he needs to hunt so they *teach* him (Wayne 2001).

hours . . . Eleven year old Fase has been busy harvesting beans . . . since morning. He works as fast as . . . his father and grown-up brother . . . and only takes a rest when they [do] . . . Fase is a fully competent . . . with regard to harvesting beans. He even takes on the role of supervising his younger brothers and checks their performance from time to time. (Polak 2003: 130, 132)

Lastly, we have the "fishing" curriculum. On the small, scattered islands of Micronesia, villagers enjoy a rich diet of marine products. Palauans name 300 distinct species, and can describe dozens of capture techniques.[6] As Johannes documents, becoming expert may take years. On Tobia, boys begin fishing at seven. Prior to the introduction of metal, fishhooks were precious and a boy first practiced with a baited line. Or the line would be looped and used to lasso small creatures in tide-pools. This long period of intense, small-scale exploration developed both dexterity and a broad knowledge of the marine environment (Johannes 1981). Working diligently, a boy might gradually master the art of making fishhooks from shell and bone. "The final stage in this period, when the boys had reached late adolescence, involved learning how to cast out beyond the reef crest to catch larger fish living on the outer reef slope" (Johannes 1981: 88–89). Many specialized fishing techniques were considered private property, jealously guarded. Still, a young man was expected to attempt to "steal" them (Johannes 1981) and advance in the fishers' pecking order.

Unlike the lock-step, standardized *academic* curriculum, the chore curriculum is highly elastic within[7] and across cultures. A nine-year-old girl likely carries more of a burden for household tasks if she's the oldest of four children than if she's the youngest of four. She'll have less responsibility in a larger household (Munroe *et al.* 1984) where "many hands make light work." In an Iraqi Kurdish village, a nine-year-old has near complete responsibility in the domestic sphere (Friedl 1992: 36), whereas in a Berber village in Morocco she would be eleven or twelve (Cross 1995: 70). A nine-year-old in a *foraging* society will be relatively unburdened compared with her counterpart in a *farming* or *pastoralist* community (Kogel *et al.* 1983: 364).

Equally importantly, we will rarely see evidence of *teaching*. In the Congo, once released from the protective custody of female caretakers, boys of the Kuba tribe are drawn to areas where men are working on craft production, including blacksmithing and weaving of cloth, but no one troubles to teach

---

[6] Elsewhere in the Pacific, ethnographers have also noted the huge information store a competent fisher must acquire and accompanying folk wisdom that children will take years to master the repertoire fully. Mandok Island: Pomponio (1992); Ponam Island: Lancy (1983); Wogeo Island: Hogbin (1970b).

[7] There are some exceptions. The Kwoma are very rank conscious and tasks (clearing the bush before planting) are graded. Boys, especially, are prevented from engaging in certain tasks until they've achieved sufficient age/status (Whiting 1941).

them, they must learn on their own (Binkley 2006: 106). According to Charles Wagley, when a Tapirapé (Brazil)

boy became *churangi* (young adolescent)... [and] moved from the family dwelling to the *takana*... he was supposed to learn... how to weave baskets, how to make a bow and straight arrows, how to fabricate the spirit masks that the men wore... However, I never witnessed any express attempt... to teach a young boy such pursuits. On the other hand, the *takana* was the place where adult men generally worked, and a boy had ample chance to watch them at it... Older men found boys of this age rather amusing in their attempts to carry out adult activities. (Wagley 1977: 149–150)

From the foregoing, it should be obvious that the chore curriculum can be highly individualized. That is, slow and fast learners can be readily accommodated as can those with latent talent in some areas only. This flexibility also extends to the intensity of effort. Kids are expected to be kids, to mix in play with their work.

All work and no play?

Anthropologists... have found that the separation of work and play (labor and leisure), which is characteristic of industrialized societies, is frequently absent in non-industrialized cultures. (Schwartzman 1978: 5)

... role play was particularly low in Nyansongo [Kenya] probably because children there participated earliest and most heavily in real adult work and therefore did not need to "practice" through acting out. (Edwards 2005: 94)

Child watchers are often impressed by their ability to shift gears quickly, illustrated in this vignette from Bolivia:

[as her] mother had taken lunch to her husband working in some distant fields, Marianela, as the oldest sibling present, *stopped playing with the dolls* and automatically assumed a parental type role. She served lunch... [while] ordering her younger siblings about in a competent, organized way. (Punch 2003: 283 – emphasis added)

In a village near Kisoro, southern Uganda, I watched a curious game of tag. Four girls carrying infants held to their backs by a length of cloth chased each other around a cleared area. To "tag" someone your baby had to touch their baby. Of course, if you ran or tagged too vigorously, your charge might start crying, ending your participation. Sara Harkness and Charlie Super describe young Kipsigis (also in East Africa) shepherds playing tag among their flocks and tree-climbers keeping a wary eye on their charges below (Harkness and Super 1986: 99). Another common chore, particularly for boys, is to keep pests from attacking the ripening crops. But what could be more effective deterrents than a well-aimed slingshot, boisterous noise-making (Punch 2003: 288), or racing around the field in a game of tag?

The Hadza children who lift the burden of provisioning from their parents by finding their own food

> engage in foraging with a spirit of adventure, joy, fun, and achievement. Their foraging is interrupted by chat, joking and gentle teasing, resting, grooming, singing, and rushing about, all accompanied with smiles and laughter. Their foraging seldom appears to be a response to instructions from adults, and even if adults leave them with instructions, they have no way to know whether the children followed them. Children often leave camp to forage long after the women have gone, and men are often out of sight at "the men's place," and the food that children get is usually all eaten up by the time the women return. (Blurton-Jones *et al.* 1997: 282–283)

In the Sudan, children capture birds with nets and consume or sell their catch. However, bird trapping was pursued "for its own intrinsic value and not for economic gain or to provide household subsistence" (Maxwell Katz 1986: 48). On Madagascar, Mikea children "learn at their own leisurely pace. Their objectives when foraging may be primarily social and recreational" (Tucker and Young 2005: 169).

The age at which children transition from mostly playing to mostly working varies widely. Generally speaking, farming and pastoralist societies are able to exploit children as workers at far earlier ages than are foragers. For foragers, their food sources may lie far from camp, there may be severe environmental dangers, and foraging itself may require considerable skill and physical maturity, all of which mitigate against child workers (Hames and Draper 2004: 325, 334). By contrast, at age four, Kipsigis (farmer) children are more involved in work than play; by age eight they're working five hours for every hour of play (Harkness and Super 1986). This pattern is replicated in Mayan communities and is probably representative for subsistence farming communities (Gaskins *et al.* 2007). However, in Khalapur, India – a more prosperous farming society – children are at leisure until age six, the earliest that animal tending and household chores are assigned (Edwards 2005: 90).

One of the first signs of the divergent life-course of boys and girls revolves around the play-to-work transition. In a series of observational studies conducted at village sites around the world, girls consistently spent more of their day doing chores, including sib-care, housework, and gardening. "Boys spend relatively more of their time playing. These sex differences are seen from age three onwards" (Edwards 2005: 87). While girls seem firmly attached to their mothers and function from an early age as their assistants, boys are much less often in close proximity to their fathers. Kerkenni (Tunisia) boys "do not socialize with their fathers or their fathers' peers. This would be disrespectful" (Platt 1988: 282). And while many of a woman's burdens can be shared with a child, men's work tends to demand physical strength (clearing bush), finely honed skills (bow-hunting), or erudition – not attributes possessed by little boys.

These gender differences are maintained even as societies modernize.[8]

About half of Moroccan adolescents in Zawaiya attend school . . . a typical adolescent girl attends school for about three hours, then goes home for chores such as fetching water, washing laundry, taking care of younger siblings, household cleaning, and cooking . . . [their] leisure time is scarce . . . The typical boy was occupied with school classes, prayer, homework, hanging out with friends, playing soccer, and watching television. (Gibbons 2004: 261)

Not only do girls begin the transition to working earlier than boys, their work/play ratio is higher (2:1 among the Giriama – Wenger 1989: 98–99) and they earn different assignments (maize-hulling vs herding – Wenger 1989: 98–99). Generally speaking, a girl's working sphere coincides with that of her mother – the household, kitchen, nursery, laundry, and garden. Boys range further afield, running errands, patrolling distant fields, and hunting in the bush. To outside observers, boy's "work" often looks more like play while girl's work looks like – work. Even in contemporary US society, this pattern holds. Teenage girls work about six hours per week, whereas boys work fewer than four hours. Girls work indoors as their chores include cleaning and babysitting. Boys work outdoors, taking out garbage or mowing the lawn (Blair 1992: 179).

Close study of Hadza children's foraging illustrates the way in which girls "get serious" at an age when boys are acting rather frivolously, with significant consequences. From the age of ten, girls are gathering more food than they consume. Boys, on the other hand, concentrate on exciting but low-return foods such as honey and small game. They harvest far fewer calories than they consume (Blurton-Jones *et al.* 1997: 291, 304, 306).

A number of anthropologists have noted that the onset of gender segregation has it origins in chore assignments. With rare exceptions,[9] tasks are gender-specific. Hopi girls "will begin to grind corn [and] accompany their mothers to the spring for water" (Schlegel 1973: 453). Giriama boys "do no 'carrying' (of water, produce, and firewood) – tasks traditionally regarded as women's . . . the most frequent chore boys . . . perform is the running of errands" (Wenger 1989: 100). In the Kerala (India) region:

Female tasks such as cooking and washing children's clothes cannot be performed by a male without incurring the risk of ridicule . . . Male tasks such as receiving guests and visitors, asking for loans and searching for wage work outside the immediate vicinity of the home, conversely, cannot be performed by females without the entire family losing face. (Nieuwenhuys 1994: 69)

---

[8] In a recent, and as yet unpublished, survey of Muslim countries, the authors found much evidence of change in areas affecting children and youth *except* in the area of gender roles (Gielen and Ramada 2007).

[9] "Efe boys and girls overlap to a remarkable degree in the types of infant care activities they perform" (Henry *et al.* 2005: 200).

One often learns of prescribed gender role assignments when they are *violated*. Joseph Lijembe, a Kenyan from an Abaluyia-speaking area, poignantly describes, in his autobiography, how he was "obliged, though still a very young child myself, to become the day-to-day 'nurse' for [my] baby sister." Of course, as a boy, this chore was "unnatural" and his "mother to make me succeed in this function, had to train me" (Lijembe 1967: 5). In a Luo-speaking community in Kenya, the shortage of daughters was community-wide and Carol Ember discovered that "Approximately half the boys in the community had been assigned 'feminine' work... because the ratio of boys to girls... was almost three to two... at the time of the study" (Ember 1973: 425–426).

The timing of the play-to-work transition can also be affected by environmental conditions. Play among squirrel monkeys drops sharply when food is scarce and juveniles are forced to spend long periods of time foraging (Baldwin and Baldwin 1976). Among humans, the loss of the father or mother either permanently or temporarily owing to illness or pregnancy can rapidly escalate the child's workload. In the next section we will examine numerous cases where children are seen to pick up skills in a quite relaxed, casual manner, but even at a fairly young age are able to activate and intensify those skills to become more productive, if the need arises.

Productivity and proficiency

How much experience do Meriam children need before they become efficient reef foragers? Evidently very little. (D. Bird and R. Bird 2002: 291)

[In Kerala, a girl's] socialization into the world of coir begins as soon as she can be of some use to the older women. (Nieuwenhuys 1994: 135)

Current debate in the USA on children's learning often pivots on President G. W. Bush's "No Child Left Behind" (NCLB) initiative. Clearly the NCLB program is based on concern for children who are being "left behind" – those whose progress through the curriculum our society prescribes for the attainment of independent and successful adulthood is too slow or uncertain. The NCLB mandate to use highly structured teaching materials and frequent assessment[10] conveys an image of rapt concentration and marathon-like endurance.

In a similar vein, scholars of human evolution, when they take note of children, see the prolonged period of semi-dependency and the long-delayed onset of puberty and mating as providing a sheltered learning environment. They reason that the human adaptive model requires the gradual acquisition of an entire curriculum of increasingly more challenging skills. Hill Kaplan and colleagues have provided a recent version of this proposal (Kaplan *et al.*

[10] Information obtained from www.ed.gov/nclb; accessed 4.19.07.

2000: 156). They offer an impressive catalog of the enormous variety of wild resources of which humans have taken advantage through a dazzling array of often Rube Goldberg-worthy capture, collection, and processing strategies. They further cite evidence that for many of these resource-acquisition skills, such as large mammal hunting, honey extraction, and finding and removing certain edible roots, expert practitioners are found only among those in their late twenties and thirties. The implication is that, as with NCLB, children must be busy practicing these skills or learning the component skills for *years* prior to mastery (Diamond 1992: 69). However, there's now a rapidly growing body of research which suggests that's *not* happening, at least not in every society.

In the late 1970s, along with several colleagues, I undertook a comparative analysis of child development in nine contrasting societies – ranging from forest-dwelling foragers (Kiwai Island, Fly River), to swidden (slash and burn) horticulturalists (Kewa tribe, Southern Highlands) to maritime fishers and traders (Ponam Island, Bismarck Sea) in Papua New Guinea. A variety of evidence suggested that, unlike the highly standardized public school curriculum in place, the village curriculum ranged from fairly demanding to quite undemanding.

Children . . . are expected to share or mimic adult responsibilities from an early age. For Kewa children this means digging and weeding in the garden, weaving *bilums* (net-bags), carrying firewood and little else. On Ponam, by contrast, children are engaged in a host of multifaceted activities. They help to build and then learn to handle various size canoes, and they work various sections of the reef with different tools and techniques. They [learn to] make rope; work with wood; make a variety of traditional ornaments, costumes and *bilums*, and make various nets, spears and other fishing gear . . . Furthermore, maritime . . . gathering as a way of life is unstable and will change continuously in the direction of greater complexity [while] Highlands horticulture and pig husbandry have persisted virtually unchanged for centuries. (Lancy 1983: 121–122)[11]

From the Papua New Guinea study, we concluded that it would take much longer to master what an adult forager knew than what an adult farmer might need to know. But as the accounts of more recent anthropological studies of child development suggest, even among foragers, achieving competence may not be all that demanding; for example, Inuit "children produce a large percentage of their own food supply by gathering shellfish" (Zeller 1987: 545).

---

[11] The absence of a lengthy chore curriculum in the Kewa case should not blind us to the many other demands for learning that societies impose on children. In particular, "middle childhood is a critical point of change in abilities that allows for the internalization of a particular cultural stance (which is of significant complexity in all cultures), so that the child becomes a bearer of culture (in an individual, psychological sense) rather than just a habitual participant" (Suzanne Gaskins, personal communication, August 8, 2006).

Figure 22 Kewa boy digging in family plot

Additional examples of "precocity" from recent research include, first, from the rainforest of Paraguay:

Both sexes . . . learn to follow the signs indicating that Ache have walked through an area. These signs, which are almost invisible to the untutored, consist of bent leaves, twigs, and shrubs that the Ache call a *kuere* or "trail." Following these trails is one of the most important forest skills, and *most children are successful by about eight years of age.* This enables children to navigate between camps without always being in the sight of adults, and it allows boys to begin small hunting forays without getting lost. (Hill and Hurtado 1996: 223 – emphasis added)

Zapotec (Mexico) children's excellent command of ethnobotany is described as "everyday knowledge acquired without apparent effort at an early age by virtually everyone in town" (Hunn 2002).

From Mer in the Torres Straits Islands:

Four-year old children... don't really forage: they have knowledge of appropriate reef prey, but they are easily distracted and spend time pursuing items that are inedible or associated with extremely low foraging returns. They are also extremely slow and tire easily when the substrate is difficult to negotiate... they may play the role of retriever in picking up [mollusks] spotted by adults... The learning process involves little or no direct adult instruction [rather by] forag[ing] in groups with older children, observing intently their prey choice and processing strategies... *by age six, children have become fairly efficient foragers.* (D. Bird and R. Bird 2002: 291 – emphasis added)

Children begin spearfishing with toddler-sized spears as soon as they begin walking, using them at first to spear sardines along the foreshore for bait... they carry their spears when they begin shellfish collecting on the reef between ages 6 and 7. *Those children that choose to invest in spearfishing practice reach the same efficiency as the most practiced adult by ages 10–14.* (R. Bird and D. Bird 2002: 262 – emphasis added)

From the Western Australian desert:

An ethos of self-sufficiency surrounds Martu children. Desert-born adults recall a child-hood spent foraging with other children to keep themselves fed while [parents were off hunting]. Women hunt on foot with digging stick, and they often remark that children are too slow to keep pace while they are searching and tracking... men would never take children on foot hunts... Once Martu children systematically begin to hunt for goanna lizards, they are already well practiced... the youngest hunters can be nearly as efficient as the older children. (Bird and Bird 2005: 135, 142)

In Tibet,

Children as young as six or seven... look after herds of goats, sheep, dzo, and yaks in the mountains... a major responsibility since much of the wealth of nomadic families is invested in these animals. It can also be a very scary and lonely activity since wolves, snow leopards, and eagles regularly attack the sheep and goats. Using a slingshot to control the animals, *boys at seven or eight years of age are considered to be effective herders.* (Gielen 1993: 426 – emphasis added)

In the Central African Republic, Aka foragers deploy more than fifty different skills in acquiring the means to survive. Aka children, as is the case in many foraging bands, aren't under any pressure to provision themselves or the community. Nevertheless, "*at age 10... both sexes... know the majority of foraging skills* [and] If need be, [can] make a living in the forest" (Hewlett and Cavalli-Sforza 1986: 930 – emphasis added).

Hadza children not only start foraging at an early age, but they quickly develop competence in fruit and tuber acquisition and processing. Boys are able to "bring home the bacon" with bow and snare from an early age and losing practice opportunities while away from home (at boarding school) imposes no retardation of skill. Nevertheless, they don't use poison arrows before fourteen and archery skill grows throughout adulthood (Blurton-Jones and Marlowe 2002). Most Ache and Hadza men are married with children long before they reach their peak hunting efficiency (Blurton-Jones 2005: 107). Ache girls don't learn basketry until after marriage, while men aren't able to make bows and arrows until middle age (Hill and Hurtado 1996: 223).[12] !Kung children are "late bloomers" by comparison with peers in other foraging groups. Their parents *discourage* them from leaving camp to forage (Blurton-Jones *et al.* 1997: 307). Once they start following the groups leaving camp each day, they quickly pick up what they need to know to become self-sufficient.

This pattern, of sometimes quite early skill mastery and sometimes quite late mastery, is characterized by John Bock as "punctuated development." He finds that, for some tasks, experience is the best predictor of proficiency; for others, strength is critical. At one extreme, such as processing baobab fruits, the technique requires neither great strength nor skill and can be undertaken by four-year-olds. Mongongo nut processing requires both, and Bock finds that the most proficient women are twenty-five to fifty-five years old. He concludes that, where strength and maturity are critical, the onset of learning will be delayed (Bock 2002b).

Karen Kramer reviews a wealth of data on children's productivity to show that farming children (Mayan[13]) become net producers (produce more than they consume) on average five to ten years earlier than their counterparts in two South American foraging groups (Machiguenga and Piro: Kramer 2005: 135).[14] Hames and Draper explain why this large gap in net production between farmers and foragers might occur. They argue that hunters and gatherers, generally, work alone and must therefore deploy a complete, well-honed skill set. Farming tasks, on the other hand, "can be distributed over time and among laborers of different types and skills . . . [including] children" (Hames and Draper 2004: 336).

Another factor that adds complexity to this picture might be termed "learning versus performance." I recall an ingenious experiment from the 1960s that was used to demonstrate this phenomenon. Rats were placed in a maze where they

---

[12] In a documentary film on a previously uncontacted Brazilian group known as the Korubo (they refer to themselves as Dslala), a boy of approximately fourteen years of age stands by and holds the blowgun while an adult hunter readies a dart. He is present during the hunt but does not himself hunt. The boy *watches* game being plucked and cleaned, and he *assists* with creating a sling to carry the game but does no carrying (New Atlantis 2005). A very similar pattern has been observed among the !Kung (Maxwell Katz and Konner 1981: 167).

[13] For comparable results from the Q'equchi Maya in Belize, see Zarger (2002).

[14] A very recent, fine-grained study of the growth of hunting prowess among the Tsimane of Bolivia shows that improved returns are driven by the long, gradual acquisition of tracking skill – as well as by increased strength and endurance. However, the study also showed that, with the adoption of new techniques such as flashlights and dogs, the importance of such skill decreases (Gurven *et al.* 2006).

wandered around, seemingly at random. Then, a food reward was placed in one of the end compartments of the maze. Rats that had the opportunity to explore had consistently faster times to the prize than rats without such experience. Clearly the aimlessly wandering rats *had* been learning the maze and were waiting only for an incentive to apply what they'd learned.

We see the same thing with children. On the reef, they seem happy-go-lucky and casual in contrast to adult foragers who move rapidly with intense concentration. The anthropologists "were always surprised by the wealth of knowledge Meriam children had about reef ecology, prey characteristics, search techniques, and handling strategies . . . many were skilled shellfishers" (D. Bird and R. Bird 2002: 276).[15] I was treated to a similar excursion in Gbarngasuakwelle as I was led into the bush on a mushroom-hunting expedition by a group of children barely out of toddler-hood. The atmosphere was entirely playful, yet the children were able to locate and gather mushrooms that were completely invisible to me (Lancy 1996: 156). Neither the shellfish nor mushroom collectors are making a significant contribution to the stewpot – yet! However, as their role within the household economy shifts, sometimes abruptly with the arrival of a new baby – thus reducing the mother's food-getting opportunities – they can ratchet up their productivity quickly and execute efficiently those skills they've been perfecting through playful work.

The trigger that releases a child's untapped productivity is often pulled by an overworked parent. I'll discuss the transition from strictly voluntary, child-initiated work to adult-directed, compulsory labor later in the chapter. Now, however, I want to introduce the reader to less common and more complex skill acquisition by children. While the chore curriculum is considered mandatory with differentiation by age and gender, the craft skills we'll examine in the following two sections are much more restricted in distribution, almost "extra-curricular."

Learning crafts

. . . novice [flint-knapping] takes place in areas peripheral to the production areas of skilled [neolithic] toolmakers . . . inexperienced toolmakers use raw materials of lower quality than those used by skilled toolmakers at the same site. (Baxter 2005: 54)

. . . the sum of . . . knowledge [on Pohnpei] is not given out to all . . . members, nor is it divided equally and parceled out. (Falgout 1992: 37)

For the past hundred years in the West, ideas like a standardized curriculum in a state-supported school with compulsory attendance have been widely accepted

---

[15] Pomponio (1992: 72) had exactly the same reaction to the Mandok child reef foragers she accompanied and attempted to emulate. Other studies document subsistence foraging by low-caste Bengali girls (Rohner and Chaki-Sircar 1988) and Mayan children's acquisition of locally relevant botanical information (Zarger and Stepp 2004).

as reflecting good economic and social policy. The state takes responsibility for insuring that every child – irrespective of his talents or his motivation – should be "educated" to some, officially determined, level. However, when first introduced, these ideas were strongly resisted. As we'll see, parents may seek a greater return on their investment by putting children to work rather than sending them to school (Neill 1983: 48). A second objection is less obvious and that is the belief that, for advanced and less commonly practiced skills, children must be allowed to display the proper aptitude and willingness to learn before a skilled practitioner/teacher should take time to instruct them.

I was very surprised to discover that, in Gbarngasuakwelle, there is a wide gulf between the chore curriculum and what we might call the craft curriculum. The former is often compulsory – a child may be severely chastised or beaten for failure to complete appropriate chores satisfactorily. The latter is not only entirely voluntary, children seem to be offered little encouragement. Indeed, they may be actively discouraged from trying to learn a craft or otherwise complex trade.[16] I explored this issue at considerable length with my Kpelle informants in order to understand their perspective. First, they tend to treat skills as having some fungible value and, indeed, it is customary to make a token gift to an expert practitioner when seeking guidance or advice. Second, there is the sense that the learner must go very far on her own[17] observing, trying, and practicing diligently before an expert – even her own mother – will consent to critique or correct her handiwork. In *Playing on the Mother Ground*, I provide an extended example, of mother Sua and daughter Nyenpu each weaving a fishnet, the point of which is to show how little interest Sua has in getting involved in Nyenpu's weaving. Sua claimed that her stance was typical and replicated her own mother's attitude when she was learning net-weaving. Several other informants told me of approaching experts for help and being rebuffed (Lancy 1996).

And I don't think the Kpelle are especially callous or indifferent to aspirant craftspeople; I believe their perspective is quite typical. A Talensi cap maker told Meyer Fortes: "he learned his craft, as a youth . . . by carefully watching [a capmaker] at work. When he was young, he explained, he had 'very good eyes'" (Fortes 1938: 23). Carolyn Pope Edwards recounts this scene from Khalapur, India:

---

[16] In coastal Indian villages, coconut husk is spun and woven into coir products such as mats. It is a woman's craft and not difficult to learn. The fact that girls aren't encouraged to learn the craft until their mid-teens is accounted for by the "shared opinion that girls should not threaten the income opportunities of adult women" (Nieuwenhuys 1994: 137).

[17] The component skills of the West African *griot* – such as *sabar* drumming – can be attempted and practiced by children. Indeed, this early interest and dedication is seen as a forecast of future potential (Tang 2006: 107).

a 6-year-old girl was trying to embroider a little piece of cloth. Her aunt and grandmother were nearby but did not help her. She threaded the needle after many tries, and then followed the lines of a design, carefully counting the stitches and correcting her mistakes. After 5 minutes, her aunt and grandmother inspected her work and told her to take it all out because she was ruining the cloth. [Nevertheless] the girl continued to work on and try to correct her mistakes . . . [the observer, noting that] actually she had done quite well for a first try. (Edwards 2005: 91)

Patty Crown's survey of twenty-five societies in which pottery making is an important activity found that in half the cases, children acquired their craft through observation and practice; fewer than a third of the cases would be described as a formal apprenticeship. Puebloan girls in the southwestern USA took the initiative to learn the craft, observing and imitating their mothers or other competent female relatives. Girls were discouraged from pursuing ceramics until they'd mastered all the "mandatory" chores associated with the domestic sphere. Adults spared little time to serve as teachers.

Questioning was discouraged, and if brief instructions were given, they were offered only once. Adults are quoted as stating that children understood the process more thoroughly when they learned through trial and error . . . Learning apparently followed a sequence that mirrored the production process . . . with the progression largely driven by the child's interest and skill level. There is no mention of children aiding adults in making or decorating pots. (Crown 2002: 109)[18]

Complementary surveys of Puebloan ceramics from museum collections fill in more details of the picture. Children seem to have started out making toy figurines and vessels from clay.[19] Measuring fingerprints left on them, one can determine that the youngest artisans may have been four years old (Kamp 2002: 87). In a small number of cases, evidence of high and lower skill on the same vessel suggests joint adult–child production. In skillfully made vessels, children might contribute by doing the simpler part of the decoration, thus enhancing the adult's output. In well-made vessels with childish decoration, Crown avers: "The finished pieces were not enhanced by the child's contribution. Indeed, the degree of adult effort on these vessels suggests indulgence of young children or attempts to keep them occupied rather than instruction" (Crown 2002: 117).

In Africa also, pottery making is often practiced exclusively by women and, in at least one ethnic group in Cameroon, it is restricted to the wives and daughters of blacksmiths (Wallaert-Pêtre 2001: 473). In more conservative

---

[18] Closely parallel observations have been made of novice potters in the Andes region (Sillar 1994: 52).

[19] Parenthetically, I should point out that, as with the chore curriculum, virtually all children who learn a craft would have passed through an earlier stage during which they observed and emulated craftspersons in their make-believe play. I reported on one extended and vivid example from Gbarngasuakwelle, namely the dramatization of the life and work of the town blacksmith (Lancy 1980a: 271).

areas, mothers train their daughters via a formal apprenticeship that begins as early as seven and ends, with a ceremony, at about fifteen: "the 'newborn' potter is blessed by her parents in front of the community members and receives her own tools" (Wallaert-Pêtre 2001: 475). In effect, mothers benefit from their daughter's production until they lose them to marriage.

However, culture change may dramatically impact this process. In another Cameroonian pottery-making area, Wallaert-Pêtre found that many of the traditions had disappeared as young women began producing ceramics *for sale*.

Here, anyone can learn to make pottery, and [most of] the female population practice it. Training . . . lasts an average of two years . . . and no particular ritual marks the end of the learning period . . . [Fali] potters were always ready to attempt new tasks, even if they knew they did not have the ability to succeed . . . believ[ing] that something can be learned even through failure . . . Personal gratification is important and overrides the judgment of other potters . . . leading to a diversity of production and style. (Wallaert-Pêtre 2001: 476, 483, 489)

A strikingly parallel case has been documented by Patricia Greenfield and colleagues among Tzotzil Maya weavers in the Chiapas Highlands.[20] In this area, women weave, and, traditionally, mothers actively trained their daughters,[21] using methods handed down over generations, to produce a limited repertoire of essential items. The substitution of cheap, machine-made clothing for locally woven items coupled with tourist demand for new products and innovative styles led to the emancipation of young weavers. They now master the art through their own trial and error – only occasionally seeking a mother's input (Greenfield *et al.* 1995). It appears that young weavers also market their own products, and, perhaps, the fruits of their skill now accrue more directly to themselves rather than primarily augmenting their mother's output as in the past.

The chore curriculum, with its emphasis on wholly self-guided, self-taught skill acquisition, changes subtly as craft skills are introduced into the picture. The acquisition process often involves greater structure and the attention of an expert, and, importantly, not all children are expected to learn particular crafts. Apprenticeship moves further along the continuum towards the kind of formal schooling that is ubiquitous in modern society. While Conambo girls learning pottery at their mother's elbow are encouraged to create new decorative motifs

---

[20] No case of craft skill acquisition has been so thoroughly studied. Another interesting finding is that traditional weaving is undertaken in a kneeling position so, from an early age, girls mimic the kneeling posture of older women as they care for babies and prepare food. This early and persistent posture facilitates a physical adaptation which maintains the ease with which kneeling can be sustained (Maynard *et al.* 1999).

[21] My sense is that the direct instruction originally observed in Chiapas is rare. More typically, Quechua "children are not taught to spin or weave. Rather, they observe family members who have mastered these crafts and imitate them directly" (Bolin 2006: 99).

(Bowser and Patton 2008), among the Nigerian Hausa, such license would be frowned on in what is clearly a very formal weaving apprenticeship.[22]

Where the "chore curriculum" can be quite flexible, in the *apprenticeship* undertaken by aspirant potters in Cameroon,

> the *chaîne opératoire* is not divulged as a whole to the beginner, but rather is presented in short sequences of actions evolving with the stages of apprenticeship . . . beginner apprentices . . . limit their production to miniatures: simple shapes with no design . . . Even gifted apprentices . . . maintain a low level of practice to fit with the established structure and to respect the "normal" duration of apprenticeship. (Wallaert-Pêtre 2001: 484)

Along with greater structure and rigidity, the apprenticeship also depends on a restricted "admissions" policy in that an apprentice must rely upon family to arrange and pay for training.

Apprenticeship

One Japanese term for apprenticeship is *minari*, literally one who learns by observation. (Singleton 1989: 29)

The . . . apprentice [Tukolor weaver] learns . . . not only the necessary skills in weaving . . . but also the mystical and religious aspects of craft lore. (Dilley 1989: 190)

One of the criteria that distinguishes apprenticeship from less formal means of skill transmission is that parents are expected to pay a fee up front to induce the master to accept their child. In ancient Rome, a father wanting his son to learn the weaving trade would pay a fee *and* his son's room and board. The son is "bound" for a year, unable to leave his master for this minimum term (Shelton 1998: 111–112). Also, the apprentice typically lives with his master's family, insuring his availability for menial chores like sweeping out the workshop at the end of the day.

An apprentice may be quite young, as all apprenticeships include a lengthy period of menial service. Tukolor (West African farmers) apprentice weavers are "asked to wind bobbins for each weaver as needed . . . other duties are to

---

[22] Two points deserve some clarification. First, in the literature on children and youth acquiring adult skills, the term "apprenticeship" is used in both a loose and a much tighter sense. I will define the stricter version shortly. Second, I do not know why, in the same general region, a given craft, like weaving, may be seen as strictly women's work versus strictly men's work nor why a craft should sometimes be viewed as requiring a structured, formal apprenticeship and, in other societies, be seen as buried in the chore curriculum. One underlying factor may be the degree to which mastery of the craft is associated with a guild-like status differential. If practitioners are regarded as having inherently higher status, then it would behoove them to block access to all but the most worthy. This is certainly the case with blacksmithing in West Africa.

undo and prepare hanks for rewinding, fetch water for the other weavers, and perform any other menial tasks that are required" (Dilley 1989:187).

In Tanon's thorough study of the Dioula (Ivory Coast) weaving apprenticeship, what is striking is the severe restriction imposed on what the apprentice can and cannot assay. The novice weaver is constrained to advance his skill in "baby steps" to reduce the likelihood of mistakes that an expert would need to rectify. Hence, while the ethnographer learns to weave in an intense period of rapid learning (Tanon 1994: 34),[23] the apprentice at eight is preparing bobbins; a few years later he's weaving plain white bands on a loom an expert has set up for him. A year or two later finds him weaving patterned blankets of larger and larger dimensions until, perhaps at eighteen, the "apprentice will learn to set up his first warp under the close scrutiny of his master" (Tanon 1994: 26).

Menial work in the earliest stage matches the apprentice's ability level, provides a kind of pre-payment for the apprenticeship opportunity, and, most importantly, offers a measure – for the master to evaluate – of the apprentice's level of motivation. To become a potter in Japan, according to John Singleton, requires "a single-minded, wholehearted dedication to the craft . . . talent is to be developed through persistence, it is not considered to be inherited or innate" (Singleton 1989: 29).

In a typical apprenticeship, the master will probably *not* be the boy's father because a common ingredient is the verbal and physical abuse of the apprentice by the master.[24] A parent is considered incapable of imposing the required level of discipline (Coy 1989: 120; Aronson 1989).[25] Tukolor "fathers prefer that another weaver . . . train their sons . . . since they feel that they will not exert enough discipline in training" (Dilley 1989: 188). Gonja (Ghana) believe that familiarity breeds contempt and that sons wouldn't show sufficient respect towards their fathers to learn from them (Goody 2006: 254).

The apprentice does not expect to be "taught" beyond the master pointing out some aspect of the process that is not obvious. "When an apprentice presumes to ask the master a question, he will be asked why he has not been watching the potter at work, or the answer would be obvious" (Singleton 1989: 26). Nor is praise likely. The apprentice Japanese potter knows he's making progress when the master selects some of his pots for firing, rather than destroying them (Singleton 1989: 28).

---

[23] The majority of ethnographic accounts of apprenticeship derive from *participant* observation in which the anthropologist rapidly learns a skill which the apprentice is expected to take years to master. I find this a subtle affirmation of the argument made throughout the chapter regarding the undemanding nature of the village curriculum.

[24] An extremely well-known proverb from ancient Egypt says: "The student has ears on his back," meaning that to get anything across to him, the master must beat it into him.

[25] John Locke warned that a parent's fondness for a child renders them incapable of being effective teachers (Locke 1693/1964).

There is much in the master's practice that falls under the heading of lore. The African blacksmith, in particular, is invested with special knowledge and may be empowered to perform certain rituals (Lancy 1980a). Peter McNaughton, an American who served as a blacksmith's apprentice in Mali, describes the craft as floating "on a sea of secret expertise" (McNaughton 1988: xvi). Tukolor weaving lore "called *gandal* . . . can be used . . . to protect the weaver from spiritual forces associated with the craft and . . . as a means of defense against the malicious intention of other . . . weavers" (Dilley 1989: 195). None of this lore is freely given to the apprentice and a truly worthy apprentice is expected to "steal" as much of these more subtle aspects of the craft as he can winkle out.

As the apprentice develops expertise, he can be expected to continue working under the master for a further, often lengthy, term. All of his finished goods belong to the master as payment for the opportunity to learn a trade.[26] In Gbarngasuakwelle, Chief Wolliekollie watched and assisted his father weaving and mastered the craft under the watchful eye of his brother, who, even as close kin, expected a substantial portion of his first year's production as payment (Lancy 1996: 164).

Studies of apprenticeship in more modern, urban settings show remarkable continuity with these village practices. Jean Lave's study of Monrovia (Liberia) apprentice tailors shows them making a direct contribution to the success of the master even as they learn rudimentary skills like hemming trousers (Lave 1990: 314). Apprentice shoemakers in Naples contribute to the shop even if they don't progress beyond the first and most basic task – applying a layer of glue to the edges of the to-be-joined pieces of leather (Goddard 1985: 19).

In Michael Herzfeld's observations of (male) Greek apprenticeships, kin are not taken on as apprentices because "the bonds of kinship are too easily exploited" (Herzfeld 1995: 136). Instruction or even discussion of the process is minimal; mostly the apprentice is teased and insulted (Herzfeld 1995: 137) and, again, "apprentices are expected to 'steal' their masters' ideas and techniques" (Herzfeld 1995: 131).

In a recent book-length analysis of the training of master minaret builders in Yemen – where the process has achieved high art – Marchand identifies themes touched on earlier. For instance, many are called, few chosen. Among young men taken on as builders, it is the rare individual who actually achieves the level of masonry skill, zeal, and initiative to be treated as an apprentice. A thick skin doesn't hurt, either:

Curses and derogatory remarks were the most common form of communication from "teacher" to "learner" either in the assignment of tasks or in the correction of ones in

---

[26] Unspoken may be the master's desire to keep his apprentice from direct competition as long as possible.

progress. As opposed to explanation, this form of abuse served as a potent disciplinary tool, effectively reinforcing the existing hierarchy amongst the builders. (Marchand 2001: 144)

However, Marchand makes a telling point: "Although the distinct status of that builder which I recognized as an 'apprentice' was plainly acknowledged by all, there was seemingly no special terminology to designate it" (Marchand 2001: 136). It is my sense that this anomaly is true for all the cases reviewed in this section and the reason is that, fundamentally, the process of becoming a minaret designer/builder, a weaver, or potter is not seen by the community as all that different from learning to herd goats or harvest beans. All these accomplishments are seen to rest on elementary principles: maturity (sense, strength); ability to pay attention; ability to copy faithfully; willingness to work hard and practice; respect for experts; and, in some cases, ambition to excel. Teaching – as active intervention and explanation by an expert – and learning – as a distinct internal, cognitive process – aren't seen as essential to the successful apprenticeship or any other skill learned in the village.

Becoming a navigator

The stars are taught by placing a circle of pebbles on the ground, each standing for a star which the student must learn to name. (Gladwin 1970: 130)

The senior navigators often discourage young men from trying because they are fairly sure they will not make it. (Gladwin 1970: 127)

The single exception I have found to the generalization made at the end of the last section is the training of navigators on Puluwat Island. The process was recorded by Thomas Gladwin in *East is a Big Bird*, possibly my favorite work in the entire corpus of ethnography. Like most of the anthropologists cited in the discussion on apprenticeship, Gladwin put himself forward as an apprentice navigator, having already logged years of open ocean sailing and navigation. Starting with an area of the Pacific characterized by vast distances between tiny specks of land, he zeroed in on the most storied long-distance sailors still plying the waves, the mariners of Puluwat in the Caroline chain.

Puluwatans are blessed with abundant calories from gardens and the sea. They have the leisure and motivation to make frequent long-ranging voyages to distant islands – largely for the fun of it. There are some "objectives" they may have in setting out, like going to Pikelot Island to hunt turtles – more numerous there than around Puluwat – but, mostly, they just love being at sea. And, before European contact and pacification, "when wars were fought between islands . . . the Puluwatans were the scourge and terror of the Central Carolines" (Gladwin 1970: 16).

Unlike the *laissez faire* attitude we've encountered so far in the chapter, Puluwat adults "push" their children to learn sea-faring. Children experience their first extended voyage at five, "despite the objections of their worried mothers, so that they will early in their lives get to know and to enjoy life at sea" (Gladwin 1970: 48). Each voyage takes on the character of an "adventure cruise" and, not surprisingly, "almost every young man seems still to aspire to become a navigator. Only a handful make it, but those who fall by the way-side are willing to settle for the lesser glory of being a crew member" (Gladwin 1970: 36–37). Aside from the rarified position of navigator – there were only six on the island during Gladwin's stay – an ambitious young man can apprentice as a canoe builder.

A young man . . . asks one of the active canoe-builders for instruction. If the latter is willing and the pupil apt they work together until the young man is ready to start building canoes on his own. This may take several years. Often the apprenticeship begins with the younger man watching the older at work, asking questions, helping at first only with routine chores and then gradually with tasks which require increasing degrees of skill. However informal in its inception, the relation between student and teacher becomes formalized when the apprentice undertakes the supervised construction of his first canoe with a hull contoured for sailing. (Gladwin 1970: 71)

Learning to build ocean-going canoes closely resembles the apprenticeships discussed earlier, even to the secret lore.[27] Learning to navigate is strikingly different, however, because of the enormous amount of "theory" or, for lack of a better term, "book-learning," and the corollary necessity for active teaching.

Formal instruction begins on land. It demands that great masses of factual information be committed to memory. This information is detailed, specific, and potentially of life-or-death importance. It is taught by a senior navigator to one or several students . . . they sit together in the canoe house, perhaps making little diagrams with pebbles on the mats which cover the sandy floor. The pebbles usually represent stars, but they are also used to illustrate islands and how the islands "move" as they pass the canoe on one side or the other . . . There [is] much magic and esoteric knowledge . . . known only by the privileged few . . . navigational skills were and still are valuable property . . . taught . . . for a stiff price. (Gladwin 1970: 128–129)

The theory consists of an intimate knowledge of the celestial or star chart and the courses followed by the stars during the night – at different times of the year. Each journey between any pair of islands (the Puluwatan universe consists of at least thirty islands spread over hundreds of miles of sea) has its own program, so to speak. That is, in the course of the journey, the guide star or stars for this particular route will follow a predictable trajectory which can be learned.

---

[27] Rob Borofsky describes the transmission of canoe-making (actually repairing an older canoe) expertise on Pukapuka, a remote atoll in the Cook Islands, as a casual affair – lacking the attributes of an apprenticeship (Borofsky 1987).

This core curriculum is augmented by a developing understanding of waves, currents, and other aspects of particular sea lanes. Then there is knowledge and intuition about weather patterns and how to sail in a storm, and "*etak*, the system used for keeping track of distance traveled" (Gladwin 1970: 131–132). Like trigonometry or Latin grammar,

No one could possibly learn [navigation] except through the most painstaking and lengthy instruction... memorized through endless reiteration and testing... not complete until the student at his instructor's request can start with any island in the known ocean and rattle off the stars both going and returning between that island and all the others. (Gladwin 1970: 131)

Naturally, sessions of "classroom" instruction are interspersed with many voyages to test the apprentice's seamanship as well as his navigation ability. On his "final exam," Rapqui "set out with his aging... instructor Angora on... the direct 130-mile run to tiny Satawal" (Gladwin 1970: 127).

At this point in the chapter, we also change course. Consistently, we have observed children *voluntarily* seeking to acquire and practice the skills of their older and more experienced relatives and neighbors. In extreme cases, only the most ambitious and highly motivated will master a very specialized trade, like navigation. For the remainder of the chapter, we will examine cases where the child's participation in work may not be entirely voluntary and where the enthusiasm we've observed so far may, understandably, be lacking.

Milk debt

In accord with the belief that lactation uses up maternally irreplaceable body substances, it is seen [in rural Mexico] as incurring debts on the part of children, who thus are obligated to attend their mother's wants in old age. (Millard and Graham 1985: 72)

... initial efforts at subsistence work are recognized by giving them food, enthusiastic praise and by calling other people's attention to a child's effort... [Murik] mothers [thus] encourage a strong association between work, recognition, and being fed. (Barlow 2001: 86–87)

... parents exercise a considerable amount of coercive control over children's time. (Bock 2002a: 211)

Throughout the chapter, we have watched the autonomous child observing and imitating adults and older siblings, volunteering to help out, sometimes being rebuffed where its involvement might diminish the productivity of those more competent (Kramer 2002a). But anthropologists also find lots of evidence that parents, especially mothers, see their children as providing critical labor inputs. Compelling children to do their fair share is seen as part of the child's socialization as a citizen *and* as paying its mother back the "milk debt." In central Mexico, "pregnancy, childbirth, and breastfeeding are... seen as sacrifices ... to be paid back later as the child matures and assumes household responsibility" (Millard and Graham 1985: 63).

A Giriama mother who demands obedience and hard work from her children earns the community's respect (Wenger 1989: 93). For the Sebei of Uganda, a girl

is taught to do exactly as her mother does, so that when the mother goes anywhere, she will return home to find the work done. If the mother finds the work improperly done, she ... abuses the girl ... saying: "I hope that you have stomach pains and dysentery." Mothers are concerned that their daughters learn proper housekeeping so that their husbands will not beat them for neglecting their duties, and so it will not be said that they failed to learn proper behavior from their mother. (Goldschmidt 1976: 259)

Kpelle women "view their children ... as resources ... whose labor will lighten their burdens and offer them security in their old age" (Bledsoe 1980b: 3). A Papel mother laments: "Because I do not have the heart to beat my children they never help me ... I have to do all the work myself" (Einarsdottir 2004: 95).

In trying to understand how Thai parents can earn money from their children's prostitution, Montgomery explains that:

according to the Thai Buddhist moral scale, parents are entitled to be "moral creditors" (*phu mii phra khun*) because of their presumably self-sacrificing labour of bearing and rearing children ... while children are moral debtors ... one raises a child in expectation of explicit returns. A daughter repays the debt to her mother by remaining in the parental household to care for her parents in old age, while a son ordains as a Buddhist monk to pay his mother back for her breast milk. (Montgomery 2001b: 73)

Tom Weisner has done a masterful job of contrasting the ever-solicitous parent depicted in Western child development textbooks – with what he observed in an Abaluyia farming village in East Africa. Parents and adults rarely assist children with tasks. More often help is provided by other children and even this token aid is "often indirect and delayed" (Weisner 1989: 72). The only direct communication is to assign the child its chores; indirect communication also includes teasing and aggression. "Food is used consistently to reward and acknowledge the child's contribution and vice-versa, recalcitrance is rewarded by food denial" (Weisner 1989: 78).

We find *some* evidence of positive appraisal: Hopi "girls are ... early to grind [maize], and they are often prevailed upon to display their accomplishment before visitors" (Hough 1915: 63). "Mothers sweeten the burdensome task by telling their daughters that grinding brings the blood to their cheeks and makes them pretty" (Schlegel 1973: 456).

Many communities – perhaps a growing majority – depend heavily on children's labor for basic survival. "Without the contributions of their children, Maya parents would have to double or triple their work levels beyond observed values" (Kramer 2005: 168). Reviewing her thorough study of children's labor, Olga Nieuwenhuys writes: "Does the Kerala [India] economy at large need the work of children? My contention is that is does. The livelihood of the rural poor in both fisheries and coir is realized within an economic set-up that requires large numbers of either unpaid or marginally remunerated workers" (Nieuwenhuys 1994: 200). Parents often suppress the child's attempt to master a more complex skill to reassign them a more critical task they've already mastered (Bock 2002a: 211). The parent–child relationship takes on the character of overseer–laborer.[28] A related issue – one we will more fully explore in chapter 9 – is parents' control over the child's access to schooling. For example, Bock finds in Botswana that in farming communities, girls, who can free their mothers to work in fields by doing household chores, are less likely to be sent to school. In herding societies, boys are preferred as livestock tenders, and are, hence, less often sent to school than their sisters (Bock 2002a: 218).

The very careful management of the child's time that we see in these cases is quite characteristic of societies that depend on very labor-intensive forms of agriculture. Fertility is high, weaning is relatively early, and children are transitioned from play to work as soon as they can be useful (Ember 1983). Among foragers, parents often have much lower expectations of their children: "the attitude of [Chewong] adults is . . . permissive . . . They do not seek actively to teach anything at all . . . [children are left to] their own devices . . . On the other hand, it is assumed that every maiden and bachelor will have mastered the customary tasks by the time they approach marriage, and most in fact do so" (Howell 1988: 160). Even into the modern period in the West, we have ample evidence of parents managing their children for their own ends. Comfortably ensconced in a middle-class family, Charles Dickens showed early signs of promise. His career as a scholar was abruptly terminated when his impecunious father could no longer stave off creditors. Of the children still at home, "Alfred, at two, Frederick, at four, and Leticia, at eight, were too young to help. At almost twelve, Charles was employable in a society in which child labor provided an opportunity for additional income for hard-pressed families and capital advantage for eager employers" (Kaplan 1988: 38). Sent to work in a boot "blacking" factory,

The future was snatched away, the dreams and visions of his youth thrown off . . . This is the haunted place of Dickens's imagination . . . he was to take the bottles of blacking and prepare them for sale . . . When he had finished a few gross of these, "I was to paste on each a printed label." He worked for ten hours a day . . . his childhood came suddenly to an end, together with that world of reading and of imagination . . . But it was not gone . . . Instead it was suspended entire in the amber of Dickens's rich memory. (Ackroyd 1990: 59, 68)

---

[28] See also Munroe and Munroe (1972).

Until he died, Dickens was embittered by what he saw as a great injustice perpetrated by his parents. The common denominator in all these examples is the parent or guardian exercising the prerogative to maximize the child's value to themselves and the family. Another "modern" context in which children's labor was essential to the family's survival was the westward expansion in North America.

Little buckaroos

Children... were... the most accomplished and versatile workers of the farming frontier. (West 1992: 30)

Childhood, as depicted in the contemporary mass media, looks totally different than childhood in the village societies we've been discussing. And yet we need not go too far back in our own history to discover parallels to Papua New Guinea or the Yucatan. Were we to give a man-on-the-street survey in the USA, asking folks to complete the sentence "_____won the West," "Children" wouldn't make it into the top 100 choices. Yet the labor of children was critical in this enterprise.

"In 1877 Curt and Mary Norton left their Illinois farm to homestead near Fort Larned in western Kansas, with them came their eight children" (West 1992: 31). As Elliot West shows, very large families were essential for the enormous task of "taming" the frontier. Children willingly pitched in to help out wherever they were needed and they were largely self-taught. From numerous diaries we can construct word pictures of children farming, managing stock, hunting, fishing, marketing, transporting foods – all in the absence of adults. And children also contributed to family survival through wage employment: "Nine-year-old Cliff Newland was hired to haul supplies every week to cowboys in line camps, a round-trip of seventy-five miles. Cliff knew that the pay – fifty cents a day – helped him and his widowed father pay for necessities on their small West Texas ranch" (West 1992: 37).

Members of the emerging sect who called themselves Latter Day Saints took this process a step further by promoting polygyny[29] – so anxious were they to populate the heretofore uninhabited (except by the native people, of course) inter-mountain West (Harris 1990: 196). Brigham Young claimed a huge area for his "peculiar people" that included present-day Utah and significant portions of what became Colorado, Wyoming, Nevada, Arizona, and Idaho and gave it the ambitious title – Kingdom of Deseret. To accelerate the process of colonization, Young promoted polygyny (a practice embraced by the founder

---

[29] Anthropologists use the term *polygamy* to describe customary family arrangements where there are multiple spouses. *Polyandry* describes the one wife, multiple husband case and *polygyny* the far more common, one husband, multiple wives case.

of the church, Joseph Smith) to insure that every female of breeding age would, in fact, bear as many offspring as possible. Young, himself, set the example with his twenty-seven wives and more than fifty children.[30]

Homesteaders in the nineteenth and early twentieth century did not have to depend entirely on their own fecundity to increase the farm labor supply. Known as the "largest children's migration in history," so-called "orphan trains" carried about 200,000 children (Warren 2001: 4) from orphanages and foundling homes in eastern coastal cities to families in the Midwest (Kay 2003: iii) and West.

Demand was greater for younger, female children who were more easily trained or "tractable" than older children and boys (Gordon 2000: 17). And most were not, strictly speaking, orphans. They still had living parents or relatives but were "surplus" to the poor, urban families into which they were born. Flyers were sent out to communities along the railroad lines to bring more people out to see the children "paraded" (Warren 2001: 14) at train stations to prospective "parents" or employers (O'Conner 2001: xvi). This viewing by future families was recalled as a "horror" by the children, interviewed as adults (Warren 2001: 13). The Sisters of Charity proudly refused to display the children, giving each child a number that corresponded to a tag sent to the prospective parents (Gordon 1999: 37).[31]

The orphan trains continued until 1929 (Warren 2001: 20) which indicates how very recently our fundamental conception of children as chattel changed to viewing them as cherubs. In much of the Third World today, this transition has yet to take place.

Poverty and children's labor

[In Zimbabwe] Girls are good at panning. From as young as seven they are much better than boys are. Boys are too lazy and rough. They are better at helping in the shaft. (McIvor 2000: 182)

[Landowners in Pakistan think] Children are cheaper to run than tractors and smarter than oxen. (Silvers 1996: 82)[32]

---

[30] At age sixty-two Young married a twenty-five-year-old, at sixty-four he added a twenty-one-year-old wife on whom he sired his last child at the age of seventy (Moynihan 2002: 623). In the latter part of the nineteenth century, children's labor became even more critical in bringing this vast area into agricultural use as the male head of household was usually absent on trips outside the region to convert and recruit new settlers. From about 1890, males had a further reason for staying away from their homes as polygamy had been outlawed and they were subject to imprisonment if seen living openly with multiple wives (Kinkead 1996).

[31] Note also that overcrowded European orphanages in the seventeenth century were emptied when "children were shipped to labor-hungry America" (Sommerville 1982: 103).

[32] Comment of a landowner who employs children as young as four as farm laborers in Rawalpindi, Pakistan.

In many parts of the less-developed areas of the world, decreases in the carrying capacity of the land have not corresponded to a decline in fertility. In worst-case scenarios, like Guinea-Bissau, mothers who can barely feed themselves continue to obey the dictum: "you never have too many children" (Einarsdottir 2004: 63). And children suffer the consequences of this Malthusian dilemma. Parents go to desperate lengths to unburden themselves of child maintenance and/or to earn even a pittance from the child's labor. A Kyrgyz (Central Asia) boy of twelve is sent from his village to the city of Osh where he earns $1.50 a day, saving $ 0.25 per day to remit to his family (*The Times of Central Asia*, June 15, 2007: 3).

In Mexico, "Children between the ages of 7–14 make up 30 percent of the agricultural labour force . . . and are responsible for earning up to a third of their family's income" (Gamlin 2005: 2). On coffee plantations,

Children accompany their parents to the plantations from infancy . . . from around 5 years of age children are given their own small buckets and begin learning to pick . . . Their . . . work is an integral part of the survival strategies of these very poor families. By the time they are 7 or 8 years old they [are] expected to spend several hours a day picking intensively . . . Coffee plants are rarely higher than 1.5m, making the task of picking ripe coffee berries ideal for children. (Gamlin 2005: 6–8)[33]

In some areas of Zimbabwe (once one of the most prosperous countries in the developing world),

there are many signs that the population is becoming too great for the available land and that the natural environment is being threatened. People are now cultivating land traditionally set aside for grazing, as well as stony land on the steep sides of hills and sandy patches incapable of yielding meaningful returns on agricultural activity. (Chirwa and Bourdillon 2000: 128)

Under the circumstances, farmers not only cease paying school fees, but they may send children to farms where productivity can accommodate further labor inputs. They are rid of the child and the employing farmer has acquired an inexpensive worker. When queried the parties may claim a kin tie but these are often, or usually, fictitious. Employment conditions can be grim. A typical case is eleven-year-old Pedzisai. Sent to work on a more prosperous farm, his work day begins at 5.30 a.m. and ends at dusk. He has a 7 kilometer walk between his

---

[33] See also de Suremain (2000: 234). The reader might well ask, "How is this different than the bean farming scenario described earlier?" I would say there are two differences. I don't think the coffee pickers can choose *not* to participate whereas there appears little compulsion in the children's involvement with bean cultivation. Second, the Malian children are not prevented from attending school, whereas I believe that to be the case in the coffee-growing area described here. On the other hand, from the perspective of parents, these distinctions may not be apparent or important. One of the reasons for the ease with which child "labor" has become a worldwide phenomenon of vast proportion is that it sits on a firm foundation of the ubiquitous chore curricula.

morning job of weeding and his afternoon goat-tending assignment. Paid little, he is sent home, periodically, with his wages tied in a cloth, to be delivered upon arrival to his father (Chirwa and Bourdillon 2000: 134).

Elsewhere in Zimbabwe, impoverished parents whose farms can no longer provide food for the family force their children to work long hours in chrome and gold mining. Mining areas are characterized by "extreme environmental degradation" (McIvor 2000: 176). While younger children collect chrome from the surface and pan for gold, children above fifteen work in the mine shafts, at night, and longer than eight hours: "in order to overcome their fear, [they] smoke 'dagga' (cannabis) to give them courage . . . one claimed that 'they age early'" (McIvor 2000: 179).

Families in neighboring Mozambique, facing even more dire circumstances – due largely to decades of civil war – send their children, as young as nine, illegally, to work on small-scale tea farms in Zimbabwe. The lack of legal protection permits the farmers to withhold any payment to the children beyond their keep without fear of reprisal (Bourdillon 2000: 168).

Of course, there is mass migration to cities where families eke out a living by pooling their earnings. In Harare, the typical homeless family is fatherless, headed by a female whose ties with her natal village and extended family have been forcibly sundered. She will have borne six or more surviving children without whose labor none would survive (Mapedzahama and Bourdillon 2000).

In Burkina Faso, outside agencies have funded an expansion of cotton farming, providing resources to expand acreage and output. This has led to a labor shortage in the region which has been met by importing child workers from impoverished villages in the arid north. Boys over ten are recruited by an agent and trucked 200 miles to the cotton-growing area. They may not return home for at least a year. Lucky boys are treated well, fed, clothed, and sent back home after one year with a new bicycle. Unlucky ones are beaten, starved, and sent home without a bicycle because they "didn't work hard enough." Despite the abuse, long odds on earning a bike, and the horror stories, boys willingly volunteer, and parents encourage them to go. They are pleased to find that, after what amounts to a year's hard labor, their children come home much more servile and more willing to labor on the family's plot (de Lange 2005).

Virtual child slavery is not only cloaked by the benign tradition of fosterage – through creating fictive kin ties – it is also cloaked by labeling the work "apprenticeship." In Lomé, the capital of Togo, there are an estimated 25,000 plus "apprentices." Substantial fees in cash and liquor are demanded up front from potential apprentices. In reality, most apprentices "supply free, relatively unskilled labour . . . and . . . renew the workshop capital [through their] fees" (Marguerat 2000: 241). According to Marguerat (2000): "some bosses take on an unbelievable number of apprentices . . . as many as . . . twenty working on two sewing machines at a tailor's" (p. 243). After supplying years of free labor, the apprentice is "released" lacking critical skills so that he will be unable to compete for clients effectively (Marguerat 2000: 244).

In Thailand, rural women seem unhesitant about sending their daughters off to serve as prostitutes in urban areas. Indeed, economic surveys of rural villages show higher family incomes where daughters are in the sex trade (Taylor 2002). Similarly, in Chile, child prostitutes are able to buy things that are more luxurious than anything else the family owns. Hence, they are self-assured, with little sense of guilt (Silva 1981: 170).

In densely populated India, child labor is commonplace. In the lock industry, children use potassium cyanide and other toxic chemicals. Exposure to toxic fumes leads to pulmonary diseases. Intense heat is the norm in the glass industry where children must carry ingots of molten glass (Larson and Suman 1999: 710). Thousands of children, from the age of five, work ten-hour shifts in the match industry of Tamil Nadu. The Factories Act of 1948 outlawed child workers in the carpet industry, so manufacturing shifted from factories to the houses of the master weavers – effectively circumventing the restriction. In Gujarat, boys work in the diamond-cutting industry; their eyes are at great risk. "In the tea gardens of Assam, where the employment of children . . . is prohibited by law . . . a little girl is able to contribute 1 to 5 kg to her mother's basket every afternoon" (Dube 1981: 195–196, 199).

Impoverished Himalayan villages export children to Kathmandu for employment in carpet factories. The children may go unpaid for months during a "training period," and when and if they receive wages, they will be expected to send them back home. Indeed, many work up to sixteen hours a day to assist families saving for a festival celebration (Bray *et al.* 2002: 39). Other poor families may send boys as young as eleven to the recruiters to begin work as paid porters. They carry loads up to 48 kg, equivalent to 134 percent of their body weight (Malville 1999: 8).

Overpopulated rural villages in southern Pakistan export their children to serve as sex workers, entertainers, and camel jockeys (15,000 to date according to one estimate: Sabir-Farhat 2005). The latter are typically around four years old, and they are sent to the Gulf States where they may be treated abysmally in spite of the popularity and expense lavished on camel racing. In one survey, the great majority of children had experienced physical, including sexual, abuse. The researchers traced the network of agents from urban centers through intermediate towns to sub-agents in the village. Records from 1985 show that, initially, parents were paid a fee up front for the child. But so many were eager to place their children in the commercial sector – even though they rarely received the promised payments – that today they must *pay* a fee to get the agents to take their children. As laws are passed to protect children, traffickers easily finesse them. There's a whole industry in Pakistan producing fake birth

Figure 23 Fish sellers, Hodeidah, Yemen

and marriage certificates and passports. Officials are bribed to look the other way (Bokhari 2005).

In northern Pakistan, children are hardly sheltered from the tribal and sectarian violence endemic to the region. A video shown on the *National Geographic* website reveals family gun-making workshops in the Pashtun area. Four brothers ages eight to ten are working on hand-guns, filing, polishing, and cutting metal pieces with a hacksaw. In another room – adorned with a poster depicting Osama Bin Laden – boys work with milling machinery.[34] While international agencies may have adopted the child-centered morality of the West, locally traditional values – which identify children as chattel of their parents – prevail.

[34] National Geographic News, December 2004: http://magma.nationalgeographic.com; accessed 4.24.07.

In Colombia (in fact throughout the Andes) parents benefit from the earnings of their child (coal) miners:

children are preferred for ore extraction in the deepest, narrowest parts of the gallery because they are so small and agile. They work in hot, humid, contaminated spaces with no ventilation and constant exposure to lung-damaging toxic gases and dust. [They] start...from as young as six years old [able] to work as soon as they can pick up objects and drag them along. The smallest children work at the pithead: sorting coal, carrying wood, tools, water, and food. Older ones do jobs that demand a greater degree of resistance. Working hours usually extend from 1 or 2 a.m. through 8 or 9 a.m. when the children are released for school before later going to work in the fields. (Sastre and Meyer 2000: 87–88)

The child miners' health, not surprisingly, is very poor. They show signs of evident malnutrition with accompanying parasites, anaemia, and decaying teeth. Diseases associated specifically with mining include pharyngitis, tonsillitis, sinusitis, influenza, pulmonary ailments, and silicosis. Skin and limb infections as well as deformity are evident in long-term employees (Sastre and Meyer 2000: 89).

As China embraces free market principles and the economy booms, eager entrepreneurs readily use child laborers to gain a competitive advantage. As rural areas lose agricultural subsidies, farm families must put their children to work in dangerous industrial settings to survive. Stories of children injured or poisoned in industrial accidents are flooding the media. In one tragedy, five girls were killed when their fireworks assembly workplace exploded. Another sensational case involved a large-scale kidnapping operation in Guizhou Province to supply child laborers to assemble Christmas tree lights (Ching-Ching 2005: A1).

TVE sponsored a widely broadcast film to expose the fate of children in the village-based fireworks industry in Guatemala. Grinding poverty, brought on by overpopulation – the focal family had eight offspring – means children must start working by age six. Their little fingers are well suited to the delicate task of rapidly inserting wicks into tiny firecrackers, all the while inhaling gunpowder and risking horrific burns or death from an accident. They earn 50 cents for every finished string of 160 crackers (Marlow 2002).

Throughout, we've looked at children through different lenses, avoiding the tendency to evaluate childhood in one society by the ideals espoused in another. But it goes without saying that the lives of impoverished children in the Third World are miserable compared with contemporary children in the developed world – including those living in relative poverty in urban ghettos or rural hideaways. But I don't think I fall prey to the "noble savage" myth when I assert that children in traditional villages not yet blighted by overpopulation and outside influence also enjoy lives that are idyllic compared with the children we've just been reading about. Yet another lens we might use is historical and here we see many children whose experiences were akin to contemporary child miners and prostitutes.

Plus ça change...

Daughters working with their mothers [in Naples] are unlikely to get any wages at all, and their contribution to the household is made directly through their labour. (Goddard 1985: 19)

It is sobering to realize that the horror stories I've just been recounting would have been commonplace in the West until quite recently. Epitaphs from ancient Rome convey eloquently the child's economic importance to their parents:

In memory of Viccentia, a very sweet girl, a worker in gold. She lived nine years.

In memory of Pieris a hairdresser. She lived nine years. Her mother Hilara put up this tombstone. (Shelton 1998: 112)

In Stella's unvarnished history of child labor in Europe[35] just prior to the industrial revolution, he finds that apprentices rarely became masters; most ended up as laborers. Apprenticeship appears to have been less an educational medium than an avenue for craftspersons to acquire cheap labor and families to shed surplus children, particularly upon the death of one or both parents (Stella 2000). On the other hand, children born free whose parents couldn't care for them often ended up as slaves.

Nominally, girls went into domestic service as a kind of apprenticeship, and might save up enough money for a dowry, marry, and start a family. That was the ideal. More commonly, they remained in domestic service their whole lives, did not marry, but did bear children as a consequence of the sexual service they provided their master. These bastard children often ended up as slaves or indentured servants.

During the industrial revolution, the situation went from bad to worse. Even landless and homeless families might find work for their children in the mills where small size wasn't always a disadvantage, especially for close-work. Filthy, dangerous, and mind-numbing tasks occupied children as young as eight for up to sixteen hours a day. The birth-rate actually increased as parents saw new opportunities to gain value from their offspring (Sommerville 1982: 180).

An initial wave of reform aimed at children in the nineteenth century was actually less concerned with child labor (considered a good thing) than with

---

[35] While apprenticeships have changed over time in Europe, making them much more favorable for the apprentice, they're still highly structured and a very popular option for adolescents, especially in the German-speaking countries (Alice Schlegel, personal communication, April 5, 2007).

Figure 24 Spinners and doffers in Mollahan Mills

children who were "vagrants" (Zelizer 1985: 61), who'd somehow broken free of their families and the constrictions of the factory, like the boys in Dickens' *Oliver Twist*. The termination of child labor was strongly resisted, mostly by parents as an infringement on their economic interests in their children and, in many cases, as a loss of critical family income. In a US study of child labor conducted in 1895, it turned out that, while the children came from homes with a father present, he was usually unable to support the family. Most forms of blue-collar work were so taxing that men were likely to be "superannuated early in their forties" (Hine 1999: 125).

Demand for child laborers was curtailed primarily by improvements in technology that eliminated some of the more perfunctory, menial chores children were so good at. "During the 1870s one in three Macy's employees were cash boys or girls. Department stores were the largest single employers of city [children]. But the cash girls and boys were a short-lived army. In 1902 Macy's installed eighteen miles of brass pneumatic tubes and rendered [them] obsolete" (Hine 1999: 128). As new machines were more sophisticated, it behooved a company to employ more mature, stable, and better-educated workers (Hine 1999: 171). Ultimately, in the USA, it was the Depression that sounded the death knell for children as factory laborers. "Finding jobs for men who were married with children was the top priority [and] 1.5 million youths lost their jobs" (Hine 1999: 206). Children's labor will, no doubt, continue to be a contentious issue. I agree with Victoria Goddard's (1985) condemnation, with respect to children working, of the "tendency to take a moralistic standpoint . . . and uncritically transpose European urban middle-class expectations" (p. 18). Her subjects are actually from Western Europe, albeit in southern Italy, until recently one of the poorer regions of the continent.

Even the briefest visit to Naples will reveal to the often surprised tourist the existence of child workers. As you sit in any café you will see a nine or ten-year-old boy flit in and out of office buildings carrying his tray of cups of coffees, or hanging around during his work-break, with a cigarette dangling from his mouth in expert fashion. A more adventurous visitor, exploring the narrow streets of the old quarters of the city, will see small boys covered in grease helping out at a car mechanic's workshop or bicycle-shop. (Goddard 1985: 18)

But Goddard (1985) notes that the aggressive enforcement of child labor laws may drive children from well-regulated businesses to "the small workshop or sweatshop, unnoticed by either public or State, and cramped into unhygienic conditions by its lack of capital" (p. 18).

In Naples at least, parents who aspire to middle-class status for their children have made an important shift. Many now

opt for having two, or no more than three, children so that they can provide for them adequately and give them a solid basis for their adult lives. They look down upon couples who have many children [as] uncaring and selfish. [They] do not wish their own fate on their children: they find their own work tiring and dull, and want something better for their offspring. (Goddard 1985: 19)

Would this were an international trend of tidal-wave dimension.

8   Living in limbo

Introduction

Adolescent psychology is a Eurocentric enterprise. (Nsamenang 2002: 61)

... circumcision begins the process of separation from the old status known in Mende as *kpowa*... "fool, or stupid one"... into the new status of responsible, informed adult. (Day 1998: 65)

In humans, adolescence is associated with dramatic physiological change, notably puberty and a rapid growth spurt (Bogin 1994). As we will see, first menses is often treated as an important milestone, sometimes triggering an elaborate series of rites to mark the change in a young woman's status. Other physiological markers may be treated as culturally salient.

The period of youth on Vanatinai begins at about age fourteen, or when the signs of puberty... are visible to onlookers. For a girl that is when her breast buds are noticeable "the size of betel nuts," and for a boy when his voice begins to change... The term for young males is *zeva*, and for young females it is *gamaina*, which translates literally as "child female." (Lepowsky 1998: 128)

But societies vary in the alacrity with which they crown the achievement of biological maturity with the status of social maturity. In the West, the long hiatus between puberty and marriage/family formation has spawned an entire youth culture (Harris 1998: 275). And this culture has become so attractive to Americans that Hine claims: "Ours is a culture that is perpetually adolescent: always becoming but never mature" (Hine 1999: 10).

By contrast, in the Muslim Middle East, "adolescence, as perceived in modern Western thought, scarcely existed" (Fernea 1991: 453). In rural Morocco, marriage follows soon after puberty and, with this rite of passage, adulthood is conferred (Davis and Davis 1989: 59). Similarly, "Rural India lacks an adolescent culture. The burden of adult responsibilities falls quickly on young people" (Deka 1993: 132). Among the traditionally hunting and fishing North American Copper Inuit, girls "would often be married and performing many adult roles even before reaching sexual maturity" (Condon 1987: 67). The following analysis of adolescence in a Chinese fishing village fits thousands of villages around the globe:

> problems of adolescent adjustment appear to be minimal, especially for boys ... children grow up with a clear idea of exactly what their place in the socio-economic system [will] be ... the necessary skills ... acquired gradually and at home; marriages ... arranged when the children were about sixteen years old ... the ceremony of marriage conferred adulthood publicly and without any doubt [giving] adolescent sexual activity both limitation and legitimation ... there were virtually no alternatives offered to adolescents, no choices they could make ... no sharp discontinuities at any stage. (Ward 1970: 115)

In most societies, however, a discernible gap appears between puberty and the age at which young people are considered competent to create a family and household, thus affording an adolescent period – however brief (Schlegel and Barry 1991: 18). Throughout much of European history, the length of adolescence waxed and waned. During periods of relative plenty, children were better nourished, reached puberty sooner, and teenage marriages were the rule. In lean times, it took longer for couples to accrue sufficient resources to establish themselves and marriage was delayed well into their third decade. Similarly, among contemporary societies, age of menarche or onset of puberty ranges from twelve among wealthy, well-nourished Europeans through fourteen in poorer but reasonably well-nourished populations (Egypt) to seventeen in the least well-nourished areas (Nepal, Central Africa, New Guinea Highlands; Eveleth and Tanner 1990: 170). Further, during the past hundred years, with improved nutrition, the onset of menarche has steadily advanced: in Japan, for example, by a year each decade from 1950 onwards (Eveleth and Tanner 1990: 171).

Adolescence is also affected by the nature of the subsistence system. We have often noted that, in agrarian societies, children's economic contributions may be significant, and childhood is curtailed. As a corollary, adolescence might be brief or non-existent as children are put to work. However, among foragers, children may not become economically self-sufficient until their late teens so one sees a distinct adolescent period (Hewlett 1992: 229–230). However, it is rare to find a society that supports an adolescent period as long as that found among the modern executive class, typically a decade at least. In the past forty years, the number of offspring aged over twenty still living at home has increased dramatically. Demographers label this group "emerging adults," suggesting that, while they are biologically and legally adult, they are "unmarried, financially dependent and still being cared for by their parents" (Armstrong 2004). Similarly, Japan is now experiencing rapid growth in the population of "parasitic singles." By staying at home, older children save the cost of rent and continue to enjoy their mother's devoted service (Kingston 2004: 274).

A contemporary teenage "couple" is biologically capable of conceiving and bearing a child, and our legal system can confer legitimacy on their union.

Wealthy Western nations can insure that this young family has a roof over its head and doesn't starve. And, of course, the teenagers[1] themselves are driven by powerful forces to create and consummate heterosexual unions. Yet, all these forces must somehow be held in check during the ever-lengthening "student" years (Arnett 2002: 321). This is incendiary material awaiting spontaneous combustion. And yet, it doesn't happen often because society goes to enormous trouble to insure that teenagers are exercising their brains and not their libidos. The result: a significant segment of our society lives in a state of limbo – neither child nor adult. Not surprisingly, therefore, conflict is "higher in the West than in traditional cultures, largely because parents and adolescents ... [daily] grapple ... with ... parental authority and the borders of adolescent autonomy" (Arnett 2002: 312).[2]

Hangin'

You know, like if you came here and didn't hang around with us [High School clique], I wouldn't even know you. (Cusick 1973: 67)[3]

Many young [Tongan] boys are eager to move into the boys' huts, to be associated with the older boys, and to experience their comparative freedom. (Morton 1996: 112)

Boy, 15, is electrocuted scaling a transformer with his high-school pals. (*Salt Lake Tribune*, October 14, 2007: A1)

In most societies, boys and girls mingle freely during childhood until the pre-teen years. The Fore of PNG are typical: "Up to about the age of seven years, the activities of both boys and girls were much the same" (Sorenson 1976: 191). However, at nine, children spontaneously segregate. "First the girls and then the boys show a decided preference for same-sex playmates during this 'gang stage' " (Weisfeld 1999: 113).[4]

Also, from a very wide range of primate studies comes the common obser-vation that juvenile males form a distinct sub-set of the troop. Juvenile females

---

[1] The term "teenager" dates only from World War II (Hine 1999: 223).

[2] Parents are not the only authority figures that adolescents must contend with, as legislators also wade into the fray. In Utah, the "age of consent" for sex is eighteen. A woman of seventeen in a consensual relationship with a man ten years or more her senior is considered a victim of statutory rape. On the other hand, the "age of consent" to marriage, implying both sex *and* childbearing, is fourteen. Obviously, official concern for "sin" trumps any concerns for the adolescent's wellbeing or her offspring. Information from http://marriage.about.com, accessed 4.21.07; www.ageofconsent.com, accessed 4.21.07. The prevailing mores in Utah go back to antiquity. The legendary John Chrysostom of Byzantium urged his followers in the fourth century CE to marry their children off before puberty so that their virginity would not be compromised (Eyben 1991: 135).

[3] Comment by one of Phil Cusick's high school informants.

[4] See also Wilder (1970: 230). Pellegrini relates this segregation to the onset of ecologically divergent lifestyles of men and women, especially in foraging societies (Pellegrini 2004).

are attached to their mothers, eagerly seizing opportunities to allomother their younger siblings and groom high-ranking females (Baldwin and Baldwin 1977: 364) who might be future allies when they have offspring of their own. Their more limited socializing with peers is confined to a few friends (Schlegel 1995). But the young males, chased away by both ranking males and females, find security and entertainment (they're play partners) in hanging out together (Mitchell 1981). Mature males want to protect their breeding rights, and females want to protect their young from the boisterous attentions of their clumsy older sons; hence, the juveniles form what amounts to an outcast cohort or gang. For their part, the young males don't seem to resent their outcast status; on the contrary, they relish it.

The literature is replete with scenes like these:

[Ache] males of this age . . . often engage in obnoxious or high-risk behavior in order to gain attention. Although they often swagger in an exaggerated manner when among age mates or women and children, these adolescent boys also show clear signs of intimidation when fully mature adult males are present. (Hill and Hurtado 1996: 226)

Out of the range of parental authority, [US] adolescents often revel in their independence, cultivating in-group norms, slang expressions, distinctive clothing styles, and so forth to further separate themselves from adults. If they have some disposable income, they can further isolate themselves in cars and other settings. A favorite ploy is to retreat behind a sound barrier of "music" that is insufferable to adults. The same adolescents often engage in a variety of delinquent behaviors, as though they have adopted the adolescent culture *in favor* of the adult one. (Weisfeld 1999: 106 – emphasis added)

However, while our society might deplore this "anti-social" behavior and attempt to restrain it, elsewhere it is accepted philosophically. In the ultra-conservative Amish sect, for example, males "running wild" is tolerated as a brief but necessary interlude just prior to marriage (Hostetler 1964: 192). In much of the Pacific and in parts of Africa (Read 1960: 94) as well, adolescent males may be formally segregated in dormitory-like accommodations. We also see cases, like the Hopi, where boys move into the *khiva*, or men's house (Schlegel and Barry 1991: 70).

Even though these adolescent male associations may be referred to in the literature as "gangs" (Howard 1970), this may be misleading. While given a great deal of freedom, young Rotuman males, for example, "form the nucleus of communal labor in every village" (p. 66–67). That is, while they hang out and have fun together, Rotuman youth also relish the solidarity of working collectively for the community. Adolescent male associations can coalesce into civil defense forces on fairly short notice as apparently happened on a regular basis in medieval Europe (Mitterauer 1992: 164).

Scholars have explored the adaptive value of such adolescent male groups. Proposed benefits of adolescent "dispersal" include "that the likelihood of close kin mating is reduced . . . [and that it reduces the] concentration of animals that would degrade the local habitat" (Schlegel and Barry 1991: 20). Another possibility occurs in societies where hunting is cooperative, a situation found among chimpanzees as well as among many human groups. In these cases, the close fraternal relations within a cohort of young males just might establish the coordinated reflexes that will yield significant caloric payoffs in adulthood (Sugiyama and Chacon 2005). Successful hunting or, indeed, the opportunistic discovery of new food sources may be inherently risky. The juvenile group, human or non-human, travels away from "camp" in search of adventure where they may find food – or a predator may find *them*.

Dozens of studies have documented the heightened likelihood of sensation-seeking (Zuckerman 1984) or risk-taking by adolescent males in groups. For example, sub-adult "vervet monkeys were more likely to approach humans in the field and also approach strange males, enter a new area, or approach novel objects than were younger monkeys or adults" (Burghardt 2005: 390). Studies consistently find that juvenile curiosity or experimentation may lead to the discovery or spread of novel ideas such as the ability to use stone tools to crack open nuts (Whiten *et al.* 1999: 284). On the downside, among Japanese macaques, the adult sex ratio is five females to one male, and this is attributed entirely to males lost to risky behavior (for example, playing on roads; Fedigan and Zohar 1997).

Playful, rapid locomotion through a terrestrial environment, just like high-speed driving at night on winding roads, can have fatal consequences. Male-on-male fighting is not without risk. Mortality among primate male juveniles is high (Walter 1987: 359); however, Geary sees a potential payoff to the sensation-seeker in enhanced social rank and increased mating opportunities (Geary 1998: 63). Glenn Weisfeld has, in several studies, documented the relationship between an adolescent male's standing in the peer group (place in the dominance hierarchy), athletic prowess, physical attractiveness, and appeal to the opposite sex. (Weisfeld 1999: 215).

Among contemporary adolescents, the costs of risky endeavors abetted by peers may be more evident than the benefits. Lives are cut short or blighted by substance abuse, STDs, vehicle accidents, suicide,[5] and, notably, homicide. This last is a particular problem in the USA because of the near absence of restrictions on firearm purchase, storage, and use – "what might be a fist fight between young men in London or Paris easily becomes murder in Chicago or Washington, D.C." (Arnett 2002: 331).

Research portrays American adolescents as "not very concerned with the fulfillment of attachment or care giving needs . . . Instead, their focus is on who

---

[5] Suicide rates are particularly high among Native American and Amish youth (Associated Press, March 6, 2005); Hostetler (1964: 191–192).

they are, how attractive they are . . . and *how it all looks to their peer group"*
(Sax 2005: 133). Worse, peers can override the guidance of parents and teachers.[6] Studies document that peer influence can enhance or depress academic
performance (Kindermann 1993). Among African-Americans, Signithia Fordham and the late John Ogbu have shown how bright, academically talented
students are harassed by their peers – who accuse them of "acting white,"
of being "braniacs" or "gay." And these efforts are often successful: capable
students do reduce their effort to avoid out-shining their peers academically
(Fordham and Ogbu 1986; Ogbu 2003: 105).

Observing adolescent culture in the West we might note a subtle irony. As
discussed in this and the previous chapter, around the world adolescents are
chastened[7] or urged into responsible adulthood via initiation rites that may
involve painful minor surgeries and body-marking (Vizedom and Zais 1976).
The irony occurs when contemporary adolescents, living beyond the close
scrutiny of parents, *pay* to have their bodies pierced and tattooed to declare
their allegiance to the peer culture and *defiance* of adult authority (Myers 1992:
295).

In the next section, we'll see that the attributes of male adolescence that
may make young men a burden to their communities become distinct assets in
warrior societies.

Creating warriors

. . . during the period of seclusion [Sebei boys] engaged in stick-fighting duels and
practiced spear throwing and other military arts. (Goldschmidt 1986: 105)

[In Papua New Guinea] warfare, marriage, and initiation were interlocking institutions.
(Herdt 2001: 163)

Contemporary industrialized society would appear to dictate a lengthy period
of adolescence as youth take ever longer to complete the preparation necessary
for successful adulthood including adequately paid employment.[8] But in the
pre-modern world, *male* adolescence also extended well into the third decade
in societies that depended on maintaining what was, in effect, a standing army.
The best known of these societies was that of the Spartans who left nothing

---

[6] It is a commonplace observation in modern society that teenagers are "embarrassed" to be seen
by peers in company with their parents. The humor columnist Dave Barry tells a story about
a teenage daughter overheard "begging" her father, renowned crooner Billy Joel, not to sing in
public and embarrass her (Barry 1996).

[7] For example, "When an adolescent child flouts parental authority and has become a cause of
public annoyance, father and mother agree that he should be curbed by the *kisusa* rite" (Raum
1940: 303).

[8] Indeed, in a very recent study in the USA, even a college degree is no guarantee of competence
in our increasingly information-rich and complex society (Baer *et al.* 2006).

to chance in preparing the *ephebos*, including putting to death all but the most robust infants. Intense training began at seven when boys were transferred from their homes to a dormitory, remaining until they were twenty. Boys were exposed to extremes of physical endurance, and their emotional toughness was fostered by "a process of hazing and ridicule" (Sommerville 1982: 24–25).[9] Parents cheered on their sons during flogging competitions. "If a boy died during such a competition without making a sound, he became a hero" (Peisner 1989: 120).

As noted above, a significant element in Spartan training is the removal of the boy from his home (Shapiro 2003: 107). Seclusion from the domestic society of the village and/or home may be a critical element in effecting the "separation" that Van Gennep identified as the first stage in the *rite of passage* (Van Gennep 1908/1960: 62). In the past, Kpelle pre-adolescents in same-sex cohorts were dramatically removed from the village by masked figures and sequestered for months or years in specially constructed villages in the bush (deep forest) to enforce a transition from "carefree" childhood to responsible adulthood (Erchak 1977).[10]

Other societies where boys, especially,[11] leave their homes to reside with other adolescents and/or senior males include the Tapirapé (boys move to the *takana*; Wagley 1977: 149); Igbo boys move to the bachelors' house (Ottenberg 1989: 49), Ngoni boys move to a dormitory (Read 1960: 94), Wogeo boys move into what Hogbin (1970a) refers to as a "clubhouse" (p. 103), Trobrianders move to the *bukumatula* (Malinowski 1929), and in the Sepik River area of PNG, it is the *Haus Tambaran* (Tuzin 1980).

A few societies impose complete isolation on initiates. Following first menstruation, a Mehinacu (Brazilian rainforest) maiden will remain secluded for a year. Her male counterpart will be isolated in a small cell, his social circle limited to family members with whom he has brief whispered exchanges. He must refrain from physical activity or displays of emotional intensity. All this is "necessary if he is to grow up into a strong man and become a good wrestler, a clever hunter, and a successful fisherman" (Gregor 1970: 243).

---

[9] Up until fairly recently, elite English boarding schools (and their USA counterparts) for males weren't all that different in terms of the constant hazing of younger by older boys, the emphasis on physical deprivation and removal from family, and daily engagement in team sports. This is probably what prompted Arthur Wellesley, the Duke of Wellington, to remark: "The battle of Waterloo was won on the playing-fields of Eton."

[10] For comparable Mende (Sierra Leone) practices, see Little (1970).

[11] One reason that boys are much more likely to be removed from their homes than girls and subjected to severe pain and privation during initiation – aside from toughening them up to be warriors – is the very widespread notion that boys cannot grow into men without the systematic *removal* of female essence acquired during gestation, birth, and infancy. These ideas are also found in societies that embrace the Christian concept of original sin (of Eve), hence the need for infant baptism.

Inca society was similar to Sparta in its determination to turn well-born boys into fearless warriors. After years of rigorous training that included, for example, carrying "heavy loads of firewood to build their strength" (Shein 1992), they were put through the culminating tests during the great *capac raymi* festival. Aside from marking the transition to adulthood, the ceremonies tested the boys' resistance to suffering through fasting, running long, arduous marathons, and sleeping on the ground in the high mountains. Those who persisted had their earlobes perforated in the *tocochicoy* rite and received the large ear-plugs characteristic of South American warriors. Finally, the last test was a footrace down from the mountain which usually resulted in a few crippling injuries as all sought to become the "first boy to reach the bottom and drink the *chicha* proffered by the girls" (Shein 1992: 77).

The *Codex Mendoza* is a sixteenth-century manuscript prepared by Aztec scribes and commissioned by then Mexican governor Mendoza. Much of the third part, about twenty pages, deals with youth. In colorful pictures and accompanying text in Spanish and Nauhatl, the scribes detailed Aztec (or Mexica) childrearing practices. The most noteworthy aspect of this is the frequent depiction and description of severe corporal punishment and the threat of the same inflicted on boys and girls as young as eight. The severity gradually escalates and includes, for the recalcitrant eleven-year-old, being forced to inhale chili smoke. Novice priests who are wayward are shown festooned with maguey spikes jabbed into their skin by the angry priests. Young soldiers are shown having their hair cut off and their scalp singed by a firebrand (Berdan and Anawalt 1997).

Historically, pastoralist societies in Africa were noted for their ready willingness to attack neighboring groups in raids to secure cattle and women. In turn, we frequently see the creation of distinct warrior sub-cultures into which young men are indoctrinated (Gilmore 2001: 209). Among the Dinka of the Sudan, boys were initiated between the ages of sixteen and eighteen and given gifts of well-designed spears symbolizing the military function of youth (Deng 1972). The pastoralist Masaai are also notorious warriors. The process of joining the warrior elite, becoming a *moran*, begins with a rite of passage.[12] The principal test of a boy's worthiness is the circumcision during which a "flinch or even the bat of an eyelid as primitive razor sears into flesh is interpreted . . . as a desire to run away and [this loss of] honour . . . can never be redeemed" (Spencer 1970: 134).

After the circumcision ceremony, the initiates spend a period . . . under strict ritual prohibitions [in] close company with other initiates. These prohibitions end with a further ceremony at which the initiates formally become moran; they start to grow

---

[12] More recent research finds a close association between the effort invested in rites of passage for boys and the importance of promoting a warrior mentality (Sosis *et al.* 2007).

their hair, and to plait it and embellish it with red ochre. This is the first of a series of ceremonies known as *ilmugit*, and the initiate vows . . . not to eat any meat seen by a woman . . . [rather] meat of the bush where the moran belong and where they share one another's company . . . [while avoiding that of] young . . . women. (Spencer 1970: 137)

Not surprisingly, the *moran* are looked on with awe, especially by young boys. They are admired and feared[13] but, at the same time, their physical and symbolic isolation from the community insures that older men can maintain their control over access to the tribe's young women. They decide when and to whom a *moran* will finally, at age thirty to thirty-five, be allowed to marry.

In Polynesia, boys became men during, sometimes protracted, rites which demonstrated their courage, including either the removal or the incising of the foreskin. Before they rejoined society, they would be tattooed extensively. Thus, like the *moran*'s unique hairdo, their new status was obvious to all. Indeed, on Tonga, males who'd not yet been cut did not take meals with the household and "would be spurned by the girls . . . teased that they [were] unclean and still young boys" (Morton 1996: 112).

The warrior societies native to North America employed a number of similar tactics to prepare young men for the rigors of armed conflict. The Creek of North America inflicted bloody wounds to punish mischievous boys but also "the profusion of blood . . . serves to convince the child that the loss of it is not attended with danger, or loss of life: that when he becomes . . . a warrior, he need not shrink from an enemy" (Swanton 1928: 363). Navajo boys were awakened in the middle of the night and made to roll naked in the snow (Leighton and Kluckhohn 1948: 56). Among the Plains Indians, aspirant warriors were sent off to fast in the wilderness as part of their "vision quest" (Delaney 1995). Indian youth attached a boulder to their bodies with hooks dragging it considerable distances to demonstrate courage and endurance.

Another bastion of the warrior cult can be found in several regions of Papua New Guinea (Strathern 1970).[14] Gil Herdt, working among the "Sambia," has contributed to our understanding of the shaping of boys into misogynist warriors. Elaborate rituals and rites of passage separate boys from their mothers and make them "manly," teach them to despise and lord it over women and enemy tribesmen. The first stage in this initiation includes days of hazing, fasting, beating, sleeplessness, and sudden surprises. This is followed by forced nosebleeding to remove female contaminants.

The first boy is quickly grabbed. He struggles and shouts but is held down by three men . . . before [he] can catch his breath the initiator rolls up cane-grasses and, as

---

[13] Interestingly, *moran* bravery and endurance are augmented by the use of various drugs, including stimulants (Lehmann and Mihalyi 1982: 345).

[14] Also: "Kuma initiations are about male dominance, clan prestige, the appeasement of spirits, and warfare" (Reay 1959: 172).

the novice's head is held back, pushes them down repeatedly into the boy's nose. Tears and blood flow as the boy is held...then another boy...is grasped and bled. One lad tries to run away but is grabbed...he is...bled harder and longer than the others...Another boy is penetrated until blood flows profusely; and after each instance of this, the collectivity of men raise the ritual/war chant. (Herdt 1990: 376)

Similarly, among the Mende of Sierra Leone,

Each boy is seized in turn by a number of the men...stripped naked and his clothes kept to wipe away the blood which flows from the cuts. Then he is thrown roughly on to the ground, and the appropriate marks are made, either by a hook, which raises the skin, or by a razor. If he shows fright, or tries to run away, his head is pushed into a hole which has already been dug for the purpose. During the operation, the "spirit" plays loudly on his pipe and there is a clapping of hands, which drowns the noise of the boys' cries and prevents them being overhead by passers-by, especially women and children. (Little 1970: 214)

One element that looms large in the training of male adolescents in much of Africa (Little 1970: 218–219; Goldschmidt 1986; Konner 2005: 30) and PNG is misogyny, as noted above. There is a distinct focus on teaching boys to feel superior towards and contemptuous of women. The "text" of many messages conveyed to initiates is replete with references to women's physical weakness relative to men and their power to pollute through menstrual and puerperal blood. Another tool in the men's arsenal is the use of "secrets," including sacred terms, rituals, locations, and objects such as masks. These "secrets" are denied to women on pain of death.[15] For the Arapesh (Sepik Region, PNG), "initiation ceremonies [include] an ordeal followed by the novices being shown the secret paraphernalia...flutes, frims, paintings, statues, bullroarers" (Tuzin 1980: 26).

Denying female access to powerful spirit forces aids in maintaining male hegemony. A Mehinacu girl "cannot learn the basic myths because the words 'will not stay in her stomach'" (Gregor 1990: 484). Among the Igbo of southestern Nigeria, boys are moved through a series of ceremonial stages that simultaneously distance them from women and bind them to senior males. From an early age, boys are gradually invested with the trappings of their authority, including boys' masquerades, their transfer to the boys' house, and various rituals – all of which were taboo to females (Ottenberg 2006: 117–119).

However, in some societies, notably in Africa, gender and rank are "contested" openly. Hence, initiation rites, focused on adolescents who'll soon

---

[15] During fieldwork in Gbarngasuakwelle one evening, I had gathered a small group consisting of a woman and three or four children in order to record folk-tales. A bell rang (although I didn't hear it) and my informants almost literally turned white with fear and immediately raced to their homes, warning me to douse the lantern and go to sleep. I learned the next day that the bell had signaled the imminent arrival of a masked "devil" into the village to look upon whom would mean instant death for anyone other than males already initiated into the *Poro* secret society (Lancy 1996: 99).

become principal players, reflect these conflicting claims for hegemony. The Chewa (southern Africa farmers) case is particularly interesting. There are "junior" secret societies, associations that build and use versions of the senior, adult masks and costumes and initiation rites for boys *and* girls. Children are taught to guard zealously the respective secrets taught by their female and male elders such as the identity of the *Nyau Yolemba* masked spirit figure. For their ceremonies, males and females are costumed differently and conduct their rites in bush and village, respectively.[16] Ultimately, children are taught the fundamental complementarity of their community's ethos.

It is clear that the major concern of *chinamwali* [initiation rite] is reproduction. This is in sharp contrast to the men's *nyau* association, which is in charge of funerary ritual. The men of the nyau actually say, "Because women make a secret of birth, we make a secret of death." Chewa men are excluded from witnessing births and are never told openly how a child is born. (Yoshida 2006: 234)

We might also want to briefly look at the training of warriors in more complex societies. In Japan, the preparation of Samurai included puberty rites featuring severe ordeals (Sofue 1965: 156–157). During World War II, the training of suicidal *kamikazè* pilots involved *seishin kyoiku* – rigorous physical and spiritual training to build character (Rohlen 1996: 50). The Hitler Youth and Soviet Young Pioneers both capitalized on the idealism and fanaticism characteristic of adolescence (Valsiner 2000: 295).[17] During the Cultural Revolution, Chinese authorities used the naturally "anti-social," rebellious nature of adolescents in recruiting, training, and then setting them loose as "Red Guards" to destroy bourgeoisie, Western, or intellectual elements of Chinese society. Today, Palestinian terrorist organizations easily recruit male and female adolescents to serve as suicide bombers. Again, there are fundamental biological and psychological aspects of adolescence that render them susceptible to group-think mentality. Normal standards of human decency are suspended, allowing them to commit crimes in the name of the group.

Even when the goal of training is to convert the faithless through missionary work and not kill them, the training regimen and use of adolescent psychology may be similar (Dutcher 2000). The charismatic religious reformer friar Savonarola, operating in Florence in the fifteenth century, successfully seduced the youth of the city to aid his cause:

Children informed on parents who kept books on magic or indecent paintings, dice, or beauty aids at home. They were even protected by police while breaking into houses to look for such things to add to the great bonfires of "vanities." When the traditional rulers of Florence were able to reassert themselves and execute the reformer, they naturally destroyed the political organizations of the young. (Sommerville 1982: 96)

[16] See also Kratz (1990: 456).   [17] See also Lupher (1995).

Spencer's observations on the Masaai have wide applicability: "brainwashing for religious and political ends can be effectively done by finding a 'sore spot' in the victim's experience and working away at it" (Spencer 1970: 149). Don Tuzin provides a vivid illustration of the use of such psychology by Arapesh (Sepik Region of PNG) males to enthrall initiates in the *Falanga* rite:

immediately following it [the ordeal], the initiators drop their razors, spears, cudgels or what have you, and comfort the boys with lavish displays of tender emotion. What resentment the latter may have been harboring instantly dissipates, replaced by a palpable warmth and affection for the men who, moments before, had been seemingly bent on their destruction. As their confidence recovers itself, the novices become giddy with the realization that they have surmounted the ordeal. (Tuzin 1980: 78)

As we've seen, many initiation ceremonies include contests or military-like exercises that were central to the preparation of warriors. And these have given us much of our modern repertoire of organized sports. Cudgel fighting was common among East African pastoralists (Read 1960: 95). Xhosa informants suggested that, while cudgel games are now "just a sport," earlier they were considered central to a warrior's training.[18] Still, "a *mtshotsho* boy who fights well and fearlessly will be admired [and] respected" (Mayer and Mayer 1970: 168). In West Africa, cudgel fighting gives way to wrestling which seems to have transitioned smoothly from its role in warrior training to become a popular (cheering spectators, side betting, weight and skill levels) sport (Ottenberg 1989: 85–86; Stevens 1996). In East Asia the "martial arts" have also evolved from warrior training into competitive sports (Donohue 1994).

In the absence of a warrior sub-culture and the energy-absorbing pursuit of athletic glory, adults may yet feel the necessity of curbing or taming their obstreperous and "self-centered" adolescents.[19] Canela tribesmen from Brazil publicly chastise and humiliate wayward youth. A senior male might call his "nephew" to stand before the assembled village while he stomps

on the youth's insteps, yank[s] him off the ground by his sideburns, and give[s] him a blistering lecture, describing his shameful infractions for all the women to hear . . . [rakes] the . . . youth's legs with rodents' teeth until they bleed . . . forces pepper into his mouth, and . . . draws back his foreskin for the assembled men and women to see the glans of his penis. Girls who had violated the norms of sexual and dietary restraint [are] shamed in this ceremony by having their leaf aprons torn off and their genitalia exposed. (Crocker and Crocker 1994: 37).

The Hopi of the southwestern USA were not known as particularly warlike, especially compared with their Navajo neighbors. But male initiation could be quite severe. In Don Talayesva's autobiography, he confesses to being quite

[18] For the Zulu as well (Edgerton 1988: 179).

[19] These "typical adolescent personality traits are widely reported and may have adaptive value" (Weisfeld 1999: 106).

"naughty" as a boy. So, when he was initiated into the Katchina society with his age group, his father arranged for him to be taught a lesson by having the Whipper Katsinas give him extra blows with the sharp-spined ocotillo whips to "drive the evil from [his] mind, so that he may grow up to be a good and wise man" (Simmons 1942: 80). Tapirapé young men who were "known to be having sexual relations, or [were] getting too imperious [were] scratched over [the] thighs and arms with the teeth of the agouti until the blood flowed freely" (Wagley 1977: 151).

However, more commonly, the Tapirapé coming of age ceremony is dignified, solemn, and nostalgia provoking. The initiate's hair and body are carefully decorated, "chest and arms ... covered with soft white bird down, glued to [the] body with a sticky sap" (Wagley 1977: 153–154). A large headdress is placed on his head. Under the gaze of his community, he will dance for many hours on end with little relief until, finally, retiring from the plaza with honor.

Note the similarity to an age-old European rite that I experienced first hand as a high school exchange student in Germany.

Traditionally the acquisition of good manners is closely related to learning to dance. The classical dancing school claimed to provide training in both. For young people from the upper classes, the first dance meant far more than participation in youthful pursuits. It meant being introduced to "society," which presupposed that one had mastered its conventions. The dancing school provided a preparation for this important stage of growing up. We may regard attendance at dancing school as one of the "initiation rites" of the bourgeois society. (Mitterauer 1992: 43).

To conclude this section, let us consider one of the most intriguing theories for the famous Paleolithic-era cave paintings in France and Spain. The paintings, dramatic and often colorful renderings of large mammals (wooly mammoths, bears, rhinoceros, bulls, horses), are typically found deep inside a cave system. Visitors would have to travel a considerable distance on tortuous passageways, possibly in complete darkness. Then, sudden light from oil lamps would reveal the vivid images to a cohort of extremely vulnerable and frightened young men. The most compelling evidence for this idea stems from the fact that, in more recently discovered caves, where the passageways were thoroughly studied before a horde of visitors came tramping through, the footprints of dozens of slowly treading adolescent males are clearly outlined (Johnson 1989: 246).

Sexuality

[Rotuman boys] are expected to pursue sexual gratification ... whereas girls are discouraged and in most cases closely guarded. (Howard 1970: 71)

It is clear that when no property accompanies the marriage, virginity is of little interest. (Schlegel 1991: 725)

In 1904, G. Stanley Hall published the first comprehensive treatment of adolescence. This work was to have enormous influence on psychology and on anthropology as well. Ironically, rather than seeing the "problems" of adolescence as due to delayed or thwarted sexuality, Hall, rather puritanically, saw modern society as creating a "hothouse atmosphere" in which sexual "ripening" was accelerated (Hall 1904). Nevertheless, he argued that adolescence was universally a stressful period fueled by the individual's emerging sexuality.[20] Urged on by her mentor, Franz Boas, Margaret Mead took up this gauntlet and traveled to Samoa to study adolescence in a "primitive," non-Western society.

Mead concluded that Hall was wrong – adolescent stress was culturally constructed rather than biologically based – because Samoan adolescents were relaxed about sex and everything else. This single negative instance Mead argued was enough to undermine Hall's universality claim (Mead 1928). Mead's claim, in turn, was challenged – posthumously – by Derek Freeman. His work – *Margaret Mead and Samoa: The Making and Unmaking of an Anthropological Myth* – embroiled American anthropology for years. Freeman offers a multilayered and thorough documentation of adolescent stress and restricted sexuality in Samoa beginning with the earliest travelers' reports from the islands. Far from the easy and casual approach to sex described by Mead,[21] Freeman describes an ancient and still powerful "cult of virginity," present in Samoa and throughout western Polynesia:

taupous, or ceremonial virgins, occupied positions of great social importance and virginity at marriage was very highly prized . . . young chieftains would vie for the special prestige associated with the deflowering of a *taupou* . . . in public . . . If no proof of the bride's virginity was obtained, she was sorely abused by her friends, called prostitute . . . exposed as a nonvirgin, her brother, or even her father . . . rushed upon her with their clubs, and dispatched her. (Freeman 1983: 227, 229, 231).

Freeman goes on to describe the less spectacular but nevertheless pervasive restrictions on adolescent sexuality brought to Samoa by the Victorian-era Christian missionaries who, for example, hounded the appropriately dressed-for-the-climate Samoan women into wearing chaste, full-body-covering *mumus*. Margaret Mead might have had better luck in working with Quechua speakers in the Vilcanota Valley of Peru. Long-term ethnographer Inge Bolin concludes that adolescent anxiety is rare because a "degree of promiscuity is not frowned upon until marriage or a firm commitment has been

---

[20] To the present, our society has remained deeply divided on the issue of whether teenagers are harmed emotionally and physically by sexual activity or the reverse, harmed by being prevented from fulfilling their sexual needs (Levine 2002).

[21] Alice Schlegel suggested to me that Freeman focused mainly on aristocratic Samoan culture while Mead may have been interacting primarily with very low-status girls with consequently different mores (personal communication, November 2005).

made" (Bolin 2006: 142). In the Massim area of PNG, including the Trobriand and Vanatinai Islands, where matrilineality prevails, adolescent sexuality is considered healthy and normal. Adolescents are expected to become distracted and preoccupied by their physical appearance and sexual attractiveness, and adults willingly share their love potions with them (Lepowsky 1998: 133).

The "Red" Xhosa in southern Africa are yet more liberal. Sex play is tolerated in childhood, and *metsha,* or external sexual intercourse, is encouraged in adolescence. Indeed, girls who spurn sex are thought to become stiff and eventually turn into witches. And "a male who has not had sweethearts – an *isishumana* – is unlikely to enjoy prestige in the youth organization" (Mayer and Mayer 1970: 175). As a result, youth "problems" are minimal, and "traditional" girls – because they practice *metsha* – are less often pregnant than "'School' (Christian) or urban Xhosa girls" (Mayer and Mayer 1970: 163).

A surprising number of societies, including the prim and proper Balinese, tolerate sexual play among very young children (Covarrubias 1937: 137).[22] The Muria from central India move their children into a dorm-like structure from late childhood to the end of adolescence. This *ghotul* is coed and girls and boys are encouraged to form short-term but mutually satisfying relationships. In effect the Muria seem to be bowing to the inevitable (Elwin 1947).[23] Similarly, in the Nicobar Islands, boys and girls have the sexual freedom to find a good match, and these unions are fully legitimated by their families and the community (Mann 1979: 99). In Tamang communities in the Himalayas, adolescents are expected to enjoy sexual relations discretely during celebratory occasions such as night-long shamanistic rituals and community-wide dances (Fricke 1994: 102).

Among the Ache, a girl may have as many as four different sexual partners *before* menarche. The Yuqui, another group of South American forest dwellers, believe that "it is only by having intercourse with a ... number of men that [a girl] is able to achieve sexual maturity, or ... to be able to bear children" (Stearman 1989: 93). Similar beliefs, while not common, are found scattered around the globe and include, for example, the Lepcha of Sikkim (Gorer 1967: 175). Jane Lancaster surveys research showing that apes don't necessarily become fertile immediately post-menarche; humans are sub-fertile for at least two years. Hence, "although sexual activity almost invariably follows menarche, the likelihood of pregnancy is very low for the first few years" (Lancaster 1986: 25). She also identifies many possible benefits of pre-marital promiscuity including

[22] See also Goldschmidt (1986: 97).
[23] For a lengthy discussion of present-day adolescent cohabitation among the Kond in Orissa (western India), see Hardenberg (2006).

the development of strategies to attract a mate and the ability to discern the value of potential future spouses (Lancaster 1984).[24]

In broad areas of New Guinea including the Highlands and the Sepik, it is *male* reproductive potency that must be developed, and sexual relations, per se, are inadequate for this task. There is the "conviction that maleness, unlike femaleness, is not a biological given. It must be artificially induced through secret ritual" (Herdt 2001: 165). One impediment is the boy's femininity, acquired as he is born of, nursed, and raised by women. The Anga of the Eastern Highlands counter this threat by a rite in which eight- to twelve-year-olds are smeared (by their mother's brother) with red pandanus seeds and red ocher (representing blood) and pushed through narrow structures decorated with red leaves representing the uterus and vulva. The drama continues through the ritual daubing with yellow mud, which all newborns receive, and the boys are now reborn as males, capable of reproduction (Bonnemere 2006).

Canela (Brazilian foragers) society occupies a kind of middle ground between *laissez faire* and restrictive. Young men can expect to draw sexual satisfaction and strength from intercourse with much older women – as contrasted with the alleged strength-depleting effect of sex with their peers (Crocker and Crocker 1994: 33). Adolescent girls, on the other hand, should copulate with older men to *gain* strength and vitality (Crocker and Crocker 1994: 34).

While a relaxed attitude towards pre-adult sexuality may be the rule in foraging and some pastoralist societies,[25] it is seen as problematic in more complex, patriarchal societies (Hotvedt 1990; Barry III 2005; Broude and Greene 1976). A woman's value as a provider may be diminished[26] thus, by default, enhancing her value as a breeder. Consequently, others control the young woman's sexuality, as a means of confidently verifying the paternity of her offspring. Virginity is a key factor in a daughter's marriageability, and it behooves families to guard it vigorously: "a [Rotuman] girl's sexuality was 'owned' by her local kinship group; it was they who benefited by a favorable marital transaction" (Howard 1970: 72).[27] Among the Gebusi, living in an area of Papua New Guinea bisected by the Fly River, "adult kinswomen . . . adopt a strong protective relationship towards adolescent girls in regard to male sexual conduct" (Cantrell 1998: 96).

An extreme case is provided by the Guajiro pastoralist peoples of northern Colombia. From toddlerhood, girls are warned to keep their distance from all males and told that sex is evil. Later, they will be severely scolded for conversing with boys and, if they persist, the "mother may place the tip of a hot branding iron on [her] vagina [as] a convincing object lesson" (Watson 1972: 151).

---

[24] Perhaps as a result of undernutrition, "too-early" pregnancy does not appear to be a conspicuous problem among societies where sexual relations begin at the onset of adolescence, or earlier.

[25] Nor is this parental and community tolerance extended only to *heterosexual* relations among pre-adults (Blackwood 2001).

[26] (See chapter 2, p. 30).   [27] See also Caldwell *et al.* (1998: 143).

The rationale for this repressive treatment lies in the fact that the groom and his kin must assemble bride-price in the form of livestock and jewelry which is seen as "purchasing . . . the bride's sexual integrity for the exclusive pleasure and delight of her husband" (Watson 1972: 153). Similarly, in Turkey, separation of the sexes and women's limited power is justified in the name of honor (*namus*). *Namus* requires that "men control the sexuality of their women . . . wives, daughters, sisters, and other female relatives" (Kagitçibasi and Sunar 1992: 78).

One aspect of the large complex of customs surrounding young women's sexuality that has become a *cause célèbre* is clitoridectomy.[28] In spite of very widespread and persistent international condemnation of the practice (Rajman and Toubia 2000; Gruenbaum 1982),[29] it shows no signs of abating and, indeed, is most vigorously defended by the very women who have been "mutilated." Originating in Egypt,[30] it is still practiced on the majority of Muslim and Christian Egyptian girls. It is also common throughout much of Africa and in areas where Muslims are in the majority, affecting upwards of 100 million women (Matias 1996: 2). The most commonly voiced rationale for clitoridectomy is to curtail the woman's sex drive, reducing the risk that she will fornicate or be tempted into adultery.

Another indicator of how deep-seated these attitudes are is the popularity in the Middle East of the recently introduced Barbie-like doll, "Fulla." Described as "Barbie with Muslim Values," Fulla comes wearing a full-length black *abaya* and scarf. A pink felt prayer rug is included as an accessory. Less busty than the previously shunned Barbie and with long *black* hair, Fulla is, commercially, a Barbie clone with an extensive, flashy wardrobe (sold separately) (New York Times, September 22, 2005: A4). More seriously, girls are prevented from going very far in school in much of the Muslim world, ostensibly to prevent them from forming even the most fleeting relationship with a boy (Davis and Davis 1989: 61). Attitudes are gradually liberalizing but, in the 1960s in Baalbeck, Lebanon, Prothro (1961) found universal prohibition on girls' schooling for fear that, by becoming literate, they could engage in illicit communication (p. 15).[31] A similar rationale was used in Taliban-controlled Afghanistan to block women from schooling.[32]

---

[28]   Information from www.equalitynow.org; accessed 4.21.07.

[29]   Attitudes are slow to change but, according to Nadia Lancy, many African governments have outlawed the practice and are promoting alternative rituals to mark the rite of passage to womanhood: "Female genital mutilation," *Inside Africa*, CNN International, November 11, 2006.

[30]   Evidence for circumcision rites are found in various Egyptian sources beginning with a scene of ritual (male) circumcision from a sixth dynasty (twenty-fourth-century BCE) *mastaba* tomb (King 2006: 48–49).

[31]   See also Williams (1968: 49).

[32]   The Taliban were equally vigilant over the morality of boys, ending the long-standing Pashtun custom of senior males acquiring boys as sexual playmates. A reporter recently observed,

Figure 25 Yemeni schoolgirl with Fulla backpack

Sociologists have charted important differences in cultural prescriptions for
adolescents' sexuality even between otherwise similar societies. In Europe
the attitude of authority figures tends to be relatively permissive. Students are
given accurate information in school regarding reproduction and ready access
to contraception. In the USA, the political influence of the Religious Right has

however, that "the streets of Kandahar are now full of bearded men (usually married with
families), walking openly accompanied by 15- or 16-year-old boys": *Pravda*, March 27, 2002,
http://english.pravda.ru; accessed 04.21.07.

led to repressive policies.[33] For example, Hine (1999) describes parent teacher association (PTA) members in North Carolina diligently excising portions of the ninth- grade health textbook that discussed sex, contraception, and AIDS (p. 23). Hence, while the level of sexual activity varies little between the USA and Europe, poorly informed US adolescents are far more likely to suffer harmful effects – for example, unplanned pregnancy and sexually transmitted disease – than their Western European counterparts (Arnett 2002: 317).[34]

Another cross-cultural divide exists among immigrants from less-developed regions living in the developed countries.[35] Barbara Miller (1995) has studied Hindu communities in the USA where the parents go to great lengths to inculcate values imported from India (p. 74). The results are mixed: many young women resist parental dictates to dress modestly, preferring to assimilate. And, while many adolescents are forbidden from dating, they do so surreptitiously. With contempt, one informant asserted: "Nobody really takes chastity seriously anymore" (Miller 1995: 76).

Restrictive attitudes regarding women's sexual activity often go hand in hand with the contrasting expectation for young males[36] to display machismo through conquests.[37] Sebei (East African pastoralist) youth "will bleed their penises with a thorn 'to make them sharp,' so they can penetrate a virgin" (Goldschmidt 1986: 105). Among the Lepcha, "Almost all boys and young men get their first real sexual experience and training from an older married woman"

---

[33] However, I would agree that "No clear mores currently exist in American society concerning the sexual behavior of unmarried young people in their teens" (Arnett 1999: 320). One reason for this ambiguity – unique in the world – is that, even among fundamentalist Christians such as the Mormons, there is the notion that young women can, indeed *should*, be "sexy" *and* chaste. For example, in Utah, junior and high school "spirit squads" are extremely popular. Essentially, pubertal girls wearing revealing, skin-tight outfits perform, ensemble, suggestive Las Vegas-style dance routines at half-time during athletic contests. In spite of the potent sexuality projected by these young women, the overt messages are all about fitness, teamwork, patriotism – anything but sex! Similarly, we find even very young girls using "make-up," and by "fourth and fifth grades some girls own their own cosmetics which they often freely share . . . " (Thorne 1993: 148).

[34] The ideological purity of "abstinence only" sex education in the USA comes with an enormous price tag. One estimate of the annual cost of teen pregnancy in the country is $7 billion (Adams 2005b). Teenage mothers are almost inevitably on the public dole and their babies are likely to be born premature with greatly increased antenatal expenses. Then, too, both mother and child have extremely poor educational prospects, hence the long-term cost to taxpayers of inadequate pregnancy prevention programs will be far higher than the figure just mentioned.

[35] And between morally restrictive sub-cultures, such as the Amish, and the mainstream. See for example, Hostetler (1964: 188).

[36] While this imbalance almost inevitably favors males, rare cases where women are expected to initiate sexual contact while men are intimidated by sex have been found. The Kaulong of Papua New Guinea are perhaps the best known example (Goodale 1980: 135).

[37] " . . . boys in Guajiro society are taught surreptitiously by male socializers to be sexually aggressive and to seek sexual conquests as long as this activity poses no risk to themselves or to their families. A girl must therefore, contend with the active, seductive sexual interest of boys whenever she is in their company" (Watson 1972: 152). Further examples: Booth (2002: 211); Lewis (1961: 38).

(Gorer 1967: 161). In the movie *Monsieur Ibrahim*, set in 1960s France, the local prostitutes take pity on a pubescent boy and offer him a discount (Dupeyron and Schmitt 2003). They are no doubt seen as performing a social service by deflecting the movie's protagonist from deflowering "good" girls.

In ancient Greece, girls from "good" families (those with full citizenship rights) were expected to remain chaste until marriage and were largely sequestered inside their homes after marriage. Boys, on the other hand, had an extended period of adolescence to complete their formal education, physical fitness preparation in a *gymnasion*, and military service as a *hoplite* (Beaumont 2000). While they might not marry until thirty (Golden 2003: 25), they were expected to be active sexually throughout adolescence. Two avenues towards this end were socially sanctioned: visiting a brothel and homosexuality. Vase paintings depict fathers delivering their sons to the brothel owner for their initiation (Shapiro 2003: 98). However, far to be preferred was the establishment of a mentor relationship between the youth and an older, wiser male lover.[38] Such relationships are frequently shown on vase paintings where an artistic convention was employed in which the younger partner is shown beardless – but otherwise physically mature – while the older partner – still in his physical prime – sports a full beard.[39]

Another culture area where homosexuality is endorsed as an essential stage in normal adolescent development is in southwestern PNG, such as among the Keraki (Williams 1936). The pattern of sexual relations between boys and slightly older men is carefully scripted to enhance the boy's physical maturity, primarily through the ingestion of semen during fellatio.[40]

The major impetus to restrict adolescent sexuality in the modern era has been the need to postpone family formation until one's formal education is complete. The Boy Scout movement, for example, was founded in the early twentieth century with the explicit goal of prolonging boyhood (Hine 1999: 167). During the same period, girls were being cautioned against the consumption of meat "because they thought it stimulated sexual appetites, and even led to nymphomania" (Hine 1999: 181). Many who followed this advice became chloritic and acquired a greenish cast to their complexion.

More recently in the USA, Scouting has been joined by a huge array of highly structured extra-curricular activities for (children and) adolescents that,

---

[38] Cartledge comments that such a relationship was virtually mandatory for Spartan youth, but "sex was by no means the only or even the major object [rather, the relationship had a definite] pedagogic dimension . . . " (Cartledge 2003: 69).

[39] Attic black figure cup, Boston: Museum of Fine Arts, 08.292. Shapiro (2003: 99).

[40] Due to the low protein diet, children reach puberty very late and women, with the greater demands imposed on their bodies by hard physical labor (men are politicians, hunters, and warriors) and childbearing, waste early. So men take great pains to encourage the growth of strength, courage, and masculinity in boys via special taboos, initiation rituals, and homosexual relations (Gray 1994). These practices are by no means rare, as Creed notes: "the practice of homosexuality in New Guinea is widespread, highly structured, and culturally regulated" (Creed 1984: 158).

in effect, keep them under the constant scrutiny of adults. And, according to survey results, contemporary adolescents rarely resist! Most see the alternatives to adult-managed recreation as boredom and getting into trouble (Duffett and Johnson 2004: 9–10).

While we've seen wide variation in the treatment of adolescent sexuality and variation in how closely or loosely adolescents are bound to their natal families, there is far less autonomy[41] when it comes to marriage. A few societies may let youngsters select their own mates. For instance, among the Tapirapé,

There was no marriage ceremony, nor a bride price. When a young man reached an understanding with a young woman he would carry a load of firewood across the village plaza and deposit it at her family dwelling. This was a public announcement of his union with the girl. He then moved his hammock next to hers and became an economic participant in her household. First marriages between young men and young women were proverbially brittle – almost trial marriages. (Wagley 1977: 157)

More commonly, "match-making" is done by one's kin. An important factor to consider is that, depending on inheritance and residence patterns, a family will, in marriage, be losing or gaining a potentially valuable worker (Schlegel and Barry 1991: 106). In Mayan farming communities, adolescents are restrained from marriage until relatively late (nineteen for females, twenty-two for males) as their contribution to the household economy is so valuable (Kramer 2002b: 314). More typically, Moroccan mothers eagerly play match-maker to marry off their sons to girls who'll be good homemakers and responsive to their mother-in-law (Davis and Davis 1989: 77). And a daughter is supported by her family in the quest to place her with a man with "prospects" from a "good" family (Sellen 1998b: 330). I would venture that there are societies where parents – especially fathers – spend far more time in negotiating the details of their offspring's marriage (dowry, bride-price, housing, land tenure) than they ever did in childcare.[42] They want the best for their son or daughter *and* their grandchildren.[43]

---

[41] Somewhat cynically, it may be noted that adolescent freedom may be more apparent than real. There are multiple cases in this chapter of adults using adolescents. To quote Schlegel and Barry "adults use adolescents in the furthering of their own ends – as laborers, pawns in marriage negotiations, performers in dance or sports . . . " (Schlegel and Barry 1991: 6–7).

[42] The central crisis of Sholom Aleichem's stories (*Fiddler on the Roof*) is the fate of a man with too many daughters to marry off and not enough wealth to meet the dowry requirements (Aleichem 1990).

[43] Blurton-Jones has pointed out that it is in the best genetic interest of parents to make a good match for their offspring to increase the likelihood of getting well-cared-for grandchildren who will carry their genes into the next generation (Blurton-Jones 1993: 406). The term "daughter guarding" has been coined to describe a process whereby a girl's parents monitor her associates closely to prevent her from making a bad match or diminishing her prospects by unchaste behavior (Flinn 1988: 195). See also Wilder (1970: 230).

Figure 26 Brides-to-be, Luang Prabang, Laos

It is also rare for a society to treat pregnancy out of wedlock with equanimity. Non-mainstream communities in North America where marriages are tentative and somewhat optional provide exceptions. In a black community in North Carolina, "from 1969 through 1986, no girl . . . completed the teenage years without having at least 1 baby. The particular father . . . mattered little . . . the neighborhood seemed glad to have a child" (Heath 1990: 502). In Holman, a remote Inuit community with plentiful resources, a teenage girl can be assured both that her own family will assist in rearing her child and that extended family members would come forward offering to adopt should she decide to give up the baby (Condon 1987: 98). Likewise, in poor white Appalachian communities, pregnancy in one's teenage daughter or a son's impending paternity may be seen in a positive light. The hope is that caring for a child will have a maturing effect (Fitchen 1981: 128).

More commonly, marriage is viewed as a tension-laden piece of diplomacy where the marriageable daughter courts disaster for herself and her family. In matrilineal Hopi society, young men are reluctant to leave the comfort and ease of their family home to labor long and hard on behalf of their wife's family. Luring a good son-in-law into the family is unlikely if one's daughter is lazy or promiscuous (Schlegel 1973: 457). Among the Bajau fishermen of the Sulu Sea, whose dwellings are their boats, a girl may enjoy discreet sexual relations, but if she's perceived as too free with her favors, she will be "unable to command a high bride-price and may have to settle for a less desirable mate" (Nimmo 1970: 255). In patrilineal Teso (Uganda) society, a post-pubescent girl who isn't married is a source of anxiety to her father because on her reputation rests "his hopes for bridewealth cattle, cattle that he will need in order to marry [off] his sons" (de Berry 2004: 56).

Marriage is viewed as an opportunity to secure a "good" match for one's offspring or to endow them with family wealth – to aid in their household formation and the creation of a suitable home for grandchildren. Alice Schlegel, in a brilliant study, explicates this phenomenon. Societies that dower their daughters need to guard against ne'er-do-well, social-climbing males (exemplified by Wickham in *Pride and Prejudice*) who would advance their fortunes through seduction; hence, a premium is placed on female chastity before marriage (Schlegel 1991: 724).

Finally, there are a number of societies that value chastity so highly that, at the earliest sign of puberty, daughters are married off (Whiting *et al.* 1986: 287).

Coming of age

[Among !Ko Bushman] Puberty rites may be regarded as a crash course in adulthood. (Weisfeld 1999: 110)

In approximately a third of the societies in the ethnographic record, adolescents must pass through an initiation process (Schlegel and Barry 1979) which, in effect, certifies them as ready to begin mating and forming their own family (Vizedom and Zais 1976). Many of the male initiation rites discussed earlier in the chapter may serve this "gateway to adulthood" function,[44] among others, but it is the most likely function of the initiation of young women.[45] Among pastoralist groups, such as the East African Sebei, a girl's circumcision may carry much the same meaning as a boy's – admission to adult status – not as a deterrent to sexual pleasure.[46] As such, girls eagerly submit to the ordeal, and despite the absence of sanitary conditions, deaths from the operation are rare. "The dominant theme of the initiation is that of an ordeal – trial and proof of maturity" (Goldschmidt 1986: 95–96).[47]

Among West African Mende farmers, the girls' initiation is organized by the *Sande* women's secret society (boys' by the male equivalent – *Poro*[48]):

girls first go through a portal, into a cleared place in the forest . . . ritually separated [for two to three years] from the social context in which they were girls. One of the most dramatic ritual elements . . . is clitoridectomy . . . Sande women explain that this makes women "clean" [also] the pain . . . is a metaphor for the pain of childbirth . . . Womanhood is symbolically achieved in clitoridectomy and confirmed, under the midwife's hand in childbirth. [Another] important element in the ritual process of Sande initiation is fattening. Beauty, prosperity, health and fertility are explicitly linked to fatness . . . The opposite of fat is . . . dry, connoting among other things a dry and barren uterus. (Mac-Cormack 1994: 111–112)

Schlegel and Barry's review finds the theme of "fattening" – to prepare for the rigors of childbearing – quite common (Schlegel and Barry 1980). Girls are held in seclusion and kept well fed so that they "fill out," and thus display their

---

[44] In a few societies, the gateway to adulthood is not through a military-like boot camp, but rather through training in priestly duties. All Mormon males are expected to marry after completing two years of missionary service, proselytizing their faith. In India, high-caste youth go through the lengthy *upanayana* rite during which, with shaved heads, they wander as an ascetic, begging monk (Rohner and Chaki-Sircar 1988: 85).

[45] Not surprisingly, given the privation and pain that usually accompanies initiation, parents are rarely involved with the initiation of their own children (Hotvedt 1990: 167–168).

[46] Initiation rites aren't only (or, in some cases, not even primarily) for the "benefit" of the initiate. For the Rauto of PNG, the initiation rite – like costly weddings in some strata of contemporary society – is seen as an opportunity to acquire and display wealth and status, viz. "The menarcheal rites cannot begin until the girl's family has amassed sufficient wealth in the form of pigs, taro, and shell valuables to pay for the ritual services that will be provided . . . " (Maschio 1995: 137). A second example is the Japanese maiden's "coming of age" ceremony, the focus of which will be her expensive kimono, make-up, and accessories – conspicuous display designed to enhance her family's public image (Goldstein-Gidoni 1999).

[47] Goldschmidt makes clear that the youths themselves press adults to sponsor the initiation rites which sound like a big frat party.

[48] Historically, *Poro* prepared Mende youth to become warriors, defending the village and raiding neighboring villages to capture slaves (Rosen 2005: 64).

readiness for mating (Gleason and Ibubuya 1991). Paiela (PNG Highlands) girls are aided by an array of magical plants and procedures to enlarge their breasts (Biersack 1998: 74–75). For the Bemba of Zimbabwe, the girls' initiation process, *chisungu*, is replete with sexual imagery:

> women... snatch at a *mufungo* bush for leaves... (which) they fold into cones to resemble small conical fish traps. They sing a song about setting fish traps and... pretend to catch each other's fingers in the leaf traps... The traps and fingers represent the female and male sexual organs and a song "The fish has many children and so will the girl" is sung. (Richards 1956: 65).

Also in southern Africa, Chewa girls go through the *chinamwali* initiation in which they dance around various clay figures, including a python "that is thought to be in control of fertility of the land and human beings" (Yoshida 2006: 234).

While these examples showcase the positive aspects of a woman's emerging fertility,[49] for many societies, menstruation, intercourse, pregnancy, and childbirth are seen as potentially harmful to the community. For the Ndu of the Sepik area of PNG, women's *narandanwa* rites are episodic and designed to "detoxify" the pollution accompanying these physiological processes (Roscoe 1995).

Another common theme of women's "coming of age" rites is the role of the woman as provider.[50] A Hopi girl's first menstruation signals the onset of ritual events, such as the corn-grinding ceremony, and her hair is reshaped into the "butterfly whorl" style. At the same time, her tether is shortened as she will now be expected to remain in close proximity to her mother and apply herself to learning all aspects of the woman's domestic repertoire (Schlegel 1973: 455–456). For the Makiritare peoples of the Orinocco basin,

> the *ahishto hiyacado* is begun with the first signs of... menstruation... the whole village is alerted... inside a *conuco* beside the village... the women simulate all the tasks the girl will be responsible for during her lifetime inside the garden... some elders gather around her and... start singing songs to encourage her to be a hard worker. (Guss 1982: 264).

---

[49] Somewhat ironically, while adolescent initiation ceremonies signal the youths' readiness for mating, they may also signal a broader segregation of the sexes. That is, in many cases, girls and boys have been free to associate but initiation begins a rapid process whereby, once married, men and women live in separate spheres with different role assignments, recreational pursuits, and even, in many cases, residence. While this pattern is not uncommon, it has been most thoroughly described for the Kipsigis (Kenya) (Harkness and Super 1985: 222).

[50] In the case of foraging societies, a young male's demonstration of his ability as a provider is noted – such as an Inuit's youth's first caribou or seal – but not necessarily with a full-fledged initiation *ceremony* (Condon 1987: 56).

Those on the threshold of adulthood may experience various forms of some-times painful body modification other than circumcision. Abelam (agricultur-alists of the Sepik Region, PNG) girls are "scarified at their first menstru-ation . . . standardized patterns (*ramoni*) are cut on their breasts, bellies, and upper arms" (Hauser-Schaublin 1995: 40). Mehinacu and Canela nine-year-olds have their ears pierced to hold wooden plugs (Gregor 1970: 242; Crocker and Crocker 1994: 116). Tapirapé boys acquire a prominent lip plug (Wagley 1977: 149). Young Tapirapé women, just prior to their first pregnancy, pass through a rite which includes decorative scarification:

This traditionally consisted of a quarter-moon design on each cheek and a half-moon design under the chin . . . only women who carried that design on their face were truly beautiful. The design was drawn in charcoal and then cut into the face with crisscross lacerations using the sharp incisor teeth of the agouti or paca . . . into these wounds ginipap juice was rubbed so that it would become permanently black. (Wagley 1977: 163)[51]

The teeth are often subject to modification. Aka youth have their incisors filed to points (Konner 2005: 51). Adolescent Japanese girls, during the Tokugawa period, had their teeth blackened (Sofue 1965: 156). Balinese children have their teeth filed *and* blackened (*mesangi, mepandes*) during their coming of age ceremony, viz.:

The patient is laid on . . . offerings, the head resting on a pillow which is covered with . . . one of the magic cloths . . . The body is wrapped in new white cloth and assistants hold down the victim by the hands and feet. The tooth-filer . . . inscribes magic syllables (*aksara*) on the teeth about to be filed with a ruby set in a gold ring. The filing then proceeds, taking from fifteen minutes to a half-hour, endured stoically with clenched hands and goose-flesh, but without even a noise from the patient. (Covarrubias 1937: 135–136)

In a few cases, the initiation *follows* or occurs almost simultaneously with parenthood. In certain Ijo (Nigerian) villages the clitoridectomy, which "ini-tiates" the process of becoming a woman, is performed in the seventh month of pregnancy.[52] Following delivery and recovery, the new mother dances in "the *seigbein*, a twelve-day celebration of the ancestors and a purging of bad spirits from the town" (Hollos and Leis 1989: 75). This completes the process of becoming an adult.

For the Sambia, adulthood (*aatmwunu*), for both sexes, is not conferred until two pregnancies have been brought to a successful conclusion. However,

[51] In addition to *visible* symbols, nomenclature may also accompany the change in status. Tapirapé girls are *kotantani*, becoming *kuchamoko* after their first menses (Wagley 1977: 150).

[52] "None of the female subjects, regardless of their future plans and aspirations, voiced any objection to the procedure, and most of them eagerly looked forward to it as to a graduation ceremony into adulthood. The clitoridectomy fees are paid by the father of the woman's unborn child, which established the paternity of the child" (Hollos and Leis 1989: 125).

ceremonial recognition of the man's potency continues through the fourth birth, after which "there is no reason to belabor what is by now obvious: a man has proved himself competent in reproduction" (Herdt 2001: 164). In Thailand, "land is often given to a couple at the birth of their first child, rather than on marriage, as it is parenthood and not marriage that is a sign of the couple's maturity" (Montgomery 2001a: 60). On Vanatinai Island, neither marriage nor the birth of a child is sufficient to claim full adult status, which is only conferred once the individual (in their late twenties) has settled into a "stable" marriage (Lepowsky 1998: 127).

As we've seen, marriage per se may *not* be treated as an important rite of passage. Typically, of course, marriage *is* a rite of passage (Van Gennep 1908/1960), but like the initiation ceremony, a primary function may be to curtail the unregulated activities of adolescents. Earlier, I noted the way in which the transfer of property at marriage might be used to add weight to the prohibition on adolescent female sexual activity. But unruly male adolescents can also be brought to heel by the threat of kinsmen to withhold support for their marriage.[53] Among the Kaugel of the New Guinea Highlands, young men who fail to fall into line and demonstrate the proper deference accorded to senior members of the tribe risk permanent bachelorhood as they can't possibly acquire on their own the enormous resources required to make an adequate bride-price payment (Bowers 1965). Schapera (1996) describes a parallel case in southeastern Africa where senior Tswana men own the cattle that junior men need in order to acquire a bride.

However, as the next section reveals, rapid social change is having a dramatic impact on these customs. To take just this last example, the availability of wage employment permits adolescent males to finesse the approval of senior males by acquiring resources to marry and start a household of their own (Caldwell *et al.* 1998: 139).

Adolescence and social change in traditional societies

By handing over [Teso] girls to soldiers, the middlemen destroyed the claim of their fathers for bridewealth. (de Berry 2004: 56)

Adolescents are often found along the leading edge of social change. In Sadolparo village in India, the Garo people practice an "animist" faith called

---

[53] Although this doesn't seem to be discussed much in the literature, adults customarily make critical decisions in the lives of adolescents – allocating them land, school fees, donating their service to organized religion, sending them off to soldier or labor or apprentice, pairing them with a spouse. These decisions strike me as closely parallel to the decision-making that occurs upon the birth of a child that was discussed in chapters 2 and 3. That is, the parent is acting strategically to maximize both genetic and material returns from their offspring.

Sansarek. However, the Christian church service is entirely populated by adolescents who reject and admit to being ashamed of Sansarek (Stafford and Nair 2003). Earlier, we noted that adolescent males are expected to roam more widely, beyond the family pale. And, in recent history, that has often meant that they are the first members of the village to venture forth to the big city or commercial enclave (plantation, mine). Returning, they bear gifts and radical ideas.[54] Less frequently but still in significant numbers, adolescent females migrate to urban areas in search of schooling and/or employment as sex workers (Rubenson *et al.* 2005).

China has witnessed a dramatic change in rural society as adolescents flee from the stultifying control of traditional authorities to take advantage of new employment opportunities in huge industrial enclaves that have sprung up (Stevenson and Zusho 2002: 141). One of the most recognizable consequences of these shifts is the breakdown of the village social structure. In Gbarngasuakwelle, young men returning from the town imported playing cards and the Ludo boardgame, eschewing the traditional *malang* game. Since senior males are the acknowledged masters and own the often intricately carved *malang* boards, this change effectively closed off yet another opportunity elder males used to assert their superiority over the young (Lancy 1977).

In a remote area of the PNG Highlands, Aletta Biersack has documented the breakdown of the lengthy and elaborate bride-price negotiation/display as young men bypass these traditions in obtaining wives. She warns:

What drops out of the picture with a loss of these practices is not just... ritual... but... the very social order that the ritual was meant to construct and maintain. The loss of these practices could well be one of several symptoms that collective life in this part of the highlands is currently on the wane. (Biersack 1998: 87).

Throughout much of contemporary PNG, young males are referred to in Melanesian pidgin as *bikhet* (or, in an urban context, *rascal*). Christian missions offer them the opportunity to escape the restrictions imposed by traditional rites associated, for example in the Sepik area, with the men's *Haus Tambaran*, without actually socializing them to embrace Western/Christian values. Similarly, in attending government schools, they signal their abandonment of the traditional agrarian economy without actually learning enough to secure a job in the modern economy. In short, they have been led to believe they are superior

---

[54] No doubt in the first wave of urbanization, adolescents chose to migrate – often against the wishes of their families. Today, in much of the Third World, overpopulation and the declining productivity of rural farms means that adolescents are *compelled* to migrate because they cannot support themselves through agricultural labor.

to the senior men, yet bring no significant resources to the community, hence – *bikhets* (Leavitt 1998).[55]

Clearly, vestiges of urbanization will find their way to the hinterlands and adolescents are often the quickest to adapt and respond. Compounds provided for forest-dwelling tribal people in South America often incorporate medical facilities, schools, commercial outlets, and foreign religious institutions. Some Ache were induced to settle on a reservation where younger tribesmen adapted more rapidly to the changed circumstances. As a consequence, "the traditional power structure was turned upside down... young men [acquired] more wives and children than they had been able to acquire in the forest" (Hill and Hurtado 1996: 53).

When men migrate from the village, their absence leaves women and, especially children, with a greater burden (LeVine 1966: 188). Not surprisingly, women may become eager to follow the men's lead and escape rural poverty. Lee describes how the decline in subsidized agriculture in China has made women a liability in rural areas just as factory employment is expanding in the cities. Young women trade close parental control and the boredom of the village for freedom, big city bright lights, and a meager wage (Lee 1998). Traditional match-making and family formation, naturally, go by the board as "heterosexual dating has become increasingly frequent in China" (Stevenson and Zusho 2002: 149). Farmers, of course, now find it extremely hard to find a spouse. In Africa

acculturation seems to be downgrading the significance of initiation, vaginal inspection... and infibulation, cultural practices that were powerful sources of sexual control in adolescents as they marked specific developmental transitions... In addition, traditional education through initiation rites, chaperones, folklore, and the orientation of adolescents to acceptable sexual behaviors by grandparents, through oral traditions, seems to be losing its relevance rather rapidly. (Nsamenang 2002: 84–85)

In much-publicized cases from contemporary Muslim states, both legal statues and vigilante justice combine to deny women opportunities for independence[56] and the traditional patriarchy is maintained, but elsewhere, such as Barbados (Stoffle 1977) and Sri Lanka (Caldwell *et al.* 1998: 144), barriers are falling. During this profound and protracted transition, a girl's chances of continuing her education or economic advancement may depend on her access to contraception to avoid the pregnancy that, custom demands, will end her single status (Caldwell *et al.* 1998: 141). Elsewhere, pregnancy may not be seen as

---

[55] More generally, Schlegel traces delinquency in the village to loosening of ties between adolescents and adults, including members of one's lineage. Where kin ties are strong, adults, other than parents, also exert a socializing influence (Schlegel 2000b).

[56] In Bangladesh these twin forces, government-inspired modernization which promotes female emancipation and a vigorous, Taliban-like fundamentalist movement, are in deep contention.

an impediment as the baby can be placed with relatives in the village (Hollos and Leis 1989: 73);[57] however, "higher school fees encourage schoolgirls to earn money through sex or seek sugar daddies, dangerous behavior in an era of AIDS" (Caldwell *et al.* 1998: 143).

Recently, a shift has begun whereby employers are preferentially hiring women who are more reliable and cheaper than men. In Costa Rica, the decline in coffee prices has eliminated a reliable source of employment for rural men while women's employment in manufacturing has increased dramatically. Hence men find themselves unable to fulfill the traditional breadwinner role and are, in effect, unable to achieve adult status (Mannon and Kemp 2005: 11). If young men cannot find the means to support wives and offspring while women *can* earn a living and care for offspring, perhaps with the assistance of their mothers, it follows that the nuclear family will decline in importance. More ominously, poverty and civil strife may sweep adolescents into the ranks of impromptu militias. One well-studied case is Tajikistan, where overpopulation has created a huge cadre of unemployed youth who, repeatedly, go on the rampage (C. Harris 2006: 29).

David Rosen provides a catalog of cases – paralleling those from the totalitarian societies in the middle of the twentieth century discussed earlier – in which contemporary governments, and "rebel" or terrorist organizations, continue to exploit, often willing, adolescents for nefarious purposes. Terrorist-trainers capitalize on the peculiarities of adolescent psychology, brought on in part by "living in limbo," to create pliable fanatics (Rosen 2005: 157). Rosen also notes the continuity between traditional Mende warrior training, described earlier in this chapter, and the recruitment and training of child soldiers.

The RUF [Revolutionary United Front] also made use of... *Poro*-like rituals. RUF recruits were often sworn to secrecy and took oaths of loyalty, the violation of which was said to result in the magical death of the violator... many fighting groups seized on these powerful symbols as a means to organize and control youth... [who willingly]... set people on fire, burned down their houses, shot children, paraded citizens about naked and beat them, brought opponents before youth-run kangaroo courts, and hacked men and women to death with machetes. (Rosen 2005: 72, 78)

Disaffected West African students, their hopes for white-collar jobs dashed by stagnant economies, become easy targets (Lancy 1996: 198). The current government in the Ivory Coast is widely accused of fostering an army of young thugs and, periodically, arousing them to "spontaneous" street demonstrations

---

[57] The relevant large-scale demographic trends in Africa show the age of marriage rising, as adolescent women seek education and employment in lieu of marriage; however, the age of first pregnancy is not appreciably rising, perhaps due to the non-availability of contraception (Bledsoe and Cohen 1993).

(riots) in support of the government as a deterrent to political opposition (Washington Post, January 22, 2006: A25).

In the developed societies, remote rural and impoverished urban enclaves foster the same sort of anomie – with comparable results. Adolescent males living in run-down US inner cities are extremely likely to be incarcerated, infected with HIV/AIDS, addicted, or end their lives as homicide or suicide victims (Rose and McClain 1990). Similarly, adolescent males living on Indian reservations suffer mortality and suicide rates three times the national average. On Red Lake Reservation (North America), the locus for a devastating mass murder/suicide by a despondent teenager in 2005, a third of those eligible aren't in school and gang violence and drug abuse are endemic (*Associated Press* March 6, 2005; Washington Post, March 24, 2005: B1).

Political and economic forces are combining to create conditions in which adolescent limbo threatens to become a life-long state. The agricultural economy, whether small-scale village-based farming or plantation-scale agribusiness, is in stagnation or decline. Manufacturing is, indeed, migrating "downward" from wealthy nations in Europe, Asia, and North America to rapidly modernizing countries. But this spreading wage economy is hardly penetrating the poorer countries including most of Africa, Oceania, and large sectors of the Western Hemisphere and Southeast Asia.

As rare as adolescence may have been in the past, there is considerable irony in the fact that modern economic forces have created two very different kinds of adolescence. We've just been reviewing the fate of individuals who, as a result of economic insecurity, seem not to be able to exit adolescence and cross the threshold into community-supported family formation. In the concluding section, we will consider individuals who must remain in adolescence to take advantage of economic opportunities that are only available to the well educated.

Adolescents as students and consumers

... students in secondary school learn about a life state called adolescence, so for some school has "created" the concept as well as the expectation of behaviors associated with it. (Davis and Davis 1989: 59)

... overwhelming messages from popular culture, parents, and teachers make it clear that the prom is an important cultural rite of passage (Best 2000: 18)

In the Philippines, there is a growing gulf between urban, educated adolescents and their lower-class or rural counterparts. Relative to the latter, the former are delaying marriage and family formation as children are seen as an economic liability (Santa Maria 2002: 184). Surveys show that, where the pathway from school to wage employment is relatively secure, "parents are found to work harder and longer hours to replace the loss of children's labor" (Larson and Suman 1999: 708).

Students may make little contribution to the household. Across Europe, adolescent "chores" consume no more than 10–40 minutes a day, on average (Larson and Suman 1999: 705). Parents may need to pay, often high, school fees. In Morocco, "it cost . . . 400 dirhams ($66) each year to attend school, which is about what a woman would earn working as a field laborer . . . for a whole month" (Davis and Davis 1989: 62). In "some countries, such as Egypt, private schools have become more numerous and popular among those who can afford them, as public schools become more crowded and less effective" (Booth 2002: 223).

The expectation, of course, is that for students, schoolwork is their "job":

schoolwork fills close to half of waking hours among Korean adolescents, a third of waking hours for a sample of Japanese adolescents and samples of adolescents in an elite Italian high school . . . In East Asia, the school day is 8 hours long, and students attend an extra half day on Saturday . . . homework was found to take . . . 2.5 hours per day for samples of Polish, Romanian, and Russian adolescents . . . 3.0 hours per day among Korean high school students . . . in Taiwan . . . 11th graders report spending an average of 3.7 hours per day on homework. (Larson and Suman 1999: 712–713)[58]

However, besides schoolwork, it is common for adolescents to be provided with supervised extra-curricular activities. In Europe, music lessons and practice are the norm. In the USA, competitive athletic activity soaks up adolescents' time and their parents' dollars (Larson and Suman 1999: 720–721).

While the need to engage in the decades-long apprenticeship known as formal education is the most important factor in the creation of modern adolescence as a distinct life-stage, the *culture* of adolescence is largely a product of the discretionary income of youth. The USA leads the way in every respect: our adolescents are much more likely to be employed, their earnings are spent almost 100 percent on themselves, and parents who prevent their children from working – correctly fearing the negative impact on their schoolwork – must compensate by providing an allowance. As a result, "They spend about $100 billion a year, just on things for themselves. Two thirds of this comes from their own earnings, the rest from their parents" Hine 1999: 23). American adolescents have the means to fuel an entire market devoted to their needs, including movies, music, television, clothing, cosmetics, home furnishings (beyond North America and Western Europe, adolescents do not, generally, have their own rooms), electronics, and automobiles. Indeed, earning a driver's license is treated as a major rite of passage (Chang 1992: 106).

---

[58] The USA is anomalous in these surveys because averages for schoolwork and homework are much lower than in other modern, industrial countries. This is at least partly because admission to two- and four-year post-secondary institutions (which educate and credential one for the workforce) is comparatively more liberal.

And this commercial culture has been taken up, in varying degrees depending on family size and income, around the globe, including Japan (White 1993). In South Africa, "Coca-Cola kids ... [have] ... embraced Western values of individualism, competition, and materialism ... In rural north China, intergenerational squabbles have emerged over the young people's embrace of materialistic values, their display of new clothes, leather shoes, expensive cigarettes, and cassettes" (Gibbons 2004: 258). The "airwaves of Morocco are filled with songs of romantic passion – in Arabic, French, and English" (Davis and Davis 1989: 133) while "upper-class youth in the large cities like Casablanca may live lives similar to urban Americans, with dating and discos a regular part of their experience" (Davis and Davis 1989: 209). "St. Valentine's Day has sprung up as a day of celebration, a 'sweetheart's day,' spreading rapidly through the college-preparatory schools of cities and towns all over Poland" (Schlegel 2000a: 80).

My own epiphany regarding the spread of this international "youth culture" occurred during a Galapagos visit in 2004. A thousand kilometers from the coast of South America, the Galapagos epitomize remote and exotic. The only urban enclave is quiet, little Puerto Ayora, a town of 8,000 on Santa Cruz Island. Nevertheless, in a small, commercial computer center, we encountered a bevy of children busily playing video games against competitors from around the world. Their dress, the music blasting over the speakers, and the Cokes they were consuming were all too familiar.

9   How schools can raise property values

Introduction: a tale of two Lincolns

"It's absolutely the schools, no question," says Maria Segal, a local real-estate agent . . . it means a difference of hundreds and hundreds of thousands of dollars over comparable houses in other locations. (Boyer 2005: 62)

The prevalence of mass education is a striking feature of the modern world. (Boli *et al.* 1985: 145)

The story of childhood that has unfolded in this book contains many scenes, but classrooms are conspicuously absent. Children across cultures and through time have managed to grow to adulthood and learn to become functioning members of their society without the necessity of schooling. Fast-forward to the twenty-first century and we find a world where childhood without schooling is unthinkable. Modern children may spend more waking hours in school than in their homes, more time with teachers than with parents. They are students for the bulk of each day with residual time left for leisure, family, and chores. And, as we saw in chapter 6, leisure (as in organized sports, violin lessons, boy scouts) is often as tightly organized and "developmental" as school. Indeed, there's a veritable library of scolding diatribes urging us to "reclaim childhood" (Elkind 2001; Rosenfeld and Wise 2000; Crain 2004).

However strong these "lighten up" messages may be, parents are, through the medium of mass communication, given daily reminders that childhood is a "race" in which the winners may enjoy the good life while the losers may be shot in a drug deal gone wrong (*Washington Post Health*, December 18, 1990: 17). And, in the USA, we seem increasingly committed to the idea that winners and losers should be "handicapped"[1] earlier and earlier, even before the race has truly begun.

The State of California maintains a website to report its mandated evaluation of every public school in the state. Schools are rated on a scale from, roughly,

---

[1] Handicapping refers to the various methods by which spectators can predict and quantify the results of a sporting match. The term is also applied to the practice of predicting the result of a competition, such as for purposes of betting against the point spread. Information from http://en.wikipedia.org; accessed 4.20.07.

400 to 1,000, based on a composite of the several state-wide achievement tests that are administered annually. Essentially, test scores earned by individual students determine a school's rating.

Lincoln Elementary School in Compton, California – in Los Angeles County – has a racial mix of 45 percent African-American, 55 percent Hispanic, and 100 percent of its students are designated as "socioeconomically disadvantaged." Its composite score for 2005 was 583, quite low. Many students are likely residents of Ujima Village, a federally subsidized housing project for the poor, managed by the Los Angeles County Housing Authority.[2] Lincoln Elementary School in Cupertino, California (Silicon Valley) – in Santa Clara County – has a racial mix of 0.01 percent African-American, 0.02 percent Hispanic, 25 percent white, 72 percent Asian, and 0.03 percent of its students are designated as "socioeconomically disadvantaged." Its composite score for 2005 was 920, quite high.[3]

We shouldn't be surprised to learn, then, that:

for many, acquiring a Cupertino address is an important factor in planning their families. The address comes at a premium, with houses bearing an average price of nearly a million dollars . . . Larry Woodard, a computer-networking executive . . . and his wife had found their home in Cupertino by handing their real-estate agent a school-district map showing the school's boundaries, and saying, "Those are your parameters." (Boyer 2005: 62)

In an ethnographic study in a comparable northern California community,[4] the authors report that parents of children in "Forestview" had closely evaluated schools and plotted district boundaries to determine where to search for a home. And the principal freely acknowledged that one role his school played "in the community was to 'raise property values' " (Lewis and Forman 2002: 65). In a parallel study of parental attitudes in an urban ghetto, a mother explains why she plans to move when her children reach school age because the neighborhood school is "ranked third worst in our district . . . unsafe, in terms of violence and drugs, weapons coming into the school" (Kusserow 2004: 62). Unlike this mother, the wealthy can choose to shelter their children behind the walls of a "gated community," isolating them from perceived threats to their safety and wellbeing (Low 2003: 11). "Currently, one-third of all new communities in southern California are gated" (Low 2003: 15).

---

[2] Information from www.lacdc.org; accessed 4.20.07.

[3] Information from www.cde.ca.gov; accessed 4.20.07. This wide disparity grows even wider through middle school and high school. Hemmings studied three high schools ranging along a low to high SES continuum. At the high end, 90 percent of the high school seniors passed the exit exam, at the low end, only 14 percent passed (Hemmings 2004: 13).

[4] This phenomenon is readily apparent outside the USA as well: "In London . . . estate agents advertise properties as being within the catchment area of 'good' schools, and there is a . . . correlation between property prices and school results or reputations" (Buckingham and Scanlon 2003: 150).

Meanwhile, a few thousand miles to the southwest on Tonga, Helen Morton describes similar themes:

Overcrowding in classrooms is a problem, and most schools have an acute shortage of educational resources. Despite the high value placed on education, teaching is a fairly low-status profession in Tonga, and the working conditions are poor. Funded from overseas, Mormon and Seventh Day Adventist schools – with their sports facilities, new buildings, modern equipment and textbooks, and extracurricular activities for students – provide a sharp contrast to the other Tongan schools. School fees and other school-related expenses place a great financial strain on many families, and most rely on remittances from overseas relatives to cover these expenses. (Morton 1996: 39)

Two prominent issues in this chapter, therefore, are the emergence of universal schooling (Benavot *et al.* 1992: 41) as the *sine qua non* of childhood and the divide this has opened up between the "haves" and the "have nots."

The ubiquity of schooling in the lives of modern children must be set against its absence or relative unimportance throughout much of Western history and in the myriad societies documented by anthropologists. One consequence has been that, while access to some form of public schooling has spread rapidly, there has not been a corollary growth in an educated workforce – especially in the Third World. In fact, most students end up "failing" by any number of criteria. And, not surprisingly, village parents are reluctant to trade a successful farmworker for an unsuccessful student. We will examine the many obstacles, especially for girls, that have turned hopeful educational institutions into potentially harmful indoctrination rites.

In Asia, the "academic grind" entered the culture much earlier than in the West and has continued to exert a powerful influence on the socialization of children. Families – mothers, in particular – carry a heavy burden of responsibility to support their children's preparation for "examination hell." The tactics developed over centuries have also proved successful as Asian families migrate to Europe and the USA, allowing students to excel in spite of language, cultural, and social barriers.

While Asian and other recent immigrants to the USA beat the odds, other sub-cultures that lack family traditions that support academic success watch, in disappointment, as the benefits of education elude their grasp. Globally, educational policy is moving rapidly towards a triage model which rewards families – regardless of income – who own the cultural routines that are effective. The chapter concludes by examining the economic and ethical consequences of writing off the hopeless cases implied by triage policies.

The rise of schooling

Boys needed some occupation; as Aristotle puts it picturesquely, education is an older child's rattle. (Golden 1990: 64)

Luther did not hold with the adage that ignorance is the mother of devotion...he believed ignorance was the mother of superstition, so he wanted...to encourage enlightenment by enforcing school attendance, even against parental resistance. (Sommerville 1982: 92).

...the...ideal in Confucian society was that any son – like the popular symbol of a carp leaping over the rocks to become a dragon – could become, through studying hard and passing civil examinations, a scholar and government official. (Berliner 2003: 13).

This section offers two contrasting narratives. In the West, we see schooling for the elite instituted gradually over centuries. Only in the very recent past has schooling become universal – with very mixed results. In Asia, schooling has considerable antiquity and has had an unwavering and clear-cut objective – the training *and* selection of a competent civil service. Little attempt has ever been made to "universalize" schooling so that it serves the needs of all children.

The earliest indications of "schooling" would have been for the training of scribes in ancient Sumer. Classes in the *edduba* or "tablet house," named for the clay tablet writing medium, would look quite familiar to us – save for the absence of females (Kramer 1963; Frayne 1999).[5] Artifactual remains suggest that Egyptian scribes passed through an apprenticeship stage as we find discarded ostraca with text fragments copied over and over as practice and other fragments in black ink with overwritten *corrections* in red ink by a different hand. However, the formal training of scribes in classroom-like settings was probably uncommon. Rather, fathers passed down the scribe's trade to their sons and may have been the principal teachers – through example. A famous proverb claims that scribes have ears on their backs, implying that aspirant scribes must be beaten regularly or they won't listen. And the number of errors in the ancient texts suggests that many scribes may have been mere artisans, and not actually literate (Strouhal 1992: 35–37). It is not clear, then, that "schooling" in Egypt was even remotely similar to modern practice.

Classical Greece invented the "humanities," rich traditions of study and creativity in the arts, philosophy, and literature sustained through their deliberate transmission to the next generation. In a blackware vase painting on a kylix crater from the Antikensammlung Berlin we see various depictions of teaching and learning with a tutor and pupil reciting verse, playing the flute and lyre, and writing on a wax tablet (Neils and Oakley 2003: 66).[6] Also very commonly depicted are scenes of athleticism. Boys were sent daily to the *gymnasion* to exercise and learn the various routines that are still found

---

[5] Information from www.sumerian.org; accessed 4.23.07.

[6] Other common scenes on Greek vases are depictions of slave girls doing heavy labor and boys serving men wine and holding a pot for them to piss in (Neils and Oakley 2003).

in the modern Olympics. Schools for learning the arts and *grammata* (literary studies and writing) were private, tuition-based. As the epigraph quoting Aristotle suggests, boys were not being trained for a career in the usual sense but were socialized into the ideal adult role as someone who displayed both refined sensibilities and, as the occasion demanded, the skills and demeanor of a warrior. To that end, any show of disrespect for the masters was rewarded with a beating: "*paideuo*, 'I teach,' also has the meaning 'I correct, I discipline' in classical Attic" (Golden 1990: 64).

The term *paidagogos* originally referred to the slave who accompanied the boy to and from his home and other public institutions, to protect him from lewd attention or other harmful experiences. Girls were considered too vulnerable to go out in public, even with a guardian.

Elite Roman society continued with the role of *paedagogue*, usually a Greek slave, but with expanded duties, including the sort of school readiness training that today we assign to parents and pre-schools. As education seemed to be an avenue for upward mobility, less wealthy families started sending their boys to private schools. Schooling was offered at three levels: first, the 3 Rs, including heavy doses of memorization of classic texts; second, intense study "with a *grammaticus* [who] refined the student's style of writing and speaking, taught him to analyze poetry, and taught him Greek" (Shelton 1998: 103); and third, training by a *rhetor* in the skills required of a public office-holder.

Schools were privately financed and varied widely in quality.... [the school might occupy] a small room in an apartment building or a little street-level shop. However, many teachers met their students outdoors and held classes on the sidewalks or in piazzas. There were, of course, many disadvantages for the students, and traffic noise and street crowds must have been very distracting for the students, and inclement weather was surely a problem. However, sidewalk schools avoided rent and lighting costs. (Shelton 1998: 103–104)

Schools, as bad as they may have been, disappeared with the fall of Rome and did not reappear in the West for more than a thousand years. The upper class in Western Europe depended for its success on dynastic marriages and deeds of valor and "saw no need for literacy" (Sommerville 1982: 60–61). Commerce and government were rudimentary, obviating the need for an educated bureaucracy. Literacy became the provenance of the church. However, the mass of clergy weren't even literate, let alone "educated" in the Roman sense. On the contrary, as Freeman notes: "faith . . . achieved prominence over reason" (Freeman 2004). Even though children might be taken into the monastery as young as three in order to "train" them to sing in the choir, instruction was by rote. Choirboys did not learn from music texts, and "If they made mistakes . . . corporal punishments such as whipping were common" (Boynton and Cochelin 2006: 16–17).

Gradually, the ecclesiastical curriculum expanded and lengthened. Still, there was no sense that everyone, not even particularly members of the ruling class, should be literate. Literacy itself was seen as a means to acquire the modest trade of scribe which included working-class women among its practioners (Ariès 1962: 334). Scribes were trained in the difficult art of writing on parchment with a quill pen (Shahar 1990: 187). They were craftsmen, not scholars.

The Renaissance and, with much greater impetus, the Reformation introduced new ideas and inventions that gave tremendous energy to the development of widespread basic or general education. With the growth of secular knowledge and the demand of commerce for educated labor, grammar schools multiplied in number. Still, "young scholars were administered large doses of moralism with their letters" (Borstelmann 1983: 13). The great philosopher Erasmus published two works in 1529 and 1530 that are among the earliest "modern" statements about children and their education.[7] He wrote: "Why should we leave little children to their mothers and nurses, who do nothing but coddle and spoil them? It is better to teach them to read and write as soon as possible, for children have excellent memories when they are young."[8]

The invention of the printing press eventually led to the publication of textbooks, an incalculable boon because it increased the teacher's productivity. Adrian von Ostade depicted classrooms he saw in late seventeenth-century Netherlands. In one engraving, a schoolmaster is seated at his desk, surrounded by three boys as they share a glimpse of the single book lying on the desk (von Ostade nd). The availability of cheaply produced texts permitted the "radical pedagogical innovation" (Olson 2003: 197) of whole-class instruction in the eighteenth century. In 1716, the Emperor of Prussia made schooling for village children compulsory (Boli 1987) but a hundred years later, Prussia had to institute labor restrictions such "that children could not work regularly in a factory, mine or foundry [without] documentation of three years schooling" (Mitterauer 1992: 70–71).

In the USA at the turn of the twentieth century, only children of the elite attended high school. Most of the population left school by the ninth grade and the quality of education in the typical rural school was low (Kantor and Lowe 2004: 7). However, as compulsory schooling spread to include more of the population, evidence of academic failure grew apace. School officials in Atlanta, Georgia, for example, began to contend with this problem as early as 1898. In January of that year, Superintendent William F. Slaton called on the city's board of education to adopt a regulation to "prevent children of dull minds and weak intellects from remaining 3 or 4 years in the same grade"

---

[7] However, doubts arose about the spread of education. A century after Erasmus and Luther, Cardinal Richelieu "expressed fears of the overabundance of intellectuals, and a shortage of manual labor" (Ariès 1962: 335).

[8] Cited in Koops and Zuckerman (2003: 54).

(Franklin 1998: 31). In other words, since 1898, it has been recognized that not all students respond equally well to the "treatment" of formal education.

Education in Asia has its origins in the almost messianic teachings of Confucius (K'ung-fu-tzu, 551–479 BCE). The net effect of Confucianism was to create in China the earliest meritocracy: a government run by learned and morally sound bureaucrats. Hence, formal education in East Asia has a much longer and less checkered history than it does in the West. Luther's and Erasmus' philosophical counterpart was Xunzi who lived in the fourth century BCE. He offered the idea that education might bring out the child's potential, and, more practically, good public schools supported "the establishment of the civil service, which required an honest and educated staff to run the bureaucracy" (Kinney 1995: 18–19).

The cornerstone of this system was the imperial examination for entry and placement in the civil service. In the late fourteenth century CE, for example, exams lasted from twenty-four to seventy-two hours and were held in spare, isolated halls. Each candidate was issued an ID number and his answers were rewritten by a scribe so that the examinee's calligraphy wouldn't reveal his identity to the exam reader.[9]

Virtually any male could pursue the arduous path to success via this series of exams. Stories of individuals of humble origin rising to prominence through merit are legendary, such as that of Huang Fu.

A native of the small and remote village of *Huang Cun*, Huang Fu first passed the provincial civil examination... and, [then] succeeded in the far more difficult, and prestigious, feat of passing the national civil examination in the eighth year of the Jianjing reign (1529 CE). The... emperor... ordered that a grand hall... called *Jin Shi Di*... be built in honor of Huang Fu. The respect accorded to [him] and his rise to officialdom in his own village is evident... by the continual reverence accorded to him and the continual maintenance and endurance of *Jin Shi Di*. Today, it stands in the center... and is the most-tended building in the village. (Berliner 2003: 14)

As Chinese influence permeated Asia and Western civilization was imposed on the Western and Southern Hemispheres, schooling, with set curricula, designated teachers, and classrooms, slowly penetrated every corner of the globe.

Bush schools

Formal education in the initiations is minimal, as it is only occasionally desirable in everyday Afikpo life. There really is no "school in the bush," the specific knowledge that the boys acquire is not extensive. (Ottenberg 1989: 237)

---

[9] Information from http://en.wikipedia.org; accessed 4.20.07.

One reason for the rapid spread of this foreign institution is that there were no competing institutions which offered any resistance.[10] In Africa, the initiation rites for youth described in the previous chapter have long been referred to as "bush schools." However, the emphasis seems to have been on indoctrination, not education (Lancy 1975).[11] *Chisungu*, the lengthy girls' initiation in Bemba (Zimbabwe) society, includes "rites representing hoeing, sowing, cooking, gathering firewood . . . but, instruction, in the European sense, was quite unnecessary in such subjects" (Richards 1956: 161).

Kuttab schools have been around a long time and are found wherever Islam has taken hold. However, instruction consists primarily of reciting and ultimately memorizing the Qur'an, for which literacy is not essential (Fernea 1991: 452). Secondarily, these schools aim to indoctrinate pupils in a specific moral code (Moore 2006: 113). Similar emphases on rigid discipline and memorization of texts are found in religious schools serving Hindu (Broyon 2004) and Coptic (Levine 1965: 267) students.

We can also find a few examples of school-like settings for acquiring particular skills or areas of expertise, such as instruction in the traditional Balinese *gamelan* instruments. However, to a Westerner, although there is a classroom and a teacher, it does not look like "education." The teacher models correct performance, otherwise it is up to the pupils' initiative. He "explains nothing, since for him there is nothing to explain. If there are mistakes, he corrects them" (McPhee 1955). In Yemen, the training of a master builder is long and demanding as there are many skills to be acquired. Nevertheless, Yemeni minaret builders disavow any reliance on schooling as we know it (Marchand 2001: 219). So, no matter where we may look, we will not see communities where there are existing institutions that can be adapted or seen as analogues for the introduced schools derived from Western or Eastern models.

The lack of school-like institutions is compounded by the sharp divide between everyday knowledge and academic knowledge. As we have seen, historically, literacy and education were not inseparable. Except in rare instances that separation has disappeared. One of those cases can be found in the Vai tribe of Liberia who had adopted an alphabet and the practice of writing many years in advance of the arrival of schools in their area. Sylvia Scribner and Michael Cole compared unschooled villagers who were able to use the Vai script for limited purposes, such as writing letters and keeping accounts, with Vai public school students who'd become literate in English. School-based

---

[10] Only recently have we seen a growing resistance to secular education and outright conflict between public schools and Qur'anic schools in some Muslim areas, such as northern Cameroon (Moore 2006: 114).

[11] An interesting exception occurred in Sierra Leone where, for a few years from 1943, the government coopted the *Sande* bush school (see chapter 8) to teach what used to be called "home economics" (Day 1998: 57).

literacy supported the development of an array of cognitive skills (for example, metalinguistic discourse) that the more limited and task-oriented village literacy did not (Scribner and Cole 1981).

Several studies have also been undertaken to compare the math used in the village setting with mathematics used in school. One finding is that traditional principles underlying math in the village are often among the first casualties of outside contact where, for example, native counting and measurement tools are abandoned in favor of more efficient foreign methods (Lancy 1983: 109). A second finding is that village math, like village literacy, shares few unifying principles (Gay and Cole 1967). Essentially, *mathematics* does not exist to a villager who sees instead a series of discrete problems and discrete solutions.[12] One very general principle might be, "keep it simple."[13] A third finding is that the math used to solve everyday problems – especially the calculations employed by urban street sellers – does not *transfer* to school math (Saxe 1990; Rampal 2003).[14] And, in spite of hundreds of attempts (Demmert and Towner 2003) to alter the curriculum to create bridges between village and school ways of thinking, the successful efforts have been rare and costly (Lipka *et al.* 2005).

Indeed, observers have often noted resistance on the part of villagers to the inclusion of material from the indigenous culture into lessons: "a teacher in Chaing Rai [Thailand] bemoans the fact that . . . they do not want to waste time studying . . . [their] culture but would rather concentrate on such things as computers" (Montgomery 2001a: 148). In an Inuit community, parents balked at the incorporation of Inuktitut lessons into the classroom. Many requested "that their children be withdrawn from cultural inclusion programs" (Condon 1987: 160).

Hence, the village child on his first day of school really does resemble Locke's *tabula rasa* (Locke 1693/1994).

Village schools

The future is for those who know how to hold a pencil. (Nicolaisen 1988: 203)[15]

Liberia was ruled by soldiers, by weapons, and by those most often rejected by society, namely, those who had angry power rather than education. (Gay 2005: 23)

---

[12] The villager behaves like a *bricoleur* (Lévi-Strauss 1966).

[13] For example, Ghanaian fish "sellers probably do not utilize all supply and demand information and do not combine such information to arrive at an overall assessment of market condition because, like all other decision makers, they avoid complex calculations" (Quinn 1978: 214).

[14] However, a study in Liberia *did* find that village arithmetic strategies were successfully applied in school (Brenner 1985: 182).

[15] Sentiments of Punan Bah (Borneo) informant.

[Teachers in Guinea believe] "Il faut suffrir pour apprendre" (to learn one must suffer). (Anderson-Levitt 2005: 988)[16]

On every continent, it is now unusual *not* to see an example of Western or Asian-inspired public schools in every village. But a closer look doesn't inspire confidence. Even a casual observer will note the crowding, the lack of materials, the teacher droning in a language the pupils aren't following very well, and his clear preference for chastisement over praise (Borofsky 1987: 94; Anderson-Levitt 2005). The massive international investment in human capital has yielded a low return, and we will examine some of the reason why that's the case.

In the late 1960s, I had the opportunity to observe village schools in Liberia serving children of the Kpelle tribe. One in Sinyeé – a village near a major road, hospital, and mission-run liberal arts college – was well constructed and equipped. The building, contents, and teachers all represented investments by the Liberian and US governments – USAID funded the buildings, the US Peace Corps supplied hundreds of teachers. The goals were primarily to promote improvements in the quality of life at the village level including enhanced health, agricultural production, and entrepreneurship. Secondarily, there was the desire to build an educated workforce that would provide the human capital upon which a modern economy could be built.[17] And, third, like much of post-colonial Africa, nationalism rarely went beyond the capital as tribal groups in the interior were largely in ignorance of the national government and had little reason to adopt a Liberian identity.[18] These initiatives with the same objectives were undertaken with great fanfare and optimism in the so-called "Third" or "Underdeveloped" World from the early 1960s to the 1990s.

However, I did not observe a great deal of learning in the school and felt that conditions were more akin to the "Bush School," that is, an initiation rite (Lancy 1975: 375) as described in the previous chapter. Aside from the severe problems imposed by pupils' near-zero knowledge of English, which was the language of instruction, I saw "no books in Kpelle homes to learn from, no library, no "Sesame Street." Parents, almost all of whom are illiterate, cannot

---

[16] Attitude expressed by village teachers in Guinea.

[17] At that time, Liberia's economy, while robust in dollar terms, was considered fragile as it depended on extraction of non-renewable resources (iron, old-growth timber) and production of raw commodities (rubber) with zero in-country manufacturing or secondary production (Clower *et al.* 1966).

[18] For a thorough treatment of the Ghanaian government's use of the schools to create a national identity, see Coe (2005). The use of the schools to promote national over local or tribal identity is not limited to emerging nations. Public education systems in Europe were developed with that as a primary goal (Boli 1987:4) while, more recently, public education has been conscripted in the push to *preserve* local culture and identity, such as the decentralization of schools in Belgium and the imposition of Welsh language in the schools of Wales (Schriewer *et al.* 2000: 16).

teach their children what they are expected to learn in school. The school, like the initiation ritual, exercises complete control over the access to knowledge" (Lancy 1975: 378). My colleagues John Gay and Michael Cole, looking at the same school, concluded that its efforts were largely wasted (Gay and Cole 1967: 35). None of the lofty goals enumerated above was ever achieved. Indeed, the Liberian government was viewed as skimming off the cream of the limited economy, and there were no jobs for well-educated Liberians – let alone the thousands of "school leavers."[19] As a result, the country, in effect, collapsed into anarchy in the early 1980s, a state from which it is just now emerging after almost twenty-five years. The goals were perfectly reasonable, but the means provided to achieve them were patently inadequate.

I witnessed much the same scenario in Papua New Guinea a decade later. In the Gapun village school, for example,

Children learn very little during their first two or three years . . . due . . . to their inability to cope with instruction in English . . . Outside of school . . . literacy skills are almost never used . . . after they leave school at ages fourteen to fifteen, many of these young people may never read and will almost certainly never write again. (Kulick and Stroud 1993: 32)

In PNG, government and foreign aid was significantly augmented by Christian missions. Also, a shift in emphasis had occurred. Universal primary education – considered by the United Nations the *sine qua non* of modernity – was now embraced as a means to promote *rural development*.[20] This was not a message that parents wanted to hear (Lancy 1979). But this redefinition of purpose has continued to be adopted in many areas of the Third World, provoking a similar response. In Uganda in the late 1990s, top-down attempts to "ruralize" or "vocationalize" the curriculum were resisted. At the local level, people continued to view the school as preparing students for non-rural, upwardly mobile futures. The "image of the dirty 'village child' or 'primitive farmer' [was juxtaposed with] 'looking proper' and 'smart' in a school uniform" (Meinert 2003: 189).

As we travel around the globe, these and other problems emerge as anthropologists look at the school in the village. In Chillihuani village where hamlets are dispersed over a valley running from 3,800 to 5,000 meters, children's

---

[19] The term "school leaver" is used in preference to the US term "drop-out." It has broader connotations and can include students who've completed ("graduated") whatever level of education was available to them but without transitioning into the modern economic sector. It conveys the notion of someone who started the process of schooling in order to leave the subsistence sector but who was, for any number of reasons, unsuccessful.

[20] I suspect a more effective approach to rural development is to deliver very focused (hygiene, new seed varieties, fuel sources) training directly to the adults who'll be making the changes (or not) and let the kids continue to acquire the traditional culture, informally, the way they always have.

attendance at school is limited by the harsh climate and the great distance they must cover during the journey from home to school (Bolin 2006: 85). The monolingual Quechua children struggle with Spanish as the traditional language of instruction and the fact that the classroom is overcrowded and many must sit on the floor. In spite of a sympathetic teacher locally, Bolin notes that, generally, Indian children suffer harassment and other forms of abuse at the hands of *mestizo* teachers and students (Bolin 2006: 87).

Pupils in the Mayan village in the Chiapas Highlands of Mexico studied by Nancy Modiano in the early 1970s were beaten and made to kneel on pebbles or fruit pits to drive lessons home. It is no wonder that "Indian parents did all they could to save their children from the terrible fate of attending school" (Modiano 1973: 87).

In Central Africa, pygmy school-children are harassed and bullied by children from more powerful Bantu tribes, and government officials speak of them with evident racism and contempt. The obstacles they face mean that, according to a sympathetic teacher: "They sometimes take three to four years to complete a single year of normal schooling" (Raffaele 2003: 132). In Bangladesh, village children begin schooling quite late – on their own initiative – and their attendance is erratic. Hence, by adolescence, the average child has completed only three years of education (Nath and Hadi 2000).

On Malaita Island in Melanesia, the teacher corps is poorly trained, not fluent in the language of instruction (English), and turns over frequently. Materials are outdated and full of culturally inappropriate references. Children "memorize the singsong phrases required of them for oral recitation without understanding what the sentences mean" (Watson-Gegeo and Gegeo 1992: 18–19). On Pulap Island (Micronesia) Flinn observed the following incompatible culture mix:

Although the educational system ostensibly derives from an American model ... many aspects nonetheless continue to transmit Pulapese culture ... the atmosphere at the school is very lax and permissive to an American observer ... The cupboards and shelves of the classrooms are in disarray ... The bells marking the periods ring at haphazard times – resulting in periods of irregular and unpredictable length and a recess that lasts two or three times the designated length ... Much of the seemingly chaotic behavior is consistent with other aspects of life on Pulap. No one follows a clock or is concerned with tardiness, and no island event scheduled for a particular time ever begins at that time. (Flinn 1992: 52).

Moore observed a similar clash in Cameroonian village schools between the modern, constructivist teaching methods promoted by the Ministry of Education and teachers' adherence to a traditional, authoritarian teaching style that stressed discipline and rote memorization (Moore 2006: 115).[21]

---

[21] For a parallel account of conflict between traditional teaching styles and government-sponsored reform from (formerly French Equatorial) Guinea, see Anderson-Levitt and Diallo (2003).

For children of the Shipbo tribe in Peru, schooling leads them into a kind of twilight zone because it keeps "them from learning their environment and own culture, [yet gives] them only minimal skills for life in town" (Hern 1992: 36). While in school they are removed from opportunities to observe and emulate their elders – who will not stop to remedy this loss by actively teaching them.[22] Furthermore, their heads will be turned, their attention diverted from the village where their future probably lies to the town, where the poor quality of their education hobbles them.[23]

As depressing as these scenes are[24] – and they could easily be multiplied – we must bear in mind that, from the child's perspective, school may look quite different. If the alternative is lugging around a cranky baby brother or weeding the garden or sticking around home all day helping mother, then spending a few hours in the company of peers, even under otherwise adverse circumstances, might not seem so bad.[25] Furthermore, in my conversations with village students in Liberia, PNG, and Trinidad, the males, at least, freely expect that this reprieve from farm labor will be permanent. They expect to follow the yellow brick road of public schooling right to a well-paid white-collar job in the capital city.

However, many, perhaps the majority, discover that the road ends well short of their goal. In Zawiya, Morocco, for example, fewer than 3 percent of the age cohort complete high school, and even college graduates face poor job prospects. This has led to "increasing frustration and cynicism among Zawiyans and Moroccans generally" (Davis and Davis 1989: 141–142). This malaise is by now quite widespread. Universal primary schooling has created "an avalanche of failed aspirations throughout the third world" (LeVine and White 1986: 193) where schools find themselves "in the business of producing failures" (Serpell

[22] Among the Cree, because parents don't see themselves as teachers, they take no special pains to alter their foraging behavior to accommodate children's school attendance. They *could* schedule bush collecting trips for weekends or holiday periods so children could accompany them and continue to learn from observation, but they do not. As a result, traditional subsistence knowledge is not being passed on (Ohmagari and Berkes 1997). Similarly, "Young Lacandones (Maya) tend to know much less about the forest than their fathers . . . " (Ross 2002: 592).

[23] Nsamenang characterized all of Africa in these terms, for example, "the school system in much of Africa has so spiraled out of control that it mainly churns out unemployed youth who can read and write but who are totally dependent and cannot even create or utilize local knowledge" (Nsamenang 2002: 91).

[24] It's worth remarking that learning *can* occur under what appear to be very adverse circumstances. Some readers no doubt shared my experience of attending a one-room, multi-graded primary school with no plumbing and little heat. European immigrant children, especially working-class Jews in New York in the early years of the twentieth century, attended horrible, overcrowded schools. There was no accommodation for non-English speakers; in fact, students were punished for using Yiddish by having their mouths washed out with (kosher) soap. In spite of achieving successful integration and even prosperity, as adults, the Jewish students still recalled their suffering and acute embarrassment (Berrol 1992: 45, 54–55).

[25] In Guinea, for instance, "Students wanted to be in school and certainly preferred school to being home, where they would have to do chores. That is why the big punishment was to be '*bâni*' (banished), turned away from school" (Anderson-Levitt 2005: 988).

1993: 10). Particularly in Africa, frustrated "school leavers" of the 1960s and '70s became the brutal "rebels" of the 1980s and '90s (Honwana 2005; Utas (2005).

And there is absolutely no mystery about why this happened. It is due to the utter failure of the developed world's intelligentsia (for example, agencies like USAID, International Monetary Fund, World Bank, United Nations Development Program) to recognize the need to spend far *more* to educate children from societies with no traditions of formal education than we spend per pupil in the developed world. As we'll see in sections that follow, successful schooling in modern society depends crucially on parents acting as their children's first, best, and enduring teachers. When parents are unable or unwilling to play this role, the state must close the gap with subsidized pre-school, compensatory education, and "special" education services.

Schooling and children's work

... children are kept out of school [in rural Lebanon] whenever there is work to be done at home or in the fields. (Williams 1968: 52)

Parents, in effect, substitute a strategy of rearing only a few well-educated but potentially well-paid and influential children for a strategy of raising a lot of poorly educated farm hands. (Harris 1990: 218–219)

As discussed in chapters 3 and 7, in most of the world, children have no intrinsic value but have great potential worth as future workers and as caretakers for their elderly parents. The introduction of schooling into the traditional society may not, therefore, be embraced with unbridled enthusiasm, as it implies both direct costs and the opportunity costs associated with the loss of the child's labor. In this section we'll learn how canny parents carefully assess the costs and benefits of their children's schooling.

Compared with children, parents' views on the value of schooling are more varied, if not more sophisticated. Working for the Ministry of Education, I traveled widely in PNG during a period (1976–1980) when the number of school places was expanding even as the number of new salaried positions was shrinking rapidly. In the civil service sector (including schools), the transition from Australian expatriate staff to native replacements was nearly complete and the only paying jobs in the private sector were for unskilled workers on plantations and in mines. I had numerous conversations with parents whose generation was the first in the region to learn of the modern world. They were, nevertheless, convinced that, by attending the rudimentary (in every sense) school in the village, their son would travel the *rot bilong mani* (road to riches) to a life of ease – just like the *whitepela*.

When I asked if they were taking special pains on weekends to insure that their children in school would "catch up" on what they were *not* learning about village life, they responded, in effect, "What for? They won't ever live in the village."[26] Other sites that I visited had had a longer period of association with schooling. There I met adults, now sadly wiser, who angrily denounced the *bikhets* (big-heads) – school leavers who had returned to the village without jobs, nor with any appreciation for or tools to succeed in village life.

In fact, Ali Pomponio and I took advantage of the gradual spread of public schooling in Papua New Guinea – from coastal areas inland – to systematically compare parental perspectives. In the Southern Highlands where their children were the first cohort to gain access to schooling, Imbonggu parents willingly paid school fees and sent the majority of their sons to school, eagerly anticipating the eventual windfall of remitted wages when their children became salaried civil servants. In the Siassi Islands, parents had enjoyed such a windfall from their children who were among the first to gain access to secondary education in the 1960s and who did find ready employment in government jobs that were opening up.[27] But, by 1979, the expense of sending children through to secondary school had climbed, while the returns had declined: graduates were no longer finding jobs. Hence, enrollment in local elementary schools had dropped dramatically as parents recognized that schooling was no longer a good investment (Pomponio and Lancy 1986: 45–47).[28] They realized that they would achieve a greater return from their children if they kept them busy in gardens or collecting on the reef (Pomponio 1992).[29]

One common theme in the narratives gathered by ethnographers is that the school has little to do with *traditional* village life (Nieuwenhuys 2003: 106). Among the Inuit and the Navajo:[30]

Children who previously spent their days helping parents with hunting, trapping, fishing, skin preparation, and general household chores now spend much of the day in an institutional setting learning skills unrelated, and sometimes antithetical, to those emphasized at home. (Condon 1987: 157)

---

[26] While village parents around the world seem eager to send their children off down the yellow brick road to earn their fortune, studies of Native American communities in the USA present a very different picture. Here, parents strenuously resist any notion that their children will use schooling as an "exit" strategy to move away from family and the reservation. This "resistance" is cited as one of the major causes of very low academic success by Native American students (Deyhle 1991: 294; 1992; Condon 1987: 162).

[27] A similar pattern can be found on Rotuman (Howard 1970: 63) and Ponam Islands (Carrier 1981: 239).

[28] Elsewhere in PNG, the story is the same.

[29] However, there appear to be a growing number of cases in the Third World where the lack of suitable cropland – obviating the need for child workers – forces parents to send children to school in the hope that this will lead them to greener pastures elsewhere (Stambach 1998: 193).

[30] Other North American examples of resistance to the demands of the school ethos include the Amish (Hostetler and Huntington (1971/1992: 3) and Hopi (Simmons (1942: 100).

Not all parents understood or accepted the idea of homework. A Navajo . . . teacher at the elementary school said, "The Navajo way is that you are in school all day . . . at home you have other things to do; haul water, chop wood, help with the children." (Deyhle 1991: 288)

If parents[31] believe their children have economic opportunities outside the village that education can help them realize, they'll send them to school, buy the uniforms and books, and pay the fees.[32] Otherwise, they'll refuse to make these sacrifices (Akabayashi and Psacharopoulos 1999). Yemeni adolescent boys are "actively discouraged by parents and peers from pursuing studies as there were no perceived gains and prolonged education was viewed as an impediment to early marriage" (Marchand 2001: 102). Similarly among the lowland Maya, "no jobs are available for which formal education is a prerequisite. On the other hand, children can assist with maize production with little training, so why waste limited resources on schooling?" (Kramer 2002b 305).[33]

The Touaregs, famous desert caravaners studied by Gerd Spittler, refused to send their children to a new school even though attendance was compulsory. Some even went so far as to purchase potions from the shaman to make them appear stupid (Spittler 1998: 16). Others claimed that only poor parents without the means to employ children in herding or fruit harvesting send them to school (Spittler 1998: 33). Reports of strong resistance to schooling come from rural communities in Asia (Montgomery 2001a: 67; Nash 1970: 308) as well.

Some governments have taken the extraordinary step of compensating families directly for the loss of children's labor. This has happened in Jordan with some Bedouin groups (Spicer 2005: 2171). And Turkey has recently launched a program – "Will you be my parents?" – in which private donors are solicited for funds to permit peasant children to attend school in lieu of working in the cotton fields of Anatolia (*The New Anatolian*, May 18, 2006: 12). While it may be difficult to persuade villagers to invest in schooling, parents who do hold aspirations for their children may discover that the government is coming up short in its investment in education. Village parents may elect to send children to serve in the households of distant kinsmen, in hopes that they will gain access to superior urban schools. This example is from Liberia:

---

[31] I use the term "parents" for convenience. In my reading of the literature, the decision to send a child to school, and provision of the source(s) of funds to do so, is just as diffuse a responsibility as any other aspect of childrearing, as discussed in chapter 4.

[32] Not surprisingly, villagers in China (Taiwan, in one study) are the exception, in emphasizing the importance of schooling over other obligations including chores and religious ceremonies. Migrating from the village to seek employment before completing one's education is discouraged. Schoolteachers are held up as models for students to emulate (Stafford 1995). In Shandong zeal for schooling – village students outscore urban students on national exams – comes from the desire to escape the stigma of being a peasant (Kipnis 2001: 17).

[33] See also Barber (2002: 364).

many children must support themselves through school as wards in the households of people who live near schools. Parents realize their children may be overworked, underfed, or beaten in other people's households but they hope for a minimum of mistreatment in exchange for a chance to have an educated child. The potential income from an educated child with a good job warrants the risks involved. (Bledsoe 1980a: 35)

In places as different as Egypt (Booth 2002: 223, 226)[34] and Micronesia (Falgout 1992: 39; Hashim 2005), aspiring parents are hoarding funds to send their children to private schools. Hardly swank, they are, however, vastly superior to the available public institutions. In Pakistan, public and private resources are being redirected towards private schools as "a strong wealthy modernizing elite continues to impose its goals on a relatively poorer, traditional mass of common people" (Jalil and McGinn 1992: 105). In Tanzania, the recent proliferation of private schools has "served further to differentiate wealthy communities from poor" (Stambach 1998: 196). Pervasive economic woe is no impediment to the creation of "haves and have nots," as shown in a comparison of urban private and rural public schools in Ethiopia (Poluha 2004).

In the upper echelon of Mexican society, maids and house-boys replace the labor normally provided by children of the household. In turn, they "consider themselves above any manual labor and above those who must perform it . . . their time should be spent in schooling and in entertainment" (Modiano 1973: 85). In South Asian Bengali villages, the labor of low-caste families provides the added wealth and leisure that permits high-caste children to succeed in school, often with the aid of paid tutors (Rohner and Chaki-Sircar 1988: 75).

The provision of resources by the central government to villages to "educate" their children has not only been wholly inadequate in terms of preparing students to enter the wage sector, it has not even insured that some segment of the village is sufficiently educated to take on the multi-national corporations. Pomponio documents the ease with which rural Papua New Guineans are hoodwinked into giving away precious natural resources (old-growth timber) for a pittance (Pomponio 1981). Similarly,

Rural Solomon Islanders are increasingly under pressure to sign contracts with multinational corporations allowing lumbering, mining, or plantations on their land. The kind of schooling currently available in the Solomons is not preparing islanders to make principled decisions on the issues such as these . . . The growing split between urban and rural areas in quality of schooling and educational opportunities has also effectively disenfranchised villagers from political power in the Solomons. Educated Solomon Islanders sent to villages by government offices or development agencies to present information

---

[34] Also in Egypt, at least some public schools display very uneven distribution of resources with high-achieving students served in a section of the school with clean, modern facilities compared with the remainder (Saad 2006: 92).

Figure 27 Private school students exiting antiquities museum, Istanbul

or introduce new projects often treat villagers with arrogance, refusing to speak the local language when they know it, and define essential concepts. (Watson-Gegeo and Gegeo 1992: 19)

Pandya describes the Indian government's institution of a public school in an Ongee (Andaman Island) village. In a multi-year account, we learn how the community struggles to find something useful or meaningful in the curriculum that's been imported *in toto* from Hindu-speaking, urban India. After twenty years "five boys who had been in the school off and on for about eight years ... could not read or write" (Pandya 2005: 400). The villagers are, effectively, mute as the forest – their home and their livelihood – is rapidly cut in large-scale logging.

It's a necessary first step for parents to acquiesce to their children's schooling and find funds to cover the inevitable expenses, even to the point of paying for private schooling. But, in the First World, a cornerstone of current theories of education and child development is the necessity for parents to *involve themselves* directly in their children's education, virtually from birth.[35] The evidence we've seen so far suggests that this may be another of the obstacles on the road to success for village children (Harris 2006: 91).

Parents as teachers

In contrast to American parents, who seem to feel that knowledge is something like medicine – it's good for the child and must be crammed down his throat even if he does not like it – Rotuman parents acted as if learning were inevitable because the child wants to learn. (Howard 1970: 37)

Instead of seeing parents as either bad or good, it is more useful to recognize that their level of investment in children varies greatly. (Barber 2000: 1)

One of the major themes of chapter 5 – Making sense – is that village adults rarely see the necessity of *teaching* children; rather that children are expected (and rarely fail to meet that expectation) to observe and emulate the behavior of more competent community members, practicing until they, too, are competent. In the concluding section of the chapter, I contrasted the intensive and elaborate language socialization employed by modern, middle-class mothers with its absence elsewhere and linked this to the need to prepare the child for school.[36]

This contrast between adult–child language interaction patterns in the village and those found in schools and the cultures that spawned them has received a great deal of attention. Susan Phillips and others have shown that Native American children use patterns of communication at home that are different than those expected in the classroom and this accounts in part for their failure to meet the school's academic expectations (Phillips 1983).[37] Cazden discusses the conflict that arises in US public schools when children are asked to "share" or "show and tell" a personal narrative. While mainstream children have no difficulty with this rhetoric, poor, African-American children have had little exposure to or practice with it. In fact their stories tend to be episodic. Teachers

---

[35] In a large-scale survey undertaken in the USA, "Mothers ranked teaching as their most prominent strength" (Strom *et al.* 2004: 681).

[36] For a thorough overview of the contrast between the "folk" pedagogy of the village and the academic pedagogy of the school, see Rogoff *et al.* (2003).

[37] Another study that documents differences between village and school participation rules was undertaken on Kosrae (Michalchik 1997). For a discussion of the *congruence* between home and school in middle-class society – in Italy and the USA – see Sterponi and Santagata (2000).

are less accepting of episodic narrative and try to steer children around to topic-centered narratives because they want the child to "construct an oral text that is as similar as possible to a written composition" (Cazden 1988: 14; Michaels and Cazden 1986: 136).

In a Tongan *classroom*, teachers may well expect students to volunteer information, ask questions, or eagerly answer the teacher's academic questions. In a Tongan *village*, children are to learn through observation alone.

When children are present during adult conversations they are expected to remain silent . . . adults either ignore them or treat them with impatience or anger[38] . . . Children who interrupt or offer advice to adults without being asked may be accused of being *fie poto* (thinking themselves clever) . . . Even at mealtimes when, in most households, the whole family sits together, the adults do not usually include the children in their conversations. (Morton 1996: 166, 90, 170)

In Kenya, LeVine and colleagues observed that:

Gusii mothers . . . expected their infants and toddlers to comply with their wishes . . . They rarely praised their infants or asked them questions but tended to issue commands and threats in communicating with them . . . many of the interrogatives were rhetorical questions that have the force of commands or even threats: "Why are you crying?" or "Do you want me to beat you?" (LeVine 2004: 156)

These village norms have real consequences in terms of the mindset children bring to the classroom, as demonstrated in an ingenious experiment. Mayan children were compared with middle-class American counterparts in a novel origami-folding task. The village-reared children were much more attentive to the demonstration and to the activities of others in the setting, especially adults. Unlike the Anglo children, they did not seek additional information to aid them in completing the task (Correa-Chavez and Rogoff 2005: 9).[39] Parallel results were observed in a study comparing native Hawaiian and *Haole* (Anglo) students where the latter were much more likely to request adult assistance and, consequently, were more successful at the task (Gallimore *et al.* 1969).

Paula Levin, from her fieldwork with native Hawaiians, uncovers the conflict that arises when village mothers attempt to act as teachers. Direct instruction, while "considered appropriate for acquiring school skills . . . is the strategy of last resort [in] learning household chores" (Levin 1992: 67).

[38] For comparable observations from Tanna Island, see Lindstrom (1990: 114).

[39] In a parallel study in the USA, groups of children whose immigrant mothers were relatively well educated or poorly educated behaved differently when shown how to make origami figures. The latter group relied solely on observation whereas the former sought additional information through questioning the teacher (Mejia-Arauz *et al.* 2005). See also Correa-Chavez and Rogoff (2005). Another study demonstrated that Mayan mothers in Mexico with twelve or more years of schooling behaved much more like schoolteachers in interacting with children than did mothers with two or fewer years of schooling (Chavajay 2006).

Village parents may use punitive means to shape children's behavior, a tactic at variance with modern notions of appropriate teacher behavior (Wolf 1972: 68). Observers of children in urban slums also see adults imposing harsh discipline. A mother in a *favela* of Rio de Janeiro knows "intuitively that in order for her children to survive, toughness, obedience, subservience, and street smarts are necessary; otherwise, the child can end up dead" (Goldstein 1998: 395).

A radically different scene confronts an observer in Sweden where parents strive to "enter and understand the child's world... to ensure their children's participation in decision making" (Dahlberg 1992: 132–133).Western parents emulate teachers[40] in offering children inducements and praise or a show of excitement – behavior absent in village mother–child relations (Rohner and Chaki-Sircar 1988: 77). Such praise "may serve to motivate children to engage in activities in which they otherwise might not choose to participate" (Rogoff 2003: 306–307). As noted in chapter 5, children *want* to learn their culture and may need no more than the occasional tongue-lashing to remain diligent in their pursuit of adult competence. But school subjects are often of far less interest and children require incentives to raise their motivation to adequate levels.

Another source of conflict noted by many anthropologists is the school's emphasis on individualism, on students taking *individual* responsibility, on earning *their* grade, on paying attention to the teacher and not their peers. This contrasts with a village emphasis on collectivism, especially where children are concerned. "Children are more likely to be trained to become people like *us*, rather than a person like *me*" (Ritchie and Ritchie 1979: 65). Here is a concrete manifestation of this attitude at work in Poomkara (south India) village:

pre-puberty children could be everywhere in the house but could claim none of the spaces as theirs. Children had no rooms of their own in the tiny huts. Schoolbooks were often simply stuck under the palm roof and children's clothes hung on a rope. Children did their homework sitting on the same mat on which they slept at night. Even this mat was often shared with others. (Nieuwenhuys 2003: 103)

This vignette also suggests that village parents don't feel much need to make adjustments in domestic arrangements on behalf of their schoolchildren. In our society, by contrast, there are warehouses full of child-specific furnishings, many of which explicitly wear an "educational" label (Sutton-Smith 1986: 33). Here's an interesting Japanese invention:

The home-study desk bought by most parents for their smaller children symbolizes the hovering care and intensity of the mother's involvement: all models have a high front and half-sides, cutting out distractions and enclosing the workspace in womb-like

---

[40] And schools *expect* them to, as shown in studies from Norway and France (Liden 2003: 127; Wylie 1957: 60).

protection. There is a built-in study light, shelves, a clock, electric pencil sharpener and built-in calculator. The most popular recent model included a push button connecting to a buzzer in the kitchen to summon mother for help or for a snack. (LeVine and White 1986: 123)

In this section, many conflicts between village strategies for enculturation and the ethos of the public school have been enumerated. Parents and the community at large have access to well-developed cultural routines to replicate themselves and raise well-adjusted, productive community members. But they lack, and seem unprepared to easily acquire, student-preparedness routines that are often *assumed* by school authorities to be already in place.

An educated woman

Roman men did not appreciate well-educated women. (Colón, with Colón 2001: 105).

[In post-industrial society] women are coming on much stronger, often leapfrogging the men to the academic finish. (Lewin 2006: 1).

To this point in the chapter, boys were explicitly identified as students or this has been largely assumed, because, from both the historical and cross-cultural perspectives, girls have rarely had access to schooling. That imbalance is beginning to disappear.

In ancient Egypt, some girls were taught to read and write and the hieroglyph for scribe, with the determinative for female added, is found from the Middle Kingdom (beginning of the second millennium BCE). No such practice existed at the time in Mesopotamia (Colón, with Colón 2001: 28).

In classical Greek civilization, girls did not go to school, and the extent of any education they may have encountered in the homes of their parents was probably limited. Girls were referred to as *pais* (child) until they married, whereas boys left that inferior (slaves were also *pais*) state when they came of age (Golden 2003: 14). Further, post-pubertal women were considered extremely dangerous because of their almost uncontrollable sexuality (Reeder 1995). In combination these views clearly made the idea of education for women unthinkable.

Some Roman girls attended school; however, because they were married in their teens, their studies were limited compared with boys. As in Greece, the few well-read and erudite Roman women were likely to be courtesans (Shelton 1998: 105). This was true in China as well where it was understood that, in a properly run household, females were not only segregated from males but excluded from cultural events and intellectual life as well. Exposure to and training in the arts and literature were available only to courtesans (Dardess 1991: 83–84).

In the early modern era (the eighteenth and nineteenth centuries), schooling for middle- and upper-class girls became the norm, but was aimed primarily at preparing them for society and to insure their virtue. Unlike boys, they weren't taught Greek or Latin or other "higher" subjects designed to prepare students for employment and/or leadership (Pollock 1983: 251). This attitude persists today. In many modern, well-off communities, while boys are expected to excel and use college as the means to an outstanding career, girls pursue post-secondary schooling to make themselves a more attractive mate and more competent mother.[41]

In the village, the impediments to boys' education are trebled for girls. In Turkey, as in so much of the world, "A girl is regarded as the 'property of strangers,' since when she marries she will contribute to the welfare of her husband's family, not her own" (Kagitçibasi and Sunar 1992: 77). This equation nullifies any profit parents might find in sending daughters to school.

A second and related issue is the need to keep daughters chaste to preserve their value as wives. Girls on Madagascar are withdrawn from school at puberty, no matter how well they're doing, "because their parents are so fearful of their involvement in what is assumed to be a highly sexualized urban world" (Sharp 2002: 227).[42]

Third, numerous anthropologists have observed the discouraging treatment of schoolgirls – by boys and the teachers, as well. In Guinea, for example, girls – but not boys – are expected to clean the classrooms daily and are punished for not doing an adequate job (Anderson-Levitt 2005). In Nigeria, the sexual harassment of female students has reached epidemic proportions.[43]

Fourth, girls are perceived as much more useful adjuncts to the household. They are preferred as child-minders and as their mother's helpmates in farming and the domestic sphere. While Ijo (Nigeria) girls may now go to school, this has hardly lessened their contribution to the household, while boys may roam about the village – as they always have – after school (Hollos and Leis 1989: 70).

These arguments can be heard throughout the Third World, and, indeed, it is extremely rare that village parents provide the same level of support for girls' and boys' schooling (Bolin 2006: 108). In Nepal, girls are forced to leave school early, and Sarah LeVine found that they

spoke of their truncated education with convincing bitterness. Regardless of academic talent, many had been pulled out of school to work in the house and on the family farm, or . . . to work as domestic servants or as laborers on construction sites. Their parents,

---

[41] This would be the perspective of the majority of young women in Utah who belong to the LDS (Latter Day Saint or Mormon) church. See also Holland and Eisenhart (1990) and La Russo (1988: 145). However, I believe that these cases are vestigial. The majority of middle-class women, in future, will aspire to professional careers.

[42] See also C. Harris (2006: 105).

[43] "Pressure by teachers for sex reported in Nigeria's Schools," *Seattle Times Online*, March 26, 2007: http://archives.seattletimes.nwsource.com; accessed 4.24.07.

to whom they gave their wages, had sometimes used the money to pay their brothers' school expenses. (LeVine 2006: 37)

Despite their negative feelings, this study was able to demonstrate that, even with limited schooling and literacy, these young women were distinguishable from their unschooled or less literate compatriots.[44] They were more savvy when it came to their own and their children's health care[45] and were more effective at supporting their own children's formal education (LeVine *et al.* 2004: 875). Indeed, private schools in India deny admission to students whose mothers aren't educated for just these reasons.[46] Their children will be much harder to educate. For years, worldwide surveys have shown that children's prospects are improved if their mothers have been schooled (Schultz 1994), and anthropologists are trying to uncover more specific reasons for this relationship. For example, schooled mothers may make more effective teachers of their pre-schoolers, adopting more school-like modes of discourse with them (Mejia-Arauz *et al.* 2005: 290).

In the West, gradual social change has elevated the status of women, and schooling has been instrumental in this process.[47] In Finland, for example, the majority of adult women are wage-earners and have slightly more education than men (Husu and Niemela 1993: 61). And among the Chaga, a relatively prosperous enclave in Tanzania, young women are so successful as students and, later, wage-earners that they are forgoing marriage (Stambach 1998).[48] There is, in fact, diverse evidence that the "information society" may favor female students.[49]

Nevertheless, schooling, generally, and academic literacy, in particular, call upon numerous skills and a mindset that do not seem to emerge naturally in the course of the child's development. Unlike social learning and make-believe play, which do come to the child's aid as marvelous systems for acquiring his/her

---

[44] Given the discussion earlier in the chapter of schooling as indoctrination, it's not clear whether these mothers' successful adaptation to modern institutions is primarily due to the knowledge and skills acquired at school or to the change in their self-image and in how others perceive them. Had they been educated or indoctrinated (Vavrus and Larsen 2003)?

[45] See also Lee and Mason (2005).

[46] Anita Rampal (personal communication, April 2004).

[47] Reports of progress in girls' education have surfaced from India (Roopnarine and Hoosain 1992), Korea (Cho 1995: 160), and Pohnpei (Falgout 1992: 40).

[48] Educated African women who do marry have fewer children and are less likely to be in a polygynous household (Hollos 1998: 255).

[49] As barriers are torn down and a female advantage in education starts to emerge, scholars have found suggestive evidence for a biological basis for this superiority. Little girls are better than boys at reading facial expressions and detecting emotion (Boyatzis *et al.* 1993). They have more acute hearing (Cassidy and Ditty 2001). Young female chimpanzees are much more attentive to adults, their mothers, in particular. While males spend more time playing, females are busy observing and practicing. They are, therefore, quicker to pick up useful skills, such as termiting (Lonsdorf 2005: 680).

culture, the tools to decode and absorb school subjects must be inculcated by a patient teacher, perhaps over several years *prior* to the start of school itself.

Bedtime stories as cultural capital

Adults jump at openings their children give them for pursuing talk about books and reading. (Heath 1982: 52)

Children learn to "talk like a book" before they learn to read. (Martini 1995: 58)

For working-class and poor families, the cultural logic of childrearing at home is out of synch with the standards of institutions. (Lareau 2003: 3)

To provoke an interest in reading on the part of boys, it helps to read them stories at bedtime. The linguistic anthropologist Shirley Brice Heath conducted a long-term ethnographic project with families in North Carolina in the 1970s. Her goal was to understand how different communities interact with literacy, especially where children were concerned. In a poor African-American community, "Tracton," use of books (other than the Bible) and printed material was limited, and parents did not engage in elaborate conversations with their young children, nor did they see it as their responsibility to act as the child's first teacher. She recorded sentiments that echo those recorded by anthropologists in villages throughout the world.

"He [her grandson] gotta learn to *know* 'bout dis world, can't nobody tell 'im. Now just how crazy is dat? White folks uh hear dey kids say sump'n, dey say it back to 'em, dey aks 'em 'gain 'n 'gain 'bout things . . . He just gotta be kéen, keep his eyes open . . . Gotta watch hisself by watchin' other folks. Ain't no use me tellin' 'im: "learn dis, learn dat" . . . He just gotta léarn . . . he see one thing one place one time, he know how it go, see sump'n like it again, maybe it be de same, maybe it won't. He hafta try it out." (Heath 1983: 84)

In a nearby, predominantly white, middle-class community, "Maintown," Heath sees a different picture.[50] Here homes are saturated with literacy as are the lives of children – from an early age. Aside from bedtime stories, which appear to be a nearly foolproof strategy to enhance children's learning to read (Teale 1978),

as early as 6 months of age, children give attention to books and information derived from books. Their rooms contain bookcases and are decorated with murals, bedspreads, mobiles, and stuffed animals that represent characters found in books . . . Adults expand nonverbal responses and vocalizations from infants into fully formed grammatical sentences. When children begin to verbalize about the contents of books, adults extend their

---

[50] McNaughton has found directly parallel results working with Pacific Islanders and *pakeha* (Anglo) communities in New Zealand (McNaughton 1996: 194–195).

Figure 28 Rocky and his mom reading in the hammock

question from simple requests for labels . . . to ask about the attributes of these items ("What does the doggie say?" "What color is the ball?"). (Heath 1982: 52)

Subsequent work by Catherine Snow and colleagues provided many additional cases of literary and non-literary home environments.[51] Scenes representing the latter condition included homes without any books, magazines, or newspapers, parents who claimed never to read and who had no awareness of or involvement in the children's homework. Ms. Pagliucca "knew Derek went to the bookmobile . . . but she never asked to see his books or talked to him about what he was reading" (Snow *et al.* 1991: 76). Not surprisingly, the dominant family pastime was TV viewing.

This continuum between Tracton and Maintown can be extended further by considering the situation in East Asian society. Here prevailing custom is quite explicit in designating the mother as the child's pre-school teacher, including insuring the child is literate *before* s/he starts school. Consequently, "the majority of Japanese children can read from around the age of 3 or 4" (Jolivet 1997: 43).

The routines (Lancy 1996: 15) that parents employ to insure school readiness, including, especially, involving children with books and literate speech,

[51] See also Purcell-Gates (1994).

have been referred to as a form of "cultural capital" (Bourdieu 1973). "In this view, home preparation is seen as essential, making it difficult for low-income children, who don't receive such preparation, to succeed in school, even if teaching is excellent" (Martini 1995: 50). The gap in the amount of pre-school language stimulation between lower- and middle-class homes can be extremely wide. In one comprehensive study, children of professional parents were exposed to three times the verbal stimulation as those of parents on welfare and the children's own vocabulary was twice as large. Vocabulary, in turn, is highly predictive of school success (Hart and Risley 1995; 2003).

These findings have prompted attempts to transfer middle-class routines to families lacking these resources (Delgado-Gaitan 1994b; Buckingham and Scanlon 2003: 6): "several European countries such as Belgium, the Netherlands, and France have set up programs designed to compensate for children's initial disadvantages in linguistic and cultural capital and to increase parental competence in dealing with homework and curricular activities" (Duru-Bellat and van Zaten 2000: 152). Government and NGOs routinely use mass media to try and "sell" parents on early reading and language-development activities. The *Salt Lake Tribune* had such an exhortatory piece that listed fourteen discrete pre-reading skills (for example, "Labels objects in books") a three-year-old should have – none of which they are likely to acquire unaided. But the obstacles are formidable (Mattingly *et al.* 2002; Grubb and Lazerson 1982: 226), chiefly that the very idea of being one's child's teacher is so strange to many, if not most, parents. Here's the reaction of one (English) parent to government-sponsored guidance efforts: "You know, I'd never say to Peter, 'Ooh, you're learning about Romans, let's go in the kitchen and make some "sweet wine cakes."' That just wouldn't happen. You know, the practical side of it, we just wouldn't do it. Playing games and making cakes and all that sort of thing – no" (Buckingham and Scanlon 2003: 183). Equally unpromising, the targeted parents did not enjoy much success as students themselves, and their interest in personal reading may be nil. Lastly, parents who've immigrated from a village culture where schooling was of little value may not even recognize the need to inform themselves of the childrearing practices that are required for their child to succeed as a student. They rely on information within the immigrant community, which fits the child for village life (Bornstein and Cote 2005). In short, the *Salt Lake Tribune* article and others like it probably preach to the choir.

Insuring that *pre-school* teachers can deploy these techniques with three- and four-year-olds in their charge may be more efficient than trying to train parents (who may be resistant) (Snow *et al.* 1998: 147). High-quality, literacy-rich pre-school programs have shown extremely positive results (Dickinson and Smith 1994; Neuman 1996). However, as a major survey revealed, the quality of pre-schools varies enormously (Snow *et al.* 1998: 329).[52] The high level of training evinced by teachers and the high teacher/pupil ratio in the excellent and widely available pre-schools in Europe (Corsaro 1996: 427; Dahlberg 1992), for example, are rarely matched in US pre-schools serving poverty-class children. A comparative analysis of a nursery school serving white suburban children and a Head Start pre-school for black inner-city children revealed that adult–child language and literacy practices are *imported* from the community (Lubeck 1984).

That is, black Head Start teachers treated the students as Tracton parents treat their children and white nursery school teachers behaved just like Maintown mothers. These programs appear then to *reproduce* existing literacy patterns in society and do not function in a compensatory manner (Lancy 1994a).

Earlier in this chapter, I asserted that universal primary education had been a failure in transforming Third World countries or, individually, many of their citizens. The reason, I argued, was that the resources allocated to this task were inadequate. Based on the amount of cultural capital that middle-class parents have at their disposal – as discussed in this and the next section – to invest in their children's successful education, it appears that public expenditure on "compensatory" education in the developed countries has also fallen far short.

"Dry cleaner" parents and "helicopter" parents

. . . you shouldn't baby them too much, give them too much praise. You don't want them to be too soft. (Kusserow 2004: 37)[53]

For many [US] parents . . . children are an extension of themselves, a means of self-fulfillment, and an important part of their self-image. (Fitchen 1981: 109).

As the home and school occupy almost non-overlapping cultures in the village, comparable separation may be the norm in many communities in the developed world as well. In an impoverished rural community in northern Appalachia, parents care greatly for their children to the point of digging themselves deeply into debt to purchase them impressive Christmas presents. They are concerned for their children's future but fail to cultivate a sense of ambition. They assert that

If you teach your children right and wrong, if you bring them up knowing how to behave themselves and how to get along with other people, if they learn to take care of themselves and mind their manners, then if they're given a chance, they'll be able to show that they're just as good as anybody else. (Fitchen 1981: 143)[54]

---

[52] More recently, see Magnuson *et al.* (2004).

[53] Comments of an urban working class parent.

[54] Psychologists have found that parental pressure towards conformity – of the sort described here – is negatively correlated with academic achievement (Okagaki and Sternberg 1993).

Further, these parents lack the requisite cultural capital to insure their children's success in school – where they themselves were unsuccessful. They don't routinely take their children to libraries, museums, or other cultural institutions. Children, therefore, lack the "mental pictures to go with the words in . . . school books" (Fitchen 1981: 142). As a result

we watch a child emerge from an innocent newborn to a sad, defeated youngster, conscious that he just can't seem to do anything right in school; from an eager kindergartner to an eighth-grade truant [another] victim of the bitter cycle of economic, social, and psychological problems that has crushed the hopes of one generation after another in these rural depressed areas. (Fitchen 1981: 125)

On US Indian reservations, where only one-third of the population completes high school, parents pay little attention to their children's schooling: "This noninterference approach is typical of some traditional Northern America Cheyenne parents who allow adolescents more freedom in making decisions than is characteristic of American middle-class culture" (Ward 2005: 124). Lareau's cross-class comparative ethnography identifies similar attitudes from a typical working-class community. Mrs. Morris, a mother from Colton, saw her son Tommy's education beginning when she "turned over responsibility" for him to the school. Afterwards, she remained largely in ignorance of his progress and was surprised to be called to the school and informed that he was doing poorly (Lareau 1989: 41). Teachers refer to mothers like Mrs. Morris as "'dry-cleaner parents' who drop their rambunctious kids off in the morning and expect them to be returned at the end of the day all clean and proper and practically sealed in plastic" (Gibbs 2005: 47).

John Ogbu used a "beer mug" metaphor to describe the behavior of his African-American informants in a middle-class community. The child's academic success does not depend on anything a parent might do. Nor is the child responsible – he is seen as a passive vessel – "students learn and perform well if the teacher pours knowledge well" (Ogbu 2003: 236). When beer mug parents *are* contacted by teachers expressing concern about their children, the response, typically, is to blame the teacher for being discriminatory, overly demanding, and critical (Lareau 2003: 193, 195),[55] or to promise to punish the child (Ogbu 2003: 233). It is just not part of their mental model of parenting to act as the child's academic tutor or mentor. Also, knowing how to approach and talk to authority figures – teachers in particular – is part of the portfolio of cultural capital not readily available to members of the proletariat: "The McAllisters, like other poor and working-class families, display caution and at times distrust

---

[55] One Catch-22 that is apparent from the literature is that beer mug parents only monitor the child's grades, and when s/he has a B on a report card they assume the child is doing well. But, due to social concerns about mediocre grades lowering a student's self-esteem, a B may, in fact, reflect very poor performance (Ogbu 2003: 247).

Figure 29 Honors student bumper sticker

towards individuals in positions of authority in dominant institutions" (Lareau 2003: 157).

In dramatic contrast to Mrs. Morris and Ms. McAllister are the mothers teachers refer to as "'helicopter parents,' who hover over the school at all times, waiting to drop in at the least sign of trouble" (Gibbs 2005: 44). I first heard the term "helicopter parents" in connection with the registration of new Honors freshmen.[56] So ubiquitous and intrusive were some of the parents that our admissions and counseling staff had to create separate parent activities and insist that students go through orientation and registration sans parents.

Alexandra Robbins' recent exposé, *The Overachievers*, is replete with such cases, including mothers who attend their children's math classes so they can be better tutors, those who write their children's essays and then complain about the essay receiving a low grade, parents who readily pay $16,000 annual pre-school tuition and later $33,000 for two years of pre-college grooming from "IvyWise" (Robbins 2006). While the number of such parents may be relatively small, through their example, lobbying, and political activism, they set the bar for everyone else.

Helicopters, humming birds, and anxious parents seem to be in constant motion. In one study,

the pace of life was different for middle-class families compared to working-class and poor families. In the middle-class, life was hectic. Parents were racing from activity to activity . . . children's activities determined the schedule for the entire family. Adults' leisure time was absorbed by children's activities. Children also spent much of their time in the company of adults or being directed by adults. (Lareau 2003: 35)

Anthropologist Elinor Ochs and colleagues at the UCLA/Sloan Center on Everyday Lives of Families[57] have been following thirty-two families to

---

[56] I was directing our university's Honors program at the time.
[57] Information from www.celf.ucla.edu; accessed 4.20.07.

document just how hectic middle-class life can be. As Ochs comments in an *Associated Press* story: "With all the scheduling, family life begins to resemble running a small business" (*The Herald Journal*, March 20, 2005: A10).

"Mom Taxi" trips present opportunities that aren't to be wasted. The ride to and from hockey practice serves as a forum for parent and child(ren) to reprise the day's school lessons. The parent uses these accounts to spot trouble brewing, to acknowledge praiseworthy achievements, and, ultimately, to enact a speech lesson. A subtle message consistently conveyed is that the child will assume a commanding position in society, perhaps as early as elementary school. This is revealed in the comments of bourgeois parents, interviewed by Adrie Kusserow, who think "that it was somehow demeaning to treat the child in a childlike way." "We give our children the right to choose what activity they want to do... so it's not, "I'm going to read you the book about such and such," but "Why don't you pick a book that you'd like me to read?" It lets them have some ownership of the situation and that's good" (Kusserow 2004: 105, 108). By contrast, working-class families remind children of their inferior status.

Queens parents... did not feel it was... inhibiting the child's development if they asserted their power... over the child. Hierarchy was part of life, the way things were, and something the child would have to accept... the child's lower status [is] manifested in... not having access to all parts of the house or pieces of furniture... having to use a respectful tone of voice in talking with parents, and... parents not... knock[ing] on the child's door before entering. (Kusserow 2004: 51–52)

Kusserow's Manhattan parents tolerate "stubbornness and willfulness" while her Queens' parents curb what they see as a "fresh" attitude (Kusserow 2004: 101). As we will observe, children raised to be independent and assertive are more likely to be immune from the potentially harmful influence of peers.

In the upwardly mobile communities where "pushy" parents rule,[58] the Mom Taxi is likely to be driven by the father: "[Mr. Tallinger] stays behind to take the children to school and to attend 'donuts with Dad,' an event sponsored by the parent–teachers organization" (Lareau 2003: 51). This finding of heightened involvement by fathers in their children's education has emerged in several studies, including middle-class African-American (Roopnarine *et al.* 2005), Caribbean (Rooparine *et al.* 2006), and Indian (Verma and Saraswathi 2002:

---

[58] My father was so "pushy," he assigned me two hours of homework a day because he didn't think the teachers were demanding enough. Eventually, he grew so disgusted with the public schools, he sent me to parochial school. By the standards of elite schools, the average student is "lazy" and has to be pushed. To express this in more academic terms, "individuals... seek... answers that are good enough to allow them to get by, and not necessarily the best answers overall..." (Barrett *et al.* 2002: 278).

109) communities.[59] In Sweden, fathers are "expected to be as capable and interested in active caretaking of offspring, including infants, as are the mothers. This 'soft' (*mjuk*) side of manhood has affectionately been called the velveteen daddy phenomenon" (Welles-Nyström 1996: 197–198).[60]

Sometimes the helicopter parent is more concerned about preventing *downward social mobility*. "Attentive parents study the faculty like stock tables, looking for the best performer and then lobbying to get their kids into that teacher's class" (Gibbs 2005: 46). Mothers are intimately aware of their children's progress in school. As Lareau notes, "parents' activities shape the degree to which children receive a 'generic' or a 'customized' educational experience" (Lareau 1989: 123). Mrs. Harris observes Alan's (lack of) progress in spelling as she serves a volunteer stint in the classroom. She asks for and is granted spelling materials to work (successfully) with Alan at home. Another family found out that their son needed occupational therapy for fine muscle control, which they willingly paid for, and the child experienced "dramatic improvement in his posture, his handwriting, and his motor coordination in soccer" (Lareau 1989: 117). Indeed, this is one of Lareau's most striking findings, that "the most intense family–school relationships were not for the highest achieving students in upper-middle-class families. These occurred in families whose children were at the *bottom* of their class" (Lareau 1989: 129).[61]

Helicopter parents aren't just concerned with choosing a "good" school and good teacher; equally important is the careful screening of the child's peers (J. R. Harris 2006: 233).

The fact that Alex Williams is a young African American male also shaped various aspects of his life in important ways. He belonged to an all-Black church, and he had regular opportunities to form friendships with other Black children. His parents carefully scrutinized his social environment, always seeking, as Ms. Williams said, to keep him in the company of individuals who were also "cultured." (Lareau 2003: 132–133)

As they transition from one set of peers to another, subtle changes occur in students' attitudes towards and performance in school (Kindermann 1993). A parent's knowledge of this phenomenon is, again, part of the stock portfolio we've been labeling "cultural capital." In selecting their homes based on an assessment of school quality, middle-class families are also, as a bonus, insuring that their children's neighborhood playmates will share the values they espouse. In working-class communities, children "have more autonomy from adults than their middle-class counterparts" (Lareau 2003: 151).

---

[59] In the USA, research indicates that children with non-involved fathers may "fail at school, develop behavioral and emotional problems, get into trouble with the law, engage in early and promiscuous sexual activity, or become welfare dependent later in life" (Horn 2003: 129).

[60] In point of fact, policies providing very generous childcare leave for fathers in much of Scandinavia have been largely spurned by the beneficiaries, see Gillis (2000: 233).

[61] See also Pomerantz and Moorman (2007).

Nowhere is the management of the child's peer relations more evident than among recent immigrant families in the USA: "among immigrant students the peer group... serves to reinforce a positive school adaptation pattern and to support compliance with school norms" (Gibson 1988: 178). Like their mainstream counterparts, immigrant parents also command an array of routines to undergird their children's education. But the tactics and values aren't identical to those of middle-class helicopter parents. For example, immigrant families are probably less likely to invest in girls' education or in schooling for a handicapped or "learning disabled" child. They want to back sure winners in the race to lucrative and secure employment.

Against all odds

... ideas about schooling (internal working models) migrate with... parents to the United States. (Roopnarine *et al.* 2004: 332)

The most noteworthy aspect of the Scripps (US) National Spelling Bee in 2004 was that a child of Indian immigrant parents did *not* win it. Indians had won the coveted prize in four of the previous five years. Thirty of the 249 finalists in 2004 were Indian-American. However, Akshay Buddiga *was* the runner-up. His older brother Pratyush had been the big winner in 2000, correctly spelling "prospicience" to take the prize. Pratyush's accomplishment was all the more remarkable given the fact that at his public middle school in Colorado Springs, he was teased almost daily for his dark skin, Indian heritage, uncircumcised penis, and nerdiness. Upon returning to school following the contest, he expected to be beaten up in gym class.[62]

These extraordinary overachievers are featured in the marvelous documentary *Spellbound* made about the lives of participants in the 1999 National Spelling Bee. For example, Neil Kadakia's performance was assisted by the efforts of a thousand Indian villagers his grandfather had paid to chant on his behalf. Perhaps more practically, he was aided by the hundreds of hours of training overseen by parents. One of the highlights of *Spellbound* is Neil's father's detailed explication of the complex and intense regimen they had developed for Neil (Blitz 2002).

The spelling bee success of first-generation East Indian students is the tip of a large iceberg that anthropologists have been examining for nearly two decades.[63] One of the first studies was carried out by Greta Gibson, who

[62] Information from www.bobfromaccounting.com; accessed 4.20.07.

[63] In contrast to recent immigrants who see their children's successful education and subsequent career as the path to improved family well being, most earlier immigrants from Europe had other priorities. They improved their lot through industrial employment and, consequently, did not "push" their children to excel in school (La Russo 1988: 143–144).

focused on a community of Sikh immigrants from the Punjab (northern India) living in California. The Punjabis chose to work just as hard as they had as farmers in India but, in the USA, they have been able to experience significant upward mobility. There were opportunities for factory employment, and by living frugally, they acquired farmland (particularly orchards) with their savings. Pushing their children to excel in school, the graduates found high-paying jobs in technical fields and shared earnings with the family.

Punjabi teenagers experienced a great deal of conflict in school centered on religion, values, dress, customs, and lifestyle. They were subject to racist taunts and had to communicate and learn in what was for them a second language. Nevertheless, on a variety of measures of academic success, Punjabi students did better than Mexican-American and Anglo students. "Parents were not naïve about the difficulties their children faced in school. They simply brooked no excuses for poor performance" (Gibson 1988: 293).[64] They couldn't blame teachers or the "system." If students fell out of line, parents forced them into early marriage and/or put them to work in fruit orchards. The primary method by which Punjabi parents facilitated their children's success was by insisting that they conform rigidly to the academic demands imposed by the school. And the children implicitly accepted their parents' views. They worked hard, did homework before watching TV, stayed out of fights, and obeyed and respected their teachers. Students did not want to follow their parents into the orchards but aspired to well-paid white-collar professions. Punjabi parents declare that "American" kids have too much freedom and too little responsibility. The Punjabi children weren't permitted to participate in extra-curricular activities such as sports, hold jobs, or date – since marriages are arranged.[65]

By contrast, only 12 percent of the Punjabi students' Anglo classmates take college prep courses, and parents and students seem to share a low estimate of the value of schooling. Similarly,

principals observed that the Mexican American children seemed to have less sense of purpose and direction in school than the Punjabis... Mexican American parents... looked to the schools for assistance in helping children develop and maintain their Spanish skills, while the Punjabi parents favored all-English instruction. (Gibson 1988: 107)

---

[64] This general attitude is what propels Asian students to success in spite of poorly endowed school systems. For example, Korean students outperform US students by a wide margin on objective tests of achievement, despite the government spending less than half the funds and despite much larger class sizes. One of the clues to understanding these differences is that "Guilt in Korea has a positive aspect... that promotes filial piety [and] achievement motivation" (Park and Kim 2006: 424).

[65] Interestingly, in the UK, where high schools can be much more academically oriented than they are in the USA, successful Sikh students are those who quickly *assimilate* to the dominant culture (Hall 2002: 111).

This and other evidence from Gibson's study suggest that parents in the three groups view schooling quite differently. They convey their differing values to their children and to the school authorities, and these values significantly influence student–school interaction patterns. Her findings closely parallel those found in an ethnography of Southeast Asian "boat people," who escaped after the fall of Saigon in 1975 (Caplan *et al.* 1991; Finnan 1987).

Meanwhile, evidence accrues that other, non-Asiatic immigrant groups with high aspirations also import some successful strategies for insuring their children's academic success. Caribbean (Roopnarine *et al.* 2004: 332), Central American (Suarez-Orozco 1989), and Russian (Delgado-Gaitan 1994a) immigrant students have vaulted over their neighbors whose US ancestry may go back many generations (Ogbu 1987). Indeed, in Hemmings' ethnography of three high schools, recent immigrants, who may come from diverse points on the globe, form a distinct clique based on shared values. One informant told her that

her best friend was Japanese-American. The two were inseparable, often walking arm-in-arm through the hallways. Her other friends included a Pakistani Muslim girl, a Russian immigrant, and a girl from India. Christina said the girls had become close friends because they came from families that were different from those of preppies. "Our families are really, really strict about things. Like we're not allowed to go on dates and church is the center of our lives." (Hemmings 2004: 29)

Immigrant families seem acutely conscious of the perils of their adolescent children "in limbo." They impose a model of adolescence on them – lacking jobs, money, sports, romance, sex, music, and cars – completely at odds with mainstream American values.

Examination hell

[Korean mothers] think of their children's scores as their own . . . [they are ever vigilant] in order to prevent their children from collapsing or falling behind in the war. (Cho 1995: 151).

The reader will have noted the many references in this chapter to the extraordinary success of children of Asian origin in US schools and universities. The tools used by families to construct such success have been forged in the fires of the widely acknowledged "examination hell." In the education systems of Asia, even in nursery school, the Confucian legacy lives on in an exam-driven obstacle course in which survivors can expect the lifetime security of salaried employment (Allison 1991: 199).

In China, the child receives constant reminders of the high expectations for academic excellence. Even when the child is doing "well," parents fret that this level won't be sustained. The child's inclination to help out, to do chores, is thwarted by mothers who would be broken-hearted if their child became distracted from schoolwork. Indeed, mothers reported spending an average of five hours per week helping their child with homework. Another survey found that "more than 90 percent of Chinese families buy books for their children" (Stevenson *et al.* 1992: 29–30).

Similar attitudes prevail across East Asia. In South Korea a mother is expected to carefully select infant toys that stimulate left-brain development. She will invest in pre-school and supplementary classes in music, painting, math, calligraphy, and foreign languages (Cho 1995: 148). When she visits her child's teacher, the conscientious mother will discreetly leave a cash-filled envelope to insure good treatment for her child. She networks with the school and other parents to keep abreast of changes in the college entrance examinations, the better to prepare her child for the critical event of its life – and hers! "For the last hundred days and on the very day of the examination, all mothers go to their religious centers to pray and cry together. It is a moving scene that every television news show displays as the examination date comes near" (Cho 1995: 158–159).

While American teachers may feel intimidated by helicopter parents, in Japan the school system actively socializes the mother, preparing her to do her part in the child's education. When American anthropologist Ann Allison placed her son in a private Japanese nursery school (*yochien*), she learned that she'd need to spend hours each day preparing a home-made, beautifully arranged, thoroughly Japanese, multi-item lunch-box. This meal is called *obentō*, and it serves as a test of the child's rapid acquisition of school culture – eat your whole lunch quickly without grumbling – and of the mother's dedication to her child's academic success. "*Obentō* guidelines issued by the school and sent home . . . [mean that] Motherhood is not only watched and manipulated by the state but made by it into a conduit of ideological indoctrination" (Allison 1991: 202, 206). It is thus, unsurprising, that Asian students of immigrant families don't simply "adapt" to a "foreign" situation. They excel. In one long-term comparison of Chinese-American and European-American children's math achievement during the elementary grades, a widening gap opened up favoring the Chinese. Further, the gap was associated with an even more dramatic difference in the amount of time spent by parents in deliberate, structured teaching of math at home (Huntsinger *et al.* 2000). However, as smooth as the transition might be for Asian families, there is one major difference between schools in Asia and in the USA. In the USA bright, compliant students are called "Nerds." This is not a complimentary term unless used as a badge of solidarity by the Nerds themselves. In the next section, we will gain a better understanding of why US secondary schools aren't always comfortable for academically oriented students.

Nerds, Jocks, Fluff Chicks, Breakers, and Homeboys

... if they're followers, doin' what their friends are doing ... they can't be themselves. (Kusserow 2004: 70)

... in high school, the big thing, for guys, is to give the appearance of not doing much work, trying to excel at sports and shine socially. (*New York Times*, July 9, 2006)[66]

The USA has, since early in its history, been socially diverse. Importing an aristocratic class from Britain, it also imported slaves from Africa. Immigrants from around the globe brought their cultures with them, and distinctly different ecologies created regional cultures. This diversity is particularly evident in the large public secondary schools found throughout the country. Against this diversity, juxtapose Asia's "one-size fits all" examination hell, a phenomenon quite foreign to the US secondary school ethos. This contrastive ethos is reflected in the fact that "grade-point averages are rising at a rate of about 0.15 points every decade" (*Washington Post*, January 28, 2003: A2).

As Kantor and Lowe point out in surveying the history of public schooling in the USA, "if quality education is taken to mean a strong academic curriculum taught by engaged, engaging, and well-educated teachers in schools committed to the promotion of intellectual development, we simply cannot locate much of it in the past" (Kantor and Lowe 2004: 6). Contrast this state of affairs with China, where "The sea of learning knows no bounds; only through diligence may its shores be reached" (Ho 1994: 296). Jin Li has carried out an interesting analysis of the terminology employed in China and the USA to discuss teaching and learning. Vocabulary that was prominent in Chinese discourse on education – hard work, effort, persistence, desire, and passion – is absent from comparable American discourse (Li 2003: 261–262). Schooling in Asia seems never to have strayed far from the Confucian verities whereas, in the USA, student intelligence, whether inherited or acquired, has rarely been the cornerstone of respected pedagogy as one critic of "multiple intelligences" points out (Gottfredson 2004: 42, 45). An acerbic columnist takes aim at the same social trend:

A school in Connecticut has gone so far as to ban red ink outright. Others are encouraging teachers to grade papers in "more pleasant-feeling tones" such as purple ... This parental get-the-red-out campaign is part of a larger self-esteem-based movement in grading students ... Parents should be more worried about the comments on their child's homework than the color in which they're written. Red ink will be the last of his problems when, one day, he's handed a pink slip. (*Salt Lake Tribune*, April 10, 2005: AA7)

A real-world analogue of Garrison Keillor's mythical "Lake Wobegon," where all "the children are above average," would be Muncie, Indiana, as

---

[66] Information from www.nytimes.com; accessed 4.20.07.

profiled by the Lynds in the mid-1920s. To the citizens of "Middletown," high school was represented by "dances, dramatics, and other interests . . . but . . . the 'Bearcats,' particularly the basket-ball team . . . dominate the life of the school" (Lynd and Lynd 1929: 213). By contrast, teachers, learning, and the content of books weren't particularly valued; instead, "education, appears to be desired . . . as a symbol . . . it is not primarily learning, or even intelligence, as much as character and good will which are exalted" (Lynd and Lynd 1929: 219–220). In a more recent report, we learn that, from the end of winter, "proms are the focal point of school life . . . [a welcome] break in the monotony of . . . what are often considered mundane school routines" (Best 2000: 18).

In the USA, there are manifold ways of being a "student," especially in secondary school. However, clusters of students or cliques typically demand rigid conformity. At Chaparral high school in an affluent Arizona suburb, a "Fluff Chick" talks about her coveted seat in the outdoor dining area: "'You wouldn't dare come sit out here if you didn't know the people,' said Lauren Barth, a sophomore cheerleader. 'But once you're in with the girls, everyone is really friendly to you. When I made cheerleader, it was like I was just set'" (*New York Times*, May 2, 1999: 1).[67]

Mainstream American parents do not hesitate to invest heavily in their children's sports activity, dance classes, and organized social groups like boy scouts. Investments in their appearance, such as orthodontic braces, "cool" clothes, and a respectable car, may be substantial as well. The net effect is to increase the likelihood their child will, at the very least, fit in (Chang 1992: 111), better yet, be popular, and, at best, earn an athletic or leadership scholarship.[68] On the other hand, when these tactics fail, parents may be confronted with the prospect of a very unhappy child. The popularity of advice manuals that address this issue suggest the magnitude of the problem (Wiseman 2003). And the press delivers a steady stream of horror stories that have their origin in the public school "loner" (Fox *et al.* 2005).

Larger, peri-urban high schools tend to provide a greater variety of niches or more fertile ground for the breeding of cliques. The Wikipedia entry lists nearly a hundred distinct clique names (*Washington Post*, January 28, 2003: A2).[69] Some of the most popular include Bandos (band members, musicians), Stoners (conspicuous drug users), Skaters (skateboarding fanatics), Hackers (also known as computer geeks), and Airheads (Barbie-like mannequins). However, the Jocks are both ubiquitous and paramount (Canaan, 1987: 388).

---

[67] Of course, Lauren would not refer to herself as a "Fluff Chick." As Varenne discovered, students can much more readily discuss *other* cliques and their members than their own (Varenne 1982: 218).

[68] A recent report confirms the importance of a "winning personality" in hiring decisions made by US firms (*Salt Lake Tribune*, November 6, 2007: A10).

[69] Information from http://en.wikipedia.org; accessed 4.20.07.

In a study of six ... high school classes ... athletic ability and attractiveness were significantly correlated with popularity, leadership, and dominance ... Attractive, athletic boys were also ranked as desirable dates and party guests by girls. *A boy's intelligence had little or no effect on any of these measures of social standing.* (Weisfeld 1999: 215 – emphasis added)

While Jocks and Preppies seem to rise to the top of the high school pecking order, and cliques like the Hempies (Palonsky 1975) or Stoners lie at the bottom, the status of other cliques cannot be predicted in advance. In Gary Fine's ethnography of high school debate teams, he notes that: "In some schools debate is ... a high-status pursuit – whereas at other high schools, debate is a low-status, stigmatized activity, left to social outsiders" (Fine 2001: 5–6).

Historically, Jocks are juxtaposed with Nerds, in that, to be a good athlete meant one had little time for academics, which were uncool as well. Among (non-Asian) minority students, athletics are seen as a far more promising avenue to popularity than good grades: "Black students invested so much time in sports that they had little time for their academic schoolwork" (Ogbu 2003: 156). Among Northern Cheyenne, some students whose grades rendered them ineligible to play sports transferred to another school with lower standards (Ward 2005: 137).

While Cheerleaders, Jocks, Nerds, and Preppies occupy distinct niches in the high school landscape, they hold in common that they are all – in different ways – "into school." This is decidedly not the case with many other cliques, including "Skinheads ... boys who shaved their heads, tattooed swastikas on their arms ... Head bangers mimicked rogue motorcycle gangs with their shiny black leather jackets draped in chains. Grunge looked like prison inmates with their over-sized jeans that sagged and drooped low in the behind" (Hemmings 2004: 21).

Anthropologists who have carried out in-depth studies of high schools with predominantly minority students have discovered that the antipathy towards "good" students has generalized to become a condemnation of anyone who "acts white." In a mostly black high school in Washington, DC, Signithia Fordham asked her informants to identify attributes that would indicate a student was "acting white," and, should, therefore, be ostracized. Among the many items were included "speaking standard English[70] ... going to the opera or ballet ... spending a lot of time in the library studying ... getting good grades in school (... labeled 'brainiacs') ... going to the Smithsonian ... doing volunteer work ... being on time ... reading and writing poetry" (Fordham and Ogbu 1986: 186).

Fordham and Ogbu document the powerful effect of peer pressure as students, who had been doing well academically, lessen their effort in order to

[70] They "lease" rather than attempt to gain "ownership" of standard English (Fordham 1999).

fit in.[71] "Because his friends are critically important to him and his sense of identity, Max . . . holds on to them at the expense of his academic progress" (Fordham and Ogbu 1986: 189). Male students, particularly, risk being labeled homosexual if they do well academically or take Advanced Placement (AP) classes (Fordham and Ogbu 1986: 194).[72]

In inner-city Chicago, Kotlowitz records that "Because Pharoah is studious, likes school, and does well, he's teased and taunted by classmates – in 4th grade!" (Kotlowitz 1991: 75). However, even middle-class African-American students living in an affluent community (Shaker Heights, Ohio) are not immune.[73] Ogbu recorded this conversation with a counselor who had asked a black student he knew to be bright why he acted dumb in class.

His response: "You don't have to ride home on the bus like I do." I said; "You're right, I don't." "You don't have to play in the neighborhood with all the other kids." I said, "You're right, I don't understand." He said, "I don't want 'em to know I'm smart. They'll make fun of me. I won't have any friends." I said, "So you'd rather sit there and pretend that you don't know than face kids who might say you're smart." And he even said, "Worse than that." I said, "Well, what's worse than that in your world?" He said, "Where I live, they're gonna say I'm White." (Ogbu 2003: 202).

In a racially mixed high school on the Utah–Arizona border, Navajo students are stigmatized because they are Indian and they are not represented among the academically or athletically successful cliques. So they forge their own clique based on dedication to and success at breakdancing. The "Breakers" set themselves defiantly apart from the Jocks and Preppies.[74] According to ethnographer Donna Deyhle, the creation of a distinct clique with all the

[71] Several recent studies document the forces that act to forestall the need to lessen effort in order to remain accepted by peers. These include parental and school efforts to segregate high-achieving minority students using Honors, Gifted, and Advanced Placement (AP) classes (Flores-Gonzalez 2005: 625; Conchas 2006; Bergin and Cooks 2002: 130–131; Herbert and Reis 1999: 454; Stinson 2006: 498).

[72] An interesting contrastive case is provided by a Russian colleague who related a story of one of her seventh-grade students in an elite St. Petersburg school who was thrashed by his classmates because of his negative attitude towards school and ill-preparedness (Zina Generalova, personal communication, October 2006).

[73] The tragic irony here is that, while ethnically Asian students find academic success in spurning conformity to mainstream American culture, African-American students feel that doing well academically is tantamount to rejecting their ethnic identity.

[74] The obvious question here is what is the chicken, and what is the egg? Do ethnic minority students form themselves into anti-school cliques or sub-cultures because the dominant society damns them to failure in the form of teachers' racist attitudes, culturally biased curricula, and testing and grading policies that undermine their self-esteem? Or is academic failure a result of students voluntarily opting out of the demanding school culture to join a more comfortable "Breakers" or "Homeboy" clique? Deyhle would, I suspect, vote for the former, while the late John Ogbu was increasingly moving towards the latter perspective. In the Shaker Heights study, he wrote, for example, "In our observation of more than 100 classroom lessons from elementary through high school we did not record a single instance of cultural barriers preventing a student from learning the subject . . . " (Ogbu 2003: 38).

accoutrements, including dress, allowed the Navajos "a means for expressing success in an otherwise indifferent or negative school and community environment" (Deyhle 1986: 112).

Even Asian students may find themselves drawn inexorably to peer associations that are antithetical to school values if their parents lacked the cultural capital to insure their early success (Lew 2004: 304). In a very important study in an urban, multi-class, multi-ethnic school, Goto found a multiplicity of cliques illustrating the interplay of ethnicity and social class we've been discussing. The *Nerds* were hardworking, serious ethnic Chinese students. *Normal People* were those who were doing well academically but who took pains to hide it in order to fit in. *Homeboys* were the Black and Hispanic students who resisted conformity to school requirements. And, last, the *Wannabes* were Cambodian and Vietnamese students who could not keep up with the Nerds so they sought acceptance by the Homeboys (Goto 1997).

Several studies have shown that the behavior of teachers is also affected by the "not acting white" mentality. Anti-intellectual students constantly disrupt lessons by talking and fooling around. They complain and lobby teachers for easier assignments and provide a colorful array of excuses to escape even these obligations. Beleaguered teachers make "huge concessions or surrender altogether to students who spend entire class periods cavorting with their friends" (Hemmings 2004: 45–46).

However, not all minority students become trapped in the Homeboy–Wannabe crab bucket.[75] In Ogbu's study, the students who successfully resisted peer pressure in taking Honors and AP classes and earned good grades were bolstered by the close supervision of parents and through carefully choosing a few like-minded friends (Ogbu 2003: 216–217).[76]

The commitment of public school systems to student diversity is now being challenged on grounds of wasted public resources. As we've seen, diversity incorporates the possibility of being a student but not really being "into" school or classes or homework. Hence, for a significant segment of the adolescent population, school provides an – increasingly expensive – custodial function without serving any significant educational function. Reform is in the wind.

---

[75] In the proverbial crab bucket, a lone crab trying to climb out of the bucket is inevitably pulled back in by its fellows.

[76] See also Bergin (2000) and Stinson (2006) on segregating by ability. An innovative program provides intervention to assist in the creation of a "posse" – a cohort of high-achieving minority students who band together for mutual protection and support: www.possefoundation.org; accessed 9/30/2007.

Moving towards a meritocracy

...the United States faces a serious and intensifying economic challenge from abroad – we appear to be on a losing path. (Augustine 2005)

...someone said that his classmates would rather have "freedom" than "calculus". (Ogbu 2003: 21)

...parents, who are paying for private schools for their children in addition to supporting public education through their taxes, add angry fuel to the current privatization movement. (Ascher *et al.* 1996: 2)

In the previous section, the focus was on relatively voluntary segregation of students into cliques. In this section the segregation of students is shown as resulting from social forces not entirely under the control of the students themselves.[77] One of the central issues in the US civil rights movement was the racial segregation of schools. In a landmark ruling in 1954 (*Brown vs Board of Education*), the Supreme Court determined that *de jure* segregation was illegal. It based its decision at least in part on research by James Coleman and others which found that African-American students tended to perform more poorly if segregated from more successful white students (Coleman 1966). There followed several decades of remediation efforts including the busing of students from segregated neighborhoods to integrated schools. Coleman, himself, acknowledged the failure of these initiatives by showing, for example, that the schools quickly resegregated as white families escaped to all-white suburbs outside the range of busing (Coleman *et al.* 1975).[78] As early as 1976, two prominent leftist thinkers had declared that efforts to equalize educational opportunity, such as President Lyndon Johnson's Great Society programs, had failed (Bowles and Gintis 1976). Fifteen years ago, liberal social critic Jonathan Kozol wrote: "the fact of racial segregation has been, and continues to be, largely uncontested...the nation, for all practice and intent, has turned its back upon the moral implications, if not yet the legal ramifications, of the *Brown* decision...In public schooling, social policy has been turned back almost one hundred years" (Kozol 1991: 4). The concern for equity has been superceded by concerns about the nation's workforce.

Today, two broad avenues through the education system in the USA are discernible. One avenue is favored by immigrants and natives with high aspirations. We'll call this avenue "Lombard Street" – San Francisco's famously

---

[77] Relative to the USA, European public schools have not, historically, been so dramatically variant in terms of student achievement. However, owing in part to the influx of immigrants and in part to more liberal admission policies, we now see the "development of new hierarchies within European school systems" (Zymek 2000: 114).

[78] So unpopular was this news that Coleman – one of the towering giants of social science – was nearly voted out of the American Sociological Association.

steep, winding lane. A second avenue is taken by those who don't see learning either as pleasurable in itself or as an instrumental means to a desired end. We'll call this avenue "Easy Street." As we have seen, for some students, school is about learning, studying, advancing through a more and more demanding curriculum, doing homework, and so on. For others, school is a place to socialize with peers, to flirt, to develop one's athletic ability, and to participate in plays. These two ways of experiencing school – especially secondary school – indicate the operation of at least two separate worlds,[79] bisected by our two avenues.

Economic analysts seem to think that too many students are traveling on Easy Street: "If current trends continue, the proportion of US workers with high school diplomas and college degrees will decrease and the personal income of Americans will decline over the next 15 years" (Anonymous 2005: 1). Norman Augustine, chairman of a committee organized by the National Academy of Sciences, sounds the alarm regarding the low level of educational attainment in the USA. In the most recent round of international tests of secondary students, the USA finished twenty-seventh. While 60 percent or more of college graduates in East Asia earn degrees in science and engineering, the figure for the USA is 30 percent (Augustine 2005: A29).

Augustine's remarks are buttressed by numerous studies documenting the growing disparity between (low) high school and (high) college expectations (Adelman 2006; Lewin 2005: 3; Peter D. Hart Research Associates 2005: 1). The negative import of these national trends is exaggerated when we consider historically underachieving minority students. Whatever gains brought about by programs to promote greater educational fairness are now threatened. Recent reports map the landscape. "By the time they are in the 12th grade, Black students are about 2 or more years behind their White peers in reading and mathematics" (Ogbu 2003: 4). In 1998 "the Hispanic dropout rate was four times higher than that of Whites" (Lee 2002: 10). Almost 30 percent "of American Indian/Alaska Native youth . . . are not enrolled in school [nor] completed . . . twelfth grade" (Waggoner 1991: 165).

The response to the problem of Easy Street by political leaders has been to install barriers in the form of academic competency tests at various grade levels. In foregrounding examination results as the principal criterion by which students, their schools, and parents will be judged,[80] it appears as though the USA is moving towards a more Asian-style meritocracy.[81] In more and more

---

[79] Actually, in a large high school there are multiple worlds, as we've seen, but, for the sake of the ensuing argument, I'd like to focus on the two most common or expected of these worlds.

[80] Another factor driving this trend is grade inflation, where teachers are pressured not to give "low" grades and everyone's grade point average approaches the maximum (*Salt Lake Tribune*, November 23, 2006: A24).

[81] Colleges, for example, are shifting scholarship funds to those with "merit" and away from those with "need" (*New York Times*, September 27, 2005). However, in an extreme irony,

states, students can't just be socially "going to" high school; they must learn the material, as measured on newly instituted exit exams.[82] In Utah, more than six thousand (17 percent of total) students have repeatedly taken and failed to pass a basic competency test that is now required for graduation (Lynn 2005).

One consequence will be a sharp rise in the African-American drop-out rate, as "passing grades" lose their currency (Dee and Jacob 2006). The effects of higher drop-out rates will be grim as this is the pool from which the majority of the nation's homicide victims and prison inmates is drawn (Bourgois 1998: 348–349; *Christian Science Monitor*, April 17, 2006: 8).

US policymakers seem to be increasingly attracted to a Darwinian "survival of the fittest" model in dealing with social ills.[83] Via institutions like magnet and charter schools, merit scholarships, and, above all, school vouchers, their aim is to effect a kind of *triage*. Instead of doling out what are seen as generous (but ineffective) government funds to the neediest,[84] funds will be directed to those who will benefit the most. So students who are already in a gifted program in a "good" school would not benefit, nor would those whose prospects are so poor their failure is a certainty.[85] Instead, supplemental funds will benefit the children of the poor who are willing to become, in effect, helicopter parents.[86] Funds will flow to poor areas with higher than expected test scores and this dynamic will be driven by a crucial partnership between committed parents and teachers.[87] Schools where teachers and parents take a "business as usual"

China has, for several years, been implementing drastic educational reforms to de-emphasize exam preparation as the sole *raison d'être* of schooling and to emphasize, instead, a broad "liberal" education and the fostering of creativity in students (Kipnis 2001: 10–11). Also, there is evidence that European education systems, which have more closely resembled the highly competitive, highly selective Asian systems, are liberalizing standards in the face of growing failure rates: "Primary schools, secondary schools: in route to the 'bac,'" *Label France*, No. 54: www.diplomatie.gouv.fr; accessed 4.5.07.

[82] While new to the USA, such exams are endemic in the secondary education systems of Asia and Europe.

[83] For example, the 1996 welfare reform law resulted in a 60 percent drop in welfare recipients (Besharov and Germanis 2003: 2). However, it is supremely ironic that, as the theory of evolution comes under increasing attack on ideological grounds as well as through sheer ignorance, social Darwinism – roundly rejected by evolutionary thinkers – has become extremely popular.

[84] In Chicago: "Many suburban legislators representing affluent school districts use terms such as 'sinkhole' when opposing funding for Chicago's children. 'We can't keep throwing money,' said Governor Thompson in 1988, 'into a black hole'" (Kozol 1991: 53).

[85] For a left-oriented alternative, see Ladson-Billings (2006).

[86] In actuality, studies show that charter schools primarily serve as a middle-class "escape hatch." Middle-class parents have the motivation, the means, and the cultural capital necessary to wrestle with the bureaucracy to establish and run the schools. In the greater Salt Lake City area, minority enrollment is around 50 percent but minority enrollment in the district's charter schools is below 20 percent (Baker and Lyon 2006: A6).

[87] Of course, the notion that the emerging educational policy is a form of triage is not lost on middle-class parents who worry that teachers will focus on raising the scores of the majority while neglecting "to spur the strongest kids . . . " (Gibbs 2005: 45).

attitude will lose money, and they will inevitably become a dumping ground for the hopeless.

Conditions in these "dumping grounds" are already bad. In New York City there are more than 3,200 uniformed officers in the Division of School Safety – a contingent larger than the entire Boston Police Department. One school studied by Devine had a total of 110 "security personnel"; by comparison, the size of the teaching staff was 150 (Devine 1996: 76, 78). Devine points out that, as the more promising students are routinely pulled out of the lower-tier schools to attend magnet schools, the former become the equivalent of juvenile prisons. Here is one anthropologist's first impression of such a school:

As I approached the school, I was struck by how much it resembled a prison complex. The parking lot and playing fields in the back were surrounded by a chain-link fence with barbed wire strung along the top. The plain, red-brick school building had five sets of doors that were locked except for those in the front facing the street. Security guards were posted at the front doors screening everyone who went in and out. Windows were covered with bars and student bathrooms had stalls without latches and often without toilet paper. The prison-like layout reinforced Central City High's public reputation as a dangerous school overrun with Black hoodlums. (Hemmings 2004: 32).

Under the new initiatives, some children will be able to escape these prisons.[88] The beneficiaries of these new triage policies will be children like Julianna, whose mother, Lisa, although poor, clearly has some definite strengths. She speaks of

the *pull* of the wrong crowd, how individualism and strong self-esteem helped [her] child resist that and get above it all. She spoke about the survival tactics she had to teach her child: "I've even talked to her about like if she's in the play yard at school and you hear gunfire, you get down on the ground. Can you believe that I had to tell this to my child?" (Kusserow 2004: 63)

Another one of Kusserow's informants, Ellen, from a working-class neighborhood, offers a similar perspective.

Ellen described herself as not necessarily from a "lower-class" background . . . she decided to send [her kids] to a Catholic school not because it was better academically than the public school, but because the Catholic School had "a better class of people in it." "For some reason I do feel that in the Catholic school there's more mothers [or] better families . . . that do care more." (Kusserow 2004: 76).

Milwaukee, Wisconsin, public schools implemented a voucher program (Choice) relatively early, and the process has been studied carefully. Parents who took advantage of Choice to enroll their children in "better" schools

---

[88] One student of "choice" programs is not, however, very optimistic. Williams contends that such programs are usually derailed by bureaucratic inertia, unions, corruption, political ideology, and money wasted on incompetent staff and teachers (Williams 2005).

were – compared with non-enrollees – much more actively involved with the schools and with educating their children at home, including regularly reading to them. "Once enrolled in the Choice Program, their high level of involvement was likely to continue and even to intensify" (Ascher *et al.* 1996: 73).

It may be economical and expedient for the government to reward families who bring cultural capital to the table. Who wouldn't want to "back a winner"? But, as there are economic benefits to be accrued by investing in the meritorious, there are significant costs associated with neglecting the less well endowed.

The other side of the coin

A 2005 Rand Corp. study in California said each dollar spent on early childhood education every year returns $1.10 in benefits. (*Atlanta Journal-Constitution*, February 26, 2006: Q1)

Investing in preschool will reduce the amount of money you need to spend on prisons 20 years down the line. (Steven Barnett, director, National Institute for Early Education Research, Rutgers University, *Salt Lake Tribune*, September 19, 2004: B1)

As I write these words,[89] Governor Schwarzenegger is calling the California legislature into special session to address the prison-bed crisis. Already housing the largest population of any state, California's prisons are filled to twice their designed capacity.[90] For years, demographers and political analysts have been sounding an alarm regarding the "graying of America," as the ratio of retirees to employees is swelled by retiring baby boomers. But far less is said about a similar explosion of the undereducated population who readily transition into very expensive institutional living – at public expense. Even if we are somehow inured to the dead-end lives of US urban ghetto children described by Kotlowitz and Kozol or the Third World street children we visited in chapter 7, we surely must feel some anxiety about the staggering *economic* cost of this human wastage.

Head Start, founded in 1965 as part of President Johnson's War on Poverty, was designed to bring poor children up to par with their more affluent counterparts academically, to create a more level playing field. Rooted in research demonstrating that intensive, high-quality pre-school could compensate for the lack of academic preparation in the home, Head Start has, nevertheless, fallen short of its promise. While study after study has shown the efficacy of long-term, high-quality pre-schools in helping children break the cycle of poverty (Schweinhart 2004; Barnett 1995), most public pre-school programs offer "too little, too late" (Campbell *et al.* 2002). And many needy children have no access

---

[89] November 11, 2006.

[90] Growing at a rate of 900 additional inmates a week between 2003 and 2004, the USA has the highest rate of incarceration in the world (*Salt Lake Tribune*, April 25, 2005: B3).

even to a minimal school readiness program (Kozol 1991: 143; Magnuson *et al.* 2004: 119).

While an unwillingness to spend the additional dollars (perhaps as much as $10 billion) may seem to be the primary obstacle, countries with only modest economies like Hungary and Finland have succeeded in providing high-quality, universal pre-school – from infancy (Brayfield and Korintus 2005; Husu and Niemela 1993: 62). Unfortunately, "support for and attacks on Head Start have been driven by ideological beliefs far more than by evidence" (Hacsi 2002: 58).[91] So, we face a stalemate in which the political tide seems to be running against efforts to use schooling to reduce the disparity between haves and have-nots.

In California on June 6, 2006, such opposition killed the first statewide attempt to provide universal pre-school education, even though the proposed program would have been far more modest in scope than the "model" programs noted above (Hull 2006). For California's underachieving students, the "real estate" that's most relevant to their future may be one of the new prisons California's governor is proposing to build.

[91] On the grounds of "family values" (for example, mothers should stay at home as child caretakers), Republican President Richard Nixon vetoed a measure in 1971 that would have committed the federal government to providing the resources to insure that every child was adequately prepared for school (Beatty 1995: 198).

10   Suffer the children

Introduction

Anthropologists have much to contribute to our understanding of the conditions of children and youth in the 21st century. (Schwartzman 2001: 15)

... the global distribution of resources ... means that some children must work to ensure household survival whilst others can over-consume ... (Holloway and Valentine 2000: 10)

Estimates suggest that as many as 11 million Indian children and adolescents fend for themselves on the streets of metropolitan cities or large townships. (Verma and Sharma 2007: 193)

As Jill Korbin observes, the perspective taken by anthropology tends to be conservative, describing the successful adaptation of children to societies that are themselves successfully adapted to their environment and material circumstances (Korbin 1987b). But, as these patterns of cultural adaptation are stressed by global forces that overwhelm local coping strategies, the lives of children are adversely affected. Anthropologists are prominent in the corps of concerned observers working to understand the contexts in which contemporary children live and to offer ideas to improve their lot.[1]

We will see that the distinction posed at the outset between cherubs, chattel, and changelings continues to apply in the present and into the future. In the First World, the elevation of children to god-like cherubs and corollary expense shows no signs of slowing. In the Third World, parents continue to seek the means to divest themselves of unwanted changelings or to convert their offspring to usable chattel. Indeed, Olga Nieuwenhuys simultaneously condemns the export of the First World model of childhood (Nieuwenhuys 1996: 242) – turn them all into cherubs – *and* the globalization that turns Third World children into chattel on behalf of their wealthy counterparts. She argues that poorly paid children's labor in developing countries is, effectively, a subsidy

---

[1] Inge Bolin's recent report of very happy children in a poor but harmonious community in the High Andes reminds us that not all indigenous peoples are in crisis, far from it (Bolin 2006: 151).

352

which keeps the cost of goods purchased on behalf of First World children artificially low (Nieuwenhuys 2005: 178).

In this chapter, we will visit several "flash-points" in the contemporary crisis of childhood beginning with the family where supporting social mechanisms are imperiled. Unlike the casual process by which children proceed through a chore curriculum described in chapter 7, we now see an urgency – children must begin earning their keep earlier and earlier. We will see children divorced from the comforting confines of family and village, migrating, often involuntarily, to work on plantation, in factory or mine, or to the urban jungle. The ties that bind children to parents and community may be sundered by migration or the death of one or both parents. Increasingly, observers identify self-sufficient children, especially in urban areas, surviving independently from family. However, as they are caught up in urban crime or free-roving militias, children hover on a razor's edge of moral ambiguity, one minute victims, the next, aggressors.

Briefly focusing on relatively privileged children, we note that they suffer from a cultural pattern of overprotection and indulgence. This ironic contrast is well represented by images of badly abused slave children in Ivory Coast harvesting the cocoa beans that will be processed into the chocolates consumed by obese children in Los Angeles (*Salt Lake Tribune*, July 1, 2001: A9, A10). The chapter concludes with a catalog of the major conclusions we can draw from the preceding nine chapters.

Mother's choices

One cannot help wondering why [poor US] mothers continue to bear so many babies into so much suffering. (Bourgois 1998: 342)

The child labor pool [in Pakistan] is all but inexhaustible, owing . . . to a birth rate that is among the world's highest . . . (Silvers 1996: 81)

Most street children are simply "excess" kids . . . (Scheper-Hughes and Hoffman 1998: 362)

The conditions that foster the birth and development of healthy children are very well understood. However, the number of children born into adverse circumstances is rapidly increasing, relative to those born into favorable circumstances (Gielen and Chumachenko 2004: 91). For example, in much of Africa, the birth rate is very high (5.9 in Nigeria) while the adult death rate, from HIV/AIDS, malaria, and TB, is also extraordinarily high, leaving children to be raised entirely by other children (Gielen and Chumachenko 2004: 87). Traditional means to limit family size, including infanticide and the post-partum sex taboo, have been curtailed by outside moral authorities who may also oppose modern methods of contraception (Miller 1987). The resulting overpopulation in the countryside pushes villagers into urban areas; squalid slums are the fastest-growing housing category in much of the Third World (Anonymous 2006c; Cage 2006). The cosseted security of a village childhood is exchanged for the bare survival of an urban scavenger.

Scheper-Hughes and Hoffman make the case that, in Brazil, official suppression of abortion and contraception means that poor children have a "right-to-life" that is short and filled with misery (Scheper-Hughes and Hoffman 1998: 376).

Ironically, while parents in wealthy nations question their ability to "afford another child," in poor nations like Burkina Faso, parents feel almost no responsibility for the wellbeing of their children:

There are no perceived disadvantages in having lots of children. Children are never seen as a drain on resources. The availability of food is believed to be purely a product of the God-given fortune of the child, and nothing to do with the level of resources available within the household or the number of mouths to feed: *BiDDo fuu rimdatakena e tindem* = "every child is born with its own luck . . ." (Hampshire 2001: 115)

In populous northern Ghana, children are exported to the more prosperous south at an early age. Most barely survive but a very few are taken up in businesses, like auto repair, and gradually establish themselves, even able to proudly send some money back to the village. These stories spread widely, fanning the flames of hope and maintaining high birth rates (Anarfi and Kwankye 2005).

In China "The child is born to be socialized [as] . . . the future caretaker for the parent" (Potter 1987: 33).[2] The alternative is awful to contemplate. Elderly Chinese, who depend on the state for their care, live in "decrepit dwellings, with barely enough to eat, a tiny allowance of a few yuan a month . . ." (Potter 1987: 35). No surprise, then, that the "one-child" policy has been strenuously resisted as it raises the specter of old age uncomforted by even a single devoted son.

Contraception and family planning services have, therefore, a checkered history.[3] There are reports of relatively educated (LeVine *et al.* 2004: 875) or urbanized women eagerly seeking such opportunities (Pickering 2005), especially where high fertility is seen as hampering economic opportunities (Kress 2005). However, lack of funds and/or ideological opposition[4] may severely

---

[2] Indeed, one anthropologist speculates that Chinese mothers hold, indulge, and deny others access to their infants to foster dependence and loyalty that they will be able to redeem in their old age (Wolf 1972).

[3] Although reproductive choice is much more the reality in the First World than the Third World, the issue has been quite contentious in Japan, until recently, and very much so today in the USA.

[4] Influenced by the Religious Right, US President George W. Bush has consistently refused to allocate funds voted by Congress to the United Nations Population Fund, which is supported by 171 donor nations. Information from www.34millionfriends.org; accessed 4.24.07. Of course, an alternative explanation for the Republican Party's opposition to family planning may stem

limit the provision of public services which means that relatively few women are in a position to plan or limit their pregnancies.

In some communities, such as the Shipibo Indian village of Mahco Capac in the Peruvian Amazon, people are desperate for contraceptives – which they've heard about but cannot obtain. Hern's informant

Chomoshico was nearing the end of her eleventh pregnancy. She already had seven living children. Neither she nor her husband wants more. "Enough. Clothes cost," they told me. "I'm tired of having children," she said. "I almost died with the last one." Her husband has tuberculosis. In the same village, a few weeks before, a young girl died on her thirteenth birthday trying to give birth to twins. And in that girl's natal village, just up the river, I had just seen my first case of frank starvation among the Shipibo Indians, with whom I had worked . . . since 1964. (Hern 1992: 31)

Egypt is being crushed under the weight of its enormous population: 62 percent of its citizens are under fourteen (Gielen and Chumachenko 2004: 88) yet high fertility is a cornerstone of Muslim ideology. Unlike other Arab countries, Egypt has many well-educated women who can be expected to limit fertility and to raise healthy, well-educated children more effectively. However, these women are spurned by educated males who prefer less well-educated wives (Ahmed 2005: 157).

Similarly, on Tonga, the national government, recognizing that "The growing numbers of children to be cared for within a rapidly growing population . . . is straining the resources of adults and especially the elderly" (Morton 1996: 58), has taken vigorous action to promote fertility reduction. Nevertheless, the powerful Roman Catholic and Mormon churches prohibit contraception on moral grounds while Tongan husbands are opposed to their wives exercising control over reproduction, "even insisting that their wives have contraceptive devices such as IUDs removed" (Morton 1996: 53).[5]

Mothers are caught in a Catch-22. Denied the option of limiting fertility, they discover that there are far fewer helpers at the nest nowadays. The extended family "safety net" has been repeatedly dismantled by missionaries intent on promoting the nuclear family as the Christian ideal (Ballantyne 1994: 8). Glass-Coffin describes the difficulties faced by her Peruvian informant whose husband migrated for work, and eventually abandoned his family. Returning with young children to her natal home, Rigoberta did not find a warm welcome as her siblings were reluctant to share their already meager resources (Glass-Coffin 1988: 10).

from a conscious decision to foster high birth rates in the Third World, leading to reduced wages and lower-priced imports. Ideology also may prevent a mother from protecting her children, as when Islamic clerics condemn the use of measles and polio vaccines as a US plot to sterilize the population (*Salt Lake Tribune*, March 28, 2005: A4).

[5] Much the same scenario is playing out today in Chile (Gallardo 2006).

The "communities" that Peruvian villagers migrate to in search of opportunity consist of:

shifting households in shanty towns . . . of unrelated men and a few girlfriends . . . little resemblance to traditional families . . . perform few of their supportive functions . . . rife with conflict. Wives and children . . . stay in the home villages – if fortunate, among extended kin. Women left to care for numerous young children, on their own . . . [come] up short, and child neglect and abuse increase . . . children [are] . . . left with relatives too old and lacking in resources to care for them. (Martini 2005: 134)

Numerous observers have compared conditions for children's development in the city unfavorably with the village. Urban Maori children suffer far more abuse than their rural cousins, because, behind closed doors in the city, parents aren't scrutinized by neighbors (Ritchie and Ritchie 1981: 197). Studying families and children "in pain" is difficult for the anthropologist. Philippe Bourgois writes: "When the shrieks of crying children rose through the heating pipes in my tenement in East Harlem, New York, I fretted: Was I ethnocentrically misreading the . . . aggressive childrearing practices of my second generation Puerto Rican immigrant neighbors?" (Bourgois 1998: 331). Even in prosperous nations like Japan and the USA (Warner 2005), mothers (and their children) suffer from the isolating effects of modern, anonymous communities. In Japan, child abuse is becoming quite prevalent (Kingston 2004: 260). Women can't escape the mentally stultifying confines of the nursery because conservative governments refuse to fund daycare (Kingston 2004: 281). Three-generation domiciles are disappearing; grandmothers live with their children in only 12 percent of contemporary Japanese homes (Shwalb and Shwalb 2005). Public attempts to promote greater involvement of fathers in childcare have been a conspicuous failure (Kingston 2004: 283)[6] and companies have no compunction about relocating male employees without their families (Tanaka and Nakazawa 2005).

Economic and social forces dictate women's employment, but, at home, they begin a "second shift" unaided by their husbands (Townsend 2001: 120). This imbalance is blamed for the rising divorce rate and the increase in women electing to have children out of wedlock (Silverstein and Auerbach 2005: 43; Craig 2006). The result is that a growing proportion of children in the USA and worldwide are living without their biological fathers (Horn 2003: 129).

Aids to reduce the burden of childcare are attractive to harried mothers. In the Yucatan, Mayan mothers have enthusiastically adopted bottle-feeding – leading to malnourished, parasite-infected babies (Howrigan 1988) – a worldwide phenomenon that has prompted some nations to ban the sale of baby bottles and infant formula. In Pakistan, there is a thriving business in spurious breast milk tests that justify a mother's adopting bottle-feeding – leading to an often

---

[6] See also Craig (2006); Carlsen (1994).

fatal but not necessarily unwelcome outcome (Mull 1992). Early supplemental feeding, including candies and other calming sweets, is increasingly popular (Millard and Graham 1985; Slome 2003) contributing to the worldwide epidemic of obesity and diabetes (Can 2003). Overall, and in spite of international campaigns to promote breastfeeding, rates are declining in most of the Third World – where nutritious substitutes are least available (Raphael and Davis 1985: 49).

If village women[7] were committed to the ideal of raising a few healthy and well-educated children, *and* they were given the means, including contraception and protection from *machismo* partners, *then* they might be receptive to messages regarding breastfeeding and other healthful childcare practices.

Children as breadwinners

[In Mexico] the more working children a family has, the more money can be put aside. (Bey 2003: 291)

. . . we need to balance out concerns for the rights of children with a recognitions that "universal" rights are often based on ethnocentric definitions of childhood. (Holloway and Valentine 2000: 10)

Children have always been expected to assist their families but in the situations many contemporary families find themselves in, such assistance may be deadly. Heather Montgomery studied Baan Nua, a type of squatter community in Thailand which is becoming more and more common. Forced off the land because of crowding in their rural homeland, adults find that the surest source of income is through the prostitution of their children, nearly half of whom had been so employed (Montgomery 2001a: 72). In Ho Chi Minh City, girls in their later teen years join the ranks of prostitutes to earn a respectable income and to help support their families (Rubenson *et al.* 2005). In Bom Jesus da Mata, Brazil, children earn their keep in shoe factories – making a mockery of child labor laws. "The children . . . slathered intoxicating glue on the leather [fostering the] strong subculture of glue sniffing" (Scheper-Hughes and Hoffman 1998: 367). Factory wages are so low that families can only make ends meet if all able-bodied members are employed (Nieuwenhuys 2005: 178).

In southern Mexico, rural Mixtec are too numerous to all make a living off the land and earn enough cash to meet burgeoning needs for new expenses like electricity, clothing, and taxes. There is mass migration each year to the agribusiness-controlled croplands (growing, for example, tomatoes) in the north. "Any worker, whether, man, woman or child, is paid 27 pesos per

---

[7] Even among the elite, mothers use aids that aren't entirely healthy. Anthropologists suggest, for example, that the use of nursery monitors would better serve babies if they broadcast the mother's breathing and vocalization *to the baby* (Trevathan and McKenna 2003: 42).

day . . . [Children's productivity is comparable to an adult's even considering that they] "are put to work before the permitted age of 8, some parents use forged papers, claiming that, in the mountains, children do not grow" (Bey 2003: 292). It is difficult to attach blame exclusively to parents when absentee landowners, labor organizers, and bribe-taking officials together orchestrate a climate of misery in which "children are merely the last link in [the] chain of exploitation" (Bey 2003: 294).

International agencies have not been idle, and several highly touted intervention efforts exist. The International Labor Organization has been active in Pakistan where footballs stitched by children are used in televised matches watched by millions; through a combination of political pressure and outside funding, its goal is to insure that footballs are made by adults in well-managed factories while children attend school.[8] International pressure has also been brought to bear on the Pakistani practice of exporting little boys to the Gulf States to serve as camel jockeys (Asghar 2004) with the result that a Swiss firm has designed a robot jockey that Qatar will eventually use in lieu of boys (*USA Today*, April 20, 2005: A14).

However, these cases of direct intervention are rather exceptional: ILO and UN strictures on child labor are rarely observed, especially in places like China where the practice is rampant.

In principle, China is committed to ending child labor. According to the International Labor Organization, China has ratified two ILO conventions on labor practices. Convention 138 forbids minors under fifteen from working. Convention 182 bans the worst forms of child labor, including prostitution and slave labor. But this is a country where making laws is much easier than implementing them. Youths desperate to help their families or simply tired of village life can easily lie about their age and use fake identity papers. Employers eager to hire them for their nimble hands and low cost often don't bother to check (*Los Angeles Times*, May 13, 2005: A1).

One of the most thorough exposés of child labor describes conditions in "Santa's sweatshop," a vast manufacturing enclave in the Pearl River delta where thousands of young women turn out 80 percent of the word's toys. Barbie dolls, which cost $9.99 in WalMart, are purchased by Hasbro for 35 cents from manufacturers who pay employees 12 cents an hour (Clark 2007: 194, 198, 200).

Consumers can now buy oriental carpets with the *Rugmark* label certifying that children did not make the rug. But what will become of the estimated one million children employed in the industry (Manfra 2006)? In Nepal, children willingly flock to urban centers to find employment making carpets (Bray

---

[8] The ILO claims to have reduced the population of child football stitchers from 7,000 to nil (2006).

Figure 30 Suitcase makers in Kashgar

et al. 2002: 34).[9] In Bihar and Uttar Pradesh Provinces of India, the growing economy is fueled by an expansion of the carpet industry, which, in turn, is heavily dependent on child labor (Gulrajani 2000).[10]

Following children into the streets we should note that, contrary to popular opinion, not all of them are on their own. Many, perhaps the majority, return in the evening to the squatter settlements where their families live. In Mexican cities, there are deeply rooted economic niches for poor children. For example, they assist store patrons to carry their purchases to their vehicles or clean windshields in return for tips. They sell newspapers on the street corner; others perform magic and circus-type acts in public. Many street children are from intact families where the father and the mother carefully orchestrate the work of the children (Taracena and Tavera 2000).

In Kaduna, Nigeria, adult women may be forced by Islamic custom to remain hidden from the public.[11] Their children, hence, play a critical role in marketing their products or commodities. Daughters, in particular, are "expected to meet

[9] There are an estimated 5–6 million children under ten employed in Pakistani factories and "In the lowest castes, children become laborers as soon as they can walk" (Silvers 1996: 81–82).

[10] Many Third World industries would collapse without the low-cost labor provided by children. Another recently "exposed" example is the fishing industry on Lake Volta in Ghana where almost six hundred boys, as young as six, have been "rescued" from brutal labor conditions (*New York Times*, October 29, 2006); www.nytimes.com/2006/10/29/world/africa; accessed 10.29.06.

[11] In fact, it has been argued that, in those societies where women of childbearing age are kept in a state of seclusion or *purdah*, children replace the women as farmworkers (Schildkrout 1981: 84).

their prospective husbands during street trading or *talla*. The proceeds of their trade constitute part of the financial resources that their mothers use to obtain dowry" (Oloko 1994: 202).

In Quito, I observed "*chicle*" (literally Chiclets™ or other small hard candies) sellers at traffic intersections. Children of seven to nine seemed to behave like sellers, quickly moving on if rebuffed. Younger children of four to six acted more like beggars; if rebuffed, they'd hold their palm out and beg in a whining tone. They tended to be filthy and dressed poorly, but I observed that the (I presume) older brother who hovered nearby with back-up supplies of candy was clean and well dressed. My overall impression was that whole families "worked" particular locations, with mothers selling crafts and trinkets from a relatively fixed location, while child sellers were more mobile.

In the USA, immigrants from Latin America depend heavily on the economic contributions of their children, who are involved in

selling food, clothes, or other merchandise alongside adult street vendors; helping their parents to clean houses . . . cleaning tables in a *pupusería* . . . In one family, the five children (ranging in age from four to twelve) spent several hours each evening putting price stickers on "Barbie" sunglasses that were sold . . . they told me, in Toys 'R' Us . . . [Also] . . . parents in Pico Union take it for granted that children should use their English abilities [and] literacy skills to translate for them [and cope with the] . . . complex English literacy demands for daily life in Los Angeles. (Orellana 2001: 374–376, 378)

In contrast to these scenes of the survival of family life in the face of adversity, numerous observers report conflict between street children and their parents. This conflict arises because of the harsh treatment meted out by parents and their appropriation of the child's income (Verma and Sharma 2007: 194).

When child labor investigators study the situation on the ground, they see impediments to change at the village (or squatter settlement) level, chiefly the attitude that children have few or no rights compared with parents and that families cannot survive without the resources acquired through their children's employment. As a compromise, a frequent policy recommendation is to define acceptable conditions for children's labor rather than banning it outright (Blagbrough and Glynn 1999: 55). Nevertheless, the moral ambiguity in these situations is sharp and one can't help wondering whether children may be better off without parents.[12]

---

[12] In chapter 2, I discussed the situation in the African-American community where men's inability to obtain employment has led women to establish households on their own. A similar phenomenon may be emerging in much of the Third World where children – who are employed for wages – may see their parents as parasites, draining away their meager earnings, and so they elect to "escape" from their families.

Children without parents

The extended family system [is] breaking down... people cannot afford to look after their kin... (Mapedzahama and Bourdillon 2000: 39)

It is not uncommon... to find children [in Zimbabwe] as young as ten or eleven heading entire households due to the death of both parents and the absence of relatives to look after them. (McIvor 2000: 173)

Although father absence may have relatively little direct impact on young children, adolescents clearly miss the restraint imposed by the family's moral guardian. Draper and Harpending (1982) argue that the father's presence in the household models the value of enduring pair-bonds and conveys an expectation of long-term investment in one's offspring. Children in families without fathers have teenagers who become parents. Teens make poor parents, as demonstrated in studies from developing and industrialized societies (Elster and Lamb 1986: 184; Gelles 1986: 347).

The appeal of owning a creature whose destiny you can control and who offers you unconditional affection is strong: "Maria was overjoyed to be pregnant... the happiest I had ever seen her... it was precisely her wretched living conditions that made motherhood so appealing... a romantic escape" (Bourgois 1998: 342). Also the teen mother may gain status in the community:

Young Black mothers stroll up and down the street... pushing their babies in carriages... mothers and their babies were dressed "to kill," often sporting the latest athletic wear. The baby strollers were the best that money could buy....[an] opportunity... to see and be seen by neighborhood audiences. (Burton and Graham 1998: 16)

Teenage parenthood will continue to rise, but the large number of children growing up in single-parent households is now overshadowed by the growing cadre of orphans. We have seen in chapter 2 that communities take steps to insure there won't be too many children for a given set of parents or the community as a whole to nurture, but HIV/AIDS has overwhelmed these coping mechanisms as high fertility, discussed in the previous section, is coupled with unprecedented (since the Middle Ages) adult mortality. A recent study suggests also that, for a host of reasons, grandmothers can't substitute for their ill or deceased daughters (Bock and Johnson 2008).

The number of children who have lost one or both parents has reached plague dimensions. "UNICEF estimates... more than 24 million orphans in sub-Saharan Africa... Uganda alone [has] 2 million... 19 percent of [the population]" (Oleke *et al.* 2005: 267). Even when these children are absorbed into the homes of relatives, they fare badly compared with their peers whose biological ties to the family are stronger. They don't eat as well, they're assigned more chores, and they're less likely to be enrolled in school (Case *et al.* 2004: 6).

Poor Third World countries like Malawi are not prepared to offer *in loco parentis* services and, not surprisingly, "the extended family system is over-stretched and can no longer provide the necessary care for orphans" (Oleke *et al.* 2005: 268). One anthropologist argued that the traditional *laissez faire* childrearing mechanisms – described in chapter 5 – actually help prepare children better to cope with the disruptive effects of war, pestilence, and famine (Mann 2004: 8–9). Indeed, studies of Somali refugee families indicate that children's resilience allows them to withstand adverse conditions better than adults (Rousseau *et al.* 1998).

Lewis Aptekar (1991) has conducted fieldwork with street children in many cities and finds that, in the absence of parents, siblings do a more than adequate job of caring for their young kin – as we saw in chapter 4. Studies of AIDS orphans[13] in South Africa similarly reveal the "dexterity young people bring to bear in drawing on networks of kin to reconfigure a sense of place for themselves" (Henderson 2006: 322). Children are also ingenious in finding the means to make a living. Commonly, they guard parked cars from traffic police and thieves (Chirwa and Wakatama 2000: 55), they sell candy, cigarettes, and newspapers to passersby, and they "mine" the urban dump for saleable items (Waddington 2005). Of course they are vulnerable to a whole host of threats, from traffic to bullies (Nzewi 2005). And the ultimate irony occurs when AIDS orphans themselves contract the disease from selling themselves (Tanon 2005).

Passing judgment on the phenomena of AIDS orphans and street children is easily done as various bodies have declared for the "rights" of children, but as Stephens (1995) argues, "children also have rights not to be constrained within exclusionary cultural identities and not to have their bodies and minds appropriated as the unprotected terrain upon which cultural battles are fought" (p. 4). Such larger battles include civil conflicts, such as the war in Iraq, where more and more young girls are being married off to relieve their families of the need to feed and clothe them (Flintoff 2006).[14] Economic stagnation or decline drives children from their homes even in the wealthiest countries, as documented in the USA after prolonged depressions during the nineteenth (Riis 1890/1996) and twentieth centuries (Minehan 1934). Then there's the push to "modernize" the economies of poorer nations where, to take the Cuban case, one result has been the recent sudden appearance of street children in Havana (Mickelson 2000). Several investigators claim that street children may have

---

[13] Critics argue that the very term is misleading as many AIDS orphans are well looked after by extended kin while non-orphans may be in dire straits. But from a "marketing" point-of-view, aid agencies find the label very potent in soliciting donations (Meintjes and Giese 2006).

[14] Information from www.npr.org; accessed 04.21.07.

Figure 31 Siblings in Srinigar

actually improved their lot from what it had been "at home" where they may face abuse and privation (Aptekar 2004: 379; Evans 2004). And, when we see homeless children in the company of their mother (or grandmother), we shouldn't assume they are thriving under her nurturing ministrations. On the contrary, she is likely marketing their services as sex workers:

She has unequivocally told Patience and Pamela that they must not refuse to entertain those boys . . . unless they want to starve. Sometimes the girls had to entertain old men[15] who give large sums of money to their grandmother. The young girls had heard about AIDS and that it kills, but they did not seem to know much about it and had not bothered to find out, largely because of the pressure to eke out an existence. (Rurevo and Bourdillion 2003: 23)

Although street children have attracted the most attention, another group of children growing up without their parents have been left behind in the village when their parents migrated for employment. The USA and Canada, for example, have adopted immigration policies that, effectively, invite mothers from the "south" to leave their own children to travel north to work as nannies (Katz 2001). Heather Rae-Espinoza (2006) has studied these bifurcated families split between Ecuador and the USA and she also finds that the "It Takes a

---

[15] The belief that pre-pubertal girls don't harbor AIDS and are safer as sex partners is widespread (De Meyer 2001: 7).

Village" model is breaking down in the face of too many children per adult caretaker.

Children's agency

First World journalists have created a rhetoric of calamity about streetchildren...
(Valsiner 2000: 37)

... the moral condemnation of child labor assumes that children's place in modern society must perforce be one of dependency and passivity. (Nieuwenhuys 1996: 238)

When the city government in Salvador, Brazil constructed a 500-bed facility to accommodate street children, only 25 spaces were taken up (Waddington 2005). This story stands as a fable reflecting the complex reality of children in the Third World. As some anthropologists have argued recently,[16] we must see children not exclusively as the *objects* of adult influence, but as *agents* of their own destiny and it is their *voices*[17] we must attend to (Pufall and Unsworth 2004; Schwartzman 2001: 25).

Whether given a push by their parents (Khair 2005) or not (Whitehead *et al.* 2005), children are readily leaving for the city to seek employment – as vendors or domestics in Mumbai, for example. When interviewed, they don't seem too eager to rejoin the bosom of their small town or rural families (Iversen and Raghavendra 2005).[18] Some see themselves as searching for adventure in the city and a wage of 25 cents an hour puts spending money in their pocket where before there was none (Thorsen 2005).

International agencies – both public and private – would provide statutory solutions to the "problem" of child labor and children as independent agents (Nieuwenhuys 1996: 241). However, a noted authority claims: "Generally, international campaigns to stop child labor have not resulted in children going back to school and improving their situation. The more likely result is that they

---

[16] Not that these views are completely novel – Jacob Riis, writing about street children in New York: "The Street Arab has all the faults and all the virtues of the lawless life he leads. Vagabond that he is, acknowledging no authority and owing no allegiance to anybody or anything, with his grimy fist raised against society whenever it tries to coerce him, he is as bright and sharp as the weasel, which, among all the predatory beasts, he most resembles, His sturdy independence, love of freedom and absolute self-reliance, together with his rude sense of justice enables him to govern his little community . . . " (Riis 1890/1996: 188).

In Dickens' vivid narrative, we hear Sam Weller's (Mr. Pickwick's young man-of-all-work) father proudly claim credit for his son's perspicacity: "I took a good deal o' pains with his eddication, sir; let him run in the streets when he was very young, and shift for hisself. It's the only way to make a boy sharp, sir": Dickens (1836/1964: 306).

[17] However, one scholar cautions "against too simplistic and/or sensationalized a usage of the term 'voice'" (Komulainen 2007: 22).

[18] Children rescued from bone-crushing labor in stone quarries in Nigeria – where they earned 20 cents a day – were returned to the parents who'd sold them to roving labor recruiters (*Oakland Tribune*, October 24, 2003: A7).

are forced into work that is more poorly paid and more dangerous than what they were doing before" (Bourdillion 2000: 15).[19] It is particularly hypocritical for the USA to condemn child labor abroad when, under the guise of religious freedom, children provide unpaid or low-cost labor in factories and businesses run by fundamentalist Christian groups.[20] Quite recently, a Christian family made the news when they moved to Idaho from Washington State to take advantage of more lenient child labor laws (Idaho hadn't updated its statutes since the early 1900s). The family business used children to gain a competitive advantage in spite of the fact that "The boys were operating heavy equipment and riding atop moving houses. . . work that's too dangerous for youngsters" according to state inspectors (*The Herald Journal*, November 21, 2005: A5, A6).

And shouldn't the current trafficking of children, especially for the sex trade, from the former Soviet-dominated areas, for example, be treated as a serious problem (Esadze 2005)? As anthropologists, should we use "cultural relativism" and child "agency" to neutralize our aversion to stories of child prostitutes and miners? What message should we derive from statements by child sex workers who "claim that they become and remain prostitutes out of duty and love to their parents" and strenuously resist attempts to remove them from their parents' custody (Montgomery 2001a: 82)? The authors of a study of young prostitutes in Zimbabwe have trouble endorsing the "government regulation does more harm than good" mentality:

this study calls into question an approach that accepts the decisions of children to come onto the streets as a solution to serious problems elsewhere, and which points to the resilience of children and their coping mechanisms to weigh against their vulnerability. In the current situation, life on the streets means high probability of HIV infection and death from AIDS. (Rurevo and Bourdillion 2003: 61)

Another moral divide opens up when we consider how readily children can turn from victims to victimizers (Stephens 1995: 13). In Nairobi, youths threaten to plaster feces on passersby unless they're paid off (Droz 2006: 349–350). More and more violent crime is perpetrated by minors. In Rio de Janiero, the beach season was dubbed "Wilding Summer," because of dozens of attacks on bathers by young thieves (Larmer 1992: 39).

Such blatant anti-social activity, in turn, creates a climate that justifies children's "elimination" by death squads, funded by the business community (Stephens 1995: 12) to clean up this "blemish on the urban landscape"

---

[19] See also Reynolds *et al.* (2006: 291–292).

[20] The Twelve Tribes cult in New York is accused of using children in its soap- and furniture-making factories: *New York Post*, October 4; information from 2001 www.wwrn.org; accessed 04.21.07.

(Scheper-Hughes and Hoffman 1998: 353). Short of murdering them, governments may try and drive rural children out of urban centers by denying them schooling and social services because they lack a residence permit (Burr 2006: 67).

Recent violent internal conflicts on every continent save Australia have not spared children.[21] In northern Uganda the Lord's Resistance Army has abducted 18,000 children and turned many of them into willing soldiers. When captured or "rescued," these children pose a dilemma for society. Should they be treated as victims or perpetrators (Mawson 2004: 131)? In Cambodia, the Khmer Rouge consistently used children as informers and enforcers, thus provoking general paranoia and abuse of unattached children (Boyden 2004: 242).

In Colombia, one-third of the population is younger than eighteen. Roughly half of them are "internally displaced persons" (IDPs) who find a home and improved living conditions in the sheltering embrace of the armed forces or rebel militias. "For many children... joining a fighting force is a matter of survival. It renders the distinction between forced and voluntary recruitment academic" (Geisler and Roshani 2006: 1).[22] And children become enthusiastic combatants: "Armed children and youth spread unspeakable fear throughout Sierra Leone. They were responsible for thousands of murders, mutilations, and rapes, and for torture, forced labor, and sexual slavery" (Rosen 2005: 58).[23]

Building a child welfare policy based on the notion of children as autonomous and self-guided individuals may make some sense in modern society. For example, in Belgium, the government, responding to the dictates of the UN Convention on the Rights of the Child, undertook a survey to "gain insight into the housing desires of youngsters... [whose wants] subsequently led to the formulation of policy options" (Verhetsel and Witlox 2006: 205). Consider the absurdity of surveying child soldiers in Angola regarding their housing preferences. Surely it is not an infringement of the child's integrity to declare, without prior consultation, that they shouldn't be employed as soldiers or prostitutes or miners? And to prosecute vigorously those who would conscript them into these activities?

---

[21] In 1998 it was estimated that up to 300,000 children were actively involved in armed conflict. Information from www.child-soldiers.org; accessed 4.20.07. It is important to note how slight the "moral high ground" is for the West on this issue. In the Napoleonic wars in the early nineteenth century, naval ships were heavily staffed by children, lower-class boys served as stewards and "powder monkeys" exposed to the full carnage of "action," while upper-class boys served as "midshipmen," apprentice officers who went fully armed into battle. In mid-century, the US Civil War was called "the boys' war" as more than 100,000 of the combatants were under fifteen (Rosen 2005: 5).

[22] "The role of young IDPs as child soldiers," *Columbia Journal Online*, July 17, 2006; www.colombiajournal.org; accessed 04.21.07.

[23] For a vivid and probably accurate portrayal of child soldiers in Sierra Leone, see the film *Blood Diamond* (2006). Ironically, children orphaned by civil war and AIDS in Mozambique served as extras during the filming.

Figure 32 Soldier boy

Over-protection

Americans [are] eager to protect children from dirty words and pornography but not to shelter them from consumer desire. (Cross 2004: 185)

. . . some forces affecting children are simply too complicated for parents to control. (Coontz 1992/2000: 225)

It is no small irony that the enduring image of Third World children as fending for themselves in an urban jungle is juxtaposed with an image of First World children as smothered by oversolicitous parents and governments. While Third World children are being sold to slavers, swallowed up in brothels, and snuffed by death squads, First World parents' fears of harmful strangers and other threats are magnified to an irrational level (Best and Horiuchi 1985; Shutt *et al.* 2004; Glassner 1999).[24]

In Thailand, there is "no concept of any golden age of childhood . . . children are pitied because . . . they are everybody's *nong* (younger sibling/inferior)" (Montgomery 2001a: 59). For the Ifaluk, conspicuously happy children are a cause for concern and may require suppression (Lutz (1988). In contrast, we embrace the "myth of childhood happiness . . . [which] flourishes . . . because it satisfies the needs of adults" (Firestone 1971: 31). So, when our children are unhappy – an unacceptable state – we seek medical assistance, resulting in a tripling of youth on anti-depressants since 1993 (Zito *et al.* 2003).[25]

Our need to keep our children happy grants them enormous license. China's one-child policy has led to the proliferation of "Little Emperors," who are indulged in their craving for junk food to the point of obesity and heart disease (Chee 2000). In the USA, obesity is rapidly increasing, in part because parents consider it too risky to let their children "run around" the neighborhood (Seiter 1998: 306). Then, we compound the problem of obesity by denying that it exists.[26]

Overprotectiveness has other negative consequences. Twenty years ago, a handful of tragic cases prompted governments in North America to require children's toys and clothing to be fireproof. Now, the widely used fire-retardant in children's products (a chemical which "migrates" into the atmosphere) is being blamed for the enormous spike in children's hyperactivity and Canada has banned its use (Mittelstaedt 2006). The growing incidence of child asthma, eczema, allergies, and chronic illness is now being blamed on our tendency to shrink-wrap our kids in a too-clean environment. We prevent them from exposure to bacteria-rich and tolerance-inducing dirt, manure, animals, and plants (Grady 2002).[27]

In school, we are so anxious to protect the child's self-esteem we shower them with praise and withhold appropriate negative feedback. Results may be

---

[24] Fass argues that these irrational fears blind us to the real threats contemporary American children face from inadequate medical care, poor schools, and unhealthy lifestyles (Fass 1997).

[25] Another, more benign, trend is the rapid growth in demand for "organic baby food" to "protect" babies from the effects of agricultural chemicals. In fact, the average urban or suburban baby will inhale far more questionable chemicals in their homes than they'd ever ingest being fed regular baby food. Baby gas masks?

[26] Until recently, the medical profession and the Centers for Disease Control cautioned against using the terms "obese" and "overweight" in reference to children whose condition warranted such labels on the grounds of undermining their self-esteem: "Experts labeling kids obese," FoxNews.com, July 3, 2006: www.foxnews.com; accessed 04.21.07.

[27] Contrast our attitudes with those of the Swedes for whom there is "no bad weather, only bad clothing," and where "even crawling infants are encouraged to explore nature. In the summer . . . babies and young children spend days at a time completely naked, running around on the grass or beach" (Welles-Nyström 1996: 208).

the opposite of what we intend – frequently praised children lose motivation and persistence (Bronson 2007; Baumeister *et al.* 2005).

In the USA,[28] "thought police" protect children from exposure to information about sex, so, in ignorance, teenagers get pregnant and contract STDs. They also shelter students from scientific information that runs counter to holy scripture, so US students are, by international standards, scientifically illiterate (Zimmerman 2002).

But the number one scapegoat for all that troubles the youth of our society is, collectively, the popular media (Sternheimer 2003: 63). Innumerable watchdog organizations aggressively work to sanitize popular music, TV, cinema, the internet, and video games (Giroux 1998: 270). However, and in spite of millions of research dollars expended, there is little evidence of lasting harmful effects of media on children (Goldstein 1998). The most significant effects relate to the rise of sedentism and consumerism. For example, the decline in national park visitation tracks perfectly the rise in video game use (Nielson 2006). And in a study of children's "Letters to Santa . . . children who watched more television . . . were more likely to request not only more branded goods, but also more items generally . . . For most toy companies, it is only about profit. The role of children is a clear one: they are cash cows to be milked" (Clark 2007: 165).

So we close this section with a pair of images, of an American child – with an allowance to "invest" – engrossed in conversation with a parent as they consider the relative cost and merits of several soccer balls in the sports store[29] and, halfway around the world in India,[30] of another child who labors to meet her football stitching quota.

What have we learned?

Obviously poverty is not good for children. (Raphael and Davis 1985: 139)

Throughout the book, I have drawn contrasts between the childhood that is depicted in our common understanding[31] and what one sees in the ethnographic and historic records. We can summarize these discussions through a series of polemical comparisons:

- The modern "ideal" family features the biological parents and their children cohabiting under one roof. The parents, faithful to each other,

---

[28] Islamic fundamentalists exercise similar power over the curriculum in Turkey (Kaplan 2006) and Pakistan (Jalil and McGinn 1992: 101).

[29] Actual event recorded by author in August 2006.

[30] In a follow-up to the ILO intervention mentioned earlier in the chapter, it was shown that the industry moved across the border into India – and continued to employ children (Berik 2001). Cited in Palley (2002).

[31] And, to a great extent, in the pages of child development texts as well.

Figure 33 Football stitcher from Gandhi Camp

cooperate fully in the household economy and share the great burden of childrearing. This perspective can be challenged by:
- Studies of human reproductive patterns and the notes of anthropologists reveal that men rarely commit to life-long monogamy, may not reside with their wives and offspring, and, hence, may have virtually no contact with their children. The "nuclear" family is relatively rare; far more common are large extended families and households composed of mother and offspring.

• Every child is invested with tremendous inherent worth, regardless of gender. We spend millions in enhanced reproductive techniques and millions more on keeping alive even the highest risk neonates.
- Since the dawn of mankind, humans have abandoned or disposed of surplus or defective babies. Girl babies are especially vulnerable to

population limiting choices. Societies develop elaborate customs that legitimate and dignify these practices.

- Most modern societies embrace the ideal of limited fertility so that one can "afford" the high costs of raising (few) children.
  - It is far more common to find societies where high fertility – especially the production of males – is highly valued – even if children may not be. Childless individuals may be scorned.

- Unthreatened by mother or infant mortality,[32] we celebrate the child's birth with baby showers, redecorated nurseries, open houses, and christenings.
  - More commonly, the mother and baby are in a liminal state, vulnerable to infection and other medical crises as well as potential harm to and from others. Birth and the post-partum period may be characterized by secrecy and seclusion.

- We treat the child's illness as strictly a *medical* problem.
  - In the village, illness may originate in supernatural forces or familial discord that must be diagnosed and placated before the child can get well.

- In our society, the child's wellbeing is paramount; its needs trump the desires of other family members.
  - Not so elsewhere; children are the lowest ranking members of the community and are treated accordingly, fed on leavings from the adult's meal, for example.

- We believe the normal childhood state is one of happiness and act vigorously to alleviate any symptoms of unhappiness.
  - Given the child's low status, lack of skills, and resources, why should s/he be happy? Unhappiness is to be expected.

- In the West and in East Asia one commonly finds selfless mothers who lavish attention and instruction on their young well into adolescence.
  - In traditional societies, mothers pass off their infants and toddlers to sibling or granny caretakers. The mother's energies are, preferentially, devoted to subsistence or commercial activity and to preparing herself for the next birth.

- Also in the developed societies, there is the presumption that, to mature successfully, children require intellectual stimulation from birth – or even in the womb. Their caretakers aim to "optimize" the child's development to maximize their accomplishments. This perspective can be challenged by:

---

[32] Of course, the low risk doesn't prevent parents from *acting* as if the risk were quite high (Welles-Nyström 1988: 76).

> – The belief that children are without sense or the ability to learn until at least their fifth year. They are, in effect, unteachable. And, later, caretakers behave like "satisficers;"[33] "ok" is good enough.

- Our society sees children as precious and innocent, needing protection from the world of adults and exploitative labor. This perspective can be challenged by:
  - Elsewhere, parents expect an economic return from each child. They begin early to contribute to the household economy and if not needed as workers, they may be sold into slavery or donated to a monastery.

- Our childrearing manuals admonish us that children have a need and right to play. The experts fret that childhood is "hurried," play opportunities curtailed.
  - The parents anthropologists talk to see little value in play, aside from keeping children busy and out of the way. Play is often seen as antithetical to the child's fulfillment of its role as a productive contributor to the household.

- In our society, childhood, as the period when our offspring are too young to fend for themselves completely and require active nurturing, begins in infancy and may extend past college-age. This perspective contrasts with:
  - In most of the societies discussed in this book, childhood is brief.

- Our recent history shows formal schooling starting in early childhood and lasting into adulthood. Teaching the young is seen as both essential and extremely challenging.
  - Throughout the ethnographic literature, formal schooling is virtually absent. Children are supposed to learn the culture through observation and imitation. Teaching is seen as unnecessary and a waste of an adult's precious time.

- Contemporary values in modernized societies stress the malleability of gender roles: girls are encouraged to pursue everything from contact sports to careers in politics. More typically, we see:
  - Extremely rigid management of the development of gender roles where the daughter becomes a full-time assistant to her mother and boys may endure a painful initiation to divest them forcibly of any feminine traits acquired from their mothers.

- To succeed in modern society, adolescents are encouraged to practice abstinence and delay family formation until they've mastered a profession

---

[33] I draw the terms optimizer and satisficer from Simon's theory of bounded rationality (Simon 1956).

and achieved economic self-sufficiency – a process that may extend well into their third decade. These attitudes can be juxtaposed to:
– Historically and in much of the Third World today, adolescence is ephemeral. The onset of sexual relations follows closely after puberty and, by the end of her third decade, a woman may have completed her family and be on the threshold of grandmotherhood.

• Educational policy in the USA has operated under the assumption that every child can be shaped by the school into a well-educated, economically productive member of the society. This perspective can be challenged by:
– Anthropological study shows that the impact of formal schooling, independent of family influence, is limited. Parents and families – especially the lower class – often do not command the enormous cultural capital (for example, the "bedtime story" routine) needed to insure a child's academic success.

So what can be done?

Nothing much can be done to address the plight of the world's children, if we fail to take into account these radically different ways of viewing and thinking about them – as enumerated above. Let's briefly examine some pragmatic issues that might be impacted by these differences. Perhaps the most significant insight gained from using anthropology's lens to study children is to appreciate their relative value. Our society is a neontocracy where kids rule. So valuable are they to many parents, that they are overindulged and coddled – to their own detriment. Because most societies look more like a gerontocracy, as the quote above from Thailand suggests, children are the least important members of the community. At an early age, they display many liabilities and no assets. As fetuses and then neonates, they endanger and deplete the wellbeing of women, who are the workhorses of most communities. Children lack the strength and skill of adults and the wisdom of the elderly.

This implies that programs to promote child welfare must take this hierarchy into account and insure that any government intervention or change in their legal status leads to increased value added to children rather than the reverse. For example, parents cannot be expected to relinquish their children's labor and pay school fees unless there are jobs available to those who complete school successfully (Demerath 1999). If there are no jobs requiring literacy or more advanced schooling or if the quality of education provided is so poor that students can't meet the hiring criteria, then establishing public schools in the village becomes a meaningless gesture of "modernization," or "development."

A second broad conclusion might be that traditional economies are very successful at providing a comfortable standard of living and that children willingly replicate the systems that have worked in the past. There is a font of knowledge on how to adapt to a particular environment and to maintain sufficiently harmonious relations within the community so children are cared for.[34] This knowledge is made available to the rising generation which is endowed from birth with the social learning skills to acquire it – slowly but surely. Formal training of any sort isn't required. Attempts to repackage the traditional culture and deliver it to students in classrooms (Coe 2005: 82) seems perverse. They'd be far better off avoiding the classroom and hanging around working adults.

On the other hand, villagers and squatters are politically disenfranchised by the current inadequate education system. Triage is an unfortunate recognition of the limits of the generosity of "the haves" vis-à-vis the "have nots." The logical compromise is to adopt something akin to "affirmative action" for poor children. Community members will quickly appreciate the value of having a few educated "*wantoks*"[35] and will learn how to spot children with the potential to be good students. What I'm suggesting is that Third World governments should offer fewer, better-funded school places but make sure that the student population is representative of the political, ethnic, and gender diversity in the country.

All members of the child's extended family can step forward to serve as primary caretaker should the need arise. Out-migration by parents shouldn't, therefore, have an enormous impact on children. But the system is quite complex as non-parental caretakers expect some form of reciprocity. The latest figures show that women are now as likely to be migrants as men, and, while they are much more likely than men to send remittances home to the village (Alcalá 2006), their absence must have an impact on the quality of childcare. In short, it is regrettable that village children may benefit *either* from the modern economy or from close parental care but not both.[36]

Fifth, we must recognize that this economic and social infrastructure within which children were raised to take their place as productive members of society is collapsing in many Third World countries and among poor communities in the developed countries. Ironically, the most expeditious intervention that can be made to redress this collapse is through massive inputs to programs that facilitate protected sex and fertility reduction. Basically, in spite of drastic declines in rural economies and the rise of adult mortality and disability, the

---

[34] I'm grateful to John Gay for making this point forcibly in a letter (personal communication, May 2004).

[35] The Melanesian pidgin term means the speaker and designee share a common tongue and culture. Ethnicity becomes a kind of political "special interest group."

[36] Many would blame neo-liberal policies where profit trumps people for this state of affairs. But, as we watch formerly socialist countries, like Hungary and Sweden, move – democratically – to the right, popular support for *viejo*-liberal ideas seems scarce.

birth rate remains high. There are, consequently, too many children for the available supply of food, caretakers, or decent schools.

Sixth, in the absence of artificial population-limiting mechanisms like contraception, the population will be reduced through other means including diseases like malaria and child maltreatment or "selective neglect" (Korbin 1987a: 36). Economic inducements to adults to limit fertility may be a better way to allocate, historically inadequate, resources than to try and ameliorate children's suffering. Throughout the accounts of anthropologists, street children and those working under inhumane conditions are described as "surplus" (Jacquemin 2006: 391).

For children, there is no *détente*. While traditional forms of village warfare tended to arrive at a stalemate and children were relatively unaffected, today children are both the primary victims and, often, the primary perpetrators of armed violence. Attempts by the super-powers to separate and/or equalize warring factions largely fail until the carnage reaches holocaust proportions. The only diplomatic policy that will favor children is disarmament, starting with a total ban on land mines.[37] All lethal weapons should be treated as we treat opium, as inherently harmful to all humans and worthy only of contraband designation. The cherished American "right" to bear arms is nothing more than a lottery with constantly improving odds that winners – often children – will get wounded or killed.[38]

While we can discuss improvements in our interventions with children in the Third World, the First World will continue to play a minor, if not negative, role in children's lives throughout the world until we confront our own ethnocentrism. Even though we recoil from discussions of children as chattel, our current policies, in fact, turn children into commodities with a precise dollar value. Effectively, we embrace the notions that anyone can have a child, everyone can have as many children as they want, that infertility can be circumvented, that the fetus is human and deserves whatever measures are available to keep it alive, regardless of any handicaps or defects it may harbor.

Contrariwise, we erect barriers to thwart those who would prevent pregnancy and childbirth, thereby, swelling the ranks of unwanted, abused youngsters.

We see no reason to impose "conditions" or limitations on conception and birth, only on the prevention of same. But there is no celestial bank account available to fund everyone's dreams of successful progeny. The net result of our mindset is that the *marketplace* decides the fate of children. In poor countries, food shortages means many potentially sound children will suffer malnutrition and neglect. Dollars that could be sent overseas to vaccinate, educate, and feed these children are, instead, spent at home on expensive technologies and

---

[37] Website: www.banminesusa.org; accessed 4.20.07.
[38] *Kansas City Star*, October 1, 2007: www.kansascity.com; accessed 10.1.2007.

caretakers to keep alive children whose quality of life is non-existent. While sick, premature babies born to the well-off will survive through "miracles" of modern medicine, the poor will lose their otherwise healthy children to preventable diseases. The rich will purchase their way to parenthood, regardless of their biological or psychological "fitness." While we build state-of-the-art sports and computer facilities for students in wealthy school districts, our failure to fund universal pre-school access consigns poor children in the USA to perpetual "below grade level" status. Poor people nurture their employer's children while neglecting their own. Poor children working for low wages in developing countries will produce clothes and toys to enrich the lives of children in developed countries whose parents are grateful to find "bargains" for them at WalMart.

Who lives, who dies, who is healthy, who is chronically ill, who sells themselves in a brothel and who goes to school, who gets vaccinated and who doesn't, who is a victim of crime or war, who lives in comfort and safety – it's all about money. Because of our failure to address the inherent value conflicts in our *lassez faire* attitude, we have allowed children to become a commodity that is not fundamentally different from oil.

References

Achpal, Beena. 2003. Parenting concerns of European American and Puerto Rican parents. Paper presented at annual meeting, Society for Cross-Cultural Research, Charleston, SC, February

Acredolo, Linda and Goodwyn, Susan. 2002. *Baby Signs: How to Talk with Your Baby Before Your Baby Can Talk.* Chicago, IL: Contemporary Books

Adamson, Peter. 2007. Child poverty in perspective: an overview of child well-being in rich countries. *Innocenti Report Card 7.* Florence: UNICEF Innocenti Research Centre

Adelman, Clifford. 2006. *The Toolbox Revisited: Paths to Degree Completion from High School through College.* Washington, DC: US Department of Education Research Report

Adriani, Nicolaus. 1951/1997. *The Bare'e-Speaking Toradja of Central Celebes.* New Haven, CT: HRAF

Ahmed, Ramadan A. 2005. Egyptian families, in *Families in Global Perspective.* Edited by Jaipaul L. Roopnarine, pp. 151–168. Boston, MA: Pearson

Aiello, Leslie C. and Wheeler, Peter. 1995. The expensive-tissue hypothesis. *Current Anthropology,* 36(2):199–221

Ainsworth, Mary D. 1967. *Infancy in Uganda: Infant Care and the Growth of Love.* Baltimore, MD: The Johns Hopkins University Press

Akabayashi, Hideo and Psacharopoulos, George. 1999. The trade-off between child labour and human capital formation: A Tanzanian case study. *The Journal of Developmental Studies,* 35(5):120–140

Alcalá, María José. 2006. *A Passage to Hope: Women in International Migration.* New York, NY: United Nations Population Fund

Aleichem, Sholom. 1990. *Favorite Tales of Sholom Aleichem.* New York, NY: Random House

Aldis, Owen. 1975. *Playfighting.* New York, NY: Academic Press

Alexander, Richard D. 1990. *How Did Humans Evolve? Reflections on the Uniquely Unique Species.* Ann Arbor, MI: University of Michigan Museum of Zoology

Alexander, Richard D. and Noonan, Katherine M. 1979. Concealment of ovulation, parental care, and human social evolution, in *Evolutionary Biology and Human Social Behavior: An Anthropological Perspective.* Edited by Napoleon A. Chagnon and William G. Irons, pp. 436–453. North Scituate, MA: Duxbury Press

Alford, Kathleen F. 1983. Privileged play: Joking relationships between parents and children, in *The World of Play.* Edited by Frank E. Manning, pp. 170–187. West Point, NY: Leisure Press

Allison, Anne. 1991. Japanese mothers and *obentōs*: The lunch-box as ideological state apparatus. *Anthropological Quarterly*, 64(4):195–208

Allison, Marvin J. 1984. Paleopathology in Peruvian and Chilean populations, in *Paleopathology at the Origins of Agriculture*. Edited by Mark N. Cohen and George J. Armelagos, pp. 531–558. Orlando, FL: Academic Press

Allport, Susan. 1997. *A Natural History of Parenting*. New York, NY: Harmony Books

Alston, Lester. 1992. Children as chattel, in *Small Worlds: Children and Adolescents in America, 1850–1950*. Edited by Elliot West and Paula Petrik, pp. 208–231. Lawrence, KS: University Press of Kansas

Altman, Irwin and Ginat, Joseph. 1996. *Polygamous Families in Contemporary Society*. Cambridge, UK: Cambridge University Press

Altmann, Jeanne. 1980. *Baboon Mothers and Infants*. Cambridge, MA: Harvard University Press

Altorki, Soraya. 1980. Milk-kinship in Arab society: An unexplored problem in the ethnography of marriage. *Ethnology*, 19(2):233–244

Anarfi, John and Kwankye, Steven. 2005. The costs and benefits of children's independent migration from Northern to Southern Ghana. Paper presented at conference on Children and Youth in Emerging and Transforming Societies, Oslo, June

Andersen, Peder Ø. and Kampmann, Jørn. 1996. *Børns legekultur*. Copenhagen: Munksgaard International

Anderson, Kermyt G., Kaplan, Hillard, Lam, David, and Lancaster, Jane B. 1999. Paternal care by genetic fathers and stepfathers II: Reports by Xhosa high school students. *Evolution and Human Behavior*, 20(4):433–451

Anderson, Kermyt G., Kaplan, Hillard, and Lancaster, Jane B. 2007. Confidence of paternity, divorce, and investment in children by Albuquerque men. *Evolution and Human Behavior*, 28(1):1–10

Anderson-Levitt, Kathryn M. 2005. The schoolyard gate: Schooling and childhood in global perspective. *Journal of Social History*, 38(4):987–1006

Anderson-Levitt, Kathryn M. and Diallo, Boubacar Bayero. 2003. Teaching by the book in Guinea, in *Local Meanings, Global Schooling: Anthropology and World Culture Theory*. Edited by Kathryn M. Anderson-Levitt, pp. 75–97. Basingstone, UK: Palgrave Macmillan

Anonymous. 2002a. *Television: How It Affects Children*. Elk Grove, IL: American Academy of Pediatrics

Anonymous. 2005. *Income of US Workforce Projected to Decline if Education Does Not Improve*. Washington, DC: The National Center for Public Policy and Higher Education

Anonymous. 2006. *State of the World's Cities Report 2006–2007: Millennium Development Goals and Urban Sustainability – 30 Years of Shaping the Habitat Agenda*. New York, NY: United Nations Human Settlements Programme

Anonymous Venetian Diplomat. 1847. *A Relation of the Island of England*. Translated by Charlotte A. Sneyd. London, UK: Camden Society, 37:24–25

Ansar, Sarah F. D. and Martin, Vanessa. 2003. *Women, Religion and Culture in Iran*. London, UK: Curzon

Apicella, Coren L. and Marlowe, Frank W. 2004. Perceived mate fidelity and paternal resemblance predict men's investment in children. *Evolution and Human Behavior*, 25(6):371–378

Aptekar, Lewis. 1991. Are Colombian street children neglected? The contributions of ethnographic and ethnohistorical approaches to the study of children. *Anthropology and Education Quarterly*, 22(4):326–49

2004. The changing developmental dynamics of children in particularly difficult circumstances: Examples of street and war-traumatized children, in *Childhood and Adolescence: Cross-Cultural Perspectives and Applications*. Edited by Uwe P. Gielen and Jaipaul L. Roopnarine, pp. 377–410. Westport, CT: Praeger

Ariel, Shlomo and Sever, Irene. 1980. Play in the desert and play in the town: On play activities of Bedouin Arab children, in *Play and Culture*. Edited by Helen B. Schwartzman, pp. 164–174. West Point, NY: Leisure Press

Ariès, Philippe. 1962. *Centuries of Childhood*. Translated by Robert Baldick. New York, NY: Alfred A. Knopf

Armstrong, Elizabeth. 2004. Lost in transition? Young adults take longer to become emotionally and financially independent. *The Christian Science Monitor*, 96(72):15

Arnett, Jeffrey J. 1999. Adolescent storm and stress, reconsidered. *American Psychologist*, 54(5):317–326

2002. Adolescents in Western countries in the 21st century: Vast opportunities – for all?, in *The World's Youth: Adolescence in Eight Regions of the Globe*. Edited by Bradford B. Brown, Reed W. Larson, and T. S. Saraswathi, pp. 307–343. Cambridge, MA: Cambridge University Press

Arnold, Mary Jo. 2006. *Ndomo* ritual and *Sogo bo* play: Boy's masquerading among the Bamana of Mali, in *Playful Performers: African Children's Masquerades*. Edited by Simon Ottenberg and David A. Binkley, pp. 49–65. Brunswick, NJ: Transaction Publishers

Aronson, Lisa. 1989. To weave or not to weave: apprenticeship rules among the Akwete Igbo of Nigeria and the Baulé of the Ivory Coast, in *Apprenticeship: From Theory to Method and Back Again*. Edited by Michael W. Coy, pp. 149–162. Albany, NY: State University of New York Press

Arriaza, Bernardo T. 1995. *Beyond Death: The Chinchorro Mummies of Ancient Chile*. Washington, DC: Smithsonian Press

Arriaza, Bernardo T., Cardenas-Arroyo, Felipe, Kleiss, Ekkehard, and Verano, John W. 1998. South American mummies: Culture and disease, in *Mummies, Disease, and Ancient Cultures*. Edited by Aidan Cockburn, Eve Cockburn, and Theodore A. Reyman, pp. 190–234. Cambridge, MA: Cambridge University Press

Ascher, Carol, Norm Fruchter, and Robert Berne. 1996. *Hard Lessons: Public Schools and Privatization*. New York, NY: Twentieth Century Fund Press

Ascione, Frank R. 2005. *Children and Animals: Exploring the Roots of Kindness and Cruelty*. Lafayette, IN: Purdue University Press

Asghar, Syed M. 2004. *Camel Jockeys of Rahimyar Khan*. Peshawar, Pakistan and Stockholm: Save the Children

Ataka, Yuji and Ohtsuka, Ryutaro. 2006. Migration and fertility of a small island population in Manus, in *Population, Reproduction, and Fertility in Melanesia*. Edited by Stanley J. Ulijaszek, pp. 90–109. Oxford, UK: Berghahn Books

Atran, Scott and Sperber, Dan. 1991. Learning without teaching: Its place in culture, in *Culture, Schooling, and Psychological Development*. Edited by Liliana T. Landsmann, pp. 39–55. Norwood, NJ: Ablex

Aunger, Robert. 1994. Sources of variation in ethnographic interview data: Food avoidances in the Ituri forest, Zaire. *Ethnology*, 33(1):65–99

Bachman, Jerald G., Safron, Deborah J., Sy, Susan Rogala, and Schulenberg, John E. 2003. Wishing to work: New perspectives on how adolescents' part-time work intensity is linked to educational disengagement, substance use, and other problem behaviours. *International Journal of Behavioral Development*, 27(4):301–315

Baer, Justin D., Cook, Andrea L., and Baldi, Stephane. 2006. *The Literacy of America's College Students*. Washington, DC: American Institutes for Research

Bai, Limin. 2005. Children at play: A childhood beyond the Confucian shadow. *Childhood*, 12(1):9–32

Bakeman, Roger, Adamson, Lauren B., Konner, Melvin, and Barr, Ronald G. 1990. !Kung infancy: The social context of object exploration. *Child Development*, 61(4):794–809

Baker, Rachel and Panter-Brick, Catherine. 2000. A comparative perspective on children's "Careers" and abandonment in Nepal, in *Abandoned Children*. Edited by Catherine Panter-Brick and Malcom T. Smith, pp. 161–181. Cambridge, MA: Cambridge University Press

Baldwin, John D. and Baldwin, Janice I. 1972. The ecology and behavior of squirrel monkeys (*Saimiri*) in a natural forest in western Panama. *Folia Primatologica*, 18(1):161–184

1976. Effects of food ecology on social play: A laboratory simulation. *Zeitschrift der Tierpsychologie*, 40(1):1–14

1977. The role of learning phenomena in the ontogeny of exploration and play, in *Primate Bio-Social Development: Biological, Social, and Ecological Determinants*. Edited by Suzanne Chevalier-Skolnikoff and Frank E. Poirier, pp. 343–406. New York, NY: Garland

1978. Exploration and play in howler monkeys (*Aloutta palliata*). *Primates*, 19(3):411–422

Balicki, Asen. 1967. Female infanticide on the Arctic coast. *Man*, 2(4):615–625

Ballantyne, Tony. 1994. The mission station as "The Enchanter's Wand": Protestant missionaries, Maori, and the notion of the household. *Archaeological Review from Cambridge*, 13(2):1–16

Barber, Nigel. 1991. Play and regulation in mammals. *The Quarterly Review of Biology*, 66(2):129–146

2000. *Why Parents Matter: Parental Investment and Child Outcomes*. Westport, CT: Bergin and Garvey

2002. Does parental investment increase wealth, or does wealth increase parental investment? *Cross-Cultural Research*, 36(4):362–378

Bard, Katherine A. 1995. Parenting in primates, in *Handbook of Parenting*, Vol. II: *Biology and Ecology of Parenting*. Edited by Marc H. Bornstein, pp. 27–58. Mahwah, NJ: Lawrence Erlbaum Associates

Bardo, Massimo, Petto, Andrew J., and Lee-Parritz, David E. 2001. Parental failure in captive cotton-top tamarins (*Saguinus oedipus*). *American Journal of Primatology*, 54(2):159–169

Barlow, Kathleen. 2001. Working mothers and the work of culture in a Papua New Guinea society. *Ethos*, 29(1):78–107

Barnett, W. Steven. 1995. Long-term effects of early childhood programs on cognitive and school outcomes. *The Future of Children*, 5(3):25–50

Baron-Cohen, Simon. 1995. *Mindblindness: An Essay on Autism and Theory of Mind*. Cambridge, MA: MIT Press

Barrett, Louise, Dunbar, Robin, and Lycett, John. 2002. *Human Evolutionary Psychology*. Princeton, NJ: Princeton University Press

Barry, Herbert L., III. 2005. Sexual freedom for adolescent boys and girls is associated with seven cultural customs. Paper presented at 34th annual meeting, Society for Cross-Cultural Research, Santa Fe, February

Barry, Herbert L., III and Paxson, Leonora M. 1971. Infancy and early childhood: Cross-cultural codes 2. *Ethnology*, 10(3):466–508

Barth, Fredrik. 1993. *Balinese Worlds*. Chicago, IL: University of Chicago Press

Bascom, William. 1969. *The Yoruba of Southwest Nigeria*. New York, NY: Holt, Rhinehart and Winston

Basden, George T. 1966. *Niger Ibos*. London, UK: Cass

Bastian, Misty L. 2001 "The demon superstition": Abominable twins and mission culture in Onitsha history. *Ethnology*, 40(1):13–27

Batels, Lambert. 1969. Birth customs and birth songs of the Macha Galla. *Ethnology*, 8(4):406–422

Bates, Brian and Turner, Allison N. 2003. Imagery and symbolism in the birth practices of traditional cultures, in *The Manner Born: Birth Rites in Cross-Cultural Perspective*. Edited by Lauren Dundes, pp. 87–97. New York, NY: AltaMira Press

Bateson, Gregory and Mead, Margaret. 1942. *Balinese Character: A Photographic Analysis*. New York, NY: New York Academy of Sciences

Baumeister, Roy F., Campbell, Jennifer D., Krueger, Joachim I., and Vohs, Kathleen D. 2005. Exploding the self-esteem myth. *Scientific American Mind*, 16(4):50–57

Baumrind, Diana. 1971. Current patterns of parental authority. *Developmental Psychology Monographs*, 4(no. 1, part 2):1–103

Baxter, Jane Eva. 2005. *The Archaeology of Childhood*. New York, NY: AltaMira Press

Baxter, Paul T. W. 1953. *The Azande, and Related Peoples of the Anglo-Egyptian Sudan and Belgian Congo*. London, UK: International African Institute

Beach, Betty A. 2003. Rural children's play in the natural environment, in *Play and Educational Theory and Practice*. Edited by Donald E. Lytle, pp. 183–194. Westport, CT: Praeger

Beatty, Barbara. 1995. *Preschool Education in America: The Culture of Young Children from the Colonial Era to the Present*. New Haven, CT: Yale University Press

Beaumont, Lesley A. 1994. Constructing a methodology for the interpretation of childhood age in classical Athenian iconography. *Archaeological Review from Cambridge*, 13(2):81–96

2000. The social status and artistic presentation of "adolescence" in fifth-century Athens, in *Children and Material Culture*. Edited by Joanna S. Derevenski, pp. 39–49. London, UK: Routledge

Beckerman, Stephan, Lizarralde, Roberto, Ballew, Carol, Schroeder, Sissel, Fingelton, Cristina, Garrison, Angela, and Smith, Helen. 1998. The Bari partible paternity project: Preliminary results. *Current Anthropology*, 39(1):164–167

Beckerman, Stephan and Valentine, Paul. 2002. *Cultures of Multiple Fathers: The Theory and Practice of Partible Paternity in Lowland South America*. Gainesville, FL: University of Florida Press

Belaunde, Luisa E. 2001. Menstruation, birth observances and the couple's love amongst the Airo-Pai of Amazonian Peru, in *Managing Reproductive Life: Cross-Cultural Themes in Sexuality and Fertility*. Edited by Soraya Tremayne, pp. 127–139. Oxford, UK: Berghahn Books

Belo, Jane. 1980. A study of customs pertaining to twins in Bali, in *Traditional Balinese Culture*. Edited by Jane Belo. New York, NY: Columbia University Press

Belsky, Jay, Steinberg, Lawrence, and Draper, Patricia. 1991. Childhood experience, interpersonal development, and reproductive strategy: An evolutionary theory of socialization. *Child Development*, 62(4):647–670

Belton, Teresa. 2001. Television and imagination: An investigation of the medium's influence on children's story-making. *Media, Culture and Society*, 23(6):799–820

Benavot, Aaron, Cha, Yun-Kyung, Kamens, David H., Meyer, David, and Wong, Suk-Ying. 1992. Knowledge for the masses: World models and national curricula, 1920–1986, in *School Knowledge for the Masses: World Models and National Primary Curricular Categories in the Twentieth Century*. Edited by John Meyer, David H. Kamens, Aaron Benavot, Yun-Kyung Cha, and Suk-Ying Wong, pp. 40–62. Washington, DC: Falmer Press

Benedict, Ruth F. 1922. The vision in Plains Culture. *American Anthropologist*, 24(1):1–23

Bengston, Vern L., Biblarz, Timothy J., and Roberts, Robert E. L. 2002. *How Families Still Matter: A Longitudinal Study of Youth in Two Generations*. Cambridge, MA: Cambridge University Press

Berdan, Frances F. and Anawalt, Patricia Rieff. 1997. *The Essential Codex Mendoza*. Berkeley: University of California Press

Bereczkei, Tamas. 2001. Maternal trade-off in treating high-risk children. *Evolution and Human Behavior*, 22(2):197–212

Bereczkei, Tamas and Csanaky, Andras. 2001. Stressful family environment, mortality, and child socialisation: Life-history strategies among adolescents and adults from unfavourable social circumstances. *International Journal of Behavioral Development*, 25(6):501–508

Bereczkei, Tamas and Dunbar, Robin I. M. 1997. Female-biased reproductive strategies in a Hungarian Gypsy population. *Proceedings of the Royal Society of London*, Series B, 264:17–22

Bergin, David A. 2000. Academic competition among students of color: An interview study. *Urban Education*, 35(4):442–472

Bergin, David A. and Cooks, Helen C. 2002. High school students of color talk about accusations of "acting white." *The Urban Review*, 34(2):113–135

Berik, Günseli. 2001. What happened after Pakistan's soccer ball industry went child free? Paper presented at the Conference on Child Labor held at the Graduate School of Social Work, University of Utah, Salt Lake City, Utah, May. Cited in: Palley, Thomas I. (2002) The child labor problem and the need for international labor standards. *Journal of Economic Issues*, 36(3):1–15

Berk, Sarah F. 1985. *The Gender Factor: The Apportionment of Work in American Households*. New York, NY: Plenum Press

Berliner, Nancy. 2003. *Yin Yu Tang: The Architecture and Daily Life of a Chinese House*. Boston, MA: Tuttle Publishing

Berrelleza, Juan Alberto Román and Balderas, Ximena Chávez. 2006. The role of children in the ritual practices of the Great Temple of Tenochtitlan and the Great Temple of Tlatelolco, in *The Social Experience of Childhood in Ancient Mesoamerica*. Edited by Traci Adren and Scott R. Hutson, pp. 233–248. Boulder, CO: University of Colorado Press

Berrick, Jill Duerr. 1995. *Faces of Poverty: Portraits of Women and Children on Welfare.* New York, NY: Oxford University Press

Berrol, Selma. 1992. Immigrant children at school, 1880–1940: A child's eye view, in *Small Worlds: Children and Adolescents in America, 1850–1950.* Edited by Elliot West and Paula, Petrick, pp. 42–60. Lawrence, KS: University Press of Kansas

Besharov, Douglas J. and Germanis, Peter. 2003. Introduction, in *Family and Child Wellbeing After welfare Reform.* Edited by Douglas J. Besharov, pp.1–33. New Brunswick, NJ: Transaction Publishers

Best, Amy L. 2000. *Prom Night: Youth, Schools, and Popular Culture.* New York, NY: Routledge

Best, Joel and Horiuchi, Gerald T. 1985. The razor blade in the apple: The social construction of urban legends. *Social Problems,* 32(5):488–499

Bey, Marguerite. 2003. The Mexican child: from work with the family to paid employment. *Childhood,* 10(3):287–299

Biben, Maxine, Symmes, David, and Bernard, Deborah. 1989. Vigilance during play in squirrel monkeys. *American Journal of Primatology,* 17(1):41–49

Biersack, Aletta. 1998. Horticulture and hierarchy: The youthful beautification of the body in the Paiela and Porgera Valleys, in *Adolescence in Pacific Island Societies.* Edited by Gilbert H. Herdt and Stephen C. Leavitt, pp. 71–91. Pittsburgh, PA: University of Pittsburgh Press

Biesele, Megan. 1993. *"Women Like Meat": The Folklore and Foraging Ideology of the Kalahari Ju/'hoan.* Bloomington, IN: Indiana University Press

　1997. An ideal of unassisted birth: Hunting, healing, and transformation among the Kalahari Ju/'hoansi, in *Childbirth and Authoritative Knowledge.* Edited by Robbie E. Davis-Floyd and Carolyn F. Sargent, pp. 474–492. Berkeley, CA: University of California Press

Binkley, David A. 2006. From grasshoppers to Babende: The socialization of Southern Kuba boys to masquerade, in *Playful Performers: African Children's Masquerades.* Edited by Simon Ottenberg and David A. Binkley, pp. 105–115. New Brunswick, NJ: Transaction Publishers

Binser, Martin J. 2004. "Sadder but Fitter": Die evolutionäre Funktion von depressiven Symptomen nach Fehl- und Totgeburten. *Zeitschrift für Sozialpsychologie,* 35(3):157–170

Bird, Douglas W. and Bird, Rebecca Bliege. 2002. Children on the reef: Slow learning or strategic foraging? *Human Nature,* 13(2):269–297

　2005. Martu children's hunting strategies in the western desert, Australia, in *Hunter Gatherer Childhoods: Evolutionary, Developmental, and Cultural Perspectives.* Edited by Barry S. Hewlett and Michael E. Lamb, pp. 129–146. New Brunswick, NJ: AldineTransaction

Bird, Rebecca Bliege and Bird, Douglas W. 2002. Constraints of knowing or constraints of growing? Fishing and collection by the children of Mer. *Human Nature,* 13(2):239–267

Black, Maureen M., Dubowitz, Howard, and Starr, Raymond H., Jr., 1999. African American fathers in low income, urban families: Development, behavior, and home environment of their three-year-old children. *Child Development,* 70(4):967–978

Blackwood, Evelyn. 2001. Women's intimate friendships and other affairs: An ethnographic overview, in *Gender in Cross-Cultural Perspective.* Edited by Caroline B.

Brettell and Carolyn F. Sargent, pp. 237–247. Upper Saddle River, NJ: Prentice Hall

Blagbrough, Jonathan and Glynn, Edmund. 1999. Child domestic workers: Characteristics of the modern slave and approaches to ending such exploitation. *Childhood*, 6(1):51–56

Blair, Sampson Lee. 1992. The sex-typing of children's household labor: Parental influence on daughters' and sons' housework. *Youth and Society*, 24(2):178–203

Blanchard, Ray and Bogaert, Anthony F. 1997. The relation of close birth intervals to the sex of the preceding child and the sexual orientation of the succeeding child. *Journal of Biosocial Science*, 29(1):111–118

Bledsoe, Caroline H. 1980a. The manipulation of Kpelle social fatherhood. *Ethnology*, 19(1):29–45

1980b. *Women and Marriage in Kpelle Society*. Stanford, CA: Stanford University Press

2001. The bodily costs of childrearing: Western science through a West African lens, in *Children and Anthropology: Perspectives for the 21st Century*. Edited by Helen B. Schwartzman, pp. 57–81. Westport, CT: Bergin and Garvey

Bledsoe, Caroline H. and Cohen, Barney. (eds.) 1993. *Social Dynamics of Adolescent Fertility in Sub-Saharan Africa*. Washington, DC: National Research Council

Bledsoe, Caroline H. and Isiugo-Abanihe, Uche. 1989. Strategies of child-fosterage among Mende grannies in Sierra Leone, in *Reproduction and Social Organization in Sub-Saharan Africa*. Edited by Ron J. Lesthaeghe, pp. 443–474. Berkeley, CA: University of California Press

Blinn-Pike, Lynn, Kuschel, Diane, McDaniel, Annette, Mingus, Suzanne, and Mutti, Megan Poole. 1998. The process of mentoring pregnant adolescents: An exploratory study. *Family Relations*, 47(2): 119–127

Blitz, Jeffrey. (dir.) 2002. *Spellbound* (film). Los Angeles, CA: Columbia Tristar

Bloch, Marianne N. 1989. Young boys' and girls' play at home and in the community: A cultural-ecological framework, in *The Ecological Context of Children's Play*. Edited by Marianne N. Bloch and Anthony D. Pellegrini, pp. 120–154. Norwood, NJ: Ablex Publishing

Bloom-Feshbach, Jonathan. 1981. Historical perspectives on the father's role, in *The Role of the Father in Child Development*. Edited by Michael E. Lamb, pp. 71–112. New York, NY: John Wiley

Blunt, Sheryl H. 2003. A man and a woman. *Christianity Today*, 47(12):21–22

Blurton-Jones, Nicholas G. 1967. An ethological study of some aspects of social behavior of children in nursery school, in *Primate Ethology*. Edited by Desmond Morris, pp. 347–367. London, UK: Weidenfield and Nicolson

1993. The lives of hunter-gatherer children: Effects of parental behavior and parental reproduction strategy, in *Juveniles: Comparative Socioecology*. Edited by Michael Pereira and Lynn Fairbanks, pp. 405–426. Oxford, UK: Oxford University Press

2005. Why childhood? in *Hunter-Gatherer Childhoods*. Edited by Barry S. Hewlett and Michael E. Lamb, pp. 105–108. New Brunswick, NJ: AldineTransaction

Blurton-Jones, Nicholas G., Hawkes, Kirsten, and O'Connell, James F. 1997. Why do Hadza children forage?, in *Uniting Psychology and Biology: Integrative Perspectives on Human Development*. Edtied by Nancy, L. Segal, Glenn, E. Weisfeld and Carol, C. Weisfeld, pp. 279–313. Washington, DC: American Psychological Association

2005. Older Hadza men and women as helpers, in *Hunter Gatherer Childhoods: Evolutionary, Developmental, and Cultural Perspectives*. Edtied by Barry S. Hewlett and Michael E. Lamb, pp. 214–236. New Brunswick, NJ: AldineTransaction

Blurton-Jones, Nicholas G. and Konner, Melvin. 1973. Sex differences in the behavior of Bushman and London two- to five-year-olds, in *Comparative Ecology and Behavior of Primates*. Edited by Richard P. Michael and John H. Crook, pp. 689–750. New York, NY: Academic Press

Blurton-Jones, Nicholas G. and Marlowe, Frank W. 2002. Selection for delayed maturity: Does it take 20 years to learn to hunt and gather? *Human Nature*, 13(2):199–238

Blurton-Jones, Nicholas G., Marlowe, Frank W., Hawkes, Kristen, and O'Connell, James F. 2000. Paternal investment and hunter-gatherer divorce rates, in *Adaptation and Human Behavior: An Anthropological Perspective*. Edited by Lee Cronk, Napoleon Chagnon, and William Irons, pp. 69–90. New York, NY: Aldine De Gruyter

Bock, John. 2002a. Evolutionary demography and intrahousehold time allocation: School attendance and child labor among the Okavango Delta peoples of Botswana. *American Journal of Human Biology*, 14(2):206–221

2002b. Learning, life history, and productivity: Children's lives in the Okavango Delta of Botswana. *Human Nature*, 13(2):161–198

Bock, John and Johnson, Sara E. 2002. Male migration, remittances, and child outcome among the Okavango Delta peoples of Botswana, in *Handbook of Father Involvement: Multidisciplinary Perspectives*. Edited by Catherine S. Tamis-LaMonda and Natasha Cabrera, pp. 308–335. Mahwah, NJ: Erlbaum

2004. Subsistence ecology and play among the Okavango Delta peoples of Botswana. *Human Nature*, 15(1):63–82

2008 (in press) Grandmother hypothesis and the HIV/AIDS pandemic in sub-Saharan Africa. *Journal of Cross-Cultural Gerontology*, 25(1)

Bodenhorn, Barbara. 1988. Whales, souls, children, and other things that are "good to share": Core metaphors in a contemporary whaling society. *Cambridge Anthropology*, 13(1):1–19

Boesch, Christophe. 1991. Teaching in wild chimpanzees. *Animal Behaviour*, 41(4):530–532

Boesch, Christophe and Tomasello, Michael. 1998. Chimpanzee and human cultures. *Current Anthropology*, 39(5):591–614

Bogin, Barry. 1994. Adolescence in evolutionary perspective. *Acta Paediatrica Scandinavia (Suppl.)*, 406:29–35

1998. Evolutionary and biological aspects of childhood, in *Biosocial Perspectives on Children*. Edited by Catherine Panter-Brick, pp. 10–44, Cambridge, MA: Cambridge University Press

Bogin, Barry and Smith, Brian H. 1996. Evolution of the human life cycle. *American Journal of Human Biology*, 8(6):703–716

Bokhari, Shahbaz. 2005. The trafficking in children for labor and sexual exploitation in Pakistan. Paper presented at conference on Children and Youth in Emerging and Transforming Societies, Oslo, June

Boli, John. 1987. The political construction of mass schooling: European origins and worldwide institutionalization. *Sociology of Education*, 60(1): 2–17

Boli, John, Ramirez, Francisco O., and Meyer, John W. 1985. Explaining the origins of expansion of mass education. *Comparative Education Review*, 29(1):145–170

Bolin, Inge. 2006. *Growing up in a Culture of Respect: Childrearing in Highland Peru.* Austin, TX: University of Texas Press

Bonnemere, Pascale. 2006. Variations on a theme: Fertility, sexuality and masculinity in Highland New Guinea, in *Population, Reproduction, and Fertility in Melanesia.* Edited by Stanley J. Ulijaszek, pp. 201–238. Oxford, UK: Berghahn Books

Boone, James and Kessler, Karen L. 1999. More status or more children? Social status, fertility reduction, and long-term fitness. *Evolution and Human Behavior,* 20(2):257–277

Booth, Marilyn. 2002. Arab adolescents facing the future: Enduring ideals and pressure to change, in *The World's Youth: Adolescence in Eight Regions of the Globe.* Edited by Bradford B. Brown, Reed W. Larson, and T. S. Saraswathi, pp. 207–242. Cambridge, MA: Cambridge University Press

Bornstein, Marc H. and Cote, Linda. 2005. Parenting and knowledge of parenting and child development in immigrant mothers: Risk and remediation. Paper presented at annual meeting, American Anthropological Association, Washington, DC, December

Borofsky, Robert. 1987. *Making History: Pukapukan and Anthropological Constructions of Knowledge.* New York, NY: Cambridge University Press

Borries, Carola, Launhardt, Kristen, Epplen, Cornelia, Epplen, Jörg T., and Winkler, Paul. 1999. Males as infant protectors in Hanuman langurs (*Presbytis entellus*) living in multimale groups: defense pattern, paternity and sexual behaviour. *Behavioral Ecology and Sociobiology,* 46(5):350–356

Borstelmann, Lloyd J. 1983. Children before psychology: Ideas about children from antiquity to the late 1800s, in *Handbook of Child Psychology,* 4th edn. Edited by Paul M. Mussen, pp. 1–40. New York, NY: Wiley

Boserup, Ester. 1970. *Women's Role in Economic Development.* London, UK: Allen and Unwin

Boswell, John. 1988. *The Kindness of Strangers.* New York, NY: Pantheon Books

Boulton, Michael J. and Smith, Peter K. 1992. The social nature of play fighting and play chasing: Mechanisms and strategies underlying cooperation and compromise, in *The Adapted Mind: Evolutionary Psychology and the Generation of Culture.* Edited by Jerome H. Barkow, Leda Cosmides and John Tooby, pp. 429–444. New York, NY: Oxford University Press

Bourdieu, Pierre. 1973. Cultural reproduction and social reproduction, in *Knowledge, Education and Social Change.* Edited by Richard Brown, pp. 49–76. London, UK: Tavistock

Bourdillon, Michael. 2000. Children at work on tea and coffee estates, in *Earning a Life: Working Children in Zimbabwe.* Edited by Michael Bourdillon, pp. 1–24. Harare, Zimbabwe: Weaver Press

Bourgois, Philippe. 1998. Families and children in pain in the US inner city, in *Small Wars: The Cultural Politics of Childhood.* Edited by Nancy Scheper-Hughes and Carolyn F. Sargent, pp. 331–351. Berkeley, CA: University of California Press

Bove, Riley B., Valeggia, Claudia R., and Ellison, Peter T. 2002. Girl helpers and time allocation of nursing women among the Toba of Argentina. *Human Nature,* 13(4):457–472

Bowers, Nancy. 1965. Permanent bachelorhood in the Upper Kaugel Valley of Highland New Guinea. *Oceania,* 36:27–37

Bowles, Samuel and Gintis, Herbert. 1976. *Schooling in Capitalist America*. New York, NY: Basic Books

Bowser, Brenda J. and Patton, John Q. 2008 (in press). Learning and transmission of pottery style: Women's life histories and communities of practice in the Ecuadorian Amazon, in *Breaking Down Boundaries: Anthropological Approaches to Cultural Transmission, Learning, and Material Culture*. Edited by Miriam T. Stark, Brenda J. Bowser and Lee Horne. Tucson, AZ: University of Arizona Press

Boyatzis, Chris, Chazan, Elizabeth, and Ting, Carol. 1993. Preschool children's decoding of facial emotions. *Journal of Genetic Psychology*, 154(3):375–82

Boyd, Robert and Richerson, Peter J. 1996. Why culture is common, but cultural evolution is rare. *Proceedings of the British Academy*, 88:77–93

Boyden, Jo. 2004. Anthropology under fire: Ethics, researchers and children in war, in *Children and Youth on the Front Line: Ethnography, Armed Conflict and Displacement*. Edited by Jo Boyden and Joanna de Berry, pp. 237–258. New York, NY: Berghahn Books

Boyer, Peter J. 2005. Jesus in the classroom. *The New Yorker*, March 21:62–71

Boynton, Susan and Cochelin, Isabelle. 2006. The sociomusical role of child oblates in the Abbey of Cluny in the eleventh century, in *Musical Childhoods and the Culture of Youth*. Edited by Susan Boynton and Roe-Min Kok, pp. 3–24. Middletown, CT: Wesleyan University Press

Brase, Gary L. 2006. Cues of parental investment as a factor in attractiveness. *Evolution and Human Behavior*, 27(2):145–157

Bray, Rachel, Hinton, Rachel, and Nepal, Vinod K. 2002. An assessment of knowledge and practice in achieving the rights of the child. Kathmandu, Nepal: IUAES: Commission on Children, Youth, and Childhood

Brayfield, April and Korintus, Mrta. 2005. Childrearing values and the social organization of childcare in Hungary. Paper presented at conference on Children and Youth in Emerging and Transforming Societies, Oslo, June

Brenner, Mary E. 1985. The practice of arithmetic in Liberian schools. *Anthropology and Education Quarterly*, 16(3):177–186

Brenner, Suzanne. 2001. Why women rule the roost: Rethinking Javanese ideologies of gender and self-control, in Gender in Cross-Cultural Perspective. Edited by Caroline B. Brettell and Carolyn F. Sargent, pp. 135–156. Upper Saddle River, NJ: Prentice Hall

Briggs, Jean L. 1970. *Never in Anger: Portrait of an Eskimo Family*. Cambridge, MA: Harvard University Press

1990. Playwork as a tool in the socialization of an Inuit child. *Arctic Medical Research*, 49:34–38

Brison, Karen J. 1999. Hierarchy in the world of Fijian children. *Ethnology*, 38(2):97–119

Broude, Gwen J. 1975. Norms of premarital sexual behavior: A cross-cultural study. *Ethos*, 3(3):381–401

Broude, Gwen J. and Greene, Sarah J. 1976. Cross-cultural codes on twenty sexual attitudes and practices. *Ethnology*, 15(4):409–429

Broughton, Ashley. 2003. Baby discovered crawling down Orem's busy State Street at 3 a.m. *The Salt Lake Tribune*, May 30, B1, B4

Browner, Carole H. 2001. The politics of reproduction in a Mexican village, in *Gender in Cross-Cultural Perspective*. Edited by Caroline B. Brettell and Carolyn F. Sargent, pp. 460–470. Upper Saddle River, NJ: Prentice Hall

Broyon, Marie Anne. 2004. L'éducation sanskrite à Bénares, enjeu d'une société qui oscille entre traditions et transition. Paper presented at a seminar on Learning Processes and Everyday Cognition: The Role of Play and Games, April 16, Charmey, Switzerland

Bruner, Jerome S. and Sherwood, Virginia. 1976. Peekaboo and the learning of rule structure, in *Play – Its Role in Development and Evolution*. Edited by Jerome S. Bruner, Allison Jolly, and Kathy Sylva, pp. 277–286. New York, NY: Basic Books

Bucher, Julia B. and D'Amorim, Maria A. 1993. Brazil, in *International Handbook on Gender Roles*. Edited by Leonore Loeb Adler, pp. 16–27. Westport, CT: Greenwood Press

Buckingham, David and Scanlon, Margaret. 2003. *Education, Entertainment, and Learning in the Home*. Maidenhead, UK: Open University Press

Bugos, Peter E., Jr. and McCarthy, Lorraine M. 1984. Ayoreo infanticide: A case study, in *Infanticide: Comparative and Evolutionary Perspectives*. Edited by Glen Hausfater and Sarah Blaffer Hrdy, pp. 503–520. New York, NY: Aldine

Burghardt, Gordon M. 2005. *The Genesis of Animal Play*. Cambridge, MA: MIT Press

Burling, Robbins. 1963. *Rengsanggri: Family and Kinship in a Garo Village*. Philadelphia, PA: University of Pennsylvania Press

Burr, Rachael. 2006. *Vietnam's Children in a Changing World*. New Brunswick, NJ: Rutgers University Press

Burrows, Edwin G. and Shapiro, Melford E. 1957. *An Atoll Culture*. Westport, CT: Greenwood Press

Burton, Frances. 1972. The integration of biology and behavior in the socialization of *Macaca sylvana* of Gibraltar, in *Primate Socialization*. Edited by Frank Poirier, pp. 29–62. New York, NY: Random House

Burton, Linda M. and Graham, Joan E. 1998. Neighborhood rhythms and the social activities of adolescent mothers. *New Directions for Child and Adolescent Development*, 82:7–22

Buss, David M. 1994. *The Evolution of Desire*. New York, NY: Basic Books

Byers, John A. 1998. The biology of human play. *Child Development*, 69(3):599–600

Byrne, Richard. 1995. *The Thinking Ape*. Oxford, UK: Oxford University Press

Caine, Mead. T. 1977. The economic activities of children in a village in Bangladesh. *Population and Development Review*, 13(3):201–227

Caldwell, John C. 1982. *"The Great Transition": Theory of Fertility Decline*. New York, NY: Academic Press

Caldwell, John C. and Caldwell, Bruce K. 2005. Family size control by infanticide in the great agrarian societies of Asia. *Journal of Comparative Family Studies*, 36(2):205–226

Caldwell, John C., Caldwell, Pat, Caldwell, Bruce K., and Pieris, Indrani. 1998. The construction of adolescence in a changing world: Implications for sexuality, reproduction, and marriage. *Studies in Family Planning*, 29(2):137–153

Calvert, Karin. 1992. *Children in the House: The Material Culture of Early Childhood, 1600–1900*. Boston, MA: Northeastern University Press

2003. Patterns of childrearing in America, in *Beyond the Century of the Child: Cultural History and Developmental Psychology*. Edited by Willem Koops and Michael Zucherman, pp. 62–81. Philadelphia, PA: University of Pennsylvania Press

Calvert, Sandra. 2003. The value of play for children's learning in digital spaces. Paper presented at 33rd annual meeting, Jean Piaget Society, Chicago, IL, June

Campbell, Frances A., Ramey, Craig T., Pungello, Elizabeth, Sparling, Joseph, and Miller-Johnson, Shari. 2002. Early childhood education: Young adult outcomes from the Abecedarian Project. *Applied Developmental Science*, 6:42–57

Can, Delice. (ed.) 2003. *Diabetes Atlas*, 2nd edn. Brussels, Belgium: International Diabetes Federation

Canaan, Joyce. 1987. A comparative analysis of American suburban middle class, middle school, and high school teenage cliques, in *Interpretive Ethnography of Education: At Home and Abroad*. Edited by George Spindler and Louise Spindler, pp. 385–406. Hillsdale, NJ: Erlbaum

Cangelosi, James S. 2003. *Classroom Management Strategies: Gaining and Maintaining Students' Cooperation*, 5th edn. New York, NY: Wiley

Cantrell, Eileen M. 1998. Woman the sexual, a question of when: A study of Gebusi adolescence, in *Adolescence in Pacific Island Societies*. Edited by Gilbert H. Herdt and Stephen C. Leavitt, pp. 92–120. Pittsburgh, PA: University of Pittsburgh Press

Caplan, Nathan S., Whitmore, John K., and Choy, Marcella H. 1991. *Children of the Boat People: A Study of Educational Success*. Ann Arbor: The University of Michigan Press

Carey, Celia. 1999. Secrets of the sacrificed. *Discovering Archaeology*, 1(4):48–51

Carlsen, Soren. 1994. Men's utilization of paternity leave and parental leave schemes, in *The Equality Dilemma: Reconciling Working Life and Family Life, Viewed in an Equality Perspective: The Danish Example*. Edited by Soren Carlsen and Jens E. Larsen, pp. 79–90. Copenhagen, Denmark: Munksgaard International

Carrasco, David. 1999. *City of Sacrifice: The Aztec Empire and the Role of Violence in Civilization*. Boston, MA: Beacon Press

Carrier, Achsah H. 1985. Infant care and family relations on Ponam Island, Manus Province, Papua New Guinea, in *Infant Care and Feeding in the South Pacific*. Edited by Leslie B. Marshall, pp. 189–205. New York, NY: Gordon and Breach

Carrier, James G. 1981. Labour migration and labour export on Ponam Island. *Oceania*, 51:237–255

Cartledge, Paul. 2003. *The Spartans*. Woodstock, NY: The Overlook Press

Case, Anne, Paxson, Christina, and Ableidinger, Joseph. 2004. *Orphans in Africa: Parental Death, Poverty and School Enrollment*. Princeton, NJ: Princeton University Center for Health and Wellbeing Research Program in Development Studies

Cassidy, Claire. 1980. Benign neglect and toddler malnutrition, in *Social and Biological Predictors of Nutritional Status, Physical Growth, and Neurological Development*. Edited by Lawrence Greene and Francis Johnston, pp. 109–139. New York, NY: Academic Press

Cassidy, Jane and Ditty, Karen. 2001. Gender differences among newborns on a transient otoacoustic emissions test for hearing. *Journal of Music Therapy*, 37:28–35

Caudill, William. 1988. Tiny dramas: Vocal communication between mother and infant in Japanese and American families. In *Childhood Socialization*. Edited by Gerald Handel, pp. 49–72. New York, NY: Aldine

Caudill, William and Weinstein, Helen. 1969. Maternal care and infant behavior in Japan and America. *Psychiatry*, 32:12–43

Cavalli-Sforza, Luigi L. and Feldman, Marcus W. 1981. *Cultural Transmission and Evolution: A Quantitative Approach*. Princeton, NJ: Princeton University Press

Cazden, Courtney B. 1988. *Classroom Discourse: The Language of Teaching and Learning*. Portsmouth, NH: Heinemann

Centner, Therese. 1963. L'enfant africain et ses jeux. Elisabethville, Congo: CEPSI

Chadha, Gurinder. (dir.) 2002. *Bend it Like Beckham* (film) London, UK: Bend it Films

Chagnon, Napoleon A. 1968/1992. *Yanomamö: The Fierce People*. Fort Worth, TX: Harcourt Brace Jovanovich

1979. Is reproductive success equal in egalitarian societies?, in *Evolutionary Biology and Human Social Behavior: An Anthropological Perspective*. Edited by Napoleon A. Chagnon and William Irons, pp. 374–401. North Scituate, MA: Duxbury

Chang, Heewon. 1992. *Adolescent Life and Ethos: An Ethnography of a US High School*. Washington, DC: The Falmer Press

Charnov, Eric. L. 2001. Evolution of mammal life histories. *Evolutionary Ecology Research*, 3:521–535

Chaudhuri, Nupur. 1991. England, in *Children in Historical and Comparative Perspective*. Edited by Joseph M. Hawes and N. Ray Hiner, pp. 53–70. Westport, CT: Greenwood Press

Chavajay, Pablo. 2006. How Mayan mothers with different amounts of schooling organize a problem-solving discussion with children. *International Journal of Behavioral Development*, 30(4):371–382

Chee, Bernadine W. L. 2000. Eating snacks, biting pressure: Only children in Beijing, in *Feeding China's Little Emperors: Food, Children, and Social Change*. Edited by Jun Jing, pp. 48–70. Stanford, CA: Stanford University Press

Cherry, Robert Allen. 2004. *Wilt: Larger than Life*. Chicago, IL: Triumph Books

Chevalier-Skolnikoff, Suzanne. 1977. A Piagetian model for describing and comparing socialization in monkey, ape, and human infants, in *Primate Bio-Social Development: Biological, Social, and Ecological Determinants*. Edited by Suzanne Chevalier-Skolnikoff and Frank E. Poirier, pp. 159–187. New York, NY: Garland

Chick, Gary. 2001. What is play for?: Sexual selection and the evolution of play, in *Theory in Context and Out*. Edited by Stuart Reifel, pp. 3–26. Westport, CT: Ablex

Chirwa, Yotamu and Bourdillon, Michael. 2000. Small-scale commercial farming: Working children in Nyangadzi Irrigation Scheme, in *Earning a Life: Working Children in Zimbabwe*. Edited by Michael Bourdillon, pp. 127–145. Harare, Zimbabwe: Weaver Press

Chirwa, Yotamu, and Wakatama, Markim. 2000. Working street children in Harare, in *Earning a Life: Working Children in Zimbabwe*. Edited by Michael Bourdillon, pp. 45–58. Harare, Zimbabwe: Weaver Press

Chisholm, John S. 1980. Development and adaptation in infancy. *New Directions for Child Development*, 8:15–30

1983. *Navajo Infancy: An Ethological Study of Child Development.* Hawthorne, NY: Aldine de Gruyter

Cho, Hae-Joang. 1995. Children in the examination war in South Korea: A cultural analysis, in *Children and the Politics of Culture.* Edited by Sharon Stephens, pp. 141–168. Princeton, NJ: Princeton University Press

Chudacoff, Howard P. 2007. *Children at Play: An American History.* New York, NY: New York University Press

Ciaccio, Nicholas V. and el Shakry, Omnia Sayed. 1993. Egypt, in *International Handbook on Gender Roles.* Edited by Leonore Loeb Adler, pp. 46–58. Westport, CT: Greenwood Press

Clark, Eric. 2007. *The Real Toy Story: Inside the Ruthless Battle for America's Youngest Consumers.* New York, NY: Free Press

Clark, Gracia. 1995. *Onions Are My Husband: Survival and Accumulation by West African Market Women.* Chicago, IL: University of Chicago Press

Clark, Sam, Colson, Elizabeth, Lee, J., and Scudder, Thayer. 1995. Ten thousand Tonga: A longitudinal anthropological study from southern Zambia, 1956–1991. *Population Studies,* 49: 91–109

Clinton, Hillary Rodham. 1996. *It Takes a Village.* New York, NY: Simon and Schuster

Clower, Robert W., George, Dalton, Harwitz, Mitchell, Walters, A. A., Armstrong, Robert P., Cole, Johnetta, Cole, Robert E., and Lamson, George. 1966. *Growth without Development: An Economic Survey of Liberia.* Evanston, WY: Northwestern University Press

Cobo, Father Bernabe. 1653/1990. *Inca Religion and Customs.* Translated and edited by Roland. Hamilton Austin, TX: University of Texas Press

Coe, Cati. 2005. *Dilemmas of Culture in African Schools: Youth, Nationalism, and the Transformation of Knowledge.* Chicago, IL: The University of Chicago Press

Cole, Mike, Gay, John. A., Glick, Joe, Sharp, Don W., Ciborowski, Tom, Frankel, Fred, Kellemu, John, and Lancy, David F. 1971. *The Cultural Context of Learning and Thinking.* New York, NY: Basic Books

Coleman, James S. 1966. *Equality of Educational Opportunity.* Washington, DC: US Department of Health, Education and Welfare

   1976. Learning through games, in *Play: Its Role in Development and Evolution.* Edited by Jerome S. Bruner, Alison Jolly, and Kathy Sylva, pp. 460–463. New York, NY: Basic Books

Coleman, James S., Kelly, Sara D., and Moore, John A. 1975. Recent trends in school integration. Paper presented at annual meeting, American Educational Research Association, Washington, DC, April 2

Coleman, Simon. 1999. God's children: Physical and spiritual growth among evangelical Christians, in *Children in New Religions.* Edited by Susan J. Palmer and Charlotte E. Hardman, pp. 71–87. New Brunswick, NJ: Rutgers University Press

Colón, Angel R., with Colón, Patricia A. 2001. *A History of Children: A Socio-cultural Survey across Millennia.* Westport, CT: Greenwood Press

Conchas, Gilberto Q. 2006. *The Color of Success: Race and High-Achieving Urban Youth.* New York, NY: Teachers College Press

Conde-Agudelo, Agustin, Rosas-Bermudez, Anyeli, and Kafury-Goeta, Ana Cecilia. 2006. Birth spacing and risk of adverse perinatal outcomes. *Journal of the American Medical Association,* 295(15):1809–1823

Condon, Richard G. 1987. *Inuit Youth: Growth and Change in the Canadian Arctic.* New Brunswick, NJ: Rutgers University Press

Conklin, Beth A. 2001. Women's blood, warrior's blood and the conquest of vitality in Amazonia, in *Gender in Amazonia and Melanesia: An Exploration of the Comparative Method.* Edited by Thomas A. Gregor and Donald Tuzin, pp. 141–172. Berkeley, CA: University of California Press

Conkling, Winnifred. 2001. *Smart-Wiring Your Baby's Brain.* New York, NY: Harper-Collins

Coontz, Stephanie. 1992/2000. *The Way We Never Were: American Families and the Nostalgia Trap.* New York, NY: Basic Books

Cornwall, Andrea. 2001. Looking for a child: Coping with infertility in Ado-Odo, south-western Nigeria, in *Managing Reproductive Life: Cross-Cultural Themes in Sexuality and Fertility.* Edited by Soraya Tremayne, pp. 140–156. Oxford, UK: Berghahn Books

Correa-Chavez, Maricela and Rogoff, Barbara. 2005. Cultural research has transformed our ideas of cognitive development. *International Society for the Study of Behavioral Development Newsletter,* 47(1):7–10

Corsaro, William A. 1996. Transitions in early childhood: The promise of comparative, longitudinal ethnography, in *Ethnography and Human Development: Context and Meaning in Social Inquiry.* Edited by Richard Jessor, Anne Colby, and Richard A. Sweder, pp. 419–457. Chicago, IL: University of Chicago Press

Cosminsky, Sheila. 1985. Infant feeding practices in rural Kenya, in *Breastfeeding, Child Health and Birth Spacing: Cross-Cultural Perspectives.* Edited by Valeria Hull and Mayling Simpson, pp. 35–54. London, UK: Croom Helm

    1994. Childbirth and change: A Guatemalan study, in *Ethnography of Fertility and Birth.* Edited by Carol P. MacCormack, pp. 195–219. Prospect Heights, IL: Waveland Press

Counts, Dorothy A. 1985. Infant care and feeding in Kaliai, West New Britain, Papua New Guinea, in *Infant Care and Feeding in the South Pacific.* Edited by Leslie B. Marshall, pp. 155–169. New York, NY: Gordon and Breach

Covarrubias, Miguel. 1937. *Island of Bali.* New York, NY: Alfred A. Knopf

Cox, Caroline. 2007. Boy soldiers: Lessons from the American Revolution. *Society for the History of Children and Youth Newsletter,* 9(Winter):20–21

Coy, Michael W. 1989. Being what we pretend to be: The usefulness of apprenticeship as a field method, in *Apprenticeship: From Theory to Method and Back Again.* Edited by Michael W. Coy, pp. 115–135. Albany, NY: State University of New York Press

Craig, Lyn. 2006. Does father care mean father share?: A comparison of how mothers and fathers in intact families spend time with children. *Gender and Society,* 20(2):259–281

Crain, William. 2004. *Reclaiming Childhood: Letting Children Be Children in Our Achievement-Oriented Society.* New York, NY: Owl Books

Crandell, Susan. 2005. Oh, Baby. *AARP Magazine,* 48(5A):98–107

Creed, Gerald W. 1984. Sexual subordination: Institutionalized homosexuality and social control in Melanesia. *Ethnology,* 23(3):157–176

Crocker, William and Crocker, Jean. 1994. *The Canela: Bonding through Kinship, Ritual and Sex.* New York, NY: Harcourt, Brace

Crognier, Emile, Baali, A, and Hilali, Mohamed Kamal. 2001. Do "helpers-at-the-nest" increase their parents' reproductive success? *American Journal of Human Biology*, 13:365–373

Cronk, Lee. 1993. Parental favoritism toward daughters. *American Scientist*, 81(3):272–280

2000. Female-biased parental investment and growth performance among the Mukogodo, in *Adaptation and Human Behavior: An Anthropological Perspective*. Edited by Lee Cronk, Napoleon Chagnon, and William Irons, pp. 203–221 New York: Aldine

Cross, Gary. 2004. *The Cute and the Cool: Wondrous Innocence and Modern American Children's Culture*. New York, NY: Oxford University Press

Cross, Mary. 1995. *Morocco: Sahara to the Sea*. New York, NY: Abbeville Press

Crown, Patricia L. 2002. Learning and teaching in the Prehispanic American Southwest, in *Children in the Prehistoric Puebloan Southwest*. Edited by Katheryn A. Kamp, pp. 108–124. Salt Lake City, UT: The University of Utah Press

Culwick, Arthur T. 1935. *Ubena of the Rivers*. London, UK: George Allen and Unwin

Cusick, Phillip A. 1973. *Inside High School: The Student's World*. New York, NY: Holt, Rinehart and Winston

Dahlberg, Gunilla. 1992. The parent–child relationship and socialization in the context of modern childhood: The case of Sweden, in *Parent–Child Socialization in Diverse Cultures*. Edited by Jaipaul L. Roopnarine and D. Bruce Carter, pp. 121–137. Norwood, NJ: Ablex.

Daly, Martin and Wilson, Margo. 1984. A sociobiological analysis of human infanticide, in *Infanticide: Comparative and Evolutionary Perspectives*. Edited by Glenn Hausfater and Sarah Blaffer Hrdy, pp. 487–502. New York, NY: Aldine

1988. *Homicide*. New York, NY: Aldine

Danielsson, Bengt. 1952. *The Happy Island*. London, UK: George Allen and Unwin

Dardess, John. 1991. Childhood in premodern China, in *Children in Historical and Comparative Perspective*. Edited by Joseph M. Hawes and N. Ray Hiner, pp. 71–94. Westport, CT: Greenwood Press

Das Gupta, Monika. 1987. Selective discrimination against female children in rural Punjab, India. *Population and Development Review*, 13:77–100

Dasen, Pierre R., Inhelder, Barbel, Lavalée, M., and Retschitzki, Jean. 1978. *Naissance de l'intelligence chez infant Baoulè de Côte d'Ivoire*. Bern, Switzerland: Hans Huber

Davenport, R. and Rogers, C. M. 1970. Differential rearing of the chimpanzee. *The Chimpanzee*, 3:337–360

Davis, John. 1992. The anthropology of suffering. *Journal of Refugee Studies*, 5(2):149–161

Davis, Susan Schaefer and Davis, Douglas A. 1989. *Adolescence in a Moroccan Town: Making Social Sense*. New Brunswick, NJ: Rutgers University Press

Dawkins, Richard. 1989. *The Selfish Gene*. New York, NY: Oxford University Press

Day, Lynda R. 1998. Rites and reason: Precolonial education and its relevance to the current production and transmission of knowledge, in *Women and Education in Sub-Saharan Africa: Power, Opportunities, and Constraints*. Edited by Marianne Bloch, Josephine A. Beoku-Betts, and B. Robert Tabachnick, pp. 49–72. Boulder, CO: Lynne Rienner

de Berry, Joanna. 2004. The sexual vulnerability of adolescent girls during civil war in Teso, Uganda, in *Children and Youth on the Front Line: Ethnography, Armed Conflict, and Displacement*. Edited by Jo Boyden and Joanna de Berry, pp. 45–62. New York, NY: Berghahn Books

de Boeck, Filip. 2005. The divine seed: Children, gift, and witchcraft in the Democratic Republic of Congo, in *Makers and Breakers: Children and Youth in Post Colonial Africa*. Edited by Alcinda Honwana and Filip de Boeck, pp. 188–214. Trenton, NJ: Africa World Press

de Laguna, Frederica. 1972. *Under Mount Saint Elias: The History and Culture of the Yakutat Tlingit*. Washington, DC: Smithsonian Institution Press

de Lange, Albertine. 2005. Child trafficking for agricultural labour exploitation in Burkina Faso. Paper presented at conference on Children and Youth in Emerging and Transforming Societies, Oslo, Norway, June

de Leon, Lourdes. 2000. The emergent participant: Interactive patterns in the socialization of Tzotzil (Mayan) infants. *Journal of Linguistic Anthropology*, 8(2):131–161

de Marrais, Katherine B., Nelson, Patricia A., and Baker, Jill H. 1992. Meaning in mud: Yup'ik Eskimo girls at play. *Anthropology and Education Quarterly*, 23(2):120–145

de Meyer, Tim. 2001. The problem of child labour in Africa. Paper presented at OAU/UNICEF Pan-African Forum on the Future of Children, Cairo, Egypt, May 28

de Suremain, Charles-Édouard. 2000. Coffee beans and the seeds of labour: Child labour on Guatemalan plantations, in *The Exploited Child*. Edited by Bernard Schlemmer, pp. 231–238. New York, NY: Zed Books

deVries, Marten W. 1987a. Alternatives to mother–infant attachment in the neonatal period, in *The Role of Culture in Developmental Disorder*. Edited by Charles M. Super, pp. 109–130. New York, NY: Academic Press

1987b. Cry babies, culture, and catastrophe: Infant temperament among the Masai, in *Child Survival: Anthropological Perspectives on the Treatment and Maltreatment of Children*. Edited by Nancy Scheper-Hughes, pp. 165–185. Dordrecht, Netherlands: D. Reidel

de Waal, Frans. 2001. *The Ape and the Sushi Master*. New York, NY: Basic Books

Dee, Thomas S. and Jacob, Brian. 2006. Do high school exit exams influence educational attainment or labor market performance? *NBER Working Paper* No. W12199. Washington, DC: National Bureau of Economic Research

Deka, Nalini. 1993. India, in *International Handbook on Gender Roles*. Edited by Leonore Loeb Adler, pp. 122–143. Westport, CT: Greenwood Press

Delaney, Cassandra Halle. 1995. Rites of passage in adolescence. *Adolescence*, 30(120):891–898

Delgado-Gaitan, Concha. 1994a. Russian refugee families: Accommodating aspiration through education. *Anthropology and Education Quarterly*, 25(2):137–155

1994b. Socializing young children in Mexican-American families: An intergenerational perspective, in *Cross-cultural Roots of Minority Child Development*. Edited by Patricia Marks Greenfield and Rodney R. Cocking, pp. 55–86. Hillsdale, NJ: Erlbaum

deMause, Lloyd. 1974. The evolution of childhood, in *The History of Childhood*. Edited by Lloyd deMause, pp. 1–73. New York, NY: Harper and Row

Demerath, Peter. 1999. The cultural production of educational utility in Pere Village: Papua New Guinea. *Comparative Education Review*, 43(2):162–192

Demmert, William G., Jr. and Towner, John C. 2003. *A Review of the Research Literature on the Influence of Culturally Based Education on the Academic Performance of Native American Students*. Portland, OR: Northwest Regional Lab

Demuth, Katherine. 1986. Prompting routines in the language socialization of Basotho children, in *Language Socialization across Cultures*. Edited by Bambi B. Schiefflin and Elinor Ochs, pp. 51–79. New York, NY: Cambridge University Press

Deng, Francis M. 1972. *The Dinka of the Sudan*. Prospect Heights, IL: Waveland Press

Dentan, Robert Knox. 1978. Notes on childhood in a nonviolent context: The Semai case, in *Learning Non-Aggression: The Experience of Non-Literate Societies*. Edited by Ashley Montague, pp. 94–143. New York, NY: Oxford University Press

Dettwyler, Katherine A. 1994. *Dancing Skeletons: Life and Death in West Africa*. Prospect Heights, IL: Waveland Press

Devereux, Edward C. 1976. Backyard versus Little League baseball: The impoverishment of children's games, in *Social Problems in Athletics*. Edited by Daniel M. Landers, pp. 37–58. Urbana, IL: University of Illinois Press

Devine, John. 1996. *Maximum Security: The Culture of Violence in Inner-City Schools*. Chicago, IL: University of Chicago Press

Deyhle, Donna. 1986. Break dancing and breaking out: Anglos, Utes and Navajos in a border reservation high school. *Anthropology and Education Quarterly*, 17(2):111–127

1991. Empowerment and cultural conflict: Navajo parents and the schooling of their children. *Qualitative Studies in Education*, 4:277–297

1992. Constructing failure and maintaining cultural identity: Navajo and Ute school leavers. *Journal of American Indian Education*, 31:24–47

Diamond, Jared. 1992. *The Third Chimpanzee: The Evolution and Future of the Human Animal*. New York, NY: HarperCollins

1997. *Guns, Germs and Steel*. New York, NY: W. W. Norton

Dickeman, Mildred. 1975. Demographic consequences of infanticide in man. *Annual Review of Ecology and Systematics*, 6:107–137

1979. Female infanticide, reproductive strategies, and social stratification: A preliminary model, in *Evolutionary Biology and Human Social Behavior: An Anthropological Perspective*. Edited by Napoleon A. Chagnon and William G. Irons, pp. 321–367. North Scituate, MA: Duxbury Press

Dickens, Charles. 1836/1964. *The Pickwick Papers*. New York, NY: New American Library.

Dickinson, David K. and Smith, Miriam W. 1994. Long-term effects of preschool teachers' book readings on low-income children's vocabulary and story comprehension. *Reading Research Quarterly*, 29(2):104–122

Dilley, Roy M. 1989. Secrets and skills: Apprenticeship among Tukolor weavers, in *Apprenticeship: From Theory to Method and Back Again*. Edited by Michael W. Coy, pp. 181–198. Albany, NY: State University of New York Press

Divale, William T. and Harris, Marvin. 1976. Population, warfare, and the male supremacist complex. *American Anthropologist*, 78:521–538

Donohue, John J. 1994. *Warrior Dreams: The Martial Arts and the American Imagination*. Westport, CT: Bergin and Garvey

Douyon, Chavannes, Philippe, Jeanne, and Frazier, Cynthia. 1993. Haiti, in *International Handbook on Gender Roles*. Edited by Leonore Loeb Adler, pp. 98–107. Westport, CT: Greenwood Press

Draper, Patricia. 1976. Social and economic constraints on child life among the !Kung, in *Kalahari Hunter-Gatherers: Studies of the !Kung San and their Neighbors*. Edited by Richard B. Lee and Irven DeVore, pp. 199–217. Cambridge, MA: Harvard University Press

  1978. The learning environment for aggression and anti-social behavior among the !Kung, in *Learning Non-Aggression: The Experience of Non-Literate Societies*. Edited by Ashley Montague, pp. 31–53. Oxford, UK: Oxford University Press

  1989. African marriage systems: perspective from evolutionary ecology. *Ethology and Sociobiology*, 10:145–169

Draper, Patricia and Cashdan, Elinor. 1988. Technological change and child behavior among the !Kung. *Ethnology*, 27:339–365

Draper, Patricia and Harpending, Henry. 1982. Father absence and reproductive strategy: An evolutionary perspective. *Journal of Anthropological Research*, 38:255–273

Droz, Yvan. 2006. Street children and the work ethic: New policy for an old moral, Nairobi (Kenya). *Childhood*, 13(3):349–363

Dube, Leela. 1981. The economic roles of children in India: Methodological issues, in *Child Work, Poverty, and Underdevelopment*. Edited by Gerry Rodgers and Guy Standing, pp. 179–213. Geneva, Switzerland: International Labour Office

  2000. Child domestic work, in *Earning a Life: Working Children in Zimbabwe*. Edited by Michael Bourdillon, pp. 95–107. Harare, Zimbabwe: Weaver Press

DuBois, Cora. 1944. *The People of Alor: A Social-Psychological Study of an East Indian Island*. Minneapolis, MN: University of Minnesota Press

Duffett, Ann and Johnson, Jean. 2004. *All Work and No Play: Listening to What KIDS and PARENTS Really Want from Out-of-School Time*. Washington, DC: Public Agenda

Dugatkin, Lee A. and Bekoff, Marc. 2003. Play and the evolution of fairness: A game theory model. *Behavioural Processes*, 60:209–214

Dunbar, Robin I. M. 1999. *Grooming, Gossip, and the Evolution of Language*. London, UK: Faber and Faber

Dunn, Patrick. 1974. "That enemy is the baby": childhood in imperial Russia, in *The History of Childhood*. Edited by Lloyd deMause, pp. 383–405. New York, NY: Harper and Row

Dupeyron, François and Schmitt, Eric-Emmanuel (dirs.). 2003. *Monsieur Ibrahim* (film). Los Angeles, CA: Sony Pictures

Dupire, M. 1963. The position of women in pastoral society (the Fulani WoDaaBee, nomads of the Niger), in *Women of Tropical Africa*. Edited by Denise Paulme, pp. 47–92. Berkeley, CA: University of California Press

Duru-Bellat, Marie and van Zaten, Agnes. 2000. The impact of family socialization processes and educational strategies on the adaptation and academic success of students, in *Problems and Prospects in European Education*. Edited by Elizabeth Sherman Swing, Jurgen Schriewer, and François Orvil, pp. 143–165. Westport, CT: Praeger

Dutcher, Richard 2000. *God's Army* (Film). Provo, UT: Zion Films

Dybdhal, Ragnhild and Hundeide, Karsten. 1998. Childhood in the Somali context: Mothers' and children's ideas about childhood and parenthood. *Psychology and Developing Societies*, 10(2):131–145

Dyhouse, Carol. 1978. Working-class mothers and infant mortality in England, 1895–1914. *Journal of Social History*, 12(2):248–267

Eberstadt, Mary. 2004. *Home Alone America: The Hidden Toll of Daycare, Behavioral Drugs, and Other Parent Substitutes*. New York, NY: Penguin

Eco, Umberto. 2000. *Baudolino*. Translated by Warren Weaver. New York, NY: Harcourt

Edgerton, Robert B. 1988. *Like Lions They Fought: The Zulu War and the Last Black Empire in South Africa*. New York, NY: Collier-Macmillan
    1992. *Sick Societies: Challenging the Myth of Primitive Harmony*. New York, NY: The Free Press

Edwards, Carolyn Pope. 2005. Children's play in cross-cultural perspective: A new look at the Six Culture Study, in *Play: An Interdisciplinary Synthesis*. Edited by Felicia F. McMahon, Donald E. Lytle, and Brian Sutton Smith, pp. 81–96. Lanham, MD: University Press of America

Edwards, Caroline Pope and Whiting, Beatrice B. 1980. Differential socialization of girls and boys in light of cross-cultural research. *New Directions for Child Development*, 8:45–57

Eggan, Dorothy. 1956. Instruction and affect in Hopi cultural continuity. *Southwestern Journal of Anthropology*, 12(4):347–370

Eibl-Eibesfeldt, Irenäus. 1983. Patterns of parent–child interaction in a cross-cultural perspective, in *The Behavior of Human Infants*. Edited by Alberto Oliverio, pp. 177–217. New York, NY: Plenum Press
    1989. *Human Ethology*. New York: Aldine de Gruyter

Eifermann, Rivka. 1971. Social play in childhood, in *Child's Play*. Edited by Robert E. Herron and Brian Sutton-Smith, pp. 270–297. New York, NY: J. Wiley

Einarsdottir, Jonina. 2004. *Tired of Weeping: Mother Love, Child Death, and Poverty in Guinea-Bissau*. Madison, WI: University of Wisconsin Press

Eisman, Fred B. 1989. *Bali: Sekala and Niskala*. Berkeley, CA: Periplus Edition

Elder, Glen. 1969. Appearance and education in marriage mobility. *American Sociological Review*, 34:519–533

Elkind, David. 2001. *The Hurried Child: Growing Up Too Fast Too Soon*. 3rd edn. New York, NY: Perseus Books

Elmendorf, Mary L. 1976. *Nine Mayan Women: A Village Faces Change*. Cambridge, MA: Schenkman

Elster, Arthur B. and Lamb, Michael E. 1986. Adolescent fathers: The under-studied side of adolescent pregnancy, in *School-Age Pregnancy and Parenthood: Biosocial Dimensions*. Edited by Jane B. Lancaster and Beatrix A. Hamburg, pp. 177–190. New York, NY: Aldine de Gruyter

Elwin, Verrier. 1947. *The Muria and their Ghotul*. Calcutta: Oxford University Press

Ember, Carol R. 1973. Feminine task assignment and the social behavior of boys. *Ethos*, 1(4):424–439
    1983. The relative decline of women's contribution to agriculture with intensification. *American Anthropologist*, 85:285–304

Ember, Carol R. and Ember, Melvin. 1994. War, socialization, and interpersonal violence: A cross-cultural study. *Journal of Conflict Resolution*, 38:620–646

2005. Explaining corporal punishment of children: A cross-cultural study. *American Anthropologist*, 107:609–619

2007. Effects of war and peace socialization: Comparing evolutionary models. Paper presented at annual meeting, Society for Cross-Cultural Research, San Antonio, TX, February 21–24

Endicott, Karen Lampell. 1992. Fathering in an egalitarian society, in *Father–Child Relations: Cultural and Biosocial Contexts*. Edited by Barry S. Hewlett, pp. 291–295. New York, NY: Aldine

Erchak, Gerald M. 1977. *Full Respect: Kpelle Children in Adaptation*. New Haven, CT: Hraflex Books

1980. The acquisition of cultural rules by Kpelle children. *Ethos*, 8:40–44

1992. *The Anthropology of Self and Behavior*. New Brunswick, NJ: Rutgers University Press

Esadze, Londa. 2005. Trafficking in children: A case study of Georgia. Paper presented at conference on Children and Youth in Emerging and Transforming Societies, Oslo, Norway, June

Evans, Ruth M. C. 2004. Tanzanian childhoods: Street children's narratives of "home." *Journal of Contemporary African Studies*, 22(1):69–92

Eveleth, Phyllis B. and Tanner, James M. 1990. *Worldwide Variation in Human Growth*. Cambridge, UK: Cambridge University Press

Eyben, Emiel. 1991. Fathers and sons, in *Marriage, Divorce, and Children in Ancient Rome*. Edited by Beryl Rawson, pp. 114–143. Canberra: Clarendon Press

Fabian, Stephen M. 1990. *Space-time of the Bororo of Brazil*. Gainesville, FL: University Press of Florida

Faerman, Marina, Bar-Gal, Gila Kahila, Filon, Dvora, Greenblatt, Charles L., Stager, Lawrence, Oppenheim, Ariella, and Smith, Patricia. 1998. Determining the sex of infanticide victims from the late Roman era through ancient DNA analysis. *Journal of Archeological Science*, 25:861–865

Fagen, Robert. 1981. *Animal Play Behavior*. New York, NY: Oxford University Press

Fairbanks, Lynn A. 1990. Reciprocal benefits of allomothering for female vervet monkeys. *Animal Behaviour*, 40:553–562

1995. Developmental timing of primate play, in *Biology, Brains, and Behavior: The Evolution of Human Development*. Edited by Sue Taylor Parker, Jonas Langer, and Michael L. McKinney, Pp 131–158. Santa Fe, NM: School of American Research Press

Falgout, Suzanne. 1992. Hierarchy vs. democracy: Two management strategies for the management of knowledge in Pohnpei. *Anthropology and Education Quarterly*, 23(1):30–43

Farver, Jo Ann M. 1993. Cultural differences in scaffolding pretend play: A comparison of American and Mexican mother–child and sibling–child pairs, in *Parent–Child Play: Descriptions and Implications*. Edited by Kevin MacDonald, pp. 349–366. Albany, NY: State University of New York Press

Farver, Jo Ann M. and Howes, C. 1993. Cultural differences in American and Mexican mother–child pretend play. *Merrill-Palmer Quarterly*, 39:344–358

Fass, Paula. 1997. *Kidnapped: Child Abduction in America.* New York: Oxford University Press.

Father Bernabe. 1653/1990. *Inca Religion and Customs.* Translated and edited by Roland Hamilton: Austin, TX: University of Texas Press

Fedigan, Linda M. and Zohar, Sandra. 1997. Sex differences in mortality of Japanese macaques: Twenty-one years of data from Arashiyama West population. *American Journal of Physical Anthropology*, 102(2):161–175

Fermé, Mariane C. 2001. *The Underneath of Things: Violence, History, and the Everyday in Sierra Leone.* Berkeley, CA: University of California Press

Fernald, Anne. 1992. Human maternal vocalizations to infants as biologically relevant signals: An evolutionary perspective, in *The Adapted Mind: Evolutionary Psychology and the Generation of Culture.* Edited by Jerome H. Barkow, Leda Cosmides, and John Tooby, pp. 391–428. New York, NY: Oxford University Press

Fernea, Elizabeth. 1991. Muslim Middle East, in *Children in Historical and Comparative Perspective.* Edited by Joseph M. Hawes and N. Ray Hiner, pp. 447–470. Westport, CT: Greenwood Press

Field, Margaret Joyce. 1970. *Search for Security: An Ethno-Psychiatric Study of Rural Ghana.* New York, NY: W. W. Norton

Field, Tiffany M., Shostak, A. Marjorie, Vietze, P., and Leiderman, Phillip H. 1981. *Culture and Early Interactions.* Hillsdale, NJ: Lawrence Erlbaum Associates

Field, Tiffany M., Widmayer, Susan M., Adler, Sherilyn, and de Cubas, Mercedes. 1992. Mother–infant interactions of Haitian immigrants and Black Americans living in Miami, in *Parent–Child Socialization in Diverse Cultures.* Edited by Jaipaul L. Roopnarine and D. Bruce Carter, pp. 173–184. Norwood, NJ: Ablex

Fine, Gary Alan. 1987. *With the Boys: Little League Baseball and Preadolescent Culture.* Chicago, IL: University of Chicago Press

2001. *Gifted Tongues: High School Debate and Adolescent Culture.* Princeton, NJ: Princeton University Press

2002. *Shared Fantasy: Role-Playing Games as Social World.* Chicago, IL: University of Chicago Press

Finkelstein, Marni. 2005. *With No Direction Home: Homeless Youth on the Road and in the Streets.* Belmont, CA: Thompson Wadsworth

Finnan, Christine Robinson. 1987. The influence of the ethnic community on the adjustment of Vietnamese refugees, in *Interpretive Ethnography of Education: At Home and Abroad.* Edited by George Spindler and Louise Spindler, pp. 313–330. Hillsdale, NJ: Lawrence Erlbaum

Firestone, Shulamith. 1971. *The Dialectic of Sex: The Case for Feminist Revolution.* London, UK: Jonathan Cape

Firth, Raymond. 1970. Education in Tikopia, in *From Child to Adult.* Edited by John Middleton, pp. 75–90. Garden City, NY: Natural History Press

Fisher, Ann. 1963. Reproduction in Truk. *Ethnology*, 2(4):526–540

Fisher, Edward P. 1992. The impact of play on development: A meta-analysis. *Play and Culture*, 5(2):159–181

Fiske, Alan Page. 1997. Learning a culture the way informants do: Observing, imitating, and participating. Unpublished MS, February 27

Fitchen, Janet M. 1981. *Poverty in Rural America: A Case Study.* Boulder, CO: Westview Press

Flinn, Juliana. 1992. Transmitting traditional values in new schools: Elementary education of Pulap Atoll. *Anthropology and Education Quarterly*, 23(1):44–58

Flinn, Mark V. 1988. Parent–offspring interactions in a Caribbean village: Daughter guarding, in *Human Reproductive Behavior: A Darwinian Perspective*. Edited by Laura Betzig, Monique Borgerhoff Mulder, and Paul Turke, pp. 189–200. Cambridge, MA: Cambridge University Press

  1989. Household composition and female reproductive strategies, in *The Sociobiology of Sexual and Reproductive Strategies*. Edited by Anne E. Rasa, Christian Vogel, and Eckart Voland, pp. 206–233. London, UK: Chapman and Hall

Flinn, Mark V. and England, Barry G. 1995. Childhood stress and family environment. *Current Anthropology*, 36(5):854–866

Flinn, Mark V., Geary, David C., and Ward, Carol V. 2005. Ecological dominance, social competition, and coalitionary arms races: Why humans evolved extraordinary intelligence. *Evolution and Human Behavior*, 26:10–46

Flores-Gonzalez, Nilda. 2005. Popularity versus respect: School structure, peer groups and Latino academic achievement. *International Journal of Qualitative Studies in Education*, 18(5):625–642

Fodor, Eva. 2003. *Working Difference: Women's Working Lives in Hungary and Austria, 1945–1995*. Durham, NC: Duke University Press

Fogel, Allen, Barratt, Marguerite Stevenson, and Messinger, Daniel. 1992. A comparison of the parent–child relationship in Japan and the United States, in *Parent–Child Socialization in Diverse Cultures*. Edited by Jaipaul L. Roopnarine and D. Bruce Carter, pp. 35–51. Norwood, NJ: Ablex

Fogiel-Bijaoui, Sylvie. 2005. Familism, postmodernity, and the state: The case of Israel, in *Families in Global Perspective*. Edited by Jaipaul L. Roopnarine, pp. 184–204. Boston, MA: Pearson

Ford, Clellan S. 1964. *A Comparative Study of Human Reproduction*. New Haven, CT: Yale University Publications in Anthropology, Human Relations Area Files Press

Fordham, Signithia. 1999. "Dissin' the standard": Ebonics as guerilla warfare at Capital High. *Anthropology and Education Quarterly*, 30(3):272–293

Fordham, Signithia and Ogbu, John U. 1986. Black students' school success: Coping with the burden of "Acting White." *The Urban Review*, 18(3):176–206

Formanek-Brunell, Miriam. 1992. Sugar and spite: The politics of doll play in nineteenth-century America, in *Small Worlds: Children and Adolescents in America, 1850–1950*. Edited by Elliott West and Paula Petrik, pp. 107–124. Lawrence, KS: University Press of Kansas

Fortes, Meyer. 1938. *Social and Psychological Aspects of Education in Taleland*. Oxford, UK: Oxford University Press

  1950. Kinship and marriage among the Ashanti, in *African Systems of Kinship and Marriage*. Edited by A. R. Radcliffe-Brown and Daryll Forde, pp. 252–284. London, UK: Oxford University Press

  1970. Social and psychological aspects of education in Taleland, in *From Child to Adult*. Edited by John Middleton, pp. 14–74. Garden City, NY: Natural History Press

Fosburg, Steven. 1982. Family day care: The role of surrogate mother, in *Families as Learning Environments for Children*. Edited by Luis M. Laosa and Irving E. Sigel, pp. 223–260. New York, NY: Plenum Press

Fouts, Hillary N. 2004a. Social contexts of weaning: The importance of cross-cultural studies, in *Childhood and Adolescence: Cross-Cultural Perspectives and Applications*. Edited by Uwe P. Gielen and Jaipaul L. Roopnarine, pp. 133–148. Westport, CT: Praeger

2004b. Social and emotional contexts of weaning among Bofi farmers and foragers. *Ethnology*, 43:65–81

2005. Families in Central Africa: A comparison of Bofi farmer and forager families, in *Families in Global Perspective*. Edited by Jaipaul L. Roopnarine, pp. 347–363. Boston, MA: Pearson

2007. Aka and Bofi forager father involvement with young children: Is there a forager fathering style? Paper presented at annual meeting, Society for Cross-Cultural Research, San Antonio, February 21–24

Fouts, Hillary N., Hewlett, Barry S., and Lamb, Michael E. 2001. Weaning and the nature of early childhood interactions among Bofi foragers in Central Africa. *Human Nature*, 12(1):27–46

Fox, Cybelle, Harding, David J., Mehta, Jai, Roth, Wendy, and Newman, Katherine S. (eds.). 2005. *Rampage: The Social Roots of School Shootings*. New York, NY: Basic Books

Fox, Robin. 1972. Alliance and constraint: Sexual selection in the evolution of human kinship systems, in *Sexual Selection and the Descent of Man*. Edited by Bernard Campbell, pp. 283–331. Chicago, IL: Aldine

Franklin, Barry M. 1998. Low-achieving children and teacher heroism: A genealogical examination, in *When Children Don't Learn: Student Failure and the Culture of Teaching*. Edited by Barry M. Franklin, pp. 28–51. New York, NY: Teachers College Press

Frayne, Douglas R. 1999. Scribal education in ancient Babylonia. Lecture given at Ontario Institute for Studies in Education, Toronto, October

Freed, Ruth S. and Freed, Stanley. A. 1981. Enculturation and education in Shanti Nagar. *Anthropological Papers of the American Museum of Natural History*, 57(2):149–154

Freedman, Daniel G. 1974. *Human Infancy: An Evolutionary Perspective*. New York, NY: John Wiley

2003. Ethnic differences in babies, in *The Manner Born: Birth Rites in Cross-Cultural Perspective*. Edited by Lauren Dundes, pp. 221–232. New York, NY: AltaMira Press

Freely, John. 1996. *Istanbul: The Imperial City*. London, UK: Penguin

Freeman, Charles. 2004. *The Closing of the Western Mind*. New York, NY: Alfred A. Knopf

Freeman, Derek. 1983. *Margaret Mead and Samoa: The Making and Unmaking of an Anthropological Myth*. Cambridge, MA: Harvard University Press

Freie, Carrie. 1999. Rules in children's games and play, in *Play Contexts Revisited*. Edited by Stuart Reifel, pp. 83–100. Stamford, CT: Ablex

French, Valerie. 1991. Children in antiquity, in *Children in Historical and Comparative Perspective*. Edited by Joseph M. Hawes and N. Ray Hiner, pp. 13–29. Westport, CT: Greenwood Press

Fricke, Tom. 1994. *Himalayan Households: Tamang Demography and Domestic Process*. New York, NY: Columbia University Press

Friedl, Ernestine. 1992. Moonrose watched through a sunny day. *Natural History*, 101(8):34–44

Fry, Douglas P. 1987. Differences between playfighting and serious fights among Zapotec children. *Ethology and Sociobiology*, 8:285–306

2005. Rough-and-tumble social play in humans, in *The Nature of Play: Great Apes and Humans*. Edited by Anthony D. Pellegrini and Peter K. Smith, pp. 54–85. New York: Guilford Press

Fujioka, Takako, Ross, Bernhard, Kakigi, Ryusuke, Pantev, Christo, and Trainor, Laurel J. 2006. One year of musical training affects development of auditory cortical-evoked fields in young children. *Brain*, 129(10):2593–2608

Fung, Heidi. 1999. Becoming a moral child: The socialization of shame among young Chinese children. *Ethos*, 27(2):180–209

Gail, A. 1988. Fertility, infant feeding, and change in Yucatan, in *Parental Behavior in Diverse Societies*. Edited by Robert A. LeVine, Patrice M. Miller, and Mary M. West. *New Directions for Child Development*, 40:37–50

Gallimore, Ronald, Howard, Alan, and Jordan, Cathie. 1969. Independence training among Hawaiians: A cross cultural study, in *Contemporary Research in Social Psychology*. Edited by Henry Clay Lindgren, pp. 392–397. New York, NY: John Wiley

Gamlin, Jennie. 2005. The normality of child labour on a coffee plantation in Mexico. Presented at conference on Children and Youth in Emerging and Transforming Societies, Oslo, Norway, June

Gardner, Robert and Heider, Karl G. 1969. *Gardens of War: Life and Death in the New Guinea Stone Age*. New York, NY: Random House

Gaskins, Suzanne. 2003. All in a day's work. Paper presented at symposium on the Cultural Construction of Play, Jean Piaget Society Annual Meeting, Chicago, IL, June 5

2006. Cultural perspectives on infant–caregiver interaction, in *The Roots of Human Sociality: Culture, Cognition, and Human Interaction*. Edited by Nicholas J. Enfield and Steven C. Levinson, pp. 279–298. New York, NY: Berg Press

Gaskins, Suzanne and Göncü, Artin. 1992. Cultural variation in play: A challenge to Piaget and Vygotsky. *Quarterly Newsletter of the Laboratory of Comparative Human Cognition*, 14(2):31–41

Gaskins, Suzanne, Haight, Wendy, and Lancy, David F. 2007. The cultural construction of play, in *Play and Development: Evolutionary, Sociocultural, and Functional Perspectives*. Edited by Artin Göncü and Suzanne Gaskins, pp. 179–202. Mahwah, NJ: Erlbaum

Gaskins, Suzanne and Miller, Peggy J. 2002. The cultural roles of emotions in pretend play. Paper presented at annual meeting, Association for the Study of Play, Santa Fe, NM, February

In press. The cultural roles of emotions in pretend play, in *Play and Culture Studies*, Volume IX, Edited by Cindy Dell Clark. Westport, CT: Ablex

Gaulin, Stephen J. C. and Robbins, Carole J. 1991. Trivers–Willard effect in contemporary North American society. *American Journal of Physical Anthropology*, 85:61–69

Gauvain, Mary. 2001. *The Social Context of Cognitive Development*. New York, NY: The Guilford Press

Gavitt, Phillip. 1990. *Charity and Children in Renaissance Florence: The Ospedale degli Innocenti, 1410–1536*. Ann Arbor, MI: The University of Michigan Press

Gay, John. 2005. Liberia's choices and regional stability. Working Paper No. 251. Boston, MA: Boston University African Studies Center

Gay, John and Cole, Michael. 1967. *The New Mathematics and an Old Culture: A Study of Learning among the Kpelle*. New York, NY: Holt, Rinehart and Winston

Geary, David C. 1998. *Male, Female: The Evolution of Human Sex Differences*. Washington, DC: American Psychological Association

Gegeo, David Welchman and Watson-Gegeo, Karen Ann. 1985. Kwara'ae mothers and infants: changing family practices in health, work, and childrearing, in *Infant Care and Feeding in the South Pacific*. Edited by Leslie B. Marshall, pp. 235–253. New York, NY: Gordon and Breach Science

Gelles, Richard J. 1986. School-age parents and child abuse, in *School-Age Pregnancy and Parenthood: Biosocial Dimensions*. Edited by Jane B. Lancaster and Beatrix A. Hamburg, pp. 347–359. New York, NY: Aldine de Gruyter

Geronimus, Arline T. 1992. The weathering hypothesis and the health of African-American women and infants: Evidence and speculations. *Ethnicity and Disease*, 2:207–221

1996. What teen mothers know. *Human Nature*, 7(4):323–352

Gibbons, Judith L. 2004. Adolescents in the developing world, in *Childhood and Adolescence: Cross-Cultural Perspectives and Applications*. Edited by Uwe P. Gielen and Jaipaul L. Roopnarine, pp. 255–276. Westport, CT: Praeger

Gibbs, Nancy. 2005. Parents behaving badly. *Time Magazine*, 165(8):40–49

Gibson, Margaret. 1988. *Accommodation without Assimilation: Sikh Immigrants in an American High School*. Ithaca, NY: Cornell University Press

Gibson, Mhairi A. and Mace, Ruth. 2005. Helpful grandmothers in rural Ethiopia: A study of the effect of kin on child survival and growth. *Evolution and Human Behavior*, 26(6):469–482

Gielen, Uwe P. 1993. Traditional Tibetan societies, in *International Handbook on Gender Roles*. Edited by Leonore Loeb Adler, pp. 413–437. Westport, CT: Greenwood Press

2004. The cross-cultural study of human development: An opinionated historical introduction, in *Childhood and Adolescence: Cross-Cultural Perspectives and Applications*. Edited by Uwe P. Gielen and Jaipaul L. Roopnarine, pp. 3–45. Westport, CT: Praeger

Gielen, Uwe P. and Chumachenko, Oksana. 2004. All the world's children: The impact of global demographic trends and economic disparities, in *Childhood and Adolescence: Cross-Cultural Perspectives and Applications*. Edited by Uwe P. Gielen and Jaipaul L. Roopnarine, pp. 81–109. Westport, CT: Praeger

Gielen, Uwe P. and Ramada, A. Ahmed. 2007. Children and adolescents in the Arab world. Paper presented at annual meeting, Society for Cross-Cultural Research, San Antonio, TX, February 21–24

Gies, Frances and Gies, Joseph. 1987. *Marriage and the Family in the Middle Ages*. New York, NY: Harper and Row

Gillis, John R. 2000. Marginalization of fatherhood in western countries. *Childhood*, 7(2):225–238

404   References

2003. The birth of the virtual child: A Victorian progeny, in *Beyond the Century of the Child: Cultural History and Developmental Psychology*. Edited by Willem Koops and Michael Zuckerman, pp. 82–95. Philadelphia, PA: University of Pennsylvania Press

Gilmore, David D. 2001. The manhood puzzle, in *Gender in Cross-Cultural Perspective*. Edited by Caroline B. Brettell and Carolyn F. Sargent, pp. 207–220. Upper Saddle River, NJ: Prentice Hall

Giroux, Henry A. 1998. Stealing innocence: The politics of child beauty pageants, in *The Children's Culture Reader*. Edited by Henry Jenkins, pp. 265–282. New York: New York University Press

Gladwin, Thomas. 1970. *East is a Big Bird: Navigation and Logic on Puluwat Atoll*. Cambridge, MA: Harvard University Press

Glass-Coffin, Bonnie. 1988. *The Gift of Life: Female Spirituality and Healing in Northern Peru*. Albuquerque, NM: University of New Mexico Press

Glassner, Barry. 1999. *The Culture of Fear*. New York, NY: Basic Books

Gleason, Judith and Ibubuya, Allison. 1991. My year reached, we heard ourselves singing: Dawn songs of girls becoming women in Ogbogbo, Okirka, Rivers State, Nigeria. *Research in African Literature*, 2:135–147

Goddard, Victoria. 1985. Child labour in Naples: The case of outwork. *Anthropology Today*, 1(5):18–21

Golden, Mark. 1990. *Children and Childhood in Classical Athens*. Baltimore, MD: The Johns Hopkins University Press

2003. Childhood in ancient Greece, in *Coming of Age in Ancient Greece*. Edited by Jennifer Neils and John H. Oakley, pp. 13–29. New Haven, CT: Yale University Press

Goldschmidt, Walter. 1976. *Culture and Behavior of the Sebei*. Berkeley, CA: University of California Press

1986. *The Sebei: A Study in Adaptation*. New York, NY: Holt, Rinehart and Winston

Goldstein, Donna M. 1998. Nothing bad intended: Child discipline, punishment, and survival in Shantytown in Rio de Janeiro, Brazil, in *Small Wars: The Cultural Politics of Childhood*. Edited by Nancy Scheper-Hughes and Carolyn F. Sargent, pp. 389–415. Berkeley, CA: University of California Press

Goldstein, Jeffrey. 1998. Why we watch, in *Why We Watch: The Attractions of Violent Entertainment*. Edited by Jeffery Goldstein, pp. 212–226. New York, NY: Oxford University Press

Goldstein-Gidoni, Ofra. 1999. Kimono and the construction of gendered and cultural identities. *Ethnology*, 38(4):351–370

Göncü, Artin. 2004. Interpreting children's play as cultural activity. Paper presented at a seminar on Learning Processes and Everyday Cognition: The Role of Play and Games, Charmey, Switzerland, April 16

Göncü, Artin, Mistry, Jayanthi, and Mosier, Christine. 2000. Cultural variations in the play of toddlers. *International Journal of Behavioral Development*, 24(3):321–329

Goodale, Jane C. 1980. Gender, sexuality, and marriage: A Kaulong model of nature and culture, in *Nature, Culture and Gender*. Edited by Carol P. MacCormack, pp. 119–143. Cambridge, MA: Cambridge University Press

Goodkind, Daniel. 1996. On substituting sex preference strategies in East Asia: Does prenatal sex selection reduce postnatal discrimination? *Population and Development Review*, 22:111–125

Goodnow, Jacqueline J. 1990. The socialization of cognition, in *Cultural Psychology*. Edited by James W. Stigler, Richard A. Shweder, and Gilbert H. Herdt, pp. 259–286. Cambridge, MA: Cambridge University Press

   1996. From household practices to parents' ideas about work and interpersonal relationships, in *Parents' Cultural Belief Systems: Their Origins, Expressions, and Consequences*. Edited by Sara Harkness and Charles M. Super, pp. 313–344. New York, NY: The Guilford Press

Goodwin, Grenville. 1942. *The Social Organization of the Western Apache*. Chicago, IL: University of Chicago Press

Goodwin, Marjorie Harness. 1998. Games of stance: Conflict and footing in hopscotch, in *Kids Talk: Strategic Language Use in Later Childhood*. Edited by Susan M. Hoyle and Carolyn Temple Adger, pp. 23–46. New York, NY: Oxford University Press

   2006. *The Hidden Life of Girls: Games of Stance, Status, and Exclusion*. Oxford, UK: Blackwell

Goody, Esther N. 1982. *Parenthood and Social Reproduction*. Cambridge, MA: Cambridge University Press

   1992. From play to work: Adults and peers as scaffolders of adult role skills in northern Ghana. Paper presented at the 91st Annual Meeting, American Anthropological Association, San Francisco, CA, December

   2006. Dynamics of the emergence of sociocultural institutional practices, in *Technology, Literacy, and the Evolution of Society*. Edited by David R. Olson and Michael Cole, pp. 241–264. Nahwah, NJ: Erlbaum

Gordon, Linda. 1999. *The Great Arizona Orphan Abduction*. Cambridge, MA: Harvard University Press

Gorer, Geoffrey. 1967. *Himalayan Village: An Account of the Lepchas of Sikkim*. New York, NY: Basic Books

Gosso, Yumi, Otta, Emma, De Lima, Maria, Morais, Salum, E. Ribeiro, Fernando Jose Leite, and Raad Bussab, Vera Silvaia. 2005. Play in hunter-gatherer society, in *The Nature of Play: Great Apes and Humans*. Edited by Anthony D. Pellegrini and Peter K. Smith, pp. 213–253. New York, NY: The Guilford Press

Goto, Stanford T. 1997. Nerds, normal people and homeboys: Accommodation and resistance among Chinese-American students. *Anthropology and Education Quarterly*, 28(1):70–84

Gottfredson, Linda S. 2004. Schools and the *g* factor. *The Wilson Quarterly*, 28(3):35–45

Gottlieb, Alma. 1992. *Under the Kapok Tree: Identity and Difference in Beng Thought*. Bloomington, IN: Indiana University Press

   2000. Luring your child into this life: A Beng path for infant care, in *A World of Babies: Imagined Childcare Guides for Seven Societies*. Edited by Judy DeLoache and Alma Gottlieb, pp. 55–90. Cambridge, MA: Cambridge University Press

Grammer, Karl, Kruck, Kirsten, Juette, Astrid, and Fink, Bernhard. 2000. Non-verbal behavior as courtship signals: The role of control and choice in selecting partners. *Evolution and Human Behavior*, 21:371–390

Gray, Brenda M. 1994. Enga birth, maturation and survival: Physiological characteristics of the life cycle in the New Guinea Highlands, in *Ethnography of Fertility and Birth*. Edited by Carol P. MacCormack, pp. 65–103. Prospect Heights, IL: Waveland Press

Green, Miranda A. 1999. Human sacrifice in Iron Age Europe. *Discovering Archeology*, 1(2):56–80

Greenfield, Patricia M., Brazelton, T. Barry, and Childs, Carla P. 1989. From birth to maturity in Zinacantan: Ontogenesis in cultural context, in *Ethnographic Encounters in Southern Mesoamerica: Celebratory Essays in Honor of Evon Z. Vogt*. Edited by Victoria Bricker and Gary Gosen, pp. 177–216. Albany, NY: State University of New York Press

Greenfield, Patricia M., Maynard, Ashley E., Boehm, Christopher, and Schmidtling, Emily Yut. 1995. Cultural Apprenticeship and Cultural Change, in *Biology, Brains, and Behavior: The Evolution of Human Development*. Edited by Sue Taylor Parker, Jonas Langer, and Michael L. McKinney, pp. 237–277. Santa Fe, NM: SAR Press

Greenfield, Patricia M., Yut, Emily, Chung, Mabel, Land, Deborah, Kreider, Holly, Pantoja, Maurice, and Horsley, Kris. 1990. The program-length commercial: A study of the effects of television toy tie-ins on imaginative play. *Psychology and Marketing*, 7(4):237–255

Gregor, Thomas. 1970. Exposure and seclusion: A study of institutionalized isolation among the Mehinacu Indians of Brazil. *Ethnology*, 9(3):234–250

1988. *Mehinacu: The Drama of Daily Life in a Brazilian Indian Village*. Chicago, IL: University of Chicago Press

1990. Male dominance and sexual coercion, in *Cultural Psychology*. Edited by James W. Stigler, Richard A. Shweder, and Gilbert H. Herdt, pp. 477–495. New York, NY: Cambridge University Press

Griffin, P. Bion and Griffin, Marcus B. 1992. Fathers and childcare among the Cagayan Agta, in *Father–Child Relations: Cultural and Biosocial Contexts*. Edited by Berry S. Hewlett, pp. 297–320. New York, NY: Aldine

Grindal, Bruce. 1972. *Growing Up in Two Worlds: Education and Transition among the Sisala of Northern Ghana*. New York, NY: Holt, Rinehart and Winston

Groos, Karl. 1898/1976. *The Play of Animals*. Translated by E. L. Baldwin. New York, NY: Appleton

Gross, Dana, Horst, Kate, and Kyle, Barbara. 2003. Parent–child interaction in a parent education program for adolescent parents. Paper presented at annual meeting, Association for the Study of Play, Charleston, SC, February

Grubb, W. Norton and Lazerson, Marvin. 1982. *Broken Promises: How Americans Fail their Children*. Chicago, IL: University of Chicago Press

Gruenbaum, Ellen. 1982. The movement against clitoridectomy and infibulation in Sudan: Public health policy and the women's movement. *Medical Anthropology Newsletter*, 13(2):4–12

Guemple, D. Lee. 1969. The Eskimo ritual sponsor: A problem in the fusion of semantic domains. *Ethnology*, 8(4):468–483

1979. Inuit socialization: A study of children as social actors in an Eskimo community, in *Childhood and Adolescence in Canada*. Edited by Ishwaran Karigoudar, pp. 39–71. Toronto, Canada: McGraw-Hill Ryerson

Gulrajani, Mohini. 2000. Child labour and the export sector in the Indian carpet industry, in *The Exploited Child*. Edited by Bernard Schlemmer, pp. 51–66. New York, NY: Zed Books

Gurven, Michael, Kaplan, Hillard, and Gutierrez, Maguin. 2006. How long does it take to become a proficient hunter? Implications for the evolution of extended development and long life span. *Journal of Human Evolution*, 51:454–470

Gusinde, Martin. 1937. *The Yahgan: The Life and Thought of the Water Nomads of Cape Horn*. Mödling bei Wien, Austria: Anthropos-Bibliothek

Guss, David M. 1982. The enculturation of Makiritare women. *Ethnology*, 21(3):259–269

Hacsi, Timothy A. 2002. *Children as Pawns: The Politics of Educational Reform*. Cambridge, MA: Harvard University Press

Haffter, Carl. 1986. The changeling: History and psychodynamics of attitudes to handicapped children in European folklore. *Journal of the History of Behavioral Sciences*, 4:55–61

Hagen, Edward H. 1999. The functions of post-partum depression. *Evolution and Human Behavior*, 20:325–359

Haight, Wendy. 2003. When play is the child's work: The cultural construction of pretend play in Taiwanese and European American families. Paper presented at symposium on the Cultural Construction of Play, Jean Piaget Society Annual Meeting, Chicago, IL, June 5

Haight, Wendy L. and Miller, Peggy J. 1993. *Pretending at Home: Early Development in a Sociocultural Context*. Albany, NY: State University of New York Press

Haight, Wendy, Wang, Xiao-lei, Fung, Heidi Han-tih, Williams, Kimberley, and Mintz, Judith. 1999. Universal, developmental, and variable aspects of young children's play: A cross-cultural comparison of pretending at home. *Child Development*, 70(6):1477–1488

Halioua, Bruno and Ziskind, Bernard. 2005. *Medicine in the Days of the Pharaohs*. Cambridge, MA: Harvard University Press

Hall, Granville Stanley. 1904. *Adolescence: Its Psychology and its Relations to Physiology, Anthropology, Sociology, Sex, Crime, Religion, and Education*. New York, NY: D. Appleton and Company

Hall, K. R. L. 1963. Variations in the ecology of the chacma baboon (*Papio ursinus*). *Symposium of the Zoological Society of London*, 1(1):1–28

Hall, Kathleen D. 2002. *Lives in Translation: Sikh Youth as British Citizens*. Philadelphia, PA: University of Pennsylvania Press

Hames, Raymond. 1992. Time allocation, in *Evolutionary Ecology and Human Behavior*. Edited by Eric Alders Smith and Bruce Winterhalder, pp. 203–235. Hawthorne, NY: Aldine de Gruyter

Hames, Raymond and Draper, Patricia. 2004. Women's work, childcare, and helpers-at-the-nest in a hunter-gatherer society. *Human Nature*, 15(4):319–341

Hampshire, Kate. 2001. The impact of male migration on fertility decisions and outcomes in northern Burkina Faso, in *Managing Reproductive Life: Cross-Cultural Themes in Sexuality and Fertility*. Edited by Soraya Tremayne, pp. 107–125. Oxford, UK: Berghahn Books

Hanawalt, Barbara A. 1986. *The Ties that Bound*. Oxford: Oxford University Press

2003. The child in the Middle Ages and the Renaissance, in *Beyond the Century of the Child: Cultural History and Developmental Psychology*. Edited by Willem Koops and Michael Zuckerman, pp. 21–42. Philadelphia, PA: University of Pennsylvania Press

Hardenberg, Roland. 2006. Hut of the young girls: Transition from childhood to adolescence in a middle Indian tribal society, in *Childhoods in South Asia*. Edited by Deepak K. Behera, pp. 65–81, Singapore: Pearson Education

Hardman, Charlotte. 1980. Can there be an anthropology of children? *Journal of the Anthropological Society of Oxford*, 4:85–89

Harkness, Sara and Super, Charles M. 1985. The cultural context of gender segregation in children's peer groups. *Child Development*, 56:219–224

1986. The cultural structuring of children's play in a rural African community, in *The Many Faces of Play*. Edited by Kendall Blanchard, pp. 96–103. Champaign, IL: Human Kinetics

1991. East Africa, in *Children in Historical and Comparative Perspective*. Edited by Joseph M. Hawes and N. Ray Hiner, pp. 217–239. Westport, CT: Greenwood Press

Harkness, Sara, Super, Charles M., and Keefer, Constance H. 1992. Learning to be an American parent: How cultural models gain directive force, in *Human Motives and Cultural Models*. Edited by Roy D'Andrade and Claudia Strauss, pp. 163–178. Cambridge, MA: Cambridge University Press

Harkness, Sara, Super, Charles M., Keefer, Constance H., Raghavan, Chemba S., and Campbell, Elizabeth Kipp. 1996. Ask the doctor: The negotiation of cultural models in American parent–pediatrician discourse, in *Parents' Cultural Belief Systems: Their Origins, Expressions, and Consequences*. Edited by Sara Harkness and Charles M. Super, pp. 289–310. New York, NY: The Guilford Press

Harkness, Sara, Super, Charles M., Parmar, Parmindar, Hidalgo, Victoria, and Welles-Nystrom, Barbara. 2006. The isolated nuclear family – how isolated? How nuclear? A study in seven Western cultures. Paper presented at 35th annual meeting, Society for Cross-Cultural Research, Savannah, GA, February 24

Harris, Colette. 2006. *Muslim Youth: Tensions and Transitions in Tajikistan*. Boulder, CO: Westview Press

Harris, Judith Rich. 1998. *The Nurture Assumption: Why Children Turn Out the Way They Do*. New York, NY: Free Press

2006. *No Two Alike: Human Nature and Human Individuality*. New York, NY: W. W. Norton and Company

Harris, Marvin. 1990. *Our Kind: Who We Are, Where We Came From, Where We Are Going*. New York, NY: Harper and Row

Hart, Betty and Risley, Todd. 1995. *Meaningful Differences in the Everyday Experience of Young American Children*. Baltimore, MD: Paul H. Brookes

2003. The early catastrophe: The 30 million word gap. *American Educator*, 27(1): 4–9

Hart, Don V. 1965. From pregnancy through birth in a Bisayan Filipino village, in *Southeast Asian Birth Customs*. Edited by Don V. Hart and Richard I. Coughlin. Behavior Science Monographs, New Haven, CT: HRAF Press

Hashim, Imam. 2005. Exploring the inter-linkages between children's independent migration and education: Evidence from Ghana. Paper presented at conference on Children and Youth in Emerging and Transforming Societies, Oslo, Norway, June

Hassig, Ros. 1945. *Aztec Warfare*. Norman, OK: University of Oklahoma Press

Hauser-Schaublin, Brigitta. 1995. Puberty rites, women's Naven, and initiation: Women's rituals of transition in Abelam and Iatmul culture, in *Gender Rituals: Female Initiation in Melanesia*. Edited by Nancy C. Lutkehaus and Paul B. Roscoe, pp. 33–53. London, UK: Routledge

Hausfater, Glenn and Hrdy, Sarah Blaffer. 1984. Preface, in *Infanticide: Comparative and Evolutionary Perspectives*. Edited by Glenn Hausfater and Sarah Blaffer Hrdy, pp. xi–xxxv. New York, NY: Aldine

Hawcroft, Jennie and Dennell, Robin. 2000. Neanderthal cognitive life history and its implications for material culture, in *Children and Material Culture*. Edited by Joanna Sofaer Derevenski, pp. 89–99. London, UK: Routledge

Hawkes, Kristen. 1991. 'Showing off: Tests of another hypothesis about men's foraging goals'. *Ethology and Sociobiology*, 11:29–54

Hawkes, Kristen, O'Connell, James F., and Blurton-Jones, Nicholas G. 1997. Hadza women's time allocation, offspring provisioning, and the evolutions of long post-menopausal life spans. *Current Anthropology*, 38:551–577

Hawkes, Kristen, O'Connell, James F., Blurton-Jones, Nicholas G., Alvarez, Helen, and Charnov, Eric L. 2000. The grandmother hypothesis and human evolution. In *Adaptation and Human Behavior: An Anthropological Perspective*. Edited by Lee Cronk, Napoleon Chagnon, and William Irons, pp. 237–258. Hawthorne, NY: Aldine de Gruyter.

Hazel, Ashley. 2007. Ecological underpinnings of women's reproductive lives. Paper presented at annual meeting, Society for Cross-Cultural Research, San Antonio, TX, February 21–24

Heath, Shirley Brice. 1982. What no bedtime story means: Narrative skills at home and school. *Language in Society*, 11:49–76

1983. *Ways with Words*. Cambridge, MA: Cambridge University Press

1990. The children of Tracton's children, in *Cultural Psychology*. Edited by James W. Stigler, Richard A. Shweder, and Gilbert H. Herdt, pp. 496–519. Cambridge, MA: Cambridge University Press

Heaton, Tom B. 1988. Four c's of the Mormon family: Chastity, conjugality, children, and chauvinism, in *The Religion and Family Connection: Social Science Perspectives*. Edited by Darwin L. Thomas, pp. 107–124. Salt Lake City, UT: Bookcraft

Heider, Karl G. 1976. Dani children's development of competency in social structural concepts. *Ethnology*, 15(1):47–62

Hemmings, Annette B. 2004. *Coming of Age in US High Schools: Economic, Kinship, Religious, and Political Crosscurrents*. Mahwah, NJ: Lawrence Erlbaum

Henderson, Patricia C. 2006. South African AIDS orphans: Examining assumptions around vulnerability from the perspective of rural children and youth. *Childhood*, 13(3):303–327

Henrich, Joseph 2001. Cultural transmission and the diffusion of innovations: Adoption dynamics indicate that biased cultural transmission is the predominate force in behavioral change. *American Anthropologist*, 103(4):992–1013

Henrich, Joseph, McElreath, Richard, Barr, Abigail, Ensminger, Jean, Barrett, Clark, Bolyanatz, Alexander, Cardenas, Juan Camilo, Gurven, Michael, Gwako, Edwins,

Henrich, Natalie, Lesorogol, Carolyn, Marlowe, Frank, Tracer, David, and Ziker, John. 2006. Costly punishment across human societies. *Science*, 312:1767–1770

Henry, Paula I., Morelli, Gilda A., and Tronick, Edward Z. 2005. Child caretakers among Efe foragers of the Itruri Forest, in *Hunter Gatherer Childhoods: Evolutionary, Developmental, and Cultural Perspectives*. Edited by Barry S. Hewlett and Michael E. Lamb, pp. 191–213. New Brunswick, NJ: AldineTransaction

Herbert, Thomas P. and Reis, Sally M. 1999. Culturally diverse high-achieving students in an urban high school. *Urban Education*, 34(4):438–457

Herdt, Gilbert H. 1990. Sambia nosebleeding rites and male proximity to women, in *Cultural Psychology*. Edited by James W. Stigler, Richard A. Shweder, and Gilbert H. Herdt, pp. 366–400. New York, NY: Cambridge University Press

2001. Rituals in manhood: Male initiation in Papua New Guinea, in *Gender in Cross-Cultural Perspective*. Edited by Caroline B. Brettell and Carolyn F. Sargent, pp. 162–166. Upper Saddle River, NJ: Prentice Hall

Hern, Warren M. 1992. Family planning, Amazon style. *Natural History*, 101(12):30–37

Herzfeld, Michael. 1995. It takes one to know one: Collective resentment and mutual recognition among Greeks in local and global contexts, in *Counterworks: Managing the Diversity of Knowledge*. Edited by Richard Fardon, pp. 124–142. London, UK: Routledge

Hewlett, Barry S. 1986. Intimate fathers: paternal patterns of holding among Aka Pygmies, in *Father's Role in Cross-Cultural Perspective*. Edited by Michael E. Lamb, pp. 34–61. New York, NY: Erlbaum

1988. Sexual selection and paternal investment among Aka Pygmies, in *Human Reproductive Behavior: A Darwinian Perspective*. Edited by L. Betzing, M. Borgerhoff Mulder, and P. Turke, pp. 263–276. Cambridge, MA: Cambridge University Press

1991. *Intimate Fathers: The Nature and Context of Aka Pygmy Paternal-Infant Care*. Ann Arbor, MI: University of Michigan Press

1992. The parent–infant relationship and social-emotional development among Aka Pygmies, in *Parent–Child Socialization in Diverse Cultures*. Edited by Jaipaul L. Roopnarine and D. Bruce Carter, pp. 223–243. Norwood, NJ: Ablex

2001. The cultural nexus of father–infant bonding, in *Gender in Cross-Cultural Perspective*. Edited by Caroline B. Brettell and Carolyn F. Sargent, pp. 45–56. Upper Saddle River, NJ: Prentice Hall

Hewlett, Barry S. and Cavalli-Sforza, Luca L. 1986. Cultural transmission among Aka Pygmies. *American Anthropologist*, 88:922–934

Hewlett, Barry S., Lamb, Michael E., Leyendecker, Birgit, and Schölmerich, Axel. 2000. Parental investment strategies among Aka foragers, Ngandu farmers, and Euro-American urban-industrialists, in *Adaptation and Human Behavior: An Anthropological Perspective*. Edited by Lee Cronk, Napoleon Chagnon, and William Irons, pp. 155–178. New York, NY: Aldine de Gruyter

Hewlett, Barry S., Lamb, Michael E., Shannon, Donald, Leyendecker, Birgit, and Schölmerich, Helge. 1998. Culture and infancy among Central African foragers and farmers. *Developmental Psychology*, 34(4):653–661

Hill, Kim and Hurtado, A. Magdalena. 1996. *Ache Life History: The Ecology and Demography of a Foraging People*. New York, NY: Aldine de Gruyter

Hill, Sarah E. and Reeve, H. Kern. 2004. Mating games: The evolution of human mating transactions. *Behavioral Ecology*, 15(5):748–756

Hine, Thomas. 1999. *The Rise and Fall of the American Teenager*. New York, NY: HarperCollins

Hirschfeld, Lawrence E. 2002. Why don't anthropologists like children? *American Anthropologist*, 104(2):611–627

Ho, David Y. F. 1994. Cognitive socialization in Confucian heritage cultures, in *Cross-Cultural Roots of Minority Child Development*. Edited by Patricia M. Greenfield and Rodney R. Cocking, pp. 285–313. Hillsdale, NJ: Erlbaum

Hobart, Angela. 1988. The shadow play and operetta as mediums of education in Bali, in *Acquiring Culture: Cross-Cultural Studies in Child Development*. Edited by Gustav Jahoda and Ioan M. Lewis, pp. 113–144. London, UK: Croom Helm

Hobart, Angela, Ramseyer, Urs, and Leeman, Albert. 1996. *The Peoples of Bali*. Cambridge, MA: Blackwell

Hodges, Glenn. 2003. Mongolian crossing, *National Geographic*, 204(4):102–121

Hofferth, Sandra, Brayfield, April, Deich, Sharon G., and Holcomb, Pamela. 1991. *National Childcare Survey 1990*. Washington, DC: The Urban Institute Press

Hoffman, Lois Wladis. 1988. Cross-cultural differences in childrearing goals, in *Parental Behavior in Diverse Societies*. Edited by Robert A. LeVine, Patricia M. Miller, and Mary M. West, *New Directions for Child Development*, 40:99–122

Hogbin, H. Ian. 1970a. *The Island of Menstruating Men*. Scranton, PA: Chandler

Hogbin, H. Ian. 1970b. A New Guinea childhood: From weaning till the eighth year in Wogeo, in *From Child to Adult*. Edited by John Middleton, pp. 134–162. Garden City, NY: The Natural History Press

Holman, Thomas B. 2002. Choosing and being the right spouse. *Ensign*, 32(9):62–67

Holland, Dorothy C. and Eisenhart, Margaret A. 1990. *Educated in Romance: Women, Achievement and College Culture*. Chicago, IL: University of Chicago Press

Hollos, Marida. 1998. The status of women in southern Nigeria: Is education a help or a hindrance? in *Women and Education in Sub-Saharan Africa: Power, Opportunities, and Constraints*. Edited by Marianne Bloch, Josephine A. Beoku-Betts, and B. Robert Tabachnick, pp. 247–276. Boulder, CO: Lynne Rienner

Hollos, Marida and Leis, Philip E. 1989. *Becoming Nigerian in Ijo Society*. New Brunswick, NJ: Rutgers University Press

Holloway, Sarah L. and Valentine, Gill. 2000. Children's geographies and the new social studies of childhood, in *Children's Geographies: Playing, Living, Learning*. Edited by Sarah L. Holloway and Gill Valentine, pp.1–26. London, UK: Routledge

Holmes, Hilary. 1994. Pregnancy and birth as rites of passage for two groups of women in Britain, in *Ethnography of Fertility and Birth*. Edited by Carol P. MacCormack, pp. 221–258. Prospect Heights, IL: Waveland Press

Honwana, Alcinda. 2005. The pain of agency: The agency of pain, in *Makers and Breakers: Children and Youth in Post Colonial Africa*. Edited by Alcinda Honwana and Filip de Boeck, pp. 31–52. Trenton, NJ: Africa World Press

Hopcroft, Rosemary L. 2006. Sex, status, reproductive success in the contemporary United States. *Evolution and Human Behavior*, 27:104–120

Horn, Wade F. 2003. Fatherhood, cohabitation, and marriage, in *Family and Child Wellbeing after Welfare Reform*. Edited by Douglas J. Besharov, pp. 129–144. New Brunswick, NJ: Transaction Publishers

Horr, David Agee. 1977. Orang-utan maturation: Growing up in a female world, in *Primate Bio-Social Development: Biological, Social, and Ecological Determinants*. Edited by Suzanne Chevalier-Skolnikoff and Frank E. Poirier, pp. 289–321. London, UK: Garland

Hostetler, John A. 1964. Persistence and change patterns in Amish society. *Ethnology*, 3(2):185–198

Hostetler, John A. and Huntington, Gertrude E. 1971/1992. *Amish Children: Education in the Family, School, and the Community*, 2nd edn. Orlando, FL: Harcourt Brace Jovanovich

Hotvedt, Mary E. 1990. Emerging and submerging adolescent sexuality: Culture and sexual orientation, in *Adolescence and Puberty*. Edited by John Bancroft and June M. Reinisch, pp. 157–172. New York, NY: Oxford University Press

Houby-Nielsen, Sanne. 2000. Child burials in ancient Athens, in *Children and Material Culture*. Edited by Joanna S. Derevenski, pp. 151–166. London, UK: Routledge

Hough, Walter. 1915. *The Hopi Indians*. Cedar Rapids, IA: Torch Press

Howard, Alan. 1970. *Learning to be Rotuman*. New York, NY: Teachers College Press

Howell, Nancy. 1979. *Demography of the Dobe !Kung*. New York, NY: Academic Press

Howell, Signe. 1988. From child to human: Chewong concepts of self, in *Acquiring Culture: Cross Cultural Studies in Child Development*. Edited by Gustav Jahoda and Ioan M. Lewis, pp. 147–168. London, UK: Croom Helm

Howrigan, Gail A. 1988. Fertility, infant feeding, and change in Yucatan, in *Parental Behavior in Diverse Societies*. Edited by Robert A. LeVine, Patricia M. Miller, and Mary Maxwell West. *New Directions for Child Development*, 40:37–50

Hrdy, Sarah Blaffer. 1976. Care and exploitation of nonhuman primate infants by conspecifics other than the mother. *Advances in the Study of Behavior*, 6:101–158

1992. Fitness tradeoffs in the history and evolution of delegated mothering with special reference to wet-nursing, abandonment, and infanticide. *Ethology and Sociobiology*, 13:409–442

1999. *Mother Nature: Maternal Instincts and How They Shape the Human Species*. New York, NY: Ballantine

2005. Comes the child before man: How cooperative breeding and prolonged postweaning dependence shaped human potential, in *Hunter Gatherer Childhoods: Evolutionary, Developmental, and Cultural Perspectives*. Edited by Barry S. Hewlett and Michael E. Lamb, pp. 65–91. New Brunswick, NJ: AldineTransaction

Hua, Cai. 2001. *A Society without Fathers or Husbands: The Na of China*. Translated by Asti Hustvedt. Brooklyn, NY: Zone Books

Huber, Brad R. 2006. Kinship laterality, paternal certainty, and direct care made by kin during childbirth. Paper presented at 35th annual meeting, Society for Cross-Cultural Research, Savannah, GA, February 24

2007. Evolutionary theory, kinship, and childbirth in cross-cultural perspective. *Cross-Cultural Research*, 41(2):196–219

Hudson, Valerie M. and Boer, Andrea M. Den. 2005. *Bare Branches: The Security Implications of Asia's Surplus Male Population*. Cambridge, MA: MIT Press

Hunn, Eugene S. 2002. Evidence for the precocious acquisition of plant knowledge by Zapotec children, in *Ethnobiology and Biocultural Diversity: Proceedings of the Seventh International Congress of Ethnobiology*. Edited by John R. Stepp, Felice

S. Wyndham, and Rebecca K. Zarger, pp. 604–613. Athens, GA: University of Georgia Press

Huntsinger, Carol S., Jose, Paul E., Larson, Shari L., Kreig, Dana B., and Shaligram, Chitra. 2000. Mathematics, vocabulary, and reading development in Chinese American and European American children over the primary school years. *Journal of Educational Psychology*, 92(4):745–760

Husu, Lisa and Niemela, Pirkko. 1993. Finland, in *International Handbook on Gender Roles*. Edited by Leonore Loeb Adler, pp. 59–76. Westport, CT: Greenwood Press

Huxley, Aldous. 1931/1998. *Brave New World*. New York, NY: Harper

Inhorn, Marcia C. 2005. Religion and reproductive technologies. *Anthropology News*, 4(2):14, 18

Irons, William. 2000. Why do the Yomut raise more sons than daughters?, in *Adaptation and Human Behavior: An Anthropological Perspective*. Edited by Lee Cronk, Napoleon Chagnon, and William Irons, pp. 223–236. New York, NY: Aldine

Irvine, Judith T. 1978. Wolof "magical thinking": Culture and conservation revisited. *Journal of Cross-Cultural Psychology*, 9:300–310

Isaac, Barry L. and Conrad, Shelby R. 1982. Child fosterage among the Mende of Upper Bambara Chiefdom, Sierra Leone: Rural–urban and occupational comparisons. *Ethnology*, 21(3):243–247

Isaac, Barry L. and Feinberg, William E. 1982. Marital form and infant survival among the Mende of rural Upper Bambara Chiefdom, Sierra Leone. *Human Biology*, 54(3):627–634

Isaacson, Nicole. 2002. Preterm babies in the "Mother Machine": Metaphoric reasoning and bureaucratic rituals that finish the "unfinished infant," in *Culture in Mind: Toward a Sociology of Culture and Cognition*. Edited by Karen A. Cerulo, pp. 89–100. New York, NY: Routledge

Iversen, Vegard and Raghavendra, P. S. 2005. Work and hardship, friendship and learning. Paper presented at conference on Children and Youth in Emerging and Transforming Societies, Oslo, Norway, June

Jacquemin, Mélanie Y. 2004. Children's domestic work in Abidjan, Côte d'Ivoire: The petites bonnes have the floor. *Childhood*, 11(3):383–397

2006. Can the language of rights get hold of the complex realities of child domestic work? *Childhood*, 13(3):389–406

Jalil, Nasir and McGinn, Noel F. 1992. Pakistan, in *Education's Role in National Development Plans: Ten Country Cases*. Edited by R. Murray Thomas, pp. 89–108. New York, NY: Praeger

Jameton, Andrew L. 1995. Paediatric nursing ethics, in *Ethics and Perinatology*. Edited by Amnon Goldworth, William Silverman, David K. Stevenson, Ernlé W. D. Young, and Rodney Rivers, pp. 427–443. Oxford, UK: Oxford University Press

Jamin, Jacqueline Rabain. 1994. Language and socialization of the child in African families living in France, in *Cross-cultural Roots of Minority Child Development*. Edited by Patricia M. Greenfield and Rodney R. Cocking, pp. 147–167. Hillsdale, NJ: Lawrence Erlbaum Associates

Janssen, Rosalind M. and Janssen, Jac J. 1990. *Growing Up in Ancient Egypt*. London, UK: The Rubicon Press

Jelliffe, D. B, Woodburn, J., Bennett, F. J., and Jelliffe, E. F. B. 1962. The children of Hadza hunters. *Tropical Pediatrics*, 60(2):907–913

Jenkins, Carol L., Orr-Ewing, Alison K., and Heywood, Peter F. 1985. Cultural aspects of early childhood growth and nutrition among the Amele of Lowland Papua New Guinea, in *Infant Care and Feeding in the South Pacific*. Edited by Leslie B. Marshall, pp. 29–50. New York, NY: Gordon and Breach

Jensen, Gordon D. and Suryani, Luh Ketut. 1992. *The Balinese People: A Reinvestigation of Character*. Singapore: Oxford University Press

Jensen de López, Kristine. 2003. Weddings, funerals and other important games: Zapotec (Southern Mexico) children's sociodramatic play. Paper presented to the Jean Piaget Society, Chicago, IL, June

Johannes, Robert E. 1981. *Words of the Lagoon: Fishing and Marine Lore in the Palau District of Micronesia*. Berkeley, CA: University of California Press

Johansen, Henriette. 2007. Human sacrifice in early Bronze Age Umm el-Marra, Syria? *Minerva*, 18(1):5

Johnson, George Ellsworth. 1916. *Education through Recreation*. Cleveland, OH: Survey Committee of the Cleveland Foundation

Johnson, Kay Ann. 2004. *Wanting a Daughter, Needing a Son*. St. Paul, MN: Yeong and Yeong

Johnson, Norris B. 1989. Prehistoric European decorated caves: Structured earth environments, initiation, and rites of passage, in *Child Development within Culturally Structured Environments*, Vol. II. Edited by Jaan Valsiner, pp. 227–267. Norwood, NJ: Ablex

Johnson, Sara E. and Bock, John. 2004. Trade-offs in skill acquisition and time allocation among juvenile Chacma baboons. *Human Nature*, 15(1):45–62

Jolivet, Muriel. 1997. *Japan: The Childless Society? The Crisis of Motherhood*. London, UK: Routledge

Josephson, Steven C. 1993. Status, reproductive success, and marrying polygynously. *Ethology and Sociobiology*, 14:391–396

2002. Fathering as reproductive investment, in *Handbook of Father Involvement: Multidisciplinary Perspectives*. Edited by Catherine S. Tamis-LeMonda and Natasha Cabrera, pp. 359–382. Mahwah, NJ: Erlbaum

Junod, Henri A. 1927. *The Life of a South African Tribe*. London, UK: Macmilllan

Kagitçibasi, Çigdem and Sunar, Diane. 1992. Family and socialization in Turkey, in *Parent–Child Socialization in Diverse Cultures*. Edited by Jaipaul L. Roopnarine and D. Bruce Carter, pp. 75–88. Norwood, NJ: Ablex

Kamp, Kathryn A. 2002. Working for a living, in *Children in the Prehistoric Puebloan Southwest*. Edited by Kathryn A. Kamp, pp. 71–89. Salt Lake City, UT: University of Utah Press

Kamp, Kathryn A. and Whittaker, John C. 2002. Prehistoric Puebloan children in archaeology and art, in *Children in the Prehistoric Puebloan Southwest*. Edited by Kathryn A. Kamp, pp. 14–40. Salt Lake City, UT: University of Utah Press

Kanazawa, Satoshi and Still, Mary C. 2000. Parental investment as a game of chicken. *Politics and the Life Sciences*, 10(1):17–26

Kantor, Harvey and Lowe, Robert. 2004. Reflections on history and quality education. *Educational Researcher*, 33(5):6–10

Kaplan, Fred. 1988. *Dickens: A Biography*. New York, NY: William Morrow and Company

Kaplan, Hillard. 1994. Evolutionary and wealth flows theories of fertility: Empirical tests and new models. *Population and Development Review*, 20:753–791

Kaplan, Hillard and Dove, Heather. 1987. Infant development among the Ache of eastern Paraguay. *Developmental Psychology*, 23:190–198

Kaplan, Hillard and Hill, Kim. 1992. The evolutionary ecology of food acquisition, in *Evolutionary Ecology and Human Behavior*. Edited by Eric A. Smith and Bruce Winterhalder, pp. 167–201. New York, NY: Aldine

Kaplan, Hillard, Hill, Kim, Lancaster, Jane B., and Hurtado, A. Magdalena. 2000. A theory of human life history evolution: Brains, learning, and longevity. *Evolutionary Anthropology*, 9:156–185

Kaplan, Hillard and Lancaster, Jane B. 2000. The evolutionary economics and psychology of the demographic transition to low fertility, in *Adaptation and Human Behavior: An Anthropological Perspective*. Edited by Lee Cronk, Napoleon Chagnon, and William Irons, pp. 283–322. New York, NY: Aldine

Kaplan, Hillard, Lancaster, Jane B., and Anderson, Kermyt G. 1998. Human parental investment and fertility: The life histories of men in Albuquerque, in *Men in Families: When Do They Get Involved? What Difference Does It Make?* Edited by Allan Booth and Ann C. Crouter, pp. 55–111. Hillsdale, NJ: Erlbaum

Kaplan, Sam. 2006. *The Pedagogical State: Education and the Politics of National Culture in Post-1980 Turkey*. Palo Alto, CA: Stanford University Press

Karsten, Lia. 2003. Children's use of public space: The gendered world of the playground. *Childhood*, 10(4):457–473

Katz, Cindi. 1986. Children and the environment: Work, play and learning in rural Sudan. *Children's Environment Quarterly*, 3(4):43–51

2001. Vagabond capitalism and the necessity of social reproduction. *Antipode*, 33:709–728

2005. The terrors of hypervigilance: Security and the compromised spaces of contemporary childhood, in *Studies in Modern Childhood*. Edited by Jens Qvortrup, pp. 99–114. Houndmills, UK: Palgrave Macmillan

Katz, Richard. 1981. Education is transformation: Becoming a healer among the !Kung and the Fijians. *Harvard Education Review*, 51(1):57–78

Kay, Verla. 2003. *Orphan Train*. New York, NY: G. P. Putnam's Sons

Keller, Heidi and Lamm, Bettina. 2005. Parenting as an expression of sociohistorical time: The case of German individualization. *International Journal of Behavioral Development*, 29(3):238–246

Kerrigan, John F., Aleck, Kirk A., Tarby, Theodore J., Bird, C. Roger, and Heidenreich, Randall A. 2000. Fumaric aciduria: Clinical and imaging features. *Annals of Neurology*, 47(5):583–588

Kertzer, David 1993. *Sacrificed for Honor: Italian Infant Abandonment and the Politics of Reproductive Control*. Boston, MA: Beacon Press

Kessen, William. 1978. Rousseau's children. *Daedalus*, 107(3):13–26

Khair, Sumaiya. 2005. Voluntary autonomous child migration: Perspectives from Bangladesh. Paper presented at conference on Children and Youth in Emerging and Transforming Societies, Oslo, Norway, June

Kilbride, Janet E. 1975. Sitting and smiling behavior of Baganda infants: The influence of culturally constituted experience. *Journal of Cross-Cultural Psychology*, 6(1):88–107

Kilbride, Philip L. 1974. Sociocultural factors and the early manifestation of sociobility behavior among Baganda infants. *Ethos*, 2(3):296–314

Kilbride, Philip L. and Kilbride, Janet C. 1990. *Changing Family Life in East Africa: Women and Children at Risk*. University Park, PA: Penn State University Press

Kim, Kwang-Woong. 2007. Hyo and parenting in Korea, in *Parenting Beliefs, Behavior and Parent–Child Relationships: A Cross-Cultural Perspective*. Edited by Kenneth H. Rubin and Ock Boon Chung, pp. 207–222. New York, NY: Psychology Press

Kim, Tae Lyon. 1993. Korea, in *International Handbook on Gender Roles*. Edited by Leonore Loeb Adler, pp. 187–198. Westport, CT: Greenwood Press

Kim, Uichol and Choi, So-Hyang. 1994. Individualism, collectivism, and child development: A Korean perspective, in *Cross-Cultural Roots of Minority Child Development*. Edited by Patricia M. Greenfield and Rodney R. Cocking, pp. 227–259. Hillsdale, NJ: Erlbaum

Kindermann, Thomas A. 1993. Natural peer groups as contexts for individual development: The case of children's development within natural peer contexts. *Developmental Psychology*, 29:970–977

King, Barbara J. 1999. New directions in the study of primate learning, in *Mammalian Social Learning: Comparative and Ecological Perspectives*. Edited by Hilary O. Box and Kathleen R. Gibson, pp. 17–32. Cambridge, UK: Cambridge University Press

　　2005. How gorillas and chimpanzees can help our children. *Anthropology News*, 46(3):9

King, Phillip J. 2006. Who did it, who didn't and why: Circumcision. *Biblical Archaeology Review*, 32(4):48–55

King, Stacie M. 2006. The coming of age in ancient coastal Oaxaca, in *The Social Experience of Childhood in Ancient Mesoamerica*. Edited by Traci Adren and Scott R. Hutson, pp. 169–200. Boulder, CO: University of Colorado Press

Kingston, Jeff. 2004. *Japan's Quiet Transformation: Social Change and Civil Society in the Twenty-first Century*. Abingdon, Canada: Routledge Curzon

Kinkead, Joyce A. (ed.) 1996. *A Schoolmarm all my Life: Personal Narratives from Frontier Utah*. Salt Lake City, UT: Signature Books

Kinney, Anne B. 1995. Dyed silk: Han notions of the moral development of children, in *Chinese Views of Childhood*. Edited by Anne B. Kinney, pp. 17–56. Honolulu, HI: University of Hawai'i Press

Kipling, Rudyard. 1901/2003. *Kim*. New York: Barnes and Noble

Kipnis, Andrew. 2001. The disturbing educational discipline of "peasants." *The China Journal*, 46:1–24

Klapisch-Zuber, Christiane. 1985. *Women, Family, and Ritual in Renaissance Italy*. Translated by Lydia Cochrane. Chicago, IL: University of Chicago Press

Kloek, Els. 2003. Early modern childhood in the Dutch context, in *Beyond the Century of the Child: Cultural History and Developmental Psychology*. Edited by Willem Koops and Michael Zucherman, pp. 43–61. Philadelphia, PA: University of Pennsylvania Press

Knott, Cheryl. 2003. Code red. *National Geographic*, 204(4):76–81

Kogel, Amy, Bolton, Ralph, and Bolton, Charlene. 1983. Time allocation in four societies. *Ethnology*, 22(4):355–370

Kojima, Hideo. 2003. The history of children and youth in Japan, in *Beyond the Century of the Child: Cultural History and Developmental Psychology*. Edited by Willem Koops and Michael Zucherman, pp. 112–135. Philadelphia, PA: University of Pennsylvania Press

Komulainen, Sirkka. 2007. The ambiguity of the child's voice in social research. *Childhood*, 14(1):11–28

Konner, Melvin. 2005. Hunter-gatherer infancy and childhood, in *Hunter Gatherer Childhoods: Evolutionary, Developmental, and Cultural Perspectives*. Edited by Barry S. Hewlett and Michael E. Lamb, pp. 19–64. New Brunswick, NJ: Aldine-Transaction

Konner, Melvin and Carol, Worthman. 1980. Nursing frequency, gonadal function and birth spacing among !Kung hunter-gatherers. *Science*, 207:788–91

Koops, Willem and Zuckerman, Michael (eds.). 2003. *Beyond the Century of the Child: Cultural History and Developmental Psychology*. Philadelphia: University of Pennsylvania Press

Kopp, Claire B., Khoka, Ellen W., and Sigman, Marian. 1977. A comparison of sensorimotor development among infants in India and the United States. *Journal of Cross-Cultural Psychology*, 8(4):435–451

Korbin, Jill E. 1987a. Child maltreatment in cross-cultural perspective: Vulnerable children and circumstances, in *Child Abuse and Neglect: Biosocial Dimensions*. Edited by Richard J. Gelles and Jane B. Lancaster, pp. 31–56. New York, NY: Aldine de Gruyter

1987b. Child sexual abuse: Implications from the cross-cultural record, in *Child Survival: Anthropological Perspectives on the Treatment and Maltreatment of children*. Edited by Nancy Scheper-Hughes, pp. 247–265. Dordrecht, Holland: D. Reidel

Kotlowitz, Alex. 1991. *There Are No Children Here*. New York, NY: Doubleday

Kozol, Jonathan. 1991. *Savage Inequalities: Children in America's Schools*. New York, NY: Crown

Kramer, Karen L. 2002a. Demographic changes and the timing of wealth flows across the life cycle of Maya families. Paper presented at symposium on New Research in Human Behavior Ecology, American Anthropological Association, New Orleans, LA, November

2002b. Variation in juvenile dependence: Helping behavior among Maya children. *Human Nature*, 13(2):299–325

2005. *Maya Children: Helpers on the Farm*. Cambridge, MA: Harvard University Press

Kramer, Samuel N. 1963. *The Sumerians: Their History, Culture and Character*. Chicago, IL: University of Chicago Press

Kratz, Corinne. A. 1990. Sexual solidarity and the secrets of sight and sound: Shifting gender relations and their ceremonial constitution. *American Ethnologist*, 17(3):449–469

Kress, Howard. 2005. The role of culture, economics, and education in reproductive decision making in Otavalo, Ecuador. Paper presented at annual meeting, American Anthropological Association, Washington, DC, December.

2007. An evaluation of infant mortality and embodied capital models of fertility transition in Otavalo, Ecuador. Paper presented at 36th annual meeting, Society for Cross-Cultural Research, and Third General Meeting, Society for Scientific Anthropology, San Antonio, TX, February 21–24

Krige, Eileen J. 1965/2005. *The Social System of the Zulus*. Pietermaritzburg, South Africa: Shuter and Shooter; New Haven, CT: HRAF

Kulick, Don. 1992. *Language Shift and Cultural Reproduction: Socialization, Self, and Syncretism in a Papua New Guinea Village*. Cambridge, UK: Cambridge University Press

Kulick, Don and Stroud, Christopher. 1993. Conceptions and uses of literacy in a Papua New Guinean village, in *Cross-Cultural Approaches to Literacy*. Edited by Brian Street, pp. 30–61. Cambridge, UK: Cambridge University Press

Kusserow, Adrie S. 2004. *American Individualisms: Child Rearing and Social Class in Three Neighborhoods*. New York: Palgrave Macmillan

La Russo, Maria G. 1988. A portrait of third generation Italian-American family life: Interviews and observations with six families. Ann Arbor, MI: University Microfilms

Ladson-Billings, Gloria. 2006. Presidential address. From the achievement gap to the education debt: Understanding achievement in US schools. *Educational Researcher*, 35(7):3–12

Lambert, James D. and Thomasson, Gordon C. 1997. Mormon American families, in *Families in Cultural Context: Strengths and Challenges in Diversity*. Edited by Mary Kay DeGenova, pp. 85–106. Mountain View, CA: Mayfield

Lancaster, Jane B. 1984. Evolutionary perspectives on sex differences in the higher primates, in *Gender and the Life Course*. Edited by Alice Rossi, pp. 3–28. New York, NY: Aldine

   1986. Human adolescence and reproduction: Evolutionary perspectives, in *School-Age Pregnancy and Parenthood: Biosocial Dimensions*. Edited by Jane B. Lancaster and Beatrix A. Hamburg, pp. 17–37. New York, NY: Aldine

Lancaster, Jane B. and Kaplan, Hillard S. 2000. Parenting other men's children: Costs, benefits, and consequences, in *Adaptation and Human Behavior: An Anthropological Perspective*. Edited by Lee, Cronk, Napoleon, Chagnon and William, Irons, pp. 179–201. New York, NY: Aldine

Lancaster, Jane B. and Lancaster, Chet. S. 1983. Parental investment: The hominid adaptation, in *How Humans Adapt*. Edited by Douglas J. Ortner, pp. 33–65. Washington, DC: Smithsonian Institution Press

Lancy, David F. 1975. The social organization of learning: Initiation rituals and public schools. *Human Organization*, 34:371–380

   1976. The play behavior of Kpelle children during rapid cultural change, in *The Anthropological Study of Play: Problems and Prospects*. Edited by David F. Lancy and B. Alan Tindall, pp. 72–79. West Point, NY: Leisure Press

   1977. The impact of the modern world on village life: Gbarngasuakwelle. *Papua New Guinea Journal of Education*, 13(1):36–44

   (ed.). 1979. Introduction, in *The Community School. Papua New Guinea Journal of Education* (special issue), 15(1):1–9

   1980a. Becoming a blacksmith in Gbarngasuakwelle. *Anthropology and Education Quarterly*, 11:266–274

   1980b. Play in species adaptation, in *Annual Review of Anthropology*. Edited by Bernard J. Siegel, 9:471–495

1980c. Speech events in a West African court. *Communication and Cognition*, 13(4):397–412

1982a. Socio-dramatic play and the acquisition of occupational roles. *Review Journal of Philosophy and Social Science*, 7:285–295

1982b. Some missed opportunities in theories of play. *The Behavioral and Brain Sciences*, 5:165–166

1983. *Cross-Cultural Studies in Cognition and Mathematics*. New York, NY: Academic Press

1984. Play in anthropological perspective, in *Play in Animals and Humans*. Edited by Peter K. Smith, pp. 295–304. London, UK: Basil Blackwell

1989. An information processing framework for the study of culture and thought, in *Thinking Across Cultures*. Edited by Donald Topping, Doris Crowell, and Victor Kobayashi, pp. 13–26. Hillsdale, NJ: Erlbaum

1994a. Anthropological study of literacy and numeracy, in *International Encyclopedia of Education*. Edited by Torsten Husén and T. Neville Postlethwaite, pp. 3346–3453. London, UK: Pergamon

1994b. The conditions that support emergent literacy, in *Children's Emergent Literacy: From Research to Practice*. Edited by Davd F. Lancy, pp. 1–19. Westport, CT: Praeger

1996. *Playing on the Mother Ground: Cultural Routines for Children's Development*. New York, NY: Guilford

2001. Cultural constraints on children's play. *Play and Culture Studies*, 4:3–62

2004. The anthropology of children. Invited presentation for a seminar on Learning Processes and Everyday Cognition: The Role of Play and Games, Charmey, Switzerland, April 16

2007a. Accounting for the presence/absence of mother–child play. *American Anthropologist*, 109(2):273–284

2007b. Toddler rejection. Paper presented at annual meeting, Society for Cross-Cultural Research and Society for Anthropological Sciences, San Antonio, TX, February 21–24

Lancy, David F. and Grove, M. Annette. 2006. "Baby-parading": Childcare or showing off? Paper presented at symposium on Defining Childhood: Cross-cultural Perspectives at annual meeting, the Society for Anthropological Sciences, Savannah, GA, February

Lancy, David F. and Madsen, Millard C. 1981. Cultural patterns and the social behavior of children: Two studies from Papua New Guinea. *Ethos*, 9:201–216

Lancy, David F. and Strathern, Andrew J. 1981. Making-twos: Pairing as an alternative to the taxonomic mode of representation. *American Anthropologist*, 81:773–795

Lange, Garret and Rodman, Hyman. 1992. Family relationships and patterns of child-rearing in the Caribbean, in *Parent–Child Socialization in Diverse Cultures*. Edited by Jaipaul L. Roopnarine and D. Bruce Carter, pp. 185–198. Norwood, NJ: Ablex

Lange, Karen E. 2007. Full circle. *National Geographic*, 212(4):28

Langer, William L. 1973–1974. Infanticide: A historical survey. *History of Childhood Quarterly: The Journal of Psychohistory*, 1:353–365

Langness, Louis L. 1981. Child abuse and cultural values: The case of New Guinea, in *Child Abuse and Neglect: Cross-Cultural Perspectives*. Edited by Jill E. Korbin, pp. 13–34. Berkeley, CA: University of California Press

Lansing, J. Stephen. 1994. *The Balinese*. Fort Worth, TX: Harcourt Brace

LaPlante, Matthew D. 2005. Prosecutors helpless to fight currently legal child erotica. *The Salt Lake Tribune*, February 7, A1, A7

Lareau, Annette. 1989. *Home Advantage: Social Class and Parental Intervention in Elementary Education*. New York, NY: Falmer

2003. *Unequal Childhoods; Class, Race, and Family Life*. Berkley, CA: University of California Press

LeFevre, Andrew T. 2004. *Report Card on American Education*. Washington, D.C. American Legislative Exchange Council

Larmer, Brook. 1992. Dead end kids. *Newsweek*. May 25:38–40

Larson, Reed W. and Suman, Verma. 1999. How children and adolescents spend time across the world: Work, play, and development opportunities. *Psychological Bulletin*, 125(6):701–736

Lave, Jean. 1990. The culture of acquisition and the practice of understanding, in *Cultural Psychology*. Edited by James W. Stigler, Richard A. Shweder, and Gilbert H. Herdt, pp. 309–327. Cambridge, MA: Cambridge University Press

Le, Huynh-Nhu. 2000. Never leave your little one alone: Raising an Ifaluk child, in *A World of Babies: Imagined Childcare Guides for Seven Societies*. Edited by J. DeLoache and A. Gottlieb, pp. 199–220. Cambridge: Cambridge University Press

Leavitt, Stephen C. 1998. The *bikhet* mystique: Masculine identity and patterns of rebellion among Bumbita adolescent males, in *Adolescence in Pacific Island Societies*. Edited by Gilbert H. Herdt and Stephen Leavitt, pp. 173–194. Pittsburgh, PA: University of Pittsburgh Press

Lebra, Takie Sugiyama. 1994. Mother and child in Japanese socialization: A Japan–US comparison, in *Cross-Cultural Roots of Minority Child Development*. Edited by Patricia M. Greenfield and Rodney R. Cocking, pp. 259–274. Hillsdale, NJ: Erlbaum

Lee, Jaekyung. 2002. Racial and ethnic achievement gap trends: Reversing the progress toward equity? *Educational Researcher*, 31(1):3–12

Lee, K. Alexandra. 1994. Attitudes and prejudices towards infanticide: Carthage, Rome and today. *Archaeological Review from Cambridge*, 13:65–79

Lee, Kwan Ching. 1998. *Gender and the South China Miracle: Two Worlds of Factory Women*. Berkeley, CA: University of California Press

Lee, Phyllis C. 1996. The meanings of weaning: Growth, lactation, and life history. *Evolutionary Anthropology*, 5:87–96

Lee, Richard Borshay. 1979. *The !Kung San: Men, Women and Work in a Foraging Society*. Cambridge, MA: Cambridge University Press

Lee, Sang-hyop and Mason, Andrew. 2005. Mother's education, learning-by-doing, and child health care in rural India. *Comparative Education Review*, 49(4):534–551

Lehmann, Arthur C. and Mihalyi, Louis. 1982. Aggression, bravery, endurance, and drugs: A radical re-evaluation and analysis of the Masai Warrior Complex. *Ethnology*, 21(4):335–347

Leighton, Dorothea and Kluckhohn, Clyde C. 1948. *Children of the People*. Cambridge, MA: Harvard University Press

Leis, Phillip E. 1982. The not-so-supernatural power of Ijaw children, in *African Religious Groups and Beliefs*. Edited by Simon Ottenberg, pp. 151–169. Meerut, India: Folklore Institute

Lepowsky, Maria A. 1985. Food taboos, malaria and dietary change: Infant feeding and cultural adaptation on a Papua New Guinea Island, in *Infant Care and Feeding in the South Pacific*. Edited by Leslie B. Marshall, pp. 51–81. New York, NY: Gordon and Breach

1987. Food taboos and child survival: A case study from the Coral Sea, in *Child Survival: Anthropological Perspectives on the Treatment and Maltreatment of Children*. Edited by Nancy Scheper-Hughes, pp. 71–92. Dordrecht, Netherlands: D. Reidel

1998. Coming of age on Vanatinai: Gender, sexuality, and power, in *Adolescence in Pacific Island Societies*. Edited by Gilbert H. Herdt and Stephen C. Leavitt, pp. 123–147. Pittsburgh, PA: University of Pittsburgh Press

Lerer, Leonard B. 1998. Who is the rogue? Hunger, death, and circumstance in John Mampe Square, in *Small Wars: The Cultural Politics of Childhood*. Edited by Nancy Scheper-Hughes and Carolyn F. Sargent, pp. 228–250. Berkeley, CA: University of California Press

Leung, Angela Ki Che. 1995. Relief institutions for children in nineteenth-century China, in *Chinese Views of Childhood*. Edited by Anne B. Kinney, pp. 251–278. Honolulu, HI: University of Hawai'i Press

Levenson, Jon D. 1993. *The Death and Resurrection of the Beloved Son: The Transformation of Child Sacrifice in Judaism and Christianity*. New Haven, CT: Yale University Press

Levenstein, Phyllis. 1976. Cognitive development through verbalized play: The mother–child home programme, in *Play – Its Role in Development and Evolution*. Edited by Jerome S. Bruner, Alison Jolly, and Kathy Sylva, pp. 286–297. New York, NY: Basic Books

Lever, Janet. 1978a. Sex differences in the complexity of children's play and games. *American Sociological Review*, 43:471–483

1978b. Sex differences in the games children play. *Social Problems*, 23:487–87

Levin, Paula. 1992. The impact of preschool teaching and learning in Hawaiian families. *Anthropology and Education Quarterly*, 23(1):59–72

Levine, Donald N. 1965. *Wax and Gold: Tradition and Innovation in Ethiopian Culture*. Chicago, IL: University of Chicago Press

Levine, Judith. 2002. *Harmful to Minors: The Perils of Protecting Children from Sex*. Minneapolis, MN: University of Minnesota Press

LeVine, Robert A. 1966. Sex roles and economic change in Africa. *Ethnology*, 5(2):186–193

1973. Patterns of personality in Africa. *Ethos*, 1(2):123–152

1974. Children's kinship concepts: Cognitive development and early experience among the Hausa. *Ethnology*, 13(1):25–44

1988. Human parental care: universal goals, cultural strategies, individual behavior. *New Directions for Child Development*, 40:3–11

2004. Challenging expert knowledge: Findings from an African study of infant care and development, in *Childhood and Adolescence: Cross-Cultural Perspectives and Applications*. Edited by Uwe P. Gielen and Jaipaul L. Roopnarine, pp. 149–165. Westport, CT: Praeger

2007. Ethnographic studies of childhood: A historical overview. *American Anthropologist*, 109(2):247–260

LeVine, Robert A. and LeVine, Sarah E. 1988. Parental strategies among the Gusii of Kenya, in *Parental Behavior in Diverse Societies*. Edited by Robert A. LeVine, Patricia M. Miller, and Mary Maxwell West. *New Directions for Child Development*, 40:27–36

LeVine, Robert A., LeVine, Sarah, Dixon, Suzanne, Richman, Amy, Leiderman, P. Herbert, Keefer, Constance H., and Brazelton, T. Berry. 1994. *Child Care and Culture: Lessons from Africa*. Cambridge, MA: Cambridge University Press

LeVine, Robert A., LeVine, Sarah E., Rowe, Meredith L., and Anzola-Schnell, Beatrice. 2004. Maternal literacy and health behavior: A Nepalese case study. *Social Science and Medicine*, 58:863–877

LeVine, Robert A. and White, Merrie I. 1986. *Human Conditions*. New York, NY: Routledge and Kegan Paul

LeVine, Sarah. 2006. Getting in, dropping out, and staying on: Determinants of girls' school attendance in the Kathmandu Valley in Nepal. *Anthropology and Education Quarterly*, 37(1): 21–41

LeVine, Sarah and LeVine, Robert A. 1981. Child abuse and neglect in sub-Saharan Africa, in *Child Abuse and Neglect*. Edited by Jill E. Korbin, pp. 35–55. Berkeley, CA: University of California Press

Lévi-Strauss, Claude. 1966. *The Savage Mind*. Chicago, IL: University of Chicago Press

Levy, Robert I. 1973. *The Tahitians*. Chicago, IL: University of Chicago Press

1996. Essential contrasts: Differences in parental ideas about learners and teaching in Tahiti and Nepal, in *Parents' Cultural Belief Systems: Their Origins, Expressions, and Consequences*. Edited by Sara Harkness and Charles M. Super, pp. 123–142. New York, NY: The Guilford Press

Lew, Jamie. 2004. The "other" story of model minorities: Korean American high school dropouts in an urban context. *Anthropology and Education Quarterly*, 35(3):303–323

Lewis, Amanda E. and Forman, Tyrone A. 2002. Contestation or collaboration?: A comparative study of home–school relations. *Anthropology and Education Quarterly*, 33(1):60–89

Lewis, Kerrie P. and Barton, Robert A. 2004. Playing for keeps: Evolutionary relationships between social play and the cerebellum in nonhuman primates. *Human Nature*, 15(1):5–21

Lewis, Oscar. 1961. *The Children of the Sanchez*. New York, NY: Random House

Li, Jin. 2003. US and Chinese cultural beliefs about learning. *Journal of Educational Psychology*, 95(2):258–267

Li, Jin, Wang, Lianquin, and Fischer, Kurt W. 2004. The organization of Chinese shame concepts. *Cognition and Emotion*, 18(6):767–797

Liapis, Vayos. 2004. Choes, Anthesteria, and the dead: A re-appraisal. Paper presented at the American Philological Association annual meeting, San Francisco, CA, January

Liden, Hilde. 2003. Common neighbourhoods, diversified lives: Growing up in urban Norway, in *Children's Places: Cross-Cultural Perspectives*. Edited by Karen Fog Olwig and Eva Gullov, pp. 119–137. New York, NY: Routledge

Lijembe, Joseph. 1967. The valley between: A Muluyia's story, in *East African Childhood*. Edited by Lorene Fox, pp. 4–7. Nairobi, Kenya: Oxford University Press

Lindenbaum, Shirley. 1973. Sorcerers, ghosts, and polluting women: An analysis of religious beliefs and population control. *Ethnology*, 2(3):241–253

Lindstrom, Lamont. 1990. *Knowledge and Power in a South Pacific Society*. Washington, DC: Smithsonian Institution Press

Lipka, Jerry, Hogan, Maureen P., Webster, Joan Parker, Yanez, Evelyn, Adams, Barbara, Clark, Stacy, and Lacy, Doreen. 2005. Math in a cultural context: Two case studies of a successfully culturally based math project. *Anthropology Education Quarterly*, 26(4):367–385

Little, Kenneth. 1970. The social cycle and initiation among the Mende, in *From Child to Adult*. Edited by John Middleton, pp. 207–225. Garden City, NY: Natural History Press

Locke, John J. 1693/1994. *Some Thoughts on Education*. Edited by Frances W. Garforth. Woodbury, NY: Barron's Education Series

Lonsdorf, Elizabeth. 2005. Sex differences in the development of termite-fishing skills in the wild chimpanzees, *Pan troglodytes schweinfurthii,* of Gombe National Park, Tanzania. *Animal Behavior*, 70:673–683

Lorenz, John M., Paneth, Nigel, Jetton, James R., Ouden, Lyaden, and Tyson, Jon E. 2001. Comparison of management strategies for extreme prematurity in New Jersey and the Netherlands: Outcomes and resource expenditure. *Pediatrics*, 108:1269–1274

Lorenz, Konrad. 1943. Die angeborenen formen möglicher erfahrung. *Zeitschrift der Tierpsychologie*, 5:235–409

Loudon, John. B. 1970. Teasing and socialization on Tristan da Cunha, in *Socialization: The Approach from Social Anthropology*. Edited by Phillip Mayer, pp. 293–332. London, UK: Tavistock

Low, Bobbi S. 1989. Cross-cultural patterns in the training of children: An evolutionary perspective. *Journal of Comparative Psychology*, 103(4): 311–319

2000. Sex, wealth, and fertility: old rules, new environments, in *Adaptation and Human Behavior: An Anthropological Perspective*. Edited by Lee Cronk, Napoleon Chagnon, and William Irons, pp. 323–344. New York, NY: Aldine de Gruyter

2005. Families: An evolutionary anthropological perspective, in *Families in Global Perspective*. Edited by Jaipaul L. Roopnarine, pp. 14–32. Boston, MA: Pearson

Low, Bobbi S., Parker, Nicolas, and Hazel, Ashley. 2007. Ecological underpinnings of women's reproductive lives. Paper presented at annual meeting, Society for Cross-Cultural Research, San Antonio, TX, February 21–24

Low, Setha. 2003. *Behind the Gates: Life, Security, and the Pursuit of Happiness in Fortress America*. New York, NY: Routledge

Lown, Jean M. and Rowe, Barbara R. 2003. A profile of Utah consumer bankruptcy petitioners. *Journal of Law and Family Studies*, 5:113–130

Loy, John. 1970. Behavioral responses of free-ranging rhesus monkeys to food shortage. *American Journal of Physical Anthropology*, 33(2):263–272

Lozoff, Betsy and Brittenham, Gary. 1979. Infant care: Cache or carry. *Journal of Pediatrics*, 95(3):478–483

Lubeck, Sally. 1984. Kinship and classrooms: An ethnographic perspective on education as cultural transmission. *Sociology of Education*, 57:219–232

Lucy, Sam. 1994. Children in early medieval cemeteries. *Archaeological Review from Cambridge*, 13(2):24–37

Lupher, Mark. 1995. Revolutionary little red devils: The social psychology of rebel youth, 1966–1967, in *Chinese Views of Childhood*. Edited by Anne B. Kinney, pp. 321–343. Honolulu, HI: University of Hawai'i Press

Lutz, Catherine A. 1983. Parental goals, ethnopsychology, and the development of emotional meaning. *Ethos*, 11(4):246–262

1985. Cultural patterns and individual differences in the child's emotional meaning system, in *The Socialization of Emotions*. Edited by M. Lewis and C. Saarni. Chicago, IL: University of Chicago Press

1988. *Unnatural Emotions: Everyday Sentiments on a Micronesian Atoll and their Challenge to Western Theory*. Chicago, IL: University of Chicago Press

Lutz, Catherine A. and LeVine, R. A. 1983. Culture and intelligence in infancy: An ethnopsychological view, in *Origins of Intelligence*. Edited by M. Lewis, pp. 327–346. New York, NY: Plenum

Lynd, Robert S. and Lynd, Helen Merrell. 1929. *Middletown: A Study in American Culture*. New York, NY: Harcourt, Brace and Company

Lytton, Hugh and Romney, David. 1991. Parents' differential socialization of boys and girls: A meta-analysis. *Psychological Bulletin*, 109:267–296

Mabilia, Mara. 2005. *Breast Feeding and Sexuality: Beliefs and Taboos among the Gogo Mothers in Tanzania*. Oxford, UK: Berghahn Books

Maccoby, Michael. 1976. *The Gamesman*. New York, NY: Simon and Schuster

MacCormack, Carol P. 1994. Health, fertility and birth in Moyamba District, Sierra Leone, in *Ethnography of Fertility and Birth*. Edited by Carol, P. MacCormack, pp. 105–129. Prospect Heights, IL: Waveland Press

McCafferty, Geoffery G. and McCafferty, Sharisse D. 2006. Boys and girls interrupted: Mortuary evidence of children from postclassical Cholula, Puebla, in *The Social Experience of Childhood in Ancient Mesoamerica*. Edited by Traci Adren and Scott R. Hutson, pp. 25–82. Boulder, CO: University of Colorado Press

McElreath, Richard. 2004. Social learning and the maintenance of cultural variation: An evolutionary model and data from East Africa. *American Anthropologist*, 106(2):308–321

McGilvray, Dennis B. 1994. Sexual power and fertility in Sri Lanka: Batticaloa Tamils and Moors, in *Ethnography of Fertility and Birth*. Edited by Carol P. MacCormack, pp. 15–63. Prospect Heights, IL: Waveland Press

McGrew, William C. 1977. Socialization and object manipulation of wild chimpanzees, in *Primate Bio-Social Development: Biological, Social, and Ecological Determinants*. Edited by Suzanne Chevalier-Skolnikoff and Frank E. Poirier, pp. 261–288. New York, NY: Garland

McIvor, Chris. 2000. Child labour in informal mines in Zimbabwe, in *Earning a Life: Working Children in Zimbabwe*. Edited by Michael Bourdillon, pp. 173–185. Harare, Zimbabwe: Weaver Press

McLaren, Peter. 1980. *Cries from the Corridor*. Toronto, Ont.: Methuen

Maclean, Una. 1994. Folk medicine and fertility: Aspects of Yoruba medical practice affecting women, in *Ethnography of Fertility and Birth*. Edited by Carol P. MacCormack, pp. 151–169. Prospect Heights, IL: Waveland Press

McNaughton, Peter R. 1988. *The Mande Blacksmiths*. Bloomington, IN: Indiana University Press

McNaughton, Stuart. 1996. Ways of parenting and cultural identity. *Culture and Psychology*, 2:173–201

McPhee, Colin. 1955. Children and music in Bali, in *Childhood in Contemporary Cultures*. Edited by Margaret Mead and Martha Wolfenstein, pp. 70–98. Chicago, IL: University of Chicago Press

Madsen, Millard C. 1971. Developmental and cross-cultural differences in the cooperation and competitive behavior of young children. *Journal of Cross-Cultural Psychology*, 2:365–371

Maestripieri, Dario. 1994. Social structure, infant handling, and mothering styles in group-living Old World monkeys. *International Journal of Primatology*, 15:531–553

Maestripieri, Dario and Pelka, Suzanne. 2001. Sex differences in interest in infants across the lifespan: A biological adaptation for parenting? *Human Nature*, 13(3):327–344

Magnuson, Katherine A., Meyers, Marcia K., Rhum, Christopher J., and Waldfogel, Jane. 2004. Inequality in preschool education and school readiness. *American Education Research Journal*, 41:115–157

Makey, Wade C. 1983. A preliminary test for the validation of the adult male–child bond as a species-characteristic trait. *American Anthropologist*, 85:391–402

Malinowski, Bronislaw. 1929. *The Sexual Life of Savages*. New York, NY: Harcourt, Brace
    1932. *The Sexual Life of Savages in North-western Melanesia; An Ethnographic Account of Courtship, Marriage, and Family Life among the Natives of the Trobriand Islands, British New Guinea*. London, UK: Routledge

Malville, Nancy J. 1999. Porters of the eastern hills of Nepal: body size and load weight. *American Journal of Human Biology*, 11:1–11

Manderson, Lenore. 2003. Roasting, smoking, and dieting in response to birth: Malay confinement in cross-cultural perspective, in *The Manner Born: Birth Rites in Cross-Cultural Perspective*. Edited by Lauren Dundes, pp. 137–159. New York, NY: AltaMira Press

Manfra, Laurie. 2006. The ethics of rugs. *Metropolis*, 25(6):82–83

Mann, Gillian. 2004. Separated children: Care and support in context, in *Children and Youth on the Front Line: Ethnography, Armed Conflict and Displacement*. Edited by Jo Boyden and Joanna de Berry, pp. 3–22. New York, NY: Berghahn Books

Mann, Janet. 2002. Nurturance or negligence: Maternal psychology and behavioral preference among preterm twins, in *The Adapted Mind: Evolutionary Psychology and the Generation of Culture*. Edited by James Tooby, Leeda Cosmides, and Jerome Barkow, pp. 367–390. Oxford, UK: Oxford University Press

Mann, Rann Singh. 1979. *The Bay Islander*. Calcutta: Institute of Social Research and Applied Anthropology

Mannon, Susan E. and Kemp, Egan. 2005. Male youth employment in Costa Rica. Paper presented at the Pacific Sociological Association annual meetings, Portland, OR, April

Mapedzahama, Virginia and Bourdillon, Michael 2000. Street workers in a Harare suburb, in *Earning a Life: Working Children in Zimbabwe*. Edited by Michael Bourdillon, pp. 25–44. Harare, Zimbabwe: Weaver Press

Marchand, Trevor H. J. 2001. *Minaret Building and Apprenticeship in Yemen*. Richmond, UK: Curzon Press

Marguerat, Yves. 2000. The exploitation of apprentices in Togo, in *The Exploited Child*. Edited by Bernard Schlemmer, pp. 239–247. New York, NY: Zed Books

Mariko, Fujita. 1989. "It's All Mother's Fault": Childcare and the Socialization of Working Mothers in Japan. *Journal of Japanese Studies*, 15(1):67–91

Marks, Jonathan. 2003. *What It Means to be 98% Chimpanzee: Apes, People and their Genes*. Berkeley, CA: University of California Press

Marlow, Emily. 2002. *Danger: Children at Work* (DVD). London, UK: Television Trust for the Environment (TVE)

Marlowe, Frank W. 1999. Showoffs or providers? The Parenting effort of Hadza men. *Evolution and Human Behavior*, 20:391–404

   2004. Mate preferences among Hadza hunter-gatherers. *Human Nature*, 15(4):365–376

   2005. Who tends Hadza children?, in *Hunter Gatherer Childhoods: Evolutionary, Developmental, and Cultural Perspectives*. Edited by Barry S. Hewlett and Michael E. Lamb, pp. 177–190. New Brunswick, NJ: AldineTransaction

   2007. Hunting and gathering: The human sexual division of foraging labor. *Cross-Cultural Research*, 41(2):170–195

Marshall, John. 1972. *Playing with Scorpions* (film). Watertown, MA: Documentary Educational Resources

Martin, Diana. 2001. The meaning of children in Hong Kong, in *Managing Reproductive Life: Cross-Cultural Themes in Sexuality and Fertility*. Edited by Soraya Tremayne, pp. 157–171. Oxford, UK: Berghahn Books

Martin, Joyce A., Kochanek, Kenneth D., Strobino, Donna M., Guyer, Bernard, and MacDorman, Marian F. 2005. Annual summary of vital statistics: 2003. *Pediatrics*, 115(3):619–634

Martin, Kay and Voorhies, Barbara. 1975. *Female of the Species*. New York, NY: Columbia University Press

Martini, Mary. 1994. Peer interactions in Polynesia: A view from the Marquesas, in *Children's Play in Diverse Cultures*. Edited by Jaipaul L. Roopnarine, James E. Jonson, and Frank H. Hooper, pp. 73–103. Albany, NY: State University of New York Press

   1995. Features of home environments associated with children's school success. *Early Child Development and Care*, 111:49–68

   1996. "What's new?" at the dinner table: Family dynamics during mealtimes in two cultural groups in Hawaii. *Early Development and Parenting*, 5(1):23–34

   2005. Family development in two island cultures in the changing Pacific, in *Families in Global Perspective*. Edited by Jaipaul L. Roopnarine, pp. 120–147. Boston, MA: Pearson

Martini, Mary and Kirkpatrick, John. 1981. Early interaction in the Marquesas Islands, in *Culture and Early Interactions*. Edited by Tiffany M. Field, Anita M. Sostek, Peter Vietze, and P. Herbert Leiderman. Hillsdale, NJ: Lawrence Erlbaum.

   1992. Parenting in Polynesia: A view from the Marquesas, in *Parent–Child Socialization in Diverse Cultures*, Vol. V: *Annual Advances in Applied Developmental Psychology*. Edited by Jaipaul L. Roopnarine and D. Bruce Carter, pp. 199–222. Norwood, NJ: Ablex

Marvin, Harris. 1990. *Our Kind*. New York, NY: Harper and Row

Maschio, Thomas. 1995. Mythic images and objects of myth in Rauto female puberty ritual, in *Gender Rituals: Female Initiation in Melanesia*. Edited by Nancy C. Lutkehaus and Paul B. Roscoe, pp. 131–161. London, UK: Routledge

Mathews, Harold. F. 1992. The directive force of morality tales in a Mexican community, in *Human Motives and Cultural Models*. Edited by Roy D'Andrade and Claudia Strauss, pp. 127–162. New York, NY: Cambridge University Press

Matias, Aisha Samad. 1996. Female circumcision in Africa. *Africa Update*, 3(2)

Matsuzawa, Tetsuro. 1994. Field experiments on use of stone tools by chimpanzees in the wild, in *Chimpanzee Cultures*. Edited by Richard Wrangham, William C. McGrew, Frans B. M. de Waal, and Paul G. Heltne, pp. 351–370. Cambridge, MA: Harvard University Press

Mattingly, Doreen J., Prislin, Radmila, McKenzie, Thomas L., Rodriguez, James L., and Kayzar, Brenda. 2002. Evaluating evaluations: The case of parent involvement programs. *Review of Educational Research*, 72(4):549–576

Mawson, Andrew. 2004. Children, impunity and justice: Some dilemmas from northern Uganda, in *Children and Youth on the Front Line: Ethnography, Armed Conflict and Displacement*. Edited by Jo Boyden and Joanna de Berry, pp. 130–141. New York, NY: Berghahn Books

Maxwell Katz (West), Mary. 1985. Infant care in a group of outer Fiji islands, in *Infant Care and Feeding in the South Pacific*. Edited by Leslie B. Marshall, pp. 269–292. New York, NY: Gordon and Breach Science

Maxwell Katz (West), Mary and Konner, Melvin J. 1981. The role of the father: An anthropological perspective, in *The Role of the Father in Child Development*. Edited by Michael E. Lamb, pp. 155–218. New York, NY: Wiley

Maxwell West (Katz), Mary. 1988. Parental values and behavior in the outer Fiji islands, in *Parental Behaviour in Diverse Societies*. Edited by Robert LeVine, Patrice M. Miller, and Mary Maxwell West. *New Directions for Child Development*, 40:13–26

Mayer, Philip and Mayer, Iona. 1970. Socialization by peers: The youth organization of the Red Xhosa, in *Socialization: The Approach from Social Anthropology*. Edited by Philip Mayer, pp. 159–189. London, UK: Tavistock Publications

Maynard, Ashley E. 2004. Sibling interactions, in *Childhood and Adolescence: Cross-Cultural Perspectives and Applications*. Edited by Uwe P. Gielen and Jaipaul L. Roopnarine, pp. 229–252. Westport, CT: Praeger

Maynard, Ashley E., Greenfield, Patricia M., and Childs, Carla P. 1999. Culture, history, biology and body: Native and non-native acquisition of technological skill. *Ethos*, 27(3):379–402

Mays, Sam. 2000. The archaeology and history of infanticide, and its occurrence in earlier British populations, in *Children and Material Culture*. Edited by Joanna S. Derevenski, pp. 180–190. London, UK: Routledge

Mbilinyi, Marjorie. 1998. Searching for Utopia: The politics of gender and education in Tanzania, in *Women and Education in Sub-Saharan Africa: Power, Opportunities, and Constraints*. Edited by Marianne Bloch, Josephine A. Beoku-Betts, and B. Robert Tabachnick, pp. 277–295. Boulder, CO: Lynne Rienner

Mead, Margaret. 1928/1961. *Coming of Age in Samoa*. New York, NY: New American Library

1955. Children and ritual in Bali, in *Childhood in Contemporary Cultures*. Edited by Margaret Mead and Martha, Wolfenstein, pp. 40–51. Chicago: IL: University of Chicago Press

1972. *Blackberry Winter: My Earlier Years*. New York, NY: Kondansha International

Mechling, Jay. 2001. *On My Honor: Boy Scouts and the Making of American Youth*. Chicago, IL: University of Chicago Press

Mederer, Helen J. 1993. Division of labor in two-earner homes: Task accomplishment versus household management as critical variables in perceptions about family work. *Journal of Marriage and the Family*, 55(1):133–145

Meehan, Courtney L. 2005. The effects of residential locality on parental and allo-parental investment among the Aka foragers of the Central African Republic. *Human Nature*, 16:58–80

Meinert, Lotte. 2003. Sweet and bitter places: The politics of schoolchildren's orientation in rural Uganda, in *Children's Places: Cross-Cultural Perspectives*. Edited by Karen Fog Olwig and Eva Gullov, pp. 179–196. New York, NY: Routledge

Meintjes, Helen and Giese, Sonja. 2006. Spinning the epidemic: The making of mythologies of orphanhood in the context of AIDS. *Childhood*, 13(3):407–430

Mejia-Arauz, Rebecca, Rogoff, Barbara, and Paradise, Ruth. (2005). Cultural variation in children's observation during a demonstration. *International Journal of Behavioral Development*, 29(4):282–291

Menon, Shanti. 1996. To appease the mountain. *Discovery*, 17(1):22–23

2001. Male authority and female autonomy: A study of the matrilineal Nayars of Kerala, south India, in *Gender in Cross-Cultural Perspective*. Edited by Caroline B. Brettell and Carolyn F. Sargent, pp. 352–361. Upper Saddle River, NJ: Prentice Hall

Mergen, Bernard. 1992. Made, bought, and stolen: Toys and the culture of childhood, in *Small Worlds: Children and Adolescents in America, 1850–1950*. Edited by Elliott West and Paula Petrik, pp. 86–106. Lawrence, KS: University Press of Kansas

Meskell, Lynn. 1994. Dying young: The experience of death at Deir el Medina. *Archaeological Review from Cambridge*, 13:35–45

Messing, Simon D. 1985. *Highland Plateau Amhara of Ethiopia*. New Haven, CT: Human Relations Area Files

Michaels, Sarah and Cazden, Courtney B. 1986. Teacher/child collaboration as oral preparation for literacy, in *The Acquisition of Literacy: Ethnographic Perspectives*. Edited by Bambi B. Schiefflin and Perry Gilmore, pp. 132–154. Norwood, NJ: Ablex

Michalchik, Vera S. 1997. The display of cultural knowledge in cultural transmission: Models of participation from the Pacific Island of Kosrae, in *Education and Cultural Process: Anthropological Approaches*. Edited by George D. Spindler, pp. 393–426. Prospect Heights, IL: Waveland Press

Mickelson, Roslyn A. 2000. Globalization, childhood poverty and education in the Americas, in *Children on the Streets of the Americas: Globalization, Homelessness, and Education in the United States, Brazil, and Cuba*. Edited by Roslyn A. Mickelson, pp. 11–42. New York, NY: Routledge

Millard, Ann V. and Graham, Margaret A. 1985. Breastfeeding in two Mexican villages: Social and demographic perspectives, in *Breastfeeding, Child Health and Birth Spacing: Cross-Cultural Perspectives*. Edited by Valerie Hull and Mayling Simpson, pp. 55–74. London, UK: Croom Helm

Miller, Barbara D. 1987. Female infanticide and child neglect in rural north India, in *Child Survival: Anthropological Perspectives on the Treatment and Maltreatment of Children*. Edited by Nancy Scheper-Hughes, pp. 95–112. Dordrecht, Holland: D. Reidel

    1995. Precepts and practices: Researching identity formation among Indian Hindu adolescents in the United States, in *Cultural Practices as Contexts for Development*. Edited by Jacqueline J. Goodnow, Peggy J. Miller, and Frank Kessel, pp. 71–90. San Francisco, CA: Jossey-Bass

Miller, Brent C., Leavitt, Spencer C., Merrill, Junius K., and Park, Kyung-Eun. 2005. Marriages and families in the United States, in *Families in Global Perspective*. Edited by Jaipaul L. Roopnarine, pp. 293–310. Boston, MA: Pearson

Minehan, Thomas. 1934. *Boy and Girl Tramps of America*. New York, NY: Farrar and Rinehart

Mitchell, George. 1981. *Human Sex Differences: A Primatologists' Perspective*. New York, NY: Van Nostrand Reinhold

Mittelstaedt, Martin. 2006. Ottawa plans to snuff out flame retardants: Researchers link common chemicals to hyperactivity. Workopolis.com, May 30

Mitterauer, Michael. 1992. *A History of Youth*. Oxford, UK: Blackwell

Mock, Douglas W. 2004. *More than Kin and Less than Kind: The Evolution of Family Conflict*. Cambridge, MA: Harvard University Press

Modiano, Nancy. 1973. *Indian Education in the Chiapas Highlands*. New York, NY: Holt, Rinehart, and Winston

Mohammad, Patel H. 1997. Child rearing and socialization among the Savaras. *Man and Life*, 23:173–182

Monberg, Torben. 1970. Determinants of choice in adoption and fosterage on Bella Island. *Ethnology*, 9(2):99–136

Montague, Susan P. 1985. Infant feeding and health care in Kaduwaga Village, the Trobriand Islands, in *Infant Care and Feeding in the South Pacific*. Edited by Leslie B. Marshall, pp. 83–96. New York, NY: Gordon and Breach

Montgomery, Heather. 2001a. *Modern Babylon: Prostituting Children in Thailand*. Oxford, UK: Berghahn Books

    2001b. Motherhood, fertility and ambivalence among young prostitutes in Thailand, in *Managing Reproductive Life: Cross-Cultural Themes in Sexuality and Fertility*. Edited by Soraya Tremayne, pp. 71–84. Oxford, UK: Berghahn Books

Moore, Leslie C. 2006. Learning by heart in Qur'anic and public schools in northern Cameroon. *Social Analysis: The International Journal of Cultural and Social Practice*, 50(3):109–126

Morais, Maria and Gosso, Yumii. 2003. Pretend play of Brazilian children: A window into different cultural worlds. Paper presented at 33rd annual meeting, Jean Piaget Society, Chicago, June

Morelli, Gilda A., Rogoff, Barbara, and Angelillo, Cathy. 2003. Cultural variation in young children's access to work or involvement in specialized child-focused activities. *International Journal of Behavioral Development*, 27(3):264–274

Morelli, Gilda A. and Tronick, Edward Z. 1991. Parenting and child development in the Efe foragers and Lese farmers of Zaire, in *Cultural Approaches to Parenting*. Edited by Mark H. Bornstein, pp. 91–113. Hillsdale, NJ: Erlbaum

Morgan, Lynn M. 1998 Ambiguities lost: fashioning the fetus into a child in Ecuador and the United States, in *Small Wars: The Cultural Politics of Childhood*. Edited by Nancy Scheper-Hughes and Carolyn F. Sargent, pp. 58–74. Berkeley, CA: University of California Press

Morton, Helen. 1996. *Becoming Tongan: An Ethnography of Childhood*. Honolulu, HI: University of Hawai'i Press

Moynihan, Brian. 2002. *The Faith: A History of Christianity*. New York, NY: Doubleday

Mulder, Monique Borgerhoff. 1992. Reproductive decisions, in *Evolutionary Ecology and Human Behavior*. Edited by Eric Alden Smith and Bruce Winterhalder, pp. 339–374. New York, NY: Aldine

Mull, Dorothy S. 1992. Mother's milk and pseudoscientific breastmilk testing in Pakistan. *Social Science and Medicine*, 34:1277–1290

Mull, Dorothy S. and Mull, J. Dennis. 1987. Infanticide among the Tarahumara of the Mexican Sierra Madre, in *Child Survival: Anthropological Perspectives on the Treatment and Maltreatment of Children*. Edited by Nancy Scheper-Hughes, pp. 113–132. Dordrecht, Holland: D. Reidel

Munroe, Lee. 2005. Fatherhood and effects on children in four cultures. Paper presented at 34th annual meeting, Society for Cross-Cultural Research, Santa Fe, February 25

Munroe, Robert L. and Munroe, Ruth H. 1972. Obedience among children in an East African society. *Journal of Cross-Cultural Psychology*, 3(4):395–400

    1992. Fathers in children's environments: A four culture study, in *Father–Child Relations: Cultural and Biosocial Contexts*. Edited by Barry S. Hewlett, pp. 213–229. New York, NY: Aldine de Gruyter

Munroe, Ruth H., Munroe, Robert L., and Shimmin, Harold S. 1984. Children's work in four cultures: Determinants and consequences. *American Anthropologist*, 86:369–379

Murdock, George P. 1967. *Ethnographic Atlas*. Pittsburg, PA: University of Pittsburgh Press

Murphy, Elizabeth. 2007. Images of childhood in mothers' accounts of contemporary childrearing. *Childhood*, 14(1):105–127

Musil, Alois. 1928. *The Manners and Customs of the Rwala Bedouin*. New York: American Geographical Society

Myers, James. 1992. Non-mainstream body modifications: Genital piercing, branding, burning, and cutting. *Journal of Contemporary Ethnography*, 21(3):267–306

Nag, Moni, White, Benjamin N. F., and Peet, R. Creighton. 1978. An anthropological approach to the study of the economic value of children in Java and Nepal. *Current Anthropology*, 19(2):293–306

Naito, Takashi and Gielen, Uwe P. 2005. The changing Japanese family: A psychological portrait, in *Families in Global Perspective*. Edited by Jaipaul L. Roopnarine, pp. 63–84. Boston, MA: Pearson

Nasaw, David. 1992. Children and commercial culture, in *Small Worlds: Children and Adolescents in America, 1850–1950*. Edited by Elliott West and Paula Petrik, pp. 14–25. Lawrence, KS: University Press of Kansas

Nash, Manning. 1970. Education in a new nation: the village school in upper Burma, in *From Child to Adult*. Edited by John Middleton, pp. 301–313. Garden City, NY: The Natural History Press

Nath, Samir R. and Hadi, Abdullahel. 2000. Role of education in reducing child labour: Evidence from rural Bangaladesh. *Journal of Biosocial Science*, 32:301–313

Neel, James V. 1970. Lessons from a "primitive" people. *Science*, 170:815–22

Neill, Sean R. 1983. Children's social relationships and education: An evolutionary effect? *Social Biology and Human Affairs*, 47:48–55

Neils, Jennifer and Oakley, John H. 2003. *Coming of Age in Ancient Greece* (DVD). Cincinnati, OH: Institute of Mediterranean Studies

Nerlove, Sarah B. 1974. Women's workload and infant feeding practices: A relationship with demographic implications. *Ethnology*, 13:207–214

Nerlove, Sarah B. and Roberts, John M. 1974. Natural indicators of cognitive development: An observational study of rural Guatemalan children. *Ethos*, 2:265–295

Neuman, Susan B. 1996. *Evaluation of the Books Aloud Project: An Executive Summary*. Philadelphia, PA: William Penn Foundation

New Atlantis. 2005. *The Korubo People of Amazonia* (film). Princeton, NJ: Films for the Humanities and Sciences

New, Rebecca S. 1994. Child's play – *una cosa naturale*: An Italian perspective, in *Children's Play in Diverse Cultures*. Edited by Jaipaul L. Roopnarine, James E. Johnson, and Frank H. Hooper, pp. 123–147. Albany, NY: State University of New York Press

Nicholls, Robert W. 2006. *Omepa* and *Onyeweh* children's masquerades, in *Playful Performers: African Children's Masquerades*. Edited by Simon Ottenberg and David A. Binkley, pp. 129–150. New Brunswick, NJ: Transaction Publishers

Nicolaisen, Ida. 1988. Concepts and learning among the Punan Bah of Sarawak, in *Acquiring Culture: Cross Cultural Studies in Child Development*. Edited by Gustav Jahoda and Ioan Lewis, pp. 193–221. London, UK: Croom Helm

Nicolas, David. 1991. Children in medieval Europe, in *Children in Historical and Comparative Perspective*. Edited by Joseph M. Hawes and N. Ray Hiner, pp. 31–52. Westport, CT: Greenwood Press

Nicolson, Nancy A. 1977. A comparison of early behavioral development in wild and captive chimpanzees, in *Primate Bio-Social Development: Biological, Social, and Ecological Determinants*. Edited by Suzanne Chevalier-Skolnikoff and Frank E. Poirier, pp. 529–600. New York, NY: Garland

Nieuwenhuys, Olga. 1994. *Children's Lifeworlds: Gender, Welfare, and Labour in the Developing World*. London, UK: Routledge

1996. The paradox of child labor and anthropology. *Annual Review of Anthropology*, 25:237–251

2003. Growing up between places of work and non-places of childhood: The uneasy relationship, in *Children's Places: Cross-Cultural Perspectives*. Edited by Karen Fog Olwig and Eva Gullov, pp. 99–118. New York, NY: Routledge

2005. The wealth of children: Reconsidering the child labor debate, in *Studies in Modern Childhood*. Edited by Jens Qvortrup, pp. 167–183. Houndsmills, UK: Palgrave Macmillian

Nimmo, H. Arlo. 1970. Bajau sex and reproduction. *Ethnology*, 9(3):251–262

Noonan, John T. 1970. An almost absolute value in history, in *The Morality of Abortion: Legal and Historical Perspectives*. Edited by John T. Noonan, pp. 1–59. Cambridge, MA: Harvard University Press

Nsamenang, Bame A. 1992. *Human Development in Cultural Context: A Third-World Perspective*. Newbury Park, CA: Sage

2002. Adolescence in sub-Saharan Africa: An image constructed from Africa's triple inheritance, in *The World's Youth: Adolescence in Eight Regions of the Globe*. Edited by Bradford B. Brown, Reed W. Larson, and T. S. Saraswathi, pp. 61–105. Cambridge, MA: Cambridge University Press

Nwokah, Evangeline E. and Ikekonwu, Clara. 1998. A sociocultural comparison of Nigerian and American children's games, in *Diversions and Divergences in Fields of Play*. Edited by Margaret C. Duncan, Garry Chick, and Alan Aycock, pp. 59–76. Westport, CT: Ablex

Nzewi, Esther. 2005. "Street peddling" and the risks for sexual trauma in African children mediated by culture and social class. Paper presented at 34th Annual Meeting, Society for Cross-Cultural Research, Santa Fe, February

O'Brien, Catherine. 2003. The nature of childhood through history revealed in artworks? *Childhood*, 10(3):362–378

O'Conner, Stephen. 2001. *Orphan Trains: The Story of Charles Loring Brace and the Children He Saved and Failed*. Boston. MA: Houghton Mifflin

O'Neill-Wagner, Peggy. 2003. Play, exploration and program attentiveness of monkeys introduced to audio-visual entertainment. Paper presented at annual meeting, Association for the Study of Play, Charleston, SC, February

Ochs, Elinor. 1988. *Culture and Language Development: Language Socialization and Language Acquisition in a Samoan Village*. Cambridge, UK: Cambridge University Press

Ochs, Elinor and Schieffelin, Bambi B. 1984. Language acquisition and socialization: Three developmental stories and their implications, in *Culture Theory: Essays on Mind, Self and Society*. Edited by Richard A. Shweder and Robert A. LeVine, pp. 276–320. New York, NY: Cambridge University Press

Ochs, Elinor, Taylor, Carolyn, Rudolph, Dina, and Smith, Ruth. 1992. Storytelling as a theory-building activity. *Discourse Processes*, 15:37–72

Ogbu, John U. 1987. Variability in minority school performance: A problem in search of an explanation. *Anthropology and Education Quarterly*, 18(4):312–334

2003. *Black American Students in an Affluent Suburb: A Study of Academic Disengagement*. Mahwah, NJ: Lawrence Erlbaum Associates

Ohmagari, Kayo and Berkes, Fikret. 1997. Transmission of indigenous knowledge and bush skills among the Western James Bay Cree women of subarctic Canada. *Human Ecology*, 23(2):197–222

Okagaki, Lynn and Sternberg, Robert J. 1993. Parental beliefs and children's school performance. *Child Development*, 64:36–56

Oleke, Christopher, Blystad, Astrid, Moland, Karen Marie, Rekdal, Ole Bjorn, and Heggenhougen, Kristian. 2005. The varying vulnerability of African orphans: The case of the Langi, northern Uganda. *Childhood*, 13(2):267–284

Oloko, Beatrice A. 1994. Children's street work in urban Nigeria: Dilemma of modernizing tradition, in *Cross-Cultural Roots of Minority Child Development*. Edited by Patricia M. Greenfield and Rodney R. Cocking, pp. 197–224. Hillsdale, NJ: Erlbaum

Olson, David R. 2003. *Psychological Theory and Educational Reform: How School Remakes Mind and Society*. New York, NY: Cambridge University Press

Olusanya, P.O. 1989. Human reproduction in Africa: Fact, myth and the martyr syndrome. *Research for Development*, 6:69–97

Oonk, Gerard. 2000. *The Dark Side of Football*. Amsterdam: Indian Committee of the Netherlands

Opie, Iona and Opie, Peter. 1969. *Children's Games in Street and Playground*. Oxford, UK: Clarendon Press

1997. *Children's Games with Things*. Oxford, UK: Oxford University Press

Orellana, Marjorie Faulstich. 2001. The work kids do: Mexican and Central American immigrant children's contributions to households and schools in California. *Harvard Educational Review*, 71(3):366–389

Ottenberg, Simon. 1968. *Double Descent in an African Society: The Afikpo Village-group*. Seattle, WA: University of Washington Press

1989. *Boyhood Rituals in an African Society: An Interpretation*. Seattle, WA: University of Washington Press

2006. Emulation in boy's masquerades: The Afikpo case, in *Playful Performers: African Children's Masquerades*. Edited by Simon Ottenberg and David A. Binkley, pp. 117–127. New Brunswick, NJ: Transaction Publishers

Overing, Joanna. 1988. Personal autonomy and the domestication of the self in Piaroa society, in *Acquiring Culture: Cross-Cultural Studies in Child Development*. Edited by Gustav Jahod and Ioan M. Lewis, pp. 169–192. London, UK: Croom Helm

Packer, Boyd K. 1993. For time and all eternity. *Ensign*, January: 21–25

Palley, Thomas I. 2002. The child labor problem and the need for international labor standards. *Journal of Economic Issues*, 36(3):1–15

Palmeri, Christopher. 2005. In hot pursuit of Yoga Mama. *Business Week*, 3958:128

Palonsky, Stuart B. 1975. Hempies and squeaks, truckers and cruisers: A participant observer study in a city high school. *Educational Administration Quarterly*, 11(2):86–103

Pan, Hui-ling Wendy. 1994. Children's play in Taiwan, in *Children's Play in Diverse Cultures*. Edited by Jaipaul L. Roopnarine, James E. Johnson, and Frank H. Hooper, pp. 31–72. Albany, NY: State University of New York Press

Pandya, Vishvajit. 1992. Gukwelonone: The game of hiding fathers and seeking sons among the Ongee of Little Andaman, in *Father–Child Relations: Cultural and Biosocial Contexts*. Edited by Barry S. Hewlett, pp. 263–279. New York, NY: Aldine

2005. Deforesting among Adamanese children, in *Hunter Gatherer Childhoods: Evolutionary, Developmental, and Cultural Perspectives*. Edited by Barry S. Hewlett and Michael E. Lamb, pp. 385–406. New Brunswick, NJ: AldineTransaction

Parin, Paul. 1963. *The Whites Think Too Much: Psychoanalytic Investigations among the Dogon in West Africa*. Zurich, Switzerland: Atlantis Verlag

Park, Young-Shin and Kim, Uichol. 2006. Family, parent–child relationship, and academic achievement in Korea: Indigenous, cultural, and psychological analysis, in *Indigenous and Cultural Psychology: Understanding People in Context*. Edited by

Uichol Kim, Kuo-Shu Yang, and Kwang-Kuo Hwang, pp. 421–443. New York: Springer.

Parker, Sue Taylor. 1984. Playing for keeps: An evolutionary perspective on human games, in *Play in Animals and Humans*. Edited by Peter K. Smith, pp. 271–294. London, UK: Basil Blackwell

Patterson, Cynthia. 1985. "Not worth rearing": The causes of infant exposure in ancient Greece. *Transactions of the American Philological Association*, 115:103–123

Paulli, Julia. 2005. "We didn't grow up together!" Relatedness among the Damara/Nama of Fransfontein, Namibia. Paper presented at Familie und Verwandtschaft conference, Bayreuth, July

Paulme, Denise. 1940. *Social Organization of the Dogon*. Paris, France: Éditions Domat-Montchrestien

Pearsall, Marion. 1950. *Klamath Childhood and Education*. Berkeley, CA: University of California Press

Pederson, Jon. 1987. Plantation women and children: Wage labor, adoption, and fertility in the Seychelles. *Ethnology*, 26(1):51–61

Peisner, Ellen S. 1989. To spare or not to spare the rod: A cultural-historical view of child discipline, in *Child Development in Cultural Context*. Edited by Jaan Valsiner, pp. 111–141. Lewiston, NY: Hogrefe and Huber

Peissel, Michel. 1992. *Mustang: A Lost Tibetan Kingdom*. Delhi, India: South Asia Books

Pellegrini, Anthony D. 1984–1985. The effects of exploration and play on young children's associative fluency. *Imagination, Cognition, and Personality*, 4:29–40

    2002. Rough-and-tumble play from childhood through adolescence: Development and possible functions, in *Blackwell Handbook of Childhood Social Development*. Edited by Peter K. Smith and Craig H. Hart, pp. 438–474. Malden, UK: Blackwell Publishers

    2003. Perceptions and possible functions of play and real fighting in early adolescence. *Child Development*, 74:1552–1533

    2004. Sexual segregation in childhood: A review of evidence for two hypotheses. *Animal Behaviour* 68(3):435–443

Pellegrini, Anthony D. and Bjorkland, David F. 2004. The ontogeny and phylogeny of children's object and fantasy play. *Human Nature*, 15(1):23–43

Pennington, Renee and Harpending, Henry. 1993. *The Structure of an African Pastoralist Community: Demography, History, and Ecology of the Ngamiland Herero*. Oxford, UK: Oxford University Press

Peter D. Hart Research Associates. 2005. *Rising to the Challenge: Are High School Graduates Prepared for College and Work?* Washington, DC: Achieve

Peters, John F. 1998. *Life among the Yanomami: The Story of Change among the Xilixana on the Mucajai River in Brazil*. Orchard Park, NY: Broadview Press

Philbrick, Nathaniel. 2000. *In the Heart of the Sea*. London, UK: HarperCollins

Phillips, Susan U. 1983. *Invisible Culture: Communication in Classroom and Community on the Warm Springs Indian Reservation*. White Plains, NY: Longman

Piaget, Jean. 1932/1965. *The Moral Judgment of the Child*. Translated by Marjorie Gabain. New York, NY: Free Press

    1951. *Play Dreams and Imitation in Childhood*. New York, NY: W. W. Norton

Pickering, Apryle J. 2005. Individual agency in the context of powerful cultural forces: Fertility strategies in contemporary Nepal. Paper presented at annual meeting, American Anthropological Association, Washington, DC, December

Pine, Karen J. and Nash, Avril. 2002. Dear Santa: The effects of television advertising on young children. *International Journal of Behavioral Development*, 26(6):529–539

Pitock, Trevor. 1996. Dreaming of Michaela. *Tikkun*, 11(6):54

Platt, Katherine. 1988. Cognitive development and sex roles of the Kerkennah Islands of Tunisia, in *Acquiring Culture: Cross-Cultural Studies in Child Development*. Edited by Gustav Jahoda and Ioan M. Lewis, pp. 271–287. London, UK: Croom Helm

Plooij, Frans. 1979. How wild chimpanzee babies trigger the onset of mother–infant play and what the mother makes of it, in *Before Speech: The Beginning of Interpersonal Communication*. Edited by Margaret Bullowa, pp. 223–243. Cambridge, MA: Cambridge University Press

Poirier, Frank E. 1977. Introduction, in *Primate Bio-Social Development: Biological, Social, and Ecological Determinants*. Edited by Suzanne Chevalier-Skolnikoff and Frank E. Poirier, pp. 1–39. New York, NY: Garland

Polak, Barbara. 2003. Little peasants: On the importance of reliability in child labour, in *Le travail en Afrique noire: Représentations et pratiques à l'époque contemporaine*. Edited by Hèléne D'Almeida-Topor, Monique Lakroum, and Gerd Spittler, pp. 125–136. Paris, France: Karthala

Pollock, Linda A. 1983. *Forgotten Children: Parent–Child Relations from 1500 to 1900*. Cambridge, MA: Cambridge University Press

Poluha, Eva. 2004. *The Power of Continuity: Ethiopia through the Eyes of its Children*. Stockholm, Sweden: Nordiska Afrikainstitutet

Pomerantz, Eva M. and Moorman, Elizabeth A. 2007. The how, whom, and why of parental involvement in children's academic lives: More is not always better. *Review of Educational Research*, 77(3):373–410

Pomponio, Alice. 1981. School, fish and timber: Economic development and culture change on Mandok Island, Siassi Sub District, Morobe Province. Seminar presented to the Papua New Guinea Institute of Applied Social and Economic Research, Port Moresby, Papua New Guinea, March

1992. *Seagulls Don't Fly into the Bush*. Belmont, CA: Wadsworth

Pomponio, Alice and Lancy, David F. 1986. A pen or a bush knife: School, work and personal investment in Papua New Guinea. *Anthropology and Education Quarterly*, 17:40–61

Pontecorvo, Clotilde, Fasulo, Allesandra, and Sterponi, Laura. 2001. Mutual apprentices: The making of parenthood and childhood in family dinner conversations. *Human Development*, 44:340–361

Portes, Pedro, Dunham, Richard M., King, F. J., and Kidwell, Jeannie S. 1988. Early age intervention and parent-child interaction: Their relation to student achievement. *Journal of Research and Development in Education*, 21(4):78–86

Potter, Sulamith Heins. 1987. Birth planning in rural China: A cultural account, in *Child Survival: Anthropological Perspectives on the Treatment and Maltreatment of Children*. Edited by Nancy Scheper-Hughes, pp. 33–58. Dordrecht, Holland: D. Reidel

Potts, Malcolm and Short, Roger. 1999. *Ever since Adam and Eve: The Evolution of Human Sexuality.* Cambridge, UK: Cambridge University Press

Power, Thomas G. 2000. *Play and Exploration in Children and Animals.* Mahwah, NJ: Lawrence Erlbaum Associates

Power, Thomas G. and Ross, D. Parke. 1982. Play as a context for early learning: Lab and home analyses, in *Families as Learning Environments for Children.* Edited by Luis M. Laosa and Irving E. Sigel, pp. 147–178. New York, NY: Plenum Press

Prosser, G.V., Hutt, Corinne, Hutt, Stephen J., Mahindadasa, K. J., and Goonetilleke, M. D. J. 1986. Children's play in Sri Lanka: A cross-cultural study. *The British Psychological Society,* 4:179–186

Prothro, Edwin Terry. 1961. *Child Rearing in the Lebanon.* Cambridge, MA: Harvard University Press

Pufall, Peter B. and Unsworth, Richard P. 2004. The imperative and the process for rethinking childhood, in *Rethinking Childhood.* Edited by Peter B. Pufall and Richard P. Unsworth, pp. 1–21. New Brunswick, NJ: Rutgers University Press

Punch, Samantha. 2003. Childhoods in the majority world: Miniature adults or tribal children? *Sociology,* 37(2):277–295

Purcell-Gates, Victoria. 1994. Nonliterate homes and emergent literacy, in *Children's Emergent Literacy: From Research to Practice.* Edited by David F. Lancy, pp. 41–52. Westport, CT: Praeger

Qin, Wen-jie. (dir.) 1997. *We are Not Beggars* (film). Watertown, MA: Documentary Educational Resources

Quinn, Naomi. 1978. Do Mfantse fish sellers estimate probability in their heads? *American Ethnologist,* 5(2):206–226

2005. Universals of child rearing. *Anthropological Theory,* 5(4):477–516

Rabain, Jean. 1979. *L'enfant du lignage: Du sevrage á la classe d'âge.* Paris, France: Payot

Rae-Espinoza, Heather. 2006. Methodological techniques in the psychological evaluation of the children left behind. Paper presented at 35th annual meeting, Society for Cross-Cultural Research, Savannah, GA, February 23

Raffaele, Paul. 2003. *The Last Tribes on Earth: Journeys among the World's Most Threatened Cultures.* Sydney, Australia: Pan Macmillan

2005. Born into bondage. *Smithsonian Magazine,* 36(6):64–73

2006. Sleeping with cannibals. *Smithsonian Magazine,* 37(8):10–11

Ragone, Helena. 2001. Surrogate motherhood: Rethinking biological models, kinship, and family, in *Gender in Cross-Cultural Perspective.* Edited by Caroline B. Brettell and Carolyn F. Sargent, pp. 470–480. Upper Saddle River, NJ: Prentice Hall

Raitt, Margaret and Lancy, David F. 1988. Rhinestone cowgirl: The education of a rodeo queen. *Play and Culture,* 1(4):267–281

Rajman, Anika and Toubia, Nahid. 2000. Background and history, in *Female Genital Mutilation: A Guide to Laws and Policies Worldwide.* London: Zed Books

Rampal, Anita. 2003. The meaning of numbers: Understanding street and folk mathematics, in *Reading Beyond the Alphabet: Innovations in Lifelong Literacy.* Edited by Brij Kothari, P. G. Vijaya, Sherry Chand, and Michael Norton, pp. 241–258. New Delhi, India: Sage.

Randerson, James. 2002. Asia's biotech tiger. *New Scientist,* 175:54–55

Ransel, David. 1988. *Mothers of Misery: Child Abandonment in Russia*. Princeton, NJ: Princeton University Press

Rao, Vijay. 1993. The rising price of husbands: A hedonic analysis of dowry increases in rural India. *Journal of Political Economy*, 101:666–677

1997. Wife-beating in rural south India: A qualitative and econometric analysis. *Journal of Sociology, Science and Medicine*, 44:1169–1180

Raphael, Dana L. 1966. The lactation-suckling process within a matrix of supportive behavior. Unpublished Ph.D. dissertation, New York: Columbia University

Raphael, Dana and Davis, Flora. 1985. *Only Mothers Know: Patterns of Infant Feeding in Traditional Cultures*. Westport, CT: Greenwood Press

Rappaport, Roy A. 1967. *Pigs for the Ancestors: Ritual in the Ecology of a New Guinea People*. New Haven, CT: Yale University Press

Rattray, Robert S. 1927. *Religion and Art in Ashanti*. Oxford, UK: Clarendon Press

Raum, Otto F. 1940. *Chaga Childhood*. London, UK: Oxford University Press

Ravololomanga, Bodo and Schlemmer, Bernard. 2000. "Unexploited" labour: Social transition in Madagascar, in *The Exploited Child*. Edited by Bernard Schlemmer, pp. 300–313. New York, NY: Zed Books

Rawson, Beryl. 1991. Adult–child relationships in Roman society, in *Marriage, Divorce, and Children in Ancient Rome*. Edited by Beryl Rawson, pp. 7–30. Canberra, Australia: Clarendon Press

Read, Margaret. 1960. *Children of their Fathers: Growing up among the Ngoni of Malawi*. New Haven, CT: Yale University Press

Reay, Marie. 1959. *The Kuma: Freedom and Conformity in the New Guinea Highlands*. Melbourne, Australia: Melbourne University Press

Rebeck, Theresa. 2003. *Bad Dates*. New York, NY: Dramatists Play Service

Reeder, Ellen D. 1995. Women as the metaphor of wild animals, in *Pandora: Women in Classical Greece*. Edited by Ellen D. Reeder, pp. 299–372. Baltimore: Walters Art Gallery

Reese, Debbie. 2000. A parenting manual, with words of advice for Puritan mothers, in *A World of Babies: Imagined Childcare Guides for Seven Societies*. Edited by Judy DeLoache and Alma Gottlieb, pp. 29–54. Cambridge, MA: Cambridge University Press

Renne, Elisha P. 2002. Childhood memories and contemporary parenting in Ekiti, Nigeria. Paper presented at annual meeting, American Anthropological Association, New Orleans, LA, November

Retschitzki, Jean. 1990. *Stratégies des jouers d'Awélé*. Paris, France: Harmattan

Reynolds, Gretchen. 2005. Will we grow babies outside their mothers' bodies? *Popular Science*. September:72–78

Reynolds, Pamela, Nieuwenhuys, Olga, and Hanson, Karl. 2006. Refractions of children's rights in development practice: A view from anthropology – introduction. *Childhood*, 13(3):291–302

Richards, Audrey I. 1956. *Chisungu*. London, UK: Faber and Faber

Richerson, Peter J. and Boyd, Robert. 1992. Cultural inheritance and evolutionary ecology, in *Evolutionary Ecology and Human Behavior*. Edited by Eric Alden Smith and Bruce Winterhalder, pp. 61–92. New York, NY: Aldine de Gruyter

Riches, David. 1974. The Netsilik Eskimo: A special case of selective female infanticide. *Ethnology*, 13(4):351–361

Richman, Amy L., M. Miller, Patrice, and Johnson Solomon, Margaret. 1988. The socialization of infants in suburban Boston, in *Parental Behavior in Diverse Societies*. Edited by Robert A. LeVine, Peggy M. Miller, and Mary Maxwell West. New Directions for Child Development. 40:65–74

Riesman, Paul. 1992. *First Find Yourself a Good Mother*. New Brunswick, NJ: Rutgers University Press

Riis, Jacob. 1890/1996. *How the Other Half Lives*. New York, NY: Penguin Classics

Rindstedt, Camilla and Aronsson, Karin. 2003. ¿Quieres bañar? Sibling caretaking, play and perspective-taking in an Andean community. Paper presented at 33rd annual meeting, Jean Piaget Society, Chicago, IL, June 5

Ritchie, James and Ritchie, Jane. 1981. Child rearing and child abuse: The Polynesian context, in *Child Abuse and Neglect: Cross Cultural Perspective*. Edited by Jill E. Korbin, pp. 186–204. Berkeley, CA: University of California Press

Ritchie, Jane and Ritchie, James. 1979. *Growing up in Polynesia*. Sydney, Australia: George Allen and Unwin

Ritter, Philip. 1981. Adoption on Kosrae Island: Solidarity and sterility. *Ethnology*, 20(1):45–61

Robbins, Alexandra. 2006. *The Overachievers: The Secret Lives of Driven Kids*. New York: Hyperion

Roberts, John M. 1964. The self-management of cultures, in *Explorations in Cultural Anthropology*. Edited by Ward H. Goodenough, pp. 433–454. New York, NY: McGraw-Hill

Roberts, John M. and Sutton-Smith, Brian. 1962. Child training and game involvement. *Ethnology*, 2:166–185

Robinson, Julie Ann. 1988. What we've got here is a failure to communicate: The culture context of meaning, in *Child Development within Culturally Structured Environments*, Vol. II. Edited by Jaan Valsiner, pp. 137–198. Norwood, NJ: Ablex

Robson, Arthur J. and Kaplan, Hillard S. 2003. The evolution of human life expectancy and intelligence in hunter-gatherer economies. *American Economic Review*, 93(1):150–169

Rogers, Alan R. 1989. Does biology constrain culture? *American Anthropologist*, 90(4):819–831

Rogoff, Barbara. 1990. *Apprenticeship in Thinking: Cognitive Development in Social Context*. New York, NY: Oxford University Press

  2003. *The Cultural Nature of Human Development*. Oxford, NY: Oxford University Press

Rogoff, Barbara, Mistry, Jayanthi, Göncü, Artin, and Mosier, Christine. 1991. Cultural variation in the role relations of toddlers and their families, in *Cultural Approaches to Parenting*. Edited by Mark H. Bornstein, pp. 173–183. Hillsdale, NJ: Erlbaum

  1993. Guided participation in cultural activity by toddlers and caregivers. *Monographs of the Society for Research in Child Development*, 58(8/236):v, vi, 1–183

Rogoff, Barbara, Paradise, Ruth, Arauz, Rebeca M., Correa-Chávez, Maricela, and Angelillo, Cathy. 2003. Firsthand learning through intent participation. *Annual Review of Psychology*, 54:175–203

Rogoff, Barbara, Sellers, Martha J., Pirotta, Sergio, Fox, Nathan, and White, Sheldon H. 1975. Age of assignment of roles and responsibilities to children. *Human Development*, 18:353–369

Rohlen, Thomas P. 1996. Building character, in *Teaching and Learning in Japan.* Edited by Thomas P. Rohlen and Gerald K. LeTendre, pp. 50–74. New York, NY: Cambridge University Press

Rohner, Ronald P. and Chaki-Sircar, Manjusri. 1988. *Women and Children in a Bengali Village.* Hanover, NH: University Press of New England

Roopnarine, Jaipaul L., Bynoe, Pauline F., and Singh, Ronald. 2004. Factors tied to the schooling of children of English-speaking Caribbean immigrants in the United States, in *Childhood and Adolescence: Cross-Cultural Perspectives and Applications.* Edited by Uwe P. Gielen and Jaipaul L. Roopnarine, pp. 319–349. Westport, CT: Praeger

Roopnarine, Jaipaul L., Fouts, Hilary N., Lamb, Michael E., and Lewis, Tracey. 2005. Mothers' and fathers' behaviors towards their 3–4 month-old infants in low-, middle- and upper-socioeconomic African American families. Paper presented at 34th annual meeting, Society for Cross Cultural Research, Santa Fe, February

Roopnarine, Jaipaul L. and Hoosain, Ziarat. 1992. Parent–child interaction patterns in urban Indian families in New Delhi: Are they changing?, in *Parent–Child Socialization in Diverse Cultures.* Edited by Jaipaul L. Roopnarine and D. Bruce Carter, pp. 1–16. Norwood, NJ: Ablex

Roopnarine, Jaipaul L., Hossain, Ziarat, Gill, Preeti, and Brophy, Holly. 1994. Play in the east Indian context, in *Children's Play in Diverse Cultures.* Edited by Jaipaul L. Roopnarine, James E. Johnson, and Frank H. Hooper, pp. 9–30. Albany, NY: State University of New York Press

Roopnarine, Jaipaul L., Johnson, James E., and Hooper, Frank H. (eds.) 1994. *Children's Play in Diverse Cultures.* Albany, NY: State University of New York Press

Roopnarine, Jaipaul L., Krishnakumar, Ambika, Metindogan, Aysegul, and Evans, Melanie. 2006. Links between parenting styles, parent–child interaction, parent–school interaction, and early academic skills and social behaviors in young children of English-speaking Caribbean. *Early Childhood Research Quarterly*, 21(2):238–252

Roscoe, Paul B. 1995. In the shadow of the Tambaran: Female initiation among the Ndu of the Sepik Basin, in *Gender Rituals: Female Initiation in Melanesia.* Edited by Nancy C. Lutkehaus and Paul B. Roscoe, pp. 55–82. London. UK: Routledge

Roscoe, Paul B. and Telban, Borut. 2004. The people of the lower Arafundi: Tropical foragers of the New Guinea rainforest. *Ethnology*, 43:93–115

Rose, Harold M. and McClain, Paula D. 1990. *Race, Place, and Risk: Black Homicide in Urban America.* Albany, NY: State University of New York Press

Rosen, David M. 2005. *Armies of the Young: Child Soldiers in War and Terrorism.* New Brunswick, NJ: Rutgers University Press

Rosenfeld, Alvin and Wise, Nicole. 2000. *The Over-Scheduled Child: Avoiding the Hyper-Parenting Trap.* New York, NY: St. Martin's Press

Roskos, Kathy and Newman, Susan. 1994. Play settings as literacy environments: Their effects on children's literacy behaviors, in *Emergent Literacy: From Research to Practice.* Edited by David F. Lancy, pp. 251–264. Westport, CT: Praeger

Ross, Norbert O. 2002. Lacandon Maya intergenerational change and the erosion of folk biological knowledge, in *Ethnobiology and Biocultural Diversity: Proceedings of the Seventh International Congress of Ethnobiology.* Edited by John R. Stepp, Felice S. Wyndham, and Rebecca K. Zarger, pp. 585–592. Athens, GA: University of Georgia Press

Roth, Ann Macy. 2002. The meaning of menial labor: "Servant statues" in Old Kingdom serdabs. *Journal of the American Research Center in Egypt*, 39:103–121

Rousseau, Cecile, Said, Taher, M., Gagné, Marie-Josee, and Bibeau, Gilles. 1998. Resilience in unaccompanied minors from the north of Somalia. *Psychoanalytic Review*, 85:615–637

Rubenson, Birgitta, Hanh, Le Thi, Höjer, Bengt, and Johansson, Eva. 2005. Young sex-workers in Ho Chi Minh City telling their life stories. *Childhood*, 12(3):391–401

Rurevo, Rumbidazi and Bourdillion, Michael. 2003. *Girls on the Street*. Harare, Zimbabwe: Weaver Press

Saad, Ahmed Youssof. 2006. Subsistence education: Schooling in a context of urban poverty, in *Cultures of Arab Schooling: Critical Ethnographies from Egypt*. Edited by Linda Herrara and Carolos Alberto Torres, pp. 83–107. Albany, NY: State University of New York Press

Sabir-Farhat, Sabir. 2005. Children trafficked to Gulf States employed as camel jockeys from southern region of Pakistan. Paper presented at conference on Children and Youth in Emerging and Transforming Societies, Oslo, Norway, June

Sachs, Dana and Le, Quang Vu. 2005. Vietnam unearths its royal past. *National Geographic*, 207(6):3

Sahagun, Fray Bernardino de. 1829/1978. *General History of the Things of Spain*, 2nd edn. Edited by Arthur J. O. Anderson and Charles E. Dibble. Santa Fe, NM: School of American Research

Santa Maria, Madelene. 2002. Youth in Southeast Asia: Living within the continuity of tradition and the turbulence of change, in *The World's Youth: Adolescence in Eight Regions of the Globe*. Edited by Bradford B. Brown, Reed W. Larson and T. S. Saraswathi, pp. 171–206. Cambridge, MA: Cambridge University Press

Sargent, Carolyn F. and Harris, Michael. 1998. Bad boys and good girls: The implications of gender ideology for child health in Jamaica, in *Small Wars: The Cultural Politics of Childhood*. Edited by Nancy Scheper-Hughes and Carolyn F. Sargent, pp. 202–227. Berkeley, CA: University of California Press

Sargent, Laurie W. 2003. *The Power of Parent–Child Play*. Wheaton, IL: Tynedale House

Sastre, Béatriz S. Céspedes and Meyer, María-Isabel Zarama V. 2000. Living and working conditions: Child labour in the coal mines of Colombia, in *The Exploited Child*. Edited by Bernard Schlemmer, pp. 83–92. New York, NY: Zed Books

Savage, Anne, Ziegler, Toni E., and Snowdon, Charles T. 1988. Sociosexual development, pair bond formation, and mechanisms of fertility suppression in female cotton-top tamarins (*Saguinus oedipus oedipus*). *American Journal of Primatology*, 14:345–359

Savage-Rumbaugh, Sue, and Lewin, Roger. 1994. *Kanzi: The Ape at the Brink of the Human Mind*. New York, NY: John Wiley

Sawhill, Isabel V. 2003. Teenage sex, pregnancy, and nonmarital births, in *Family and Child Well-Being after Welfare Reform*. Edited by Douglas J. Besharov, pp. 145–157. New Brunswick, NJ: Transaction

Sax, Leonard. 2005. *Why Gender Matters: What Parents and Teachers Need to Know about the Emerging Science of Sex Differences*. New York, NY: Doubleday

Saxe, Geoffrey. 1990. *Culture and Cognitive Development: Studies in Mathematical Understanding*. Mahwah, NJ: Erlbaum

Scarr, Sandra. 1997. Why child care has little impact on most children's development. *Current Directions in Psychological Science*, 6:143–148

Schaller, George B. 1976. *The Serengeti Lion: A Study of Predator–Prey Relations*. Chicago, IL: University of Chicago Press

Schapera, Isaac. 1930. *The Khoisan People of South Africa*. London, UK: Routledge and Kegan Paul

1966. *Married Life in an African Tribe*. Evanston, IL: Northwestern University Press

Scheper-Hughes, Nancy. 1987a. "Basic strangeness": Maternal estrangement and infant death – A critique of bonding theory, in *The Role of Culture in Developmental Disorder*. Edited by Charles M. Super, pp. 131–151. New York, NY: Academic Press

Scheper-Hughes, Nancy. 1987b. Cultures, scarcity, and maternal thinking: Mother love and child death in northeast Brazil, in *Child Survival: Anthropological Perspectives on the Treatment and Maltreatment of Children*. Edited by Nancy Scheper-Hughes, pp. 187–208. Dordrecht, Holland: D. Reidel

Scheper-Hughes, Nancy and Hoffman, Daniel. 1998. Brazilian apartheid: Street kids and the struggle for urban space, in *Small Wars: The Cultural Politics of Childhood*. Edited by Nancy Scheper-Hughes and Carolyn F. Sargent, pp. 352–388. Berkeley, CA: University of California Press

Schick, Kathy D. and Toth, Nicholas. 1993. *Making Silent Stones Speak: Human Evolution and the Dawn of Technology*. New York, NY: Simon and Schuster

Schiefenhovel, Wulf. 1989. Reproduction and sex-ratio manipulation through preferential female infanticide among the Eipo, in the highlands of western New Guinea, in *The Sociobiology of Sexual and Reproductive Strategies*. Edited by Anne E. Rasa, Christian Vogel, and Eckart Voland, pp. 170–93. New York, NY: Chapman and Hall

Schieffelin, Bambi B. 1986. Teasing and shaming in Kaluli children's interactions, in *Language Socialization across Cultures*. Edited by Bambi B. Schiefflin and Elinor Ochs, pp. 165–181. New York, NY: Cambridge University Press

1990. *The Give and Take of Everyday Life: Language Socialization of Kaluli Children*. Cambridge, MA: Cambridge University Press

Schildkrout, Enid. 1981. The employment of children in Kano (Nigeria), in *Child Work, Poverty, and Underdevelopment*. Edited by Gerry Rodgers and Guy Standing, pp. 81–112. Geneva, Switzerland: International Labour Office

1990. Children's roles, the young traders of northern Nigeria, in *Conformity amd Conflict*. Edited by James P. Spradley and Davie W. McCurdy, pp. 221–228. Glenview, IL: Scott Foresman

Schlegel, Alice. 1973. The adolescent socialization of the Hopi girl. *Ethnology*, 12(4):449–462

1991. Status, property, and the value on virginity. *American Ethnologist*, 18(4):719–734

1995. A cross-cultural approach to adolescence. *Ethos*, 23:15–32

2000a. The global spread of adolescence in times of social change, in *Negotiating Adolescence in Times of Social Change*. Edited by Lisa J. Crockett and Rainer K. Silbereisen, pp. 71–88. New York, NY: Cambridge University Press

2000b. Strangers or friends?: The need of adults in the life of adolescents. *Paideuma*, 46:137–148

Schlegel, Alice and Barry, Herbert L., III. 1979. Adolescent initiation ceremonies: A cross-cultural code. *Ethnology*, 18(2):199–210

1980. The evolutionary significance of adolescent initiation ceremonies. *American Ethnologist*, 7(4):696–715

1991. *Adolescence: An Anthropological Inquiry*. New York, NY: The Free Press

Schriewer, Jurgen, Orvil, François, and Swing, Elizabeth Sherman. 2000. European educational systems: The framework of tradition, systemic expansion, and challenges for restructuring, in *Problems and Prospects in European Education*. Edited by Elizabeth Sherman Swing, Jurgen Schriewer, and François Orvil, pp. 1–20. Westport, CT: Praeger

Schultz, T. Paul. 1994. *Human Capital Investment in Woman and Men*. San Francisco, CA: ICS Press

Schwartzman, Helen. 1976. Children's play: A sideways glance at make-believe, in *The Anthropological Study of Play: Problems and Prospects*. Edited by David F. Lancy and B. Allan Tindall, pp. 198–205. Cornwall, NY: Leisure Press

1978. *Transformations: The Anthropology of Children's Play*. New York, NY: Plenum

2001. Children and anthropology: A century of studies, in *Children and Anthropology: Perspectives for the 21st Century*. Edited by Helen B. Schwartzman, pp. 15–37. Westport, CT: Bergin and Garvey

Schweinhart, Lawrence J. 2004. *The High/Scope Perry Preschool Study through Age 40*. Ypsilanti, MI: High/Scope Educational Foundation

Scribner, Sylvia and Cole, Michael. 1981. *The Psychology of Literacy*. Cambridge, MA: Harvard University Press

Scrimshaw, Susan C. M. 1978. Infant mortality and behavior in the regulation of family size. *Population and Development Review*, 4(3):383–403

1984. Infanticide in human populations: Societal and individual concerns, in *Infanticide: Comparative and Evolutionary Perspectives*. Edited by Gerald Hausfater and Sarah Blaffer Hrdy, pp. 439–462. New York, NY: Aldine

Sear, Rebecca, Mace, Ruth, and McGregor, Ian A. 2003. The effects of kin on female fertility in rural Gambia. *Evolution and Human Behavior*, 24:25–42

Sears, Robert R., Maccoby, Eleanor E., and Levin, Harold. 1957. *Patterns of Child Rearing*. Evanston, IL: Row, Peterson

Seiter, Ellen. 1998. Children's desires/mothers' dilemmas: The social contexts of consumption, in *The Children's Culture Reader*. Edited by Henry Jenkins, pp. 297–317. New York, NY: New York University Press

Sellen, Daniel W. 1995. The socioecology of young child growth among the Datoga pastoralists of northern Kenya. Ph.D. dissertation, Department of Anthropology, University of California, Davis

1998a. Infant and young child feeding practices among African pastoralists: The Datoga of Tanzania. *Journal of Biosocial Science*, 3:481–499

1998b. Polygyny and child growth ina traditional pastoral society: The case of the Datoga of Tanzania. *Human Nature*, 10(4):329–371

2005. Promoting optimal young child feeding practices: Bringing the past into the present. Paper presented at annual meeting, American Anthropological Association, Washington, DC, December

Sellen, Daniel W. and Mace, Ruth. 1997. Fertility and mode of subsistence: A phylogenetic analysis. *Current Anthropology*, 38(5):878–889

Serpell, Robert. 1993. *The Significance of Schooling: Life Journeys in an African Society*. Cambridge, MA: Cambridge University Press

Shack, Dorothy N. 1969. Nutritional processes and personality development among the Gurage of Ethopia. *Ethnology*, 8(3):293–300

Shahar, Shulaminth. 1990. *Childhood in the Middle Ages*. London, UK: Routledge

Shapiro, H. A. 2003. Fathers and sons, men and boys, in *Coming of Age in Ancient Greece*. Edited by Jennifer Neils and John H. Oakley, pp. 85–112. New Haven, CT: Yale University Press

Sharer, Robert J. 1994. *The Ancient Maya*, 5th edn. Stanford, CA: Stanford University Press

Sharp, Lesley A. 2002. *The Sacrificed Generation: Youth, History, and the Colonized Mind*. Berkeley, CA: University of California Press

Shein, Max. 1992. *The Precolumbian Child*. Culver City, CA: Labyrinthos

Shelton, Jo-Ann. 1998. *As the Romans Did: A Sourcebook in Roman Social History*. New York, NY: Oxford University Press

Shostak, Marjorie. 1976. A !Kung woman's memories of childhood, in *Kalahri Hunter-Gatherers*. Edited by Richard B. Lee and Irvin DeVore, pp. 246–278. Cambridge, MA: Harvard University Press

Shutt, Eagle J., Miller, Mitchell J., Schreck, Christopher J., and Brown, Nancy K. 2004. Reconsidering the leading myths of stranger child abduction. *Criminal Justice Studies*, 17(1): 127–134

Shwalb, David and Shwalb, Barbara. 2005. Fathers and pre-schoolers in Japan and the US: Daily life settings, relationships and activities. Paper presented at 34th annual meeting, Society for Cross Cultural Research, Santa Fe, NM, February

Shwalb, David W., Shwalb, Barbara J., and Shoji, Junichi. 1996. Japanese mothers' ideas about infants and temperament, in *Parents' Cultural Belief Systems: Their Origins, Expressions, and Consequences*. Edited by Sara Harkness and Charles M. Super, pp. 169–191. New York, NY: The Guilford Press

Sigman, Marian, Neumann, Charlotte, Carter, Eric, Cattle, Dorothy J., D'Souza, Susan, and Bwibo, Nimrod. 1988. Home interactions and the development of Embu toddlers in Kenya. *Child Development*, 59:1251–1261

Silk, Joan B. 1980. Adoption and kinship in Oceania. *American Anthropologist*, 82: 799–820

1987. Adoption among the Inuit. *Ethos*, 15:320–330

2002. Kin selection in primate groups. *International Journal of Primatology*, 23(4):849–875

Silk, Joan B., Alberts, Susan C., and Altmann, Jeanne. 2003. Social bonds of female baboons enhance infant survival. *Science*, 302(5648):1231–1235

Sillar, Bill. 1994. Playing with God: Cultural perceptions of children, play, and miniatures in the Andes. *Archaeological Review from Cambridge*, 13:47–63

Silva, Maria dela Luz. 1981. Urban poverty and child work: Elements for the analysis of child work in Chile, in *Child Work, Poverty, and Underdevelopment*. Edited by Gerry Rodgers and Guy Standing, pp. 159–177. Geneva, Switzerland: International Labour Office

Silverman, William A. 2004. Compassion or opportunism? *Pediatrics*, 113:402–403

Silvers, Jonathan. 1996. Child labor in Pakistan. *Atlantic Monthly*, February: 79–85

Silverstein, Louise. B. and Auerbach, Carl F. 2005. (Post) Modern families, in *Families in Global Perspective*. Edited by Jaipaul L. Roopnarine, pp. 33–47. Boston, MA: Pearson

Simmons, Leo W. (ed.) 1942. *Sun Chief: The Autobiography of a Hopi Indian*. New Haven, CT: Yale University Press

Simon, Herbert A. 1956. Rational choice and the structure of the environment. *Psychological Review*, 63(1):129–138

Singleton, John. 1989. Japanese folkcraft pottery apprenticeship: Cultural patterns of an educational institution, in *Apprenticeship: From Theory to Method and Back Again*. Edited by Michael W. Coy, pp. 13–30. Albany, NY: State University of New York Press

Siskind, Amy. 1999. In whose interest?: Separating children from mothers in the Sullivan Institute/Fourth Wall community, in *Children in New Religions*. Edited by Susan J. Palmer and Charlotte E. Hardman, pp. 51–68. New Brunswick, NJ: Rutgers University Press

Sjögren-De Beauchaine, Annick. 1998. *The Bourgeoisie in the Dining Room: Meal Ritual and Cultural Process in Parisian Families of Today*. Stockholm: Institutet for Folkslivsforskining. Cited in Marie-Anne Suizo, 2002. French parents' cultural models and childrearing beliefs. *International Journal of Behavioral Development*, 26(4):297–307

Skoufias, Emmanuel. 1994. Market wages, family composition and the time allocation of children in agricultural households. *The Journal of Developmental Studies*, 30(2):335–360

Slome, Cecil. 2003. Culture and the problem of weaning, in *The Manner Born: Birth Rites in Cross-Cultural Perspective*. Edited by Lauren Dundes, pp. 193–208. New York, NY: AltaMira Press

Small, Meredith F. 1998. *Our Babies, Ourselves: How Biology and Culture Shape the Way We Parent*. New York, NY: Anchor Books

Smilansky, Sarah. 1968. *The Effects of Sociodramatic Play on Disadvantaged Preschool Children*. New York, NY: Wiley

Smith, Patricia and Kahila, Gila. 1992. Identification of infanticide in archeological sites: A case study from the late Roman–early Byzantine periods at Ashkelon, Israel. *Journal of Archeological Science*, 19:667–675

Smith, Peter K. 2002. Pretend play, meta-representation and theory of mind, in *Pretending, and Imagination in Animals and Children*. Edited by Robert W. Mitchell, pp. 129–141. Cambridge, MA: Cambridge University Press

Smith, Peter K. and Simon, Tony. 1984. Object play, problem-solving and creativity in children, in *Play in Animals and Humans*. Edited by Peter K. Smith, pp. 199–216. Oxford, UK: Basil Blackwell

Snow, Catherine E., Barnes, Wendy S., Chandler, Jean, Goodman, Irene F., and Hemphill, Lowry. 1991. *Unfulfilled Expectations: Home and School Influences on Literacy*. Cambridge, MA: Harvard University Press

Snow, Catherine E., Burns, M. Susan, and Griffin, Peg. (ed.) 1998. *Preventing Reading Difficulties in Young Children*. Washington, DC: National Academies Press

Snow, Catherine E., De Blauw, Akke, and Van Roosmalen, Ghislaine. 1979. Talking and playing with babies: The role of ideologies of child-rearing, in *Before Speech:*

The Beginnings of Interpersonal Communication. Edited by Margaret Bullowa, pp. 269–288. Cambridge, MA: Cambridge University Press

Sobolik, Kristin D. 2002. Children's health in the prehistoric Southwest, in *Children in the Prehistoric Puebloan Southwest.* Edited by Kathryn A. Kamp, pp. 125–151. Salt Lake City, UT: University of Utah Press

Sofue, Takao. 1965. Childhood ceremonies in Japan: Regional and local variations. *Ethnology,* 4(2):148–164

Sokolove, Michael. 2004. Constructing a teen phenom. *New York Times Magazine,* November 28:80–85

Sommer, Volker and Mendoza-Granados, Domingo. 1995. Play as indicator of habitat quality: A field study of langur monkeys (*Presbytis entellus*). *Ethology,* 99:177–192

Sommerville, John C. 1982. *The Rise and Fall of Childhood.* Sage Library of Social Research, Vol. 140. Beverly Hills, CA: Sage

Soren, David. 2000. Carthage must be destroyed. *Archaeology Odyssey,* 3(6):16–17

Sorenson, E. Richard. 1976. *The Edge of the Forest: Land, Childhood and Change in a New Guinea Protoagricultural Society.* Washington, DC: Smithsonian Institution Press

Sosis, Richard, Kress, Howard C., and Boster, James S. 2007. Scars for war: Evaluating alternative signaling explanations for cross-cultural variance in ritual costs. *Evolution and Human Behavior,* 28(4):234–247

Spencer, Paul. 1970. The function of ritual in the socialization of the Samburu Moran, in *Socialization: The Approach from Social Anthropology.* Edited by Philip Mayer, pp. 127–157. London: Tavistock Publications

Spicer, Neil J. 2005. Sedentarization and children's health: Changing discourses in the northeast Badia of Jordan. *Social Science and Medicine,* 61(10):2165–2176

Spilsbury, James C. and Korbin, Jill E. 2004. Negotiating the dance: Social capital from the perspective of neighborhood children and adults, in *Rethinking Childhood.* Edited by Peter B. Pufall and Richard P. Unsworth, pp. 191–206. New Brunswick, NJ: Rutgers University Press

Spittler, Gerd. 1998. *Hirtenarbeit.* Cologne: Rüdiger Köppe

Springer, John. 2007. Woman defends decision to give birth at 60. New York: MSNBC, May 24th

Stack, Carol B. 1974. *All Our Kin.* New York, NY: Harper and Row

Stafford, Charles. 1995. *The Roads of Chinese Childhood.* New York, NY: Cambridge University Press

Stafford, Dinaz and Nair, Mira. 2003. *Still the Children are Here.* Mumbai, India: Mirabai Films

Stager, Lawrence E. 1982. Carthage: A view from the Tophet, in *Phönizer im Western.* Edited by Hans Georg Niemeyer, pp. 155–66. Mainz am Rhein; Philipp von Zabern

Stager, Lawrence E. and Greene, Joseph A. 2000. Were living children sacrificed to the gods? *Archeology Odyssey,* 3(6):29–31

Stager, Lawrence E. and Wolff, Samuel R. 1984. Child sacrifice at Carthage: Religious rite or population control? *Biblical Archaeology Review,* 10(1):31–51

Stambach, Amy. 1998. "Education is my husband": Marriage, gender, and reproduction in northern Tanzania, in *Women and Education in Sub-Saharan Africa: Power,*

Opportunities, and Constraints. Edited by Marianne Bloch, Josephine A. Beoku-Betts, and B. Robert Tabachnick, pp. 185–200. Boulder, CO: Lynne Rienner

Stearman, Allyn Maclean. 1989. *Yuqui: Forest Nomads in a Changing World.* Chicago, IL: Holt, Rinehart, and Winston

Stella, Alessandro. 2000. Introduction: A history of exploited children in Europe, in *The Exploited Child.* Edited by Bernard Schlemmer, pp. 21–38. New York, NY: Zed Books

Stephens, Sharon. 1995. Introduction: Children and the politics of culture in "Late Capitalism," in *Children and the Politics of Culture.* Edited by Sharon Stephens, pp. 3–48. Princeton, NJ: Princeton University Press

Sternglanz, Sarah Hall, Gran, James L., and Murakami, Melvin. 1977. Adult preferences for infantile facial features: An ethnological approach. *Animal Behavior,* 1977(25):108–115

Sternheimer, Karen. 2003. *It's Not the Media: The Truth about Pop Culture's Influence on Children.* Boulder, CO: Westview Press

Sterponi, Laura. 2003. Account episodes in family discourse: The making of morality in everyday interaction. *Discourse Studies,* 5(1):79–100

Sterponi, Laura and Santagata, Rossella. 2000. Mistakes in the classroom and at the dinner table: A comparison between socialization practices in Italy and the United States. *Crossroads of Language, Interaction and Culture,* 3(1):57–72

Stevens, Phillips, Jr., 1996. Traditional sport in Africa: Wrestling among the Bachama of Nigeria, in *Traditional Sport in the Twenty-First Century.* Edited by Tsuneo Sogawa, pp. 83–114. Tokyo, Japan: Taishukun-Shoten

Stevenson, Harold, W., Chen, Chuansheng, and Lee, Shinying. 1992. Chinese families, in *Parent–Child Socialization in Diverse Cultures.* Edited by Jaipaul L. Roopnarine and D. Bruce Carter, pp. 17–33. Norwood, NJ: Ablex

Stevenson, Harold W. and Zusho, Akane. 2002. Adolescence in China and Japan: Adapting to a changing environment, in *The World's Youth: Adolescence in Eight Regions of the Globe.* Edited by Bradford B. Brown, Reed W. Larson, and T. S. Saraswathi, pp. 141–170. Cambridge, MA: Cambridge University Press

Stinson, David W. 2006. African American male adolescents, schooling (and mathematics): Deficiency, rejection, and achievement. *Review of Educational Research,* 76(4):477–506

Stipek, Deborah. 1995. The development of pride and shame in toddlers, in *Self-Conscious Emotions: The Psychology of Shame, Guilt, Embarrassment, and Pride.* Edited by June P. Tangney and Kurt W. Fischer, pp. 237–254. New York, NY: The Guilford Press

Stoffle, Richard W. 1977. Industrial impact on family formation in Barbados, West Indies. *Ethnology,* 16(3):253–267

Stone, Linda and James, Caroline. 1995. Dowry, bride-burning, and female power in India. *Women's Studies International Forum,* 18(2):125–135

Strassmann, Beverly I. 1993. Menstrual hut visits by Dogon women: A hormonal test distinguishes deceit from honest signaling. *Behavioral Ecology,* 7(3):304–315

1997. Polygyny as a risk factor for child mortality among the Dogon. *Current Anthropology,* 38:688–695

Strathern, Andrew. 1970. Male initiation in New Guinea Highlands societies. *Ethnology,* 9(4):373–379

Strathern, Marilyn. 1992. *Reproducing the Future: Anthropology, Kinship and the New Reproductive Technologies*. Manchester, UK: Manchester University Press

Strier, Karen B. 2003. *Primate Behavioral Ecology*, 2nd edn. Boston, MA: Allyn and Bacon

Strom, Robert D., Strom, Paris S., Strom, Shirley K., Shen, Yuh-Ling, and Beckert, Troy E. 2004. Black, Hispanic, and White American mothers of adolescents: Construction of a national standard. *Adolescence*, 39:669–685

Strouhal, Eugen. 1990. Life of ancient Egyptian children according to archaeological sources, in *Children and Exercise*. Edited by Gaston P. Beunen, pp. 184–196. Stuttgart, Germany: Enke

  1992. *Life of the Ancient Egyptians*. Norman, OK: University of Oklahoma Press

Suarez-Orozco, Marcelo M. 1989. *Central American Refugees and US High Schools: A Psycho-social Study of Motivation and Achievement*. Stanford, CA: Stanford University Press

Sugiyama, Lawrence S. and Chacon, Richard. 2005. Juvenile responses to household ecology among the Yora of Peruvian Amazonia, in *Hunter Gatherer Childhoods: Evolutionary, Developmental, and Cultural Perspectives*. Edited by Barry S. Hewlett and Michael E. Lamb, pp. 237–261. New Brunswick, NJ: AldineTransaction

Sugiyama, Yukimaru. 1967. Social organization of Hanuman langurs, in *Social Communication among Primates*. Edited by Steven A. Altmann, pp. 221–253. Chicago, IL: University of Chicago Press

Suizo, Marie-Anne. 2002. French parents' cultural models and childrearing beliefs. *International Journal of Behavioral Development*, 26(4): 297–307

Sundberg, Mark. 2006. *Global Monitoring Report: Millennium Development Goals: Strengthening Mutual Accountability, Aid, Trade, and Governance*. Washington, DC: The International Bank for Reconstruction and Development/The World Bank

Sunley, Robert. 1955. Early nineteenth-century American literature on child rearing, in *Childhood in Contemporary Cultures*. Edited by Margaret Mead and Martha Wolfenstein, pp. 150–167. Chicago, IL: University of Chicago Press

Suomi, Stephen J. 2005. Gene–environment interactions and risk behaviors in primates. Paper presented at annual meeting, American Anthropological Association, Washington, DC, December

Super, Charles M. and Harkness, Sara. 1986. The developmental niche: A conceptualization at the interface of child and culture. *International Journal of Behavioral Development*, 9:545–569

Suryani, Luh Ketut. 1984. Culture and mental disorder: The case of Bebainan in Bali. *Culture, Medicine and Psychiatry*, 8(1):95–114

Sussman, George. 1982. *Selling Mother's Milk: The Wet-Nursing Business in France, 1715–1914*. Urbana, IL: University of Illinois Press

Sussman, Robert W. 1977. Socialization, social structure, and ecology of the two sympatric species of *Lemur*, in *Primate Bio-Social Development: Biological, Social, and Ecological Determinants*. Edited by Suzanne Chevalier-Skolnikoff and Frank E. Poirier, pp. 515–528. New York, NY: Garland

Sutton-Smith, Brian. 1971. The role of play in cognitive development, in *Child's Play*. Edited by R. E. Heron and Brian Sutton-Smith, pp. 252–260. New York, NY: John Wiley

1977. Commentary. *Current Anthropology*, 18(2):184–185

1986. *Toys as Culture*. New York, NY: Gardner Press

Sutton-Smith, Brian and Rosenborg, Barak G. 1961. Sixty years of historical change in the game preferences of American children. *Journal of American Folklore*, 74:17–46

Swan, Raymond W. and Stavros, Helen. 1973. Child-rearing practices associated with the development of cognitive skills of children in low socio-economic areas. *Early Child Development and Care*, 1:23–38

Swanton, John R. 1928. Social organization and the social usages of the Creek confederacy, in *United States Bureau of American Ethnology. Forty Second Annual Report*, pp. 23–472. Washington, DC: Government Printing Office

Swift, Jonathan. 1729/1996. *A Modest Proposal*. Mineola, NY: Dover Publications

Symons, Donald. 1978. *Play and Aggression: A Study of Rhesus Monkeys*. New York, NY: Columbia University Press

Takada, Akira. 2005. Mother–infant interactions among the !Xun: Analysis of gymnastic and breastfeeding behaviors, in *Hunter Gatherer Childhoods: Evolutionary, Developmental, and Cultural Perspectives*. Edited by Barry S. Hewlett and Michael E. Lamb, pp. 289–308. New Brunswick, NJ: AldineTransaction

Tanaka, Yuko and Nakazawa, Jun. 2005. Job-related temporary father absence (*Tanshinfunin*) and child development, in *Applied Developmental Psychology: Theory, Practice, and Research from Japan*. Edited by David W. Shwalb, Jun Nakazawa, and Barbara, J. Shwalb, pp. 241–260. Greenwich, CT: Information Age Publishing

Tanner, N. Eldon. 1974. No greater honor: The woman's role. *Ensign*, 3(4):7–11

Tang, Patricia. 2006. Memory, childhood, and the construction of modern Griot identity, in *Musical Childhoods and the Culture of Youth*. Edited by Susan Boynton and Roe-Min Kok, pp. 105–120. Middletown, CT: Wesleyan University Press

1980. Celestial marriages and eternal families. *Ensign* (May): 15–18

Tanon, Fabienne. 1994. *A Cultural View on Planning: The Case of Weaving in Ivory Coast*. Tillburg, Netherlands: Tilburg University Press

2005. Collaborative research on street children in three African cities. Paper presented at 34th annual meeting, Society for Cross Cultural Research, Santa Fe, NM, February

Taracena, Elvira and Tavera, Maria-Luisa. 2000. Stigmatization versus identity: Child street-workers in Mexico, in *The Exploited Child*. Edited by Bernard Schlemmer, pp. 93–105. New York, NY: Zed Books

Taylor, Denny. 1983. *Family Literacy*. Portsmouth, NH: Heinemann

Taylor, Lisa Rende. 2002. Dangerous trade-offs: The behavioral ecology of child labor and prostitution in Thailand. Paper presented at symposium on New Research in Human Behavior Ecology, American Anthropological Association, New Orleans, LA, November

Teale, William H. 1978. Positive environments for learning to read: What studies of early readers tell us. *Language Arts*, 55:922–932

Thévenon, Emmanuel. 2004. Primary schools, secondary schools: en route to the "bac." *Label France*, No. 54.

Thiessen, Erik D., Hill, Emily A., and Saffran, Jenny R. 2005. Infant-directed speech facilitates word segmentation. *Infancy*, 7(1):53–71

Thomas, Evan. 2001. I killed my children: What made Andrea Yates snap? *Newsweek*, June 2, 20–25

Thompson, Laura. 1940. *Fijian Frontier*. San Francisco, CA: American Council, Institute of Pacific Relations

Thorne, Barrie. 1993. *Gender Play: Girls and Boys in School*. New Brunswick, NJ: Rutgers University Press

Thorsen, Dorte. 2005. Child migrants in transit strategies to becoming adult in Burkina Faso. Paper presented at conference on Children and Youth in Emerging and Transforming Societies, Oslo, Norway, June

Tietjen, Anne Marie. 1985. Infant care and feeding practices and the beginnings of socialization among the Maisin of Papua New Guinea, in *Infant Care and Feeding in the South Pacific*. Edited by Leslie B. Marshall, pp. 121–135. New York, NY: Gordon and Breach

Timaeus, Ian and Graham, Wendy. 1989. Labour circulation, marriage and fertility in southern Africa, in *Reproduction and Social Organization in Sub-Saharan Africa*. Edited by Ronald J. Lesthaeghe, pp. 364–400. Berkeley, CA: University of California Press

Tingey, Holly, Kiger, Gary, and Riley, Pamela J. 1996. Juggling multiple roles: Perceptions of working mothers. *Social Science Journal*, 33(2):183–191

Tobin, Joseph. 2004. *Pikachu's Global Adventure: The Rise and Fall of Pokémon*. Durham, NC: Duke University Press

Tomasello, Michael. 2001. Cultural transmission: A view from chimpanzees and human infants. *Journal of Cross-Cultural Psychology*, 32(2):135–146

Toney, Michael B., Golesorkhi, Banu, and Stinner, William F. 1985. Residence exposure and fertility expectations of young Mormon and non-Mormon women in Utah. *Journal of Marriage and the Family*, 47(2):459–465

Toren, Christina. 1988. Children's perceptions of gender and hierarchy in Fiji, in *Acquiring Culture: Cross-Cultural Studies in Child Development*. Edited by Gustav Jahoda and Ioan M. Lewis, pp. 225–270. London, UK: Croom Helm

1990. *Making Sense of Hierarchy: Cognition as Social Process in Fiji*. Houndsmills, UK: Palgrave-Macmillan

1993. Making history: The significance of childhood cognition for a comparative anthropology of mind. *Man*, 28(3):461–478

2001. The child mind, in *The Debated Mind: Evolutionary Psychology versus Ethnography*. Edited by Harvey Whitehouse, pp. 155–179. Oxford, UK: Berg

Toshisada, Nishida. 2003. Individuality and flexibility of cultural behavior patterns in chimpanzees, in *Animal Social Complexity: Intelligence, Culture, and Individualized Societies*. Edited by Frans B. M. de Waal and Peter L. Tyack, pp. 392–413. Cambridge, MA: Harvard University Press

Toufexis, Anastasia and Bjerklie, David. 1994. When is crib death a cover for murder? *Time Magazine*, 143(15):63–64

Townsend, Nicholas. 2001. Fatherhood and the mediating role of women, in *Gender in Cross-Cultural Perspective*. Edited by Caroline B. Brettell and Carolyn F. Sargent, pp. 120–135. Upper Saddle River, NJ: Prentice Hall

Trenholm, Christopher, Devaney, Barbara, Fortson, Ken, Quay, Lisa, Wheeler, Justin, and Clark, Melissa. 2007. *Impacts of Four Title V, Section 510 Abstinence Education Programs Final Report*. Princeton, NJ: Mathematica Policy Research

Trevarthen, Colwyn. 1983. Interpersonal abilities of infants as generators for transmission of language and culture, in *The Behavior of Human Infants*. Edited by Alberto Oliverio, pp. 145–176. New York, NY: Plenum Press

1988. Univeral co-operative motives: How infants begin to know the language and culture of their parents, in *Acquiring Culture: Cross Cultural Studies in Child Development*. Edited by Gustav Jahoda and Ioan M., Lewis, pp. 37–90. London, UK: Croom Helm

Trevathan, Wenda R. and McKenna, James J. 2003. Evolutionary environments of human birth and infancy: Insights to apply to contemporary life, in *The Manner Born: Birth Rites in Cross-Cultural Perspective*. Edited by Lauren Dundes, pp. 33–52. New York, NY: AltaMira Press

Trivers, Robert, L. 1972. Parental investment and sexual selection, in *Sexual Selection and the Descent of Man*. Edited by Bernard Campbell, pp 136–179. Chicago, IL: Aldine

Trivers, Robert L. 1974. Parent–offspring conflict. *American Zoologist*, 14:249–264

Tronick, Edward Z., Morelli, Gilda A., and Winn, Steven. 1987. Multiple caretaking of Efe (Pygmy) infants. *American Anthropologist*, 89:96–106

Tronick, Edward Z., Thomas, R. Brook, and Daltabuit, Magali. 1994. The Quechua manta pouch: A caretaking practice for buffering the Peruvian infant against the multiple stressors of high altitude. *Child Development*, 65:1005–1013

Tsogbe, Koffi. 2001. *Measles Campaign Cost Effective Analysis: Rwanda Measles Campaign*. Nairobi, Kenya: UNICEF

Tucker, Bram and Young, Alyson G. 2005. Growing up Mikea: Children's time allocation and tuber foraging in Southwestern Madagascar, in *Hunter Gatherer Childhoods: Evolutionary, Developmental, and Cultural Perspectives*. Edited by Barry S. Hewlett and Michael E. Lamb, pp. 147–171. New Brunswick, NJ: AldineTransaction

Turke, Paul, W. 1988. Helpers at the nest: Childcare networks on Ifaluk, in *Human Reproductive Behavior*. Edited by Laura Betzig Monique Borgerhoff Mulder, and Paul Turke, pp. 173–188. Cambridge, MA: Cambridge University Press

1989. Evolution and the demand for children. *Population and Development Review*, 15(1):61–90

Turnbull, Colin M. 1978. The politics of non-aggression, in *Learning Non-Aggression: The Experience of Non-Literate Societies*. Edited by Ashley Montague, pp. 161–221. New York, NY: Oxford University Press

Tuzin, Donald. 1980. *The Voice of the Tambaran: Truth and Illusion in Ilahita Arapesh Religion*. Los Angeles, CA: University of California Press

UNICEF. 2004. *Progress for Children: A Child Survival Report Card*, Vol. I. New York, NY: United Nations

Unnithan-Kumar, Maya. 2001. Emotion, agency and access to healthcare: Women's experiences of reproduction in Jaipur, in *Managing Reproductive Life: Cross-Cultural Themes in Sexuality and Fertility*. Edited by Soraya Tremayne, pp. 27–51. Oxford, UK: Berghahn Books

Uno, Kathleen S. 1991. Japan, in *Children in Historical and Comparative Perspective*. Edited by Joseph M. Hawes and N. Ray Hiner, pp. 389–419. Westport, CT: Greenwood Press

Uribe, F. Medardo, Uribe, Tapia, LeVine, Robert A., and LeVine, Sarah E. 1994. Maternal behavior in a Mexican community: The changing environments of children, in *Cross-Cultural Roots of Minority Child Development*. Edited by Patricia M. Greenfield and Rodney R. Cocking, pp. 41–54. Hillsdale, NJ: Erlbaum

Utas, Mats. 2005. Agency of victims: Young women in the Liberian civil war, in *Makers and Breakers: Children and Youth in Post Colonial Africa*. Edited by Alcinda Honwana and Filip de Boeck, pp. 53–80. Trenton, NJ: Africa World Press

Valsiner, Jaan. 2000. *Culture and Human Development*. Thousand Oaks, CA: Sage

Van Gennep, Arnold. 1908/1960. *The Rites of Passage*. Chicago, IL: University of Chicago Press

van Lawick-Goodall, Jane. 1973. Behavior of chimpanzees in their natural habitat. *American Journal of Psychiatry*, 130(1):1–12

    1976a. Chimpanzee locomotor play, in *Play – Its Role in Development and Evolution*. Edited by Jerome S. Bruner, Alison Jolly, and Kathy Sylva, pp. 156–160. New York, NY: Basic Books

    1976b. Mother chimpanzees' play with their infants, in *Play – Its Role in Development and Evolution*. Edited by Jerome S. Bruner, Alison Jolly, and Kathy Sylva, pp. 262–267. New York, NY: Basic Books

van Ostade, Adrian. nd. *The Schoolmaster*. Achenbach Foundation for Graphic Arts

Van Stone, James W. 1965. *The Changing Culture of the Snowdrift Chipewyan*. Ottawa, ON: National Museum of Canada

Varenne, Hervé. 1982. Jocks and freaks, in *Doing the Ethnography of Schooling*. Edited by George D. Spindler, pp. 210–239. New York, NY: Holt, Rinehart and Winston

Vavrus, Francis and Larsen, Ulla. 2003. Girls' education and fertility transitions: An analysis of recent trends in Tanzania and Uganda. *Economic Development and Cultural Change*, 51(4):945–976

Verhetsel, Ann and Witlox, Frank. 2006. Children and housing: "Only the best is good enough": Some evidence from Belgium. *Childhood*, 13(2):205–224

Verma, Suman and Saraswathi, T. S. 2002. Adolescence in India: Street urchins or Silicon Valley millionaires?, in *The World's Youth: Adolescence in Eight Regions of the Globe*. Edited by Bradford B. Brown, Reed W. Larson, and T. S. Saraswathi, pp. 105–140. Cambridge, MA: Cambridge University Press

Verma, Suman and Sharma, Deepali. 2007. Cultural dynamics of family relations among Indian adolescents in varied contexts, in *Parenting Beliefs, Behavior and Parent–Child Relationships: A Cross–Cultural Perspective*. Edited by Kenneth H. Rubin and Ock Boon Chung. pp. 185–205. New York, NY: Psychology Press

Vidal, Fernando. 1994. *Piaget before Piaget*. Cambridge, MA: Harvard University Press

Visalberghi, Elisabetta and Addessi, Elsa. nd. Food for thought: Social learning and feeding behavior in capuchin monkeys, insights from the laboratory. Unpublished MS

Visalberghi, Elisabetta and Fragasky, Dorothy M. 1990. Do monkeys ape?, in *Language and Intelligence in Monkeys and Apes*. Edited by Sue Taylor Parker and Katherine R. Gibson, pp. 247–73. Cambridge, MA: Cambridge University Press

Vizedom, Monika and Zais, James P. 1976. *Rites and Relationships: Rites of Passage and Contemporary Anthropology*. Beverly Hills, CA: Sage

Volk, Anthony and Quinsey, Vernon L. 2002. The influence of infant facial cues on adoption preferences. *Human Nature*, 13(4):437–455

Waddington, Clare. 2005. Young people's strategies and experiences of social change following migration from rural areas to Salvador, Northeast Brazil. Paper presented at conference on Children and Youth in Emerging and Transforming Societies, Oslo, Norway, June

Waggoner, Dorothy. 1991. *Undereducation in America: The Demography of High School Dropouts*. Westport, CT: Auburn House

Wagley, Charles. 1977. *Welcome of Tears: The Tapirapé Indians of Central Brazil*. New York, NY: Oxford University Press

Wallaert-Pêtre, Hélène. 2001. Learning how to make the right pots: Apprenticeship strategies and material culture, a case study in handmade pottery from Cameroon. *Journal of Anthropological Research*, 57:471–493

Walsh, Daniel J. 2004. Frog boy and the American monkey: The body in Japanese early schooling, in *Knowing Bodies, Moving Minds*. Edited by Liora Bresler, pp. 97–109. Dardrecht, Netherlands: Kluwer Academic

Walter, Jeffrey R. 1987. Transition to adulthood, in *Primate Societies*. Edited by Barbara B. Smuts, Dorothy L. Cheney, Robert M. Seyfarth, Richard W. Wrangham, and Thomas T. Struhsaker, pp. 358–369. Chicago, IL: University of Chicago Press

Waltner, Ann. 1995. Infanticide and dowry in Ming and early Qing China, in *Chinese Views of Childhood*. Edited by Anne B. Kinney, pp. 193–217. Honolulu, HI: University of Hawai'i Press

Ward, Barbara E. 1970. Temper tantrums in Kau Sai: Some speculations upon their effects, in *Socialization: The Approach from Social Anthropology*. Edited by Philip Mayer, pp. 107–125. London, UK: Tavistock Publications

Ward, Carol J. 2005. *Native Americans in the School System: Family, Community, and Academic Achievement*. Lanham, MD: AltaMira Press

Ward, Martha Coonfield. 1971. *Them Children: A Study in Language Learning*. New York, NY: Holt, Rinehart and Winston

Warner, Judith. 2005. *Perfect Madness: Motherhood in the Age of Anxiety*. New York, NY: Riverhead Books

Warren, Andrea. 2001. *We Rode the Orphan Trains*. Boston, MA: Houghton Mifflin

Watson, James L. 1976. Chattel slavery in Chinese peasant society: A comparative analysis. *Ethnology*, 15(4):361–375

Watson, Lawrence C. 1972. Sexual socialization in Guajiro society. *Ethnology*, 2(2):150–156

Watson-Gegeo, Karen Ann and Gegeo, David Welchman. 1989. The role of sibling interaction in child socialization, in *Sibling Interaction across Cultures*. Edited by Patricia G. Zukow, pp. 54–76. New York, NY: Springer-Verlag

1992. Schooling, knowledge, and power: Social transformation in the Solomon Islands. *Anthropology and Education Quarterly*, 23(1):10–29

2001. "That's what children do": Perspectives on work and play in Kwara'ae. Paper presented at annual meeting, Association for the Study of Play, San Diego, CA, February

Wax, Murray L. 2002. The school classroom as frontier. *Anthropology and Education Quarterly*, 33(1):118–130

Wayne, Derrick. 2001. *Bushman of the Kalahari: A Bushman Story*. Princeton, NJ: Discovery Channel Video

Wee, Vivienne. 1992. Children, population policy, and the state in Singapore, in *Children and the Politics of Culture*. Edited by Sharon Stephens, pp. 184–217. Princeton, NJ: Princeton University Press

Weeden, Jason, Abrams, Michael J., Green, Melanie C., and Sabini, John. 2006. Do high-status people really have fewer children?: Education, income, and fertility in the contemporary United States. *Human Nature*, 17(4):377–392

Weisfeld, Glenn E. 1999. *Evolutionary Principles of Human Adolescence*. New York, NY: Basic Books

Weisfeld, Glenn E. and Linkey, Harold E. 1985. Dominance displays as indicators of a social success motive, in *Power, Dominance, and Nonverbal Behavior*. Edited by Steve L. Ellyson and John F. Dovidio, pp. 109–128. New York, NY: Springer-Verlag

Weisner, Thomas S. 1989. Cultural and universal aspects of social support for children: Evidence from the Abaluyia of Kenya, in *Children's Social Networks and Social Supports*. Edited by Deborah Belle, pp. 70–90. New York, NY: John Wiley

Weisner, Thomas S. and Gallimore, Ronald. 1977. My brother's keeper: Child and sibling caretaking. *Current Anthropology*, 18(2):169–190

Welles-Nyström, Barbara. 1988. Parenthood and infancy in Sweden. *New Direction for Child Development*, 40:75–96

1996. Scenes from a marriage: Equality ideology in Swedish family policy, maternal ethnotheories, and practice, in *Parents' Cultural Belief Systems: Their Origins, Expressions, and Consequences*. Edited by Sara Harkness and Charles M. Super, pp. 192–214. New York, NY: The Guilford Press

Wenger, Martha. 1989. Work, play and social relationships among children in a Giriama community, in *Children's Social Networks and Social Supports*. Edited by Deborah Belle, pp. 91–115. New York, NY: John Wiley

West, Elliott. 1992. Children on the plains frontier, in *Small Worlds: Children and Adolescents in America, 1850–1950*. Edited by Elliott West and Paula Petrik, pp. 26–41. Lawrence, KS: University Press of Kansas

White, Merry I. 1993. *The Material Child: Coming of Age in Japan and America*. New York, NY: Free Press

2002. *Perfectly Japanese: Making Families in an Era of Upheaval*. Berkeley, CA: University of California Press

White, Robert W. 1959. Motivation reconsidered: The concept of competence. *Psychological Review*, 66:297–333

Whitehead, Ann, Hashim, Imam, and Iversen, Vegard. 2005. Child agency and intergenerational relations. Paper presented at conference on Children and Youth in Emerging and Transforming Societies, Oslo, Norway, June

Whiten, Andrew, Goodall, Jane, McGrew, William C., Nishida, T., Reynolds, Vernon, Sugiyama, Yakimaru, Tutin, Caroline E. G., Wrangham, Richard W., and Boesch, Christophe. 1999. Culture in chimpanzees. *Nature*, 399:682–685

Whiten, Andrew, Horner, Victoria, and de Waal, Frans B. M. 2005. Conformity to cultural norms of tool use in chimpanzees. *Nature*, 437:737–740

Whiting, Beatrice B. and Pope-Edwards, Carolyn. 1988a. *Children of Different Worlds: The Formation of Social Behavior*. Cambridge, MA: Harvard University Press

1988b. A cross-cultural analysis of sex differences in the behavior of children aged 3 through 11, in *Childhood Socialization*. Edited by Gerald Handel, pp. 281–297. New York, NY: Aldine

Whiting, Beatrice B. and Whiting, John W. M. 1975. *Children of Six Cultures*. Cambridge, MA: Harvard University Press

Whiting, John W. M. 1941. *Becoming a Kwoma*. New Haven, CT: Yale University Press
1977. Infanticide. Paper presented at the Society for Research in Cross-Cultural Research, Ann Arbor, MI, February

Whiting, John W. M., Burbank, Victoria, K., and Ratner, Mitchell S. 1986. The duration of maidenhood across cultures, in *School-Age Pregnancy and Parenthood: Biosocial Dimensions*. Edited by Jane B. Lancaster and Beatrix A. Hamburg, pp. 273–302. New York, NY: Aldine de Gruyter

Whittemore, Robert Dunster. 1989. Child caregiving and socialization to the Mandinka Way: Toward an ethnography of childhood. Unpublished Ph.D dissertation UCLA, Los Angeles, CA.

Whittlesey, Stephanie M. 2002. The cradle of death: Mortuary practices, bioarchaeology, and the children of Grasshopper Pueblo, in *Children in the Prehistoric Puebloan Southwest*. Edited by Kathryn A. Kamp, pp. 152–168. Salt Lake City, UT: University of Utah Press

Wiedemann, Thomas. 1989. *Adults and Children in the Roman Empire*. New Haven, CT: Yale University Press

Wilcox, Linda P. 1987. Mormon motherhood: Official images, in *Sisters in Spirit: Mormon Women in Historical and Cultural Perspective*. Edited by Maureen Beecher, pp. 208–226. Urbana/Champaign, IL: University of Illinois Press

Wilder, William. 1970. Socialization and social structure in a Malay village, in *Socialization: The Approach from Social Anthropology*. Edited by Philip Mayer, pp. 215–268. London, UK: Tavistock Publications

Wiley, Andrea S. 2004. *An Ecology of High-Altitude Infancy*. New York, NY: Cambridge University Press

Wilkie, David S. and Morelli, Gilda A. 1991. Coming of age in the Ituri. *Natural History*, 100(10):54–62

Wilkins, Sally. 2002. *Sports and Games of Medieval Cultures*. Westport, CT: Greenwood Press

Williams, Francis E. 1936. *Papuans of the Trans-Fly*. Oxford, UK: Clarendon Press

Williams, Joe. 2005. *Cheating Our Kids: How Politics and Greed Ruin Education*. New York, NY: Palgrave Macmillan

Williams, Judith R. 1968. *The Youth of Haouch El Harimi, a Lebanese Village*. Cambridge, MA: Harvard University Press

Williams, Thomas R. 1969. *A Borneo Childhood*. New York, NY: Holt, Rinehart and Winston
1983. *Socialization*. Englewood Cliffs, NJ: Prentice-Hall

Wilson, Margo and Daly, Martin. 2002. The man who mistook his wife for a chattel, in *The Adapted Mind: Evolutionary Psychology and the Generation of Culture*. Edited by James Tooby, Leeda Cosmides, and Jerome Barkow, pp. 289–322. New York, NY: Oxford University Press

Wiseman, Rosalind. 2003. *Queen Bees and Wannabes: Helping Your Daughter Survive Cliques, Gossip, Boyfriends, and Other Realities of Adolescence*. New York, NY: Three Rivers Press

Wober, Mallory M. 1972. Culture and the concept of intelligence: A case in Uganda. *Journal of Cross-Cultural Psychology*, 3:327–328

Wolf, Margery. 1972. *Woman and the Family in Rural Taiwan*. Stanford, CA: Stanford University Press

Wolfenstein, Martha. 1955. Fun morality: An analysis of recent American child-training literature, in *Childhood in Contemporary Cultures*. Margaret Mead and Martha Wolfenstein, pp. 168–178. Chicago, IL: University of Chicago Press

Wright, Robert. 1994. *The Moral Animal*. New York, NY: Vintage

Wu, Pei Yi. 1995. Childhood remembered: Parents and children in China, 800 to 1700, in *Chinese Views of Childhood*. Edited by Anne B. Kinney, pp. 129–156. Honolulu, HI: University of Hawai'i Press

Wu, Peixia, Robinson, Clyde C., Yang, Chongming, Hart, Craig H., Olsen, Susanne F., Porter, Christin L., Jin, Shenghua, Wo, Jianzhong, and Wu, Xinzi. 2002. Similarities and differences in mothers' parenting of preschoolers in China and the United States. *International Journal of Behavioural Development*, 26(6):481–491

Wylie, Laurence. 1957. *Village in the Vaucluse*. New York, NY: Harper and Row

Yakin, Boaz. 1994. *Fresh* (film). New York: Miramax Films

Yimou, Zhang. 1991. *Raise the Red Lantern* (film). New York: Miramax Films

Yoshida, Kenji. 2006. Kalumbu and Chisudzo: Boys' and girls' masquerades among the Chewa, in *Playful Performers: African Children's Masquerades*. Edited by Simon Ottenberg and David A. Binkley, pp. 221–236. New Brunswick, NJ: Transaction

Young, James. 2006. The invisible infant: Strategies for coping with high infant mortality. Paper presented at symposium on Defining Childhood: Cross-cultural Perspectives, annual meeting of the Society for Anthropological Sciences, Savannah, GA, February

Zarger, Rebecca K. 2002. Acquisition and transmission of subsistence knowledge by Q'equchi' Maya in Belize, in *Ethnobiology and Biocultural Diversity*. Edited by John R. Stepp, Felice S. Wyndham, and Rebecca K. Zarger, pp. 593–603. Athens, GA: University of Georgia Press

Zarger, Rebecca K. and Stepp, John R. 2004. Persistence of botanical knowledge among Tzeltal Maya children. *Current Anthropology*, 45(3):413–418

Zaslavsky, Claudia. 1973. *Africa Counts*. Boston, MA: Prindle, Weber and Schmidt

Zeitlin, Marian. 1996. My child is my crown: Yoruba parental theories and practices in early childhood, in *Parents' Cultural Belief Systems: Their Origins, Expressions, and Consequences*. Edited by Sara Harkness and Charles M. Super, pp. 407–427. New York, NY: The Guilford Press

Zelizer, Viviana A. 1985. *Pricing the Priceless Child: The Changing Social Value of Children*. New York, NY: Basic Books

Zeller, Anthony C. 1987. A role for children in hominid evolution. *Man*, 22:528–557

Ziegler, Toni E., Savage, Anne, Scheffler, Guenther, and Snowdon, Charles T. 1987. The endocrinology of puberty and reproductive functioning in female cotton-top tamarins (*Saguinus odipus*). *Biology of Reproduction*, 37:618–627

Zimmerman, Jonathan. 2002. *Whose America? Culture Wars in the Public Schools*. Cambridge, MA: Harvard University Press

Zipf, George K. 1949. *Human Behavior and the Principle of Least Effort: An Introduction to Human Ecology*. Cambridge, MA: Addison-Wesley

Zito, Julie Mango, Safer, Daniel J., dos Reis, Susan, Gardner, James F., Magder, Laurence, Soeken, Karen, Boles, Myde, Lynch, Frances, and Riddle, Mark A. 2003. Psychotropic practice patterns in youth. *Archives of Pediatrics and Adolescent Medicine*, 157(1):17–25

Zuckerman, Michael. 1984. Sensation-seeking: A comparative approach to a human trait. *Behavioral and Brain Sciences*, 7:413–471

Zukow, Patricia G. 1989. Siblings as effective socializing agents: Evidence from central Mexico, in *Sibling Interaction across Cultures*. Edited by Patricia G. Zukow, pp. 79–105. New York, NY: Springer-Verlag

Zymek, Bernd. 2000. Equality of opportunity: Expansion of European school systems since the Second World War, in *Problems and Prospects in European Education*. Edited by Elizabeth Sherman Swing, Jurgen Schriewer, and François Orvil, pp. 99–117. Westport, CT: Praeger

Author index

Topic index

Society index

17639804R00270

Made in the USA
Middletown, DE
02 February 2015